THE ROUTLEDGE HANDBOOK OF RESEARCH METHODS IN THE STUDY OF RELIGION

D1595172

This is the first comprehensive survey in English of research methods in the field of religious studies. It is designed to enable non-specialists and students at upper undergraduate and graduate levels to understand the variety of research methods used in the field. The aim is to create awareness of the relevant methods currently available and to stimulate an active interest in exploring unfamiliar methods, encouraging their use in research and enabling students and scholars to evaluate academic work with reference to methodological issues. A distinguished team of contributors cover a broad spectrum of topics, from research ethics, hermeneutics and interviewing, to Internet research and video-analysis. Each chapter covers practical issues and challenges, the theoretical basis of the respective method, and the way it has been used in religious studies (illustrated by case studies).

Michael Stausberg is Professor of Religion at the University of Bergen, Norway. He is author of *Religion and Tourism: Crossroads, Destinations and Encounters*, editor of *Contemporary Theories of Religion* and European editor of the journal *Religion*.

Steven Engler is Associate Professor of Religious Studies at Mount Royal University, Canada. He is a co-editor of *Historicizing 'Tradition' in the Study of Religion* and North American editor of the journal *Religion*.

THE ROUTLEDGE HANDBOOK OF RESEARCH METHODS IN THE STUDY OF RELIGION

Edited by Michael Stausberg and Steven Engler

LONDON AND NEW YORK

First published in paperback in 2014
First published in 2011
by Routledge
2 Park Square, Milton Park, Abingdon, Oxon OX14 4RN

and by Routledge
711 Third Avenue, New York, NY 10017

Routledge is an imprint of the Taylor & Francis Group, an informa business

British Library Cataloguing in Publication Data
A catalogue record for this book is available from the British Library

Library of Congress Cataloging in Publication Data
The Routledge handbook of research methods in the study of religion /
edited by Michael Stausberg and Steven Engler.
p. cm.
Includes bibliographical references and index.
1. Religion—Methodology. I. Stausberg, Michael. II. Engler, Steven.
III. Title: Handbook of research methods in the study of religion.
BL41.R686 2011
200.72—dc23

2011021788

ISBN: 978-0-415-55920-1 (hbk)
ISBN: 978-0-415-71844-8 (pbk)
ISBN: 978-0-203-15428-1 (ebk)

Typeset in Bembo
by RefineCatch Limited, Bungay, Suffolk

CONTENTS

Contents

LIST OF FIGURES AND PLATES

Figures

Plates

LIST OF TABLES

LIST OF BOXES

CONTRIBUTORS

jimi adams is Assistant Professor, School of Social and Family Dynamics, Arizona State University, USA. His main areas of work are social networks and the diffusion of ideas/ diseases. His work has been published in *Social Networks*; *Field Methods*; *Demographic Research* and the *Handbook of Medical Sociology*.

Justin L. Barrett is Thrive Chair of Applied Developmental Psychology and Professor of Psychology at Fuller Theological Seminary, and Research Associate of the University of Oxford's Centre for Anthropology and Mind. He works in the areas of cognitive anthropology, cognitive science of religion, psychology of religion, and cognitive, religious and character development. Main publications include *Why Would Anyone Believe in God?* (2004); *Cognitive Science, Religion, & Theology* (2011) and *Born Believers* (2011). He is book review editor of the *Journal of Cognition & Culture*, a consulting editor of *Psychology of Religion & Spirituality* and an editorial board member of *Religion, Brain, and Behavior*.

Frederick Bird is Research Professor in the Department of Political Science at the University of Waterloo in Ontario, Canada. He is also a Distinguished Professor Emeritus at Concordia University in Montréal, Québec, Canada, where he was a professor in the Department of Religion and held a Concordia University Research Chair in Comparative Ethics. His publications include *Voices from the Voluntary Sector: perspectives on leadership challenges* (co-edited with Frances Westley, 2010); *Just Business: practices in a diverse and developing world* (co-edited with Manuel Velasquez, 2006); *International Business and the Dilemmas of Development* (co-edited with Emmanuel Raufflet and Joseph Smucker, 2005); *International Businesses and the Challenges of Poverty in the Developing World* (co-edited with Stewart W. Herman, 2004); *Ritual and Ethnic Identity: a comparative study of liturgical ritual in synagogues* (co-authored with Jack N. Lightstone *et al.*, 1996). For a number of years he chaired the university's Human Research Ethics Committee.

Kendal C. Boyd is Associate Professor of Psychology at Loma Linda University, USA. His research areas include medically unexplained symptoms, chronic pain, post-traumatic stress disorder, sports fan dynamics, the psychology of religion, and statistics/methodology. In addition to his dissertation being a Monte Carlo study on the number of factors criteria in exploratory factor analysis, he has published factor analytic studies in the area of medically unexplained symptoms. He is a clinical psychologist who also holds an MA in Theology from Fuller Theological Seminary. He recently authored a chapter in the edited volume *A Christian Worldview and Mental Health: Adventist perspectives*.

Anna Davidsson Bremborg (PhD Lund University, Sweden), is a sociologist of religion. Her main areas of research are death studies and pilgrimages. She has published two books: *Yrke: begravningsentreprenör* [Occupation: funeral director] (2002) and *Pilgrimsvandring på svenska* [Pilgrimages, the Swedish way] (2010). She has published articles in several edited books and in journals such as the *Journal of Empirical Theology*, *Mortality* and *Social Compass*.

Richard M. Carp is Vice Provost for Undergraduate Academics at St. Mary's College of California. He works in the interstices of the academic study of religion, performance, semiotics, anthropology, and visual art and design, as well as theory and method of interdisciplinarity. He is the director and editor of *The Image Bank for Teaching World Religion* (1992). He has published in various edited volumes and journals including *Teaching Theology and Religion*, *Issues in Integrative Studies* and *Historical Reflections/Réflexions historiques*. With Rebecca Sachs Norris he is editor of *Studies in Body and Religion: a series*.

Erik H. Cohen is Associate Professor of Sociology at the School of Education, Bar Ilan University, Israel. His main areas of work are Jewish identity, youth culture, tourism and migration, and Facet Theory research methodology. He is the author of *Youth Tourism to Israel: educational experiences of the diaspora* (2008). His work has been published in *Religion*, *Current Sociology* and *Annals of Tourism Research*. He is the co-founder and editor of the *International Journal of Jewish Education Research*.

Douglas E. Cowan is Professor of Religious Studies at Renison University College, the University of Waterloo, in Ontario, Canada. His current areas of interest include religion and film, religion and popular culture, and religion and technology. His major publications include *Sacred Space: The Quest for Transcendence in Science Fiction Film and Television* (2010); *Sacred Terror: religion and horror on the silver screen* (2008); *Cults and New Religions: a brief history* (with David G. Bromley, 2008), and *Cyberhenge: modern Pagans on the Internet* (2005). He is formerly a co-general editor of *Nova Religio: The Journal of Alternative and Emergent Religions* and is currently the New Religious Movements section editor for *Religion Compass*.

Grace Davie is Professor emerita in the Sociology of Religion in the University of Exeter (UK). Her work is principally concerned with the changing place of religion in European and other societies, and the pressing need for new ways of working in the social sciences in order to understand this. She is the author of *Religion in Britain since 1945* (1994); *Religion in Modern Europe* (2000); *Europe: the exceptional case* (2002); *The Sociology of Religion* (Sage 2007). She is co-author of *Religious America, Secular Europe* (2008), and co-editor of *Welfare and Religion in 21st Century Europe* (2 vols; 2010 and 2011).

Steven Engler is Associate Professor of Religious Studies at Mount Royal University and Affiliate Associate Professor of Religion at Concordia University, Canada. He works on religion in Brazil and theory of religion. He is co-editor (with Gregory Price Grieve) of *Historicizing 'Tradition' in the Study of Religion* (2005). He is North American editor of the journal *Religion*, co-edits the book series *Studies in the History of Religions* and edits the book series *Key Thinkers in the Study of Religion*. He has recent and forthcoming articles (some co-authored with Mark Q. Gardiner) in *Journal of Ritual Studies, Method & Theory in the Study of Religion, Nova Religio: The Journal of Alternative and Emergent Religions, Numen, Religion, Religious Studies, Revista de Estudos da Religião (Rever)* and *Studies in Religion\Sciences religieuses*.

Ingvild Sælid Gilhus is Professor of Religion at the University of Bergen, Norway. She works in the areas of religions in late antiquity and new religious movements. Main publications include *Laughing Gods, Weeping Virgins: laughter in the history of religions* (1997) and *Animals, Gods and Humans: changing attitudes to animals in Greek, Roman and early Christian ideas* (2006). She is book review editor of *Numen* and is editorial board member of *Temenos*.

Rosalind I.J. Hackett is Professor and Head of Religious Studies at the University of Tennessee, Knoxville, USA. In 2010 she was re-elected President of the International Association for the History of Religions (until 2015). She has published widely on religion in Africa, notably on new religious movements, and religion and conflict in Nigeria. Her most recent books are (as editor) *Proselytization Revisited: rights talk, free markets, and culture wars* (2008) and *Displacing the State: religion and conflict in a neoliberal Africa* (co-edited with James H. Smith, 2011). She serves on numerous editorial boards, such as *Religion, Method and Theory in the Study of Religion, Culture and Religion* and the *Journal of Religion in Africa*.

Graham Harvey is Reader in Religious Studies, The Open University, UK. His research interests are primarily in the lived realities and performances of contemporary Paganisms and indigenous religions, but he has also researched ancient Jewish textual issues. His edited publications include *Religions in Focus: new approaches to tradition and contemporary practices* (2009). He is the author of *Listening People, Speaking Earth: contemporary Paganism* (2nd edn 2006) and *Animism: respecting the living world* (2005). He is co-editor of the *Vitality of Indigenous Religions* series.

John Harvey is Professor of Art and Director of the Centre for Studies in the Visual Culture of Religion, The School of Art, Aberystwyth University, UK. He is an historian of art and visual culture and a practitioner in visual and sonic fine art. His research field is the visual culture of religion. He has written several books including *Photography & Spirit* (2007); *The Appearance of Evil: apparitions of spirits in Wales* (2003); *Image of the Invisible: the visualization of religion in the Welsh Nonconformist tradition* (1999); and *The Art of Piety: the visual culture of Welsh Nonconformity* (1995). His art practice is represented in *The Pictorial Bible* (2000, 2007, 2011), and *The Aural Bible* (2011) series of exhibitions, performances and texts. He is a member of the editorial board for the journal of *Biblical Reception* (2010).

Titus Hjelm is Lecturer in Finnish Society and Culture at University College London, UK. His main areas of expertise are cultural sociology, sociology of religion, social problems, social theory, media and popular culture. His research focuses on the role of minority religions in contemporary societies and the media treatment of alternative religion. He is editor of *Religion and Social Problems* (2011) and co-editor of the *Journal of Religion in Europe*. He has published several book in Finnish and articles in journals such as *Social Compass* and *Journal of Contemporary Religion*.

Jeppe Sinding Jensen is Associate Professor in the Department for the Study of Religion, Associated Researcher, at MIND*lab*, and co-ordinator in the research unit Religion,

Cognition and Culture, all at Aarhus University, Denmark. Current main areas of interest include the philosophy of science for the study of religion and culture, post-analytic philosophy and semantics, theories of narrative and discourse, the relations between cognition and culture, cultural and moral psychology, and method and theory in the study of religion. Major book publications include: *Rationality and the Study of Religion* (ed. with Luther H. Martin 2003), *The Study of Religion in a New Key* (2003), *Myths and Mythologies: a reader* (2009). Forthcoming is *Meaning – in religion, cognition and culture*. He is an editorial board member of *Method & Theory in the Study of Religion* and editor of the book series *Religion, Cognition, and Culture*.

Hubert Knoblauch is professor of General Sociology at the Technical University of Berlin, Germany. His main areas of work are the sociology of knowledge, communication and religion. His books selected include *Populäre Religion* [Popular Religion] 2009; *Visual Analysis: new developments in the interpretative analysis of video and photography* (co-edited with Alejandro Baer, Eric Laurier, Sabine Petschke and Bernt Schnettler, a special issue of *Forum Qualitative Social Research* 3 (2008)); *Video Analysis: methodology and methods – qualitative audiovisual data analysis in sociology* (co-edited with Bernt Schnettler, Jürgen Raab and Hans-Georg Soeffner 2006; 2nd edn 2009); *Qualitative Methoden der Religionsforschung* [Qualitative Methods in Religious Studies] 2003; *Religionssoziologie* [Sociology of Religion] 1999.

Kim Knott is Professor of Religious Studies at Lancaster University, UK, and until recently was Director of a major UK research programme on 'Diasporas, Migration and Identities'. She works in the fields of religion, space and place, and religion and public life, and, with Elizabeth Poole and Teemu Taira, is completing a book on *Media Portrayals of Religion and the Secular Sacred*. Her books include *Diasporas: concepts, intersections, identities* (ed. with Seán McLoughlin, 2010), *The Location of Religion: a spatial analysis* (2005), and *Hinduism: a very short introduction* (2000). She is on the editorial boards of *Religion, South Asian Diasporas* and *Journal of Contemporary Religion*.

Barry A. Kosmin is Research Professor in the Public Policy and Law Program at Trinity College, USA, and Founding Director of the Institute for the Study of Secularism in Society and Culture. He is a sociologist and has been a principal investigator of the American Religious Identification Survey series since its inception in 1990 as well as national social surveys in Europe, Africa and Asia. His publications include *One Nation Under God: religion in contemporary American society* (1993) and *Religion in a Free Market* (2006). He is a former joint editor of the journal *Patterns of Prejudice*.

Seth D. Kunin is Professor in the Anthropology of Religion and Pro-Vice-Chancellor (Arts and Humanities) at Durham University, UK. His main areas of work are Neo-Structuralism, identity, crypto-Judaism (particularly in New Mexico) and biblical and rabbinic myth and ritual. His main publications include *Juggling Identities* (2010), *We Think What We Eat* (2004), *Religion: the modern theories* (2003) and *The Logic of Incest* (1995). His work has been published in journals such as *Religion, Temenos* and *Journal for the Study of the Old Testament*.

Esa Lehtinen is Professor of Modern Finnish at the University of Vaasa, Finland. He has conducted research on spoken interaction in religious, medical and organizational settings. He has published in various journals, e.g. *Journal of Pragmatics, Human Studies, Religion, Sociology of Health & Illness* and *Text*.

Juhem Navarro-Rivera is a Research Fellow at the Institute for the Study of Secularism in Society and Culture in Trinity College and adjunct professor of Latino Studies at the Puerto Rican and Latino Studies Institute at the University of Connecticut, USA. A political scientist, he has worked on surveys and designed questionnaires for research in Puerto Rico and the USA on political behavior, public health and religious identification. His publications include chapters in *New Drugs on the Street: changing patterns of illicit consumption* (2005) and *Secularism and Science in the 21st Century* (2008) and articles in the *Journal of Ethnicity in Substance Abuse* and *Human Organization*. He is the main analyst of the 2008 American Religious Identification Survey.

Mary Jo Neitz is Professor of Women's and Gender Studies at the University of Missouri, USA. She is a sociologist of religion and culture with interests in methodology, gender and sexuality. She is interested in changing religious practices of ordinary people in relation to religious institutions and the dynamics of global changes. She is the author of *Sociology on Culture* (with John Hall and Marshall Battani, 2003); *Culture: Sociological Perspectives* (with John Hall, 1993; Chinese edition, 2002); *Charisma and Community: a study of religious commitment within the Catholic Charismatic Renewal* (1987); *Feminist Narratives and the Sociology of Religion* (ed. with Nancy Nason-Clark, 2001) and *Sex, Lies and Sanctity: religion and deviance in contemporary North America* (ed. with Marion S. Goldman, 1995).

Chad Nelson holds an MA in Communication from Spring Arbor University, USA. His research interests include co-cultures and intercultural communication.

Wade Clark Roof is J.F. Rowny Professor of Religion and Society at the University of California at Santa Barbara, USA, and Director of the Walter H. Capps Center for the Study of Ethics, Religion and Public Life. A sociologist of religion, his interests currently focus upon the challenges of global religious pluralism and progressive change in American religion. His books include *American Mainline Religion* (with William McKinney, 1987), *A Generation of Seekers* (1994), *Spiritual Marketplace* (1999), and *Bridging Divided Worlds* (with Jackson W. Carroll, 2002); he is co-editing (with Mark Juergensmeyer) a three-volume *Encyclopedia of Global Religions*.

Jörg Rüpke is Fellow for the History of Religion at the Max Weber Centre, University of Erfurt, Germany, and co-director of the research group 'Religious individualization in historical perspective'. His work focuses on the ancient Mediterranean, in particular Roman religion and the history of scholarship. His books include *Religion of the Romans* (2001); *Fasti sacerdotum: a prosopography of Pagan, Jewish, and Christian religious officials in the city of Rome* (2005); *The Roman Calendar from Numa to Constantine: time, history, and the fasti* (2011); *Rationalization and Religious Change in Republican Rome* (forthcoming). He is co-editor of the journal *Archiv für Religionsgeschichte*.

Laurie Lamoureux Scholes is a PhD candidate in the Department of Religion at Concordia University in Montréal, Canada. Using primarily qualitative research techniques, her doctorate explores social responses to interfaith encounters and exchanges in Canada. She teaches fieldwork research techniques to undergraduates in religion.

James V. Spickard is Professor in the Department of Sociology and Anthropology at the University of Redlands, California, where he teaches Research Methods, Social Theory, and the Sociology of Religion. He has published extensively on such topics as sociological theory and methods, the sociology of religious experience, ritual, human rights, globalization and religious social activism. He is the senior editor of *Personal Knowledge and Beyond* (2002) and the co-editor of *Religion Crossing Boundaries* (2010).

Michael Stausberg is Professor of Religion at the University of Bergen, Norway. He is the author of *Religion and Tourism* (2011) and *Zarathustra and Zoroastrianism* (2008). His edited work in English includes *Contemporary Theories of Religion* (2009), *Theorizing Rituals* (with Jens Kreinath and Jan Snoek, 2 vols, 2006–07), and *Zoroastrian Rituals in Context* (2004). He is the European editor of the journal *Religion* and co-edits the book series *Religion and Reason* and *Critical Studies in Religion/Religionswissenschaft*.

Einar Thomassen is Professor of Religion at the University of Bergen, Norway. His special area of research is Gnosticism and Nag Hammadi, but he has also published and regularly teaches on the religions of classical antiquity and the Near East, early Christianity, aspects of Islam, and methodological and comparative issues. His books include *Le Traité Tripartite* (with Louis Painchaud, 1989), *The Spiritual Seed: the church of the 'Valentinians'* (2006), *L'Interprétation de la gnose* (with Wolf-Peter Funk and Louis Painchaud, 2010), and he edited or co-edited *The Letters of Ahmad b. Idris* (1993), *The World of Ancient Magic* (1999) and *Canon and Canonicity: essays on the formation and use of scripture* (2010). He was editor of *Numen* 2000–08 and now edits the *Nag Hammadi and Manichaean Studies* book series.

Alan Williams is Professor of Iranian Studies and Comparative Religion and Chair of the Department of Religions and Theology, in the School of Arts Histories and Cultures at the University of Manchester, UK. He is a specialist in Iranian languages, religions and literature, and has a more general interest in comparative literature, translation theory and poetics. Main publications (all including translations) are *The Pahlavi Rivāyat Accompanying the Dādestān ī Dēnīg* (1990); *Spiritual Verses: the first book of the* Masnavi-ye Ma'navi *of Jalāloddin Rumi* (2006); *In the Mirror of the Stream (Dar Āyine-ye Rud)* (2008); *The Zoroastrian Myth of Migration from Iran and Settlement in the Indian Diaspora* (2009). He is the co-editor (with John R. Hinnells) of *Parsis in India and the Diaspora* (2007). He is on the editorial board of the *Mevlana Rumi Review*.

Robert H. Woods, Jr is Associate Professor of Communication at Spring Arbor University, Spring Arbor, Michigan, USA, where he teaches media ethics and research in the graduate programme. He is co-editor of *Understanding Evangelical Media: the changing face of Christian communication* (2008), and *The Message in the Music: studying contemporary praise and worship* (2007); he is co-author of *Prophetically Incorrect: A Christian Introduction to Media Criticism* (2010). He has published articles in the *Review of Religious Research, Journal of Media and Religion, Christian Scholar's Review* and *Christian Higher Education*. He is the former President of the Religious Communication Association.

David Wyatt is a PhD student at Egenis, the ESRC Centre for Genomics in Society at the University of Exeter, UK. His doctorate considers the role and use of science in everyday police practice. He has a broad interest in cultural sociology, including the sociology of religion, and qualitative research methods.

Robert A. Yelle is Assistant Professor in the Department of History and the Helen Hardin Honors Program at the University of Memphis, USA. His main areas of research are the semiotics of religion, secularization, law and religion, classical Hinduism and British Protestantism. He is the author of *Explaining Mantras: ritual, rhetoric, and the dream of a natural language in Hindu tantra* (2003) and the co-editor, with Winnifred Sullivan and Mateo Taussig-Rubbo, of *After Secular Law* (2011). He is on the editorial board of *Studies in Religion\Sciences religieuses*.

PREFACE

Michael Stausberg and Steven Engler

Why this book?

The introductory essay explains why we think that research methods and methodologies are crucial for the future of the study of religion\s. We find it symptomatic of the state of affairs in our discipline that this *Handbook* is the first volume on research methods in the study of religion\s ever published in English. In the introduction we suggest some hypothetical explanations for this curious and embarrassing neglect.

When faculty at one of our departments (Stausberg's) decided to split the customary graduate-level theory and methods course into two separate courses, the lack of relevant literature in English became obvious. (Fortunately, two colleagues had just edited a volume in Norwegian.) One of the aims of this particular course on research methods is to help students to prepare the ground for their research dissertations (which play a relatively great role in the Norwegian graduate programmes). We hope that the present volume will stimulate the development of similar courses.

Neither of the editors can, nor wishes to, claim to have started this editorial project as an expert in methodological affairs, but preparing this volume has definitely helped us to improve and we have learned a lot. We are grateful to all contributors for sharing their expertise and for their patience in dealing with our various queries and requests for revision, which were typically meant to make technical points clearer to novices (like ourselves). We now hope that others, not least graduate students, will take part in this learning process. We sincerely feel that this may indeed be of critical importance for the further development of our discipline.

Neither of us had the benefit of extensive training in research methods as part of our education in the study of religion\s. In that sense, our own careers are symptomatic of the lack that this volume is meant to begin to address. In other ways, our backgrounds are somewhat atypical. We share an interest in the suspect domains of theory and metatheory, be it theories of religion, theories of ritual, or the importance of philosophies of language and meaning for the study of religion\s. At the same time, we belong to an even more exotic subspecies: theoreticians who are also committed to empirical research. We also share six more specific characteristics. We do historical and field-based work. We work on early modern European religious history and on non-European religions (Zoroastrianism in India and Iran;

spirit-possession religions in Brazil). We are concerned with the importance of theoretical models in the study of these religions. We find ourselves traversing boundaries between histories of specific religions, the history of studies of these religions and the study of religion\s in general (including its theoretical legacies). We both enjoy navigating academic discourses in different languages—a tendency reflected in the multinational authorship of this book. Last, but not least, as we explain in our joint introduction, we believe that methods mark the middle ground between theory and 'data'—and so our exploring methods in greater detail seemed a natural step. In addition, we both have experience with the collegial give-and-take that is involved in co-editing and co-authoring, including our having previously engaged in both these activities together.

Our own standpoint can be described as collaborative, critical, reflexive and reasonably conservative though open-minded. We have, of course, not engaged personally in more than a handful of the methods represented in this book; so far, for example, neither of us has done experimental work nor conducted engaged, committed or activist research, though we see value in both approaches. As scholars of religion\s we wish to retain a certain distance from religious discourses, but we are aware that the scholarly and the non-scholarly discourses are densely interwoven and that (we as) scholars of religion are not only observers but invariably actors on the religious field; moreover we don't indulge ourselves in the illusion that our views are any less ideological or value-free than those of others.

If some methods are not covered in the present *Handbook*, this is not because we wanted to create a canon and exclude other options. The inevitable lacunae are the result of a combination of our own limited perspectives, constraints on space and time, and our inability to find authors in cases where we would have liked to include additional chapters. To our eyes, there are no inherently good or bad methods or methodologies, but there are better or worse options relative to given theoretical stances, research questions and sources. Even if there are no inherently good or bad methods, there are differences in quality and productivity when methods are actually put to use—and we hope that this *Handbook* will help to improve these and to stimulate creativity in the discipline. We believe also that it is important to choose theoretical stances in an informed manner and to be critical and reflexive towards these. We envision scholarship that is transparent in method, dense in theory, rich in data, and clear in presentation/writing.

Work on this *Handbook* went off surprisingly smoothly. Apart from a single chapter that did not materialize, all the authors delivered their pieces on time or within reasonable limits, and all were very tolerant with our suggested editorial changes. Their collective collaboration is more than just greatly appreciated. Our editorial efforts established a plan and laid a foundation, but their work makes up the edifice that you see before you.

Michael Stausberg
Steven Engler

PART I

Methodology

1.1

INTRODUCTION

Research methods in the study of religion\s

Michael Stausberg and Steven Engler

It is generally agreed that **methods**, together with **theories, concepts** and **categories**,[1] are foundational for modern science: knowledge accepted as 'scientific' must be based on empirical materials (**data**) gathered by using methods that are accepted as 'scientific', and their analysis must proceed following rules based on 'scientific' methods by engaging concepts and theories accepted by the respective academic community. Scholars' dreams, for example, are not accepted as scientific data; allegorical interpretation of such dreams is not accepted as a scientific method; illumination is not generally accepted as a scientific category; and astrology is not accepted as a scientific theory.[2] Of course, rules for what qualifies as scientific data, methods, categories and theories are subject to change. The discussions and critiques that motivate such change are a basic task of scholarship. In addition, scientific data, findings and theories are constantly challenged by non-scholars. Conversely, the borderlines between what is science and what is non-science, or pseudo-science, are matters of ongoing debate and negotiation.

The past decades have seen vivid debates about conceptual and theoretical issues in the study of religion\s. The very concept of 'religion' has been challenged as a valid theoretical category; feminism, postmodernism, poststructuralism, postcolonialism, philosophy of language, evolutionary theory, the cognitive sciences and other intellectual developments have raised a number of epistemological, semantic and methodological issues (i.e. questions regarding the nature, construction, foundations and production of knowledge and meaning); there has been a wave of new theories of religion (Stausberg 2009). So far, however, these debates have remained curiously distant from issues of methodology.

The neglect of method in the study of religion\s

Issues of research methods are seldom addressed at conferences. Very few articles on methods have been published by leading journals, even in the one that has 'method' in its title.[3] Methods are rarely discussed in introductory textbooks[4] and separate courses on research methods are seldom included in religious studies programs.[5] In this respect, the study of religion\s stands in marked contrast to other disciplines, which put great emphasis on training in research methods—often in the first year—and which have a strong record of published work on methods, including journal articles, handbooks and specialist volumes. There are no discussions in the study of religion\s that can compete with the level of technical sophistication established in many other disciplines.[6] The present volume is intended as a significant step toward putting research methods more firmly on the agenda of the study of religion\s, especially for graduate students.

There are several reasons for the general neglect of research methods in the study of religion\s. A major one is the fragmentary situation of our research landscape, in which some scholars learn textual methods while others become familiar with qualitative social inquiry as part of their training. This relates to the often-heard claim that the study of religion\s is different from other disciplines because it has no research methods of its own. The fact that the field has no *sui generis* methods is true, and obviously so: almost no discipline does. The analysis of compositions in music comes to mind as a distinct method, but even the study of music uses a range of common methods such as historiography and source criticism or fieldwork. All academic disciplines use a wide variety of methods, most of which they share with others. Fieldwork has never been the exclusive domain of anthropology, and sociologists are not the only scholars who conduct surveys. It is therefore a misconception to think that the study of religion\s is significantly different from other disciplines in its use of a variety of methods; what is different is the scarcity of explicit reflection on methods in the study of religion\s.

Conversely, one often hears that the study of religion\s is a multi- or pluri-methodological discipline. Again, this amounts to merely stating the obvious. How could it be otherwise? Given the complex nature of most of the things, facts or affairs that are studied in the humanities and the social sciences, there simply are no disciplines that could afford to rely on one method only. There is, in fact, a general consensus (at least outside of the study of religion\s) that different methods should, if possible, be combined in order to achieve stronger results. A multi- or pluri-methodological approach is far from an anomaly. What is anomalous is the implicit conclusion derived from this insight, namely that issues of methods do not require attention (because there is no one method anyway). Actually, unless one mistakenly identifies **methodological pluralism** with methodological laissez-faire and dilettantism or with the belief that all methods are equally good for all purposes, one would anticipate precisely the opposite conclusion: that the challenge of having to work with and train students in a variety of different research methods requires substantial and explicit attention and commitment to issues of research methods. Given the nature of the discipline of the study of religion\s, then, we would expect to find a deep and abiding interest in training students in methodology, in refining research methods and in methodological creativity. This is clearly not the case. Rather, method use in the study of religion\s continues to be relatively unsophisticated and surprisingly uniform. It is time for this to change. For a relatively well-established discipline such as the study of religion\s, it is more than a little embarrassing that the present volume appears to be the first handbook of research methods ever published in English.[7]

Methods

As indicated above, the present volume starts from the basic assumption that methods are the rules of the game in scholarly work. Resonating the Greek etymology of the word (from *meta* 'after' and *odos* 'way'), the concept is understood here as a metaphor to refer to a (planned) 'way', a specific way of doing things, an organized procedure. A scientific method, in very broad terms, is the generally accepted mode of procedure in the sciences in a broader sense (including the humanities). In the light of theories, methods construct, collect and/or generate the data for scholarly work. Data are not simply 'out there', independent of the observer and the observation. There are no data without methods and theories. Methods help us to analyze reality but, at the same time, they, in part, produce the data that are to be analyzed. In that sense, by partially producing the realities they then go about to analyze, methods are performative (Law 2004: 143). Methods, and the concepts that inform them and describe them, also have a history, changing across scholarly generations (see Platt 1999: 44–52). The goal of this volume is to give a sense of current methods and discussions of method in the study of religion\s.

It is clear that some methods are more helpful than others (for given purposes and within given contexts), that different types of scholarly work make more productive use of some methods than others, and that all methods impose limited perspectives and select empirical materials (data). These obvious facts, however, do not make methods dispensable, for there is no scholarly (or scientific) work without method(s). This should not be misunderstood as saying that there is one special method that guarantees success, that following a method guarantees success, that methods are beyond critique, or that established scientific methods are the only way of obtaining relevant knowledge (though scientific methods are the only generally recognized way of obtaining *scientific* knowledge). Methods are not a straitjacket; they allow for creativity and new vision. Not everything can be planned out, of course, and not every plan can be put into practice. In fact, scholarly work is often steered more by external constraints, by improvisation and by *bricolage* than by a master plan. While methodological competence will yield solid work, brilliant work is often the result of serendipity. Creative scholarly work does not go against method, but creatively uses methods; as all good tools, methods are refined in use: some wear out and are replaced by others; some are broadened or reoriented in light of their limitations or when facing the threat of perceived methodological hegemony or imperialism (Law 2004).

In a formal sense, research methods are techniques for collecting and analyzing, or enacting (Law 2004) data in scientific or scholarly research. While there is always some degree of improvisation, these procedures or techniques typically follow a plan, a routine or a scheme. These established procedures should not be misunderstood as immutable laws, but as guidelines and examples of established or best practice (which is not to deny the dynamism of practices). Accordingly, the present volume does not intend to regulate or standardize research practice in the study of religion\s but to improve research and to stimulate its further development by providing reflection and suggesting alternatives.

Some key methodological issues

The application and discussion of the underlying principles of these procedures is called methodology. **Methodology** refers both to general technical issues regarding methods (i.e., case or sample selection, data collection and analysis), and to the theory and conceptualization of methods. We will address each of these in turn.

Research design

The first, technical sense of 'methodology' incorporates several issues: e.g. research design; relations and tensions between qualitative and quantitative methods; selection of methods; and means of validating results, including the use of different methods in conjunction.

Research design is covered in a separate chapter in this volume (see Chapter 1.5). Here we will confine ourselves to listing some of the basic steps involved in effective research design:[8]

- Identifying the core research question or problem and the series of specific questions or hypotheses that will investigate, support or elaborate that core issue (What is the goal of the study? What lacuna is it meant to fill? What motivates the desire to generate knowledge on this particular issue? What more specific issues will serve as stepping stones to generating that knowledge?).

- Reviewing the relevant literature (What has been published that is comparable in terms of substantive focus, methods and range of theoretical approaches used with similar issues and materials? What will the proposed study add? Are there experts in the area with whom one can consult?).
- Choosing a basic strategy (What sort of study seems best suited to addressing the core research question [comparative, retrospective, longitudinal, case-based]? Does a qualitative, quantitative or mixed-methods approach seem more promising? [see also below]).
- Deciding on the place of theory (e.g. Is the choice of theory established from the start, as when applying or testing a theory, or will one or more theoretical frames emerge during analysis?).
- Specifying methods of data collection and analysis (Which precise method(s) will be used? How will this/these address the research question and hypotheses? How will a case or sample be chosen, and how does this choice relate to other questions on this list? Is a pilot study or a pre-test of the data collection instrument(s) warranted? How will data be managed?).
- Dealing with logistical constraints (How will limited resources of money, time, assistance be distributed?).
- Assessing the value of the results (To what extent are the results of the study repeatable? What is the integrity of the results? Are the conclusions applicable to other contexts? [these issues are addressed in greater detail below]).
- Identifying ethical values, issues and potential problems (Is the topic researchable or is it too sensitive? Are any additional ethical principles and/or risks potentially involved in the research? What is the relevant institutional procedure for obtaining ethics approval? [this issue is addressed in a separate chapter on research ethics in this volume—see Chapter 1.6]).
- Planning ahead for dissemination (How will the results be presented for peer review? What genre(s) of scholarly presentation/writing will be used? Will these choices impact other aspects of the study, e.g. requiring especially reflective field notes in order to write in a more reflexive ethnographic style?).

Quantitative and qualitative methods

One of the most significant of debates in methodology concerns the use of **quantitative** versus **qualitative** methods. To simplify, quantitative methods employ numerical measurement while qualitative researchers do not. Disagreements reflect basic positions on research design: some advocates of qualitative approaches argue that certain things are simply not amenable to measurement; while some advocates of quantitative methods criticize the subjective nature of qualitative work.[9]

However, it has also become clear that there is significant overlap and that the distinction sometimes breaks down. Quantitative and qualitative methods are often combined in mixed-method research designs.[10] Beyond the sociology and to some extent the psychology of religion, quantitative approaches are currently not very popular among scholars of religion, who appear, as a group, somewhat biased against such approaches. However, one should not ignore the crucial interpretive dimensions of quantitative work such as the construction of variables to measure concepts—think of the intricate question of how to measure 'religiosity'. Moreover, scholars of religious groups—in particular of marginal ones—often neglect to provide elementary quantitative data, which would be very useful for other and later scholars (Pitchford *et al.* 2001). While there are some prototypical quantitative or qualitative methods such as statistical surveys (quantitative) and unstructured participant observation (qualitative), one finds quantitative and qualitative varieties *within* the scope of most research methods (e.g. content analysis, discourse analysis, interviews, etc.).

The distinction between these two types of methods remains widely used, but it is interpreted in different ways. At best, the distinction may be useful to distinguish tendencies and general perspectives on research interests and strategies:

- quantitative methods are often more focused on precision (e.g. closed-ended or categorical questions), qualitative methods on richness (e.g. open-ended questions);
- quantitative methods are often more concerned with generalization, qualitative methods with description;
- quantitative research is often more structured (e.g. emphasizing the use of data collection instruments), while qualitative research is more flexible (e.g. emphasizing the selection of observation sites);
- quantitative methods tend to address relations between variables, while qualitative methods tend to investigate the meaning that individuals and groups ascribe to human or social phenomena;
- quantitative methods often have a more distant relationship to their objects, while qualitative methods presuppose a closer relationship to their subjects;
- quantitative methods generally produce results that are amenable to statistical analysis, while qualitative methods necessarily use less formalized techniques, for example in potentially assessing the representativeness of samples or the validity and significance of results; and
- quantitative methods are generally associated with very structured forms of scholarly writing in the dissemination of results (including literature review, method(s), results and discussion/conclusion), while qualitative methods are associated with a much wider, more flexible and often creative range of genres and styles.

Criteria of excellence

Three well-known criteria for evaluating the goodness of research data are their **reliability, validity** and **generalizability**. In a general sense, reliability refers to the consistency or stability of data or measure of a concept; validity refers to whether an indicator (or a set of indicators) accurately reflects (or measures) the concepts it was designed to reflect or, alternatively, whether it accurately predicts relevant outcomes; and generalizability refers to the applicability of findings beyond the sample of a given study.

The literature distinguishes between different forms of reliability and validity, and methodological research has developed methods for judging and improving the achieved degree of these criteria of excellence (at least for some methods). This has led to the elaboration of various fine-tuned conceptual distinctions. These are best addressed in relation to specific sets of methods in given frameworks of studies (i.e. research designs).

These concepts raise important issues that are relevant when conducting and assessing research. Regarding reliability one might ask, for example:

- To what extent would the findings be different had the data been collected at a different date, with a different sub-group, or based on different source material?

- Would two or more observers or interpreters come to the same, or at least similar, results when looking at the same data (and would two or more researchers have produced the same, or at least similar, data in the first place)?

Regarding validity one might, for example, pose the following questions:

- Are the constructed data sufficiently relevant and specific for the object of study?
- Would findings still be accepted if other relevant theoretical criteria were applied?
- To what degree do the findings relate to people's ordinary lives beyond the context of the study itself ('ecological validity')?
- Would the analysis stand if data collected with other methods were considered? (E.g. would the analysis of a ritual based on a philological analysis of the textual sources yield the same interpretation as one based on participant observation? Would an interpretation based on interviews with the main actors yield the same interpretation as the interviews with observers?)
- To what extent can findings be generalized across the social settings studied ('external validity')?

Regarding generalizability one might ask, for example:

- Is the chosen case or sample sufficiently representative, typical, exemplary or compelling that the findings are likely to apply to relevant broader groups?
- To what extent and in what ways does the analyzed case fit with other cases? Can it be translated to other cases?
- To what extent is the analysis relevant for broader (systematic and theoretical) issues in the study of religion\s?
- What degree of generalizability is appropriate or desirable (from sample to population, or even more broadly to similar populations)? Is this a micro-study that addresses only a particular case?

Obviously, questions such as these are pertinent to research in the study of religion\s. Scholars have suggested several strategies for increasing the validity of research. For engaged or ideologically committed scholarship, findings can be validated in a catalytic manner, i.e. if the study helps the concerned people to improve their situation. In mainstream scholarship, a central form of validation is academic communication, for example by discussion and peer review. Another more specific strategy is known as respondent (or member) validation: in order to receive feedback, scholars present their findings to the people with or about whom they have conducted research. This strategy (which can be practiced in various forms and is only available when studying living groups) can be used as a way to corroborate research findings, as a further step in the collection and analysis of data and/or as a way to enhance reflections on the research process by the researcher. While this strategy can save one from errors and generate new insights, corroboration by the subjects (which can sometimes be unintentional, such as when informants implicitly confirm an interpretation by rejecting it) is not itself sufficient to validate research. Subjects may not understand the scholarly terminology and mode of discourse and may not even have the time to read long texts and—perhaps not only for them—often tedious arguments. While potentially helpful, it can result in conflicts either between the researcher and the group or among the people themselves. In many cases, however, the people we study are genuinely interested in seeing research findings, and such requests should not be ignored.

Another strategy for validating research is **triangulation**.[11] This refers to the use of more than one method and/or more than one source (or type) of empirical materials in a study. The metaphor of the triangle points to the multiplicity of perspectives on method and data.[12] Apart from involving different (or different variations of) methods and data, the concept also refers to engaging more than one researcher (observer) and/or theory. This reflects the view that differences between methods and their various implications need to be actively accounted for. Triangulation is often regarded as part of mixed-methods research. Even if this is not practicable for most single research projects in the humanities, which are typically conducted by one investigator with strictly limited time and resources, integrating elements of triangulation are useful for smaller projects as well. Methodological pluralism does not teach that all methods are equally good or bad for each and every task. In any case, the selection of appropriate research methods is an important methodological issue, which all researchers will need to address.

The concepts of reliability, validity and generalizability underline the necessity of reflecting on the quality of research regardless of the general approach one takes. Yet, these concepts have also been challenged during past decades because of their implicit affiliation to (post) positivist views of science and methodology.[13] Accordingly, other views of science invoke other criteria for evaluating research. Constructivist views, for example, have pointed to credibility, authenticity, confirmability and transferability of research (Guba and Lincoln 1994; Auerbach and Silverstein 2003). Recall also the committed or engaged research mentioned above. Ethnic, feminist or queer theoreticians, on the other hand, would point to concepts such as accountability, caring, dialogue or reflexivity as criteria for the goodness of research (Denzin and Lincoln 2005: 24). Feminist critics, for example, argue that 'validity' and related concepts tend to be interpreted in universalizing and hegemonic terms, failing to recognize the situated and co-constructed nature of truth. That is, the premise that research should be vetted as 'trustworthy' by establishing its fidelity to some objective social 'reality' defines truth as a universal relation to reality 'out there'. This constructs a mode of access to knowledge that is policed by those whose institutional positions are invested in ideological norms like 'validity'; it denies the ways in which the nature and legitimacy of knowledge is a function of situated, and power-laden, interpersonal relations.

Data, theories and methods

This leads us to the second, 'philosophical', sense of the term methodology, which is intimately connected to wider discussions in the philosophy of science and epistemology (see Chapter 1.3 on the latter in this volume). There are some important underlying philosophical (ontological and epistemological) issues, the most general of these being, 'what is reality and how can we obtain knowledge of it?' More specifically, taking methodology seriously forces us to ask hard questions about our research processes, questions that scholars of religion\s avoid at the risk of producing substandard research. At the same time, it is important to recognize that there is no neat correspondence between epistemological positions (e.g. on how we come to know about the world) and methodological stances (Platt 1999: 110–11).

A fundamental lesson from the philosophical end of the methodological spectrum is that data and theory are closely related.[14] Addressing this issue clarifies the place of method. Qualitative scholars often prefer the term 'empirical materials' to 'data', rejecting the positivist legacy of the latter concept. We prefer 'data', for the most part, granted the qualification that the current methodological and theoretical landscape takes a variety of stances on this concept.

One value of the traditional term is to clarify the legacy of Jonathan Z. Smith's often-quoted, but misleading claim that *'there is no data for religion'* (Smith 1982: xi; original emphasis).[15] In one sense, Smith reminds us of one implication of the rejection of logical positivism. As Charles Taylor notes, that early twentieth-century attempt to define meaning in terms of what was verifiable drew a distinction between interpreted data and 'brute data': 'Verification must be grounded ultimately in the acquisition of brute data [. . . i.e.] data whose validity cannot be questioned by offering another interpretation or reading.' This distinction is best rejected, not least due to 'the perpetual threat of skepticism and solipsism inseparable from a conception of the basic data of knowledge as brute data, beyond investigation' (Taylor 1971: 8). If we read 'data' as 'brute data' in this sense, then Smith's claim is misleading because it reinforces the specialness of 'religion' even as it attempts to undermine it. That is, by noting that there are no (brute) data, Smith repeats a well-known but important lesson; however, by speaking of 'data for religion', he seems to imply that there is something special about the religious case. Two issues must be kept separate here: the claim that there are no brute data *period*, for religion or anything else;[16] and the claim that there are no *essentially religious* facts, the religiosity of which is independent of our scholarly operations. The latter, however, is merely a specification of the same point, in effect the other side of the same logical coin; once again, 'religion' is not special in this sense. Granted that all data are interpreted (not just interpretable), this aspect of Smith's famous claim points to one way in which that interpretation takes place in all cases where theory is central, not just in the study of religion\s. There are no essentially religious facts in the same sense that there are no essentially economic or essentially political facts: 'religious', 'economic' and 'political' are terms that scholars (but not *only* scholars!) use to delimit a set of phenomena of interest. That is, there clearly are *data* for religion, i.e. phenomena that have come to be classified as 'religious' through the conceptual/theoretical work of scholars of religion\s, among others.[17] In essence, once we distinguish between 'facts' out there and observational 'data', Smith's famous claim effectively says the opposite of what it seems to say: i.e. 'there is *nothing but data* for religion'. That is, the empirical materials that are accepted as data in scientific (scholarly or academic) communication in the study of religion\s are constructed, collected or produced by methods accepted as scientific, the goodness of which has been evaluated by using some of the criteria mentioned above.

Theory plays a different role in different research designs, and this impacts the role of methods. We can distinguish roughly between different models along an often-disputed continuum of scholarly praxis, which cannot be discussed here in any detail. At opposite ends of the spectrum are the models of theory testing (scientific method) and theory building (grounded theory). In scientific method, a theory refers to a body of statements (axioms and hypotheses), which are constantly being tested and revised, through empirical verification and falsification. Experiments are the classical method of that type of inquiry, while surveys and other quantitative methods play an analogue function in the social sciences. Grounded theory, on the other hand, refers to a model of scholarly practice which does not use data to test theory, but which builds concepts, categories and, ultimately, theory from a dynamic interplay between the collection and analysis of data (see Chapter 2.10).

Between these two extreme models, there are differences as to where exactly theory enters the scene. In our discipline, many projects select empirical materials or cases not because of some theoretical issue or problem that the respective case or material is expected to illuminate, but because students or scholars are excited by some phenomenon that they have encountered, often among friends, in the media, or on their travels. They then start reframing this as a topic worthy of scholarly attention. All too often, the theoretical relevance of the case is then projected on the case *a posteriori*, maybe out of a tentative first analysis, and one or the other theoretical perspective is then applied. The recipe reads: choose a case; choose a theory; add rhetoric and stir.

This, however, is problematic with respect to both theory and method. If we presuppose that data are just 'out there' in the world—like insects sought by an entomologist—then theory and method are relatively minor issues of choosing a net and learning how to wield it. The case is very different when we recognize that the complex interplay between theory, methods and data not only shapes our resulting collection of bugs but plays a basic role in orienting the choice to search for these particular things, in constructing the categories that frame these 'objects' (e.g. 'species', 'insect', 'butterfly', 'wing'), and in guiding our hand at each step of our search.

Apart from being a result of analysis—or sets of statements to be tested—theory is present in the research process in various manners and on different levels. On the one hand, scholarship often operates within shared theoretical horizons, grand theories, or Grand Narratives. Almost any religious fact from the present and the past century, for example, is reflexively interpreted as a symptom of 'modernity' or 'postmodernity' and often linked to the affiliated theory of secularization (or its alternatives such as resacralization). These horizons are metatheoretical because they can be explored by using various theoretical frameworks (critical theory, poststructuralism, systems theory, etc.), which make for a different level of theory. These theories put a theoretical vocabulary at the disposal of scholars, who often combine terms with various theoretical legacies in their redescriptions of empirical materials. Descriptive vocabularies provide yet another level of theoretical imprint. While scholars of religion\s share a wide range of their vocabulary with the non-academic world (starting with the very category of religion), scholarly communication requires a specific form of articulation, which insists on a reflexive approach to our vocabulary and to its definitional and theoretical dimensions. The term 'ritual', for example, is used widely in every possible corner of public discourse, but at the same time it is subject to a wide body of scholarly theorizing (Kreinath *et al.* 2006, 2007), and one expects scholarly uses to reflect the latter in order to pass as scholarly discourse. When analyzing empirical cases, this critical engagement of a theoretical vocabulary within given theoretical horizons and frameworks is a methodological challenge, which amounts to a kind of reciprocal translation between data and theory. Concepts and categories need to be made workable (operationalized) for analysis, and in analyzing cases, theory and data infiltrate each other and can no longer be separated from each other (granted they ever were separable). Of course, different concepts of and theories of religion influence the kind of data and methods that one considers legitimate for use in the study of religion\s. It is through methods that data and theory speak to each other and become part of a shared horizon. Failure to recognize this middle-ground role of methods in framing the complex interplay between empirical materials and theory is likely a further reason that methodology is neglected in the study of religion\s.

Aims and structure

Like all handbooks, the present volume seeks to distill knowledge currently available in the field; it takes stock of past and present practices and aims to help shape the future. Not least because the study of religion\s lags behind other disciplines with respect to methodology, the present *Handbook* does not aim to provide sophisticated technical discussions of methodological details, nor does it aim to address all possible methodological options that might be available for scholars of religion\s. One practical reason for the latter limitation was the difficulty of finding scholars of religion\s who could serve as authors, based upon their having actually used certain methods we considered for inclusion.

A variety of neighboring fields are reflected in the range of methods discussed (e.g. field-work's relation to anthropology, surveys' relation to sociology, and philology's and semiotics' status as separate fields). In the case of most methods discussed in this volume, a wide range of works has been published on the use of those methods in other disciplines, and all chapters provide suggestions for further reading. Given the scarcity of published work on research methods specific to the study of religion\s, our ambition is to prepare the ground for a closer engagement with research methods. Many chapters are the first published work on a given research method by scholars of religion\s. This has been a challenge for the authors (from nine countries) who were selected because of their active familiarity with the respective research methods and their sensitivity to methodological issues.

Compared to a range of other disciplines, not only has there been a lack of interest in research methods among scholars of religion\s, but there also seems to be only a limited interest in actively exploring new methodological options. Accordingly, one of the main aims of the present volume is to sensitize scholars of religion\s to the range of methodological options and the many choices that have been and can be employed in scholarship, as well as to their various limitations. It is hoped that the book will stimulate an appropriate and creative use of research methods and help researchers in avoiding methodological pitfalls. At the same time, the chapters in this volume will help readers to evaluate scholarly work and to develop a critical awareness of strong and weak research. Given the centrality of methods for science and scholarly work, reflections on methods and methodological issues are crucial to determine and improve the quality of academic work. The present *Handbook* thus aims to be of both practical and critical value.

This introductory essay is followed by five chapters that set the stage by addressing some fundamental issues for any kind of research. These include discussions of epistemological problems (Jeppe Sinding Jensen), research ethics (Frederick Bird and Laurie Lamoureux Scholes), research design (Wade Clark Roof), and comparison (Michael Stausberg). Issues addressed in these chapters resonate throughout the rest of the volume.

The other chapter included in the introductory section, on feminist methodologies (Mary Jo Neitz), is not a method in a strict sense but a methodological position that suggests ways of using methods as means to empowerment. Standpoint feminism (highlighted in the present volume), resonates with hermeneutics by pointing to the epistemological implications of bias, yet it does not seek to overcome this but rather to turn it into a constructive tool. Apart from entailing a politicization of research, feminist methodologies put a premium on reflexivity, which is also a key issue in several other chapters. There is very little sense of methodology as empowerment in the study of religion\s. This marginalization of activist, committed, concerned, compassionate, critical, engaged and poetic tendencies in qualitative research in the discipline may well reflect its foundational, customary rejection of confessional, theological approaches.[18] In some cases, however, scholars of religion\s actively support the religious groups with which they are working, for example by sharing advice, supporting them by serving as expert witnesses, or by helping them to deal with state bureaucracies.

The second section of the book offers a sort of methodological menu, allowing readers to choose a method, or contemplate the inter-relations between more than one, at their leisure. The chapters are arranged in alphabetical order (other possible lines of division—e.g. quantitative vs. qualitative, social sciences vs. humanities; text- vs. observation-based, obtrusive vs. unobtrusive, classical vs. recent—all seemed more misleading than helpful). Clearly, there is no particular reason to read all chapters or to read them in this order. We assume that most readers, based on their own perceived interests and needs, will navigate their own course through this book. In order to facilitate this process, each chapter ends with a list of chapters on methods that are 'related' in different ways: those that have a clear affinity with a given method; those that have, in practice, often been used with that method; and those that share common ground in terms of more general issues (e.g. comparison, epistemology, research ethics or research design). This is intended to allow readers to explore their own pluri-methodological networks—to compose their own multi-course meals from the rich menu—and it reflects the fact that methods tend to be neither clearly demarcated nor mutually exclusive. In research practice, methods overlap, even in projects not designed to take advantage of a mixed methods approach.[19]

In composing this methodological menu, we took the current practice of the discipline as our starting point. Readers will notice that some chapters are longer than others, namely the ones on field research and participant observation (Graham Harvey), historiography (Jörg Rüpke), and surveys and questionnaires (Juhem Navarro-Rivera and Barry A. Kosmin). We assigned more space to these chapters since much research currently done in the study of religion\s engages one of these methodological approaches. Even in these cases, however, it turned out that very little discipline-specific technical literature on these methods was available.

Some of the chapters in this volume address methods that are seldom used in the study of religion\s. We include them here in order, ideally, to facilitate their wider reception given their great potential value for scholars of religion\s. While experiments (Justin L. Barrett) are widely used in disciplines such as psychology, they are seldom used in the study of religion\s, with one key exception: the cognitive science/study of religion. Another relatively long chapter—underlining potential value—introduces two methods related to a school of data analysis known as facet theory (Erik H. Cohen). These are techniques for data analysis facilitated by computer software. Network analysis (jimi adams) is little practiced in the mainstream study of religion\s, despite the social nature of religious groups and networks. It also comprises techniques for data collection and data analysis.

In addition, some methods are often invoked by name but rarely put into practice by scholars of religion\s. The notion of discourse, for example, has become prominent in the vocabulary of the study of religion\s. However, this rhetorical preference has not been translated into methodological terms: despite much talk of 'discourse', few scholars of religion\s have used the methodological tools of discourse analysis (Titus Hjelm). Something similar occurs with grounded theory (Steven Engler), which is both a method and a more general (methodological) view on the relationship between theory, data and method: extant work by scholars of religion\s often appeals to grounded theory without actually engaging it. It is hoped that this practice of 'methodological metonymy' (Engler) will eventually give way to more coherent methodological practice in line with standards established in other fields.

Other chapters address a methodological scenario rather than a single method in a stricter sense: field research (Graham Harvey) is a lived context where different kinds of data can be generated, and historiography also uses different ways to collect data which are then scrutinized in source criticism and ultimately framed to form an historical narrative.

Given the centrality of texts to the study of religion, several of the methods discussed in this book address aspects of work with such texts, including transcriptions of oral sources. Philology and textual studies (Einar Thomassen) produce data by analyzing textual sources. While philology is often referred to as a traditional method in the study of religion\s (now in decline, given increasing interest in contemporary religions and decreasing interest in the study of languages), very little has been published about this method by scholars of religion\s.

Since scholars of religion often deal with sources in foreign languages, translation is a key challenge; different problems and issues are here reviewed by an experienced translator (Alan Williams). Conversation analysis (Esa Lehtinen) is mainly a method of analysis of spoken (inter)action. Given the primary importance of verbal (inter)action in most religions one should think that this method would be relevant for a greater share of scholarly work in the study of religion\s. Another variety of textual analysis is content analysis (Chad Nelson and Robert H. Woods, Jr), which has a strong record of application in studies on religion but is relatively little known among mainstream scholars of religion\s.

Other methods offer primarily tools for the collection of data: interviewing (Anna Davidsson Bremborg), structured observation (Michael Stausberg) and free-listing (Michael Stausberg) are primarily used to collect (or construct) data for analysis—in the latter case with a focus on categories. Some methodological innovations depend on technological innovations. The development of video cameras, for example, has allowed a much more fine-grained type of analysis of religious actions, interactions and rituals (Hubert Knoblauch on videography). While questionnaires are devised to collect data, survey methodologies also include techniques for analyzing the data. Factor analysis (Kendal C. Boyd) is an established statistical tool to analyze the inter-relationship between variables and to review the conceptualization of theoretical constructs.

Ultimately, each research method carries a specific philosophical baggage, and by constructing a certain kind of data, all research methods facilitate certain kinds of analysis and thereby privilege certain kinds of perspectives. With some methods, the various philosophical and theoretical backgrounds remain more visible than with others (and sometimes, as in the case of discourse analysis, the theoretical background has become diversified and partly obscured once the methods were used more extensively). The methods sometimes appear as practical applications of the theoretical paradigms (but there normally are different theoretical varieties within such paradigms). Structuralism (Seth D. Kunin), for example, is based on a family of linguistic theories which have been adopted by anthropologists, whose analyses of cultures and religions in turn have inspired scholars of religion\s. Semiotic analysis (Robert A. Yelle) has a related yet distinct historical and philosophical background; in the present context, the focus is on the methodological analysis yielded by these paradigms and theories when applied to empirical materials rather than their significance for theories of religion\s. Hermeneutics (Ingvild S. Gilhus) and phenomenology (James V. Spickard) likewise have long and strong philosophical roots, which have fertilized the study of religion\s throughout its history. Since hermeneutics addresses the crucial matter of interpretation, it has had a wide impact on the humanities and the social sciences; the chapter in the present volume provides some practical advice for scholars on how to approach texts hermeneutically. Phenomenology, in particular, has been one of the foundational paradigms for the early study of religion\s (besides comparative linguistics and anthropology); in the present volume, it is presented as a method of empirical analysis.

During the past decade or so, some areas of inquiry have emerged that pose interesting challenges in methodological terms. These are characterized, to some extent, by specific sorts of data or sources and are related to a series of 'turns' that have changed the shape of the study of religion\s along with other disciplines: e.g. the linguistic turn, the performative turn, the postcolonial turn, the iconic turn, the translation turn, the spatial turn, etc. The impact of several of these 'turns' is felt in the chapters collected in the third section. The methodological dimension of the spatial turn is addressed in a chapter by a scholar (Kim Knott) who has been at the forefront of translating the ramifications of studying religion in its spatial locations to work in the field. Her spatial approach proposes a series of analyses of data collected by a variety of methods. Material culture (Richard M. Carp) and visual culture (John Harvey) have emerged as key dimensions of religion, and both authors emphasize the broad range of phenomena falling within their respective domains. Among the most recent 'turns' is the auditory turn, and Rosalind I.J. Hackett discusses its impact on the study of religion\s. These areas are characterized by interdisciplinarity and, for obvious reasons, by pluri-methodological research designs. However, while the study of music and art history have developed methods for the study of auditory and visual materials, respectively, these cannot be simply copied for the purposes of the study of religion\s. Finally, our lives, including our working lives, can hardly be imagined without the Internet, yet dealing with the promises and perils of this medium in a methodologically appropriate way requires some rethinking (Douglas E. Cowan).

In sum, this book is meant to contribute to progress along the path of methodological reflection and sensitivity in the study of religion. As readers will soon realize, the selection of methods offered and the detail in which they are explored represent some solid strides, but a long road lies ahead. We hope that others will be assisted or inspired by this collective work to continue the journey on their own. In order to recall the steps taken during this initial sortie, and to offer further guidance, all chapters are provided with glossaries of key concepts and sections of annotated readings.

Notes

1 Here and throughout the volume, concepts printed in **bold** are defined in the key concepts section at the end of the respective chapter. We refer to the study of 'religion\s' (following Stausberg 2010a) in order to index a series of theoretical and meta-theoretical questions regarding the referents and framing of 'religion' and 'religions.'

Thanks to Mark Q. Gardiner for helpful comments on a previous draft.

2 The case that astrology is not a science is argued on various grounds: because of the esoteric nature of its subject matter (i.e. on ontological grounds); because it is unfalsifiable (i.e. on methodological grounds); or because its claims are vague to the point of meaninglessness (i.e. on semantic grounds). Moreover, astrological accounts of the characteristics of individuals are so rich and complex that it would be impossible to find sufficient common cases for a double-blind analysis (von Stuckrad 2007: 357–58, 365).

3 Lincoln (1996) is one of the few texts published in *Method & Theory in the Study of Religion* with a focus on methods. Despite the title of this essay, Lincoln's view on methods is remarkably uniform: 'history is the method and religion the object of study' (Lincoln 1996: 225). While this may be so for the history of religions in a narrow sense, the present shape of the study of religion\s requires a wider methodological arsenal.

4 Chryssides and Geaves (2007) is a notable exception. See also Svensson and Arvidsson (2010) in the 'further reading' section.

5 There are many 'methods and theories' courses, but typically methods play at most a minor role.

6 A noted sociologist of religion recently commented that he 'as a reviewer of papers submitted to journals [. . . is] often disappointed and sometimes appalled by the lack of specific information provided about the data and methods employed in their analyses' (Smith 2010: 589). We agree with Smith (2010: 591) when he states: 'Data and methods are not minor technicalities that we should impatiently rush past in order to get to our analyses and findings. They are crucial disciplinary matters that help validate the very worth of our analyses and findings.'

7 Works published in other languages are briefly summarized in the 'further reading' section following the chapter. Stone (2000) edited an interesting collection in which prominent American scholars reflect on their work and the methods they have used.

8 The following points are meant to reflect roughly the chronology of a typical research design process. However, some of these elements presuppose earlier decisions (e.g. the choice to use a survey supported by interviews coming after the choice to use a mixed methods approach, or the decision to allocate money for transcription coming after the choice to work with interviews).

9 Qualitative methods have been criticized for failing to live up to the standards set by quantitative methods, which offer more formalized measures of various criteria for assessing the value of research findings. The kinds of studies common in the study of religion\s (e.g. rhetorical analysis, interviews

and ethnographic fieldwork) have been criticized as ungeneralizable: because it is difficult to generalize from one or a small number of cases; and because data collection, the conceptual frames used to interpret data, and the 'application' of theory tend to be somewhat idiosyncratic. Qualitative researchers, on the other hand, tend to emphasize the constructed, negotiated and situational character of reality and the reciprocal relationships between subjects and objects of inquiry. To some extent, this undermines the ground on which quantitative research often is built.

10 Brink 1995 advocates the use of both quantitative and qualitative methods in religious studies.

11 Some regard triangulation as an alternative to, rather than as a strategy of, validation.

12 In more recent discussions of qualitative research, it has been suggested that the metaphor of the triangle should be replaced by that of the crystal. This also takes account of the centrality of writing styles as forms of inquiry; mixed-genre texts (e.g. combining elements of fiction, autobiography, field notes and more traditional kinds of scientific prose) have become more common in recent qualitative research (Denzin and Lincoln 2005: 5–6).

13 Postpositivism (not to be confused with postmodernism) is a term referring to a number of philosophical challenges to logical positivism; some main challenges include the ideas that theories cannot be reduced to observations, that observation is not theory-neutral, that data are theory-laden, that theories do not cumulate logically, and that science is isolated neither from human agency nor from society (see Zammito 2004 for a review). Postpositivism impacted the social sciences in large part through a relativistic reading of Thomas Kuhn's concept of 'paradigm shifts', though his prompt retraction of this interpretation led to his ideas having relatively little impact in the philosophy of science. More lasting impact in the latter field emerged from attention to the problem of induction and the Quine-Duhem thesis (the underdetermination of theory by data problem).

14 Of course, post-positivist epistemology (e.g. Quine) calls into question the distinction between synthetic and analytic, and hence ultimately between observational and theoretical. Donald Davidson's critique of the scheme/content distinction has similar implications. In effect this relativizes the distinction between data and theory (see Chapter 2.10 on grounded theory, this volume).

15 On epistemological and semantic issues associated with a related emphasis of the map-territory metaphor in the study of religion\s, see Gardiner and Engler (2010).

16 The issue, as always, is more subtle. Taylor grants that certain, in his view, inadequate social scientific approaches could be developed on the basis of what are seen as brute data. The price to be paid would be the inability to explain the intersubjective and common meanings that 'are constitutive of social reality'. In order to get at them we have to drop the basic premise that social reality is made up of brute data alone (Taylor 1971: 29).

17 Smith's often-cited claim has thus served as an influential prototypical statement of 'reverse-*sui-generis* rhetoric': 'When one tacitly talks about religion as if it were an inherently more problematic concept than others, indeed an anomalous one, one therefore tacitly claims that religion is unique while on the surface denying such a claim [. . . T]he logical implication must be that religion is inherently different from all other categories, because it is clear that *all* concepts used in academic language are constructed, contextualized, fabricated, invented, selective, part of schemes of classification, and what else. Furthermore, all concepts [. . .] that operate on a similar level of abstraction are to a greater or lesser extent 'contaminated' by their entanglement in political and other social processes. Religion is not different in this respect' (Stausberg 2010b: 364–65).

18 See Droogers (2010) for a recent attempt to advance the concerned study of religion\s.

19 Michael Pye makes an important statement of this point in his call for methodological integration in the study of religion\s (Pye 1999). Pye holds that 'the discipline of the study of religions requires its own particular gathering, or as we might better say, clustering of methods' (Pye 1999: 190). In his essay he discusses several methodological requirements of such a clustering, namely that they must be adequate to the subject matter (i.e. religions); that they must cross-relate to its alleged four elementary aspects (i.e. the behavioral, conceptual, subjective and social aspects of religions); and that they should be 'recognitional' (i.e. that 'the integral meaning of the subject-matter for the believers or participants in question should be recognised in its own right' (ibid.: 198) even though allowing for tensions, the self-understandings of the believers/participants). Pye argues against the exclusive supremacy of the historical–philological methods and calls for 'the correlation of fieldwork methods with historical methods' (ibid.: 204). There is no space here to discuss this program in any detail, but the crucial issue, in our view, is that the selection and clustering of methods is not determined by the requirements of 'the discipline' but a matter of research design of single studies and must be situated in the data-method-theory triangle for each case (as discussed above).

References

Auerbach, C.F. and Silverstein, L.B., 2003. *Qualitative Data: an introduction to coding and analysis*. New York University Press, New York, London.

Austin, W.H., 1998. Explanatory pluralism. *Journal of the American Academy of Religion* 66(1): 13–37.

Brink, T.L., 1995. Quantitative and/or qualitative methods in the scientific study of religion. *Zygon* 30(3): 461–75.

Chryssides, G.D. and Geaves, R., 2007. *The Study of Religion: an introduction to key ideas and methods*. Continuum, London, New York.

Droogers, A., 2010. Towards the concerned study of religion: exploring the double power-play disparity. *Religion* 40(4): 227–38.

Gardiner, M.Q. and Engler, S., 2010. Charting the map metaphor in theories of religion. *Religion* 40(1): 1–13.

Guba, E.G. and Lincoln, Y.S., 1994. *Competing paradigms in qualitative research*. In: Denzin, N.K. and Lincoln, Y.S. (eds), *Handbook of Qualitative Research*. SAGE, London, Thousand Oaks, CA, pp. 105–17.

Kreinath, J., Snoek, J. and Stausberg, M. (eds), 2006. *Theorizing Rituals. Vol. 1: Issues, Topics, Approaches, Concepts*. Brill, Leiden, Boston.

—— 2007. *Theorizing Rituals. Vol. 2: Annotated Bibliography of Ritual Theory, 1966–2005*. Brill, Leiden, Boston.

Law, J., 2004. *After Method: mess in social science research*. Routledge, London, New York.

Lincoln, B., 1996. Theses on method. *Method and Theory in the Study of Religion* 8(3): 225–27.

Pitchford, S., Bader, C. and Stark, R., 2001. Doing field studies of religious movements: an agenda. *Journal for the Scientific Study of Religion* 40(3): 379–92.

Platt, J., 1999. *A History of Sociological Research Methods in America, 1920–1960*. Cambridge University Press, Cambridge.

Pye, M., 1999. Methodological integration in the study of religions. In: Ahlbäck, T. (ed.), *Approaching religion: based on papers read at the symposium on methodology in the study of religions held at Åbo, Finland, on 4–7 August 1997. Part 1*. Donner Institute for Research in Religious and Cultural History [Donnerska institutet för religionshistorisk och kulturhistorisk forskning] /Almqvist & Wiksell International, Åbo, Stockholm, pp. 189–205.

Smith, C., 2010. Five proposals for reforming article publishing in the social scientific study of religion (especially quantitative): improving the quality, value, and cumulativeness of our scholarship. *Journal for the Scientific Study of Religion* 49(4): 583–95.

Smith, J.Z., 1982. *Imagining Religion: from Babylon to Jonestown*. University of Chicago Press, Chicago.

Stausberg, M. (ed.), 2009. *Contemporary Theories of Religion: a critical companion*. Routledge, London, New York.

—— 2010a. Prospects in theories of religion. *Method and Theory in the Study of Religion* 22(4): 223–38.

—— 2010b. Distinctions, differentiations, ontology, and non-humans in theories of religion. *Method and Theory in the Study of Religion* 22(4): 346–66.

Stone, J.R. (ed.), 2000 [1998]. *The Craft of Religious Studies*. Palgrave, New York, Houndmills.

Taylor, C., 1971. Interpretation and the sciences of man. *The Review of Metaphysics* 25(1): 3–51.

von Stuckrad, K., 2007 [2003]. *Geschichte der Astrologie. Von den Anfängen bis zur Gegenwart*. 2nd edn. C.H. Beck, Munich.

Zammito, J.H., 2004. *A Nice Derangement of Epistemes: post-positivism in the study of science from Quine to Latour*. University of Chicago Press, Chicago, London.

Further reading

Earlier works on methods in the study of religion\s (in chronological order)

Pinard de la Boullaye, H., 1925. *L'étude comparée des religions: Essay critique. II. Ses méthodes*. [The comparative study of religions: a critical essay. II: Its methods.] G. Beauchesne, Paris. (In French, 522 pp.)

The most extensive and systematic treatment of methods and methodology in the study of religion\s ever published. The first chapter discusses fundamental issues such as the arrangement of materials, the definition of religion, the *scientific aim and three stages of the comparative study of religion\s (description: hiérographie; classification: hiérologie; speculation: hiérologie), the distinction between method and opinion, and the three subjective requirements of scholars of religion (sympathy, personal experience, impartiality). The following chapters present comparison (which is fundamental), history, philology, older (evolutionary) anthropology, new anthropology and psychological methods. The concluding chapter discusses 'the solidarity of methods' (i.e. their mutual enhancement), the necessity of detailed monographic work, and criteria for achievements; the book concludes with reflections on the problem of truth.*

Hultkrantz, Å., 1973. *Metodvägar inom den jämförande religionsforskning.* [Methodological pathways in comparative religion.] Esselte Studium, Stockholm. (In Swedish, 227 pp.)

In the introduction, the Swedish scholar (known mainly for his work on Arctic and Native American religions) states that there is no specific method in the study of religion\s and that a good scholar of religion must have a double competence (in the study of religion\s and a neighboring discipline). He identifies four reasons for disagreements in methodological matters: different views on science, different areas of specialization, the impact of evolutionary theories and the range of applications of various methods. He argues that sound judgments in many cases outweigh methodological skills. The book is divided into four main parts: (1) on sources and their analysis (sources in contexts; dimensions of sources; genres and categories; field research; document research; synthetical analysis of sources); (2) problems of comparative research (monographic and comparative research; problems of terminology; types of comparative method); (3) descriptive and systematic research (phenomenology of religion; functionalism; structuralism; ecology of religion); and (4) historical and evolutionary research (comparative histories; evolutionism; archaeology of religion; acculturation).

Ahlbäck, T. (ed.), 1999. *Approaching religion/based on papers read at the Symposium on Methodology in the Study of Religions held at Åbo, Finland, on 4–7 August 1997.* 2 volumes. Donner Institute for Research in Religious and Cultural History /Almqvist & Wiksell International, Åbo. (310 + 281 pp.)

These two volumes of conference proceedings comprise several articles on methods and methodologies, such as 'Challenges in the study of religious values' (Dziedzorm Reuben Asafo); 'Ethnohermeneutics in a postmodern world' (Armin W. Geertz); 'Misreading and re-reading: interpretation in comparative religion' (René Gothóni); 'Remarks on the description and interpretation of dialogue' (Thomas Luckmann); 'On divination: an exercise in comparative method' (Jørgen Podeman Sørensen); 'Methodological integration in the study of religions' (Michael Pye); '"Bringing it all back home": mentalities, models, and the historical study of religions' (Tom Sjöblom); 'Is philology relevant?' (Einar Thomassen) [from part I]; 'Methodological choice and the study of sensitive issues' (Nora Ahlberg); 'From the native's points of view: or daddy-knows-best?' (Monica Engelhart); 'Ecology of religion: a hermeneutical model' (Erika Meyer-Dietrich); 'How to study religion in the Muslim world: reflection on a field work experience in the middle of Morocco' (Abdelrhani Moundib); 'Focusing on fieldwork: Edward Westermarck and Hilma Granqvist—before and after Bronislaw Malinowski' (Kirsti Suolinna) [from part II].

Sharma, A. (ed.), 2002. *Methodology in Religious Studies: the interface with women's studies.* State University of New York Press, New York. (XI, 253 pp.)

An edited volume comprising studies on issues of methodology in women's studies and feminism in history of religions, philosophy of religion, and theology.

Knoblauch, H., 2003. *Qualitative Religionsforschung. Religionsethnographie in der eigenen Gesellschaft.* [Qualitative Research in Religion: Ethnography of religion in one's own society.] Schöningh, Paderborn, München, Wien, Zürich. (In German.)

Inspired by grounded theory, in this book the German sociologist guides the reader through the main stages of a specific research process. With an initial chapter on understanding, judgments, measurement and subjectivity, it has chapters on research design (types of data, selection of methods and research questions of the respective study), observation and coding, interviewing, recording, analysis, and the goodness of research and its representation. The book refers to a wide range of examples, often from the author's own work.

Sørensen, J.P., 2006. *Religionshistoriens kilder. En lille metodelære.* [Sources for the history of religion\s: a brief primer on methodology.] Books on Demand, København. (In Danish, 71 pp.)

This book, by a Danish historian of religion\s, presents and exemplifies historical, philological, hermeneutic and comparative methods (textual and visual sources) followed by a glossary of analytical terms.

Kraft, S.-E. and Natvig, R.J. (eds), 2006. *Metode i religionsvitenskap.* [Method in the study of religion.] Pax, Oslo. (In Norwegian, 275 pp.)

This volume comprises 14 chapters (most written by Norwegian scholars) on the following topics: the relationship between theory and method (Clemens Cavallin), comparison (Michael Stausberg), discourse analysis (Torjer A. Olsen), philology (Einar Thomassen), biographical and autobiographical sources (Lisbeth Mikaelsson), archival research (Gina Dahl), source criticism with Internet sources (Morten Thomsen Højsgaard), field research in the study of mass-produced religious images (Hege Irene Markussen), the interpretation of images in ancient (Egyptian) religions (Jørgen Podeman Sørensen), fieldwork in religion (Richard Johan Natvig), qualitative interview and observation (Trude A. Fonneland), reflexivity (Bjørn-Ola Tafjord), and critical approaches and ethical challenges in the study of contemporary religion (Siv Ellen Kraft). The introductory essay by the editors mainly summarizes the various contributions.

Svensson, J. and Arvidsson, S. (eds), 2010. *Människor och makter: en introduktion till religionsvetenskap.* [Humans and powers: an introduction to the study of religion\s.] 2nd edn. Högskolan i Halmstad, Halmstad. (In Swedish, 188 pp; available to download at hh.diva-portal.org.)

This introductory volume written by Swedish authors has four parts: (1) religion in history and the contemporary world; (2) studies of religion and social order; (3) understanding expressions of religion; and (4) interpreting religious words and images. It has brief chapters on the following methods: history/historiography (Catharina Raudvere), field research (Anna Davidsson Bremborg), interviews (Anna Davidsson Bremborg), statistical analysis and interpretation (Curt Dahlgren), grounded theory (Antoon Geels), source criticism (Jonas Svensson), translation (Jörgen Magnusson), discourse analysis (Jonas Otterbeck), and image analysis (Karin Sjögren).

Kurth, S. and Lehmann, K. (eds), 2011. *Religionen erforschen. Kulturwissenschaftliche Methoden in der Religionswissenschaft.* [Researching Religion: methods from the study of culture in religious studies] VS Verlag, Wiesbaden. (In German, 220 pp.)

This edited volume has an introductory essay and six chapters (by German scholars) on the following methods/ materials: interpretation of textual sources (Ilinca Tanaseanu-Döbler and Marvin Döbler), interpretation of sources from material culture (Peter J. Bräunlein), statistical analysis of quantitative data (Franziska Dambacher, Sebastian Murken, and Karsten Lehmann), participant observation (Edith Franke and Verena Maske), narrative interviews (Stefan Kurth and Karsten Lehmann), videography (Bernt Schnettler), and comparison (Oliver Freiberger). Each discussion of methods is exemplified by one main case or topic.

Selected general handbooks on research methods

Bauer, M.W. and Gaskell, G. (eds), 2000. *Qualitative Researching with Text, Image and Sound: a practical handbook.* SAGE, London, Thousand Oaks, CA.

Bernard, H.R. (ed.), 1998. *Handbook of Methods in Cultural Anthropology.* AltaMira Press, Walnut Creek, CA.

—— 2006. *Research Methods in Anthropology: qualitative and quantitative approaches.* 4th edn. AltaMira Press, Lanham, MD.

Bryman, A., 2008. *Social Research Methods.* 3rd edn. Oxford University Press, Oxford, New York.

Creswell, J.W., 2009. *Research Design: qualitative, quantitative, and mixed methods approaches.* 3rd edn. SAGE, London, Thousand Oaks, CA.

Denzin, N.K. and Lincoln, Y.S. (eds), 2005. *The SAGE Handbook of Qualitative Research.* 3rd edn. SAGE, Thousand Oaks, CA.

Denzin, N.K., Lincoln, Y.S. and Smith, L.T. (eds), 2008. *Handbook of Critical and Indigenous Methodologies.* SAGE, London, Thousand Oaks, CA.

Flick, U., von Kardorff, E. and Steinke, I., 2004. *A Companion to Qualitative Research.* SAGE, London, Thousand Oaks, CA.

Jupp, V. (ed.), 2006. *The SAGE Dictionary of Social Research Methods.* SAGE, London, Thousand Oaks, CA.

Silverman, D., 2007. *A Very Short, Fairly Interesting and Reasonably Cheap Book about Qualitative Research.* SAGE, London, Thousand Oaks, CA.

Williams, M. and Vogt, W.P., 2011. *The SAGE Handbook of Innovation in Social Research Methods.* SAGE, London, Thousand Oaks, CA.

Key concepts

Categories: More general constructs and conceptions of phenomena than concepts; concepts serve as properties of categories.

Concepts: Basic units of thought with corresponding meanings and representations; building blocks of categories and theories; these can ideally be defined.

Data: Empirical information generated and recorded by scholars, as informed by scholarly concepts, categories and theories.

Generalizability: The extent to which findings are valid beyond the specific research context in which the study was produced.

Methodological pluralism: Flexible selection of those methods held to be most suitable for the case at hand and tolerance of other scholars' methodological preferences.

Methodology: Discussion and theory of methods and their philosophical implications.

Methods: Accepted modes of scholarly analysis and production of data.

Qualitative research: Studies not amenable to quantitative measurement, typically focusing on issues of interpretation and meaning.

Quantitative research: Studies seeking to produce data in numerical form and amenable to quantitative analysis.

Reliability: The extent of consistency and stability of data.

Theories: A model, a set of concepts, categories and propositions, or a set of analytical tools that is used to explain or interpret (not merely to describe) a general type of phenomena (not just a particular case). Theories can foster understanding, prediction and/or action.

Triangulation: The observation of a phenomenon from different angles (concepts, data, methods, theories, etc.).

Validity: The extent to which the phenomenon of interest is addressed properly in research.

1.2

COMPARISON

Michael Stausberg

Chapter summary

- Comparing is a commonsense routine cognitive activity; there is no way of getting around comparison.
- Far beyond being a distinct method among others, comparison is an often-unacknowledged yet undeniable part of the scholarly project of the study of religion\s in each of its various approaches.
- There are tacit and explicit comparisons. There are different aims and forms of comparison, and comparison can be performed on different levels.
- While comparison is often referred to as a method ('the comparative method'), it is more appropriate to call it a research design.
- Comparison is embedded in various research methods.

Introduction

The French historian Marc Bloch described comparison as a four-fold project, namely (1) selecting, in one or several different social environments, two or more phenomena that, at first sight, show certain analogies; (2) to describe the lines of their evolution; (3) to observe their similarities and differences; which (4), as far as possible, should be explained (Bloch 1963: 17). Comparison is widely practiced and much discussed across the sciences, including the humanities and the social sciences.

In recent decades, comparison has been a hot topic in the non-confessional study of religion\s. As we will see, this is part of a renegotiation of the identity and the legacy of the discipline. The leading journals have published relatively few examples of comparative studies, but a wide range of publications in many languages have set out to discuss the alleged 'problem' of comparison in the study of religion\s, mostly resulting in defences of comparison and some suggestions on how to improve on its bad reputation.[1] Unfortunately, there has not been much cumulative progress in this 'fractured debate' (Roscoe 2009: 26). Here are some reasons for this lack of progress:

- the majority of the available publications fail to acknowledge or even engage each other;

- these works rarely draw on the vast literature on comparison in various other disciplines and fields; and
- the debate deals with methodological aspects of comparison only on the surface, while in fact addressing underlying theoretical and ideological issues: e.g. views on human nature, on culture, on religion, with the result that '[s]ocial scientists have wasted an inordinate amount of time and ink talking past one another on comparativism' (Roscoe 2009: 43).

To my eyes, comparison as such is *not* the problem. Inadequate comparison, of course, is a problem, but so is the inadequate use of any scholarly operation; that is why all scholarly work and use of methods is subject to correction and improvement in further research. All scholarly methods can be engaged in bad faith and appropriated for various purposes, including apologetic, colonial, ideological, imperialist, racist or sexist ones. Few would blame methods such as discourse analysis, participant observation, philology or surveys if some of its practitioners were found guilty of one or several of the above-mentioned attitudes. Yet, in the case of comparison other criteria are applied, so that comparison as such is denigrated. There are several possible reasons for the apparent anomaly in evaluating comparison. To some extent, this is because the issue of comparison masks more encompassing ideological and political questions such as:

- Can and should cultures and religion be compared?
- Which political or other interests does this serve?

Moreover, the issue of comparison closely resonates with discussions about generalization and reductionism. As we will shortly see, comparison played a pivotal role in the foundational period of the study of religion\s, known in some contexts and periods as *comparative religion*. As with similar disciplines such as anthropology, the major repositioning of the field since the 1960s has cast doubt on the role played by comparison. Some main reasons for the by now widely shared concerns and problems with comparison will be discussed below, but the major theoretical challenge to the comparative project has been the denial of fundamental comparability in religious affairs: if 'religions' are merely colonial, imaginary and rhetorical inventions, if there are no shared traits that could be juxtaposed analytically, if there is no subject matter and no object of our study, then there would indeed be nothing to compare—and the study of religion would not make any sense (Jensen 2001). This, however, is not a methodological critique but a theoretical one (albeit with clear methodological implications).

'Comparative religion': Early comparative projects in the study of religion\s and their continued relevance

All early approaches to the modern academic study of religion\s have been informed by different comparative research designs or methodologies.

In this section we will review some main examples, briefly characterize their research questions and methodological design, and point to continuities with more recent work.

Box 1.2.1 Early advocates of comparison in religious studies

- James G. Frazer (*The Golden Bough*)
- Edward B. Tylor (*Primitive Culture*; 'On a method of investigating the development of institutions')
- Friedrich Max Müller (*Lectures on the Science of Religion*)
- William James (*The Varieties of Religious Experience*)
- Émile Durkheim (*The Rules of Sociological Method*; *The Elementary Forms of Religious Life*)
- Max Weber (*The Protestant Ethic and the Spirit of Capitalism*; works on economic ethics of world religions)

Among the most famous, or notorious, practitioners of comparison are the Victorian anthropologists James G. Frazer and Edward B. Tylor. In addition to his comparative analyses of animism and sacrifice in *Primitive Culture*, which are widely known among scholars of religion, Tylor published an essay in which, based on data from 282 societies, he correlated the custom of ritual avoidance of mothers-in-law with matrilocal postmarital residence. This essay sparked an important debate (Tylor 1889). Frazer's *The Golden Bough* originated from his attempt to explain the local custom of succession of the priesthood of Diana at Aricia (near Rome). This attempt at explanation resulted in a large-scale comparative work that unfolded theories of magic and religion, sacred kingship, dying and reviving gods. The work scandalized the public because of its inclusion of the Christian resurrection in its comparative narrative (a connection which disappeared in later editions).[2]

Frazer's and Tylor's comparative work was closely tied to (though not dependent upon) their evolutionary theories. Contemporary evolutionary theorizing continues to rely on comparative methodology, even if this often remains unacknowledged on an explicit level:[3] the very fact of variation, which is crucial for evolutionary theory, requires a comparative assessment for its interpretation, for example in order to establish the occurrence of natural/cultural selection or adaptations.[4] For this reason most contributions to the study of religion that operate on the premises of contemporary evolutionary theory implicitly or explicitly operate in a comparative fashion.

Comparison played a key role in Friedrich Max Müller's foundational project of establishing a science of religion, which was modelled on the successful new science of language (i.e. comparative philology). In the first of his *Lectures on the Science of Religion*, Müller set out to defend comparison as a promising method, in part as the foundation of 'all higher knowledge' and in part as providing the basis for 'the widest evidence that can be obtained, on the broadest inductions that can be grasped by the human mind' (Müller 1874: 8). Müller expected the comparative approach to 'change many of the views commonly held about the origins, the character, the growth, and decay of the religions of the world' (Müller 1874: 10)—new insights of which many had reasons to be afraid. Famously, Müller wished to adopt Goethe's dictum on languages ('he who knows one language, knows none') for religion: 'He who knows one, knows none' (Müller 1874: 11). This became something like the credo of the nascent field of the study of religion\s, and Müller was quite aware of the potential challenge a comparative perspective could pose for all sorts of religious certainties:

> The very title of the Science of Religion jars on the ears of many persons, and a comparison of all the religions of the world, in which none can claim a privileged position, must seem to many reprehensible in itself, because ignoring that peculiar

reverence which everybody, down to the mere fetish worshipper, feels for his *own* religion and for his *own* God.[5]

(Müller 1874: 7)

The idea that 'no religion can claim a privileged position' is what distinguished the Science of Religion from religious projects of religious comparisons, which often are produced as taxonomies of religious aberrations or as an attempt to prove the superiority of one's own god and religion. As Müller anticipated, such projects are rejected by some religious people who consider their own religion to be incomparable and who fear the implied religious equality of being categorized in a homo-genous class of 'religions' (Strenski 2006: 273); accordingly, the discipline continues to be absent from countries dominated by some religious persuasions. Recall that the very **category** of religion as devised by Müller is necessarily a comparative construct since no one exemplar can exhaust its meaning.

Whatever else it is, comparative religion as practiced by the Science of Religion, therefore, is a fundamentally relativizing project.[6] Sometimes, scholars use this **strategy** deliberately. For a recent example, consider Bruce Lincoln's comparative analysis of the speeches given by the President of the United States (George W. Bush) and the founder of al-Qaeda (Osama bin Laden) on Sunday 7 October 2001. In his analysis, Lincoln shows how both speeches 'mirror one another, offering narratives in which the speakers, as defenders of righteousness, rallied an aggrieved people to strike back at aggressors who had done them terrible wrongs' (Lincoln 2003: 27). In addition to being a brilliant comparative analysis of the use of religious motives in political rhetoric, Lincoln's essay implicitly challenged chauvinist ideas of moral supremacy in the USA and in the Bush Administration.

Where Müller compared aspects of religious traditions such as books and canonical writings in order to arrive at 'a scientific and truly genetic classification of religions' (Müller 1874: 53) as modelled on the classification of languages, William James, in his *Varieties of Religious Experience* (1902), suggested using comparison to explore the specificity of religion. While Müller referred to comparative philology as his model science, James pointed to psychology and psychopathology, which operate by classifying unusual cases with related phenomena. Melancholy, happiness and trance-like states typically occurring in religion are only 'special cases of kinds of human experiences of a much wider scope', and even religious melancholy is first of all melancholy (James 1987: 30). The 'distinctive significance of religious melancholy and happiness, or of religious trances' can be ascertained 'by comparing them as conscientiously as we can with other varieties of melancholy, happiness, and trance' (James 1987: 30). To better understand religious phenomena one has to compare them to the 'mass of collateral phenomena' (James 1987: 31). The alternative, which was unacceptable for James, was to treat religious phenomena 'as if they were outside of nature's order altogether' (James 1987: 30). This expresses an approach to the study of religion\s nowadays termed 'naturalism'. As practiced by, for example, cognitive and evolutionary studies, comparison continues to play an important role—not least in comparisons between modes of cognition or ascriptions of experiences (Taves 2009), whether classified as 'religious' or otherwise. Ultimately, as pointed out by James, every theory of religion is based on tacit comparisons since it must be able to distinguish religion from non-religion, affairs interpreted as religious from those interpreted differently.

Émile Durkheim's main work on religion, *Les formes élémentaires de la vie religieuse* (1912) sought to analyze how religion works in the most elementary fashion by presenting a case study of the most primitive and simple known religion (according to him), namely Australian 'totemism'; this implied a form of 'tacit comparison' (Taves 1999: 277) between religion in simple and religion in complex (modern) society, where the elementary forms were altered by historical circumstances. Durkheim criticized the kind of vague, broad and unspecific comparison practiced by Frazer and, as if to anticipate later criticisms of comparison, he argued that social facts cannot be understood apart from the social system to which they belong so that social facts should not be compared merely because they bear some degree of superficial resemblance, but only when the respective societies 'resemble each other internally', i.e. when they are 'varieties of the same type' (Durkheim 2001: 80). For Durkheim it was 'essential to focus as narrowly as possible' and to base one's comparison only on such societies and civilizations for which one has 'the necessary competence' (ibid.: 80).

Comparison was pivotal for Durkheim's ambition to establish sociology as a true science, which he modelled on the example of biology. In his view—as expressed in his 1895 *Les règles de la méthode sociologique* [The Rules of Sociological Method]—sociology must conform to 'the principle of causality as it occurs in science itself' (Durkheim 1938: 128). As a result, comparison serves the function that experiments do in other sciences: it is an 'indirect experiment' (ibid.: 125).[7] For Durkheim, all sociology, in so far as it claims to be a science, has to be comparative. Analogous to biology, comparison must operate on the level of the (social) species: 'to explain a social institution belonging to a given species, one will compare its different forms, not only among peoples of that species but in all preceding species as well' (ibid.: 138). Given that for Durkheim each phenomenon (effect) can only have one (true) cause, comparatively analyzing concomitant variation (i.e. the interplay between correlation and difference) will reveal the relationships of causality, with permanent causes leading to observed correlations among social facts (ibid.: 131–34). While Durkheim did not apply these principles to the study of religion, they are a fundamental principle of contemporary variations of statistical methods (Ragin and Zaret 1983: 737).

Box 1.2.2 A comparative macro-study

In a comparative-statistical study of degrees of secularization, political scientists Pippa Norris and Ronald Inglehart point to a clear correlation between levels of societal development in terms of (1) the existential security societies can offer its members, and (2) the rate of secularization. Norris and Inglehart, who reject a Durkheimian theory of religion, observe that 'with rising levels of existential security, the publics of virtually all advanced industrial societies have been moving toward more secular orientations during at least the past fifty years' (Norris and Inglehart 2004: 240). They do not claim to have established *the* one cause behind this, and they suggest no less than six explanatory hypotheses, which they test in order to throw light on the observed concomitant variation. This is an impressive example of a large-scale comparative study sharing the methodological legacy of a focus on patterns of relations among abstract variables rather than on single historical cases. The study is based on macro-level data from 191 nations and on survey data from almost 80 societies around the globe, supplemented by several strategies to capture longitudinal trends. The comparative framework follows a so-called most different systems research design (Przeworski and Teune 1970), 'seeking to maximize contrast among a diverse range of almost eighty societies to distinguish systematic clusters of characteristics associated with different dimensions and types of religiosity' (Norris and Inglehart 2004: 37).

Durkheim's analysis of religion in *Les formes élémentaires de la vie religieuse* is based on a quasi-timeless example, yet statistical analysis looking at concomitant variation similarly allows for only limited insights into historical events and sequences that impact on the data. For this reason, causal analysis can require the identification of processes that link cause and effect. Statistical correlations are therefore often supplemented by process analysis, which can corroborate, modify or even contradict statistical findings (Mahoney 2004: 88–90). In comparative-historical research, variables can have different effects depending on their timing and duration, and 'the temporal location of events affects their impact on outcomes of interest' (Mahoney 2004: 91).

Contrary to the variable-based strategy, as represented by Durkheim, which seeks trans-historical generalizations, for Max Weber such generalizations served another goal, 'genetic explanation of historical diversity' (Ragin and Zaret 1983: 743). Where Durkheim compared in order to generalize, Weber was concerned with individual cases and compared in order to understand diversity and single cases. A well-known example is Weber's thesis that the Protestant ethic is one adequate cause (even if not the only and maybe not even the major one) of (the spirit of) modern capitalism. This thesis is unfolded in his famous book *Die prot-estantische Ethik und der Geist des Kapitalismus* [The Protestant Ethic and the Spirit of Capitalism] (1904–05, 1920). In addition, it is tested in a series of extended in–depth case studies on the economic ethics of world religions (with published essays on China, India and ancient Judaism, and planned essays on Islam, early Christianity and Russian Orthodoxy).[8] By means of intercultural comparison:

> Weber was not only able to show that, when the Protestant ethic was absent, modern capitalism as a rule did not arise [. . .] but he also indicated that similar rational-ethical influences among certain other sects in other cultural areas [. . .], although they did not produce capitalism of the modern Western kind, nevertheless resulted in economic rationalization and success [. . .] compared with the surrounding popula-tion of the same cultural areas. This seems to indicate an adequate causal relationship between the ethics of certain kinds of sects and a generalized concept of capitalism.
>
> *(Buss 1999: 326)*

Where Durkheim had sought to analyze the very nature of social facts, to Weber historical configurations were mainly of interest because of their cultural significance for the observer. Weber was not so much interested in the origin and functions of religion as such, but in the (motivational) impact of religions on human action, behavior, and the cultures created by interacting humans. While Durkheim challenged the analyst to free the mind from presup-positions, Weber acknowledged the impossibility of a science free of presuppositions, and he challenged observers to heuristically reconstruct their presuppositions into testable scholarly hypotheses. This strategy informs Weber's notion of the ideal-type, which plays a crucial role for his comparative project. An ideal-type does not mirror reality; it is a model that selects and highlights elements, from complex and messy historical reality, which the observer deems characteristic or relevant for the phenomenon under investigation. Ideal-types aid in concep-tualization and in the identification of adequate causes; they help to understand and to explain. Ideal-types are created by exaggerating selected aspects and, at the same time, by connecting diffuse and discrete phenomena; they are therefore necessarily one-sided, and it remains for research to comparatively establish the extent to which reality matches up to the ideal-type (Weber 1988: 191). Ideal-types don't occur in reality (Weber calls them 'utopian'), but reality can be compared to them. In historical reality no priests, prophets or mystics will entirely correspond to ideal-types of 'the priest', 'the prophet' or 'the mystic' as constructed by scholars, but the ideal-types can serve to analyze the historical dynamics of religions.

Box 1.2.3 An ideal-typical comparative study

A recent work on the basis of Weber's methodology is Martin Riesebrodt's comparative study of fundamentalism in the USA (early twentieth century) and Iran (mid-late twentieth century). Riesebrodt advocates a rather broad definition of fundamentalism (as a form of radical traditionalism). He elaborates a typological differentiation between different types of fundamentalism, which assists in describing historical developments (for example from an escapist subculture to a terrorist secret society) (Riesebrodt 1990: 24). Based on his analysis of the available research literature, Riesebrodt conducts a comparative analysis of American and Iranian fundamentalism with respect to similarities and differences in their profile, their ideology, their supporters and the causes for the supporters' mobilization. This results in a new interpretation of fundamentalism as radical-patriarchal movements of protest that contrast the ideal of a morally integrated religious society with that of a modern society perceived to be characterized by class and conflict (Riesebrodt 1990: 251).

An alternative to the ideal-typical approach to comparative concept analysis and formation is the prototypical approach. A prototype is not an idealized version (an ideal-type), but a best case—a central, salient, typical instance of a category as per common sense. A prototype can then serve as the starting point for comparative work.[9] An extension of prototypes is known as 'radical categories'. Radical categories have a central case (a prototype) but also a number of purely conventional deviations or variations 'which cannot be predicted by general rules' (Lakoff 1987: 84). Consider the case of 'a surrogate mother', or a tourist church (i.e. a church predominantly used and maintained for tourists). Radical categories are comparative and allow for comparisons.

Rejecting phenomenology—jettisoning comparison?

In my impression, the project of comparative religion is intimately linked, in the shared memory of many scholars, to the phenomenology of religion. It seems that comparative approaches now appear suspicious as a result of the general move away from phenomenology as the dominant model, trend or paradigm in the study of religion\s.

However, when reviewing the main work done by phenomenologists of religion, one notices that it has rarely been comparative in a technical and explicit sense. On my reading, even if Eliade's general interpretation of religion was informed by a contrast between archaic and modern religiosities, between cosmos and history, the work done by phenomenologists has typically been cross-religious and synthetic rather than comparative; the phenomenologists were interested more in the general structure, 'manifestations', 'typology', or 'anatomy' of religion and in constructing cross-religious categories than in comparing religious phenomena from different cultural contexts. Yet, somewhat paradoxically, their work has, in retrospect, implicitly served as a straw doll for attacks on the validity and reliability of comparison in religious studies.

One major objection has been an overemphasis on likeness rather than on difference; this criticism hits the assumed cross-cultural design of the phenomenologist categories, into which scholars had amassed data from a wide range of religions, basically in order to fill the categories up rather than to diversify them. Some critics find difference in general more 'interesting' than likeness (Smith 1982: 35), while others warn that even differences can become essentialized and thereby dangerous (Doniger 2000: 66–67). It all depends on the purpose of a given study: some may be more interested in interpreting and explaining similar or shared features while others are concerned with the singularity of the respective case— both interests require a (tacit or explicit) comparative stance. In observation, both likeness and difference capture attention and may require explanation, and in actual practice both will be necessarily highlighted in analysis.

Box 1.2.4 A phenomenological comparison

Rudolf Otto's book *West-östliche Mystik* [Mysticism East and West] is one of the few explicitly comparative monographs published by a scholar often identified (even if not self-identified) as being part of the phenomenological tradition. In the first part of this book Otto discusses the likeness between the German theologian Meister Eckhart and the Indian philosopher Adi Shankara (who serve as representative embodiments of West and East respectively), while the second part analyzes differences between the two.[10] In his introduction, Otto makes it clear that his comparative analysis points to an 'inner affinity of basic motives of the soul of mankind', which transcend external contexts, while he rejects the claim that mysticism would be the same everywhere (Otto 1932). While Otto's research design can certainly be criticized on several epistemological, theoretical and methodological grounds, it is not true to say that he was interested in likeness only.

Apart from rejecting the presumed phenomenological heritage, the general scepticism towards comparison also reflects another development in the study of religion\s. Whereas earlier scholars of religion\s, in line with Max Müller's above-cited statement, saw themselves as generalists (even though all invariably had some area of specialization), after the demise of phenomenology it is typically considered essential for scholars of religion to have primarily an in-depth specialist expertise, either on one religion (e.g. Islam), one area (e.g. Mediterranean religion or East Asian or Japanese religions), or in one field (e.g. New Religious Movements): 'generalization was reduced to the status of an avocation' (Smith 1995: 411).[11] With the exception of fields such as the sociology and psychology of religion, competence when dealing with primary sources in the respective languages and fields has become of paramount importance. Comparative analyses based on a literature review are often considered illegitimate (while this would be perfectly normal in many social sciences); the high demands placed on comparative work make many scholars hesitate to attempt it. However, there are also some historical fields where comparative research is more established than in others. The study of Indo-European religions, which have comparative analysis as their very raison d'être, is an extreme case. In the recent field of so-called New Religious Movements most scholars work on more than just one religious group and ask questions (e.g. sex and conflict; apocalypticism and violence) that require comparative designs. Generally, however, the 'emergent ethic of particularity' (Smith 1995: 411) has led to an emphasis on context and complexity, which have been two leitmotivs in a widely shared scepticism towards, or an occasional complete rejection of, comparative research designs.[12] Yet even an analysis of contextualized and complex cases rests on categories that are generally informed by and allow for comparative perspectives. So far, it is difficult to imagine an academic discussion entirely based on context-thick local concepts. Moreover, a rich analysis of context and complexity often requires inter- and intra-contextual comparison, for example with regard to diversity of contexts, differences between various actors, factors within the respective context, etc. Scepticism towards comparisons between religions, or aspects of different religious traditions or phenomena, is also informed by an increasing emphasis on the internal inconsistency and incoherence of religious traditions and the rejection of 'essentialism'; in a way, then, external comparisons have been replaced by internal ones. Yet, comparison can also be a very effective tool for undercutting essentialisms and for pointing to diversity and variety.

Another typical concern with comparison has been the critique, often called the deconstruction, of relevant categories—beginning with 'religion' but extending to virtually every category in the vocabulary of the discipline. Logically, even if not methodologically, these important studies cannot avoid comparative perspectives: e.g. comparing how a given concept was used in different periods, whether or not there are similar if not equivalent terms in different languages, cultures and religious traditions,[13] how these terms are used and understood in different discourses, or whether other terms might be more appropriate to analyze a given set of affairs.

Box 1.2.5 Costs of and problems with comparative designs

- Requires extensive preparations
- Can require various sorts of specialist expertise
- Time-consuming
- Difficult to find matching sets of source materials
- Prone to mistakes because of complexity
- Wide-ranging comparisons sacrifice depth for breadth
- Insensitive to contexts
- Prone to confusion because of surface similarities or differences
- Can be poorly received by specialists
- Potentially static and essentializing

One typical way of working with general categories in the post-generalist age has been the publication of edited volumes where specialists on various religions discuss relevant aspects of 'their' respective expertise in relation to the topic at hand. Most of these volumes cannot be said to be comparative in any relevant sense; they are not even cumulative or synthetic but rather additive or juxtapositional.

An ambitious exception was the Comparative Religious Ideas Project (CRIP) directed by the Boston theologian and philosopher Robert Cummings Neville, which in a dense communal inquiry brought together specialists in several Eastern and Western religious traditions with theologians and sociologists. Apart from comparing religious ideas (or rather the ideas of different religions on issues such as ultimate realities, truth and the human condition) the CRIP was set up to explore and defend the very possibilities of comparative work in religious studies (see Wildman 2006; Neville and Wildman 2001a). In formal terms, the CRIP suggests the following comparative procedure (the philosophical implications and historical applications of which cannot be addressed here):

- comparative work depends upon categories, which act as 'third terms' to which findings are related;

- these categories are not neutral but have an historical background (speaking of a human condition, for example, is rooted in twentieth-century existentialism, while many other categories are rooted in Western Christianity);
- the categories need to purified, abstracted or generalized (thus becoming usefully vague, i.e. neither so unspecific to be meaningless nor so specific as to exclude from the start a range of phenomena that might be discussed in relation to the respective categories);
- potentially relevant phenomena will then be translated to (rather than merely subsumed under) the respective category, which thereby gains greater specificity and is enriched by distinctions and differentiation (comparison 'is to say how the specifications are similar and different in terms of the category in respect to which they are compared' (Neville and Wildman 2001a: 16)); and
- comparison is less the assertion of hypotheses than it is the very process of making and refining such assertions (comparisons are therefore always provisional and never fixed).

Not only is this a potentially endless hermeneutical procedure, which at some point in time is cut off for pragmatic reasons, but it is also inherently vulnerable to correction and misunderstanding. In order to test the validity and reliability of the comparative categories, Neville and Wildman devised a phenomenological 'thick description' of the religions. This seeks to describe several factors: the respective religious idea with respect to the ways in which they are expressed by adherents ('intrinsic representation'); how the world looks from these perspectives ('perspectival understanding'); how they relate to other ideas and which implications they have ('theoretical representation'); their practical bearing ('practical representation'); and their singularity, i.e. their resistance to comparison (Neville and Wildman 2001b: 202–5). In some cases, there are even negative results: i.e. no relevant findings emerge when

---

Box 1.2.6 Two examples of in-depth micro-studies

Two substantial recent examples of two-case comparative studies, which combine in-depth philological and historical knowledge with an interest in general categories and an awareness of methodological challenges, are Barbara A. Holdrege's *Veda and Torah* (Holdrege 1996) and Oliver Freiberger's *Der Askesediskurs in der Religionsgeschichte* (Freiberger 2009, 2010). Similar to the procedure applied by the Comparative Religious Ideas Project, both works start with a category, for which the authors, given their previous studies, had reasons to expect the selected traditions to offer relevant examples and source materials. Both start with a relatively vague understanding of their key concept (respectively scripture and asceticism), develop their research question, give an introduction to the sources and devote the most substantial part of their study to the analysis of their textual sources (separated by tradition) with regard to a set of themes related to their category, such as creation, cognition/revelation and practice with regard to Veda and Torah (Holdrege), or statements on the spatial and temporal location of ascetics and their dealing with bodily needs in Brahmanic and early Christian sources (Freiberger). In a final part, the findings from the sources are translated into a more specific and differentiated model of the respective category, which in turn links these studies to more general theoretical discussions in the field. In Freiberger's case, he refines the methodology by not addressing asceticism but discourses on asceticism in Brahmanical and early Christian texts; this allows him to highlight varieties not as confounding variables but as part of variety of (perceived) behavior.

approaching a religious tradition with a specific comparative agenda; in some cases traditions may share comparable understandings of some ideas but assign a very different importance and function to such ideas (Neville and Wildman 2001b: 201).

The CRIP was interested in comparative theology. Ideas are of course only one aspect of religions that is amenable to comparison: e.g. architecture, attitudes, behavior, discourses, events, experiences, groups, institutions, objects, performances, rhetoric, roles, or the status of religions in relation to other societal systems.[14]

Holdrege's and Freiberger's books (see Box 1.2.6) compare phenomena across distinct and remote religious traditions. In both cases the scholars possess the philological expertise to work on the primary sources of these distinct religious traditions. This was an exceptional circumstance, and Freiberger writes in his introduction that the choice of topic was in fact dependent on his philological expertise rather than the reverse: he did not acquire this expertise in order to conduct his study (Freiberger 2009: 34). Because of the large amount of time and mental energy necessary to acquire these skills, historians of religion are as a rule much less inclined to select cases on the grounds of hypotheses or theories; in most cases the research questions arise from the materials rather than the other way around, as is the case in research traditions in history and the social sciences.

Comparison between religious phenomena in neighboring religious traditions—such as ancient Greece and Rome, or Tibetan, Japanese and Chinese varieties of Buddhism—are closer to hand; philological expertise is often acquired in combination. Such comparisons overlap with different geographical settings (Greece and Italy; Tibet, China and Japan) within larger spatial units (the Mediterranean; East Asia). There are, of course, comparisons between varieties of religious traditions on national, regional and local levels or with regard to different groups and institutions within given religious traditions and territories. There are also studies on the different fate of religion(s) in different countries or continents (such as North America and Europe). Moreover, the forms, functions and structures of a religion can be compared with respect to different periods of time. The list can go on,[15] but for some obscure reason most of such comparative works are not seen as falling under 'the comparative method'.

Comparison in the study of religion\s is not limited to the subject area, but also to second-order discourses such as the different historical constructions and discursive representations of religions in scholarship. Comparative analyses of different scholarly interpretations of

---

Box 1.2.7 Checklist for comparative work

- Become familiar with the relevant research literature
- Become familiar with possible primary sources
- Check with experts
- Conduct a critical analysis of earlier interpretations
- Explore the research question and its feasibility
- Translate the research question into relevant concepts, categories and variables
- Decide on appropriate cases
- Investigate valid sources and select appropriate methods
- Reflect on what the respective materials are a case of
- Re-describe and rectify descriptions in light of the comparative analysis
- Visualize cases/variables/factors (matrices, etc.) as a helpful analytical tool

---

religious affairs are part of the routine business of academic work, and comparison (of coders, interpretations, including the feedback of the subjects of research) is pivotal for the validation of research. Finally, in methodological terms, a comparative analysis of data and interpretations produced by using different methods, where applicable, is generally recommended ('triangulation').

Varieties of comparative designs

The literature offers several attempts to distinguish between different comparative research designs. In the study of religion\s, Jan Platvoet (1982) distinguishes between unlimited and limited comparisons, i.e. comparisons that are applied to all religions without distinction ('unlimited') and comparisons that are applied to religions that are geographically or historically contiguous or that belong to a similar type of religion ('limited'). Platvoet explores the limited form of comparison, which he structures around the three key notions of field, process and context, and which he applies to an analysis of ritual communication ('prayer') in three distinct religious traditions in Ghana, Suriname and the USA (Platvoet 1982).[16] More widely known and quoted is Jonathan Z. Smith's (1993, 1982) division into four classical modes or styles of comparison:

- ethnographic (frequently idiosyncratic unsystematic, based on travellers' impressions);
- encyclopaedic (cross-cultural material arranged by topics, mostly based on readings);
- morphological (logical-formal classification in terms of increased organization); and
- evolutionary (in the humanities a temporal arrangement of morphological classification).

Among these, Smith considers only morphological comparisons to have stood the test of time. To this list he adds three more recent approaches which seem to have sprung out of the classical ones: the statistical, the structural and the systemic. Smith holds that we now 'know better how to evaluate comparisons, but we have gained little over our predecessors in either the method for making comparisons or the reasons for its practice' (Smith 1982: 35). Even back in 1982, that statement may have been true only when restricting one's sample to literature produced by scholars of religion.

Various forms, modes and varieties have been distinguished by a variety of scholars from other disciplines. In his useful survey of comparative history, historian Hartmut Kaelble offers several distinctions. One is generalizing versus individualizing comparisons, with the former being interested in establishing rules of human social life valid for all or most societies and the latter seeking to explore differences and distinct paths of development in different societies (Kaelble 1999: 26).[17] There are several sub-types of these two main varieties, which are sometimes referred to as individualizing, variation finding, encompassing and universalizing; or contrasting, macro-causal, generalizing, inclusive and universalizing (Kaelble 1999: 30–33). Kaelble also refers to a comparison of totalities (such as civilizations) and the more widespread comparison of aspects of such totalities (Kaelble 1999: 36). This is often referred to as macro- versus micro-comparison. Another distinction is based on the number of cases, where N-cases (see Norris and Inglehart 2004, above) and two cases (see Freiberger, Holdrege, Otto, and Riesebrodt, above) are most widespread, but there are also examples for other numbers (such as three, four or five cases).[18]

Of a more technical nature is the distinction between the so-called most-similar systems design and the so-called most-different systems design (Przeworski and Teune 1970: 31–39). This refers to the units of analysis. Most-similar designs tend to downplay the importance of similar variables in cases that are closely related (such as Scandinavian societies) and to focus on observed differences; however, even when one assumes that contextual variables are less important, these can never be entirely ignored, and the conclusions can only be valid for restricted areas (yielding middle-range theories). If one wants to generalize beyond such areas (recall the study by Norris and Inglehart) one needs to maximize differences between cases. In such circumstances, sampling highly different cases (such as countries) may help to identify the relevant independent variables (della Porta 2008: 214–16).

Main aims and functions of comparative work

Even if one sometimes cannot help finding some phenomena to be strikingly similar, academic comparisons are not discoveries of relations given by nature; they are the products of academic work, starting with the scholarly categories that serve as their points of departure. Even if scholarly comparisons need to proceed by respecting the generally accepted rules of the trade and are of main interest to the academic community, they may well have purposes that are of interest beyond the academy (and which thereby can contribute to the cultural or societal relevance of the discipline). One of the main motivations of the early comparative study of religion\s was precisely the idea that Christianity was not over and above all other religions, but that it was embedded in specific religious and historical contexts; in this way, comparative religion went against specific truth claims established by religious institutions. Comparative work done in the spirit of liberal theologies wished to facilitate inter-religious dialogue and understanding. Critical comparative strategies can pursue other interests: they can aim at challenging different sorts of nationalist or religious chauvinisms, and they can help to challenge stereotypes and prejudices which are often directed at little-known religions. They can be de-normalizing and destabilizing. Comparative studies can both boost and challenge national or religious identities. Yet, none of this is specific to comparative research designs.

In more specific ways, comparison is of paramount importance for some key aspects of scholarly work in the study of religion\s. Some of these have already been mentioned. To begin with, the formation of analytical and theoretical categories requires comparative work. All our categories are based on concepts that have a specific historical background and the semantic and pragmatic baggage of these concepts is to a greater or lesser extent transformed into scholarly categories (but keeps on informing them). Some varieties and examples of this process have already been mentioned: e.g. ideal-types, prototypes and radical categories, the process suggested by the Comparative Religious Ideas Project, or categories such as asceticism, fundamentalism, religion and scripture. Comparative work leads to conceptual and typological distinctions. Think of distinctions between different types of charisma and authority, or between different historical varieties of dualism.[19] These categories help to describe and to analyze empirical facts and also serve as platforms for more general, cross-cultural observations and for more systematic and synthetic works, which, in the architecture of knowledge, can serve as middle-range intermediaries between the levels of historical analysis on the one hand and general theories of religion on the other. At the same time, comparisons often undercut generalizations that were taken for granted.

Comparisons are invaluable for the construction and testing of hypotheses. This applies both to intra- and inter-religious comparisons. For example, any hypothesis on relations between religion and violence (or rather specific aspects and types of religion and specific forms of violence) will remain a mere assertion unless it is refined and tested. Transforming widely held assumptions about religion\s into testable hypothesis and testing them empirically can be an important task of the study of religion\s. Testing hypotheses often results in new questions. Comparison can function as a heuristic tool. The necessity of looking at two cases (minimally) entails looking at the case at hand from other perspectives. At a more basic level, comparison is part of every process of interpretation and understanding, and a reflexive awareness of one's own interpretative points of departure and their limitations is part of established (but all too often ignored) hermeneutical standards. On a more ambitious level, as a kind of natural experiment, comparative research designs can be important strategies for causal analysis and explanation (recall also Durkheim above).[20] Last but not least, **typologies** or **taxonomies** of religious phenomena, which have been a recurrent occupation of scholars of religion, can only be constructed on the basis of comparison, and the very act of taxonomical **classification** is a comparative weighing of like and unlike, distinguishing homologies from analogies, traits that are shared (for example caused by historical genealogy) from others that are not.

Box 1.2.8 Purposes of comparative designs

* Category formation
* Generalization/systematization
* Construction and testing of hypotheses
* Interpretation
* Explanation ('natural experiment')
* Typologies/taxonomies

Comparison as research design and modus operandi of research methods

In the literature, comparison is generally referred to as a method ('the comparative method').[21] This is misleading in several respects. To begin with, comparison is not *one* method. As noted above, early practitioners of the study of religion\s already used a variety of comparative designs. In addition, a comparative perspective is often merely a mode of analysis, a way to approach a given problem.

Moreover, comparison is most often not practised as a separate method, but as a research design, i.e. as a framework for the collection and analysis of data and the analysis of research problems. Comparative research designs use different kinds of techniques or tools for the collection of data (i.e. methods in a more narrow sense), for example discourse analysis, content analysis, document analysis, philology, hermeneutics, historiography, phenomenology, surveys, etc.

Conversely, while comparative research designs engage specific methods, many methods in turn operate comparatively. It bears pointing out that comparison is part of the working routine of most methods. On this more basic level, comparison works in the most unspectacular ways and is largely uncontroversial. To begin with, the formation of **concepts** and classifications and related forms of systematization rely on comparison, which therefore is enshrined in all research methods. Moreover, comparison of data is standard practice in all scholarly methods; here are some brief specific examples (for more details see the chapters in Part II):

* conversation analysts compare cases;
* discourse analysts compare the use of rhetoric and turns in statements by different speakers;

- experimenters compare the control conditions to the experimental conditions;
- historians compare sources and data from different periods in order to construct historical interpretations and narratives;
- field workers compare their expectations with their findings in the field and they compare and register observations and statements by different informants and different versions of events;
- phenomenologists compare structures of experiences;
- philologists compare manuscripts in order to establish genealogies of texts and to establish readings;
- statisticians compare samples and populations;
- structuralists compare structures in narratives and rituals.

In other words, then, even if 'the comparative method' is no longer considered as the key method in the study of religion\s, comparison underlies most research activities,[22] informs many research designs and is embedded in standard research methods that are not usually considered or labelled as 'comparative'. There is simply no way of getting around comparison.

Notes

1 See the 'further reading' section for examples.
2 See Segal 2001, 2006 for defences of the comparative method as practiced by these scholars.
3 This may be so because 'the comparative method' refers to a specific method in evolutionary biology, which obscures the significance of comparison for all variants of evolutionary analysis.
4 Comparative methods are 'one of biology's most enduring approaches for testing hypotheses of adaptation' (Pagel 2001: 2403).
5 For the implications and religious and political interests in Müller's program see Gladigow 1997; Girardot 2002; Chidester 2004.
6 See also Ninian Smart's joking comment reported by Strenski (2006: 276), that 'comparative study of religion tends to make one comparatively religious'.
7 The idea of comparison as 'natural experiment' is still a prominent one in our days. For a recent and stimulating example see the studies in Diamond and Robinson (2010). This approach seems especially promising for research questions such as the environmental (ecological) constraints for religion.
8 Ultimately, his project aimed at understanding the uniqueness of Western modernity—a development with global impact.
9 See Saler (2000) for an application to the concept of 'religion'.
10 See Wilke (1996) for a more recent example comparing the teachings of these two figures.
11 For social anthropology, Yengoyan (2006: 141) notes a similar shift 'from a position of generalization to one of description' since the 1960s.
12 Such a position is difficult to maintain in practice; see Roscoe: 'Even opponents of comparison are closet comparativists' (Roscoe 2009: 27).
13 See Haußig (1999) for a comparative analysis of concepts of religion developed in other religious contexts.
14 See Sullivan (2008) for a comparison of the ways in which religion is theorized in two different legal regimes.
15 See Hanges (2006) for a comparison of comparative strategies within Christianities (and their partial rejection and partial appropriation of academic scholarship) and the legacy of Reformation-era comparative projects for contemporary Christians and contemporary scholarship.
16 Platvoet is the rare case of a scholar who explains his own autobiographical background as part of his book.
17 Others speak of parallel demonstration versus the contrasting type.
18 Shushan (2009) is one of the most interesting and methodologically reflective examples of comparative work in the study of religion\s. He focuses on 'a single aspect of afterlife beliefs: conceptions relating to the experiences of the disembodied consciousness of an individual following his or her

physical death, including journeys to other realms [. . .], encounters with other beings [. . .], undergoing perils and judgement, and ultimate fates [. . .]' (Shushan 2009: 2). Shushan compares five historically unrelated ancient religious and contemporary near-death experiences and engages a wide range of theories to explain the comparative findings.

19 For a (historical) typology of dualisms see Bianchi (2005) and other publications by this scholar.

20 See Mahoney (2004) for a discussion of necessary and sufficient causes in comparative-historical methods and new methodologies for testing hypotheses about necessary and sufficient causes (typological theory, Boolean algebra, fuzzy sets).

21 One of the most influential statements is Pettazzoni (1959).

22 Given that scholars of religion have a background of scholarly education that makes them more familiar with the work done in some fields—for example some being closer to anthropology, some to history, others to sociology—to some extent the scholarly practice in the study of religion\s is informed by the various comparative models as practised and discussed in these disciplines.

References

Bianchi, U., 2005. Dualism. In: Jones, L. (ed.), *Encyclopedia of Religion*, 2nd edn, 15 vols. Macmillan Reference, New York, Vol. 4, pp. 2504–17.

Bloch, M., 1963 [1928]. Pour une histoire comparée des sociétés européennes. In: Bloch, M., *Mélanges historiques*. S.E.V.P.E.N., Paris, pp. 16–40.

Buss, A., 1999. The concept of adequate causation and Max Weber's comparative sociology of religion. *The British Journal of Sociology* 50 (2): 317–29.

Chidester, D., 2004. 'Classify and conquer'. Friedrich Max Müller, indigenous religious traditions, and imperial comparative religion. In: Olupona, J.K. (ed.), *Beyond Primitivism: indigenous religious traditions and modernity*. Routledge, New York, pp. 71–88.

della Porta, D., 2008. Comparative analysis: case-oriented versus variable-oriented research. In: della Porta, D. and Keating, M. (eds), *Approaches and Methodologies in the Social Sciences: a pluralist perspective*. Cambridge University Press, Cambridge, New York, pp. 198–222.

Diamond, J.M. and Robinson, J.A. (eds), 2010. *Natural Experiments of History*. Harvard University Press, Cambridge, MA, London.

Doniger, W., 2000. Post-modern and -colonial comparisons. In: Patton, K.C. and Ray, B.C. (eds), *A Magic Still Dwells: comparative religion in the post-modern world*. University of California Press, Berkeley, Los Angeles, pp. 63–74.

Durkheim, E., 1938. *The Rules of Sociological Method*. University of Chicago Press, Chicago.

—— 2001 [1912]. *The Elementary Forms of Religious Life*. Trans. Carol Cosman. Oxford University Press, Oxford, New York.

Freiberger, O., 2009. *Der Askesediskurs in der Religionsgeschichte. Eine vergleichende Untersuchung brahmanischer und frühchristlicher Texte*. Harrassowitz, Wiesbaden.

—— 2010. Locating the ascetic's habitat: toward a microcomparison of religious discourses. *History of Religions* 50 (2): 162–92.

Girardot, N.J., 2002. Max Müller's *Sacred Books* and the Nineteenth-Century production of the comparative science of religion. *History of Religions* 41 (3): 213–50.

Gladigow, B., 1997. Vergleich und Interesse. In: Klimkeit, H.-J. (ed.), *Vergleichen und Verstehen in der Religionswissenschaft*. Harrassowitz, Wiesbaden, pp. 113–30.

Hanges, J.C., 2006. Interpreting glossolalia and the comparison of comparisons. In: Idinopulos, T.A., Hanges, J.C. and Wilson, B.C. (eds), *Comparing Religions: possibilities and perils?* Brill, Leiden, Boston, pp. 181–218.

Haußig, H.M., 1999. *Der Religionsbegriff in den Religionen. Studien zum Selbst-und Religionsverständnis in Hinduismus, Buddhismus, Judentum und Islam*. Philo Verlagsgesellschaft, Bodenheim.

Holdrege, B.A., 1996. *Veda and Torah: transcending the textuality of scripture*. State University of New York Press, Albany.

James, W., 1987 [1902]. *Writings 1902–1920*. Bruce Kuklick (ed.). Library Classics of the United States, New York.

Jensen, J.S., 2001. Universals, general terms and the comparative study of religion. *Numen* 48(3): 238–66.

Kaelble, H., 1999. *Der historische Vergleich. Eine eEinführung zum 19. und 20. Jahrhundert*. Campus Verlag, Frankfurt a.M.

Lakoff, G., 1987. *Women, Fire, and Dangerous Things: what categories reveal about the mind*. University of Chicago Press, Chicago, London.

Lincoln, B., 2003. *Holy Terrors: thinking about religion after September 11*. University of Chicago Press, Chicago, London.

Mahoney, J., 2004. Comparative-historical methodology. *Annual Review of Sociology* 30: 3081–101.

Müller, F.M., 1874. *Lectures on the Science of Religion; with a paper on Buddhist nihilism; and a translation of the dhammapada or 'path of virtue'*. Scribner, Armstrong, and Co., New York.

Neville, R.C. and Wildman, W.J., 2001a. On comparing religious ideas. In: Neville, R.C. (ed.), *The Human Condition*. State University of New York Press, Albany, pp. 9–20.

—— 2001b. On comparing religious ideas. In: Neville, R.C. (ed.), *Ultimate Realities*. State University of New York Press, Albany, NY, pp. 187–210.

Norris, P. and Inglehart, R., 2004. *Sacred and Secular: religion and politics worldwide*. Cambridge University Press, Cambridge, New York.

Otto, R., 1929. *West-östliche Mystik. Vergleich und Unterscheidung zur Wesensdeutung*. Klotz, Gotha.

—— (1932) *Mysticism East and West: a comparative analysis of the nature of mysticism*. The Macmillan Company, New York.

Pagel, M., 2001. Comparative method, in evolutionary studies. In: Smelser, N.J. and Baltes, P.B. (eds), *International Encyclopedia of the Social & Behavioral Sciences*. Pergamon, New York, pp. 2403–11.

Pettazzoni, R., 1959. Il metodo comparativo. *Numen* 6 (1): 1–14.

Platvoet, J.G., 1982. *Comparing Religions: a limitative approach: an analysis of Akan, Para-Creole, and IFO-Sananda rites and prayers*. Mouton, The Hague.

Przeworski, A. and Teune, H., 1970. *The Logic of Comparative Social Inquiry*. Wiley, New York.

Ragin, C. and Zaret, D., 1983. Theory and method in comparative research: two strategies. *Social Forces* 61 (3): 731–54.

Riesebrodt, M., 1990. *Fundamentalismus als patriarchalische Protestbewegung. Amerikanische Protestanten (1910–28) und iranische Schiiten (1961–79) im Vergleich*. J.C.B. Mohr (Paul Siebeck), Tübingen.

—— 1993. *Pious Passion: the emergence of modern fundamentalism in the United States and Iran*. University of California Press, Berkeley.

Roscoe, P., 2009. The comparative method. In: Segal, R.A. (ed.), *The Blackwell Companion to the Study of Religion*. Wiley-Blackwell, Malden, Oxford, pp. 25–46.

Saler, B., 2000 [1993]. *Conceptualizing Religion: immanent anthropologists, transcendent natives, and unbounded categories*. Berghahn Books, New York, Oxford.

Segal, R., 2001. In defence of the comparative method. *Numen* 48: 339–73.

—— 2006. Postmodernism and the comparative method. In: Idinopulos, T.A., Hanges, J.C. and Wilson, B.C. (eds), *Comparing Religions: possibilities and perils?* Brill, Leiden, Boston, pp. 249–70.

Shushan, G., 2009. *Conceptions of the Afterlife in Early Civilizations: universalism, constructivism and near-death experience*. Continuum, London, New York.

Smith, J.Z., 1982. *Imagining Religion: from Babylon to Jonestown*. University of Chicago Press, Chicago.

—— 1993 [1978]. *Map Is Not Territory: studies in the history of religions*. University of Chicago Press, Chicago.

—— 1995. Afterword: religious studies: whither (wither) and why? *Method & Theory in the Study of Religion* 7(4): 407–14.

Strenski, I., 2006. The only kind of comparison worth doing: history, epistemology, and the 'strong program' of comparative study. In: Idinopulos, T.A., Hanges, J.C. and Wilson, B.C. (eds), *Comparing Religions: possibilities and perils?* Brill, Leiden, Boston, pp. 271–92.

Sullivan, W.F., 2008. Comparing law comparing religion. In: Braun, W.B. and McCutcheon, R.T. (eds), *Introducing Religion: essays in honor of Jonathan Z. Smith*. Equinox, London, Oakville, pp. 450–66.

Taves, A., 1999. *Fits, Trances, & Visions: experiencing religion and explaining experience from Wesley to James*. Princeton University Press, Princeton.

—— 2009. *Religious Experience Reconsidered: a building-block approach to the study of religion and other special things*. Princeton University Press, Princeton, Woodstock.

Tylor, E.B., 1889. On a method of investigating the development of institutions; applied to laws of marriage and descent. *Journal of the Royal Anthropological Institute of Great Britain and Ireland* 18: 245–69, 270–72.

Weber, M., 1988. *Gesammelte Aufsätze zur Wissenschaftslehre*. Winckelmann, J. (ed.) 7th edn. J.C.B. Mohr (Paul Siebeck), Tübingen.

Wildman, W.J., 2006. Comparing religious ideas: there's method in the mob's madness. In: Idinopulos, T.A., Hanges, J.C. and Wilson, B.C. (eds), *Comparing Religions: possibilities and perils?* Brill, Leiden, Boston, pp. 51–57.

Wilke, A., 1996. *Ein Sein – ein Erkennen : Meister Eckharts Christologie und Śamkaras Lehre vom Ātman: zur (Un-)Vergleichbarkeit zweier Einheitslehren.* Peter Lang, Bern, etc.

Yengoyan, A.A., 2006. Comparison and its discontents. In: Yengoyan, A.A. (ed.), *Modes of Comparison: theory & practice.* The University of Michigan Press, Ann Arbor, pp. 137–58.

Further reading

Berg-Schlosser, D., 2001. Comparative studies: method and design. In: Smelser, N.J. and Baltes, P.B. (eds), *International Encyclopedia of the Social & Behavioral Sciences.* Pergamon, New York, pp. 2427–33.

Reviews recent methodological approaches in the social sciences.

Burger, M. and Calame, C. (eds), 2006. *Comparer les comparatismes. Perspectives sur l'histoire et les sciences des religions.* Edidit Archè, Paris, Milan.

Collection of essays by Swiss and Italian authors.

Cohen, D. and O'Connor, M. (eds), 2004, *Comparison and History: Europe in cross-national perspective.* Routledge, New York.

Contains some valuable essays on comparative history.

Idinopulos, T.A., Hanges, J.C. and Wilson, B.C. (eds), 2006. *Comparing Religions: possibilities and perils?* Brill, Leiden, Boston.

Collection of 14 essays by American scholars of religion.

Kaelble, H., 1999. *Der historische Vergleich. Eine Einführung zum 19. und 20. Jahrhundert.* Campus Verlag, Frankfurt a.M.

A survey of comparison in history written by a German social historian. The book discusses types and intentions of comparison in history, differences between comparison in history and the social sciences, and gives advice on how to design comparative strategies.

Numen 48(3) 2001.

Special journal issue on comparison.

Paden, W.E., 2004. Comparison in the study of religion. In: Antes, P., Geertz, A.W. and Warne, R.R. (eds), *New Approaches to the Study of Religion. Volume 2: textual, comparative, sociological, and cognitive approaches.* Walter de Gruyter, Berlin, New York, pp. 77–92.

Useful recapitulation of the discussion and thoughtful defence of comparison.

Patton, K.C. and Ray, B.C. (eds), 2000. *A Magic Still Dwells: comparative religion in the postmodern age.* University of California Press, Berkeley, Los Angeles, London.

Collection of essays by American scholars.

Sharma, A., 2005. *Religious Studies and Comparative Methodology: the case for reciprocal illumination.* State University of New York Press, Albany.

Reciprocal illumination is here introduced as one variety of comparison; it points to the mutual enlightenment between one religion/tradition and another, one method and another, between a tradition and a method, etc.

Sica, A. (ed.), 2006, *Comparative Methods in the Social Sciences.* SAGE, London, Thousand Oaks, New Delhi.

Four hefty volumes containing some 70 important essays from the social sciences.

Yengoyan, A.A. (ed.), 2006, *Modes of Comparison: theory & practice*. University of Michigan Press, Ann Arbor.

Some 17 essays by scholars from a range of disciplines (anthropologists, historians, etc.).

Key concepts

Category: A fundamental and distinct conception that groups together several concepts and serves to identify a class, group, list or set of phenomena.

Classification: Systematic assignment of beings (objects, animals, humans) into distinct units (classes).

Comparison: see chapter summary.

Concept: Basic unit of thought with corresponding meanings and representations; building blocks of categories and theories; can ideally be defined.

Strategy: goal-driven sequence of actions.

Taxonomy: Hierarchical system of classification on different levels.

Typology: A classification of types according to structural or other characteristics; alternatively, a two- or multilevel combination of classifications.

1.3
EPISTEMOLOGY

Jeppe Sinding Jensen

Chapter summary

- Theories of knowledge are relevant to the study of religion
- There are different kinds of knowledge production and validation
- Frequent terms of suspicion: positivism, reductionism and relativism
- Generalizations are compared and tested on the basis of theory
- Kinds and levels of explanation and interpretation are interdependent
- There are three directions of reasoning
- Models and concepts make unobservables objective
- Virtues are both epistemic and methodological

Introduction: Epistemological topics for the study of religion

'Philosophy of science is about as useful to scientists as ornithology is to birds.'[1]

This quip suggests that the philosophy of science and it components, such as epistemological issues, are quite useless to scholars 'in the field'. There is no doubt, however, that a theoretically more robust study of religion would have to give serious consideration to a number of philosophical issues. For instance: Is the study of religion closer to literature than to science? What are the characteristics of all those 'objects' that are considered relevant to the study of 'things religious'? How does one define, describe, analyze or explain those objects? Scholars of religion must not necessarily become philosophers of science, but they ought to see if they could solve some of the problems in the study of religion by looking towards the philosophy of science and epistemology in general, because 'Epistemology is concerned with the foundations of science' (Quine 1969: 69). Thus it is also concerned with the foundations of the study of religion.

Most of the topics of **epistemology** are as relevant for the study of religion as they would be in any other academic field. However, some topics deserve more specific discussion, as they are important to scientific practices in the study of religion. Probably the most salient issue is the status of religious discourse in relation to the discourses applied in the science of religion or, simply put, the questions of 'who is right?' and 'what is true?' At the outset we must simply say that religious and scientific claims to validity are of radically different orders. Religious claims with reference to transcendent truths or agents are impossible to validate scientifically, and most religious discourse is impervious to the data, explanations and interpretations of the sciences. This being said, it is equally evident that the subject matters of the study of religion can in fact be studied as human behaviors, ideas and institutions, and in that respect there seem to be no particular problems concerning truth claims. In this respect, the science of religion belongs squarely with the human and social sciences and it basically faces the same problems. Because of its academic history and its global, cross-cultural ambitions, however, there are some points that deserve mention in relation to epistemology in general. Among these are: the question of the nature of data; the modes of inferential reasoning; the consequences of relativism; reasons of argumentation and justification; the question of **'epistemic virtues'**; and the problem of 'knowledge of unobservables'.

Epistemology—the basics

Epistemology is the theory of knowledge, what it consists of, how we get it and how we may defend and justify our knowledge. Traditional epistemology includes a number of key questions: (1) What is knowledge? (2) What kinds of knowledge are there? (3) What are the sources of knowledge? (4) What is the structure of our body of knowledge? (5) What are the limits of what can be known? (6) What are the devices by which we gain knowledge? (7) How is knowledge related to belief and justification? (8) How ought we proceed in order to acquire knowledge? Two related questions along similar lines are: What is this thing called science? and Why do some human activities count as science and others not? (Chalmers 1999). Among the key epistemological problems are also: kinds of beliefs, modalities of truth, means of justification, regress ('where does our asking end?'), scepticism and ontology. However, before treating some of these in more detail below there are some '–isms' that need to be taken into account.[2]

The main approaches in epistemology are (normally) divided into: (1) Empiricism, (2) Rationalism and (3) Constructivism. The first view, **empiricism**, is the standard idea that most of us have as a 'default' psychological mechanism: the foundations of our knowledge of the world are derived from experience, through sensations on which we base beliefs, pronounce statements and thereby arrive at (some kind of) knowledge. To the empiricist the means for building knowledge proceeds by induction and the criterion of validity is provided by reference (e.g. Chalmers 1999: 1–21). The categories by which we understand the world are largely shaped by the way the world *is*. As simple as it seems and as effortlessly as it works in our daily life, most philosophers agree that this is a dubious solution, because the move from one step to the next is mostly inexplicable. The empiricist view is closely linked to various forms of realism. The current dominant view is that there is a world 'out there', and although we may not ever know it in its entirety or on its own terms, we may at least gather knowledge of it in 'critical, indirect realism': The world exists and we know it indirectly as mediated by theory and as a result of critical scrutiny (e.g. Churchland 1979).

In the second '–ism', **rationalism**, the categories by which we interpret the world are considered innate, stable and not derived directly from experience. Contrariwise, our experience and knowledge are shaped by cognitive mechanisms. This stance has certain merits because there is no doubt that our cognitive machinery processes whatever sensations and perceptions we might have, but it also easily leads to scepticism, for how can we then know how the world 'really is'? We may believe all kinds of things about the world that may be completely wrong (i.e. the impression that things just *have* colours). However, *how* things appear in our impressions are, of course, interesting subject matters to scholars of religion who study (among other things) religious thoughts and convictions.

The third '-ism', constructivism, is by now a well-known position in the human and social sciences (it is scarce in the realm of the natural sciences, though not in the philosophy and sociology of science). This view holds that social conditions and forces are responsible for our knowledge and knowledge-forming processes. Such social epistemology is less concerned with the traditional quest for certainty and justification, and it is therefore more concerned with the coherence of beliefs. It is focused less on reference and more on inter-subjectivity and pragmatic viability. However, in the radically social perspective, any belief that is institutionalized in a community may then count as knowledge in its own contexts and provide its own justification. As scholars of religion know, this may easily lead to relativism and (again) to scepticism, because how are true beliefs to be distinguished from false, and what are the criteria for truth and falsehood? The social epistemology and the social construction of knowledge paradigm gained momentum in the mid-20th century. There are various strands between the radical 'social construction of reality' and the weaker 'construction of social reality' which more modestly claims that the human representations of reality are socially constructed (Engler 2004). It makes sense to say that 'gender is a social construction' in so far as the representations that different cultures hold of gender are different, but to claim that biological gender did not exist before it was socially constructed is nonsense. However, social facts are not just social—they are also facts and so objects of study for the human and social sciences.[3] Characteristic of social constructionist epistemology is the rejection of the importance of 'foundations': there are 'no givens', and no 'single reference' for truth. Instead, coherence between beliefs, theories and what we may currently consider best evidence for our claims is all that is left from the classical epistemological toolbox.

The regress problem lives on in all three '-isms', for where does our asking end? It can go on into infinity: in empiricism with ever smaller or bigger entities and in rationalism with global brain functions or transmitter substances. In constructivism the 'buck stops' with coherence or fashion and that is equally dissatisfying. The regress problem remains a stubborn one. A skilful suggestion for a solution can be found in Susan Haack's 'compromise', which she labelled 'Foundherentism' as a providential terminological blend of 'foundation' and 'coherence' (Haack 1993). Just as in a crossword puzzle, where the fit of a word should be both horizontal and vertical, what we count as our best knowledge should fit with both available evidence and the theories we currently hold to be valid. With evidence and justification being infinite and theories being provisional, this is probably as good as it gets (Laudan 1996; Putnam 1990).

Two related '-isms' have circulated time and again in discussions about the study of religion, namely positivism and reductionism. Positivism developed as the key philosophy of scientific progress in the 19th century. The basic principle is that science should be concerned with issues of which we can have positive and reliable knowledge and so metaphysical speculation should be avoided. This is basically a very sound drive towards objectivity and neutrality. Not least, the study of religion has benefited from positivistic attitudes in research. Then again, even positivists have opinions and biases and they also subscribe to theories even if they are not aware of it. During the latter half of the 20th century, positivist thought came into disrepute, and 'positivist' and 'positivism' became pejorative terms for scholarship that is not theoretically aware of its own presuppositions. The ideal in current scholarship is then a drive to include the premises for research and so extend the reach of objectivity to scientific practice itself (e.g. Chalmers 1999: 113–23).

'Reduction', 'reductionism' and 'reductionist' are also regularly found as depreciatory terms in the study of religion, most often applied to those (opponents) who 'reduce' religion to 'something else' (e.g. politics, economy or cognition) and so miss the presumably essential religious qualities of religion. This is evidently a complicated issue, so suffice it here to say that such use of the term 'reduction' as a term of abuse is flawed. The term 'reduction' has several meanings but in science it primarily means a change of theory or of level and so produces a 'new picture of things' (Jensen 2003b: 134–39). Reductionism plays a role as soon as one says 'in other words [. . .]', because then a different explanatory framework is engaged along with related **interpretations** and **explanations**. If the study of religion were to totally avoid reduction, in this sense, the only task left would be to repeat what the believers think, say and do. In some circumstances that might be a noble undertaking, but science it is not. Briefly, there is no way to avoid reduction as long as theory is involved, so the duty of the scholar is to find the most appropriate kinds and ways of 'reducing'.

A curious phenomenon has appeared among the human and social sciences over the past decades, and it has not contributed to their authority or influence in the academic world in general. It is commonly known as 'postmodernism'. It reflects what Paul Boghossian terms the 'fear of knowledge', that is, the misunderstanding and misuse of 'constructivism' that end in social epistemology and the doctrine of 'equal validity' (Boghossian 2006: 1–5). In its most radical forms social epistemology makes it impossible to decide on the validity and soundness of propositions: Whatever is considered true by whomever and by whatever standards is then true. This is relativism in the extreme. It is difficult not to go along with Boghossian's critique for although we may agree that our current knowledge, be it scientific or common sense, is historically contingent and provisional—this does not entitle us to claim whatever we want and then demand to be taken seriously. There are indispensable standards of objectivity and reasonability that are the basis for the formation of all human social behavior (e.g. Rescher 1997).

What sciences are there?

Most of the discussions in epistemology and the philosophy of science have focused on the conditions and problems for the natural sciences in their pursuit of reliable knowledge, foundations and justifications. Knowledge formation in the human and social sciences have not been considered to the same extent, and these fields have not been considered by some to be scientific at all.[4] The history of the study of religion amply demonstrates how even erudite scholars have used their academic positions and influence to produce what was ultimately religious apologetics more than scholarly knowledge. However, this does not imply that it is in principle impossible to have a reasoned science of religion, as reasoned as any science about any other kind of human practice (Jensen 2003b). One would think that it should be easier to study 'things human', because we know from our own thought and practice what it means to be human. It has, however, long been proven invalid to ground scholarly practice in subjective, first-person introspection. Even the most introspectionist person needs language and concepts to think about her introspections and so the subjective, the intersubjective and the objective are linked and deeply interdependent (Davidson 2001).

In the study of religion scholars possess an immense array of products of human minds and practices as their data. These products are created by humans and they feed back on humans in cultures, societies and histories. If this seems to imply some measure of idealism and circularity, then such *are* the conditions for the human and social sciences as hermeneutics teaches us. Humans act for reasons, willingly or unwillingly, consciously or subconsciously, individually or collectively and so reasons *can* be causes and this makes for the interesting fact that humans are both driven by causes (as biological organisms) and reasons—as enculturated agents. Of course, this also opens the door for political, ideological, religious or economic influences and considerations when we turn to actual scientific practice, for scientists are also human beings. Scientific pursuits do not unfold in a void or proceed from nowhere. For instance, studies of religion have been under the influence of a very powerful model of religion derived from Western Christianity that is used even by non-Western scholars. Such issues are not just politically and philosophically trivial for they point to the need for reflexivity and scrutiny of our tacit knowledge and unquestioned cultural cosmology when we consider 'how ought we to proceed in order to acquire knowledge.' Theoretical reflexivity and scrutiny are among the most important epistemic tools in the human and social sciences. Hence, the need for historical and theoretical awareness is obvious.

Generalizations—testing theory by theory . . .

A generalizing science study takes concepts, **models**, hypotheses and definitions as its theoretical objects, and this holds for the study of religion as well. Theory is the necessary condition for there being any knowledge at all. Briefly stated, a fundamental difference between the natural sciences on the one hand and the human and social sciences on the other is that the natural sciences are nomothetic ('law positing'), because they search for general natural laws, whereas the human and social sciences tend to be more idiographic ('single description') because they often describe, analyze and explain singular phenomena or cases. Some social sciences (e.g. economics) occupy a middle ground in their search for generalities in human behavior. Obviously, there are many 'border-crossing' cases: cognitive linguistics is much more nomothetic, whereas numismatics in ancient history is likely to be idiographic. Also, there is a difference in the position of **generalizations**: in the natural sciences generalizations are (of course) made by scientists but the important question is how they can be tested and what the results are; whereas in the human and social sciences the relations between generalizations and data are more circular and the important issue is what the generalizations yield in epistemic terms. That is: how good are they? They are tested more for their utility than for their truth-properties. This may be explained in the following way: in a generalizing science of religion, theories are tested not simply in relation to objects; they are tested in relation to other theories. So the process is, ultimately, one of the falsification of theory by theory. For instance, there is no possibility of taking one of the theories of, say, Ernst Cassirer, Victor Turner or Dan Sperber on symbols and compare it to a non-theoretical model of symbols 'as such'. The question of what constitutes the units of comparison and generalization cannot be settled simply by reference to evidential data. This feature is called the 'under-determination of theory by evidence'.[5] Theories are *not given* by facts, but facts are produced relative to theories. The philosophy of the natural sciences has shown that inductivism is logically flawed because the theory-dependence of observation means that the idea of verification with reference to 'un-interpreted' empirical evidence is impossible (Everitt and Fisher 1995: 164–78; Chalmers 1999: 13–21). Theories *and* evidence (data) are mutually constitutive. Generalizations are the results of theoretical reflections on what is considered to count as evidence within a given theoretical definition-space. Consequently, there is no generalization or testing of hypotheses without comparative work.[6]

Kinds and levels of explanation

When introducing the complex topic of explanation it should be noted from the outset that there are obviously different kinds of explanations that operate on different levels. There is no fixed consensus on the issue. At most, there are a few prevalent conventions among philosophers of science concerning types and functions of explanations. The six most general are listed here on a scale from the nomothetic and causal to the idiographic and contextual:

- 'Covering law' explanations concern the discovery of *general laws*: An effect is explained when its cause(s) can be subsumed under a 'covering law'. This type is also called deductive-nomological explanation as it specifies a logical relationship between that to be explained (the *'explanandum'*) and the conditions that do the explaining (the *'explanans'*). Thus, something can be said to be explained if it can be demonstrably deduced as a *necessary* consequence of a general law (Greek: *'nomos'*) and a number of initial conditions. A covering law model usefully covers events in the physical world such as explaining the boiling point of water. The problem is, obviously, how to use this type of explanation in the social and human sciences. What place, if any, could it have in the science of religion? Well, explanations of this kind might provide some understanding of the biological foundations for the human abilities to have religion.
- 'Causal' explanations are closely linked to deductive-nomological explanations and they have often been considered identical. The problem seems to be that although the recurrence of given phenomena in a theory of regularities can be considered a criterion of cause and effect relations, it has become increasingly difficult to specify what actually constitutes a 'cause'. Cause is a highly metaphysical concept the reference of which is epistemologically unclear. There are causal explanations *in* religions, such as 'God created the world in six days', but this kind of explanation falls outside the scope covered by scientific theory. However, causal explanations in the cognitive science of religion would explain why humans have specific kinds of religious beliefs and representations and what are their causes.
- 'Statistical' explanations in which the general covering law is substituted by statistical frequency (sometimes called 'inductive-statistical' explanations). This kind of explanation is common in the social sciences and in the study of religion where it supports statements like 'Muslims do not eat pork because it is forbidden to them'. Thus, this type of explanation has some predictive force because it covers what generally seems to be the case. Although philosophically and logically dubious, there is enough common sense and pragmatic reason for using this type of explanation. In fact, humans do it all the time.
- 'Dispositional' explanations refer to dispositions, for example of grass to grow. When transposed to the realm of the social and the cultural they may be seen as 'intentional' or 'purposive' explanations of motives and reasons (i.e. the bases of common sense social inferences). It has been debated in philosophical logic whether reasons can be causes, but reasons are what render many human actions understandable. 'Dispositional' explanations are found, for instance, in dream analysis in psychology, in astrological discourse and in religious systems that contain ideas of cosmic regularity or of human nature (e.g. 'providence' or 'karma'). Dispositional explanations seem to have deep roots in human cognition because they are linked to evolved templates about intentions of animate beings and intuitive goal-structure perception. That is: we easily grasp what ordinary actions are about. Humans also seem to have strong dispositions to meaning- and world-making that are at the roots of religion.
- 'Contextual' or positional explanations. This type of explanation (of 'making clear') is important and widespread in the human and social sciences. It also covers descriptive explanations, e.g. ethnographic descriptions of how things are. It further emphasizes the understanding of subject matters in contexts such as, for instance, semantic structures,

narrative logic, or in history and society. Instead of focusing on causes of events or purposes of actions, such explanations may refer to underlying structures and mechanisms at various theoretical levels (as in a language grammar, in psychoanalytic dream analysis or in structuralist analyses of myth). Contextual explanations explain the role, place or the meaning of something in a context, and mostly at the same level (and so they are not reductions to lower levels). The *explanandum* may be the rules of chess or the syntax of a language, and such other instances where it is uncommon to ask for the causes, origins or purposes of such rules but rather of how they 'hang together'. An example could be the dietary purity rules in many religious traditions. Here, the explanatory process consists in placing the unknown in a context of things known, and this is an important heuristic practice in the study of religion. In the explanatory process, scholars search for those elements that fit into the narrative logic through which it is possible to (re-)produce a meaningful account of events. The 'parable' or 'story' perspective is justified as an explanatory strategy when scholars explain human actions, that is, as (mostly) purposeful and intentional.[7] In consequence, the more complex forms of human behavior may require both causal explanations of generative and selective mechanisms as well as structural explanations of functions and structures and these are different kinds of explanation.

- Functional explanations are a subset of positional explanations that abound in the study of religion, culture and society. They focus on the functional properties of entities, say, religious phenomena, in their contexts. Examples from the realm of religion could be the social functions of divination and oracles in political processes in ancient society. Functional explanations of (items of) religion often give attention to the role religion may play on the collective or individual levels, such as explaining the cosmos, maintaining social order or providing individual coping strategies. There is a caveat concerning functional explanations because they often convey the impression that the outcome or the effect of the function was originally the *cause* of it and so state that religions exist in order to fulfil the needs for individual psychological coping or societal stability. In such cases the functional explanation slides into a teleological explanation, such as if one were to say that rainclouds exist for the purpose of making plants grow. Functional explanations may often be revealing, but the cause-effect direction should be closely and critically monitored.

The more rewarding results in the human and social sciences will often come from combinations that provide as comprehensive accounts as possible of the phenomena under scrutiny. In the natural sciences, in contrast, the explanatory goal generally is to find the variables that explain the cause-effect relations (i.e. temperature and air pressure for the boiling point of water). It is a wider and more general view of inter-theoretic and interdisciplinary scientific work that scientists both need and should respect in order to obtain 'consilience' between sciences and also appreciate their respective epistemic goals.[8]

Interpretation and explanation

The distinction between explanation and interpretation (as heuristic and epistemic strategies) has traditionally been seen as simultaneously representing differences between natural sciences that explain objects and humanities that 'understand' subjects. The debates have been long and complex, but it now appears to be a matter more of definitions (or convictions) than of substance.[9] Interpretations and explanations are mutually compatible activities. Scientists in the 'hard' sciences obviously seek to explain 'the world', but they also interpret evidence, validations and hypotheses. Likewise, interpretation commonly includes a measure of explanation. A lexical definition of 'explanation' will typically understand explanation as 'to make plain or clear'. When looking at such human products as cultures, languages and religions it soon becomes obvious that they are semantic and semiotic compositions, and as such they are 'game-like', with rules and constraints for combinations and use. In order to explain and interpret a game, to make it 'plain and clear', one will most likely begin by explaining the rules. Why should the same not hold for the explanation, interpretation and understanding of religion and religious phenomena? How does one understand Karma, Puja, the Hajj, Zande witchcraft and Christian Baptism if not as part and parcel of social and cultural systems? In 1945 Lévi-Strauss explained the symbolic nature of kinship-systems in this telling passage:

> Because they are symbolic systems, kinship systems offer the anthropologist a rich field, where his efforts can almost [. . .] converge with those of the most highly developed of the social sciences, namely, linguistics [. . .] we must never lose sight of the fact that, in both anthropological and linguistic research, we are dealing strictly with symbolism. And although it may be legitimate or even inevitable to fall back upon a naturalistic interpretation in order to understand symbolic thinking, once the latter is given, the nature of the explanation must change as radically as the newly appeared phenomenon differs from those which have preceded and prepared it.
>
> *(Lévi-Strauss 1968: 51)*

So, if someone asked me to explain some point of French grammar, I would explain how the system is laid out structurally, how it functions in terms of grammar, syntax and pragmatics. On a textual analogy, the explanatory character of interpretation may be further extended as suitable for the analysis of human actions and institutions.

Data and interpretation: induction, abduction and deduction

As already noted, data are theory dependent. Data are produced and 'sifted' from the streams of experience by means of theories, concepts and models. Human life is in a flux and we are unable to perceive or understand it 'as such'. Events and actions are the stuff that human social and cultural life is 'made of' and in order to be able to represent the 'chunks' and patterns of events and actions we must be able to parse long streams of experience into sequences and represent packages of actions as meaningful, coherent and instrumental—or, in other cases, not so. Scientific analysis in the human and social sciences is a higher-order 'event representation' classification method where various kinds of behavior are seen as 'counting as' certain kinds of activity. Anything from sensible activities such as cooking, weddings and football to, at the other end of the scale, madness are what they are because there is social and cultural consensus as to what they 'count as'. Money is a prime example of this 'status function' mechanism that is the source of all social construction (e.g. Searle 2010). The science of religion can testify that all societies have norms, modes and schemata for behavior in mind, body and society.

In epistemological terms there would be no possibility for seeing what 'counts as what' in a scientific perspective if there were no concepts, models, schemata or theories, for '[. . .] scientific knowledge does not automatically arise as we observe our surroundings' (Audi 2003: 260). This is why former positivist ideals of **induction** have proven unfruitful: facts do not exist 'as such' and they cannot provide the concepts, models and theories that constitute knowledge and science as epistemic projects.[10] The other classical mode of inference is **deduction**, which is indispensable in the natural sciences as a predictive tool, but has a troubled reputation in the science of religion because of its predominance in normative issues in theology and philosophy.[11] Many scholars in studies of particular religions have been quite 'positivistic' as a result of their suspicions of these two disciplines. Theology and philosophy were considered to hold preconceived notions and biases that would distort interpretations and explanations of religions and cultures.[12]

The third mode of inference is **abduction**, which is less known. It is often simply referred to as 'inference to the best guess'. The process involved is one of making inferences and best guesses on the basis of what is known, what we may predict and what fits our models and theories best. In the human and social sciences nomothetic theories and covering-law explanations are rare, whereas probabilistic hypotheses and theories abound. Epistemic probability is related to the 'best guess' practice of abductive reasoning and so it is often of a creative nature. This we can use predictively in the science of religion, for although the number of actual variables may be daunting, we can still make guesses as to whether Jews would likely eat pork or Hindus beef (very simple examples), and we can explain the situational logic of behaviors and agents in relation to religious belief and action patterns, where and when coherence permits heuristic inferences from specific cases ('Oh—so this is why they do it!').[13]

Conceptual models

Abductive reasoning is thus also closely linked to the formation and use of the models that are used in the interpretation of data, such as whether a string of events is better classified as, for instance, divination or sacrifice. Models come in many forms and there is a proliferation of types of models in the literatures related to this subject. Models can be more or less heuristic, diagrammatic and predictive, but they are all related to theory, theory building and theory application. In many sciences, including the study of religion, models are used for the testing of hypotheses. However, in the study of religion models are more often used to conceptualize and construct theoretical objects from the mass of evidential data.[14] Models and the theories associated with them determine whether a set of actions counts as, for instance, a votive offering or a curative rite. Some models are analytic because they are true by definition, such as when 'axis mundi' is defined as the symbolic centre of a religious world. Other models are synthetic because they can be tested against evidence, be criticized and modified, and so yield confirmation as heuristic and epistemic devices. In addition, models may also be considered performative in the sense that they create the conditions under which the object becomes visible to scholars as, for instance, shamanism or cosmography. A large part of the research and debate in the science of religion has been devoted to the development and refinement of models. Some models have become obsolete, such as 'fetischism', 'pre-animism' or 'dynamism'. When an aggregate of models is assembled in the light of a theory, e.g. structuralism, a more complete paradigm emerges, one that may be likened to a conceptual scheme or a theoretical framework that opens up new modes of description, analysis and understanding in a disciplinary matrix. One may recall the discussions between Claude Lévi-Strauss and his opponents in the 1950s and 1960s in order to witness the changes brought about by a new theoretical paradigm. However, the world itself does not change. As Thomas Kuhn says about two scientists (one before and one after a paradigm shift): 'Both are looking at the world, and what they look at has not changed'; and so '[. . .] a scientist after a revolution is still looking at the same world' (Kuhn 1996: 150, 129).

Epistemic virtues—a useful catalogue

There are many ways of looking at the world, and so philosopher John Dupré suggests focusing on what he terms 'epistemic virtues' and disregarding the ideal of scientific unity, with physics serving as the 'mother' of science. According to Dupré, the discrimination between science and not-science through one single criterion (e.g. falsification) for what constitutes 'genuine scientific merit' seems to be un-resolvable (Dupré 1993: 221–23). Other criteria for characterizing science could be, e.g. coherent relations between theory and empirical data, that science is cooperative and cumulative, and the quest for general laws and principles. In the context of the present volume I am inclined to add that a scientific finding is a finding that was established on the basis of methods acknowledged as scientific. However, there are no comprehensive correlations that cover all sciences. As a solution Dupré offers a 'pluralistic epistemology' of 'promiscuous realism'.[15] This is not methodological anarchy, and the proposal may well be constructive in the study of religion, for as Dupré explains the notion of 'pluralistic epistemology':

> Science, construed simply as the set of knowledge-claiming practices that are accorded that title, is a mixed bag. The role of theory, evidence, and institutional norms will vary greatly from one area of science to the next. My suggestion that science should be seen as a family resemblance concept seems to imply not merely that no strong version of scientific unity of the kind advocated by classical reductionists can be sustained, but that there can be no possible answer to the demarcation problem [i.e.: the distinction between science and non-science].
>
> *(Dupré 1993: 243)*

Nevertheless, we do have principles for assessing the superiority of some claims over others, e.g. evolutionary theory versus creationism. Normative epistemological standards *are* available and they do not in fact look that much different from established practices; so Dupré suggests a 'virtue epistemology' consisting of:

> sensitivity to empirical fact, plausible background assumptions, coherence with other things we know, exposure to criticism from the widest variety of sources, and no doubt others. Some of the things we call 'science' have many such virtues, others very few [. . .] Many works of philosophy or literary criticism, even, will be more closely connected to empirical fact, coherent with other things we know, and exposed to criticism from different sources than large parts of, say, macroeconomics or theoretical ecology.
>
> *(Dupré 1993: 242–43)*

With Dupré, we may then consider the demarcation problem to be in some sense solved. With the 'wider' concept of science also comes the possibility for a theoretically and methodologically sound science of religion—keeping in mind that 'religion' is not a *thing*, of course. There is no reason to imitate outdated scientistic conceptions of science. Not all that looks, or used to look, like science *is* science.[16] Now, what are the implications of this tempered view of scientific rigour when it comes to methods and methodology? Briefly stated, the methodological consequences must be that methods and research procedures must also be virtuous, in the sense that objectivity, impartiality, honesty, reflexivity and self-criticism will be the foundations on which to build. Just imagine holding the opposite view. Thus, *knowing* epistemic virtues in theory ought to lead to *practicing* methodological virtues and so a methodologically well-reflected and honest investigation should be a display of 'virtue epistemology'. This may be easier said than done, but such notions ought to be the guiding motives and representations in research.

Knowledge of unobservables and the functions of concepts

A traditional problem in epistemology concerns knowledge of matters that are 'unobservable'. Historically, some important matters have been unobservable and ill understood until the right tools and theories were developed. Gravity is an example: already in antiquity vendors used scales to weigh their goods, but until the principles and concepts of gravity were discovered and 'invented', gravity remained 'unobservable'. Thus, empirical observation and theoretical knowledge go hand in hand. Electricity and nuclear radiation are other matters that come to mind. Inventions of instruments that amplify our cognitive and epistemic powers are important too: telescopes, fMRI scanners working at molecular levels and so forth.[17]

Religious traditions abound with claims about, e.g. agents and actions that are 'invisible', 'hidden', 'transcendent' and so unobservable,[18] but in that sense epistemology has nothing more to say than that some people hold such ideas, which are then no longer unobservable as soon as they become topics in language and symbolic systems and so emerge as social facts. Unobservable are also the properties ascribed to objects, persons and actions for the questions of 'what counts as', e.g. a taboo in ritual practice, a touchdown in football or a well-performed baptism of a child. These matters are unobservable for they depend on their interpretation to become what they are intended to be. 'Thick description' of intentions and meanings is the way to describe such actions. Many of the most important matters in human life are unobservable, and so the concerns about acquiring knowledge of the unobservable and knowing 'what counts as what' are central in the human and social sciences. The 'unseen' must be translated into matters that are epistemically accessible. Translations for the purpose of 'epistemic emergence' revolve around concepts, their use and their meaning in forms of language as, for instance, when we understand a ritual performance because we learn about taboos, purity and the role of the ancestors as guardians of morality. Without those concepts we would not understand anything.

Concepts are used to 'translate' observed actions, texts read, etc., into scholarly, conceptual meta-languages. These are as accessible as are natural languages although they often may require extensive training, say in philosophical logic or in molecular genetics. Human knowledge of all kinds is expanded by mediations between such 'languages'. In the 'translation' process 'raw data' become not only scientific but also social facts and 'cultural posits' (Quine 1969: 13–15; Jensen 2003b: 319–51). Scholarly concepts are constructed for the purposes of translation into theoretical languages where words may acquire *different* meanings. If my teaching is successful, my students will come to think differently of, say, 'taboo' as an element of theoretical discourse and not only of colloquial speech, because the theoretical concept of 'taboo' comes with different theories and conceptual ramifications. Concepts enable us to see things, to talk about them, to make theories about them, even if the 'things' do not *really* exist. Conversely, unobservable 'things', such as ideas, beliefs and convictions, come to life by being translated into perceptible forms. Consider a procession of Buddhist monks, an Ndembu healing ritual, a Roman-Catholic mass, or any other religious phenomenon. If not for the observable actions, the concepts involved would truly be abstract; and if not for the semantics of the concepts, these observed actions would be senseless. Mutual theoretical dependence and interpretational scope are the key.

Concluding remarks

So, here is a 'no problem' solution to many epistemological concerns: one no longer needs to be a physicist or a philosopher to know what science is, for scientific virtues are in principle quite easy to understand and use. They are extensions and continuations of the endowed human faculties that have evolved so that we would not walk into trees in the jungle. When we add to that the obligations of social life and the normativity of language use, we see the contours of scientific practice as similar to human practice in general. The same standards hold in the practice of science, and that is why I think we should prefer the 'virtues' scenario instead of adhering to a quest for a set of strict rules. Anyone can follow strict rules, but it is much more challenging to remain rational when the rules run out. There is a solution to that as well, for as the philosopher Hilary Putnam once said: '[. . .] we have an *underived*, a *primitive* obligation of some kind to be reasonable, not a "moral obligation" or an "ethical obligation", to be sure, but nevertheless a very real obligation to be reasonable' (Putnam 1987: 84, original emphasis). That is very good mind-set with which to begin the journey.

Notes

1 Attributed to Richard Feynman (1918–88) Nobel Prize winner in physics 1965.
2 I omit here any discussion about 'What is this thing called religion?'
3 See Jensen 2003a. The strong view is so counter-intuitive that it seems attractive to some, as e.g. the 'Sokal affair' (in 1996) demonstrated (Lease 2003).
4 French 'sciences humaines' or German 'Kulturwissenschaften' may sound awkward to Anglophone ears, but these designations do make good sense.
5 See e.g. Laudan 1996: 29–73, for a more technical discussion.
6 See Chapter 1.2 on comparison in this volume. In a different context I have argued that there are (probably) only four 'kinds' of comparison in the human and social sciences: comparisons of form, function, structure and (semantic) meaning (Jensen 2008, 2003b: 440).
7 See e.g. Polkinghorne (1988). Other human doings can be explained as events, that is, when they are the effects of, e.g. biological functions and causes (e.g. blood pressure, metabolism etc.).
8 Examples of comprehensive and complex accounts that cover vast reductive spans are Craver 2007 and Thagard 2010.
9 For a discussion in relation to the study of religion, see Jensen (2009: 236–41).
10 In its milder forms, inductivism has played a considerable role in the study of religion, simply because the early scholars in the field wanted to see what the texts or the believers 'really said', against the biased representations given by colonialists and religious missionaries. This 'mild induc-tivism' displays epistemic virtue, in anything from therapy to text readings. On the problem of induction, see Everitt and Fisher (1995: 145–63).
11 Most general works on epistemology contain a section on deduction, see e.g. Chalmers (1999: 8–10) for a very brief introduction and Audi (2003: 165–77) for a technical discussion.
12 Ironically, those same 'positivists' have since come under attack from postmodernist, feminist and post-colonialist critics for being biased. Such criticisms demonstrate a basic drive towards epistemic vigilance and justification: 'trying to get it as right as we can'.
13 The philosopher Charles S. Peirce, who was the creator of the term, said that to *abduce* a hypo-thetical explanation *a* from an observed surprising circumstance *b* is to infer that *a* may be true because then *b* would be a matter of course.
14 Concerning models in general, Frigg and Hartmann present a long list: 'Probing models, phenom-enological models, computational models, developmental models, explanatory models, impover-ished models, testing models, idealized models, theoretical models, scale models, heuristic models, caricature models, didactic models, fantasy models, toy models, imaginary models, mathematical models, substitute models, iconic models, formal models, analogue models and instrumental models are but some of the notions that are used to categorize models [. . .] While at first glance this abun-dance is overwhelming, it can quickly be brought under control by recognizing that these notions pertain to different problems that arise in connection with models. For example, models raise

questions in semantics (what is the representational function that models perform?), ontology (what kind of things are models?), epistemology (how do we learn with models?), and, of course, in philosophy of science (how do models relate to theory?; what are the implications of a model based approach to science for the debates over scientific realism, reductionism, explanation and laws of nature?)' (Frigg and Hartmann 2006: 1). Hodges (2009) is a more technical survey. On models in direct relation to the study of religion, see e.g. Jensen 2009.

15 As Dupré says, 'Certainly I can see no possible reason why commitment to many overlapping kinds of things should threaten the reality of any of them. A certain entity might be a real whale, a real mammal, a real top predator in the food chain, and even a real fish' (Dupré 1993: 262). 'Promiscuous realism' does not, however, comprise religious or fictitious ontologies and so Dupré's taxonomy of sea mammals does not include mermaids.

16 One example of scientist strategy for the recognition of academic or scientific status is quantification: 'That this aspect of scientism—perhaps we should call it "mathematicism"—is a sociologically significant contributor to scientific prestige seems hard to dispute. It is again perhaps best illustrated by the preeminent influence of economics, with its characteristic appeal to abstruse mathematical models of little empirical worth, among the social sciences' (Dupré 1993: 223).

17 The so-called 'E-meters' used in Scientology most likely are instruments of a different kind.

18 Notice that as such (unobservable, etc.) these 'phenomena' are also beyond the bounds of public control and reason, and so they are means by which power relations can be produced and upheld.

References

Audi, R., 2003. *Epistemology: a contemporary introduction to the theory of knowledge.* 2nd edn. Cambridge University Press, Cambridge.

Blackburn, S., 2006. *Truth: a guide for the perplexed.* Penguin Books, London.

Boghossian, P., 2006. *Fear of Knowledge: against relativism and constructionism.* Oxford University Press, Oxford.

Chalmers, A., 1999. *What Is This Thing Called Science? An assessment of the nature and status of science and its methods.* 3rd edn. Open University Press, New York.

Churchland, P., 1979. *Scientific Realism and the Plasticity of Mind.* Cambridge University Press, Cambridge.

Craver, C.F., 2007. *Explaining the Brain: mechanisms and the mosaic unity of neuroscience.* Clarendon Press, Oxford.

Dancy, J., 1994. *An Introduction to Contemporary Epistemology.* Blackwell, Oxford.

Dancy, J. and Sosa, E. (eds), 1992. *A Companion to Epistemology.* Blackwell, Oxford.

Davidson, D., 2001. *Subjective, Intersubjective, Objective.* Clarendon Press, Oxford.

Dupré, J., 1993. *The Disorder of Things: metaphysical foundations of the disunity of science.* Harvard University Press, Cambridge, MS, London.

Engler, S., 2004. Constructionism versus what? *Religion* 34(4): 291–313.

Everitt, N. and Fisher, A., 1995. *Modern Epistemology: a new introduction.* McGraw-Hill, New York.

Frigg, R. and Hartmann, S., 2006. Models in Science. In: *Stanford Encyclopedia of Philosophy.* plato.stanford.edu/entries/models-science.

Haack, S., 1993. *Evidence and Inquiry: towards reconstruction in epistemology.* Blackwell, Oxford.

Hodges, W., 2009. Model theory. In: *Stanford Encyclopedia of Philosophy.* plato.stanford.edu/entries/model-theory.

Jensen, J.S., 2003a. Social facts, metaphysics and rationality in the human sciences. In: Jensen, J.S. and Martin, L.H. (eds), *Rationality and the Study of Religion.* Routledge, London, pp. 117–35.

—— 2003b. *The Study of Religion in a New Key: theoretical and philosophical soundings in the comparative and general study of religion.* Aarhus University Press, Aarhus.

—— 2008. On how making differences makes a difference. In: Braun, W. and McCutcheon, R.T. (eds), *Introducing Religion. Essays in Honor of Jonathan Z. Smith.* Equinox, London, pp. 140–62.

—— 2009. Conceptual models in the study of religion. In: Clarke, P.B. (ed.), *The Oxford Handbook of the Sociology of Religion.* Oxford University Press, Oxford, pp. 245–62.

Jensen, J.S. and Martin, L.H. (eds), 2003. *Rationality and the Study of Religion.* Routledge, London.

Kuhn, T., 1996. *The Structure of Scientific Revolutions.* University of Chicago Press, Chicago.

Laudan, L., 1996. *Beyond Positivism and Relativism: theory, method and evidence.* Westview Press, Boulder, CO.

Lease, G., 2003. Rationality and evidence: the study of religion as a taxonomy of human natural history. In: Jensen, J.S. and Martin, L.H. (eds), *Rationality and the Study of Religion*. Routledge, London, pp.136–44.

Lévi-Strauss, C., 1968. *Structural Anthropology*. Vol.1. Trans. Claire Jacobson. Penguin, Harmondsworth.

Polkinghorne, D.E., 1988. *Narrative Knowing and the Human Sciences*. SUNY Press, Albany, NY.

Popper, K.R., 1979. *Objective Knowledge: an evolutionary approach*. Clarendon Press, Oxford.

Putnam, H., 1987. *The Many Faces of Realism*. Open Court, LaSalle, IL.

—— 1990. *Realism with a Human Face*. Harvard University Press, Cambridge, MA.

Quine, W.V., 1969. *Ontological Relativity and Other Essays*. Columbia University Press, New York.

Rescher, N., 1997. *Objectivity: the obligations of impersonal reason*. University of Notre Dame Press, Notre Dame, IN.

Searle, J.R., 2010. *Making the Social World: the structure of human civilization*. Oxford University Press, Oxford.

Thagard, P., 2010. *The Brain and the Meaning of Life*. Princeton University Press, Princeton.

Williamson, T., 2000. *Knowledge and its Limits*. Oxford University Press, Oxford.

Further reading

Blackburn, S., 2005. *Truth: a guide*. Oxford University Press, Oxford, New York.

Difficult reading made easy; a good entry into epistemology.

Chalmers, A., 1999. *What Is This Thing Called Science? An assessment of the nature and status of science and its methods*. 3rd edn. Open University Press, New York.

A highly recommended introduction to classical and modern problems in the philosophy of science.

Everitt, N. and Fisher, A., 1995. *Modern Epistemology: a new introduction*. McGraw-Hill, New York.

Specifically on epistemology and still accessible for the uninitiated.

Pritchard, D., 2006. *What is this Thing called Knowledge?* Routledge, London, New York.

Highly recommended as an updating addition to Chalmers 1999.

Key concepts

Abduction: reasoning upon prior knowledge to the 'best bet'.

Deduction: logical inference or reasoning where conclusion is based on fixed premises.

Empiricism: the theory that knowledge is produced from experience and the use of the senses.

Epistemic virtue: good conduct in the pursuit of knowledge.

Epistemology: the theory of knowledge in philosophy.

Explanation: disclosing how matters are causally connected or 'making things clear'.

Generalization: typical aspects of a group of 'things', e.g. rituals as behavior.

Induction: reasoning that proceeds from empirical premises to conclusions.

Interpretation: eliciting meanings and semantic values, e.g. from texts.

Model: a representation of one structure in relation to an analogous one: e.g. sound as waves.

Rationalism: the theory that reason *as such* can provide true knowledge.

1.4

FEMINIST METHODOLOGIES

Mary Jo Neitz

Chapter summary

- Feminist methodologies originated with researchers who were participants in the women's movement of the 1970s. They were critical of male biases in science and processes of knowledge production.
- Among feminist researchers today we find at least three different positions on the basic epistemological and ontological questions that undergird the production of knowledge: feminist empiricism, feminist standpoint and radical construction. This chapter focuses on feminist standpoint.
- Feminist standpoint epistemologies assert that all knowledge is partial and located.
- Researchers do not stand outside of the research process.
- Therefore researchers need to develop reflexive practices, and ways of incorporating multiple voices.
- Although some of the initial formulations put forward the idea of a 'privileged position' of women, current versions of feminist standpoint analysis speak about intersectional matrices of oppression. Gender is included but its centrality will vary depending on the subject of research.

Introduction

Feminists beginning in the 1960s produced powerful critiques of the male centeredness of society's institutions. Education, science and the production of knowledge did not escape. Feminists first asked 'where are the women?', but soon the question shifted to 'how do our theories and ways of doing research change, if we assume that gender is important?' For feminist anthropologists, historians, psychologists and sociologists concerned with doing research that would reduce inequality, these questions led to a critical examination of the research process. Feminist researchers argued that feminist research mandated feminist methods, informed by feminist epistemologies and methodologies. However, agreement about which methods were feminist, and what constituted feminist methodology did not emerge. Lively debates about how feminists gather data, our relationships with those who are the subjects of research, how we write and for whom, continue to inform and challenge those of us who seek to do feminist research.

Among feminist researchers today we find at least three different positions on the basic epistemological and ontological questions that undergird the production of knowledge: feminist empiricism, feminist standpoint and radical construction (see Box 1.4.2). This chapter focuses on feminist standpoint. Feminist standpoint analysis[1] in the United States originated in the 1970s out of a powerful dialectic between two kinds of knowledge, one originating in a renewed interest in historical materialism among neomarxists in the academy and the other coming out of feminist consciousness raising groups in the Women's Liberation Movement. Throughout the 1980s and 1990s feminist standpoint analysis underwent a number of revisions, responding to both post-structural and postmodernist challenges in the academy and debates among activists. In this chapter I will first introduce the main tenets of feminist standpoint analysis; second, briefly review the debates and outline how feminist standpoint changed; third, I will suggest what current versions of feminist standpoint offer for research on religion; and fourth, I will give several examplars of research that use feminist standpoint analysis.

Core concerns of feminist standpoint epistemology today

In her recent book, *Feminist Methodologies for Critical Researchers*, Joey Sprague (2005) reviews the debates of the previous 25 years, and articulates clearly and concisely a contemporary version of feminist standpoint methodology. Sprague's interpretation of what is at the core and what can be discarded follows from her critical perspective: she assumes that all knowledge is *interested*, and that mainstream social science 'tends to assume the position of privileged groups, helping to naturalize and sustain their privilege' (ibid.: 2). As a quantitative researcher who practices feminist standpoint analysis, Sprague separates the methodology of standpoint analysis from any particular method, quantitative or qualitative. This provides an important starting point for thinking about the ways that standpoint analysis can be used today.

Standpoint researchers believe that an individual's actual location in the social and physical world and the work that s/he does there shapes her/his understandings. In particular locations, inhabitants develop interests in the knowledge that supports their activities. In addition, people in different locations have different access to various discourses, and different tools for understanding and articulating their interests. Standpoint researchers believe that people in locations of relative power have an interest in maintaining their position, and that they are supported by the dominant institutions and discourses. A key issue for researchers, then, is **reflexivity** about one's own interests, and the interests of one's subjects. For Sprague, one of the distinctive qualities of feminist standpoint research is the choice to work for the disadvantaged rather than for those in power. This has ramifications for how we frame our questions, how we perform our analysis and whom we imagine as our audience. Rather than pursuing norms of objectivity, a practice which tends to support the status quo, Sprague asks social researchers to ask passionately, analyze critically and disseminate empoweringly (Sprague 2005: 199–200).

Box 1.4.1 Descriptive characteristics of standpoint methodology

- Work from the standpoint of the disadvantaged
- Ground interpretations in interests and experience
- Maintain a strategically diverse discourse
- Create knowledge that empowers the disadvantaged

(Sprague 2005: 75–80)

In common with other feminist standpoint researchers, Sprague distinguishes feminist stand-point from positivist and neopositivist methodologies, and also from radical constructionism and postmodernisms. In her view, conventional practices of doing research and reporting the results serve to deflect criticism, limit the size and scope of the audience to specialists, hide the workings of power, and deaden potential emotional responses to findings about the status quo (Sprague 2005: 167).

Box 1.4.2 Comparison across feminist methodologies

- *Feminist empiricism*. Feminist empiricists follow positivism in believing in the existence of a world outside of our experience of it, and that observations of it reveal patterns. The goal of the researcher is to objectively observe this world, in order to explain regularities and predict the future. They argue that much of previous research failed to achieve these ideals because researchers had race, class and gender biases. Feminist researchers seek to conduct research that avoids these biases (Hundleby 2007).

- *Standpoint research*: Standpoint researchers believe in the existence of a material world and emphasize starting analyses with people's practical activities in specific locations in the world, and, at the same time, integrate assumptions about the social construction of subjects. All knowers are located in time and place, and all knowledge is partial. Empathy and attachment offer pathways for understanding others. The best research is multivocal with researchers owning their own positions.

- *Postmodernism/radical constructionist*: Knowledge is socially constructed; order and/or truth are not discovered existing out in the world, but rather are produced through language and culture. One goal of researchers is to deconstruct meanings embedded in existing theories and categories, including the category 'woman'. Knowledge is a text, and there is no privileged interpretation. Researchers are no more authoritative than readers (Clough 1992; Mascia-Lees *et al.* 1989).

Sprague criticizes conventional positivist methodologies in particular for failing to ask what it is about the social order that makes social problems more likely. She objects to research employing logical dichotomies and abstract individualism. She also rejects the process of objectification, treating people as objects who have no ability to act on their own behalf. While not positivist per se, she criticizes conventional ways of reporting findings which have the effect of hiding the researcher. She cites Paget, who cautioned that 'The author's activity is displaced by the methods which act on the data for the author' (Sprague 2005: 22). Sprague argues for using active voice when writing results: active voice necessitate writing that someone is doing something to someone. This is in contrast to conventional social science writing where 'passive voice amounts to hiding the exercise of power' (ibid.: 24). The issue of voice raises the question of how to put the author in the text. For Sprague, the researcher's voice can be present as part of a multivocal text in which the researcher's voice speaks alongside the voices of others.

Sprague makes a clear distinction between feminist standpoint epistemology and the idea of 'giving voice' to under-represented people as has been advocated by some qualitative feminist researchers (e.g. Gluck and Patai 1991). She argues that this idea misrepresents the power dynamics between the researcher and the researched. Not only does this neglect consideration of the ways that the researched have power, but it also discounts the power that researchers have as authors, and often as possessors of specialized knowledge.

Furthermore, in contrast to some previous writers, for Sprague feminist standpoint is not about subjectivity; rather it is about location (Sprague 2005: 67).[2] For Sprague, a feminist standpoint refers to, first, an actual location in nature and the interests with regard to that location; second, the (shared) discourses that provide people with tools for making sense; and third, the positions in the social organization of knowledge production. This does not mean, however, that one cannot do research from a feminist standpoint and examine subjectivities; rather it is a caution against assuming that they are the same.

Finally, Sprague argues that we can increase the likelihood that we will ask critical questions, to the extent that we develop practices that move us outside of our closed academic conversations. She advocates getting involved in a community group, interrogating public discourse, studying up—starting with the experiences of people at the bottom of hierarchies rather than with the understandings of those at the top—and learning to pay attention to what is missing (Sprague 2005: 182–88).

Early expositions of standpoint theory: Hartsock and Smith

The political theorist Nancy Hartsock and sociologist Dorothy Smith independently worked early on in their careers on developing explicitly feminist epistemologies. In the late 1960s and early 1970s both were activists in the women's movement and both were finishing graduate degrees in the social sciences: Smith, a British woman who would make her career in Canada, earned her doctoral degree in sociology at the University of California at Berkeley, and Hartsock, a US scholar, was in graduate school in political science at the University of Chicago. Both observed the contradiction between their experiences as knowers in the women's movement and in the elite academic institutions where they were students: knowledge and ways of knowing validated through the women's movement were dismissed in the academy. Hartsock (1983) drew on a Marxist framework, using the tools of historical materialism to develop what she called a feminist standpoint. Hartsock wanted to show how women as knowers occupied a privileged location for understanding the gender order. She argued that women have access to the rules and understandings of the men in power, but they also have knowledge that comes out of the material conditions of their own subordinate position.[3] While women, similar to the working class for Marx, occupied a position of epistemological privilege, the knowledge does not come 'naturally' by virtue of having a body that can be recognized by oneself and others as 'female'; rather it is achieved through a collective process that Hartsock described as 'Consciousness Raising', a term with a specific reference to the practices of second-wave feminists.

In the 1970s Dorothy Smith began developing her critique of sociology, asking what sociology would look like from the feminist standpoint of women, which for her meant the actualities of women's everyday life experiences (Smith 1974, 1987). Smith was influenced by ethnomethodology, a branch of sociology 'which seeks to uncover the taken-for-granted that is prenormative and prior to discursive positing' (Smith 1997: 398).[4] This provided her with tools for understanding women's experience as identified within the women's movement as constituting a kind of tacit knowledge that could provide the starting point for a critical feminist sociology. Smith wrote about the profound dislocation she felt between her experience as a knower in the everyday world, and her experience as a social scientist in which she could be a 'knower', but only if she assumed a universalist, objective stance removed from and contradicting her experiences as a woman and mother. She described the disjuncture between her experience as a scientist/knower/subject and the treatment of women as objects in sociology as a 'line of fault' (Smith 1987: 49). Her proposal for sociology from the feminist standpoint of women offered a way to understand social organization and the relations of ruling from starting in actual experiences of people in daily life. Her project puts the authority of the inquirer on the same epistemological plane as the authority of the subjects of inquiry.

Smith and Hartsock both used the word 'feminist standpoint' and both were familiar with and drew on the language of Marxism. However, it was the philosopher of science, Sandra Harding, who brought together Smith and Hartsock (along with Hillary Rose) under a common rubric as 'feminist standpoint theorists' in her award-winning book, *The Science Question in Feminism* (Harding 1986). Harding's formalization of feminist standpoint theory became the received version, and critics internal to feminism and from the outside immediately contested the claims of feminist standpoint theory. It is the former and how they changed the shape of feminist standpoint theory that interests us here.

Challenges: difference and postmodernism

In the 1980s new social movements and identity politics bloomed in North America and Western Europe. Within the feminist movement, 'difference feminism' gained visibility. As soon as feminist scholars began to articulate an epistemology starting from 'the feminist standpoint of women', critics began to deconstruct the category of 'woman' arguing that there was no one universal 'woman' and therefore there could be no 'feminist standpoint of women'. Hartsock responded that her formulation does not posit a universal woman, and she pointed out that she emphasizes the achieved nature of a feminist standpoint. It is not given, but rather is the product of a political process of consciousness raising. Her epistemology is about a 'feminist standpoint' not a standpoint of women (Hartsock 1998). Smith's response to the critics emphasized the local and particular nature of starting with the experience of women, whereby the feminist standpoint of women always refers to the particular women and their actual experiences, and is always open to including whoever is there or may come. For Smith there is no abstracted (universal) 'feminist standpoint of women'.[5]

Postmodern critics also took issue with feminist standpoint theory. Radical deconstructionists cast away the careful claims of feminist standpoint epistemologies, along with more neopositivist ones of feminist empiricists: no knowledge claims could be privileged: all is rhetoric and persuasion. Donna Haraway, coming out of feminist science studies, responded to the postmodern arguments while maintaining an appreciation for the feminist critique of power at the heart of feminist standpoint epistemologies. She wrote of her radical desires for science:

> how to have simultaneously an account of the radical historical contingency for all knowledge claims and knowing subjects, a critical practice for recognizing our own 'semiotic technologies' for making meanings, and a no nonsense commitment to faithful accounts of a 'real' world, one that can be partially shared and friendly to earth-wide projects of finite freedom, adequate material abundance, modest meaning in suffering, and limited happiness.
>
> *(Haraway 2004: 85)*

Contemplating these desires, Haraway offered the term 'situated knowledges' to describe a view of embodied knowledge, and argued for thinking in terms of scientific knowledge as partial and located visions brought into conversations with each other and contributing to a strategically diverse discourse.

All of these issues—how to respond to the concerns about difference among women and multiple perspectives while at the same time retaining the focus on power that was at the core of the original feminist theorists—are integral to the work of Patricia Hill Collins (1986, 1997, 2000). She maintains the idea that feminist standpoint is the product of group-based experiences. Like other standpoint feminists, she argues that feminist standpoint theory is a tool for talking about how dominant groups maintain their power in part through control over culture and knowledge production. Hill Collins also developed the concept of '**inter-sectionality**'—the study of interlocking matrices of oppression.[6] This concept is crucial for how feminist standpoint researchers today theorize location. Hill Collins describes what she and hers have come to call the intersectionality paradigm, as follows:

> What we have now is increasing sophistication about how to discuss group location, not in the singular class framework proposed by Marx, nor in the early feminist frameworks arguing the primacy of gender, but within constructs of multiplicity residing in social structures themselves, and not individual women. Fluidity does not mean that groups disappear, to be replaced by an accumulation of decontextual-ized, unique women whose complexity erases politics. Instead the fluidity of bound-aries operates as a new lens that potentially deepens understanding of how the actual mechanisms of institutional power can change dramatically while continuing to reproduce long standing inequalities of race and gender and class that result in group stability.
>
> *(Hill Collins 1997: 377)*

For Hill Collins, all knowledge is partial, and she values knowledge generated outside the academy. In her work *Black Feminist Thought*, she described the position of black feminist academics as 'outsiders within' the academy and argued that black feminist academics use their marginal status to produce black feminist thought that reflects a feminist standpoint generated within African-American culture by black women. Furthermore, black feminist thought can also be generated by storytellers and blues singers, novelists and other organic intellectuals, and these local knowledges offer tools for resisting dominant knowledge (Hill Collins 1986). Acknowledging these other voices as authoritative contributes to maintaining a strategically diverse discourse, one of the core tenets of standpoint research.

Although the perspective originated in an Anglo-American political and intellectual context, postcolonial feminist scholars also contributed to feminist standpoint theory. They criticized the limitations of the 'women in development' research with its imposition of Western assumptions about gender, and some saw feminist standpoint as a perspective that could facilitate research for third world women. Feminist discourse that assumed a 'universal woman' was extremely problematic for third world writers, and some of these writers argued that standpoint analysis with its starting point in the actualities of women's lives—particularly in time and place—is a useful methodology for moving the project of decolonialization forward. Chandra Mohanty (2003) suggests that Smith's conceptualization of 'the relations of ruling' is a tool for understanding the intersectional oppressions of postcolonial social organi-zation, both at the discursive level and at the material level of daily life.[7]

All these writers advocate for the continued importance of uncovering or attending to subjugated knowledges. Harding, for example, argues that 'marginalized lives are better places from which to start asking casual and critical questions about the social order' (Harding 2004: 130). Feminist standpoint authors locate feminist standpoint in a shared consciousness that can arise out of experiences of a particular location, but, at the same time, epistemic privilege is achieved, not given. All contend that feminist standpoint epistemology connects issues of power and knowledge and see the position as a way of holding ourselves as researchers accountable as knowers. In effect, feminist standpoint theorists propose a kind of double reflexivity. In addition to epistemological reflexivity, where we reflect on how our domain assumptions about research affect our engagement in knowledge production (Gouldner 1970), feminists also reflect on how the researcher's location and experiences in the world affect what we see and know. For Harding, 'All of the kinds of objectivity-maximizing procedures focused on the nature of social relations that are the direct object of observation and reflection must also be focused on the observers and reflectors—scientists and the larger society whose assumptions they share' (Harding 2004: 136). Standpoint researchers look to see how interests and interpretations of experience—including our own—are shaped by our locations.

Finally, feminist standpoint theorists argue that it is communities and not individuals who produce knowledge, and that 'truth' is in the discourse. The subject must be multiple: maintaining a strategically diverse discourse is essential to the validity of the research (Sprague 2005: 78). Recent elaborations of standpoint analysis, including Sprague (2005) and Hawkesworth (2006), suggest strategies for accomplishing this. They discuss how to sample informants from different locations, systematically contrast viewpoints and compare them to uncover hidden assumptions, and/or maintain contact with popular culture forms and the discourse of those outside of academia.[8]

Box 1.4.3 Maintaining a diverse discourse

Feminist researchers emphasize the importance of 'questioning the questions'. Disciplinary discourses train (discipline) researchers to think along particular lines, and restrict the questions we ask. While this is very useful, critical researchers also train themselves to step outside the disciplinary discourses in the process of framing questions and searching for sources of data. Standpoint researchers assume that knowledge is partial and multiple, and that the comparison of multiple and conflicting views illuminates tacit assumptions and aids in uncovering the basis for competing claims. The following suggests several strategies for standpoint analysis:

- *Sample informants from different social locations and those expressing different positions.* Political scientist Mary Hawkesworth argues that feminist standpoint is an analytical tool, and illustrates a process of studying contentious issues through locating and engaging with competing claims. In this process one gathers all claims and samples divergent positions, comparing the theoretical assumptions and empirical claims (Hawkesworth 2006: 176–206).
- *Use popular cultural forms as data.* African-American researchers such as Patricia Hill Collins (2000) and Cheryl Gilkes (2002) are among those who advocate that scholars give serious attention to the voices of writers and activists outside of our own disciplinary locations, and examine critically the ways in which their writings can inform our understandings.
- *Get engaged in community groups.* Sprague (2005: 182–84) encourages researchers to become involved with ongoing social movements and to look for questions that get raised in those contexts.
- *Include participants in research.* Participatory Action Research asks members of groups being studies to be a part of framing the study questions. Manson *et al.* (2004) give a detailed account of the negotiation process in one such study.

Implications for the study of religion: what does power have to do with it?

One of the questions that contemporary feminist standpoint approaches raise for anyone who would like to use them is what does it mean to study from the feminist standpoint of the disadvantaged? McGuire (1983) and Beckford (1983) separately suggested several decades ago that sociologists of religion in fact neglect the study of power. Feminist standpoint analysis offers a way to make concerns about power more central to what we do. I'd like to suggest here three ways in which those of us who study religion can (and do) research from the feminist standpoint of the disadvantaged. First, there is a longstanding research tradition of studying religions that are outside of the majority or dominant culture. Research on sects and cults, for example, implicitly, and sometimes explicitly, places these smaller, less-powerful groups in relation to the dominant religious institutions in a society: the state churches and denominations. Second, a somewhat more recent development is the study of the lived experience of ordinary people (Ammerman 2007; McGuire 2008). This is a move to change the focus from looking at beliefs and dogmas as expressed by officials and institutions, to looking at the embodied practices in the daily lives of ordinary people. Beginning, as Smith would have us do, with the actualities of people's everyday/everynight worlds disrupts the theories and concepts of our disciplinary knowledge. As it turns out, official beliefs and dogmas do not necessarily prescribe or describe what people do, and to the extent that we take them as our starting point we miss what is happening in the social world, as well as fail to see the possibilities for change. Third, and closely related to my previous point, we can begin to examine ways in which people who are not in positions of power experience the structures that govern their lives.[9]

One of the contributions of adopting feminist standpoint epistemology, then, is that it provides a way to think more explicitly about power. Power for feminist standpoint theorists is not static (not structure as the girders of the building), but rather it is always relational and processual. Smith's conceptualization for example, of the 'relations of ruling' captures this idea of power/structure as constituted through, perhaps iterative and ongoing, acts that are carried out and experienced by people in the actualities of their daily lives. Feminist standpoint insists that researchers cannot be neutral and objective in studying relations of power, and that what has passed for neutrality in the past has most often ended up supporting the status quo, which means those in power. Furthermore the sensitivity to power relations extends to the research process itself.

Giving up the idea of neutrality, of the 'objective observer' is perhaps particularly fraught for those of us who study religion. The long process of disestablishment in the West moved toward various forms of separation of church and state. A similar process of secularization in the academy has at times required objectivity from scholars who studied religion, in effect asking them to remove their work from possible influences of the church. Insofar as religion itself was associated with unscientific and outdated forms of authority, legitimacy as a scholar of religion has, in some contexts, required that researchers distance themselves from belief. The resulting 'objectivity', as Rodney Stark notes in *One True God*, has seldom been truly agnostic toward religion, but rather takes a stance supporting the prevailing secular powers against religion (Stark 2001: 4–6). Native researchers or researchers who go native tend to be viewed with suspicion. However, we might think about how researchers who hold the identities and affiliations of the unmarked categories—those of the dominant groups and cultures—can and do carry their beliefs, values and feelings into the research without themselves or others noting it. They do not stand out and are unobserved. Being under the radar, however, is not the same as being objective. In a previous essay, I have argued that the problem with 'going native' is really an issue of loyalty and power. 'Going native' implied disloyalty and defection from the powerful through the act of joining with a marginal group (Neitz 2002: 42–43). Feminist standpoint epistemology helps us think critically and usefully about our history as scholars of religion. In marked contrast to those whose 'objectivity' perhaps unwittingly supports the status quo, feminist standpoint epistemologies see the voice of the marginal as a potentially critical location.

Exemplars

The following four scholars, representing different cohorts and positions within feminism, take on a variety of topics and employ a variety of methods, but all serve as exemplars of feminist standpoint analysis. They all work from the standpoint of the disadvantaged, ground interpretations in interests and experience, maintain a strategically diverse discourse, and create knowledge that empowers the disadvantaged. The brief sketches of their projects here suggest the range of topics, methods and audiences for standpoint research.

Nancy Nason-Clark is one of the first researchers to bring the feminist issue of domestic violence, and how Protestant congregations respond to it, to the attention of religious researchers. She has studied how church leaders and members, justice officials and shelter workers meet the needs of religious women who are victims of domestic violence. In two decades of research she and her co-authors have studied survivors of domestic violence, transition house and shelter workers, church members and pastors (Nason-Clark 1997). Most recently, she is following the experiences of batterers who participate in a court-mandated program (for preliminary findings see Nason-Clark *et al.* 2004). Her research uses questionnaires, interviews and observations. Nason-Clark writes passionately about her own personal commitment to this project (Nason-Clark 2002) and her advocacy as a practice of public sociology (Nason-Clark 2005). A current project, the Religion and Violence E-learning Project, brings current research and the everyday experiences of a multitude of individuals in very different locations—geographical, as well as social and cultural—to an accessible web-based format (www.theraveproject.org). In part it is designed to educate pastors and offer them tools; it also greatly extends the arena in which conversations about domestic violence take place and what is said about it.

Cheryl Townsend Gilkes works both as a sociologist and as a Womanist theologian.[10] Gilkes's research, preaching and writing focus is on the work of African-American women in generating social change and on the diverse roles of black Christian women in the 20th century. Her published essays, articles and sermons employ a wide range of methods, including interviews, observation and participation observation, and personal reflection (Gilkes 2001). Like Hill Collins, discussed above, Gilkes at times draws on non-traditional sources such as novels, integrating the data they present with more typical social science analysis to understand the experiences of African-American women (Gilkes 2002). Her research on the little-studied Church of God in Christ highlights the forms of leadership and voice available to black women in the sanctified church, despite exclusion from the role of pastor (Gilkes 2001). She shows church women feeding people, raising money, testifying and organizing. She uses her writings to challenge the reader, foster empathic understanding, and to advocate for a vision of 'healing, spiritual wholeness, celebration, and struggle' (Gilkes 2001: 194).

A somewhat different relationship to her subject can be seen in the work of Julie Ingersoll, who has studied evangelical feminists, many of whom were members of Christians for Biblical Equality. Ingersoll writes not as a sympathetic outsider, but as someone who grew up within the fold, and who since defected. Ingersoll is critical of the doctrine of women's submission and its deployment among fundamentalist Christians, and she has sought out the stories of the women who bear the costs of the gender battles. In her book, *Evangelical Christian Women: war stories in the gender battles*, Ingersoll uses interviews and personal correspondence with women who fought and lost battles in conservative churches, Christian seminaries and colleges. In her analysis, she uses the argument that gender is a contested category, and she shows how definitions of what it is to be a Christian man or woman are used to police the boundaries of evangelical culture. In Ingersoll's work we see an approach that is both critical and intentionally multivocal; she documents cases of those who oppose the dominant views, a move away from a univocal story that reinscribes hegemonic understandings (Ingersoll 2002).

The fourth examplar, Sarah McFarland Taylor, an historian of women and religious history, further expands how we understand location. She brings us back to place, asking scholars to consider situatedness, not just as social and cultural, but also as part of an ecological relationship with the land on which we live (see Taylor 2007b). Her book, *Green Sisters: a spiritual ecology* (Taylor 2007a) documents the growing movement of environmentally activist Roman Catholic religious sisters in North America. Her subjects are part of a loosely organized network, founded in 1993, called Sisters of the Earth. The groups she studied belong to ten different religious orders, and live their vision in some tension with both the church hierarchy and secular society. Using both historical sources and interviews, Taylor develops a method she calls 'historical ethnography' to show how the sisters model sustainability and conserve not just seeds, but parts of the religious tradition. Part of Taylor's work is showing how innovation is possible, even in a resistant context such as the Roman Catholic hierarchy.

Each of these authors exemplifies a feminist standpoint not just in terms of the choice of subject but also in terms of how they conduct the research and write up the results. They write not just about women subjects, but, while starting with specific groups and their concerns, they write about gender in relation to other systems of power and oppression. They do not assume a generic woman or speak with a single feminist voice. In each case the author's own interests are reflexively acknowledged, a part of the story.

Finally, I hope that it is obvious that a feminist standpoint perspective is not solely about a focus on women. In the work of these authors we see a focus on gender as a relational category and forms of power and arenas in which power relations play out. Successive reformulations and clarifications over the years have decentered the category of women, and now feminist methodologists see gender location as a constitutive element of a feminist standpoint, but not necessarily the defining element.[11]

Conclusion

Feminist standpoint contends that we as researchers cannot stand somewhere 'outside' of the context of research and produce an unbiased, objective account: we are in the world, and live in relation to everything here (Neitz 2009). There is no place 'outside' where we can stand. Given that that is the case, feminist standpoint researchers have proposed a methodology for turning what might have been seen as a flaw—a bias—under a different epistemological position, into a valuable tool for a critical research, one that holds the possibility of empowerment.

In the early years, many advocates of feminist methodology opposed the use of quantitative methods and discussed feminist methods in terms of interviews, oral histories and ethnography— methods, some argued, which allowed women subjects to speak for themselves. The ensuing discussion contributed enormously to our understanding of the complex relations between researchers and subjects. We came to understand that face-to-face methods do not eliminate researchers' power, in part because researchers choose the questions and write up the results. Others pointed out disadvantages of small samples and case studies when studying under-represented groups. The current view holds that 'methods' are neither feminist nor anti-feminist: rather, it depends on how a method is used. Feminist standpoint as an epistemology articulates a methodological position starting from the point that work begins with the interests of women. This affects the questions that are asked and how they are framed. Projects begin in the actualities of people's everyday experiences. Being attentive to location means that researchers avoid abstract and decontextualized approaches when they collect and analyze their data, quantitative or qualitative. In whatever ways they can, researchers work to diversify the discourse. Finally, seeking to create knowledge that empowers the disadvantaged means relating findings to public debates and finding outlets in policy forums. It can also mean paying attention to writing in ways that are accessible to those who are not specialists in the field. Some of these practices may be outside the conventions of much quantitative research, yet there is an identifiable body of feminist standpoint work that uses quantitative methods. While taking a feminist standpoint does not dictate a particular method, it changes the research process at every step: framing the questions, locating oneself in the same plane as the subjects, not outside of the research process, paying attention to how collectivities and social organizations are subject to the relations of ruling, how we think about the audience for the work, for whom and even how we write.

Notes

1 Feminist standpoint has been referred to as a theory (Harding), a methodology (Harding, Sprague), and a method of inquiry (Smith, Hawkesworth). As explicated by these authors, 'standpoint' implies both ontological assumptions about the nature of reality and an epistemological position about how we go about studying it, as well as the methodological consequences of that position.

2 Sprague's critical evaluation of some of the strategies of early feminist qualitative researchers as well as her support for the application of a standpoint perspective by quantitative researchers helps feminist researchers put aside any conflation of feminist standpoint methodology with qualitative methodology.

3 In her discussion of women's work of reproduction, Hartsock drew explicitly on psychoanalytic sources, bringing to her feminist project two major critical traditions of modern thought, Marxism and psychoanalysis.

4 Ethnomethodology (Garfinkel 1967) came out of the critical philosophy of science formulated in the phenomenological works of Alfred Schutz and Edmund Husserl. Smith's work is in conversation with both ethnomethodology and symbolic interactionism, arguably the two most significant of the interpretivist methodologies that challenged positivist models of science in sociology in the post-World War II period.

5 In fact, Smith distanced herself from the language of feminist standpoint theory, calling her project a 'method of inquiry'. More recently she and her followers describe what they do as 'institutional ethnography' and Smith's most recent work calls her feminist project a 'sociology for people' (Smith 2005). Smith also has insisted that some of her concerns are disciplinary with particular relevance for debates among sociologists (Smith 1997).

6 See also Crenshaw 1989.

7 Narayan (1989), however, suggests that positivism may be useful for third world feminists when oppression of women comes from other knowledges than scientific ones, especially religion.

8 Also, quantitative researchers rarely cite qualitative research in their literature reviews or when discussing their results, yet using qualitative findings is a way to include more standpoints in their discussions, another way to diversify the discourse (Sprague 2005: 116).

9 For Dorothy Smith (2005), one starts in the actualities of everyday experience in order to study what she calls 'the relations of ruling' from the bottom up rather than from the top down.

10 Womanist theology is a movement, beginning in the 1980s, of African-American women theologians and writers who regard the black Protestant church as the central historical institution in the survival of black families and communities in the United States. At the same time, they bring a critique of patriarchy and an awareness of gender relations and of the experiences of black women in the Christian traditions to the fore.

11 See also Kokushkin (2007) for an argument for the usefulness of standpoint analysis for understanding economic changes in Eastern Europe in the 1990s.

References

Ammerman, N.T. (ed.), 2007. *Everyday Religion: observing modern religious lives.* Oxford University Press, Oxford, New York.

Beckford, J., 1983. The restoration of 'power' to the sociology of religion. *Sociological Analysis* 44(1): 11–31.

Clough, P., 1992. *The End(s) of Ethnography: from realism to social criticism.* SAGE, Newbury Park.

Crenshaw, K., 1989. Demarginalizing the intersection of race and sex: a Black feminist critique of anti-discrimination doctrine, feminist theory and antiracist politics. *University of Chicago Legal Forum* 4: 139–67.

Garfinkle, H., 1967. *Studies in Ethnomethodology.* Prentice Hall, Englewood Cliffs, NJ.

Gilkes, C., 2002. A conscious connection to all that is: the color purple as subversive and critical ethnography. In: Spickard, J.V., Landres, S. and McGuire, M. (eds), *Personal Knowledge and Beyond: reshaping the ethnography of religion.* New York University Press, New York, pp. 174–95.

—— 2001. *If It Wasn't for the Women: Black women's experience and womanist culture in church and community.* Orbis Books, Maryknoll, NY.

Gluck, S.B. and Patai, D. (eds), 1991. *Women's Words: the feminist practice of oral history.* Routledge, New York, London.

Gouldner, A., 1970. *The Coming Crisis in Western Sociology.* Basic Books, New York.

Haraway, D., 2004 [1991]. Situated knowledges: the science question in feminism and the issue of partial perspectives. In: Harding, S. (ed.), *The Feminist Standpoint Reader: intellectual and political controversies.* Routledge, New York, pp. 81–101.

Harding, S., 2004. Rethinking feminist standpoint epistemology: what is strong objectivity? In: Harding, S. (ed.), *The Feminist Standpoint Reader: intellectual and political controversies.* Routledge, New York, pp.127–40.

—— 1986. *The Science Question in Feminism.* Cornell University Press, Ithaca.

Hartsock, N., 1998. *The Feminist Standpoint Revisited and Other Essays.* Westview Press, Boulder, CO.

—— 1983. The feminist standpoint: developing a ground for a specifically feminist historical materialism. In: Hintikka, M. and Harding, S. (eds), *Discovering Reality.* Kluwer Academic Publishers, Dordrecht, pp. 283–310.

Hawkesworth, M., 2006. *Feminist Inquiry: from political conviction to methodological innovation.* Rutgers University Press, New Brunswick, NJ.

Hill Collins, P., 2000. *Black Feminist Thought: knowledge, consciousness, and the politics of empowerment.* 2nd edn. Routledge, New York.

—— 1998. On book exhibits and new complexities: reflections on sociology as science. *Contemporary Sociology* 27(1): 7–12.

—— 1997. Comment on Hekman's 'truth and method: feminist standpoint theory revisited': where's the power?' *Signs* 22(21): 375–81.

—— 1986. Learning from the outsider within: the sociological significance of black feminist thought. *Social Problems* 33(6): S14–S32.

Hundleby, C., 2007. Feminist empiricism. In: Hesse-Biber, S. (ed.), *The Handbook of Feminist Research: theory and practice.* SAGE, London, Thousand Oaks, pp. 29–44.

Ingersoll, J., 2003. *Evangelical Christian Women: war stories in the gender battles.* New York University Press, New York.

—— 2002. Against univocality: re-reading ethnographies of conservative Protestant women. In: Spickard, J.V., Landres, S. and McGuire M. (eds), *Personal Knowledge and Beyond: reshaping the ethnography of religion.* New York University Press, New York, pp. 162–74.

Kokushkin, M., 2007. Standpoint Theory Is Dead, Long Live Standpoint Theory! Paper delivered at the annual meeting of the American Sociological Association. New York, NY.

McGuire, M., 2008. *Lived Religion: faith and practice in everyday life*. Oxford University Press, Oxford, New York.

—— 1983. Discovering religious power. *Sociological Analysis* 44(1): 1–9.

Manson, S., Garroutte, E., Turner Goins, R. and Nez Henderson, P., 2004. Access, relevance, and control in the research process. *Journal of Aging and Health* 16 (5 suppl.): 58S–77S.

Mascia-Lees, F., Sharpe, P. and Ballerino-Cohen, C., 1989. The postmodern turn in anthropology: cautions from a feminist perspective. *Signs* 15(7): 7–33.

Mohanty, C., 2003. *Feminism without Borders: decolonizing theory, practicing solidarity*. Duke University Press, Durham, NC.

Narayan, U., 1989. The project of feminist epistemology: perspectives from a nonwestern feminist. In: Jaggar, A. and Bordo, S. (eds), *Gender/Body/Knowledge: feminist reconstructions of being and knowing*. Rutgers University Press, New Brunswick, NJ, pp. 256–69.

Nason-Clark, N., 2005. Linking research and social action: violence, religion and the family. *Review of Religious Research* 46(3): 221–34.

—— 2002. From the heart of my lap-top: personal passion and research on violence against women. In: Spickard, J.V., Landres, S. and McGuire, M. (eds), *Personal Knowledge and Beyond: reshaping the ethnography of religion*. New York University Press, New York, pp. 27–32.

—— 1997. *The Battered Wife: how Christians confront family violence*. Westminster/John Knox Press, Louisville, KY.

Nason-Clark, N., Murphy, N., Fisher-Townsend, B. and Ruff, L., 2004. An overview of the characteristics of the clients at a faith-based batterers' intervention program. *Journal of Religion and Abuse* 5(4): 51–72.

Neitz, M., 2009. Encounters in the heartland: what studying rural churches taught me about working across differences. *Sociology of Religion* 70(4): 343–61.

—— 2002. Walking between the worlds: permeable boundaries, ambiguous identities. In: Spickard, J.V., Landres, S. and McGuire, M. (eds), *Personal Knowledge and Beyond: reshaping the ethnography of religion*. New York University Press, New York, pp. 33–46.

Smith, D., 2005. *Institutional Ethnography: a sociology for people*. Alta Mira, Walnut Creek, CA.

—— 1997. Comment on Hekman's truth and method: feminist standpoint theory revisited. *Signs* 22(21): 392–98.

—— 1992. Sociology from women's experience: a reaffirmation. *Sociological Theory* 10(1): 88–98.

—— 1987. *The Everyday World as Problematic*. Northeastern University Press, Boston.

—— 1974. Women's perspective as a radical critique of sociology. *Sociological Inquiry* 44(1): 1–13.

Sprague, J., 2005. *Feminist Methodologies for Critical Researchers*. Alta Mira, Walnut Creek, CA.

Stark, R., 2001. *One True God*. Princeton University Press, Princeton, NJ.

Taylor, S.M., 2007a. *Green Sisters: a spiritual ecology*. Harvard University Press, Cambridge, MS.

—— 2007b. What if religions had ecologies? The case for reinhabiting religious studies. *Journal for the Study of Religions, Nature and Culture* 1(1): 129–38

Further reading

Hesse-Biber, S. (ed.), 2007. *Handbook of Feminist Research: theory and praxis*. SAGE, Thousand Oaks, CA.

Up to date and comprehensive, 43 new essays by established feminist researchers across a range of methodologies with a strong section on intersectionality, difference and global research.

Mann, S. and Kelley, L., 1997. Standing at the crossroads of modernist thought: Collins, Smith and the New Feminist epistemologies. *Gender and Society* 11(4): 391–408.

Examines standpoint theory in relation to intersectionality.

Reinharz, S., 1992. *Feminist Methods in Social Science Research*. Oxford University Press, New York.

Reviews a wide spectrum of methodological positions and methods in use by feminist researchers.

Rose, H., 1983. Hand, brain and heart: a feminist epistemology for the natural sciences. *Signs* 9(1): 73–90.

Application of the epistemology of standpoint to the natural sciences.

Sandoval, C., 2000. *Methodology of the Oppressed*. University of Minnesota Press, Minneapolis, MN.

Presents US third world feminism as a 'differential consciousness' and argues for a methodology of mapping one's location in the interests of equity for marginalized people.

Sharma, A. (ed.), 2002. *Methodology in Religious Studies: the interface with women's studies*. State University of New York Press, New York.

Collection of articles discussing feminist methodologies across a range of approaches to studying religion including history of religions, phenomenology, psychology of religion, theology and hermeneutics in addition to the social sciences.

Key concepts

Interests: Desires and material benefits accruing to individuals due to inhabiting particular locations in nature. Under some circumstances individuals might take for granted the benefits of their location, and they may not be conscious of their interests. Standpoint analysis requires that researchers become aware of the interests of their subjects as well as their own interests.

Intersectionality: A way of theorizing inequality in terms of a 'matrix of oppression' whereby an individual exists in a social location at the intersection of vectors of privilege and oppression including, but not limited to, race, class and gender. It helps researchers get at the different experiences of, for example, middle-class black men as compared to middle-class black women and middle-class white women.

Multivocality: Originally the idea of mulitvocality was introduced in anthropology to indicate the essential ambiguity of symbols and their openness to interpretation. With the postmodern challenge in the social sciences the idea of multi-vocality was extended to texts, to indicate that they can be interpreted in more than one way, often with the intent of questioning the authority of any particular interpretation, including that of the author of the text. As used in this chapter, multivocality refers to interpretive practices at the level of constructing a text. It is a method of writing that intentionally incorporates different voices/interpretations into the text.

Reflexivity: Refers to cultivating a conscious awareness of how the researcher is a part of the knowledge production process. There are two kinds of reflexivity, and standpoint researchers employ them both. Epistemological reflexivity refers to critically examining one's own (usually tacit) domain assumptions about the nature of the world and how we as researchers can come to know it (Gouldner 1970). To this standpoint researchers also employ personal reflexivity about how our own experiences and locations in the world inform our research. Understanding the research process as a reflexive means seeing the researcher as a part of the research process, not standing outside of it.

1.5

RESEARCH DESIGN

Wade Clark Roof

Chapter summary

- Choosing a research design in the study of religion is made complicated by the interdisciplinary nature and history of the field and by the complexity of 'religion' itself.
- Research design—the overall plan or strategy for achieving the aim(s) of a particular inquiry—involves such issues as data, methods and modes of analysis, as well as issues of ethics and public dissemination of findings.
- Given the complexities of religion in the modern world (but even with historical work), conceptualizing a particular form of religion precedes the completed formulation of a research design. This helps to avoid interpretive pitfalls: e.g. idealism, objectification and ideology.
- A concrete example of research design, based on a cross-sectional study, highlights several issues related to units of analysis, dimensions of religious commitment, logics and approaches, and triangulation.
- Several dimensions of representation (of self and the people one studies) demand critical and reflexive awareness.
- Whether research designs are complex or simple, the critical issue is whether the research results in a convincing outcome as judged by the best research standards.

Introduction

Teaching courses in the sociology of American religion, I am often approached by students who say something like, 'I have an interesting topic for my paper in your class but I don't know how to go about researching it. Can you help me?' The gap between these two—an interesting topic and an appropriate research design—is not uncommon for students in religious studies. Partly this is because the study of religion lacks a distinct methodological approach of its own and borrows methods and logics of study from various disciplines within the humanities and social sciences, and increasingly from the evolutionary-cognitive sciences, but also the modern study of religion, as a field liberated from the confines of theological reflection, emerged as an intellectual hybrid with diverse roots in the history of phenomenology, philosophy and textual studies on the one hand, and anthropology, sociology and psychology on the other hand. There is no singular, widely accepted paradigm of study.

In addition, the phenomenon we study is elusive, hard to pin down and defies easy definition. To add to the complexity, 'religion' in the context of people's lives has both first-order and second-order meanings. There are the interpretive frames of religious believers themselves, which are often the object of study as within, say, ethnography. However, scholars look at the same phenomena and apply their own conceptual schemes and theories independently of, yet sometimes influenced by, how the participants describe their own worlds. Disputes over scholarly interpretations and analytic approaches are common, often leaving students confused as to what it is we really know about religion. As Willi Braun says:

> divergent, conflictual, even contradictory incantations of 'religion' are not only possible but vigorously alive side-by-side in hundreds of university religion departments whose knowledge is relayed for scholarly and popular consumption by an astonishing volume of publications [. . .] The field of religious studies is a bewildering jungle.
>
> *(Braun 2000: 5)*

This is true up to a point, but the situation Braun describes also makes for debate in the study of religion and forces researchers to think critically about fundamental issues: How does one go about setting up a research project? How is religion to be conceptualized and analyzed? What about logics and modes of analysis, and how these relate to particular methods of research? What protocols does one follow in carrying out the research? Can one be flexible in research, or must one follow the established rules at all costs? All these are questions for which answers are neither obvious nor straightforward; the more we probe the questions the more we realize how complex, and sometimes controversial, they can be. All the questions also bear upon considerations of **research design**, that is, the overall plan or strategy for achieving the aim(s) of a particular inquiry, which is to be distinguished from the broader topic of **methodology**, which reflects on the adequacy of research designs and the validity of research findings from the perspective of logic and philosophy of science.

Here our concern is with research design, with specific approaches and procedures for conducting an investigation. Much attention is given to research methods—tools of sorts— for selecting, collecting, classifying and analyzing observations and other types of information. Researchers assume responsibility for the choice of methods and their use in interpreting and representing findings from research. Generally, these choices should reflect the authenticity and trustworthiness of the researcher as well as meet the tests of inter-subjectivity, as Riis (2009: 239) emphasizes. The first two are fairly straightforward as personal virtues, the second implies that among two or more researchers using the same data, methods and modes of analysis, there should be a good deal of concurrence as to the findings. While there is always some room for differences in interpretation, as a principle, inter-subjective agreement is good in that it pushes in the direction of achieving greater accuracy.

As all these points suggest, research has a very public face: normally we conduct our investigations within, and in expectation of, scrutiny by a community of researchers—professional and academic societies in particular—with widely shared understandings about acceptable research procedures. Journal publications are typically peer reviewed and must meet academic standards relating to the proper fit of concepts and evidence and logic of argumentation. At times this involves ruling out alternative explanations and defense of a particular argument, but always there are protocols by which the procedures are evaluated. Even with exploratory research which, as the term implies, is less strict, investigation involves a measure of discipline and adherence to principles of research. Often the latter is a first step leading to a more comprehensive and frequently more complex research strategy in addressing a topic.

That word religion

Aside from exercising discipline, researchers need a probing imagination, one that pushes toward exploring new, promising leads into how and why things religious, or connected to the religious, hang together. Research builds upon initial questions or hunches about such connections, often expands into hypotheses in a more formal sense, but almost always becomes more involved or complicated as one begins to think about the possible complexities. Just as the social critic C. Wright Mills (1959) once spoke of a 'sociological imagination' as enabling a better understanding of the social order and of one's location within it, similarly a 'religious imagination' helps in grasping this complex thing called religion, so deeply and variously embedded in culture in ways both visible and invisible, obvious and not so obvious. Moreover, such imagination must extend beyond simply a grasp of the religious phenomenon itself to also prod reflection more generally about how a particular researcher or team of researchers in a particular time and place, the people who are researched either directly or indirectly, and the process of research are all closely intertwined.

A critical imagination is essential for several reasons. One is that the term 'religion' encompasses a complex set of forms: institutions, traditions, new movements, sacred texts, religious nationalism, alternative spiritual practices and so forth. Each form requires its own conceptualization and logic of research in relation to a particular social context. Added to this is the challenge of distinguishing between the 'religious' and the 'nonreligious' in the contemporary world. With rampant consumption and commodification of religious themes—i.e. ways in which beliefs, myths, ethical teachings and practices are drawn into commercial culture—distinguishing between the two becomes even more difficult and calls for especially creative conceptualizing. This is particularly evident in the case of movements addressing questions of spirituality, recovery, journey and personal meaning, all of which draw heavily from identity-affirming psychological languages.

Further, in the modern context, researchers have to be sensitive to privatizing and de-privatizing trends in religion (Casanova 1994). Individual belief and spirituality illustrate the first and resurgent fundamentalism the second. Overall, researchers must understand that religious traditions are reinvented, constantly changing, and that people exercise considerable choice in formulating their own religious worlds, likely far more so today than in the past. 'Lived religion' is far different from that normatively defined by religious authorities. Bourdieu's (1977: chapter 1) emphasis on 'strategic practices' and Swidler's (1986) cultural 'tool kit' metaphor both signal this more open, fluid situation of lived religious life. For example, according to a recent national poll, roughly a fourth of Americans say they believe in reincarnation and/or practice yoga, and those who do tend to be politically liberal—evidence of a global diffusion of religious and spiritual influences and also a reconfiguring of religion and politics (Pew Forum on Religion and Public Life 2009). Pointing to the complexities of religious meaning systems, religious studies scholar Robert Orsi (1997: 7) emphasizes that scholars should pay more attention to the 'hermeneutics of hybridity', which he describes as 'how particular people, in particular places and times, live in, with, through, and against the religious idioms, including (often enough) those not explicitly their own'.

Conceptualizing religion as a particular form, especially in the contemporary world, precedes the completed formulation of a research design. With historical study of religion, it is tempting to impose our own, temporally bound views on its forms and its meaning as if these fit in other times and places. Even in studying an ancient Hindu text or medieval Christian practices, there are analogous complications. Whether in philological-linguistic studies or analysis of historical ritual as Hall points out, there are interpretive pitfalls: idealism, objectification, and ideology, to name the three he mentions (Hall 1991: 95–98). Idealism leads to over-interpreting history, assuming that a particular ideal or cultural motif is working out over time in a particular direction; objectification implies over-interpretation of reality or presuming it to be more ordered than perhaps it is; and ideology suggests an interpretation justified by a particular set of ideas and/or interests on the part of the interpreter or of a prevailing school of interpretation. In each instance what this means for the study of religion is that some potential bias can be introduced to the interpretation by the researcher. As Jonathan Z. Smith (1978) likes to say, a 'map is not territory', underscoring the point that maps, or conceptual schemes, point always to religious realities in some particular form or manifestation. Researchers need to be cognizant of the fact that any conceptual framework privileges some aspects and expressions of religion and not others, and thus in approaching a research topic, an open, inquiring mind is essential.

A research project

Now, we turn to a specific research project, one an undergraduate major in religious studies at my university is conducting. It provides a springboard for discussing many aspects of research design. The project focuses on the religiosity of college students born of interfaith parents or where one parent claims to be religious and the other not, and how they are adapting religiously, or non-religiously, to these circumstances. Specifically, she is interested in the meaning-making process of students, of how in these situations they selectively create their own beliefs and practices, i.e. if they are religious, how so and why, and if not religious, in what sense not and why. As to the particular form of religion she wants to explore, it is the contemporary mixing and matching of themes drawn from religious traditions and current discussions of spirituality. She is upfront about why this latter type of religious formation is of interest: her mother is a practicing Sikh-American but who also reads mystical literature from various faith traditions; her father claims to be 'non-religious' but acknowledges that his grandparents were Norwegian Lutherans. Recognizing the complexity of her family situa-tion, she realizes that her study requires careful attention to issues of religious identity and practice, and particularly so with children of immigrants seeking to hold on to aspects of their culture of origin while integrating into a new, highly pluralist society such as the United States. She is drawn to sociological analysis of religion but wants to combine it with historical specificity of the faith groups. Hers is a **cross-sectional** research design, that is, one that looks at patterns among factors that she has identified as influencing the religious outcomes of the students based upon analysis at one point in time. A researcher draws inferences about the magnitude of influences and presumed trends from comparison of the factors within that single frame. This differs from **longitudinal** design since, as the latter suggests, it involves research at more than one point in time and is a means of identifying and measuring more precisely trends over a designated time span.

Units of analysis

Perhaps the first, and most obvious, issue in research design that surfaces in this project is the unit of analysis. This has to do with level of conceptualization, which in this instance is that of individuals—their identity as religious or nonreligious, and how so and in what ways. Unit of analysis shapes how we think of the properties that are forefronted in the research, i.e. in this instance personal beliefs and practices primarily, yet also the students' affiliations with religious groups, ethical commitments and worldviews. From this follows an interpretive logic framed for examining these basic religious characteristics, with attention to connections among them and how these vary by ethnic and religious tradition, family and background features, e.g. level of education, social class, and racial and ethnic identity.

However, the study of students' religious commitment is more complex than it might at first appear, a situation not all that uncommon in other research projects where the individual is the major unit of analysis. The religious influence of groups and cultural inheritance has an impact upon individuals, even among those who claim to be secular and who do not recognize such subtle influences. This is exemplified, in this project, by the researcher's father who claims to be nonreligious but acknowledges his Norwegian Lutheran background. One thinks as well of non-observant Jews and cultural Catholics, neither highly involved in a synagogue or church but who identify communally, some quite strongly, with their ethnic and/or religious heritages. Specifying the range and types of religious influences in today's world is challenging, particularly among those with limited outward appearance of being religious. In addition to the historical communities formed by religious traditions such as Norwegian Lutheran there are many new types of communities, some explicitly religious, others far less so, to which people belong. Communities emerging out of popular religious movements and a wide array of small sharing and seeker-oriented groups, both within and outside of organized religion, are prevalent around the world. These newer communities are important to the study of religion. Media and technology today, too, have a huge influence on religious and spiritual styles; the rise of Internet-driven special-purpose groups which draw selectively upon religious symbols, ethics and teachings are very successful in mobilizing large constituencies around a variety of compelling concerns: e.g. the global environmentalist, HIV/AIDS, and pro-life and pro-choice movements. The role of communal belonging in both traditional faith groups and the newer movements is critical to understanding types of individual religious loyalty.

Dimensions of religious commitment

The discussion of communities and their influences leads to broader attention to the various dimensions of religious commitment. Whether analyzing religious traditions or individual styles of faith and spirituality, there are major components such as ritual, myth, doctrine, experience, ethics, community and knowledge (see Smart 1999). For an earlier generation of scholars, sorting out these various components was essential to advancing a broad, well-rounded picture of religion and necessary for moving religious study beyond a theological or confessional mode to a more descriptive and comparative mode of analysis. Later on, psychologists and sociologists did much the same by looking at individuals and profiling patterns of commitment, and by identifying how clusters of dimensions hang together within and across faith traditions, and as correlated to people's life-situations. The empirical research of Rodney Stark and Charles Y. Glock (Stark and Glock 1968; see related research studies described in Roof 1979) was influential in describing these various types of religious dimensions within the American context.

Our student project here makes use of the research on dimensionality: the plan is to ask students about their religious beliefs, experiences, practices, values and knowledge of, and appreciation for, sacred texts using items that were used by earlier researchers. More than just looking at these substantive dimensions, the researcher asks a battery of questions exploring their nuances more deeply. At one level, there are the basic dimensions such as ritual, doctrine, myth, experience, practice and so forth, but each of these can also be examined on another grid with regard to selected features, depending upon their appropriateness pertaining to content, intensity of loyalty, centrality and frequency (see Verbit 1970). Attention to these sub-dimensions helps in capturing still greater insight into individual and group religious life. For example, some believers—often evangelical Christians—know fairly well the content of what they believe, hold intensely to their convictions and regard their personal relationship with God as central in their lives; however, seeing themselves as 'Jesus and me' believers, they do not feel it necessary to participate actively within a religious community. Knowing this, a researcher analyzing these believers would likely focus more on personal belief and its subjective meaning than on church attendance, which is an associational type of measure of religious commitment. Focus on belief and its centrality in this instance makes for greater precision as to what defines religiosity for this constituency. For scholarly reasons, too, it is important to single out particular emphases in religious commitment within traditions and in relation to social circumstances. Early 20th-century social theorists are remembered for their strong, forceful arguments about religion's role in society precisely because they defined which aspects of religion were most central and consequential, Durkheimians privileging ritual and its social functions, and Weberians stressing the autonomous influence of beliefs, ideas and ethical teachings, to cite two major historical schools of interpretation.

Logics and approaches

As already noted, research design refers to the overall plan of a project, a blueprint for linking the many parts in a logical process of investigation. It is guided first and foremost by the question asked in the research. For the student project this is 'How and in what ways were the students' religious (or nonreligious) views and practices influenced by growing up in mixed-religion families?' It is a simple descriptive type of investigation. She begins with a relatively short questionnaire distributed in several large lecture classes at her university, asking about students' parental religious backgrounds, gathers information on social demographics and a few attitudinal items, and inquires if they are willing to participate further in the study. With this information she will then select some students for in-depth interviews, including those both with interfaith parents and with mixed religious-nonreligious backgrounds. Next, she will analyze the interviews looking for meaning and overall patterns in order to make comparisons between students with interfaith parents and those with religious-secular backgrounds. One procedure builds upon another in a logically ordered project.

Internal logics vary for each of these research phases. First, it is crucial that the questionnaire be thought out and designed carefully before it is administered. Items must be worded as clearly as possible and framed to elicit the information necessary to carrying out the project. Second, the in-depth interviews require careful attention to picking up on information from the questionnaires and examining the dimensions and sub-dimensions of religiosity as described above. Familiarity with the research literature on student religiosity, much of which includes items that were used in other studies, is essential. Methodological resources and data banks are also available on the Internet (see 'data resources' at the end of this chapter), providing examples of questions that have been used. Using instruments from other studies allows for replication, which is very much valued in research. A pre-test of all instruments, and particularly of newly devised questions and items in questionnaires and interviews, is almost always essential. Even with previously used instruments, applicability depends in part upon the population to which they are administered as compared with their earlier usage.

Semi-structured interviews are appropriate for the research under discussion, since they combine major questions asked of everyone with open-ended, exploratory questions allowing the researcher to query in greater depth the nuances of beliefs and practices of the interviewees in this instance with an eye toward how the students are forging their own distinctive mix of inherited and improvised religious views.

Throughout all of this, there is the question of how concepts—the fundamental building block of any analysis—link to observations and empirical indicators. The latter may be thought of as quantifiable 'measures' as in social scientific research or simply as 'labels' attached to concepts, as is the case typically in humanistic research. Measures are treated as **operational definitions**, often somewhat arbitrarily, for tapping into the conceptual space presumed to be an aspect of reality to be examined, whereas labels are names simply given to concepts. Critical here are notions of validity and reliability, terms arising out of scientific methodologies but now widely absorbed into discussions of qualitative analysis and humanistic research as well (see Denzin and Lincoln 2003). Validity has to do with whether a particular method 'gets at' the object of study in a way that two or more observers can reasonably agree. 'Face validity' is a common concern, that is, does the measure or label adequately capture what is intended in the research; judgment about validity in this simple reading of the term can be little more than a researcher having an informed sense of its adequacy or, better, whether it is deemed appropriate in view of other research findings and how convincing and intuitively correct are the arguments based upon its use. Reliability is whether or not repeated uses of a measure in empirical-statistical research yield similar results; in humanistic research typically such judgment about labels of concepts refers, as with validity, on the adequacy and consistency of the conceptualization as revealed across a range of studies. Reliability implies validity, but extends it to a consideration of repeatability.

For the project under review, the researcher relies upon a review of the literature on student religiosity, looking at how other researchers have used concepts and particular measures to see how well they predict other responses, e.g. 'I believe in God' would likely correlate well with 'I believe in some ultimate purpose in life'. This is a simple, somewhat trivial example of what is known as 'predictive validity'. She also considers qualitative information from historical studies on religious traditions and the experiences of immigrant groups within the United States. To the extent possible, she plans to engage in a 'content analysis' looking at themes from the in-depth interviews relating to knowledge about, and commitment to, sacred texts. Influenced by her mother's interest in mystical writings such as those of the Adi Granth and the poet Kafir, she plans to query students about religious literature they and their parents have read, and then to explore patterns among themes and popular interpretations of students as compared with those of their parents. Here she is influenced by recent attention to religion and culture as symbolic objects, themselves structured into patterns of ideas, teachings, emphases and interpretive modes—good examples being texts, discourse, sermons, moral codes and popular religious literature (see Wuthnow 1987: 50–57). Again, the unit-of-analysis issue arises: aside from just individual meaning systems, there is the coherence of meaning systems as evident within such forms. Comparing the traditional meaning systems attached to the form by religious authorities with their more popular, often quite diverse interpretations can be an important part of this research task.

Triangulation

The principle of obtaining multiple 'soundings' on a phenomenon, using differing approaches to the study, is important in religious research, with variations in practice and applicability.

As we have seen, the student engaged in the project here uses a variety of methods to paint a portrait of student religiosity—questionnaires, interviews and analysis of meaning systems as inferred from religious texts with which they and their parents are familiar. Quantitative and qualitative methods are thus combined: the first provides a statistical overview of the broad parameters of the subject, while the second offers in-depth exploration and more nuanced detail both for individuals and for the textual materials. Thinking of these as data points, when combined they complement and to some extent offer a check upon one another. Even with a very simple exploratory study—say, of followers within a new religious movement, of progressive Catholics in a particular parish, or of people who go on retreats to meditate—it can be useful to compare demographics, beliefs and attitudes for the group under study with a larger, and often more representative, population. This is triangulation of a different type, but again data from one source serves as a check on newly gathered research information. Widely accessible data banks now allow researchers to determine how similar or dissimilar a relatively small group being studied is relative to other similar constituencies on a great variety of indicators. The principle of triangulation extends to looking at how variations among profiles of religiosity and social background for similar groups, thereby offering a better sense of the group under study in its larger religious and social context. Historians engage in a similar logic when they compare primary sources from archives with the secondary analysis and commentary of previous historians; in this way they can examine the representation of the former by the latter, and thus chart the process of writing revisionist history. This latter is something of an interpretive project unto itself. The fundamental argument for triangulation in whatever way it occurs is two-fold: first, alternative methods of study are complementary, each serving to round-out the picture of what amounts to a composite set of information; second, triangulation serves as a check on the researcher's subjectivity, the point being that the greater the number of 'soundings' relating to a research question the less likely it is that researchers can dismiss or twist evidence in favor of their own inclinations.

Representation

Simply put, representation refers to portrayal: the picture painted of the people, communities, institutions or other religious phenomena. It arises as a concern in various ways depending upon types of research projects. Representation begins with something as simple, yet basic as properly labeling a population or set of artifacts that is studied. Our student researcher faced this when selecting classes at the university in which to pass out questionnaires: she chose three large lecture classes in chemistry, history and political science and deliberately avoided including a religious studies class. There is no right or wrong here, mostly a matter of how best to define the parameters of the research and to meet that goal. Because she wanted to describe religious patterns of transmission from parents in the case of students with interfaith and religious/secular backgrounds at the university, she sought responses across science, social science and humanities courses. This allowed for comparison across the three subpopulations, adding to the richness of her study. A religious studies class was not included because she felt its students might be more knowledgeable about the topics she was exploring, and that this could introduce a bias into the findings. In addition, for practical reasons, she chose not to take on yet another comparison, in this instance between religious studies students and all others. Obviously, the latter could be an interesting research topic in itself, but it was not what she was interested in pursuing.

She also confronted the question of how many student questionnaires to collect and how many in-depth interviews to undertake. How many cases does one need in order to make reliable generalizations? In large-scale quantitative surveys this is less of a problem simply because with a sample size of several hundred, the reliability of inferences drawn is far more likely. The larger the sample the better since, according to the statistical 'law of large numbers', as the number of observations increases, the greater the probability that the mean (average) scores will reflect true estimates of the larger population; these same scores from small samples are more prone to fluctuate. Related is the question of randomness, or of having a **random sample**, meaning, in the strict sense, that each case in the larger population has an equal chance of being included in the sample. Obviously, in much research this assumption is not met, and because researchers often cannot conduct large studies given time and cost considerations, they are forced to settle for less-than-ideal sample sizes. She had a total of 186 completed questionnaires, which is ample; statisticians warn against fewer than 50 cases in drawing generalizations. With the in-depth interviews she did not worry as much about numbers: she conducted 37 interviews, 17 with students having inter-faith parents, 20 with those having religious-secular parents. Ideally, there would have been more interviews, but because she treated information gleaned from these for describing nuances and providing good quotes in the process of intergenerational transmission of religiosity, it seemed not to be an overly serious problem. (A 'good' quote here is not simply one that is intrinsically interesting or rhetorically effective: such citations from interviews are effective when they illustrate tendencies or significant exceptions and, more generally, when they instantiate a specific finding for one of the measures or labels used in the study.) Lack of more interviews did pose something of a tricky issue in the interpretation when looking at males and females separately within the two student clusters. Taking account of this factor reduced the number of cases more or less in half. This is not an uncommon problem in exploratory research of this kind. With qualitative studies of the sort more common in religious studies, issues of sampling and population are less weighty but cannot be totally dismissed.

With historical, textual and interpretive research (including in-depth interviews) where attention is given largely to describing the meanings ascribed to symbols, scripts, discourse and to describing what people say and do—especially in ethnographic research where the observer interacts and often participates with the people—the researcher's own views and sensitivities become a methodological concern. Particularly in the write-up of research, questions easily arise relating to voice and to the values and views of the researcher. Much attention in religious studies over the years has been given to the 'insider-outsider' debate, to **verstehen** (modeling individual perspectives), epoché (suspension of belief), '**bracketing**' of truth claims, 'methodological agnosticism', and, more recently, **self-reflexivity**, all in an effort to minimize bias or misinterpretation on the researcher's side. Our student researcher worried about how to present herself in the interviews if asked whether she and either of her parents were religious, fearing that whatever she said might in some way affect what respondents said themselves. She chose to be honest, quite appropriately, but to describe both of the parents where possible and thus give as much variation of religious and nonreligious identities as she could.

This latter concern is voiced especially in ethnography, where what is learned depends in great part on how researchers present themselves, and in turn on how the informants present themselves to the researchers, which potentially can alter the researchers' views. The interpretative process becomes very complicated, as shown in Box 1.5.1 where Landres (2002) describes eight '**representational moments**', as he calls them. Each is an example of where slippage in interpretation is possible. Other researchers have pointed to even more such moments, the major point in all of this being that ethnographers and others engaged in field research must take seriously how relations between the researcher and the researched, and between researchers and their professional colleagues, can potentially impact research. Problems of subjectivism and interactive bias in qualitative research can be reduced by involving several researchers in the same project, since they can provide checks upon one another's interpretations; however, this of course is often not possible, and single investigators must be conscious of the subtle issues involved and discipline themselves as best they can to addressing them.

Box 1.5.1 Representational moments in fieldwork

- The researcher represents herself to those studied
- The 'others' represent the researcher to themselves
- The 'others' represent themselves to others within their own group
- The 'others' represent themselves to the researcher
- The 'others' represent the researcher to herself
- The researcher represents the 'others' to other researchers and the public
- The researcher represents the 'others' to themselves
- The researcher represents the field researcher not only to the public but also to her fellow researchers

(Landres 2002)

Not just in ethnography but in religious studies projects generally, researchers need to be conscious of how they stand in relation to what they study. Anthropologist André Droogers sums up this situation very well:

> To assess the characteristics of religion, one must include the perspective of the scholar. The definition of religion is hardly objective—an old positivist ideal—without an appraisal of the presuppositions and hidden options. What was kept implicit or considered irrelevant needs to be made explicit[. . .] This means that scholars should look not only at the object of study but also at their own role[. . .] Instead of locating themselves outside their field, students of religion should view themselves, if only for a short time of self-examination, as actors in that field.
>
> *(Droogers 2009: 276)*

Situated in this manner, the work of the researcher, Droogers says, can be understood as a form of serious 'play' (Droogers 2009: 277). 'Play'—like 'imagination'—suggests many things: an awareness of roles, of engagement with others and their traditions, and of creative encounters. Whatever else is required of the researcher in religion, imagination, empathy and openness to possibilities are all critical. As in the study of culture generally, one must see oneself as engaged in an ongoing reflection over how best to represent what he or she studies and do so self-consciously, as Droogers says, as an actor within the field in an extended play of give and take, of assertion and counter-assertion, and of what amounts to an ever-shifting and negotiated set of interpretations.

Concluding comments

It should by now be apparent there is no single or 'right' research design for a particular project. Even with the best-designed projects, conceptually and methodologically, revision during the conduct of the research, and in particular after pre-tests, is not uncommon. Practical issues of time and cost almost inevitably arise. Shortcuts are often unavoidable but should be avoided if possible, in light of what this might mean for the quality of evidence, its validity and reliability. Research designs both simple and complex can yield excellent or, if the design is flawed, poor results. Simple designs that are parsimonious and well focused are among the best, but all depends, of course, on how well a design succeeds in capturing valid and reliable answers to the key question. The critical issue is whether the research results in a convincing outcome as judged by the best of research standards.

As we imagine the future, the possibilities for innovative research on religion are very promising. We know more now about the strengths and weaknesses of various types of research design than a decade or two ago, even though new challenges will inevitably arise as new religious forms emerge. Cross-cultural developments in religions, politics and ideology in a global world will almost certainly lead to the formation of better concepts, theories and research methodologies. Comparative analyses will advance as we rely upon better, more standardized types of data and as researchers become more sensitive to the cultural biases of particular methods and approaches to the study of religion. With the Internet, we now have more historical archives and databases on religion across countries than ever before, a resource that will undoubtedly continue to expand. Researchers are able already to share methods and findings across national borders, to explore multi-disciplinary approaches cross-culturally, and to communicate with one another on questions about concepts, measures, validity, reliability and other design issues. However, not all Internet resources meet the tests of providing good data. Some of it is compiled by partisan and ideologically driven sources; the information is often biased and unrepresentative, obviously a poor basis on which to draw reliable generalizations. Researchers thus must exercise considerable caution and good judgment as they use these materials. As resources at our disposal and opportunities for global collaboration increase, so too must our sense of professional discipline and responsibility. To quote the biblical injunction: to whom much is given, much is required.

References

Bourdieu, P., 1977. *Outline of a Theory of Practice*. Cambridge University Press, Cambridge.

Braun, W., 2000. Religion. In: Braun, W. and McCutcheon, R.T. (eds), *Guide to the Study of Religion*. Cassell, London, pp. 3–18.

Casanova, J., 1994. *Public Religions in the Modern World*. University of Chicago Press, Chicago.

Denzin, N.K. and Lincoln, Y.S. (eds), 2003. *The Landscape of Qualitative Research*. SAGE, London, Thousand Oaks, CA.

Droogers, A., 2009. Defining religion: a social science approach. In: Clarke, P.B. (ed.), *The Oxford Handbook of the Sociology of Religion*. Oxford University Press, Oxford.

Hall, J.R., 1991. Hermeneutics, social movements, and thematic religious history. In: Bromley, D.G. (ed.), *Religion and the Social Order*. JAI Press Inc., London, vol. 1, pp. 91–114.

Landres, J.S., 2002. Being (in) the field: defining ethnography in Southern California and Central Slovakia. In: Spickard, J.V., Landres, J.S. and McGuire, M.B. (eds), *Personal Knowledge and Beyond: Reshaping the Ethnography of Religion*. New York University Press, New York, pp. 100–12.

Mills, C.W., 1959. *The Sociological Imagination*. Oxford University Press, Oxford.

Orsi, R., 1997. Everyday Miracles: the study of lived religion. In: Hall, D.D. (ed.), *Lived Religion in America*. Princeton University Press, Princeton.

Riis, O.R., 2009. Methodology in the sociology of religion. In: Clarke, P.B. (ed.), *The Oxford Handbook of the Sociology of Religion*. Oxford University Press, Oxford, New York, pp. 229–44.

Roof, W.C., 1979. Concepts and indicators of religious commitment: a critical review. In Wuthnow, R. (ed.), *The Religious Dimension: new directions in quantitative research*. Academic Press, New York, pp. 17–45.

Smart, N., 1999. *Worldviews: cross-cultural exploration of human beliefs*. 3rd edn. Prentice-Hall, Englewood, NJ.

Smith, J.Z., 1978. *Map Is Not Territory: studies in the history of religion*. Brill, Leiden.

Stark, R. and Glock, C.Y., 1968. *American Piety: the nature of religious commitment*. University of California Press, Berkeley.

Swidler, A., 1986. Culture in action: symbols and strategies. *American Sociological Review* 51: 273–86.

Verbit, M.F., 1970. The components and dimensions of religious behavior: toward a reconceptualization of religiosity. In: Hammond, P.E. and Johnson, B. (eds), *American Mosaic: social patterns of religion in the United States*. New York: Random House, pp. 24–39.

Wuthnow, R., 1987. *Meaning and Moral Order: explorations in cultural analysis*. University of California Press, Berkeley.

Further reading

Alvesson, M., 2010. *Interpreting Interviews*. SAGE, London, Thousand Oaks, CA.

Very helpful in constructing and analyzing interview data.

Clarke, P.B. (ed.), 2009. *The Oxford Handbook of the Sociology of Religion*. Oxford University Press, New York.

A huge volume of essays surveying the sociological study of religion with an excellent section on methods and methodologies.

Creswell, J.W. and Clark, V.L., 2010. *Designing and Conducting Mixed Methods Research*. SAGE, London, Thousand Oaks, CA.

A general methods volume very helpful in making decisions about research designs, and of combining statistical and other types of methods.

Glaser, B.G. and Strauss, A.L., 1967. *The Discovery of Grounded Theory: strategies for qualitative research*. Aldine de Gruyter, Chicago.

A classic that examines observations, concept-formation and inductive logic.

Lofland, J. and Lofland, L.H., 1995. *Analyzing Social Settings: a guide to qualitative observation and analysis*. 3rd edn. Wadsworth, Belmont, CA.

Well-known researchers look closely at the 'leap' from observation in field studies to analysis.

O'Reilly, K., 2009. *Key Concepts in Ethnography*. SAGE, London, Thousand Oaks, CA.

As the title suggests, the book examines more than 30 key concepts relating to ethnography.

Travers, M., 2001. *Qualitative Research through Case Studies*. SAGE, London, Thousand Oaks, CA.

A comparative analysis of case studies, not focused on religion but helpful in grasping the logic of comparative research.

Williams, M., 2000. Interpretivism and generalization. *Sociology* 34 (2): 209–24.

An excellent treatment of the pitfalls of interpretation and of making responsible generalizations in research.

Data resources

adherents.com: An enormous bank of information on world religions by countries and geographical areas.

American Religion Data Archive. www.arda.com. A large archive of survey and membership data on religious bodies in the United States.

Online Texts. www.library.yale.edu/div/forfree.html#texts. A large set of textual and ethics resources.

Pew Forum on Religion and Public Life. pewforum.org. Extensive body of survey data and commentary on religion and social and political issues within the United States.

Religiousmovements.org. Information on new religious movements plus coverage of controversies and court cases involving new religions.

Search Institute. www.search-institute.org/content/web-links-faith-communities. An extensive and diverse set of information on religion.

Key concepts

Bracketing: self-awareness on the researcher's part to try to suspend one's own values and beliefs.

Cross-sectional design: Collection of data from a sample of cases at one point of time.

Hermeneutic of suspicion: critical and questioning interpretation looking beyond appearances.

Longitudinal design: Collection of data from the same sample (individuals or groups) across time.

Methodology: philosophical reflection on a research design, its appropriateness, validity and interpretation.

Operational definitions: measures used to represent concepts in empirical research.

Random sample: a selected subgroup where every person or unit of observation within a population has an equal chance of being selected.

Representational moments: times in representing the other in acts of research, especially in ethnography.

Research design: overall plan of the relationships among concepts, methods and logical inference in research.

Self-reflexivity: capacity to think critically about context and one's self in relation to the other.

Verstehen: quality of identifying and empathizing with another.

1.6

RESEARCH ETHICS

Frederick Bird and Laurie Lamoureux Scholes

Chapter summary

- This chapter offers researchers in religious studies practical advice for negotiating the ethical waters of research practices.
- The act of research requires that researchers ought to respect the basic dignity of their subjects, communicate honestly and objectively with their subjects and audiences, and exercise responsibly the diverse ethical judgements we inevitably make within all stages of the research process.
- In so far as our research involves interactions with living persons, our investigations also need to comply with an additional set of regulated ethical obligations with respect to risk-benefits analysis, informed consent, freedom to discontinue and confidentiality.

Research is first and foremost a moral activity.

(Nina Hallowell et al. *2005: 148)*

Introduction

As scholars within the field of religious studies we are inherently engaged in the study of the religious life of other people. Whether we focus our research on studies of architecture or texts, on organizations or rituals, historical or contemporary, our research is not just an exercise in literary criticism, symbolic analysis, social deconstruction or archaeological reconstruction. It is also an engagement with the people who have and do express their religious lives using these texts, actions and artifacts. As researchers, then, we gather, analyze, organize, interpret, translate, re-present and communicate information about religions. In the process we inevitably involve ourselves in several overlapping conversations—whether actual, assumed, implied or imagined—with the subjects of our research and with various audiences which may include other researchers, our colleagues, critics, assistants, project sponsors, people in positions of authority, policy-makers, media and interest groups, as well as the subjects themselves. These conversations require our ongoing attention to ensure ethical integrity in both our treatment of those we study and in our efforts to produce and disseminate knowledge about their religious life.

Generally, the practice of ethics involves efforts by humans to guide human conduct in relation to normative standards and values, variously identified in relation to outcomes, dispositions and modes of acting. With respect to research in religious studies, there are at present no widely recognized normative standards or guidelines, no professional code of ethics to set the standard for both how we should engage in our investigations and how we should communicate what we learn in the process. The absence of a professional code in part reflects the fact that those who engage in religious studies do so with quite different disciplinary approaches—for example, as historians, field researchers, psychologists, literary critics, economists, or philosophers. Scholars of religion also approach their studies from quite dissimilar orientations—as secular scholars, committed members of varied religious groups, and/or former members. Yet, within the diverse communities of scholars involved in religious research, we think that there are several basic principles for the practise of ethics with respect to religious research that can, and for the most part already are, held in common.

It is important to recognize that ethical issues/dilemmas arise in religious studies research in at least three different ways. First, sometimes ethical issues emerge because someone—researchers or the subjects—are clearly acting in violation of basic ethical or legal standards. For example, evidence is being blatantly misrepresented; works are being knowingly plagiarized; coercion or manipulation is possibly being practised on some group members; relevant information is being suppressed; private, confidential information is being exposed without permission; consent to undertake research has been manipulated. These are examples of **ethical wrongs**. Many more examples could be cited. It is useful to warn people against these prohibited activities, to identify any instances that might occur, and to prevent them from recurring, as far as possible. Most universities and professional associations have established complaint and due process procedures to confidentially review allegations of these kinds of wrongs and to determine appropriate responses, whether in the form of discipline, censure or referral to fitting public agencies. If we become aware that wrongs are being committed in the groups we are studying—such as what seems like the abuse of children or the use of manipulative recruitment practices—then we are obligated to determine whether relevant legal standards may be being violated and whether and how we might be called on to report on these activities. In some cases the discovery of what looks like wrongs may occasion serious dilemmas as we puzzle over what responses seem appropriate.

Second, many more ethical issues present themselves not as overt wrongs but as shortfalls from standards of excellence expressed either as fundamental moral principles or as institutional guidelines. For example, subjects are mostly but not fully informed. Relevant data is partially overlooked. Moral evaluations and/or religious views may cause researchers to discount important information too quickly. Researchers begin to reify the categories they are using for analysis; that is, they treat their concepts as more real than the people and activities they are studying. Observers too quickly dismiss the accounts of subjects as being either self-serving tales, echoed versions of official group stories, or simply fanciful expressions. All of these examples represent probable instances of **moral shortfalls**. Generally, more appropriate ethical behavior is typically fostered in these kinds of cases through mentoring, collegial criticism and by motivating people to seek more assistance/feedback and to exert greater caution.

Third, ethical issues with respect to research sometimes present themselves as genuine **ethical dilemmas** or debates about which it is possible to arrive at more than one ethically justified position. Consider the following questions: Is it acceptable or not to receive research funding from an organization associated with the group we intend to investigate? To what extent is it useful and legitimate to allow our studies of scriptures to be informed by theological assumptions? How much credence should we give to the accounts of religious movements provided by former members? Why have sociologists tended to provide sympathetic accounts of contemporary new religious movements and psychologists have in turn tended to provide much more critical accounts? When is it acceptable to pay informants for their time to be interviewed or complete questionnaires and survey forms? As we investigate a particular religious group, knowing that however we choose to focus we will overlook possibly relevant information, to what extent should we pay attention to broad characteristics, interesting examples, the accounts of articulate informants, and/or hearsay information? There are no inherently right or wrong answers to these kinds of questions. Research can and will be guided by diverse values and interests. Yet the public character of our reports and studies means that at the very least we invite diverse others to comment, to raise questions and to point out what they consider to be imbalanced in the way we have undertaken, analyzed and reported on our research.

Box 1.6.1 Ethical concerns in research

- Ethical wrongs
- Moral shortfalls
- Ethical dilemmas

In this chapter we explore further examples of each of the above ethical issues/dilemmas in relation to two different yet equally important kinds of ethical standards applicable to research in religion, whether in the field or in the library. First, we discuss three general guiding principles that are fundamental to all stages of the research process—before, during and after engagement with our research subjects. They in part define the practice of research as a profession, a moral activity with clear responsibilities and obligations. They act as a continual reminder that it is the ways in which we relate to and treat others that make our research ethical. Second, we examine the more precise set of ethical requirements regulated by formal research review boards. These more precise rules refer to the minimal obligations that must be met to receive formal approvals from institutional ethical reviews for research projects involving human subjects. While these rules must be followed by those undertaking these kinds of contemporary investigations, the considerations associated with these rules remain relevant to research in religious studies in general.

It is important to note that while ethical standards often appear by themselves quite obviously as overt ethical duties, obligations and values, many times the norms and values that shape the expectations of how we should act responsibly as researchers are also expressed by and integrated with standards communicated by common sense, methodological procedures and rules of etiquette. This is especially true with regards to the ethical standards with respect to research. Standards such as those that call for us to respect the dignity and privacy of our subjects or call for us to reliably reference the sources of our information are frequently communicated at the same time by methodological guidelines, legal stipulations, as well as ethical expectations. Correspondingly, as we review the basic ethical principles governing research ethics, we will at times echo normative expectations also expressed by those concerned with epistemological and methodological standards.[1]

Part one: Basic guiding ethical principles

In approaching any research project there are three general and fundamental ethical principles that guide how religious research ought to be done. These are as follows: first, researchers ought to respect and appreciate the dignity and integrity of our subjects; second, researchers ought to communicate honestly and objectively to our subjects and audiences who, depending on the character of our investigations, may be quite restricted or broad, include diverse publics and/or be members of our own religious communities; and third, researchers ought to exercise our judgements responsibly as we gather, analyze and evaluate our data, and report on our research.[2]

Unlike regulated ethical protocols, these fundamental principles primarily serve not as restraints to limit questionable research practices—though they do—but as grounds that identify the basic purposes of research. The ethical good of research is integrated with the efforts undertaken out of respect, interest and appreciation of the diverse others who are the subjects of our studies to locate new information, to identify significance, to see patterns and to communicate our accounts publicly as part of ongoing conversations with subjects and audiences—colleagues, critics, media, policy-makers, interest groups, etc. These principles remind us to exercise due caution so that we do not overlook people who are not as well represented in written sources and official accounts. We are cautioned as well not to unwittingly conflate our moral evaluations with our efforts to explain and identify representative information and cautioned not to communicate our results only to those likely to agree with us. These principles remind us that in all phases of the research process we are engaged in overlapping conversations—both real and imagined—with subjects and audiences and that we need to attend to what others communicate, directly and indirectly.[3]

Box 1.6.2 Three general ethical principles of religious research

- Respecting the dignity and integrity of others
- Communicating honestly and objectively with our subjects and audiences
- Responsibly exercising judgement

Respecting the dignity and integrity of others

Out of respect for the dignity of others, we must begin our studies taking very seriously how the others we are studying account for their symbols, rituals, texts and behaviors. That is, where such accounts are at all relevant, they must not simply be disregarded. Our initial mandate is to be attentive to these others as others, not subsuming them within our frames of reference but instead paying attention to them in relation to the expressions, accounts and stories they voice and narrate. We are called upon to describe their behavior in relation to the accounts they give of their behavior (Weber 1978: 4–5). The anthropologist Clifford Geertz accordingly cautions researchers: 'The ethnographer does not, and in my opinion cannot perceive what his informants perceive. What he perceives, and that uncertainly enough, is what they perceive "with"—or "by means of" or "through"—that is, the expressions, rituals, and artifacts that function as their means of communication' (Geertz 1983: 58).

As we engage in actual or imaginary conversations with our subjects, we may well find it difficult to comprehend their meanings. We may in fact find these others to be quite other, different, foreign and strange. In a way, this is a helpful initial response because it functions to warn us not to approach these others—especially predecessors in traditions with which we may now closely identify—without due respect for their uniqueness and the ways in which they may well differ from us (Barth 1957).

The sociologist Robert Bellah compellingly argued for this kind of orientation for studies of religion in an essay in which he criticized various social scientific accounts of religion that reduced religion to certain kinds of social functions. Even while he called attention to their immense contributions to understanding the central social role of religions in human societies, Bellah noted the way Durkheim largely viewed religions in terms of their impact on social cohesion and Weber largely analyzed religions in terms of the ways they shaped practical social ethics. Proposing an approach he referred to as 'symbolic realism', Bellah argued that religions ought to be analyzed on their own terms (Bellah 1970; Robbins *et al.* 1973; Anthony *et al.* 1974). In practical terms, this proposal does not mean that religions must be examined solely in terms of their own belief systems, but it does imply that researchers must attempt to cultivate an appreciative understanding of how religions present themselves as a fundamental feature of the social reality that we are seeking to analyze and explain.[4]

One way of guarding against overly superficial approaches to the study of religion is to recognize that religions as social realities are multidimensional. They include beliefs, rituals, social organizations, personal histories, art works, buildings, sentiments and memories. Although in our investigations we may appropriately focus on only particular aspects of this much larger whole, it is well to keep in mind not only that we are in the process looking at a part of the religious life in which several aspects play their role but also that religion itself may play a larger or smaller role in the lives of the people we are studying.

We are especially called to pay attention to these others and how they choose to express themselves, both those whose communications are easily accessed and those whose communications may only be accessed through reasonable inferences. Researchers are especially reminded that we are strangers often but not always self-invited to learn from our hosts. Even when these others communicate in ways that seem incomprehensible, researchers are called upon to exercise their abilities to listen, infer, imagine, suggest and question in order to gain a sense of what the others are communicating and by what means they do so.

In practical terms, to effectively navigate the rich multi-dimensional identities of our research subjects, researchers may need to invest significant time in language training, in cultural immersion and in studying histories of the religious tradition. Decent language skills provide the necessary foundation for communicating our research objectives and, more importantly, for listening effectively, thus leading to a deeper understanding of subtle variations in thought expressed in the field. We are well-cautioned not to be too smug in our skills as even the most proficient linguist may misinterpret local idioms when first heard, a situation that can, at a minimum, lead to embarrassment for all parties, or more seriously contribute to inaccurate representations (see Korum 2001).

Awareness of cultural and religious norms allows us to respect various etiquette and reciprocity protocols: whether to dress up or down, how we respond to acts of hospitality and how best to show our appreciation to the community. For example, over the years June McDaniel has, in the name of research, found herself in several odd situations. Her studies often take her into the field in India. During one trip, the only way she could collect an interview from a hefty *pisaca tantrika* was to 'be his mother. I had to feed him rice with my hand while he sat on my lap' (McDaniel 2001: 81). While the experience was odd, her informant was thrilled that she performed the requested act as it demonstrated her acceptance of the social position and authority of the *pisaca tantrika* while at the same time protecting her from potentially dangerous magic, given her new role as his mother (McDaniel 2001: 81). In the same article, McDaniel discussed the difficulties of meeting the ethic of reciprocity particularly in regard to thanking her assistants and informants for their work. Although she was quite willing to offer cash payments to her mostly impoverished informants as a token of appreciation for their time, many saw the gesture as an offence, the establishment of a hierarchical relationship of boss and slave. Her solution was to instead offer a donation to the local temple, shrine or deity for *puja* (McDaniel 2001: 80). Whether studying religious communities in our local community or in remote locations around the world, such actions go far in building trust, diminishing misunderstandings and demonstrating our respect for the dignity of others.

Typically, as we study the religious life of others, we undertake our research by contacting and questioning particular others who are accessible for our investigations, whether these be by means of interviews or by examining texts and artifacts. We are well cautioned to inquire whether our contacts (sources) are representative of the larger communities and ways of life we are hoping to study, for it is possible that these contacts may well not adequately represent the religious life of the larger group. For example, many of the written accounts we use to engage in historical studies of the religious life of people from our own or other cultures were written by and for literate, upper-class males. These accounts may not well represent the views and experiences of women, illiterate persons and lower-class groups. The written texts and accounts researchers typically use may well provide unrepresentative expressions of the religious life of people as they were in fact lived (Douglas and Ney 1998; Bird 1997). Likewise, when in the field, we need to take care in selecting our gatekeepers, translators and informants to ensure we have access to a diverse sample. If we are not collecting different points of view, our samples may not be balanced or large enough. This is not to suggest that it is unethical to have a bias. Biases of some sort are practically inevitable. However, researchers should reflect on the limitations associated with the sources of information they choose to use (even when no other sources seem to exist).

Out of respect for the dignity and integrity of others and how they understand themselves, we also need to be circumspect in the labels we use to identify others and their social locations. In our investigations we often use social science terms, like sect, cult, members and apostate, as well as religious names, like Christian, Hindu, fundamentalist or liberal, to identify particular people. While often subjects use these terms to self-identify, they also often use qualifiers to note how closely or loosely they think these terms apply (Glock and Stark 1967). In some cases subjects may be offended by such categorization and request a retraction or at least clarification. For example, in the 2007 issue of *Religion*, Moojan Momen published an article about apostates within the Baha'i tradition in which several of those portrayed took issue with the author. In this case the journal editors provided space in the 2008 issue for the aggrieved to respond to what they perceived as inaccurate representation (Stausberg 2008). Of course, not all research subjects have access to academic journals or alternative forums to respond to their perceived misrepresentation. Instead, in respect of the other, it is scholars' responsibility to treat these terms heuristically, and not as determinant classifications as with chemical elements or biological types.

Out of respect for the dignity and integrity of our subjects, we are especially called upon to protect their privacy. If they wish their identities to remain unknown and if they ask us not to divulge confidences, then we must respect their wishes, or we will be using them and their information as a means to our own ends. We are also called upon to securely protect confidential information so that it does not end up being used or exploited by others. If, on the other hand, subjects wish to be cited, then we must take care that we accurately and reliably cite them so that the statements they choose to make do not appear in forms that communicate quite different meanings.

In addition to these general guidelines regarding the respect and appreciative interest we owe those whose lives we are directly or indirectly studying, there are at least two minimal obligations we must also honour in so far as we have direct contact with these others.

First, recognizing others as autonomous agents, we are obligated to fully and clearly inform them with respect to our research and allow them the opportunity voluntarily to choose whether or not to participate. This obligation also asks that special care be taken in research with persons of diminished autonomy or deemed members of vulnerable groups such as children, the legally incompetent, indigenous peoples, refugees, the incarcerated or victims of violence. Typically, where subjects are appropriately not recognized as fully competent adults, then permission must be sought from guardians in order to conduct research with these persons. Within religious studies we might add, to the list of those for whom special care and attention needs to be exercised, marginalized members of religious communities, including women within conservative patriarchal traditions, and members of persecuted minority religious communities.

Ordinarily, it is expected that we will provide informants and subjects with a written description of the research and ask them to signify their consent in writing. Both researchers and subjects will then possess written statements clearly specifying the research process and any attendant risks. The basic assumption here is that, out of respect for the other, no one should be compelled to be the subject of research. It is worth noting that researchers often have to gain consent both from the organizations that are the site of our investigations as well from the individuals whom we are directly interviewing. Alternatively, our research may take us to settings in which it is preferred that consent be solicited and given in oral instead of written form. Oral consent is typically used in anthropological field research where subjects may well not be literate and/or where the written consent forms often aggravate undue suspicions. In these settings, as researchers it is expected that we fully and clearly describe our research and how it will affect those involved, solicit verbal consent, and make and keep written or recorded records of these verbal agreements. Lastly, because subjects freely consent to participate in research processes, then in principle they also have a right later to choose to discontinue their participation. Rarely do subjects exercise this right, yet nevertheless this remains a basic tenet of the consent process because it signals the voluntary character of the participation by subjects and informants. This is particularly important for long-term field-work research where relationships with research subjects can evolve into perceived and/or real friendships where the researcher/subject lines can blur (McDaniel 2001; Palmer 2001).

Second, in so far as research processes either expose others to more than ordinary risks or bring risky situations to light, then as researchers we are obligated to find adequate and appropriate means of managing or responding to these risks. Rarely does religious research expose others to physical or financial risks. However, investigations of religious phenomena can directly or indirectly occasion heightened reputational risks for those we are studying. They may feel that our analyses and interpretations raise questions about the character of their activities and motives. How we handle such cases may not be simple. We will explore these kinds of situations when further along we discuss the importance of exercising judgement responsibly. At this point, it is important to observe that in so far as we have voluntarily gained the consent from others to pursue research involving them, then we have some responsibility to minimize added risks they may face as a result of our research or to manage those risks in ways that do not force them to confront unwarranted public attacks. Nonetheless, there are clear limits in these settings. If, as a result of our investigations, we unearth evidence of intentional fraud or physical or psychological abuse of religious adherents, then, out of respect for the dignity and integrity of others, we are also correspondingly called upon to find ways of bringing appropriate attention to these problems.

Box 1.6.3 Respecting the dignity and integrity of others

- Take seriously how the others we study account for their symbols, rituals, texts and behaviors
- Religions ought to be analyzed on their own terms
- Recognize that religions as social realities are multidimensional
- Pay attention to these others and how they choose to express themselves
- Researchers may need to invest significant time in language training, cultural immersion and studying histories of the religious tradition
- Respect etiquette and reciprocity protocols
- Ensure our contacts (sources) are representative of the larger communities and ways of life we are hoping to study
- Be circumspect in the labels we use to identity others and their social locations

Additional obligations when research involves direct contact with research subjects

- Informed consent
- Adequate and appropriate responses to perceived risks

Communicating honestly and objectively with our subjects and audiences

It is assumed that when we engage in scholarly research we will communicate publicly what we learn as a result of our investigations. It is further assumed that we will communicate honestly and objectively. What does this mean, especially with respect to religious studies, in which scholars follow diverse normative models with regard to the epistemological validity claims of their investigations and write and speak variously as religiously committed and non-committed observers? Many scholars of religion undertake their studies and communicate what they have learned primarily as members of particular religions addressing fellow members. This occurs from time to time especially in fields like Biblical studies, Church history, Rabbinic studies, Islamic law, theology and religious ethics. In contrast, many religiously committed scholars, like their nonreligious colleagues, communicate assuming that their audiences have no faith commitments whatsoever. In turn, religiously committed audiences often find the research of nonreligious scholars both instructive and insightful. Thus, what is especially characteristic of religious studies is the considerable extent to which scholarly investigations are often intentionally addressed, sometimes at the same time, to communities of scholarship and communities of religious adherents and sometimes exclusively to one or the other. More than scholars in many other fields. particular religious researchers are likely to be communicating to quite different kinds of audiences, sometimes quite broadly and at other times much more focused, some in overt religious terms, and some overtly secular.

We honour the norm of honest communication, to the extent that we do not intentionally misrepresent or overlook pertinent evidence and do not deliberately evade or avoid relevant questions addressed to us. Correspondingly, we regard plagiarism—the direct utilization of the words and/or ideas of others without appropriate citation—as a fundamental wrong. While plagiarism clearly contravenes the principle of honest communication, there are other questionable practices that are more ambiguous. For example, at times scholarly communication has taken the form of 'bi-passing monologues' as scholars have responded to their own questions and ignored those raised by adversaries.[5] Although in past centuries many Catholics and Protestants seemed to have operated in keeping with this caricature, modern Protestant and Catholic scholars have become much more responsive to concerns raised by alternative traditions of research (Gustafson 1978). Minimally, the norms for honest communication call for those engaged in research to articulate intelligibly and not muffle their own positions, to attend to what their communicating partners say sufficiently so that they can at least identify the reasons others give for what they say, and to interact reciprocally, taking turns and taking up and responding to what the others say in what we in turn communicate (Bird 1996: 191–250). There is often a strong temptation to discount, to minimize the importance of, or to misrepresent information that seems to counter the primary positions we are seeking to put forward and defend. In these kinds of circumstances, the collegial and public character of scholarship provides an antidote. We invite others, known and unknown, to review what we have communicated and to challenge, to the extent it seems appropriate, to assess whether we have in significant ways misrepresented or misinterpreted relevant information.

Honest and objective accounts are not necessarily meant to function as accurate representations or mirrors of reality (see Rorty 1980). Rather, they serve as our attempts forthrightly to present what we have learned, to make sense of the data we have collected, and to develop re-presentations and frames of reference that allow others to recognize, comprehend, and utilize this knowledge in reliable ways.

In practical terms, given the opportunity to review our work, our sources/informants should be able to recognize themselves in our account of them. To begin with, in our accounts we should attempt to acknowledge how our subjects represent themselves even if, for comparative or historical purposes or because of our own assessments, we represent them in different terms and in different ways. However, it is important to note that an honest and objective account does not mean that we must agree with our subjects. To be sure, what we subsequently write about our sources may not be well received by all who read what we write. This was the case when modern Biblical scholars argued about how the Bible was written: many believers were offended by what Biblical scholars had been asserting about how and by whom the Bible was written over a number of centuries. Note well, however, that the angry response to modern Biblical research was largely but not exclusively occasioned by the positions that researchers maintained rather than by the way the research itself was conducted. To be sure, some believers objected to the secular way in which researchers treated the biblical texts. More recently, similar charges have been levied by Muslim believers against scholars applying redactive criticism to the Qur'an.

Ordinarily, as scholars, we regard accounts of research to be public, and thereby objective, to the degree that they are written, orally delivered and/or otherwise communicated to people who share different as well as similar political, ideological and moral, and religious views, to critics as well as supporters, to participants as well as those not involved, to strangers as well as colleagues. Private and privileged accounts typically are often initially unintelligible to outsiders. To outsiders they appear as closed language games, which are largely incomprehensible to those not immediately involved. However, much religious scholarship is undertaken and communicated by people who are members of particular religious communities and may correspondingly be communicating in part with others within their communities. In what ways can this kind of communication be objective and public? Is it possible to identify standards for objective and public communication of research knowledge both by secular and religiously committed scholars, writing both to the public in general and to members of their own traditions?

For communications to be regarded as public and objective—even when audiences are fellow religious members—they must fulfil three criteria. First, observations and explanations must be expressed in ways that allow them to be refuted (Barker 1995: 294). This is the reverse of saying they must be verifiable. In general terms, reports can be verified if it is possible to administer tests or observations that will either support these reports or result in their non-verification or falsification. Accounts are refutable to the degree that it is possible to identify changes in conditions that would thereby render observations and explanations untrue or undemonstrated. Second, data must be expressed in terms and measures that allow for comparative assessments. If we are to report our research publicly, then researchers must do so in ways that allow our diverse audiences to measure, calibrate or compare reported findings in relation to data with which they are already familiar. These comparisons may assume diverse forms. The readers of reports may wish to compare historical events, ritual practices or ancient legends. To the degree that as observers we give only our personal views, much as travellers do as they report on their journeys, our accounts neither invite nor readily allow for comparisons. They remain personal statements. To the degree that they utilize common measures, researchers in contrast allow and invite their audiences to undertake their own comparisons and assessments. Third, in principle public communications expect and welcome not just affirmations and agreements, but reasoned responses from observers who initially may well take different views. Recognizing that it is possible for us to err in our judgements and to misperceive in our observations, the norm of objectivity, which calls for us to make public accounts of our research, serves as a self-correcting procedure. By giving public accounts, we invite others to be on the lookout for what we might overlook or misconstrue.

Box 1.6.4 Communicating honestly and objectively with our subjects and audiences

More than scholars in many other fields, religious researchers communicate with different kinds of audiences—some broadly, some more focused, some in overt religious terms and some overtly secular.

- Do not intentionally misrepresent or overlook pertinent evidence
- Do not deliberately evade or avoid relevant questions
- Our sources/informants should be able to recognize themselves in our account of them

Three criteria for public and objective research:

- Research observations and explanations must be refutable or verifiable
- Data must be expressed in terms that allow for comparison
- Public reports welcome reasoned responses and corrections of information that may have been overlooked or misconstrued

---

Responsibly exercising judgement

As researchers, gathering and organizing information and reporting on our studies, we face a number of alternatives regarding what we pay attention to, what questions we raise, and what and how we choose to communicate. That is: we have a number of choices in terms of how we engage in the overlapping conversations that are integral to the practice of research. We use the word 'judgement' to describe how we make up our minds in relation to these alternatives. There are no automatic formulae, error-free methodologies or inherently correct ways of proceeding either in relation to our subjects or in relation to our audiences. We must consider alternatives, determine what evidence has greater weight and ponder varying degrees of significance. At several different moments in the research process, we inevitably have to exercise judgement. We are called to communicate as clearly as possible how we have arrived at the judgements we make.

Typically, the issues about which we have to exercise judgement assume the following forms:

- To what degree has a particular ethical issue emerged as an instance of moral wrong-doing, a case of a shortfall from a moral ideal, as a moral dilemma, or as complex concern involving all three different kinds of ethical issues? What particular ethical standards have greatest weight with regard to this issue? To what degree should we expend greater efforts to prevent or punish overt wrongs, encourage people to work to reduce ethical shortfalls, or resolve ethical dilemmas?
- What information shall we pay attention to and how reliable is this information? What forms of observation seem likely to be most informative, penetrating and reliable? Researchers are well advised, for example, to exercise critical judgement regarding the veracity and reliability of the information we receive from the others we are studying. Yet, to what extent can we rely on the data and terms of reference of our informants—whether they are currently living subjects or dead authors? To what degree might their accounts be self-serving or self-deceptive?
- Should we pay our informants out of respect for the time they spend or in regard to the value of the information they provide? Is paying them liable to affect the character of the information we receive? Conversely, is it appropriate to accept funding from the communities we study? When is it acceptable to accept funding from the military or from organizations like the Templeton Foundation with strong ideological agendas? Would such funding compromise the professional integrity of the research project and mark a researcher as a 'kept scholar', a moniker that new religious movement scholar Susan Palmer uses to advise against this practice (Palmer 2001: 114). What about otherworldly gifts offered by communities—prayers, blessings, salvation? Are they more acceptable? Should such gestures be included in our research findings?
- What significance should we attach to our own feelings and impressions occasioned by this information? To what degree can and should we reference our own immediate impressions as relevant direct or indirect sources of information?
- As we undertake our research, to what extent are our observations influenced by our own unacknowledged perspectives, biases and blind spots? As researchers we often proceed as representatives of privileged classes. As Peter Gottschalk observed of his fieldwork research experiences in rural India, his presence raised many suspicions. Residents wondered why a privileged American, assumed to live in luxury and convenience, would want to live alongside and study impoverished rural Indians? What would be the consequences of his

research? Was he a scholar intent on robbing their cultural treasures as the imperial powers of colonial times had previously robbed the nation? (Gottschalk 2001: 54).

- What restraints should be applied to ensure the research does not cause undue hardship for the community? This is particularly important for studies of marginalized religious communities that could be used by government authorities or powerful social organizations interested in the suppression, surveillance and/or control of the community (see discussions of portraying New Religious Movements (Palmer 2001), or Indigenous Traditions associated with political conflicts (Baum 2001)).
- How active should scholars be in the groups studied? Is it appropriate to join a group? Should a scholar train or criticize religious/ritual experts, where this possibility arises?
- How do we evaluate the religious, social, artistic and ethical significance of our findings?

Ethically, as researchers, we should inform our audiences of how and why we have chosen to handle these value-laden judgements in the way we have rather than in alternative ways. Through ongoing conversations with colleagues and others, we should seek out counsel and advice. We should provide clear, intelligible reasons for our choices in the introductory comments, statement on research methods and/or at other appropriate points in the body of our analysis. In so far as possible, we should attempt to distinguish and not conflate our judgements regarding facts, causes and reliable information from our judgements influenced by overt religious and moral values.

Box 1.6.5 Responsibly exercising judgement

- No automatic formulae, error-free methodologies or inherently correct ways
- Consider all options to determine what evidence has greater weight
- Ponder varying degrees of significance
- Seek out counsel and advice from colleagues and others
- Provide clear, intelligible reasons for our choices in the introductory comments, statement on research methods and/or at other appropriate points in the body of our analysis

---

Although the issues in relation to which we make value-laden judgements are diverse, it may be instructive to consider at greater length one example—concerning the uses of deception, in this instance in the form of covert investigations in field studies. A number of researchers have defended covert studies as a justifiable means for gaining information about extreme groups. They argue that it might otherwise be impossible to obtain reliable information because the groups are secretive and do not allow for outside research (Barrett 1987; Homan 1980; Reynolds 1982). For example, in order to gain fuller information about a right wing neo-Nazi group, Matthew Lauder pretended to act not only as an interested and sympathetic observer—which he could do without deception—but as an apparent convert. He later justified his deception in cost-benefit terms because of the information he thereby obtained (Lauder 2003).

How should we responsibly exercise judgement in these kinds of cases? After all, initial deception, followed by subsequent debriefings, is sometimes used in experimental studies so that subjects will respond spontaneously to the cues of the experiment. Moreover, frequently researchers will inform their subjects about some but not all of the objectives of their investigations so that subjects and informants respond more candidly than they would if they were more fully informed. For example, Robert Jackall told his informants that he was studying leadership in organizations because respondents tended to provide superficial and canned responses when informed that he was actually investigating how people practised ethics in organizations (Jackall 1988). Note well, in both of these examples researchers fully declare themselves to be researchers. Subjects know they are being investigated.

To exercise judgement responsibly in these kinds of cases, we need to take into account and balance a number of different and relevant considerations. First, in order to respect the autonomy and privacy of the individuals from whom we obtain information, as we noted previously in this chapter, we need to protect any information, including their identities, that they provide us in confidence. However, second, as we observe further in this chapter, even as unannounced observers we can report on activities of such groups in so far as these take place in settings open to the public. Nevertheless, third, because we are expected to provide honest and objective accounts of our research, our reports must be based on data more reliable, in this case at least, than hearsay we might obtain from covert inquiries. To be reliable, such information needs to be corroborated by other observers, other documented evidence, or the overt confirmation of other group members. How otherwise will researchers know they are not being misled by grudge informants or exceptional rather than representative information? Fourth, when researchers are seeking to expose practices that we judge to be dangerous or illegal, then in these cases minimally we can be expected to obtain from appropriate offices the scholarly equivalent of 'search warrants'. That is, as we already discussed, before we place ourselves or our subjects at greater risk because of the character of our investigations, we need to discuss with—and seek the counsel of—colleagues or institutional review boards to determine how we might best be expected to manage these risks appropriately. Finally, fifth, it is always worth considering in these kinds of settings whether the difficulties we may face in obtaining fuller accounts from our subjects may reflect our initial feelings of awkwardness and discomfort as investigators and our initial lack of skills in making subjects feel comfortable. The inclination to resort to deception might in some cases become less compelling as we discover alternative ways to gain fuller accounts from our informants.

When we exercise judgement with respect to ethical issues—with regard to research or other matters—we inevitably must address and consider the priority of five different ethical concerns. These are as follows: first, what is the right as opposed to the wrong way of acting—viewed either in relation to minimum obligations or standards of excellence (Fuller 1964)? Second, what is the good we are seeking to realize—viewed either in utilitarian terms as outcomes or Aristotelian terms as purposes? Third, how as persons can we act in ways that are morally worthwhile (virtuous) and not blameworthy? To answer this question, it is necessary to consider our motives and dispositions. Fourth, what ways of acting are expected by relevant customs, traditions and institutional norms? Finally, fifth, in relation to current structures of power and indifference, what courses of action are practical or exigent? Typically, we assign priority to certain questions—and our answers to these questions—and assume that the other questions are thereby resolved. However, because that is not always the case, we are called upon to exercise judgement.[6]

Exercising judgement as researchers calls for us to consider diverse issues and values, to reflect on the bearing of basic principles on the issues at hand, and to seek counsel from colleagues as we make up our minds. Ultimately, we need to determine which norms and values have greatest weight and the highest priority.

Part two: Institutional research ethics

Currently the term 'research ethics' often brings to mind the processes by which researchers secure formal research ethics approvals or 'certificates of ethical acceptability' before engaging in funded or non-funded research with human subjects. Not surprising, the increased demands have contributed to a growing critical discourse on this process, especially as it is applied to research in the social sciences and humanities (see Kitchen 2007; Curran 2006; Hallowell *et al.* 2005; Lincoln 2005; Corwin and Tierney 2005; Lincoln and Tierney 2004). There is a strong current of thought that sees this regulated process as just one more time-consuming bureaucratic hoop to jump through in the effort to secure funding for research, a step that for the most part is unnecessary especially for projects deemed as having minimal risk (see Lincoln and Tierney 2004; Hallowell *et al.* 2005). Other voices point to the increased demands and inconsistent application of ethical codes across institutions as having contributed to a subtle form of research censorship (Corwin and Tierney 2005; Kent *et al.* 2002). Still others support the more serious charge that the process is mired in methodological conservatism, which emphasizes a biomedical research model which has not only stifled the development of various qualitative research approaches in the social sciences but which limits the range of research available to other academics, the communities studied and to public policy forums (Kitchen 2007; Lincoln 2005; Corwin and Tierney 2005; Lincoln and Tierney 2004). Each voice raises important questions that will continue to inform revisions to ethical protocols and to the boards that govern the process.

Within the growing literature on research ethics, there is also increasing concern that the level of importance given to the narrow range of issues governed by the regulated ethics approval process has skewed our attention (O'Leary 2005; Curran 2006; Hallowell *et al.* 2005; Oliver 2003). Regulated ethics approval or the receipt of a **certificate of ethical acceptability** does not guarantee that a research project will avoid all ethical issues related to a given research endeavour, as not all ethical dilemmas can be determined *a priori*. Instead, it is important to remember that ethical dilemmas, such as the ones listed above, can and do occur at various points throughout the research experience, that they are more often than not unexpected, and that they are not necessarily easy to resolve. To that end it is important that researchers apply due diligence to uphold the general ethical principles for research discussed in the previous section throughout all stages of the research endeavour beyond simply meeting regulatory requirements.

Of course, many also see the formal research ethics review as an important process not only for ensuring that research subjects are respected and protected from undue harms, but for reminding us that research with human subjects carries with it clear ethical obligations and responsibilities. Some go so far as to recognize the regulated ethics review process as an increasingly positive and important peer-review process that legitimizes a research project through demonstrated institutional confidence with crucial aspects of the research endeavour (Curran 2006; Hallowell *et al.* 2005; O'Leary 2005; Kent *et al.* 2002).

Whether we agree or not with the goals, objectives and/or results of the process, **regulated research ethics** are here to stay and require our attention. Thus the chapter closes with a discussion of regulated research ethics, including a brief history, an overview of the minimum ethical obligations upheld by the various international and professional ethical protocols in use today, and some practical advice for negotiating this process in our own research endeavours.

A brief history

Public concern about research practices involving humans can be traced to the 19th century when questions were raised not only about the undue harms that befell biomedical research subjects but also the deceptive or coercive methods employed by researchers (see Faden *et al.* 1986). While such public debates raised awareness of the need for regulated research ethics, it was not until after the Nuremberg trials, where horrors of the abusive medical and psychological experiments conducted in the Nazi death camps were brought to light, that the first internationally recognized protocol for ethical research with human subjects was established—the Nuremberg Code (1947–49) (see summary of standards in Box 1.6.6). The ethical standards outlined in the Nuremberg Code inspired the second international research ethics code in the World Medical Association's Declaration of Helsinki (1964, latest revision 2000).

Box 1.6.6 Nuremberg Code (1947–49)

The ten standards of the Nuremberg Code are condensed as follows:

* Voluntary consent is essential to participate
* Researchers must fully inform volunteers of the character and purpose of the study
* The research must maximize benefits and minimize risks to subjects in the study
* Researchers are responsible for protecting participants against any harm
* Participants must be informed that they can withdraw from the study at any time
* Qualified researchers must lead and conduct the study
* The study should be terminated if adverse effects emerge
* Society should benefit from study findings
* Research on humans should be based on previous animal or other previous work
* A research study should never begin if there is a reason to believe that death or injury may result

---

Despite the wide adoption of these ethical protocols, abuses and exploitation of human research subjects continued. In the United States there are several touchstone cases including the Tuskegee Syphilis Study (1932–72), the Willowbrook hepatitis experiments (1963–66), the Jewish Chronic Disease Hospital Study (1963), the psychotropic drug experiments of Project Camelot (1964), Stanley Milgram's psychological deception studies, and the work of social scientists directed toward covert military purposes in Vietnam (Curran 2006; Lincoln 2005; Corwin and Tierney 2005; Milgram 1974). By 1974, the publicity surrounding these scandals pushed the United States government to pass the National Research Act which created the National Commission for the Protection of Human Subjects of Biomedical and Behavioral Research. The commission was charged: to determine the boundaries between biomedical and behavioral research; to assess risk-benefit criteria to determine the appropriateness of research; to identify appropriate guidelines for the selection of human subjects; and to define the nature and boundaries of informed consent in various research settings (OHSR 2010). The central policy document of the Commission, the Belmont Report (1979), includes principles similar to the general ethical principles of research discussed in the previous section; however, they are more narrowly defined with an emphasis on practical application. The three basic ethical principles to guide research practice in that report are: **respect for persons** as autonomous agents who voluntarily participate in the research; **beneficence** or the obligation to ensure the well-being of all research subjects throughout the research process—to maximize possible benefits and minimize possible harms; and **justice**, or fair distribution of burdens and benefits of research amongst diverse cultural, social, gender, racial and ethnic groups to eliminate any biases. These are linked to the following practical issues: **informed consent**, assessment of risks/benefits of the research methods and overall intentions of the project, and fair and equitable selection/protection of subjects (see Box 1.6.7).

Box 1.6.7 Belmont Report (USA, 1979)

Three basic ethical principles for human research

- Respect for persons: including autonomy of individuals and protection of persons with diminished autonomy
- Beneficence: respect persons' well-being, to maximize possible benefits and minimize possible harms
- Justice: benefits and risks of research must be distributed fairly

Application of the three ethical principles

- Informed consent: ensure that all research subjects are *informed* of the research project's purpose, procedure, risks and anticipated benefits; have a *clear understanding* of research objectives; and *voluntarily* agree to participate, with the option to withdraw at any time
- Assessment of risks and benefits: *ongoing assessment* of respondents' well-being with *immediate response* to any immediate or long-term risks
- Selection of subjects: ensure *fair procedures and outcomes* for selecting research subjects; and ensure all *subject information is protected* (i.e. anonymity in collection, storage of information)

These moral principles were subsequently codified as the Common Rule (1991), which offers detailed guidelines for identifying the minimal ethical obligations that must be met before proceeding with any research involving human subjects. The Common Rule also included the clear directive for universities and research institutes to establish Institutional Review Boards (IRBs) to ensure that all federally funded and increasingly non-funded research complies with research ethics regulations (Curran 2006; OHSR 2010).

The regulation of research ethics in Canada followed a similar trajectory to that of the United States. In 1978 the federally funded Medical Research Council (MRC) adopted the first ethical research guidelines in Canada (revised 1987), with the Social Sciences and Humanities Research Council (SSHRC) following suit in 1981. In 1997 the MRC and SSHRC joined together with the Natural Science and Engineering Research Council (NSERC) to adopt the Tri-Council Policy Statement: Ethical Conduct for Research Involving Humans (TCPS) (revised 2010). As with the Common Rule in the United States, the TCPS recognizes the same three minimum ethical principles and associated applications for research involving humans as identified in the Belmont Report. The TCPS also includes clear directives for the establishment, scope and power of Research Ethics Boards (REBs) in the review process. When the agencies adopted the first edition of the TCPS in 1998, it was with the commitment that it be a living or 'evolving' document that could respond to new forms of research and address any oversights. This commitment was demonstrated in the 2010 version of the document, which responds to expressed concerns regarding a perceived over-emphasis on biomedical research methods in evaluating qualitative research with the intro-duction of a dedicated chapter devoted to the distinct nature of qualitative research (Panel of Research Ethics 2010). The revised policy also offers clearer guidelines for REBs about the types of observational research that are exempt from the review process (e.g. where the obser-vation is of a public act accessible to all, such as observing a weekly religious worship service open to the public).

Box 1.6.8 Research Ethics Framework, Economic and Social Research Council (ESRC) (UK, 2005)

Six core principles:

- Research should be designed, reviewed and undertaken to ensure integrity and quality
- Research staff and subjects must be informed fully about the purpose, methods and intended possible uses of the research, what their participation in the research entails and what risks, if any, are involved
- The confidentiality of information supplied by research subjects and the anonymity of respondents must be respected
- Research participants must participate in a voluntary way, free from any coercion
- Harm to research participants must be avoided
- The independence of research must be clear, and any conflicts of interest or partiality must be explicit

It will be the responsibility of institutions to ensure that these are met. ESRC will adopt a 'light touch' approach to monitoring but will ultimately have the option to withhold funding from an institution in breach of the framework.

(Research Ethics Framework, from the ESRC website, 2010)

It was not until 2003 that the United Kingdom Economic and Social Research Council (ESRC) set out to develop the Research Ethics Framework (REF) (adopted in 2005, revised 2010). Like the TCPS, the REF is considered a 'living' document that will develop over time. As with the TCPS and the Common Rule, the REF provides a framework to guide the estab-lishment of Research Ethics Councils (RECs) to oversee the institutional review process, although with the directive that monitoring take a 'light touch' approach (ESRC 2005). The six core principles of the REF address many of the same ethical concerns noted above: namely the need for informed consent, participant confidentiality, a risks/benefit analysis regulated through a formal review process (see Box 1.6.8). Hallowell *et al.* suggest that the delay in the UK adoption of the REF for social science and humanities research was due in part to researchers relying more on a self-regulated approach that respected the ethical research codes provided by their respective professional associations, for example the British Psychological Society or the British Sociological Association (Hallowell *et al.* 2005: 143).

Box 1.6.9 Selected professional organizations that offer research ethics protocols for research involving human subjects

Australia

- Health Ethics Committee (AHEC) of the National Health and Medical Research Council
- Institute of Aboriginal and Torres Strait Islander Studies
- Law Reform Commission (ALRC)
- National Health and Medical Research Council (NHMRC)
- Research Council (ARC)

Canada

- Association of Canadian Universities for Northern Studies (ACUNS)
- Association of Universities and Colleges of Canada (AUCC)
- Canadian Association of Research Ethics Boards (CAREB)
- Canadian Association of University Research Administrators (CAURA)
- Canadian Bioethics Society
- Canadian Federation for the Humanities and Social Sciences
- Canadian Institutes of Health Research
- Canadian Sociological Association
- Health Canada—Research Ethics Board
- National Aboriginal Health Organization (NAHO)
- National Council on Ethics in Human Research (NCEHR)
- National Research Council (NRC), Biotechnology Research Institute
- Natural Sciences and Engineering Research Council of Canada (NSERC)
- Panel for Research Ethics (PRE) (Office overseeing the Tri-Council Policy Statement)
- Social Sciences and Humanities Research Council of Canada (SSHRC)

France

- Centre national de la recherche scientifique (CNRS)
- Comité d'éthique pour les sciences (COMETS)
- Conférence Nationale des Comités de Protection des Personnes en Recherche Biomédicale
- Institut National de la Santé et de la Recherche Médicale (INSERM)
- National Ethics Advisory Committee for the Life Sciences and Health

The Netherlands

- Dutch Health Law

New Zealand

- Health Research Council

Norway

- National Research Ethics Committees
- Norwegian Biotechnology Advisory Board

Sweden

- Swedish Research Councils

United Kingdom

- Department of Health
- Economic and Social Research Council (Research Ethics Framework)
- Engineering and Physical Sciences Research Council
- Medical Research Council Nuffield
- Council on Bioethics
- Social Research Association
- Wellcome Trust

United States

- Accreditation of Human Research Protection Programs (AAHRPP)
- African Studies Association (ASA)
- American Anthropological Association (AAA)
- American Association for the Advancement of Science (AAAS)
- American Association for Public Opinion Research (AAPOR)
- American Educational Research Association
- American Indian Law Center
- American Psychological Association (APA)
- American Sociological Association (ASA)
- Center for Drug Evaluation and Research (CDER)
- Health and Human Services, Office for Human Research Protections (OHRP) (Belmont Report and the Common Rule)
- National Bioethics Advisory Commission (NBAC, 1995–2001)
- National Human Research Protections Advisory Committee (NHRPAC)
- National Institutes of Health, Office of Human Subjects Research (OHSR)
- President's Council on Bioethics Public Responsibility in Medicine and Research (PRIMandR)

Multinational organizations

- Council for International Organizations of Medical Sciences (CIOMS)
- Council of Europe Convention for the Protection of Human Rights and Dignity of the Human Being with Regard to the Application of Biology and Medicine
- European Commission IST Respect Project
- An EU Code of Ethics for Socio-Economic Research
- European Forum for Good Clinical Practice

- European Group on Ethics in Science and New Technologies (EGE)
- Human Genome Organization (HUGO)
- International Conference on Harmonization of Technical Requirements of Pharmaceuticals for Human Use
- International Society of Ethnobiology
- Nordic Committee on Bioethics
- Nuremberg Code
- UNESCO Global Ethics Observatory

As the above survey suggests, regulated research ethics has become an institutionalized requirement across the academy. (See Box 1.6.9 for an extended list of regulated ethics protocols endorsed by various governments, academic and professional research organizations.) It has become standard for universities, research institutes and funding agencies to require all research involving human subjects to undergo a process of review to ensure that all proposed and current research practices meet these minimal ethics standards. Ostensibly, to the degree that their research does not directly involve human subjects, investigators undertaking historical, literary, archaeological or textual studies are not required to submit their research to these kinds of institutional review processes. Nonetheless, it is useful to know and honour these guidelines even when researchers do not have to submit their research plans for institutional review.

Negotiating the review process

In keeping with the regulated directives discussed above, universities and research institutes have established formal ethics review boards in countries around the world (e.g. IRBs in the United States; REBs in Canada; RECs in the UK), constituted by a representative group of researchers as well as qualified legal and medical professionals able as a group to determine whether proposed or current research endangers human subjects, abuses their rights, or violates legal standards. These boards are accountable to the senior administration and the universities or institutes as a whole. Negatively stated, it is their responsibility to make sure that researchers do not engage in practices that might occasion unnecessary and unjustifiable harm to research subjects and thereby put the larger institutions at risk for losing funding or allowing these unwarranted practices. Typically, there may be several ethics review boards at a given university, covering the research of different faculties, or differentiated in terms of the character and scope of the research projects. All research involving human subjects is supposed to be reviewed by these boards, whether it is funded or non-funded, whether it involves formal projects or informal class assignments, whether it takes the form of contract research or research related to graduate theses. In practice, most universities allow for more informal processes of review for more informal or minimal-risk research (see sample review flowchart in Figure 1.6.1). For the most part, this review process focuses on ethical issues in terms of possible wrongs, although in practice they may help researchers address ethical shortfalls and dilemmas.

The review process calls for researchers to fill out forms developed for this purpose. In general most institutions also host offices to support faculty and students through the process by providing the necessary forms/guidebooks and sometimes hosting workshops on how to negotiate the process. Many also host websites for easy access to necessary information. In

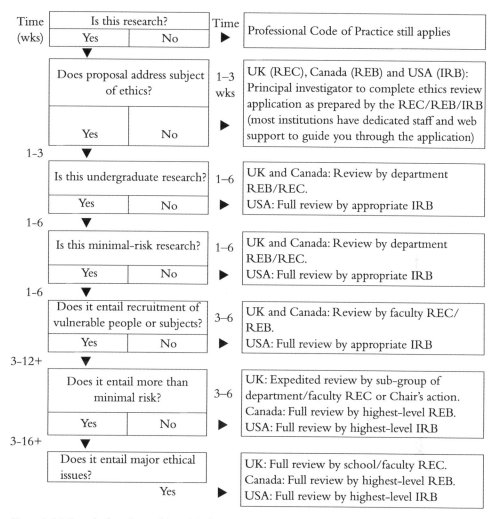

Figure 1.6.1 Sample flowchart of the ethical review process

(Adapted from the ESRC's REF Guidelines, 2010 (www.esrc.ac.uk))

keeping with the minimal obligations discussed above, for most research review applications expect researchers to:

- Describe research including methodologies and benefits of research;
- Describe the study population;
- Address specific questions regarding informed consent including uses of possible deception, right to discontinue and proposed methods for ensuring the confidentiality of all research subjects;
- Identify any potential risks the research poses to subjects and offer clear methods for minimizing the impact;
- Describe the potential for 'heinous discovery' in the research with a response plan if required;
- Define plans for securely storing the data collected;

- Offer a clear indication that the project will comply with all related governing ethical protocols, both those specific to the application process and those endorsed by related professional associations; and
- Provide copies of the proposed research instruments including sample questionnaires, interview schedules and consent forms.

The Board members in turn are expected to review this material, to look especially for missing information and questions that have not been fully answered, and to determine whether proposed research complies with basic standards. Conceived of in strict terms, Ethics Review Boards often play a policing role. After all, they are expected to be scrupulous in exercising due caution. They are expected to identify, call into question and prohibit research procedures that fail to meet the basic standards. However, it is important to recognize that these Boards do not exclusively think of themselves as agents of censure. Rather, their mandate is to facilitate ethically responsible research practices. Often in a collaborative fashion, they seek to warn researchers what is expected and to help and counsel them so that researchers design their research in appropriate ways.

Depending on the level of risk posed by proposed research, time to complete the review process can take from three weeks to several months. The extended time frames are most often related to the not uncommon request for further clarification of research methods, processes of consent or confidentiality and/or clarification of specific ethical concerns related to the research participants.

In trying to determine whether the research we are planning needs to undergo this kind of institutional review process, the long answer requires looking at the somewhat different stipulations of different universities and funding agencies. However, a shorter answer turns on how we as researchers would be able to answer two questions about public access and risk. If, for instance, the access we are using to gain information about our research topic is public—in the sense that we can gather our information at public gatherings or from public media, then ordinarily our research plans do not need to pass through the formal institutional review process. For example, a classroom-based research project that asks students to attend a public religious service falls within the minimal risk category because the research is accessing publicly available information, and it is not likely the students will be so involved with research subjects to adversely affect the subject or student through the research. Nonetheless, it is necessary to check with our institutions to confirm that this type of minimal-risk research is exempt. In some institutions the minimal risk status of projects means that the review process will be handled through a departmental review committee, a process that can often be completed within two-to-three weeks. Alternatively, studies examining religious attitudes or spiritual practices of youth or indigenous peoples typically require more scrutiny. Because both demographic groups have been identified as vulnerable or requiring special care in assessing research participation, the research proposal would automatically be placed in the more than minimal risk category, which calls for more formal review by the larger faculty or institutional board.

Notes

1   This paragraph briefly summarizes sociological and philosophical observations developed in a much longer essay on the diverse ways in which ethical ideas are communicated. Frederick Bird 'The Cultural Forms of Morality' unpublished essay.
2   Based upon our readings regarding this topic and our experiences as researchers, we have identified these three principles. We discuss a number of sub-themes related to each principle. For the sake of

simplicity, we have tried to provide an overview, organized in relation to these three principles, recognizing that it is possible to elaborate much further on a number of these sub-themes and the issues and concerns associated with them. These three principles are already widely acknowledged, although often in slightly different terms.

3   In principle, research is justifiable only in so far as it is judged to be 'good' research—that is, research that is thought out, organized and reported on in ways that are likely to produce reliable information that can be intelligibly communicated. Hence, typically the initial question asked with respect to research involving human subjects is whether colleagues and/or supervisors have already reviewed the proposed research and deemed it worth pursuing.

4   This in no way rules out functional interpretations of religious phenomena or even some interpretations that Bellah might refer to as reductionistic. Scholars can make whatever interpretations they feel called upon to make. They may argue that the accounts of their subjects are self-serving and/or self-deceptive. However, we suggest that they should, at the outset of their research, take account of how the subjects of their research choose to present themselves.

5   The phrase 'bi-passing monologues' comes from a study by Piaget (1955) of interactions between children.

6   For a fuller statement of this model of ethical decision-making see Bird and Gandz 1991; Bird 2005.

References

Anthony, D., Robbins, T. and Curtis, T.E., 1974. Reply to Bellah. *Journal for the Scientific Study of Religion* 13(4): 491–95.

Barker, E., 1995. Presidential address: the scientific study of religion? You must be joking! *Journal for the Scientific Study of Religion* 34(3): 287–310.

Barrett, S.R., 1987. *Is God a Racist? The right wing in Canada.* University of Toronto Press, Toronto.

Barth, K., 1957 [1928]. The strange new world within the Bible. In: *The Word of God and the Word of Man.* Trans. D. Horton. Harper and Brothers, New York, pp. 28–50.

Baum, R.M., 2001. The ethics of religious studies research in the context of the religious intolerance of the state: an africanist perspective. *Method and Theory in the Study of Religion* 13(1): 12–23.

Bellah, R., 1970. *Beyond Belief: essays on religion in a post-traditional world.* Harper and Row, New York.

Bird, F., 1996. *The Muted Conscience: moral silence and the practice of ethics in business.* Quorum Books, Westport, CT.

—— 2005. Dilemmas of development. In: Bird, F., Raufflet, E. and Smucker, J. (eds), *International Businesses and the Dilemmas of Development.* Palgrave Macmillan, New York, pp. 11–35.

Bird, F. and Gandz, J., 1991. Moral reasoning. In: *Good Management: business ethics in practice.* Prentice-Hall, Scarborough, ON, pp. 80–104.

Bird, P.A., 1997. *Missing Persons and Mistaken Identities: women and gender in ancient Israel.* Fortress Press, Minneapolis.

Corwin, Z. and Tierney, W., 2005. *The qualitative misfit: evaluating the interpretive complexity of IRBs.* Unpublished paper presented at the annual meeting of the American Sociological Association, Philadelphia, PA. www.allacademic.com/meta/p20109_index.html.

Curran, S.R., 2006. Ethical considerations for research in cross-cultural settings. In: Perecman, E. and Curran, S.R. (eds), *A Handbook for Social Science Field Research: essays and bibliographic sources on research design and methods.* SAGE, London, Thousand Oaks, CA, pp. 197–216.

Douglas, M. and Ney, S., 1998. *Missing Persons: a critique of social science.* University of California Press, Berkeley.

ESRC, 2005. Research ethics framework. *Economic and Social Research Council.* www.esrcsocietytoday.ac.uk/ESRCInfoCentre/about/CI/CP/Social_Sciences/issue60/research_ethics.aspx.

Faden, R.R., Beauchamp, T.L. and King, N., 1986. *A History and Theory of Informed Consent.* Oxford University Press, New York.

Fuller, L., 1964. *The Morality of Law.* Yale University Press, New Haven.

Geertz, C., 1983. *Local Knowledge: further essays in interpretive anthropology.* Basic Books, New York.

Glock, C. and Stark, R., 1967. *Religion and Society in Transition.* University of California Press, Berkeley.

Gottschalk, P., 2001. Being an 'other' other than myself: 'take it to the bridge'. *Method and Theory in the Study of Religion* 13(1): 51–57

Hallowell, N., Lawton, J. and Gregory, S., 2005. *Reflections on Research: the realities of doing research in the social sciences.* McGraw-Hill Education, New York.

Homan, R., 1980. The ethics of covert methods. *The British Journal of Sociology* 31(1): 46–59.

Jackall, R., 1988. *Moral Mazes.* Oxford University Press, New York.

Kent, J., Williamson, E., Goodenough, T. and Ashcroft, R., 2002. Social science gets the ethics treatment: research governance and ethical review. *Sociological Research Online* 7 (4). www.socresonline. org.uk/7/4/williamson.html.

Kitchen, H., 2007. *Research Ethics and the Internet: negotiating Canada's tri-council policy statement.* Fernwood Publishing, Black Point, NS.

Korum, F., 2001. Blunders, plunders and the wonders of religious ethnography: archiving tales from the field. *Method and Theory in the Study of Religion* 13(1): 58–72.

Lauder, M.A., 2003. Covert participant observation of a deviant community: justifying the use of deception. *Journal of Contemporary Religion* 18(2): 185–96.

Lincoln, Y.S., 2005. Institutional review boards and methodological conservatism: the challenge to and from phenomenological paradigms. In: Denzin N.K. and Lincoln Y.S. (eds). *The SAGE Handbook of Qualitative Research.* SAGE, London, Thousand Oaks, CA, pp. 165–81.

Lincoln, Y.S. and Tierney, W.G., 2004. Qualitative research and institutional review boards. *Qualitative Inquiry* 10(2): 219–34.

McDaniel, J., 2001. Fieldwork in Indian Religion: some notes on experience and ethics. *Method and Theory in the Study of Religion* 13(1): 78–81.

Milgram, S., 1974. *Obedience to Authority: an experimental view.* Harper & Row, New York.

OHSR, 2010. The Belmont Report Ethical Principles and Guidelines for the protection of human subjects of research. *Office of Human Subjects Research* official website. ohsr.od.nih.gov/guidelines/ belmont.html.

O'Leary, Z., 2005. Striving for integrity in the research process. *Researching Real-World Problems: a guide to methods of inquiry.* SAGE, London, Thousand Oaks, CA, pp. 61–77.

Oliver, P., 2003. *The Student's Guide to Research Ethics.* Open University Press/McGraw-Hill Education, Berkshire.

Palmer, S., 2001. Caught up in the cult wars: confessions of a Canadian researcher. In: Zablocki, B.D. and Robbins, T. (eds), *Misunderstanding Cults: searching for objectivity in a controversial field.* University of Toronto Press, Toronto, pp. 99–122.

Panel of Research Ethics (PRE), 2010. Tri-Council Policy Statement: ethical conduct for research involving humans. Official website. pre.ethics.gc.ca/eng/policy-politique/tcps-eptc/ context-contexte/#C.

Piaget, Jean. 1955. *The Language and Thought of the Child.* Trans. M. Gabain. Meridian Books, New York.

Reynolds, P.D., 1982. Moral judgments: strategies for analysis with application to covert participant observation. In: Bulmer, M. (ed.), *Social Research Ethics: an examination of the merits of covert participant observation.* Holmes and Meier, New York, pp. 185–130.

Robbins, T., Anthony, D. and Curtis, T.E., 1973. The limits of symbolic realism: problems of empathetic field observation in a sectarian context. *Journal for the Scientific Study of Religion* 12(3): 259–71.

Rorty, R. 1980. *Philosophy and the Mirror of Nature.* Blackwell Publishing, Oxford.

Stausberg, M. 2008. Challenging apostasy: responses to Moojan Momen's 'marginality and apostasy in the Baha'i community'. *Religion* 38(4): 384–85.

Weber, M., 1978. *Economy and Society.* Roth G. and Wittich, C. (eds). University of California Press, Berkeley.

Further reading

Hallowell, N., Lawton, J. and Gregory, S., 2005. *Reflections on Research: the realities of doing research in the social sciences.* Open University Press, Berkshire.

This text highlights a multitude of practical and ethical complexities that occur in our efforts to negotiate the day-to-day realities of doing social science research. While the authors tend to concentrate on research drawn primarily from the field of health care, the hundreds of examples included throughout offer a wide range of responses to some of the more personal issues each researcher encounters in fieldwork research, namely how to maintain control of the research, how to respond to emotionally charged encounters, and how to ensure appropriate ethical care of others while at the same time protecting ourselves from over-investment in the research.

Kitchen, H., 2007. *Research Ethics and the Internet: negotiating Canada's tri-council policy statement.* Fernwood Publishing, Black Point, NS.

This short text addresses some of the particular ethical concerns facing researchers whose work focuses on gathering and analyzing data collected on the Internet, including securing regulated ethics consent, informed consent and techniques for engaging your research subjects.

Robbins, T. and Zabloki. B., 2001. *Misunderstanding Cults: searching for objectivity in a controversial field.* University of Toronto Press, Toronto.

This anthology offers some candid reflections on the ethical quandaries that scholars of new religious movements may encounter. From concerns of being labelled a closet convert, hired gun or undercover agent, contributors discuss the challenges scholars encounter when fully engaged in participant/observation fieldwork research with new religious movements.

[n.a.] 2001. *Method & Theory in the Study of Religion* 13(1).

This particular issue is dedicated to the ethics of fieldwork research in religion, with contributions from scholars who have conducted traditional and non-traditional studies of religious communities around the globe.

Alver, B.G., Fjell, T.I and Øyen, Ø. (eds). 2007. *Research Ethics in Studies of Culture and Social Life.* Suomalainen Tiedeakatemia, Helsinki, Finland.

This collection of essays addresses key issues within social science research including protecting individual integrity, obtaining informed consent, special considerations for research in private or intimate arenas, research with vulnerable groups, weighing the socio-political consequences of research, cross-culture studies and assessing underlying value structures that inform research ethics.

Key concepts

Certificate of ethical acceptability: issued to research projects approved through the regulated ethics review process.

Ethical dilemmas: situations in which it is possible to arrive at more than one ethically justified position.

Ethical wrongs: ethical issues that emerge in clear violation of basic ethical or legal standards.

Fundamental regulated ethical principles:

Respect for persons: recognizes that research subjects are autonomous agents who after being supplied with adequate information about the research project, may decide to voluntarily participate in the research.

Beneficence: obliges researchers to ensure, as far as possible, the well-being of all research subjects. In other words, we have both a duty to do good or to maximize all possible benefits to the research subject while at the same time be aware of the duty to refrain from causing harm or to minimize all possible harms.

Justice: requires researchers to consider the biases that research might levy against various groups of people. More precisely, in designing the research, consideration must be given to the fair distribution of burdens and benefits of research amongst diverse cultural, social, gender, racial and ethnic groups to eliminate any biases.

Informed consent: the ethical requirement to clearly and fully inform all research subjects about the character and purposes of the research project and to solicit their voluntary consent to participate in the research process.

Moral shortfalls: not overt wrongs but shortfalls in meeting fundamental ethical principles or institutional guidelines.

Regulated research ethics: The more precise ethical research rules that refer to the minimal obligations that must be met in order to receive formal approval from institutional ethical reviews of research projects involving human subjects.

PART II

Methods

2.1

CONTENT ANALYSIS

Chad Nelson and Robert H. Woods, Jr

Chapter summary

- Content analysis is a form of textual analysis used to describe and explain characteristics of messages embedded in texts.
- Content analysis allows for both quantitative and qualitative approaches.
- Content analysis is useful as an unobtrusive method allowing researchers to manage and summarize large quantities of information, provide valuable historical and cultural insight into a research problem, and triangulate with other research methods.
- Content analysis is conducted through a process of selecting texts, unitizing message units, generating content categories, coding the text and explaining the results.
- Content analysis is utilized in religious studies to understand religious expressions and identities, evaluate religion in media, and examine religion in social institutions and culture.
- Despite several limitations of the content analysis method, it seems well suited for religious studies since it allows researchers to move beyond manifest content to latent content.

Introduction

With research methods such as experiments and surveys people respond to controlled situations or answer questions and thus provide data not formerly available. Some researchers prefer to study messages that already exist in recorded or visual form. **Textual analysis** is the method used to describe and interpret the characteristics of a recorded or visual message. 'Texts' are any object, artifact or behavior that involves symbol use. Texts can be written transcripts of speeches or conversations, written documents (letters, personnel records, newspapers, magazines, textbooks), electronic documents (audiotapes, films, videotapes, computer files), or visual texts (paintings, photographs and architecture).

There are several forms of textual analysis, including conversation and discourse analysis, hermeneutics, philology and historiography, which are addressed in other chapters in this handbook. The focus of this chapter is **content analysis**, one of the more popular forms of textual analysis in religious studies. Although the various approaches to textual analysis differ slightly in terms of purpose and technique, they all share the common focus of examining the messages embedded in texts.

In this chapter we define content analysis, explore its basic functions, consider several advantages and limitations of the method, identify its epistemological foundations and discuss practical issues related to its use, before concluding with an overview of how it is used in religious studies.

Descriptive and analytical overview

Content analysis was developed mainly as a method for describing and explaining the characteristics of messages embedded in mass mediated and public texts (although this may include messages that are private in nature or targeted to one or a few individuals). Content analysis is defined as a 'research technique for making replicable and valid inferences from texts (or other meaningful matter) to the contexts of their use' (Krippendorff 2004: 18). It includes 'any of several research techniques used to describe and systematically analyze the content of written, spoken or pictorial communication—such as books, newspapers, television programs, or interview transcripts' (Vogt 2005: 59), and it usually results in the development of objective and quantitative data, although qualitative varieties that rely primarily or exclusively on qualitative analysis and reporting are common.[1] Content analysis has its roots in religious studies and can be traced to 18th-century Sweden when scholars counted the number of religious symbols contained in a collection of 90 hymns to determine if the hymns were preaching against the church (Dovring 1954–55).

Functions

First, content analysis is useful if researchers are interested in tracking specific data to identify and understand a direction of or changes in specific phenomena over time. Dy-Liacco *et al.* (2003) reported on chapters published in *Research in the Societal Scientific Study of Religion* between 1997–2001 to describe the most common topics addressed, religious affiliations represented and methodologies used. These descriptive studies also can be used to study societal changes. For example, to demonstrate changes in religious practices and beliefs in Dutch society, Emons *et al.* (2009) studied prime-time drama programs on Dutch television between 1980 and 2005.

Second, content analysis is appropriate if researchers want to identify patterns or commonalities within a particular genre. Buddenbaum (1986) analyzed religion news coverage in three major newspapers and discovered that religion stories had become longer, fewer in number and of a more general nature.

Third, if not searching for commonalities, researchers can use content analysis to identify differences by drawing comparisons between similar types of variables in two different systems or in dissimilar contexts. Abelman (1989) compared the composition, roles and interaction between black and white families on religious and secular television programs.

Fourth, researchers can use content analysis to assess the image of particular groups in society. Ferré (1980) performed content analysis on articles published in *The New York Times* and *Washington Post* to determine if biases against Jews, Anglicans, Catholics and Evangelicals were present in religious news.

Fifth, content analysis can be used to measure a specific phenomenon against some standard in order to classify the phenomenon, make a judgment about it, or determine how close it comes to meeting a particular standard or expectation. For instance, Dyck *et al.* (2005) used statements of faith by 17 different religious groups as standards for making a judgment on the organizational structure of those groups' places of worship.

Sixth, content analysis can be used to relate certain message characteristics to other variables. Badahdah and Tiemann (2005) identified a relationship between the content of personal advertisements on a Muslim matrimonial website and mate selection practices of Muslims living in America.

Box 2.1.1 Functions of content analysis

- Tracking specific data to identify and understand a direction of or changes in specific phenomena over time.
- Identifying patterns or commonalities within a particular genre.
- Identifying differences by drawing comparisons between similar types of variables in two different systems or in dissimilar contexts.
- Assessing the image of particular groups in society.
- Measuring specific phenomena against some standard to classify the phenomena, make a judgment about them, or determine how close they come to meeting a particular standard or expectation.
- Relating certain message characteristics to other variables.

Advantages

To begin, content analysis is an unobtrusive way to measure phenomena. It studies texts that already exist rather than getting people to produce texts. The effect of the researcher's bias on the study can thus be reduced while allowing the study's subjects to operate under realistic scenarios, unlike in experiments.

Second, content analysis allows researchers to systematically manage and summarize large quantities of relatively unstructured information more easily than other research methods. For instance, Emons *et al.*'s (2009) study of Dutch television included 503 programs with a total number of 2,114 main characters. Ubanit and Tirri (2006) examined over 700 written expressions from Finnish preadolescents.

Also, because content analysis is concerned with existing texts, some of which can exist over long periods of time, the method can provide valuable historical and cultural insight into the research problem. Perkins (1984) analyzed religious content in popular American, British and Canadian publications over five decades to determine if there was a revival or decline in religious interest in these countries.

In addition, content analysis can be used to describe communication phenomena in a way that allows for triangulation with other research methods. This is helpful in increasing the validity of research results. Content analysis is often used along with other methods such as in-depth interviews, surveys and focus groups. After conducting structured qualitative interviews with 40 evangelical college students about their spiritual journeys, Knight *et al.* (2005) performed quantitative content analysis on the interview transcripts to identify gender differences in conversion narratives. Morgenthaler and Hauri-Bill (2007) followed their family religion survey of 1,344 respondents with a content analysis of open-ended survey responses. Content analysis thus allows researchers to combine what are usually thought to be antithetical modes of analysis to uncover a richer depth of data for analysis.

Epistemological basis

Despite its empirical foundations, content analysis is not a purely objective method. Texts do not have purely objective qualities; they are not 'reader-independent', explains Krippendorff (2004: 22). In the case of content analysis, meanings are brought to texts by researchers who carefully design the analysis by using particular theoretical frameworks, train independent coders to describe particular characteristics, and carefully interpret the results.

Given the reader-dependent nature of textual analysis, it is appropriate to say that meanings in texts are not discovered but constructed through the act of interpretation. Texts do not have single meanings but are dependent on a researcher's perspective and choice of operational definitions. For instance, Cooper (2005) studied images and dialogue in *The Passion of the Christ* to assess whether the film, or Mel Gibson, might be anti-Semitic. Cooper's analysis was informed, in part, by Nietzsche's perspectivism. Another analysis informed by a particular strain of Christian ethics might draw very different conclusions. Since texts rarely have a single meaning, it is not realistic or desirable to have intersubjective agreement.

Additionally, content analysis is grounded in an assumption that uniform relationships exist between symbols and their meanings. This assumption, however, overlooks various connotative meanings and cultural differences that exist in meaning making (which is one reason why content analysis is often combined with other methodologies, as explained above). The reading of texts is linked phenomenologically to something else, whether 'purely mental constructions, past or future experiences, or hidden causes' (Krippendorff 2004: 22), which researchers must identify. Analysis of the text occurs outside the physicality of the text, which in turn informs the analysis itself. Consequently, the same texts may yield different results as different analysts emphasize different contexts. Bantimaroudis's (2007) analysis of media framing of religious minorities in Greece, a country with improved performance in civil liberties and human rights, would be different in a country where lower standards of performance prevail. If researchers want content analysis to be replicable, they must explain the context that directs their analyses.

Finally, the very nature of texts and textual analysis requires that researchers draw specific **inferences** from texts to particular contexts—that is, from the text to what the text's author intended, from the text to what the text means to users, and from the text to how the text affects users. Researchers infer answers to particular research questions from texts, but those inferences can only go so far. For instance, Hirdes *et al.* (2009) used content analysis to discover that most Jesus merchandise fits the edification (personal fulfillment) category. Yet researchers could not infer whether individuals actually used the merchandise for that purpose in everyday life. Therefore, it is recommended that researchers validate results of content analysis by relating findings to audience perceptions, message uses or effects.

Basic steps

There are several basic steps in any content analysis. First, researchers must select texts relevant to their research questions. When there is a limited database, such as a particular television show or the top ten songs during a particular time period, researchers may conduct a census. Woods *et al.* (2007), for instance, conducted a census by acquiring all top 25 worship music lists from Christian Copyright Licensing International in 1989–2005.

Most often, however, content analysts face the same sampling challenges as other researchers, that is, the need to acquire a representative and sufficiently large sample. Moreover, in content analysis access to some texts may be difficult or present ethical problems, such as analyzing the content of prayers left at a war memorial, while other texts may not be recorded clearly or be available in a manner that permits analysis. Researchers who want to generalize from a sample to a population must use random sampling techniques. When these techniques are not possible, researchers must rely on non-random samples and as such could miss important matters.

Second, researchers code messages embedded in a census or sample of texts according to categories. This requires that researchers **unitize**, or identify, the proper message units to be coded. Krippendorff (1980) identifies five units that researchers study: physical (number of articles, inches of space, number of pages); syntactical (number of words, phrases or sentences); referential (the presence or absence of objects); propositional (statements or argument units); and thematic (repeating patterns of ideas or treatments). The stated research questions ultimately lead researchers to select appropriate units of analysis. In the Woods *et al.* (2007) study mentioned earlier, researchers counted the number of times certain words and phrases (syntactical units) appeared in each contemporary worship song.

Box 2.1.2 Units that can be counted in content analysis

- physical (number of articles, inches of space, number of pages)
- syntactical (number of words, phrases or sentences)
- referential (the presence or absence of objects)
- propositional (statements or argument units)
- thematic (repeating patterns of ideas or treatments)

Third, after researchers have unitized, or identified the appropriate units of analysis, nominal measurement techniques are used to generate categories into which previously identified units can be placed. The two general categories used to classify units are substance (the content of the message) and form (the way it is said) (Berelson 1952). In the Woods *et al.* (2007) study of contemporary worship music, after counting words and phrases within each song, the authors classified the substance of each song into one of three content categories: *Kerygma* (songs that preach), *Koinonia* (songs that build community), and *Leitourgia* (songs that promote individual worship toward God). The researchers could also have classified songs according to musical style or form, such as soft rock and hard rock. Regardless of the categories chosen, the classifications should be mutually exclusive and exhaustive. Classifications often include an 'other' category but the number of items in the 'other' category should be small. Coding rules for placing items in categories are established before collecting data and pre-tested by researchers, often during the coder-training stage described below.

In content analysis, **validity** refers to the appropriateness and adequacy of the **coding scheme** for the text being coded. Coding scheme validity is increased by examining previous research on the same issues and by grounding the coding scheme in theory (Potter and Levine-Donnerstein 1999). At a minimum, a categorical (coding) scheme must demonstrate face validity. On its 'face', in other words, the coding scheme must seem to capture the intended construct. To increase validity, researchers can examine content coding schemes for concurrent and construct validity. Concurrent validity is established when a new measurement for a variable, for example religiosity, is compared against an existing valid measurement of the same variable. In construct validity, a researcher asks how the measurement for a particular variable correlates with similar variables in a manner that is theoretically expected.[2] Krippendorff (2004) also recommends that researchers consider semantic validity. This reminds researchers to code content and interpret codings within the context from which the texts were selected.

Fourth, after unitizing and developing content categories, researchers train coders to identify the appropriate category for each unit. Researchers use at least two coders who work independently and place each unit into its appropriate category. Researchers then assess the **reliability** of the codings. Interobserver or intercoder reliability calculates the percentage of agreement between the observations of independent coders. If observations by two or more coders who are unaware of the purpose of the study are highly related (80 per cent agreement or more), then their ratings are considered highly reliable. Formulae such as Scott's pi take into account chance agreements. If interobserver reliability is low, then researchers can modify the classification systems and re-train observers.

Fifth, researchers must explain the results. Coding units into nominal categories produces qualitative data; counting the number of units in each category produces quantitative data. Both data types are useful for describing the message content. Most often, researchers report basic descriptive statistics followed by tests, such as chi square, to assess differences in the number of units between categories. Sometimes advanced statistical tests are used to identify key patterns. Describing results can often be troublesome. For instance, if a content analysis of prime time drama programs reveals that religious characters appear in 20 per cent of the programs, should researchers conclude this is high or low? Twenty per cent may be high when compared to religious characters appearing in sitcoms. Some benchmark for comparison is needed.

Box 2.1.3 Basic steps of content analysis

- Rationale: Does my research question call for the use of categories to produce useful data? Why is this particular message content important to study?
- Define population: How does my research question limit the communication population? Why am I selecting this particular population for analysis? What time period boundaries will I establish?
- Select sample: How does my research question limit the communication population to specific sample messages? Will my sampling allow me to make meaningful conclusions about the communication phenomena? What sampling method will I employ?
- Choose units of analysis: What communication phenomena in my sample am I going to count? Am I looking for specific words, themes or phrases? What criteria am I going to utilize to select these units for analysis?
- Select coding system: Based on my research question, what content categories will I employ to count the communication phenomena in my sample? Are my categories exhaustive, mutually exclusive and based on justifiable criteria?
- Code the text(s): Am I going to utilize a codebook or a coding form? Does the amount of data to be analyzed dictate the use of computer analysis software? How many coders are going to be involved in the research? How do I ensure intercoder reliability and validity of the measures?

Uses of content analysis in the study of religion

Religious expressions and identities

In this category, researchers focus on religious ritual practices, or the performance of (whether individual or collective) more or less invariant sequences of formal religious acts and utterances. For instance, researchers are interested in the content, structure and performance of prayers (e.g. Campbell *et al.* 2009). Sometimes prayer content is related to other variables, as in Baesler and Ladd's (2009) study that related the content of college and middle-aged adult prayer to physical, mental and spiritual health. Others study worship music and hymns. To understand the content of Presbyterian Sunday school stories and songs, Evans (1967) analyzed 32 lesson books and two hymnals.

Content analysis of conversion narratives and views of God help to identify common experiential themes that situate individual religious experiences within larger social environments. For instance, Lee (2008) analyzed conversion narratives from African-American Christian women across several denominations and demonstrated how race and gender are significant to the conversion experience. Studies on individual views of God, such as Janssen *et al.*'s (1994) content analysis of interviews with 209 Dutch secondary school students, highlight language (and the agreement of language among subjects) that is used to describe religious experience and deity.

Analyzing the content of sermons and other church documents is another way of describing institutional religious expression. Ross (1995) analyzed the sermons of Malawian Presbyterian, Anglican and Roman Catholic churches to understand the development of African Christianity. Other church documents might include bulletins, denominational publications, encyclical letters or more formal newspapers or magazines (see 'Religion in Media' below).

Other studies focus on institutional religious expressions by describing, comparing and contrasting various religions' beliefs and practices. To assess the changes to Mormon leaders' commitment rhetoric over 150 years, Shepherd and Shepherd (1984) analyzed texts from Mormon General Conferences. Sethi and Seligman (1993) analyzed sermons and liturgy from nine major religions to understand the variations in optimistic or pessimistic outlooks of individuals.

Religion in media

One category of studies explores how mainstream news media portray or frame religious individuals, groups or events. Van Driel and Richardson (1988) analyzed several newspapers and news magazines to determine the nature of their coverage of new religious movements. More recently, Cohen (2005) sought to understand how religion is covered in Israeli media by examining content of newspapers, radio programs and television.

Second, studies can focus on the presence or absence of religious content in mainstream entertainment and commercial media, often as a way to describe particular religious beliefs, identify trends or highlight biases. To understand the relationship between humorous and religious content, Lindsey and Heeren (1992) analyzed comics published in the *Los Angeles Times* from 1979–87. Mallia (2009) analyzed a variety of print, television and Internet advertisements that incorporate religious imagery and themes to assess the nature, character and implications of religion in advertising. Sometimes, mainstream media content is compared with religious media content, as in McKee and Pardun's (1996) comparison of religious and sexual imagery among rock, country and Christian music videos.

Third, researchers study religious media to determine the attitudes, beliefs, practices and identities of religious organizations or individuals. Abelman and Pettey (1988) analyzed three television episodes of the 'top ten' televangelists to identify common references to and attitudes toward specific political issues. Baab (2008) analyzed the content of six American Protestant websites to understand how churches portray their identity and what their presentations revealed about the future church.

Religion in social institutions and culture

Several studies in this area deal with government and civics. This might include the presence of religious language or imagery in elected officials' speeches (Coe and Domke 2006; Hansen 2006), or the rhetoric of groups on the Right and Left (Detweiler 1992). Other studies focus on the rhetoric surrounding certain hot-button political issues, such as abortion, environmental issues and capital punishment. Dardis *et al.* (2008: 117) conducted a content analysis of *The New York Times* in 1960–2003 and identified an emergence of an 'innocence frame' in the media's reporting of capital punishment.

Second, many studies focus on religion and its relationship to health and well-being. Narayanasamy and Owens (2001) identified four general categories of spiritual care that nurses provide, and explored the effects of spiritual care on patient well-being. Simon *et al.* (2007) attempted to understand the role of spirituality among African-American Christian women in their fight with cancer by analyzing their narratives.

Third, the intersection between religion and education generates significant interest. Romanowski (2003) analyzed religious content in the most widely used US history textbooks in US secondary schools to determine how the authors addressed the relationship between religion and history. Cardinal (2009) analyzed the similarities and differences between Christian and Muslim religious education programs in the Syrian Arab Republic by analyzing textbooks and teachers' guides.

Fourth, many researchers are interested in the role of religion in family life. Boggs (1983) focused on religion in child rearing, analyzing 32 child-rearing books, and found that the books presented the ideal child as one who has chosen to love and serve God. More recently, Morgenthaler and Hauri-Bill (2007) studied families' bedtime rituals to understand the relationship between family religion and rituals.

Finally, studies in this area focus on issues related to race and gender. To understand the use of ministerial support among African-American adults, Mattis *et al.* (2007) analyzed narratives from 13 focus groups. Regarding gender, Beal (1997) analyzed how the Promise Keepers utilize sport in their literature (e.g. *What Makes a Man* and *Seven Promises of a Promise Keeper*) to promote its specific style of masculinity, and Abdollahyan (2008) explored perceptions of women in world religions.

Conclusion

Content analysis is ideally suited for religious studies since it allows researchers to move beyond **manifest content** found in texts—the visible, surface content—to **latent content**, or interpretations about the content that imply something about the nature of communicators or effects on communicators. Yet despite its many advantages described herein, there are some limits to content analysis. First, it may be difficult to find representative samples. Second, generalizing the results of one content analysis to another is difficult since researchers may not use similar coding units or coding categories. Finally, while content analysis is useful for describing message characteristics and trends, it does not allow researchers to draw cause-and-effect conclusions as with experiments.

Box 2.1.4 Advantages and limitations of content analysis

Advantages

- An unobtrusive way to measure phenomena.
- Allows researchers to systematically manage and summarize large quantities of relatively unstructured information more easily than other research methods.
- Provide valuable historical and cultural insight into the research problem.
- Content analysis can be used to describe communication phenomena in a way that allows for triangulation with other research methods.

Limitations

- It may be difficult to find representative samples.
- Generalizing the results of one content analysis to another is difficult.
- It does not allow researchers to draw cause-and-effect conclusions as with experiments.

Future content analysis in religious studies should pay attention to the growing number of non-traditional, even unconventional, means of religious expression or experience. A growing number of sociological, anthropological and cultural perspectives explain how individuals construct religious experience from popular culture forms, everything from Elvis Presley (Reece 2006) to Star Trek (Jindra 1994). Rather than fit individual experiences within traditional frameworks, such approaches pay attention to how individuals construct religious meaning in a postmodern, post-national world. Furthermore, given that global media in a digital age are constructing trans-national religious forms, special emphasis should be given to international and intercultural cases (Horsfield *et al.* 2004). Finally, given the significant number of differences among world religions and the tension that regularly accompanies religious discourse, studies should analyze those texts that promote respectful and civil exchanges.[3]

Notes

1 Rhetorical analysis is a form of qualitative textual analysis that reports observations of texts and artifacts primarily with non-numerical (non-statistical) expressions. Rhetorical critics use any number of rhetorical frameworks or theoretical grids (everything from Aristotle's canons to Kenneth Burke's dramatistic pentad and many others) as standards for textual analysis, see Foss (2008). Also, researchers who conduct focus groups or in-depth interviews, for instance, often use content analysis to identify key patterns or themes in the data and report such patterns or themes in non-numerical (qualitative) terms. Some researchers rely on a combination of quantitative and qualitative reporting in their analysis of particular texts, as explained in this chapter.
2 For a detailed discussion of validity in content analysis, including an elaboration of concurrent and construct validity, see Krippendorff 2004: 313–38.
3 The authors thank Dr Quentin Schultze, Calvin College, for this final suggestion. See quentinschultze.com/religious-communication-scholarship.

References

Abdollahyan, H., 2008. Gender and generations modes of religiosity: locality versus globality of Iranian media. *Journal of Media & Religion* 7(1/2): 4–33.

Abelman, R., 1989. A comparison of black and white families as portrayed on religious and secular television programs. *Journal of Black Studies* 20(1): 60–79.

Abelman, R. and Pettey, G., 1988. How political is religious television? *Journalism Quarterly* 65(2/3): 313–59.

Baab, L., 2008. Portraits of the future church: a rhetorical analysis of congregational websites. *Journal of Communication & Religion* 31(2): 143–81.

Badahdah, A.M. and Tiemann, K.A., 2005. Mate selection criteria among Muslims living in America. *Evolution and Human Behavior* 26(5): 432–40.

Baesler, E. and Ladd, K., 2009. Exploring prayer contexts and health outcomes: from the chair to the pew. *Journal of Communication & Religion* 32(2): 347–74.

Bantimaroudis, P., 2007. Media framing of religious minorities in Greece: the case of the Protestants. *Journal of Media & Religion* 6(3): 219–35.

Beal, B., 1997. The promise keepers' use of sport in defining 'Christlike' masculinity. *Journal of Sport and Social Issues* 21(3): 274–84.

Berelson, B., 1952. *Content Analysis in Communications Research*. Free Press, New York.

Boggs, C.J., 1983. An analysis of selected Christian child rearing manuals. *Family Relations* 32(1): 73–80.

Buddenbaum, J., 1986. An analysis of religion news coverage in three major newspapers. *Journalism Quarterly* 63(3): 600–6.

Campbell, H., Lynch, G. and Ward, P., 2009. Can you hear the army? Exploring Evangelical discourse in Scottish youth prayer meetings. *Journal of Contemporary Religion* 24(2): 219–36.

Cardinal, M., 2009. Religious education in Syria: unity and difference. *British Journal of Religious Education* 31(2): 91–101.

Coe, K. and Domke, D., 2006. Petitioners or prophets? Presidential discourse, God, and the ascendancy of religious conservatives. *Journal of Communication* 56(2): 309–30.

Cohen, Y., 2005. Religion news in Israel. *Journal of Media & Religion* 4(3): 179–98.

Cooper, T., 2005. Of anti-Semitism, Romans de Sade, and celluloid Christianity: the cases for and against Gibson's Passion. *Journal of Media & Religion* 4(4): 251–68.

Dardis, F.E., Baumgartner, F.R., Boydstun, A.E., De Boef, S. and Shen, F., 2008. Media framing of capital punishment and its impact on individuals' cognitive responses. *Mass Communication & Society* 11(2): 115–40.

Detweiler, J.S., 1992. The religious right's battle plan in the 'civil war of values'. *Public Relations Review* 18(3): 247–55.

Dovring, K., 1954–55. Quantitative semantics in 18th century Sweden. *Public opinion Quarterly* 18: 389–94.

Dyck, B., Starke, F.A., Harder, H. and Hecht, T., 2005. Do the organizational structures of religious places of worship reflect their statements of faith? An exploratory study. *Review of Religious Research* 47(1): 51–69.

Dy-Liacco, G.S., Piedmont, R.L., Leach, M.M. and Nelson, R.W., 2003. A content analysis of research in the social scientific study of religion from 1997 to 2001: where we have been and where we hope to go. *Research in the Social Study of Religion* 14: 277–88.

Emons, P., Scheepers, P. and Wester, F., 2009. Longitudinal changes in religiosity in Dutch society and drama programs on television, 1980–2005. *Journal of Media & Religion* 8(1): 24–39.

Evans, J.F., 1967. What the church tells children in story and song. *Journalism Quarterly* 44(3): 513–19.

Ferré, J.P., 1980. Denominational biases in the American press. *Review of Religious Research* 21(3): 276–83.

Foss, S.K., 2008. *Rhetorical criticism: exploration and practice*, 4th edn. Waveland Press, Long Grove, IL.

Hansen, A., 2006. The religious text in Daniel Webster's 'First Bunker Hill address'. *Southern Communication Journal* 71(4): 383–400.

Hirdes, W., Woods, R.H. and Badzinski, D.M., 2009. A content analysis of Jesus merchandise. *Journal of Media and Religion* 8(3): 141–57.

Horsfield, P., Hess, M.E. and Medrano, A.M., 2004. *Belief in media: cultural perspectives on media and Christianity*. Ashgate, Burlington, VT.

Janssen, J., De Hart, J. and Gerardts, M., 1994. Images of God in adolescence. *International Journal for the Psychology of Religion* 4(2): 105–21.

Jindra, M., 1994. Star Trek fandom as a religious phenomenon. *Sociology of Religion* 55(1): 27–51.

Knight, D.A, Woods, R.H. and Jindra, I.W., 2005. Gender differences in the communication of Christian conversion narratives. *Review of Religious Research* 47(2): 113–34.

Krippendorff, K.H., 1980. *Content analysis: an introduction to its methodology.* Sage Publications, Thousand Oaks, California.

—— 2004. *Content analysis: an introduction to its methodology,* 2nd edn. Sage Publications, Thousand Oaks, California.

Lee, P., 2008. Christian conversion stories of African American women: a qualitative analysis. *Journal of Psychology & Christianity* 27(3): 238–52.

Lindsey, D.B. and Heeren, J., 1992. Where the sacred meets the profane: religion in the comic pages. *Review of Religious Research* 34(1): 63–77.

McKee, K.B. and Pardun, C.J., 1996. Mixed messages: the relationship between sexual and religious imagery in rock, country, and Christian videos. *Communication Reports* 9(2): 163–71.

Mallia, K., 2009. From the sacred to the profane: a critical analysis of the changing nature of religious imagery in advertising. *Journal of Media & Religion* 8(3): 172–90.

Mattis, J.S., Mitchell, N., Zapata, A., Grayman, N., Taylor, R.J., Chatters, L.M. and Neighbors, H.W., 2007. Uses of ministerial support by African Americans: a focus group study. *American Journal of Orthopsychiatry* 77(2): 249–58.

Morgenthaler, C. and Hauri-Bill, R., 2007. Tapes and tables mixed methods research on family religion. *Journal of Empirical Theology* 20(1): 77–99.

Narayanasamy, A. and Owens, J., 2001. A critical incident study of nurses' responses to the spiritual needs of their patients. *Journal of Advanced Nursing* 33(4): 446–55.

Perkins, H.W., 1984. Religious content in American, British, and Canadian popular publications from 1937 to 1979. *Sociological Analysis* 45(2): 159–65.

Potter, W.J. and Levine-Donnerstein, D., 1999. Rethinking validity and reliability in content analysis. *Journal of Applied Communication Research* 27: 258–84.

Reece, G.L., 2006. *Elvis religion: the cult of the king.* Tauris, London.

Romanowski, M.H., 2003. Religion in contemporary U.S. history textbooks. *The Social Studies* 94(1): 29–34.

Ross, K.R., 1995. Preaching in mainstream Christian churches in Malawi: a survey and analysis. *Journal of Religion in Africa* 25(1): 3–24.

Sethi, S. and Seligman, E.P., 1993. Optimism and fundamentalism. *Psychological Science* 4(4): 256–59.

Shepherd, G. and Shepherd, G., 1984. Mormon commitment rhetoric. *Journal for the Scientific Study of Religion* 23(2): 129–39.

Simon, C.E., Crowther, M. and Higgerson, H., 2007. The stage-specific role of spirituality among African American Christian women throughout the breast cancer experience. *Cultural diversity and Ethnic Minority Psychology* 13(1): 26–34.

Ubanit, M. and Tirri, K., 2006. How do Finnish preadolescents perceive religion and spirituality? *International Journal of Children's Spirituality* 11(3): 357–70.

Van Driel, B. and Richardson, J.T., 1988. Categorization of new religious movements in American print media. *Sociological Analysis* 49: 171–83.

Vogt, W.P., 2005. *Dictionary of statistics and methodology,* third edn. Sage Publications, Thousand Oaks, California.

Woods, R.H., Walrath, B. and Badzinski, D., 2007. We have come into his house: kerygma, koinonia, leitourgia—CWM that models the purpose of the church. In Woods, R.H. and Walrath, B. (eds), *The message in the music: studying contemporary praise & worship.* Abingdon Press, Nashville, TN, pp. 92–105.

Further reading

The following texts are introductory guides to the practice of content analysis. Topics such as sampling, measuring techniques, validity and reliability of the method, content classification, and resources for coding are covered:

Gerbner, G., Hosti, O.R., Krippendorff, K., Paisley, W. and Stone, P.J. (eds), 1969. *The Analysis of Communication Content.* John Wiley, New York.

Holsti, O.R., 1969. *Content Analysis for the Social Sciences and Humanities*. Addison-Wesley, Reading, Massachusetts.

Krippendorff, K.H., 1980. *Content Analysis: an introduction to its methodology*. SAGE, London, Thousand Oaks, CA.

——— 2004. *Content analysis: an introduction to its methodology*. 2nd edn. SAGE, London, Thousand Oaks, CA.

Nanenwirth, J.Z. and Weber, R.P., 1987. *Dynamics of culture*. Allen and Unwin, Winchester, Massachusetts.

Neuendorf, K.A., 2002. *The Content Analysis Guidebook*. SAGE, London, Thousand Oaks, CA.

North, R.C., Holsti, O.R., Zaninovich, M.G. and Zinnes, D.A., 1963. *Content Analysis: a handbook with applications for the study of international crises*. Northwestern University Press, Evanston, Indiana.

Weber, R.P., 1990. *Basic Content Analysis*. 2nd ed. SAGE, Newbury Park, CA.

The following websites contain comprehensive annotated bibliographies of content analysis resources, recommendations for textual analysis software, examples of content analysis, sampling codebooks and coding forms, and a host of other helpful content analysis information for researchers.

[n.a.] [n.d.] The Content Analysis Guidebook. Online academic.csuohio.edu/kneuendorf/content.

[n.a.] [n.d.] Colorado State University's Writing Guide: Content Analysis. Online writing.colostate.edu/guides/research/content/index.cfm.

[n.a.] [n.d.] SPSS computer coding software. Online www.spss.com.

The following articles discuss common questions, objections and potential problems associated with the content analysis method:

Kolbe, R.H. and Burnett, M.S., 1991. Content-analysis research: an examination of applications with directives for improving research reliability and objectivity. *The Journal of Consumer Research* 18(2): 243–50.

Krippendorff, K., 2004. Reliability in content analysis: some common misconceptions and recommendations. *Human Communication Research* 30(3): 411–33.

Lombard, M., Snyder-Duch, J. and Bracken, C.C., 2002. Content analysis in mass communication: assessment and reporting of intercoder reliability. *Human Communication Research* 28(4): 587–604.

Thomas, S., 1994. Artifactual study in the analysis of culture: a defense of content analysis in a postmodern age. *Communication Research* 21(6): 683–97.

Zollars, C., 1994. The perils of periodical indexes: some problems in constructing samples for content analysis and culture indicators research. *Communication Research* 21(6): 698–714.

Key concepts

Coding scheme: the human or computer process of dividing up message units in order to make meaningful interpretations of textual data.

Content analysis: a textual analysis method that utilizes categories to describe and analyze content by drawing inferences between texts and their specific context.

Inferences: connections and conclusions based on assumptions and carefully observed phenomena.

Latent content: interpretations about the content in texts that imply something about the nature of communicators or effects on communicators.

Manifest content: the visible, surface content found in texts.

Reliability: refers to the internal consistency of categories and coding between coders.

Texts: any object, artifact or behavior that involves symbol use. These communicated symbols can take various forms such as transcripts of speeches or conversations, paintings, photographs, films, newspapers or even political debates.

Textual analysis: a broad category of research methods which are utilized to describe and interpret the characteristics of a recorded or visual message. Other forms of textual analysis beyond content analysis include conversation and discourse analysis, hermeneutics, philology and historiography.

Unitizing: the process of identifying proper message units within a sample to be coded.

Validity: refers to the appropriateness and adequacy of the coding scheme for the text being coded.

Related chapters

2.2

CONVERSATION ANALYSIS

Esa Lehtinen

Chapter summary

- Conversation analysis is a method for the analysis of spoken interaction. It is particularly concerned with the sequential organization of talk-in-interaction and the inferential frameworks on which the participants of interaction rely.
- Conversation analysis was originated by Harvey Sacks in the 1960s. It is, most of all, influenced by the ethnomethodological sociology of Harold Garfinkel.
- Conversation analysis can be used for the microanalytic study of various kinds of religious speech events.
- The data in conversation analysis consist of video or audio recordings of naturally occurring talk-in-interaction. The analytical process typically includes transcription, initial analysis in order to find a phenomenon of interest, assembling a collection of cases of the phenomenon, and a detailed comparative analysis of the cases in the collection.
- The main strength of conversation analysis is that it comes to terms with what actually happens in religious talk-in-interaction and explicates how the participants themselves interpret each others' actions.
- Conversation analysis can be fruitfully combined with ethnographic methods.

What is conversation analysis?

Conversation analysis (henceforth CA) is a method for the analysis of spoken interaction. It is, most of all, concerned with the **sequential organization** of talk-in-interaction (Schegloff 2007). That is, it seeks to explore how actions and turns of talk follow each other in a systematic way.

An important case of sequential organization is the **adjacency pair** (Schegloff and Sacks 1973; Schegloff 2007). The adjacency pair is a term for a pair of turns that belong tightly together, such as question and answer, invitation and acceptance/rejection, greeting and greeting. When a speaker produces a first pair part, e.g. a question, it is the normative obligation of the next speaker to produce a second pair part that fits with the first pair part. The normativity of the adjacency pair means that the next speaker can be held accountable for not producing the second pair part. He/she may furnish a justification or a justification may be asked for by the speaker of the first pair part.

CA studies have also shown how sequential organization may be constrained in a special way in institutional encounters (Drew and Heritage 1992: 37–42). Questions and answers often have institutional functions. This means, first of all, that in many institutional encounters (e.g. courtrooms), turns are pre-allocated, in that one party, usually the professional, asks questions and the other answers them. Second, in many institutions there is a special kind of a third turn attached to the adjacency pair, e.g. the teacher's evaluative turn in classroom discourse.

There are three other important concepts that are closely connected to sequence organization: turn-taking, preference and repair. **Turn-taking** (Sacks *et al.* 1974) is concerned with the question of how speaker change is accomplished in talk-in-interaction. **Preference organization** (Schegloff 2007) refers to social and structural features of actions. For example, an invitation may be either accepted or declined. Accepting is the socially preferred response, and declining is dis-preferred. Dis-preferred responses usually include, e.g. delays, mitigations and justifications. **Repair organization** (see Schegloff *et al.* 1977) refers to interactants' methods for solving problems of hearing and understanding.

All of the foregoing can be seen as part of the 'sequential order' of interaction (Hutchby and Wooffitt 1998). However, CA is also interested in the 'inferential order' of interaction. In institutional encounters, in particular, there are specific 'inferential frameworks' at work (Drew and Heritage 1992). One way to analyze **inferential frameworks** is what Harvey Sacks (1992) called **membership categorization analysis**. For him, the starting point of membership categorization analysis was the idea that a person can be categorized in numerous ways. For example, a single person may be categorizable as a male, husband, father, middle-aged, white or Catholic. Thus, when a categorization is used in interaction, it is always a product of a choice. Sacks wanted to find out how categorizations are selected, used and understood in actual interaction. Thus, he was interested in the situated use of cultural resources (Hester and Eglin 1997).

Theoretical background

Although CA is nowadays practised in a multitude of disciplines, e.g. linguistics, communication studies, psychology and education, originally it is rooted in sociology. It was originated by the sociologist Harvey Sacks in the 1960s. He was, most of all, influenced by the ethnomethodological sociology of Harold Garfinkel (1967; see Heritage 1984). There is not space here for a thorough description of **ethnomethodology** (henceforth EM). I will, however, introduce some aspects of EM that are particularly important for CA.

EM can be described as the procedural study of ordinary practical action. By 'procedural' I mean that action is investigated in its situated instances. As Garfinkel (1967) says, people should not be thought of as cultural or psychological 'dopes', actors who blindly follow rules. People do use different cultural resources in doing what they do, e.g. rules, habits and background expectancies, but rules are never enough: each action is situated in a particular context, in which the actor her/himself makes the action intelligible. Garfinkel also stresses the accountability of action. This means that when norms or routines are broken, an actor can be expected to produce a justification; however, it also means that even when no norms are broken, actions are produced as accountable for the participants of the setting. They are accomplishments that rely on intersubjectivity between participants.

CA is also influenced by Erving Goffman's idea of the 'interaction order' (see Heritage 2001). This meant, for Goffman (1967), that social interaction can be treated as an institution itself, like other institutions such as family and religion. He recommended that interaction order should be approached through studying 'syntactical relations among the acts of different persons mutually present'. Goffman's 'syntax' can be seen as a predecessor of CA's focus on sequence organization.

Conversation analysis in religious studies

The main area of application for CA in religious studies is the microanalytic study of religious speech events. In any religious community there is a multitude of recurring speech events. If we take as an example a community that I have studied, Seventh-day Adventism, there are worship services, Bible study groups, youth meetings, religion lessons in Seventh-day Adventist schools, family worship, grace before meals, different forms of proselytizing, etc. Any of these events could be analyzed with CA methods. So far, CA studies of a variety of religious speech events have been published: e.g. prayer in different Christian settings (Capps and Ochs 2002), Seventh-day Adventist Bible study (Lehtinen 2005, 2009a, 2009b, 2009c), Christian church services in Bosavi, New Guinea (Schieffelin 2007), Mormon proselytizing in the Czech Republic (Sherman 2007), student-teacher interviews in a Zen monastery (Buttny and Isbell 1991), and master-student dialogues in a Bektashi Muslim community (Trix 1999).

In addition, it is possible to apply CA to religious writings. An example is Person's (1996) work on the book of Jonah. He examines how adjacency pairs are described in the biblical book.

In the following I will give two examples of CA studies of religion. The first of them is on Mormon proselytizing (Sherman 2007), the second on Seventh-day Adventist Bible study (Lehtinen 2009c). They are different in that Sherman studies interaction between a representative of a religious group and an outsider, while Lehtinen studies religious in-group interaction.

Sherman (2007) has studied 'first-contact public proselyting situations' of Mormon missionaries in the Czech Republic. These are situations where the missionaries approach strangers. As Sherman shows, there are many things the missionaries need to accomplish during a short exchange for it to be successful. The most important ones are: they need to initiate a conversation with a stranger, and they need to conduct that conversation in a way that makes it possible to establish further contact. The topic of faith need not necessarily be raised in the first encounter. Sherman describes how the missionaries accomplish their task step by step.

In the following I will concentrate on two aspects of this task: initiating contact and category work in the beginning of the conversation. Box 2.2.1 (Sherman 2007: 79) illustrates a typical case of initiating contact on the street. Sherman bases his discussion on Harvey Sacks' (1992) idea of different kinds of conversationalists. If, for example, two people are friends, they are, because of that, 'proper conversationalists'. That is, they 'have a right' to talk to each other, and they usually begin their conversation with greetings. When, however, strangers meet, they are 'non-proper conversationalists', and they have a right to talk to each other only if they, or one of them, produces a 'ticket', a socially acceptable reason for a conversation. Such conversations, instead of beginning with greetings, begin with tickets. Thus, the missionary's first and actually quite difficult problem is to find and produce a ticket that makes it possible for him to have a conversation with a stranger. He does so by producing a slightly ambivalent turn in which he asks the stranger whether he can speak with him. The recipient (line 2) shows that he or she interprets the missionary's initial turn as a pre-request and asks what the missionary 'needs'. A pre-request (Schegloff 2007) is a turn that projects an upcoming request and asks the recipient for permission to produce it. The recipient grants permission on line 2. To have a request would, of course, constitute a ticket to talk to a stranger. However, on line 3, the missionary rejects this interpretation, and produces instead an identification. It turns out (see line 9) that for the missionary the turn on line 1 is a pre-offer, not a pre-request. We can see, however, how producing a turn that is interpretable as a pre-request is suitable for his purposes: with it he gets the attention of the recipient and produces at least the appearance of having a ticket.

Box 2.2.1 Extract 1: Mormon proselytizing

01 M1: prosím vás můžu mluvit s vámi na chvilku?
     excuse me, can I speak with you for a little while?

02 C7: no: co potřebujete?
     yeah: what do you need?

03 M1: nic jenom my jsme tady jako dobrovolníci.
     nothing; we're just here as volunteers.

04 C7: no.
     yeah.

05 M1: a tady my učíme zdarma angličtinu.
     and we teach English for free here.

06 C7: no.
     yeah.

07 M1: a dnes my snažíme mluvit s lidmi o tom.
     and today we're trying to speak with people about it.

08 C7: no.
     yeah.

09 M1: já nevím jestli máte zájem? nebo jestli znáte někoho?
     I don't know if you're interested, or if you know someone?

              (Sherman 2007: 79–80; translation provided by Tamah Sherman)

The second issue that I want to point out in Sherman's study is the use of categorizations. This can also be seen in Box 2.2.1. At the beginning of a conversation between strangers, the interlocutors need to come to an understanding of what they are to each other. This is important in determining whether the conversation is worth continuing. Thus, Sherman conducted a careful comparison of how the missionaries described themselves in their encounters with strangers. Her main finding is that there is a certain order in which the missionaries use categories (Sherman 2007: 128). They use vague categories before more specific ones, categories that can be perceived as more agreeable before less agreeable ones, and familiar ones before less familiar ones. This can be seen in the extract in Box 2.2.1 where the missionary first uses a vague category 'volunteer' (line 3), and only afterwards invokes the more specific category 'English teacher' through describing the activity 'we teach English' (line 5). Also, the supposedly less agreeable religious categories like 'missionary' and 'Mormon' are not (yet) used.

My own study (Lehtinen 2005, 2009a, 2009b, 2009c) was conducted on Seventh-day Adventist Bible study in Finland. Bible study in the Seventh-day Adventist church is part of every worship service. It is led by a 'teacher' (often a layperson). It is based on an international study book that contains the texts that should be read and commentary and questions on them. As interaction, the Bible study usually consists of rounds where a text is first read or mentioned—the participants usually have a Bible with them and can thus see the verse even if it has just been mentioned; second, the participants discuss the text; and third, they apply the text into their own lives. The study concentrates on the second stage, on how the participants of Bible study talk about the text. This can be done monologically by the teacher, or through a question-answer-comment format, with the teacher doing the questioning and commenting and the other participants the answering.

For a Seventh-day Adventist, it is self-evident, in a general sense, that the Bible is relevant for the believer, that it 'speaks' to her or him. The problem for the participant of the Bible study is that he or she confronts particular passages of the Bible, and she or he must find, for each passage, how that particular passage is relevant. The study sought to explicate how this relevance was accomplished through talk by the participants of the Bible study. Thus, a conversation analytical treatise of Bible study, instead of interpreting the Bible text, analyzes talk about the text in its own right.

The main finding in the study is that already in the stage where the participants talk about the Bible text, they talk about it in a way that makes it relevant. They have methods for talking about the texts that make them 'speak'. In the following I will give an example of these methods, that of noticing (see the second extract in Box 2.2.2). In the second extract (Box 2.2.2), the participants are talking about Nehemiah 5, in which Nehemiah reprimands the leaders of Israel for their exploitation of the people. Before the extract they have talked about how Nehemiah got angry. The extract consists of a simple sequence of actions. Hilma (the teacher) first asks the participants to read a verse of the Bible. Reino then reads the verse (lines 5–10), and Hilma comments on the verse (lines 12–17). In that comment she uses a noticing. It is important to note that the commenting is made in the context of the previous turn in which the Bible verse is read.

In her turn Hilma uses the expression *ajatelkaa* 'think about it' (line 12) to draw attention to a part of a text that she presents as noticeable. The noticeable part is, in Finnish, a single word: *harkittuani* 'after considering' (line 14). She stresses it, for example, by saying it twice, lengthening sounds and raising the volume of her voice. Otherwise she just repeats part of the verse verbatim (lines 14–16, compare with lines 5–7). The important question is, however, why this particular word should be noticed in this verse. As Sacks (1992: 87–97) has shown, there is always a context-dependent reason for declaring that one has noticed something which has to do with the kinds of inferences the noticing makes available. In this case, to find these inferences, we need to look at the surrounding context and draw on cultural resources. First of all, in the text that has just been read, 'considering' is connected to 'reprimanding', it is done before the reprimanding. Second, the participants have just talked about how Nehemiah 'got angry': this issue has been given special attention. So the 'considering' is done between 'getting angry' and 'reprimanding'. The importance of considering becomes understandable in the context of conventions of getting angry and reprimanding that come into play in interpreting the biblical text. Both getting angry and reprimanding can be seen as morally delicate actions. Getting angry can entail, for example, losing control; reprimanding can be seen as rude and impolite. Most importantly, the rudeness and impoliteness of reprimanding is especially relevant when the one doing so is angry. Here we can see the moral relevance of the considering: it separates the anger from the reprimanding and thus speaks

---

Box 2.2.2 Extract 2: Seventh-day Adventist Bible study

See Box 2.2.4 for the meaning of the transcription symbols.

01 Hilma: (0.2) .hh Ja mitä hän teki

(0.2) .hh And what did he do.

02   (2.5) ((Tuija and Lea raise their hands))

03 Hilma: Seitsemäs jae.

Verse seven.

04   (9.0)

05 Reino: Ja **harkittuani** mielessäni tätä

*And **after considering** this matter*

06   asiaa (.) minä nuhtelin ylimyksiä, (0.8) ja

in my mind (.) I reprimanded the nobles, (0.8) and

07   esimiehiä ja sanoin heille .hh tehän

chiefs and said to them .hh why you

08   ↑kiskotte korkoa ↑kukiv ↑veljiltänne, (0.3)

↑practice usury↑ each of you ↑on your brothers, (0.3)

09   sittem minä panin toimeen suu:ren kokouksen]

then I arranged a bi:g assembly

10   heitä vastaan.

against them.

11   (0.5)

12 Hilma: @Nii:n@. (0.4) &Ajatelkaa hän (.) hän (.)

@Ye:s@. (0.4) &Think about it he (.) he (.)

13   sanotaan >minu e- (.) tämä että<& .h hän

it says >(-) (-)- (.) this that< .h he

14   **<harkittuani> (0.6) HAR::KITTUANI,** (1.2)

<after considering> (0.6) AFTER CONSI::DERING, (1.2)

15   mielessäni tätä asiaa (0.3) nuh:telin

this matter in my mind (0.3) I reprima:ded

16   ylimyksiä (.) >ja esimiehiä< = .h ↑onko tämä helppo

the nobles (.) >and chiefs< = .h ↑is this an easy

17   tehtävä.

task.

(Lehtinen 2009b)

---

against the possible implication that the reprimanding was done in an angry and a possibly uncontrolled state.

Thus, by drawing attention in her turn-at-talk to Nehemiah's 'considering', Hilma makes his action morally understandable. This understandability is based on moral norms and conventions that are understandable to the participants, relevant in their world. Only by relying on those same conventions can the participants see why they should notice just this expression in just this story. The story can 'speak' to them by pointing out the way in which

Nehemiah's action can provide moral guidance for them, offer an example for them to follow in similar circumstances: i.e. they should also 'consider' before 'reprimanding'.

It can be said that in both the cases described above, the analysis explicates a problem that the participants of a religious group need to solve: how to initiate and continue a conversation with a stranger, and how to make a particular Bible text 'speak' through their talk-in-interaction. Both these problems are, at least in retrospect, quite obvious to anyone who knows these religious groups. The main contribution of conversation analysis is, first of all, to show how these problems are interactional and situational in nature: they consist of choices the participants continually need to make in particular sequential positions. Second, conversation analysis can uncover the interactional methods the participants of religious groups use to accomplish their religious task, answering the question of how religious tasks are accomplished in practice.

Practical issues: How to do conversation analysis

The data in conversation analysis consist of recordings of so-called naturally occurring talk-in-interaction (Heritage 1984). This means that field notes or interviews are not considered as sufficient data. In CA the analysis needs to come to terms with minute details of actual talk, and such detail is difficult if not impossible to remember afterwards. Both audio and video recordings are used, but video recordings are preferred, since they can catch the non-verbal aspects of interaction. This type of recording data may create problems with access. There are religious groups among which it is impossible to obtain permission for recording. In these groups other methods need to be used.

Box 2.2.3 Steps to take in conversation analytical research

- video or audio recording of data
- transcription
- 'unmotivated' search for a phenomenon
- making a collection of cases
- comparison of cases
- determining the religious significance of the phenomenon

There are also ethical questions in recording interactional data. The privacy of the participants of the interaction needs to be protected. Especially when the recording is made in a non-public setting, it is necessary to obtain written informed consent from all participants. They need to be informed about the purpose of the study, the way in which the data is used and where the recordings will be viewed. In transcribing, the usual practice is to protect the privacy of the participants through changing all names, places and other details that make identification possible.[1]

In CA the recordings are always used as the primary data. However, the data also needs to be **transcribed** into written form. Since CA research is interested in detail, the transcripts are usually also very detailed. For example, pauses, overlaps, intonation, laughter, restarts and acknowledgement tokens are usually marked (see Jefferson 2004). These phenomena are important in studying, for example, turn-taking and repair. On the other hand, no matter how detailed the transcript is, it is always a product of selection.

Box 2.2.4 Transcription symbols

.	falling intonation
,	slightly falling intonation
?	rising intonation
↓	fall in pitch
↑	rise in pitch
sp<u>ea</u>k	emphasis
> speak <	faster pace than surrounding talk
< speak >	slower pace than surrounding talk
^speak^	quiet talk
SPEAK	loud talk
sp-	word cut off
spea:k	lengthening of the sound
.hhh	inbreath
hhh	outbreath
.speak	word spoken during inbreath
#speak#	creaky voice
&speak&	trembling voice
$speak$	smile voice
@speak@	unanalyzed change of tone
sp(h)eak	word produced through laugh
hehe	laughing
[	beginning of overlapping talk
]	end of overlapping talk

(Lehtinen 2009b)

In the preliminary analysis of data, conversation analysts tend to talk about 'unmotivated looking' (Sacks 1984). This means that the researcher should be open to finding unexpected phenomena in the data. 'Unmotivated' does not, however, mean that the data should be approached without any systematic method. For example, if one has a particular type of religious encounter, e.g. a worship service or a prayer meeting, my advice is to start with one instance of it and analyze it systematically, paying attention to its sequential structure. One should identify the actions that are performed, in their order, and look at how the different actions are performed. Through such preliminary analysis, one should decide on the phenomenon one wants to study. Usually the phenomenon is a particular type of turn or sequence of turns such as question and answer or request and response (Hutchby and Wooffitt 1998: 94).

When the object of analysis has been identified, the researcher should go through the data systematically and collect all instances of the phenomenon. Then the cases in the collection should be analyzed in a detailed way, especially paying attention to how the different actions are performed, and how the participants of the interaction themselves demonstrably interpret each other's actions. This means, for example, that one should not analyze questions without taking into consideration how they are answered. The goal of the analysis is to uncover recurrent patterns of action in the interaction type one studies.

It is also important to analyze the collections of cases in view of the inferential frameworks observable in them. This is especially important in determining the religious significance of the sequential patterns one studies. The researcher should ask what religious tasks the participants of the interaction accomplish and what religiously relevant 'problems' they solve through their actions. Thus, CA research can shed light on what religion is like—and what different religions are like—as practice through showing what kinds of practical problems practitioners of religion grapple with in their daily lives and how they solve them.

There is computer software available for the transcription and analysis of interactional data. It is important that the software one uses makes it possible to link clips of data to the transcription and make collections in which the link is preserved (see ten Have 2007: 112–13). Transana and CLAN, for example, have been widely used by CA researchers.

Strengths, limitations and challenges

CA involves a detailed microanalysis of data. This is both a strength and a limitation of the method. The main strength of the method is that it comes to terms with what actually happens in religious talk-in-interaction. Also, since CA is concerned with sequential analysis, it can explicate how the participants themselves interpret each others' actions. This is done through examining how actions are treated in the next turn. Thus, CA can shed light on what religious practice looks like from the standpoint of the practitioners.

However, since the analysis is so detailed, a conversation analyst must usually concentrate on just one type of a religious encounter. Thus, it can be argued that CA results give a limited picture of any religious community. Also, particularly when researchers study a religious community with which they are unfamiliar, they need cultural knowledge of the community to understand the inferential frameworks involved (see Arminen 2000). To attain such knowledge, ethnographic observation of the community needs to be conducted. Thus, a combination of ethnographic and conversation analytic methods can deliver excellent results. The best possible scenario would be to put together a research group of ethnographers and conversation analysts. The ethnographers could concentrate on giving a holistic picture of the speech community, while conversation analysts could concentrate on specific kinds of speech events (see Lehtinen 2009a).

Note

1   In the extracts in this article, all the names have been changed.

References

Arminen, I., 2000. 'On the context sensitivity of institutional interaction'. *Discourse & Society* 11, 435–58.

Buttny, R. and Isbell, T.L., 1991. 'The problem of communicating Zen understanding: a microanalysis of teacher-student interviews in a North American Zen monastery'. *Human Studies* 14, 287–309.

Capps, L. and Ochs, E., 2002. 'Cultivating prayer'. In: Ford, C.E., Fox, B.A. and Thompson, S.A. (eds), *The Language of Turn and Sequence*. Oxford University Press, Oxford, pp. 39–55.

Drew, P. and Heritage, J., 1992. 'Analyzing talk at work: an introduction'. In: Drew, P. and Heritage, J. (eds), *Talk at Work: interaction in institutional settings*. Cambridge University Press, Cambridge, pp. 3–65.

Garfinkel, H., 1967. *Studies in Ethnomethodology*. Prentice-Hall, Englewood Cliffs, NJ.

Goffman, E., 1967. *Interaction Ritual: essays on face-to-face behaviour*. Pantheon Books, New York.

Heritage, J., 1984. *Garfinkel and Ethnomethodology*. Polity Press, Cambridge.

—— 2001. 'Goffman, Garfinkel and conversation analysis'. In: Wetherell, M., Taylor, S. and Yates, S.J. (eds), *Discourse Theory and Practice: a reader*. SAGE, London, Thousand Oaks, CA, pp. 47–56.

Hester, S. and Eglin, P., 1997. 'Membership categorization analysis: an introduction'. In: Hester, S. and Eglin, P. (eds), *Culture in Action: studies in membership categorization analysis*. University Press of America, Washington, DC, pp. 1–23.

Hutchby, I. and Wooffitt, R., 1998. *Conversation Analysis: principles, practices and applications*. Polity Press, Cambridge.

Jefferson, G., 2004. 'Glossary of transcript symbols with an introduction'. In: Lerner, G. (ed.), *Conversation Analysis: studies from the first generation*. John Benjamins, Amsterdam/Philadelphia, pp. 13–31.

Lehtinen, E., 2005. 'Achieved similarity: describing experience in Seventh-day Adventist Bible study'. *Text* 25, 341–71.

—— 2009a. 'Conversation analysis and religion: practices of talking about Bible texts in Seventh-day Adventist Bible study'. *Religion* 39, 233–47.

—— 2009b. 'Practical hermeneutics: noticing in Bible study interaction'. *Human Studies* 32, 461–85.

—— 2009c. 'Sequential and inferential order in religious action: a conversation analytic perspective'. *Langage et Société* 130, 15–36.

Person, R.F., 1996. *In Conversation with Jonah: conversation analysis, literary criticism, and the book of Jonah*. Sheffield Academic Press, Sheffield.

Sacks, H., 1984. 'Notes on methodology'. In: Atkinson, J.M. and Heritage, J. (eds), *Structures of Social Action: studies in conversation analysis*. Cambridge University Press, Cambridge, pp. 21–27.

—— 1992. *Lectures on Conversation, Volume I*. Jefferson, G. (ed.) Blackwell, Oxford.

Sacks, H., Schegloff, E.A. and Jefferson, G., 1974. 'A simplest systematics for the organization of turn-taking for conversation'. *Language* 50, 696–735.

Schegloff, E.A., 2007. *Sequence Organization in Interaction: a primer in conversation analysis. Volume 1*. Cambridge University Press, Cambridge.

Schegloff, E.A. and Sacks, H., 1973. 'Opening up closings'. *Semiotica* 7, 289–327.

Schegloff, E.A., Jefferson, G. and Sacks, H., 1977. 'The preference for self-correction in the organisation of repair in conversation'. *Language* 53, 361–82.

Schieffelin, B.B., 2007. 'Found in translating: reflexive language across time and texts in Bosavi, Papua New Guinea'. In: Makihara, M. and Schieffelin, B.B. (eds), *Consequences of Contact: language ideologies and sociocultural transformations in Pacific societies*. Oxford University Press, Oxford, pp. 140–65.

Sherman, T., 2007. *Proselyting in first-contact situations*. Unpublished dissertation. Charles University, Prague.

ten Have, P., 2007. *Doing Conversation Analysis: a practical guide*. 2nd edn. SAGE, London, Thousand Oaks, CA.

Trix, F., 1999. 'Spiraling connections: the practice of repair in Bektashi Muslim discourse'. In: Kovarsky, D., Duchan, J.F. and Maxwell, M. (eds), *Constructing (In)Competence: disabling evaluations in clinical and social interaction*. Lawrence Erlbaum, Mahwah, New Jersey, pp. 149–68.

Further reading

Arminen, I., 2005. *Institutional Interaction: studies of talk at work*. Ashgate, Aldershot.

A comprehensive introduction to the study of institutional interaction.

Capps, L. and Ochs, E., 2002. 'Cultivating prayer'. In: Ford, C.E., Fox, B.A. and Thompson, S.A. (eds), *The Language of Turn and Sequence*. Oxford University Press, Oxford, pp. 39–55.

An exemplary study of religious interaction: an analysis of how prayer is interactionally organized in Christian settings.

Hutchby, I. and Wooffitt, R., 1998. *Conversation Analysis: principles, practices and applications*. Polity Press, Cambridge.

An established introductory textbook on conversation analysis. Includes a description of theoretical basis, research process and examples of studies.

Lehtinen, E., 2009. 'Conversation analysis and religion: practices of talking about Bible texts in Seventh-day Adventist Bible study'. *Religion* 39, 233–47.

A conversation analytic study of Bible study groups, with a methodological discussion on the relationship of conversation analysis and ethnography.

Peräkylä, A., 1997. 'Reliability and validity in research based on tapes and transcripts'. In: Silverman, D. (ed.), *Qualitative Research: theory, method and practice.* SAGE, London, Thousand Oaks, CA, pp. 201–20.

A discussion on conversation analytic methodology, with a particular emphasis on institutional settings.

Sacks, H., 1992. *Lectures on Conversation, Volumes I & II.* Jefferson, G. (ed.) Blackwell, Oxford.

The classical work of conversation analysis. Transcribed lectures of the founder of conversation analysis.

Schegloff, E.A., 2007. *Sequence Organization in Interaction: a primer in conversation analysis.* Vol. 1. Cambridge University Press, Cambridge.

A thorough introduction to the basic concepts and findings of conversation analysis.

Sherman, T., 2007. *Proselyting in first-contact situations.* Unpublished dissertation. Charles University, Prague.

An exemplary study on religious interaction: an analysis of Mormon proselytizing.

ten Have, P., 2007. *Doing Conversation Analysis: a practical guide.* 2nd edn. SAGE, London, Thousand Oaks, CA.

An introductory textbook on conversation analysis, with a theoretical introduction and thorough guidance on research practice.

Key concepts

Adjacency pair: a sequence of two adjacent utterances in talk-in-interaction that are normatively tied to each other, e.g. question and answer.

Ethnomethodology: a form of sociology originated by Harold Garfinkel that seeks to explicate practical action in a situated way.

Inferential framework: a set of cultural resources in a speech community that participants of interaction use in order to understand each other.

Membership categorization analysis: a mode of analysis originated by Harvey Sacks that seeks to explicate how members of a culture categorize each other in situated ways in interaction.

Preference organization: the practices that participants of talk-in-interaction use to display their orientation to the social acceptability of actions.

Repair organization: the methods that participants of talk-in-interaction use to deal with problems of hearing and understanding.

Sequence organization: the systematics in the ordering of actions in talk-in-interaction. According to conversation analysis, turns that follow each other sequentially are linked to each other in an orderly way.

Transcription: conversion of video or audio recorded data into written form. Conversation analytical transcription tries to capture both what is said and how it is said.

Turn-taking organization: the methods that participants of talk-in-interaction use to construct their turns as complete and accomplish speaker exchange.

Related chapters

- Chapter 1.5 Research design
- Chapter 1.6 Research ethics
- Chapter 2.3 Discourse analysis
- Chapter 2.8 Field research: Participant observation
- Chapter 2.11 Hermeneutics
- Chapter 2.16 Philology

2.3

DISCOURSE ANALYSIS

Titus Hjelm

Chapter summary

- Discourse analysis is the study of how to do things with words.
- Discourse analysis examines how identities, relationships, beliefs and knowledge systems are constructed in language use.
- Discourse analysis combines textual interpretation informed by social theory with linguistic analysis.
- Critical discourse analysis focuses on ideology in discourse, i.e. the reproduction and transformation of relations of domination.
- Discourse analysis is suitable for both micro- and macro-level analysis.
- In addition to the study of texts, comprehensive discursive analysis can examine the production and reception of texts, e.g. by combining discourse analysis with ethnography.
- Every discourse-analytical study needs to be designed individually; variation of emphasis and the choice of analytical 'tools' is almost unlimited.

Introduction

Discourse analysis is the study of how to do things with words (cf. Austin 1975). What consequences are there, for example, when a newspaper writes about 'Muslim terrorists'? Why don't we see 'Christian terrorists' in the news? Discourse analysis examines how actions are given meaning and how identities are produced in language use. Theoretically speaking, discourse analysts investigate processes of **social construction** (Phillips and Hardy 2002).

While quite popular in other areas of social scientific and humanistic research, religious studies or the study of religion in a broader sense has not adopted discourse analysis as a *method* in any systematic way, despite the fact that in recent years discourse has emerged as a potential key concept in the field. The more successful explorations, such as the agenda-setting articles by von Stuckrad (2003, 2010) on the 'discursive study of religion' and Russell McCutcheon's many books on the nature of religious studies (e.g. McCutcheon 1997), are examples of adopting discourse as a theoretical and metatheoretical concept (see also Murphy 2000;

Engler 2005; Lincoln 1989; Asad 1993; Brown 2009; for a critique, see Riesebrodt 2010). In sociology of religion, discourse has also been discussed in metatheoretical terms (e.g. Spickard 2005). However, sociologists of religion have also been concerned about the more practical applications of discourse theory—although as Spickard (2007: 133) notes, discourse analysis in the sense of method remains a largely untapped source. Symptomatic of this is Robert Wuthnow's (2011) promising-sounding article which, despite the title, does not engage with discourse analysis per se but with broader ethnomethodology-inspired qualitative methodology. The only book-length studies in English (of which I am aware) explicitly using a discourse-analytical framework to study religion and spirituality, by Wooffitt (2006) and Heather (2000), have gone largely unnoticed in the field.[1]

My aim in this chapter is to outline the basic premises and varieties of discourse analysis and to examine how these ideas might be put into practice in analyzing religion. While I acknowledge the above-mentioned discussions in religious studies and sociology of religion, my presentation of discourse analysis will be largely independent of them. This is because, as noted, so far the focus in religious studies has been on discussing discourse as a (meta)theoretical concept, whereas I am here mainly concerned with the application of discourse analysis as a practical method. Further, I am here interested particularly in what Fairclough refers to as 'textually oriented discourse analysis' against (although drawing in some aspects from) Michel Foucault's more abstract and broadly historical approach (for a comprehensive discussion see Fairclough 1992: 37–61). In the next sections I will explore the varieties of discourse analysis and discuss practical concerns for choosing a discourse-analytical approach. At the end of the chapter I will discuss the prospects and limitations of discourse analysis as a method in the study of religion.

What is discourse?

Discourse has been defined in various ways throughout its 'career' in the social sciences and humanities (see e.g. McDonnell 1986; Mills 2004). For the purposes of this chapter I will concentrate on the social scientific uses of the concept, which generally agree that discourse is a way of speaking that does not simply reflect or represent things 'out there', but 'constructs' or 'constitutes' them (Fairclough 1992: 3). Although discourse analysts talk about representation, they do so in a very specific sense. All descriptions of the world are by definition partial, and the variability of discourse itself is an indicator of the constructed nature of social life. The 'cult controversies' are a good example of this: how can it be that the same religious beliefs and practices are to some the way to salvation and to others deviant, harmful and evil? The answer is in the different discourses that the adherents, on the one hand, and the 'anti-cult movement', on the other, employ. It is not that either side is consciously telling lies (although sometimes that happens as well), but rather that 'while people may tell the truth, and nothing but the truth, it is impossible for anyone to tell the *whole* truth. Everyone (more or less consciously) selects what is to be included or excluded from their picture of reality according to a number of criteria—one criterion being what is relevant to their interests' (Barker 2011: 200, emphasis in original).

As the above example shows, discourse is *constitutive*—that is, it constructs social reality and relationships (see Box 2.3.1). However, discourse has a second characteristic closely connected to Barker's observation about the interests of social actors. In addition to being constitutive, discourse also has a *function* (Potter and Wetherell 1987: 32–33).[2] Discourse itself is seen as a form of social *practice*, contributing both to the reproduction of society and to social change (Fairclough 1992; Potter 1996: 105). Edwards and Potter (1992) talk about the 'action orientation' of discourse, that is, how things are *done* with discourse.[3] For example, the sentence 'it is going to drive me mad doing all those statistics by hand tonight' can be read as a simple announcement. However, if uttered in the presence of a friend in possession of a calculator, its potential meaning changes into a veiled question (Potter and Wetherell 1987: 33). The discourse of the anti-cult movement, for example, is thick with not only construc-tions of cults, but also descriptions of the ways in which cult members can be 'cured' and how the influence of cults can be prevented. This 'cult discourse' both constructs cults as a social problem and also offers solutions to dealing with the problem (see Hjelm 2009).

Box 2.3.1 The constructive effects of discourse

What is constructed in discourse?

- Social identities or 'subject positions'
- Social relationships
- Systems of knowledge and belief

(Fairclough 1992)

Although there are considerable regional, national and disciplinary differences in how academia has responded to discourse theory, the story of discourse analysis is one of increasing impact. From the late 1960s onwards both linguists and social scientists started thinking about ways of putting insights from the philosophy of language—especially the later work of Ludwig Wittgenstein—into practice. Although used in widely different senses and drawing from varying disciplinary backgrounds (see below), discourse analysis emerged as a field of interdisciplinary research in the 1970s and, boosted by the emergence of postmodernist theory, gained prominence in the 1980s. Thus, we can speak of a 'discursive turn'. Crucial to this development was the work of Michel Foucault (especially Foucault 1978, 1995), who conceptualized discourse as the defining aspect of social relations and who, consequently, saw the study of discourse as central to the study of how society is constituted in social interaction (but see above).

Discourse and cognition

Writing in the late 1980s, Teun van Dijk, one of the leading names in the development of the field, called discourse analysis a 'new, interdisciplinary field of study' (van Dijk 1988: 17). Since then discourse analysis has spread even further in academia—losing some of its initial attachment to linguistics on the way—and is now used across the social sciences and humanities. Thus the typology of three approaches (cognition, interaction, critical) that I use here is just one of many possibilities, although perhaps the most fundamental. In a way van Dijk's own work is an example of this diversification and of the fact that the different approaches overlap in many ways. The early cognitive model discussed here is less prominent in his later writings, but deserves mention here as a particular way of looking at discourse.

It should be made clear from the outset that van Dijk's model encompasses a huge variety of perspectives, from the analysis of syntax to the study of rhetoric and cognitive schemata, and a comprehensive treatment of it would require much more space than available here.

Therefore, I am concentrating on the concept of *thematic macrostructures* and their application in practical analysis. This will be unavoidably a simplified account and those interested in the full scope of the theory and method should consult van Dijk's original work (e.g. van Dijk 1980, 1988).

At the heart of van Dijk's model is the idea of social cognition: our knowledge of the world is organized into schematic structures and the aim of discourse analysis is to trace the cognitive processing of texts. Through *macroanalysis*, in van Dijk's terminology, the 'theme' or topic' of the discourse is processed and condensed from the words and sentences of the particular text. The resulting 'gist' is what van Dijk calls a *macrostructure*. Macrostructures are derived from *propositions* (*p*) that in the case of newspaper text, for example, are sentences or paragraphs. A single sentence can be considered a proposition, but complex sentences can include multiple propositions. *Macrorules* are tools of analysis that organize propositions into hierarchical macrostructures. Despite the formality of van Dijk's terminology, the process of analysis is fundamentally interpretive. Because macrorules operate with natural language, they are not grammatical rules, but interpretive tools that require contextual knowledge.

The three macrorules that van Dijk employs in his analysis of news discourse are *deletion, generalization* and *construction* (van Dijk 1988: 32).[4] The deletion rule 'deletes all those propositions of the text base which are not relevant for the interpretation of other propositions of the discourse' (van Dijk 1980: 46–47). The generalization rule abstracts more general propositions from sentences. It works similarly to the deletion rule, in that it leaves out information in the resulting macroproposition, but through abstraction and combination rather than complete deletion. Thus, Catholicism, Lutheranism, Methodism, Baptism, etc. could all be subsumed under 'Christianity'. Finally, in the construction rule, 'propositions are, so to speak, "taken together" by substituting them, as a joint sequence, by a proposition that denotes a global fact' (van Dijk 1980: 48). Prayer, liturgy, confession, Eucharist, etc., for example, constitute the 'global fact' of 'ritual'. The difference between 'generalization' and 'construction' is a fine one, as can be seen from the above.

As a result of applying these macrorules we end up with a hierarchical macrostructure like the one in Figure 2.3.1. Propositions are denoted by *p*, while first-level macropropositions are denoted by *M*, and second level macropropositions by *m*.

Basically, there is no limit to how many levels of macropropositions there can be, as long as the function of each level of analysis is to get further into the 'heart' of the topic.

As an example of the practical application of van Dijk's model, I will use a translation[5] of a news story from a Finnish Christian weekly *Kotimaa*. It is an early example of the Finnish Satanism Scare discourse (see Hjelm 2002).[6]

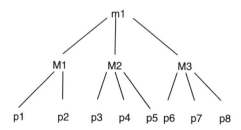

Figure 2.3.1 Macrostructure
Source: van Dijk 1988: 32–33

'Satanists in Järvenpää'[7] *(Kotimaa 29 March 1993)*

1   A youth group worshipping Satan has been exposed in Järvenpää.

2   The group consists of young girls and it is led by an older man.

3   The issue was uncovered when the girls' cutting of school classes was being investigated.

4   This is a case of a criminal drug gang, which was held on a tight leash by means of satanic rituals.

5   According to Harri Heino, the director of the Church Research Institute, groups like these have been uncovered in other parts of southern Finland as well.

6   'The pattern is quite similar to the Järvenpää case in these communities'.

7   'The group is led by one or two older men who have a criminal record and the rest of the group consists of young people', says Harri Heino.

8   The first church of Satan in the United States was established in 1966 by Anton LaVey.

9   The movement became famous when celebrities like Sammy Davis, Jr and Jayne Mansfield took part in its activities.

The process of analysis could then look like this, going through the text line by line:

1   M1 Construction
2   M1 Construction
3   Delete
4   M2 Construction
5   M1 Construction
6   M1 Construction
7   M2 Construction
8   Delete
9   Delete

The first-level macropropositions of this short article would be:

- M1 There are Satanist youth groups in southern Finland
- M2 These are criminal drug gangs

The issue of girls cutting classes is, of course, further evidence of the harmful nature of Satanism, but not central to the local context of 'discovery'. Further, while important in the broader Satanism discourse, the international nature of Satanism that the last two sentences imply (despite the fact that LaVey's organization had nothing to do with the alleged Finnish one) is not central to this discourse.

By combining M1 and M2, we would end up with a discourse that could be named 'Satanism is criminal'. Whatever else it might be, this is the aspect that comes through most forcefully in an analysis of macrostructures. Obviously, the choice (whether conscious or unconscious) to present Satanism and the youth allegedly involved in it in this particular light has important consequences when cultural artifacts like symbols and music styles are associated with Satanism. As happened in the Finnish case, many youth wearing black and listening to black metal music were labeled as either potential victims or perpetrators of crime.

While in many ways impressive in its complexity, there are many reasons why van Dijk's model is problematic from a social scientific point of view. I will discuss these below. However, I think a simplified excursus into the cognitive model of discourse analysis is important as an example of an approach that is potentially reconcilable with the emerging cognitive paradigm in the study of religion, a perspective that is often pitted against discursive and 'constructionist' methodologies.

Discourse and interaction

Although van Dijk has been very influential in establishing discourse studies as a discipline, most other approaches to discourse analysis are in many ways antithetical to his cognitive model—my own take on discourse analysis included. Perhaps the most vocal critics of the kind of cognitivism that van Dijk's model espouses have been scholars coming from a (social) psychology background. For them the concept of discourse and discourse analysis has been not just a methodological innovation, but a way to reconfigure the whole field of psychology. Hence, this approach is sometimes referred to as 'discursive psychology' (Edwards and Potter 1992; Burr 1995; Potter and Wetherell 1987).

While van Dijk's point is that we can analyze discourse by examining thematic macrostructures because texts are representations of cognitive processes, discursive psychologists and other critics of cognitive psychology argue that there is no unproblematic path to cognition, and therefore discourse should be the topic of analysis (Gergen 1994: 27; Edwards and Potter 1992: 15–16). In other words, instead of mental representations, discourse itself becomes the object of study, the 'action orientation' of discourse is defined as the prime focus of discursive psychology (Edwards and Potter 1992: 2), and discourse analysis is more broadly conceived.

Jonathan Potter, in a discussion on the discursive take on central psychological concepts such as 'memory' and 'attitude', puts it succinctly:

> Discursive psychologists ask: What does a 'memory' *do* in some interaction? How is a version of the past constructed to sustain some *action*? Or: what is an 'attitude' used to *do*? How is an evaluation built to assign blame to a minority group, say, or how is an evaluation used to persuade a reluctant adolescent to eat tuna pasta?
>
> *(Potter 2000: 35, emphasis in original)*

One of the main points of this type of discourse analysis, which focuses on language use in interaction, is to look at *variability* in discourse. In traditional psychological approaches to attitude research, according to Potter and Wetherell (1987), utterances are treated as indicators of underlying attitudes. Their research shows, however, that people are generally inconsistent, and their discourse varies dependent on what they are trying to achieve—that is, the action orientation of discourse. Their studies on the discourse of racism (Potter and Wetherell 1987; Wetherell and Potter 1992), although more than 20 years old, remain relevant for the study of religious diversification and its effects, for example. As a 'tentative' example, Potter and Wetherell analyze a short excerpt from a research interview:

> I'm not anti them at all you know, I, if they're willing to get on and be like us; but if they're just going to come here, just to be able to use our social welfares and stuff like that, then why don't they stay home?
>
> *(Potter and Wetherell 1987: 47)*

Methodologically speaking, the first statement 'I'm not anti them at all you know' could be read as a positive statement on 'them' (Polynesian immigrants in New Zealand), and on a questionnaire scale could be located at the 'sympathetic' end of the scale. The following sequence, however, paints a much less sympathetic picture. First, Potter and Wetherell point out how the expressed sympathy of the opening is qualified by organizing the discourse into 'conditionals and contrasts' (Potter and Wetherell 1987: 47): *If* (they're willing to get on and be like us), *then* (I'm not anti them), but *if* (they're just going . . . to use our social welfares), *then* (why don't they stay home). Second, the criticism of immigration/immigrants is justified rhetorically by using what the authors call an *extreme case* formulation (ibid.: 47–48). Qualifying the initial non-anti statement, the speaker says: 'if they're *just* going to come here, *just* to be able to use our social welfares'. This 'paints a picture of people whose sole purpose in coming to New Zealand is the collection of social security, a selfish motive' (ibid.: 48). Finally, the initial non-anti statement does much more than tell us about the speaker's attitude. In this case it in fact functions as a disclaimer for warding off accusations of racism, which the later they should 'stay home' implication might engender. It is a very common discursive device used in many potentially controversial topics, such as sexism and, in the case of religion, especially in order to avoid accusations of anti-Semitism or Islamophobia.

Analyzing discourse from the above perspective becomes a study of how things are accomplished discursively, how identities and social reality are constructed in interaction. Some 'interactionists' go as far as to say that, in fact, interaction is the *only* thing that we can and should study (Shotter 1993; Gergen 1994). This radical epistemology dispenses with analyses of the context of language use and focuses solely on the interaction event. It is strictly the discourse, and discourse alone, which we can analyze and make conclusions about. The critical approaches outlined below have been most critical about this kind of approach and, although characteristic of discourse analysis emerging from a social psychology framework, there are more moderate views among the representatives of this approach as well (e.g. Burr 1995).

Many studies in this vein analyze interaction also on the sequential level, that is, for example, how dialogue or group discussion is organized around taking turns in speaking and how that creates identities. In this sense the interaction perspective often comes close to conversation analysis (see Chapter 2.2 in this volume; Wooffitt 2005) in its focus on micro-level processes rather than broader social contextualization. Although the discursive psychology project is still somewhat marginal in the field of psychology, discourse analysis in the above sense has found its way into many other disciplines and become a genuinely interdisciplinary field in the process.

Discourse and power

Sometimes a distinction is made between 'constructivist'[8] and 'critical' approaches to discourse analysis. According to Phillips and Hardy, '[C]onstructivist approaches . . . produce fine-grained explorations of the way in which social reality has been constructed, and *critical* approaches . . . focus more explicitly on the dynamics of power, knowledge, and ideology that surround discursive processes' (Phillips and Hardy 2002: 20, emphasis in original). This typology should be considered flexible, since all varieties of discourse analysis are concerned with the construction of the world, identities and ideas. **Critical discourse analysis** does, however, differ from the above approaches in the sense that first, it focuses on power and ideology in discourse, and second, it acknowledges that there is a reality—physical and social—*outside* of discourse that is reproduced and changed discursively. I will discuss both of these aspects in turn.

In everyday talk **ideology** is often understood as something akin to a worldview and has sometimes been explicitly contrasted with religion (see Lease 2000). John B. Thompson neatly summarizes this view, which he calls the 'grand narrative of cultural transformation' (starting with Marx and Weber): 'the decline of religion and magic prepared the ground for the emergence of secular belief systems or "ideologies", which serve to mobilize political action without reference to other-worldly values or beings' (Thompson 1990: 77).

While the above way of using 'ideology' is rooted in the history of the concept, Thompson—one of the foremost scholars of ideology—and critical discourse analysts use it in a different sense. Therefore, for my purposes it is important to differentiate between the everyday use of the concept and the *critical conception of ideology*. For the critical tradition in social science, ideology is intimately tied with the question of power. Concisely defined, the critical tradition sees ideology as 'meaning in the service of power' (Thompson 1990: 8). Speaking in the plural, Fairclough defines ideologies as 'constructions of reality (the physical world, social relations, social identities), which are built into various dimensions of the forms/ meanings of discursive practices, and which contribute to the production, reproduction or transformation of relations of domination' (Fairclough 1992: 87).

Following Foucault, the contemporary discursive conception of ideology sees power as increasingly exercised through the use of persuasive language. When 'proper' ways of thinking about and doing things are constructed from a particular perspective—yielding a one-sided account that ignores the variety of practices—discourse is said to function *ideologically* (Chouliaraki and Fairclough 1999: 26). For example, when the characteristics of a group of people are represented as derivable from their ethnic or religious background (e.g. 'Muslim terrorists'), the discourse 'irons out' the variety of beliefs, practices and ways of thinking in the group. **Hegemony** ('hegemonic discourse') is the peak of ideology, the point when all alternative constructions are suppressed in favor of one dominating view.

In addition to what is said in discourse, it is equally important for critical discourse analysis to study what is *not* said, that is, what we take for granted. According to Fairclough, any reference to 'common sense' is 'substantially, though not entirely, *ideological*' (Fairclough 1989: 84, emphasis in original). Because common sense naturalizes our conceptions of everyday life, it is the most effective way of sustaining hegemony, that is, an exclusive interpretation of reality. This means that one of the tasks of the discursive critique of ideology is what could be called 'unmasking'. The word is problematic, of course, because it implies that the reality that the analysis unmasks is somehow false (cf. Marx's 'false consciousness'). This is not the case—and from a constructionist perspective could not be by definition. What unmasking more accurately does is to look at how 'the effect of ideologies in "ironing out" (i.e. suppressing) aspects of practices [. . .] links ideologies to "mystification" and "misrecognition"' (Chouliaraki and Fairclough 1999: 26). Therefore, unmasking and ideological analysis always means studying not only what is said, but also what is not said. 'Silences' in discourse are very effective in buffering ideology by simplifying representations of social reality.

Because critical discourse analysis is more interested in the social and political context of interaction than are either of the above approaches, the sample analysis below will, in the interests of space, be limited in many ways. As an illustration of ideology and the construction of hegemonic discourse, I offer a shortened version of Fairclough's own example from the widely read *Media Discourse* (Fairclough 1995a: 68–71). Here he analyzes a story about a British government report on hard drug abuse published in May 1985. This was at the height of the 'drug wars' in the United States, when the Thatcher government's attitude reflected those of the US counterparts. Interesting here, however, is how the viewpoints of the government report were communicated in the popular British newspaper *The Sun*. The first two lines are the headline and the third is the lead. The fourth is the first line of the actual story.

Britain faces a war to stop pedlars, warn MPs
Call up forces in drug battle!
The armed forces should be called up to fight off a massive invasion by drug pushers, MPs
demanded yesterday.
Cocaine pedlars are the greatest threat ever faced by Britain in peacetime—and
could destroy the country's way of life, they said.

In terms of meaning, the story leaves little doubt about the severity of the situation. Not only
is this a 'massive invasion', but could also 'destroy the country's way of life'. Drug policy
becomes much more than just drug policy; it becomes a struggle for survival. The war
metaphor is strong here. Being critical about this policy is being against the country's way of
life. On this level the message leaves very little room for an alternative view.

On a more linguistic level, the interesting thing here is how official language is mixed with
colloquial discourse. 'The armed forces' is official-sounding, whereas 'pedlars' (or peddlers)
and 'pushers' are more familiar from street slang. Fairclough quotes Stuart Hall *et al.* (1978: 61)
in explaining the function of this mixing: 'The translation of official viewpoints into public
idiom [. . .] makes the former more "available" to the uninitiated [and] invests them with
popular force and resonance'. In this way the news discourse legitimizes the official view and
in doing so 'helps to sustain and reproduce dominant ideological representations of the drug
issue' (Fairclough 1995a: 73).

Unlike the 'interactionist' perspective's focus on variability, the critical analysis of discourse
is interested in how variety is suppressed and hegemony produced. Critical discourse analysis
provides a powerful method for analyzing what is taken as 'common knowledge' or 'appropriate' in society and how these discursive constructions perpetuate particular ways of
thinking and practice by suppressing alternative discourses. In the field of religion, the global
'clash of civilizations' discourse, the legitimation struggles of minority religions (see Hjelm
2007) and religion and state issues are among some of the potentially fruitful objects of critical
discourse analysis.

How to choose a discourse-analytical approach

It should be clear from the above that there are many approaches within the broad field of
discourse analysis. Here I will 'diversify' the field even more. Although the three above varieties provide the most basic blueprint for navigating the field, *every discourse-analytical study needs
to be designed individually.* The research question/problem, data and method need to be aligned
in a way that enables a rich, yet practically feasible analysis. Some scholars tend to think of
discourse analysis as data-driven, but that is a simplification, because the particular constructionist framework of discourse analysis affects the formulation of research questions and so
on. At the same time, methodological fetishism should be avoided. Discourse-analytical techniques cannot make research interesting by themselves. Few discourse analysts concentrate on
the same things in their research; rather they modify and change their analytical 'toolkit' to
suit the requirements of different questions and data.

That said, the above examples are meant as a very basic pointer in the right direction.
Discourse analysts would typically work with much more substantial texts or collections of
texts, and the analysis would be more detailed and robust. As a result, the examples differ
from a typical case of discourse analysis in several ways. First, they all analyze an excerpt that
is part of a longer discussion, where a proper discourse analysis would, of course, analyze the
full text. As my interest here is mainly to demonstrate how discourse analysis works in

practice, I have chosen excerpts that are useful in illuminating the analytical frameworks outlined above. In a proper discourse analysis all passages analyzed must be explicitly considered in their fullest practicable context, unless the focus is on turn-taking and speaker positions, as in conversation analysis. Second, discourse analysts would generally spend more time describing the turns of talk in their own words, in a form of narrative paraphrase, thus contextualizing the chosen text excerpts more fully.

These points highlight a fundamental difference from the ways in which scholars of religion often work with texts. The analysis is of full and complete texts or collections of texts (e.g. complete interview transcripts) and it proceeds with a closer relation between method and theory than is often the case. That is, a typology of features of discourse—e.g. those discussed in the previous sections—emerges from theoretical concerns and is used as a schema to analyze all portions of the chosen text(s). This differs from a less formal search for portions of text that illustrate pre-determined thematic or formal concerns.[9] The previous examples are intended to illustrate the former, where the latter is characteristic of much scholarly work with texts in the study of religion.

In addition to the above, there are few hard rules about how to choose a particular approach. Needless to say, practical issues such as disciplinary background, departmental preferences and other factors not directly related to the method as such play a big part. One major issue is the difference between approaches that pay minute attention to linguistic form and those that focus on the level of meaning in text and talk. Not surprisingly, social scientists have usually been more interested in the level of meaning than in minute details of grammar, whereas a full linguistic discourse analysis can spend pages after pages discussing the nuances of a single sentence. However, as Fairclough (1992: 74) reminds us, the two approaches are interconnected: analysis on the level of meaning can gain powerful insights from more formal analysis of language, and linguistic analysis that ignores the social level has little to contribute to social and cultural research. As I argued above, the final 'research design'—that is, on which aspects of discourse the analyst will focus—depends on the requirements and goals of each research project.

As Phillips and Hardy (2002: 20) suggest, another distinction could be made between approaches that focus on variation within and between discourses on the one hand and more critical approaches that focus on how some discourses become hegemonic on the other. As mentioned above, this distinction is often blurred in practice, because as Gee (2005: 1–2) reminds us, discourse (conceptualized as language-in-use) is always political in the sense that we always choose to describe reality in some terms but not others. That choice of perspective—even if not always conscious—is a political choice from a discourse-analytical point of view. Whether and how that is foregrounded in the analysis is a choice the analyst has to make in each study.

Discourse analysis in the study of religion: prospects and challenges

Discourse analysis has proved to be a powerful tool for analyzing qualitative data, and there is no reason why it couldn't or shouldn't be used in the study of religion. From a discourse-analytical perspective religion as subject matter is no different from youth culture, crime, racism, sexuality, gender, unemployment, education, etc. (just to name some fields where discourse analysis has already been extensively used). Through their unique knowledge of the theories and contexts of religion, religious studies scholars and sociologists of religion can contribute not only to further understanding of the phenomenon of 'religion', but also to discourse theory.

143

As noted at the beginning of this chapter, 'discursive study of religion' is already emerging as a field in religious studies. Needless to say, discourse analysis can provide the method through which these discourses on religion can be examined. Another example that comes to mind is research drawing from the theoretical work of Peter Berger (see Hjelm forthcoming b). Although Berger's version of the secularization thesis has been discredited by many—including Berger himself!—many scholars in religious studies and sociology have been influenced by his broader theoretical ideas, as put forth especially in *The Social Construction of Reality*, co-authored with another well-known sociologist of religion, Thomas Luckmann (Berger and Luckmann 1967). Despite the fact that Berger and Luckmann's work is surprisingly rarely quoted in the methodological literature on discourse analysis, their basic premise of the constructed nature of social reality is at the very heart of discourse analysis, and researchers using Berger's work would certainly benefit from these methodological insights.

By way of example, there are two other substantive areas where discourse analysis seems especially relevant. First, research in the emerging field of religion and social problems (Hjelm 2009, 2011) examines how religion is constructed either as a solution to social problems or as a social problem itself. Social problems research has traditionally called this construction process 'claims-making' (e.g. Spector and Kitsuse 2001), but the field has lacked a systematic approach to the study of claims (cf. Engler 2011). If claims are seen as discourse, however, that problem can be solved. Thus, we can study how Islam is linked with terrorism in media discourse, for example.

Second, one central endeavor of scholars of religion has been the study of conversion. A lot of this research has operated with interview data, but little has been made of the systematic ways in which the experience of conversion is constructed in talk. Beckford's insightful analysis of the conversion 'accounts' of Jehovah's Witnesses (Beckford 1978) is an example of a 'proto-discursive' approach, but the study of conversion would certainly benefit from a proper discourse analysis. The study of religion and social problems and the study of conversion both touch upon the concept of *identity*, which has been central to discourse-analytical research (De Fina *et al.* 2006). This area of research could easily be broadened to include the discursive construction of all kinds of individual and communal religious identities

As stated above, from a discourse-analytical perspective the study of religion is not—or should not be—different from other areas of social and cultural research. Therefore the challenges of analyzing religious discourse are not peculiar to the study of religion. Below, I will discuss some of the main challenges, including the following:[10] the suspension of 'common sense'; the problem of causal explanation; relativization; and the time requirements of discourse-analytical research.

Anyone—whether in the humanities or social sciences—familiar with the concept of *interpretation* is told that 'the world' is never 'out there' for the researcher to find, but is always interpreted, both by our interview respondents and through the (implicit and explicit) theoretical lenses we use in our research. Despite this, the suppression of 'common sense' that a constructionist and discourse-analytical approach requires can be a challenge. What does it mean that I am discursively constructed as a man? I just *am* a man! The suppression of common sense is different from the challenge of relativization discussed below, because this is a personal, not a theoretical, challenge. I am guessing that this is especially relevant for students embarking on their first research project, but luckily they are not alone, as all academics that do broadly 'interpretative' research have had to face the same challenge. The ways in which we are treated as women and men, daughters and sons, young and old, students, scholars, religious and non-religious are (to an extent) discursively constructed, and realizing this can also be an empowering experience.

Second, for many the main problem with a discourse-analytical (and more broadly, constructionist) approach is the lack of strictly causal explanatory power (e.g. Sanderson 2001: 24–40; Little 1991: 34, 68–87; see Edwards and Potter 1992: 100). Although quite a few textbooks fail to mention this, it is safe to argue that discourse-analytical research is better equipped to answer *how* questions than *why* questions (Silverman and Gubrium 1994). To claim otherwise would be to succumb to the 'fallacy of internalism' (Thompson 1990: 24–25), that is, to claim that texts in themselves dictate the way in which they are interpreted. Even hegemonic discourse cannot tell us the practical consequences for action, because even when the variety of alternative interpretations is being suppressed within discourse, the discourse itself cannot fully tell us how it is discussed, reinterpreted and resisted in practice. Religious schism is an example of a situation where a form of hegemonic discourse is resisted to the point that abandoning the original discourse and creating an alternative discourse becomes a desirable option.

However, because good discourse analysis always analyzes discourse with reference to its social context, we can look at the history and background of events and actors and argue about the potential ways in which discourse translates into action. Looking at discourse alone, we cannot conclusively say why someone did what they did, but at least we can say that the line of action was one among a choice of actions that the discursive framework enabled—or alternatively, how the choice of action was constrained by the social and cultural framework. In Max Weber's terms this would be something akin to a 'causally adequate' explanation (Buss 1999; Ringer 2002). However, in order to make more conclusive causal claims, other types of research, such as surveys or ethnography, would be needed. In other words, it is important to think of the study of text and the study of its reception as analytically distinct categories. The study of religion and media, for example, was for a long time interested solely in discourses on religion in the media, but recent developments in research have tipped the balance towards the study of how audiences not only receive explicitly religious discourse, but also how religious discourses and identities are constructed through the use of seemingly non-religious media products (e.g. Clark 2003).

Third, discourse analysis can be extremely relativizing. If *everything* is just discourse, how is the researcher's discourse any different; and how can we say anything about 'reality' in the first place if it is in constant flux? These are common criticisms of discourse-analytical (and, again, more broadly constructionist) research that have been voiced by both 'outsiders' and discourse analysts themselves (see Parker 1998). Although there are solid arguments on both sides, I have here adopted a 'weak constructionist' approach, which emphasizes the importance of the social context in the analysis of discourse. Thus, as the above discussion on causality shows, analyzing discourse should involve examining the discourses in their social context and discussing the ways in which discourse and social action and structure are related. While this might make discourse analysis seem less all-powerful as a method (a healthy attitude towards *any* method!), it—along with the considerations of causality—helps narrow down the scope of research by focusing the formulation of research questions.

Finally, on a very practical level, discourse analysis is by definition time-consuming. The bulk of time in discourse-analytical research is spent in the actual reading and analysis of texts. That is why some studies use a seemingly limited number of sources, preferring to analyze the texts in depth. Again, there is no hard-and-fast rule about this, because, as noted, a 'lighter' discourse analysis enables broader data use. Although in principle any type of data that 'carries meaning'—regardless of medium—can be subjected to discourse analysis, most studies approach discourse as text and often convert recordings to transcripts. In terms of data types, there is a wealth of 'naturally-occurring' (Silverman 2007) texts around us that can be used. Religious books (including sacred texts), websites, radio and television speeches, recordings of sermons, etc., are all potential sources of discourse-analytical research. In addition, the researcher can analyze discourse that is 'manufactured' (Silverman 2007) in the research process, such as interviews or ethnographic field notes—all of the above within the framework of ethical research, of course (e.g. Silverman 2006: 315–35; Rapley 2007: 23–33).

Having collected the data, the discourse analyst's research process has really just begun. Unfortunately—in terms of saving time—developments in qualitative analysis software haven't made much difference for the discourse analyst. Although some of the programs (e.g. NVivo, ATLAS.ti; see Lewins and Silver 2007) can be helpful in organizing large amounts of data, the final analysis is very much hands-on work. This has two practical implications: the analyst either restricts the amount of data she analyzes, or she restricts the number of 'tools' she uses in the analysis. The choice of whether to do either or both depends on the research question and on the practical time limitations of research. An additional solution is to analyze the data with a colleague, but this is less a time-saving technique than a way of making the research more 'reliable'. Doing discourse analysis in pairs or groups is sometimes recommended for a more rounded analysis, but the process involves double (or triple, etc.) reading of the same material rather than dividing the data into smaller pieces. Thus, although struggling with time is most obviously relevant for students working on theses and dissertations, awareness of the 'bulkiness' of discourse-analytical research can also save more mature scholars from sinking into a potential analytical mire.

In conclusion, discourse analysis offers a rich and easily adaptable method for the study of religion. As mentioned above, a substantive amount of research already exists, which is based on similar principles, but which lacks the systematic analytical framework that discourse analysis can provide. Wide availability of textbooks and 'how to' guides (see 'further reading', below) make discourse analysis relatively easy to approach, but the actual application can only be learned through 'getting your hands dirty'. As also mentioned above, doing 'co-operative discourse analysis' can be helpful in learning about the process of analysis and interpretation. So far, collegial support for discourse analysts working on religion has been rather scarce, but it is my hope and belief that discourse analysis will find its way into broader application in the study of religion.

Notes

1 Wooffitt's study reads more as conversation analysis, although it uses discursive psychology (see below) as its disciplinary/methodological framework. Heather's study in turn is mostly theological in tone. Perhaps these emphases have contributed to the studies' marginal status within religious studies.
2 It is important to note that this use of the term *function* does not refer to *functionalist* ideas about society—ideas which in many ways inspired constructionist critiques, which in turn have been an inspiration for discourse analysis (see Hjelm forthcoming a).
3 The same idea is also referred to as the *performativity* of language/discourse (see Butler 1990).
4 In his earlier work van Dijk (1980: 46–49) also mentions other rules that are not relevant for the current example.
5 It has been acknowledged that writing discourse analysis in English—the *lingua franca* of academia—is problematic if the source text is in another language (Nikander 2008: 424). Fairclough (1995b: 190–191) goes so far as to suggest that the analysis should be done only in the original language. While I think this is ultimately dependent on the level of detail of the analysis, I agree that, minimally, the original version should be provided as an appendix or in footnotes. However, in the interests of space, I have not done that here.
6 Although I used van Dijk's model for my early research, I've since become quite critical of it (see below) and would characterize myself as a critical discourse analyst instead. A critical reading of the same text might be quite different.

7 Järvenpää is a small town in southern Finland. Literally translated, the headline says 'Satan worshippers in Järvenpää'. In an internationally unique development, both the media and some researchers eventually distinguished 'Satanism' and 'Satan worship' in their discourse. Here, however, I have ignored that nuance.

8 Construct*ivist* and construct*ionist* are used interchangeably here. For discussion, see Hjelm forthcoming a: chapter 1.

9 In the same vein, David Silverman, in discussing qualitative text research more broadly (Silverman 2005), recommends focusing on 'sequences' instead of 'instances' in texts.

10 Again, this is a limited choice of the potential challenges. A lot of the challenges are common to all qualitative research (see Silverman 2006). Further discussion on the challenges particular to discourse analysis can be found in the academic journals in the field, especially *Discourse and Society* and *Critical Discourse Studies*.

References

Asad, T., 1993. *Genealogies of Religion: discipline and reasons of power in Christianity and Islam.* Johns Hopkins University Press, Baltimore.

Austin, J.L., 1975. *How to Do Things with Words.* Harvard University Press, Harvard.

Barker, E., 2011. The cult as a social problem. In: Hjelm, T. (ed.), *Religion and Social Problems.* Routledge, New York, pp. 198–212.

Beckford, J.A., 1978. Accounting for conversion. *British Journal of Sociology* 29(2): 249–62.

Berger, P. and Luckmann, T. 1967 [1966]. *The Social Construction of Reality.* Anchor Books, New York.

Brown, C., 2009. *The Death of Christian Britain: understanding secularisation 1800–2000.* 2nd edn. Routledge, London.

Burr, V., 1995. *Introduction to Social Constructionism.* Routledge, London.

Buss, A., 1999. The concept of adequate causation and Max Weber's comparative sociology of religion. *British Journal of Sociology* 50(2): 317–29.

Butler, J., 1990. *Gender Trouble.* Routledge, London.

Chouliaraki, L. and Fairclough, N., 1999. *Discourse in Late Modernity.* Edinburgh University Press, Edinburgh.

Clark, L.S., 2003. *From Angels to Aliens: teenagers, the media, and the supernatural.* Oxford University Press, Oxford.

De Fina, A., Schiffrin, D., Bamberg, M. (eds), 2006. *Discourse and Identity.* Cambridge University Press, Cambridge.

Edwards, D. and Potter, J., 1992. *Discursive Psychology.* SAGE, London.

Engler, S., 2004. Constructionism versus what? *Religion* 34(4): 291–313.

—— 2005. Discourse. In: von Stuckrad, K. (ed.) (with Auffarth, C., Bernard J. and Mohr, H.), *The Brill Dictionary of Religion.* Brill, Leiden, vol. 1, pp. 516–19.

—— 2011. Other religions as social problem: the Universal Church of the Kingdom of God and Afro-Brazilian traditions. In: Hjelm, T. (ed.), *Religion and Social Problems.* Routledge, New York, pp. 213–28.

Fairclough, N., 1989. *Language and Power.* Longman, London.

—— 1992. *Discourse and Social Change.* Polity Press, Oxford.

—— 1995a. *Media Discourse.* Arnold, London.

—— 1995b. *Critical Discourse Analysis.* Longman, London.

Foucault, M., 1978. *The History of Sexuality. Vol. 1.* Penguin, London.

—— 1995 [1975]. *Discipline and Punish: the birth of the prison.* Vintage Books, New York.

Gee, J.P., 2005. *An Introduction to Discourse Analysis: theory and method.* 2nd edn. Routledge, New York.

Gergen, K., 1994. *Realities and Relationships: soundings in social construction.* Harvard University Press, Cambridge, MA.

Hall, S., Critcher, C., Jefferson, T., Clarke, J. and Roberts, B., 1978. *Policing the Crisis: mugging, the state, and law and order.* Macmillan, Basingstoke.

Heather, N., 2000. *Religious Language and Critical Discourse Analysis: Ideology and identity in Christian discourse today.* Peter Lang, Oxford.

Hjelm, T., 2002. Driven by the Devil: popular constructions of adolescent Satanist careers. *Syzygy: Journal of Alternative Religion and Culture* 11: 177–95.

—— 2007. United in diversity, divided from within: the dynamics of legitimation in contemporary witchcraft. In: Hammer, O. and von Stuckrad, K. (eds), *Polemical Encounters: Esoteric Discourse and Its Others*. Brill, Leiden.

—— 2009. Religion and social problems: a new theoretical perspective. In: Clarke, P. (ed.), *The Oxford Handbook of the Sociology of Religion*. Oxford University Press, Oxford, pp. 924–41.

—— (ed.), 2011. *Religion and Social Problems*. Routledge, New York.

—— forthcoming a. *Perspectives on Social Constructionism*. Palgrave, Basingstoke, New York.

—— forthcoming b. *Peter L. Berger on Religion: the social reality of religion*. Equinox, London.

Lease, G., 2000. Ideology. In: Braun, W. and McCutcheon, R.T. (eds), *Guide to the Study of Religion*. Cassell, London, New York, pp. 438–446.

Lewins, A. and Silver, C., 2007. *Using Software in Qualitative Research: a step-by step guide*. SAGE, London.

Lincoln, B., 1989. *Discourse and the Construction of Society: comparative studies of myth, ritual, and classification*. Oxford University Press, New York, Oxford.

Little, D., 1991. *Varieties of Social Explanation: an introduction to the philosophy of social science*. Westview Press, Boulder, CO.

McCutcheon, R.T., 1997. *Manufacturing Religion: the discourse on sui generis religion and the politics of nostalgia*. Oxford University Press, Oxford.

McDonnell, D., 1986. *Theories of Discourse*. Basil Blackwell, Oxford.

Mills, S., 2004. *Discourse*. 2nd edn. Routledge, London, New York.

Murphy, T., 2000. Discourse. In: Braun, W. and McCutcheon, R.T. (eds), *Guide to the Study of Religion*. Cassell, London, New York, pp. 396–408.

Nikander, P., 2008. Constructionism and discourse analysis. In: Holstein, J.A. and Gubrium, J.F. (eds), *Handbook of Constructionist Research*. The Guilford Press, New York, pp. 413–428.

Parker, I. (ed.), 1998. *Social Constructionism, Discourse and Realism*. SAGE, London.

Phillips, N. and Hardy, C., 2002. *Discourse Analysis: investigating processes of social construction*. SAGE, London, Thousand Oaks, CA.

Potter, J., 1996. *Representing Reality: discourse, rhetoric, and social construction*. SAGE, London.

—— 2000. Post-cognitive psychology. *Theory & Psychology* 10(1): 31–37.

Potter, J. and Wetherell, M., 1987. *Discourse and Social Psychology: beyond attitudes and behaviour*. SAGE, London.

Rapley, T., 2007. *Doing Conversation, Discourse and Document Analysis*. SAGE, London.

Riesebrodt, M., 2010. *The Promise of Salvation: a theory of religion*. University of Chicago Press, Chicago.

Ringer, F., 2002. Max Weber and causal analysis, interpretation and comparison. *History and Theory* 41(2): 163–78.

Sanderson, S.K., 2001. *The Evolution of Human Sociality: a Darwinian conflict perspective*. Rowman & Littlefield, Lanham, MD.

Shotter, J., 1993. *Conversational Realities: constructing life through language*. SAGE, London.

Silverman, D., 2006. *Interpreting Qualitative Data*. 3rd edn. SAGE, London.

—— 2007. *A Very Short, Fairly Interesting and Reasonably Cheap Book about Qualitative Research*. SAGE, London.

—— 2005. Instances or sequences? Improving the state of the art of qualitative research. *Forum: Qualitative Sozialforschung/Qualitative Research* 6(3). www.qualitative-research.net/index.php/fqs/article/view/6/14.

—— and Gubrium, J.F., 1994. Competing strategies for analyzing the contexts of social interaction. *Sociological Inquiry* 64(2): 179–98.

Spector, M. and Kitsuse, J.I., 2001 [1977]. *Constructing Social Problems*. Transaction Publishers, New Brunswick, NJ.

Spickard, J.V., 2005. Narrative versus theory in the sociology of religion: five stories of religion's place in the modern world. In: Beckford, J.A. and Wallis, J. (eds), *Theorising Religion: classical and contemporary debates*. Aldershot: Ashgate, pp. 169–181.

—— 2007. Micro qualitative approaches to the sociology of religion: phenomenologies, interviews, narratives, and ethnographies. In: Beckford, J.A. and Demerath, N.J. (eds), *The SAGE Handbook of the Sociology of Religion*. SAGE, London, pp. 121–43.

Thompson, J.B., 1990. *Ideology and Modern Culture*. Stanford University Press, Stanford.

van Dijk, T.A., 1980. *Macrostructures*. Lawrence Erlbaum Associates, Hillsdale, NJ.

—— 1988. *News as Discourse*. Lawrence Erlbaum Associates, Hillsdale, NJ.

von Stuckrad, K., 2003. Discursive study of religion: from states of the mind to communicative action. *Method & Theory in the Study of Religion* 15(3): 255–71.

—— 2010. Reflections on the limits of reflection: an invitation to the discursive study of religion. *Method & Theory in the Study of Religion* 22(2–3): 156–69.

Wetherell, M. and Potter, J., 1992. *Mapping the Language of Racism: discourse and the legitimation of exploitation.* Columbia University Press, New York.

Wooffitt, R., 2005. *Conversation Analysis and Discourse Analysis: a comparative and critical introduction.* SAGE, London.

—— 2006. *The Language of Mediums and Psychics: the social organization of everyday miracles.* Ashgate, Aldershot.

Wuthnow, R.J., 2011. Taking talk seriously: religious discourse as social practice. *Journal for the Scientific Study of Religion* 50(1): 1–21.

Further reading

Fairclough, N., 1992. *Discourse and Social Change.* Polity Press, Oxford.

This is a classic text of critical discourse analysis (CDA). The focus is on the theoretical framework of CDA, rather than practical analysis, but as a source for discussions on ideology and hegemony in discursive research, the book is indispensable.

Fairclough, N., 2003. *Analysing Discourse: textual analysis for social research.* Routledge, London.

Despite the 'how to' appearance of this book, it is quite challenging for social scientists with little or no background in linguistics. Recommended for those interested in more formal, linguistic, discourse analysis.

Gee, J.P. and Handford, M., 2011. *The Routledge Handbook of Discourse Analysis.* Routledge, London, New York.

Although the emphasis is on the linguistic aspects of discourse analysis, this handbook includes comprehensive discussion on many of the issues raised in this chapter.

Mills, S., 2004. *Discourse.* 2nd edn. Routledge, London, New York.

This is a useful, short introduction to the concept of discourse and its use in cultural studies.

Phillips, N. and Hardy, C., 2002. *Discourse Analysis: investigating processes of social construction.* SAGE. London, Thousand Oaks, CA.

Although the empirical examples are mainly from organization studies, this is a nice concise introduction to the principles of discourse analysis.

Potter, J., 1996. *Representing Reality: discourse, rhetoric, and social construction.* SAGE, London.

This book is written from a social psychology perspective, but it has a useful interdisciplinary 'history' of discursive approaches to social analysis. There is also a substantive section on rhetorical analysis.

Key concepts

Critical discourse analysis: Critical discourse analysis (or CDA) is a form of discourse analysis that focuses on the use of power in discourse. From a discursive perspective, power is not only an attribute of organizations and institutions that explicitly exercise it, but permeates all social relationships. It is also not primarily coercive, but rather persuasive, in nature. Thus, the most important 'vehicle' for power is discourse, that is, the way we speak and *do not* speak about things. See *ideology* and *hegemony*.

Discourse: Discourse is a way of speech (or an image) that does not simply reflect or represent social entities and relations, but constructs or 'constitutes' them. When language is conceived in terms of discourse it is seen as having a function, that is, 'things are done with words'.

Hegemony: When a single practice or a way of thinking becomes the *only* legitimate one, supplanting other interpretations, it has become hegemonic. Hegemony is a term coined by the influential Italian Marxist thinker Antonio Gramsci. In opposition to coercive power, hegemonic consensus is achieved by persuasion. As Fairclough (1992: 92) puts it, 'Hegemony is about constructing alliances, and integrating rather than simply dominating subordinate classes, through concessions [. . .] to win their consent'.

Ideology: The critical tradition in the social sciences sees ideology as 'meaning in the service of power' (Thompson 1990: 8). The discourse we use in interaction reproduces or transforms relations of power in society. When 'proper' ways of thinking about and doing things are constructed from a particular perspective, giving a one-sided account that ignores a variety of practices, discourse is said to function ideologically. When ideological discourse supplants (or attempts to supplant) *all* other versions of reality, it becomes hegemonic. See *hegemony*.

Social construction (constructionism): constructionism is an epistemological and theoretical perspective that sees reality as a product of human interaction. This production process is dialectical, that is, in their discourse people draw from the world, but also contribute to the reproduction and transformation of that world through discourse.

Related chapters

- ◆ Chapter 1.2 Comparison
- ◆ Chapter 1.3 Epistemology
- ◆ Chapter 1.5 Research design
- ◆ Chapter 2.10 Grounded theory
- ◆ Chapter 2.11 Hermeneutics
- ◆ Chapter 2.13 Interviewing
- ◆ Chapter 2.17 Semiotics
- ◆ Chapter 2.18 Structuralism
- ◆ Chapter 3.1 Auditory materials
- ◆ Chapter 3.2 The Internet

2.4

DOCUMENT ANALYSIS

Grace Davie and David Wyatt

Chapter summary

- Documents should be considered in terms of production, function, use and content.
- Purpose, audience, time and place are significant.
- Personal documents are an excellent source of attitudes and social values.
- Publicly available and official documents provide an insight into societal trends at specific points in time.
- Documents are a cost-effective and fruitful research material.
- There are numerous datasets available for future research, particularly electronic material.
- Electronic resources will permit new approaches to document analysis.

Introduction

This chapter draws on a wide range of literature and examples to display the considerable contribution that document analysis can make to the effective study of religion. Documents are far more than simply a resource for historians. Both recent and historic documents provide insights into peoples' lives, thoughts, beliefs and practices. Rarely, however, have they been used as a major resource in the social-scientific study of religion. Instead documents are often regarded simply as a point of reference or secondary source of information. For the reasons set out below, we commend a more positive approach: document analysis should be fully integrated into the repertoire of methods available to scholars of religion.

Documents can be deployed both quantitatively (content analysis) and qualitatively (discourse analysis). The emphasis in this chapter is on how documents are used in practice, taking as a starting point the fact that documents should be understood as more than containers of text. We begin with a brief look at how 'document' might be defined; we then set out the points to bear in mind over and above the analysis of the text itself. In so doing, we contend that documents should be considered in terms of their content, context, production and function in society. They serve purposes, have intended audiences and are created by individuals or groups within socio-historic contexts. We then draw on existing studies that make use of personal letters and official/publicly available sources, to highlight some of the strengths, limitations and practical aspects of working with documents. The chapter ends with a discussion of future possibilities with a particular emphasis on electronic examples.

Defining and using documents

The term 'document' can be used to cover an array of research materials from gravestones (Dethlefsen 1981) and epigraphy (Orr 2000) to meeting minutes (Taylor 2001, 2003) and newsletters (Hinnells 2005). Indeed, it is often unclear where to place the dividing line between what is and what is not a document. In essence, this distinction is about how the researcher *frames* an artifact and can be likened to the distinction between what is and is not art (Prior 2003). In this chapter, we employ a commonplace definition and concentrate on text-based sources on both paper and computer screen—namely personal letters and papers, publicly available material of various kinds, official documents and selected electronic resources. Although our discussion does not cover the analysis of religious texts per se, most of the points that we make are transferrable to such work.

We focus on documents that have not been solicited by the researcher and are therefore independent from the research taking place. Webb *et al.* (1966) refer to unsolicited data of this type under the heading **unobtrusive measures**. They also provide a simple typology to aid the classification of documents into two categories: ' "running records" . . . the ongoing, continuing records of a society' and ' "episodic and private records" . . . which are discontinuous and not usually part of the public record' (Webb *et al.* 1966: 53, 88).

This approach is largely helpful. The notion of unobtrusive measures prompts the researcher to consider documents beyond content alone and to think how they came into existence—including, if appropriate, the researcher's role in this process. Similarly, the distinction between running records and episodic and private records obliges the researcher to consider the relationship *between* documents. Documents can be classified by recipient, theme, institution, time, place or any mixture of these. Whatever the case, using documents successfully requires the researcher to understand how their documents fit together, or fail to do so.

A second point follows from this. Documents do not exist in a vacuum but are produced by individuals and groups who have aims and motives. In other words, documents have contexts. They are fashioned for specific purposes, for an intended audience, and often paint a picture of the authors' understanding of reality. A personal letter may convey an opinion or disperse information that the author deems important at a specific moment in time. Even documents such as private diaries have an intended audience, accepting that this may only be the author him or herself (Scott 1990: 174).

Official documents, such as meeting minutes, have a more complicated history, due both to institutional constraints and to the number of actors involved. Minutes are the authorized records of a meeting. This does not mean, however, that they are an accurate reflection of that meeting. They often contain 'integral elements of policy and administration' (Scott 1990: 84) and, like personal documents, are seldom value-free. Minutes evolve: they are drafted, edited, re-edited, amended and finally approved. The same is true for other kinds of official documents such as policies, legislation and constitutions. They remain, nonetheless, rich and very useful research material. The researcher must, however, be aware of how and why the documents they are using have been produced.

Documents must also be situated in terms of time and place—elements referred to by Foucault, in relation to **discursive formations**, as their 'condition of existence' (Foucault 1991: 61). Foucault uses this term to emphasize that language does not a have universal

Table 2.4.1 Questions to consider when using documents, taking Davie (2003) as an example*

Basic questions	Brief example responses
Where did the documents come from?	The National Gallery
Who produced the documents?	Individuals and groups, who visited the exhibition, watched the BBC2 documentary series or both.
For what purpose/function were the documents produced?	Generally to express their thanks to the Director for hosting this exhibition and to comment on the exhibition itself.
How did the documents come to be in your possession? Did you solicit the documents?	Individually, the documents were unsolicited. They were, however, requested *en bloc* from the National Gallery which passed them to the researcher. The Gallery obtained informed consent from the authors (for specific quotation) prior to publication.
Who was the intended audience?	(The Director of) the National Gallery.
What is the institutional and/or historical context of the documents?	The exhibition took place at the National Gallery in Lent 2000; the letters were received during and shortly after the exhibition.
How do the documents relate to each other (if at all)?	Related by theme (the exhibition), recipient (the Gallery's Director), time (around the time of the exhibition which took place in the Lent of the Millennium year) and place (the majority were from UK citizens and concerned a National Gallery exhibition in London, UK).

*Details of the case study can be found in the following section.

meaning. Instead, it presents an image of reality that is specific to, and situated in, a socio-historic context (Cheek 2004: 1145). It is for this reason that Scott suggests that a document should be seen as a 'situated product' (Scott 1990: 34).

Above all, we *use* documents. Some shape the way in which we conduct ourselves and how we understand our actions, while others help us to communicate our thoughts and feelings, recognizing that such uses may change over time. Documents play a central role in the way we act, interact and live in any given context. It is important, therefore, to consider how a text is read and received by the reader, which includes the researcher. As such, documents are not just 'situated products' but 'social products', given the way in which they are incorporated in social life and social action (Prior 2003: 12). They are not inanimate objects but have functions and are active agents that shape the way we traverse the social (Prior 2008: 821).

In short, working with documents involves both the analysis of content and a careful consideration of production, use and function within a specific socio–historic context (see Table 2.4.1 for a worked example of this process).

Document research in practice

In this section, we draw on a number of existing studies to illustrate the issues set out above and to highlight the strengths and limitations of documents in the study of religion.

Personal letters and papers

In one of the first studies of its kind, Thomas and Znaniecki (1918) used several hundred personal letters between Polish immigrants in the United States and their families in Poland to explore the changing nature of social and family structures. The authors were able to obtain authentic and first-hand information about a group in flux that would otherwise (for geographical reasons) have been difficult to research. At the same time, they avoided the problem of relying on the writer's memory or asking the participants themselves for information, thus sidestepping the issues of retrospective construction that are sometimes present in interviews. Quite apart from this, the study highlights that documents do not limit the researcher to the present but permit an historical approach to changing attitudes and social relations.

A well-known and specifically religious use of personal letters can be found in Towler (1984), who examined the 4,000 or so letters sent to John Robinson following the publication of *Honest to God* (1963). The letters were written in response to a well-known author, but they almost all contained a statement of the writer's own beliefs. It is these statements that constitute the core of the study. The task was considerable. Reading and re-reading a corpus of this size required the help of two research assistants who worked independently of each other. Once half the letters had been read, the emergent categories were stabilized, permitting the second half to be dealt with more quickly. It was Towler himself who determined the 'types' (essentially ideal types) from the catalogue of themes established by the researchers, distilling these on the basis of two underlying dimensions: the need for certainty and the search for meaning (the first of these became the title of the book). Five types emerged, revealing the very different ways in which a person could be a Christian in the 1960s. The five types represent five 'cognitive styles'; their respective labels capture their essence—exemplarism, conversionism, theism, gnosticism and traditionalism.

Davie (2003) used a combination of discourse and content analysis to examine the rather smaller number (461) of letters sent to the Director of the National Gallery (London) following the Spring 2000 exhibition, 'Seeing Salvation: The Image of Christ' (see Table 2.4.1). Accompanied by a BBC2 documentary series of four 50-minute programmes, this exhibition was visited by over 350,000 people, at the time a record for the National Gallery in terms of attendance and volume of responses to an exhibition (Davie 2003: 28–31). Davie worked in a similar way to Towler, bearing in mind that the task was more manageable. She read and re-read the letters until confident that their substance could be presented systematically without distorting the very personal character of the material. A number of common themes emerged in terms of both production and content. Regarding the former, these were almost all personal letters to the Gallery's Director in response to the exhibition, the BBC2 documentary series, or both. Regarding the latter, they revealed the writers' gratitude for and emotional engagement with the exhibition and/or documentary series, their frustration about the absence of a Christian presence in the celebration of the Millennium in general, and how Christianity is no longer seen as a mainstream public activity (Davie 2003: 33–35). Thus they provide insight into the subtle and different ways in which Christianity, specifically attitudes towards Christian iconography, is understood in contemporary Britain. The time and place of the exhibition were both significant; it was held in 2000 in the National Gallery (a secular public venue) and coincided with Lent, a point noted in a number of letters.

The letters, however, were far more than a repository of attitudes. Davie records the hints they gave about their writers' lives in terms of, for example, wealth, health and church affiliations/practices (Davie 2003: 32). She also raises questions about motivation: what compelled these people to write to the Gallery's Director? The letters do not provide clear-cut answers in this respect; they permit none the less interesting insights into the writers' priorities, which might have been difficult to obtain elsewhere. Regarding their physical production, very few of the letters were word-processed. Most people opted to hand-write or to use a typewriter, suggesting that the letter writers were on the whole elderly (a fact that can also be inferred from turn of phrase).

The data in both these studies are very rich. There are, however, considerable difficulties in using personal letters, not least the problem of knowing that the documents exist in the first place and obtaining access to them. It is quite possible, for example, that there are numerous caches of letters available but the academic community is unaware of them. That said, an *absence* of letters may be in itself an important indicator of attitudes, taking into account the wider social practices common at the time and place of the research. A second problem concerns the lack of researcher control in guiding their content. This has significant implications for the research design, in that the research process has to fit around the data available rather than vice versa. Third, personal letters, especially recent ones, require considerable sensitivity in terms of ethical practice. For example, in order for the researcher to obtain ethical approval from a sponsoring institution,[1] it is often necessary to obtain written consent from the document owners (this is the author and not the recipient) before the researcher can view, cite or quote the documents.[2] In Davie's case, the National Gallery obtained the authors' consent for quotation, but one cannot always rely on the goodwill of the recipient or recipient organization. In our view, however, the advantages clearly outweigh the disadvantages: appropriately used, personal, unsolicited letters reveal a great deal about societal attitudes towards religion.

Publicly available material and official documents

Turning now to publicly available material, the range is immense: the list includes a wide variety of publications (books, articles, newspapers, magazines and so on) not to mention the work of other academics. It would also include official documents of various kinds, such as constitutions, parliamentary records, minutes, policies and codes of practice. Given that they exist in the public domain, all such documents avoid the problem of invisibility, bearing in mind that some types of official material are more easily accessed than others. In general, however, if there is a *public* meeting, committee or council, one can reasonably assume that there will be a publicly available agenda, minutes and points for action. Such sources are also less problematic in terms of ethics—informed consent is seldom required for what is already publicly accessible. For all these reasons, the parameters of the research data are more easily decided by the researcher, who is free to select by type of material, by subject matter, by dates, by specific committees, or whatever.

Interestingly, a large number of studies that draw on this kind of material are discovered in doctoral theses. Why? One reason is likely to be financial: the scrutiny of texts is often less expensive than other forms of research, in that it avoids substantial travel and administration costs. A further factor may lie in the time-consuming nature of the work. As we have seen in connection with personal letters or papers, there is no way to avoid the careful reading and re-reading of a considerable volume of data that lies at the heart of both content and discourse analysis. Whether or not this is more costly in terms of time than completing, transcribing and analyzing interview transcripts is hard to say, but whatever the case, the weighting towards doctoral work is striking and is reflected in the examples that follow.

Taylor (2001), for instance, used minutes from the UK government's Inner Cities Religious Council to consider discourses on racial and religious diversity, and to highlight the increase in the use of religious terminology in public and private life, partially replacing the previous use of racial or ethnic references. The context of this shift, the moment when a question on religion was first included in the British Census (2001), should not be overlooked (Davie 2003: 39).

The *affaire du foulard*, the continuing controversy surrounding the Muslim headscarf in France, formed the subject matter of Molokotos-Liederman's thesis, which used press comments to compare French attitudes to religious dress with those in the UK (Molokotos-Liederman 2000). Her work was revealing with regard to the place of religion in neighboring European societies and, by extension, to the 'messages' passed on to new generations (Davie 2003: 40).[3] Rather similar issues are covered in the work of Hakkarainen (1978), who analyzed the content of religion and 'civics' textbooks used in the moral education of Finnish comprehensive school students, and Sinclair's (2002) study of regional and national German parliamentary debates on the issue of religious education and the religious dress of teachers.

The pros and cons of this very varied corpus should be kept in mind. Although well suited to considering the implicit and explicit discourses relating to specific topics, official documents do not allow detailed, nuanced analysis of *individual* attitudes and values. Instead, such attitudes emerge as somewhat homogenous. Such sources are more useful in uncovering general social trends rather than subjective or nuanced opinions. Other kinds of publicly available material (books, magazines, press articles, opinion pieces, etc.) are more revealing of different opinions in that the material is variously authored. An interesting study that displays a wide range of individual responses to the place of religion in the modern world can be found in Michel (1999). Michel's source is innovative: he uses the visitors' feedback comments from the St Mungo Museum of Religious Life and Art (in Glasgow) to illustrate hugely different reactions not only to the displays in the museum, but to religion itself. The St Mungo Museum exists to explore the importance of religion in people's lives across the world and across time.

Wider uses of documents and available datasets

The discussion above highlights very different uses of documents; there are, however, further possibilities to take into account. Comparative examples are particularly interesting. Such work (see Molokotos-Liederman above), requires the researcher to pay attention not only to economic, social and cultural differences, but also to specific policies and documents in order to assess how official discourses on religion infringe on, and at times alter, practices both in different places and at different times. There is scope here for in-depth, cross-cultural comparisons, for example between school textbooks used in different countries (MacNeill 2000). Comparisons across time are also possible. A notable example of the latter can be found in an on-going project which analyzes current portrayals of popular religion and the 'secular sacred' in a selection of British newspapers and TV channels. This replicates very closely the research design and methods employed in a similar project undertaken in the 1980s at the University of Leeds. Key themes discussed in 1982–83 will be re-considered, and new themes identified and analyzed.[4]

It is also possible to extend the use of more personal forms of communication, particularly the use of diaries.[5] Psychologists Boyatzis and Janicki (2003), for example, use *solicited* diaries to look more closely at children's religious socialization, paying particular attention to religious conversations between parents and young children. Rather differently, there are numerous personal accounts (some published and some not) of specific religious activities, which permit a better understanding of the experiential aspects of religion in particular socio-historic contexts. An excellent example of the latter can be found in a doctoral dissertation, which seeks to discover the 'meaning' of pilgrimage for the wide variety of people who make their way to Santiago de Compostela in Spain (De-Andrade-Chemin-Filho, forthcoming). In this case, the use of personal accounts and diaries supplements a range of other methods. It is also clear that the reception of such accounts is as important as their production.

Rather differently, there are existing research initiatives that are willing to share their data. One such, the Mass Observation Project, could be used far more widely in the study of British religiosity. Originating in the 1930s as a way of studying everyday life in the UK, Mass Observation currently uses a pool of 500 participants to solicit written responses to 'Directives' (a set of questions on a variety of themes) three times per year. It is important to remember that the participants (who volunteer to be included in the database) are not representative of the British population, and that they knowingly provide responses for the purpose of research, thus raising the possibility that participants will monitor and moderate their responses accordingly. However, if these issues can be dealt with satisfactorily, the responses allow the researcher to delve into a 'thick description' (Geertz 1973) of individual attitudes and thoughts. It is worth noting that there have been a number of Directives dealing specifically with mourning, faith and religion over the past 20 years. Also, with the possibility of commissioning a Directive, the researcher can be actively involved in constructing the question or task itself.[6]

Electronic examples

A step change in the use of documents comes with increasing accessibility of electronic data, not least in the form of blogs. Text becomes available in entirely new ways. Even a casual use of a search engine will reveal possibilities that would take months to find by other means, and electronic text can be analyzed far faster than the printed word.[7] Indeed, the associated and ever more sophisticated analytic techniques that are now widely available are as important as the new forms of text themselves. Willander and Sikström (2010), for example, exploit the possibilities of **latent semantic analysis** to grasp more fully the meanings of 'religion' and 'spirituality' as they are used in practice. Sophisticated statistical analyses are deployed to discover how words *co-occur* in freely generated texts—specifically in 220,000 Swedish blog posts on religion and spirituality. Preliminary results indicate that distinctive usage-patterns emerge in these millions of words. It is also clear that the term 'spirituality' is used in a wider range of themes than 'religion' and includes both 'holistic spirituality' and institutionalized religion. The fundamental point to grasp is that the connections between the words are drawn from the text itself. They are not imposed from outside.

Electronic material offers new possibilities; it also provokes new questions with regard to research ethics. It is reasonable to assume that if access to a blog, forum or any information owned by another is limited by a log-in, consent will be necessary, but even where access is open, the line between what is public and what is private is very easily blurred, raising important questions regarding anonymity and protection from harm.

Conclusion

Documents are multifaceted and need to be understood in terms of both their content and use in order to fulfil their potential. Documents serve a purpose, have intended audiences and are created by individuals or groups within socio-historic contexts. Significant work has been completed in this field. There are, however, huge possibilities for future research, notably with respect to electronically generated material. The sheer size of the data sets and the growing sophistication of analytical tools will permit entirely new questions to be asked of text-based material.

Table 2.4.2 Advantages and disadvantages of using unsolicited documents

	All documents	*Personal letters*	*Publicly available and official documents*	*Electronic material*
Advantages	• Easy to contain dataset • Little financial cost • Allows research data to be obtained that is less easily available through other methods • Avoids problems of retrospective narrative construction	• Authentic resource • Useful in examinations of attitudes and values	• Availability • Access • Allows consideration of explicit and implicit discourses • Researcher has some control over scope • Possibility of cross-country/-region/-time comparison	• Easily available • Ever increasing volume • Possibility of electronic analysis
Disadvantages	• Sometimes difficult to target content • Not necessarily representative—difficult to control participation • Limited by availability and access	• Non-visibility of documents • Need to obtain consent from all authors	• Official documents are not suitable for small-scale analysis of individual attitudes	• Ethical considerations (public-private distinction is blurred)

Notes

1 Normally this is the researcher's own university or professional association.
2 When the author is no longer alive, author consent is not required. Instead, consent should be obtained from the current owner of the document.
3 Molokotos–Liederman (2007) uses similar methods to research the identity card controversy in Greece.
4 See www.religionandsociety.org.uk/research_findings/projects/phase_one/large_research_projects for more details. Kim Knott at the University of Leeds is the project director.
5 Plummer (1983, 2001) is a helpful guide in the use of diaries.
6 For more information on the Mass Observation Project, see their website: www.massobs.org.uk/index.htm.
7 It is important to remember that many 'traditional' documents (newspapers, magazines, constitutions, minutes, etc.) are now available electronically, meaning that they can be searched much more quickly.

References

Boyatzis, C.J. and Janicki, D.L., 2003. Parent-child communication about religion: survey and diary data on unilateral transmission and bi-directional reciprocity styles. *Review of Religious Research* 44 (3): 252–70.
Cheek, J., 2004. At the margins? Discourse analysis and qualitative research. *Qualitative Health Research* 14 (8): 1140–50.
Davie, G., 2003. Seeing salvation: using text as data in the sociology of religion. In: Avis, P. (ed.), *Public Faith? The state of religious belief and practice in Britain*. SPCK, London, pp. 28–44.

De-Andrade-Chemin-Filho, J., forthcoming. *Pilgrimage in a Secular Age: religious and spiritual landscapes of consumer culture.* Doctoral thesis, University of Exeter.

Dethlefsen, E.S., 1981. The cemetery and cultural change: archaeological focus and ethnographic perspective. In: Gould, R.A. and Schiffer, M.B. (eds), *Modern Material Culture: the archaeology of us.* Academic Press, New York, pp. 137–59.

Foucault, M., 1991. Politics and the study of discourse. In: Burchell, G., Gordon, C. and Miller, P. (eds), *The Foucault Effect: studies in governmentality.* Harvester Wheatsheaf, London, pp. 53–72.

Geertz, C., 1973. *The Interpretation of Cultures: selected essays.* Basic Books, New York.

Hakkarainen, P., 1978. On moral education in the Finnish comprehensive school curriculum. *Journal of Moral Education* 8(1), 23–31.

Hinnells, J.R., 2005. *The Zoroastrian Diaspora: religion and migration.* Oxford University Press, Oxford.

Landauer, T., McNamara, D., Dennis, S. and Kintsch, W. (eds), 2007. *Handbook of Latent Semantic Analysis.* Psychology Press, Hove.

MacNeill, D., 2000. Religion education and national identity. *Social Compass* 47(3): 343–52.

Michel, P., 1999. *La religion au musée: croire dans l'Europe contemporaine.* L'Harmattan, Paris.

Molokotos-Liederman, L., 2000. *Pluralisme et education: l'expression de l'appartenance religieuse à l'école publique. Les cas des élèves d'origine musulmane en France et en Angleterre à travers la presse.* Doctoral thesis, Ecole Pratique des Hautes Etudes (EPHE/Sorbonne).

—— 2007. The Greek ID cards controversy: a case study on religion and national identity in a changing European Union, *Journal of Contemporary Religion* 22(2): 187–203.

Orr, L., 2000. *Donors, Devotees, and Daughters of God: temple women in medieval Tamilnadu.* Oxford University Press, Oxford.

Plummer, K., 1983. *Documents of Life: an introduction to the problems and literature of a humanistic method.* Allen & Unwin, London.

—— 2001. *Documents of Life 2: an invitation to critical humanism.* SAGE, London.

Prior, L., 2003. *Using Documents in Social Research.* SAGE, London.

—— 2008. Repositioning documents in social research. *Sociology* 42(5): 821–36.

Robinson, J.A.T., 1963. *Honest to God.* SCM, London.

Scott, J.C., 1990. *A Matter of Record: documentary sources in social research.* Polity Press, Cambridge.

Sinclair, S., 2002. *National Identity and the Politics of Religion and Education in Germany.* Doctoral thesis, Lancaster University.

Taylor, J., 2001. *After Secularism: inner-city governance and the new religious discourse.* Doctoral thesis, SOAS, University of London.

—— 2003. After Secularism: British government and the inner cities. In: Davie, G., Heelas, P. and Woodhead, L. (eds), *Predicting Religion: Christian, secular and alternative futures.* Ashgate, Farnham, pp. 120–32.

Thomas, W.I. and Znaniecki, F., 1918. *The Polish Peasant in Europe and America.* Dover Publications, New York.

Towler, R., 1984. *The Need for Certainty: a sociological study of conventional religion.* Routledge & Kegan Paul, London.

Webb, E.J., Campbell, D.T., Schwartz, R.D. and Sechrest, L., 1966. *Unobtrusive Measures: nonreactive research in the social sciences.* Rand McNally, Chicago.

Willander, E. and Sikström, S., 2010. *Public discussions on religion and spirituality: defining themes, differences and similarities.* Unpublished paper presented at the International Sociological Association, Gothenburg.

Further reading

Prior, L., 2003. *Using Documents in Social Research.* SAGE, London.

Prior provides a comprehensive overview of documents and their use, with particularly good discussions on production and function.

Plummer, K., 1983. *Documents of Life: an introduction to the problems and literature of a humanistic method.* Allen and Unwin, London.

This book covers the use of numerous different types of document. It is particularly useful for those interested in diaries and/or autobiographical documents, whether solicited or pre-existing.

Landauer, T., McNamara, D., Dennis, S. and Kintsch, W. (eds), 2007. *Handbook of Latent Semantic Analysis*. Psychology Press, Hove.

The authoritative reference for the theory behind latent semantic analysis, a mathematical method used to analyze how words make meaning.

Towler, R., 1984. *The Need for Certainty: a sociological study of conventional religion*. Routledge & Kegan Paul, London.

A seminal example of using personal letters, sent to an individual, to analyze the nature of, and ways of, believing in 1960s Britain. To be read by anyone considering using personal letters in research.

Davie, G., 2003. Seeing salvation: using text as data in the sociology of religion. In: Avis, P. (ed.), *Public Faith? The state of religious belief and practice in Britain*. SPCK, London, pp. 28–44.

Another example of using personal letters sent, this time, to an institution. Davie also provides a further discussion of the use of documents in research.

Key concepts

Discursive formations: Discursive formation is a term used by Foucault to denote the way in which discourses are ordered and how they relate to one another. For Foucault, 'discourse is constituted by the difference between what one could say . . . and what is actually said' (Foucault 1991: 63). Discursive formations are, therefore, the ways in which these discourses interrelate, contradict and overlap in specific social, historical and cultural contexts.

Latent semantic analysis: A technique in natural language processing that analyzes relationships between a set of documents and the terms they contain by producing a set of concepts related to the documents and terms. LSA aims to discover how word and passage meaning can be constructed from experience with language.

Unobtrusive measures: A method described and used by Webb *et al.* (1966) to denote the collection of research data that occurs 'naturally' without the solicitation or intrusion of the researcher into the participants' lives. A seminal example of this is the examination of the wear on floor tiles in the Chicago Museum of Science and Industry to comment on the most popular exhibits.

Related chapters

2.5

EXPERIMENTS

Justin L. Barrett

Chapter summary

- Experimental methods are important as they constitute the only tool to draw *causal* conclusions in the study of religion.
- An experiment is a comparison of a least two conditions. The **control condition** is the status quo of something (e.g. not following a religious diet), and the **experimental condition** is what happens when a given factor is added to that thing (e.g. following a religious diet).
- Experiments use two types of variables. The **dependent variable** is the phenomenon that is investigated (e.g. health), and the **independent variable** is the factor that may causally account for it (e.g. follow a religious diet).
- The main types of experimental designs are: **between-subjects, within-subjects**, and **repeated-measures**; often these types are *mixed*, or used in conjunction with *correlational* or **quasi-experimental** designs.
- Experimental methods are limited by *practical challenges* and *ethical considerations*.
- The epistemological bases of experimental methods are: *fallible realism, probabilistic causation*, **falsifiability, sampling** and *statistical analyses*, and types of **validity**; these make experimental methods an *incremental approach*.
- Although sparsely used, experimental methods have proven fruitful in the exploration of causes for religious phenomena, and as such deserve to be taken into account by scholars of religion.

Descriptive and analytical overview

Experimental methods, though relatively rarely used, have appeared in the study of religion for a very long time. One well-known experiment concerned whether a religiously dictated diet led to better health and well-being than a more robust but culturally typical diet. This experiment, conducted in the courts of Babylon under the reign of Nebuchanezzer, involved four young men in a ten-day treatment condition eating a religiously motivated vegetarian diet and an untold number of control subjects eating a different diet. The now famous finding reported in the first chapter of the Book of Daniel is that those in the 'religious diet' treatment condition were judged healthier looking and more robust after ten days. As exciting as this finding may be—particularly as it might contribute to the argument that religious practices may be adaptive in an evolutionary sense—this early experiment suffered from numerous methodological shortcomings. Nevertheless, it still serves as an illustration for experimental research methods.

Experimental methods have long had a place in the physical, natural and social sciences because of their ability to generate confident causal inferences. Correlational methods of various sorts can only tell us that two phenomena co-vary with each other—valuable information, but, as the cliché goes, 'correlation does not prove causation'. Experiments can give us license to infer causation—even if only partial, non-deterministic—and finding or claiming causal relationships between factors is a central component of the study of religion.

Causal inferences are made so commonly, and often tacitly, that they are frequently over-looked. If someone suggests that Mithraism spread through Roman maritime activities, tacitly a causal connection between Roman maritime activities and the particular distribution of Mithraism is being made. Had Roman maritime activities been different but everything else had been the same, Mithraism's distribution would still be different. Similarly, if someone suggests that women are relatively more involved in spirit-possession activities than men because possession allows them a degree of power that they would not otherwise enjoy, a causal relationship among lack of power, desire for more power and motivation to participate in spirit-possession activities is implied. It may be that scholars in the interpretive and descriptive disciplines have less interest in the particular mechanisms that make the causal relationships exist, but with the exception of purely literary or philosophical projects causal relationships are among the basic stuff of religious studies. This emphasis on causal dynamics and the ability of experimental methods to reveal causal relationships means that experimental techniques must always be in the religious studies tool kit, even if they are sparingly used.

What is an experiment?

If you are new to experimental methods, try not to cast your mind back to those grade-school science 'experiments' such as the paper-clip electric circuit or the baking-soda volcano. Those were not, technically, experiments but demonstrations rather. Experimental methods are distinguished by systematically measuring the outcome of two or more conditions that differ from each other in one dimension. Typically, one condition is the control condition, meant to represent the status quo, and one is the experimental (or treatment) condition, meant to represent what happens to the status quo when a given factor is added (or subtracted). In Daniel's experiment cited above, we have two conditions: those eating the king's prescribed diet and those eating the vegetarian diet. In a perfect experiment the diet would be the only factor that differs between the two groups. In all other dimensions the two groups would be identical. When this degree of **experimental control** is accomplished, we can infer that any difference between the two conditions is due to the factor under scrutiny (in this case, the diet). Indeed, we can conclude that there is a causal relationship between the factor that has been experimentally manipulated and the outcome measured (in this case, healthful appearance).

Unfortunately, in this and essentially all other experiments the two groups under consideration were not identical save just one varied dimension. The individuals receiving the king's diet were not identical with those receiving the vegetarian diet. Perhaps, then, Daniel and his chums were healthier from the start, or something about their physiology made their diet fine for them but it would have been a disaster for the others. Any number of factors beyond the God-fearing diet could have accounted for the difference between the groups. Ideally, Daniel and company would be sent through a duplicating machine and then their perfect replicas would be fed the king's diet while they ate veggies.

As this kind of matching each and every conceivable factor between two (or more) groups is impossible, experimentalists simply do the best they can, and the industry-accepted gold standard for group allocation is **random assignment** to conditions. If 200 young men in Nebuchanezzer's court were the 'subjects'[1] in our dietary experiment, we would randomly assign 100 to be in the king's diet condition and 100 to be in the vegetarian diet condition. In all other ways the two groups would be treated identically. The same measures of 'healthy appearance', (e.g. weight as measured by an accurate scale) would be taken for both groups directly before the start of the diet and ten days after starting it. Given a large enough sample and true random assignment (in which each individual is equally likely to be assigned to one condition or the other), we could comfortably assume that any group-level differences—such as in weight—would be the product of either the treatment or random variation. Statistical techniques give us a probability that the measured difference in weight is a product of random variation. If the probability is very low (e.g. less than 5 per cent), we infer that the difference between groups is the result of the experimental manipulation and not random variation (or any other factor). In this way we can shore up a causal relationship between two variables. For instance, we could go beyond saying that a particular diet is associated or correlated with weight, but that the differences in diets caused a difference in weight (and not the other way around).

The anatomy of an experiment

In this example and in any experiment there is at least one dependent variable that is the focal outcome of the experiment. In this case, the weight of the young men is the dependent variable. The dependent variable may take any number of forms such as a physical measure as of height or weight; a physiological measure such as blood pressure or brain activation pattern; or a behavioral measure such as eye-gaze direction, pointing or answers on a questionnaire. These dependent measures serve as an index of the factor or phenomenon that is trying to be explained.

Experiments also have one or more independent variables—the dimension that is varied in an attempt to cause a change in the dependent variable. The dependent variable is dependent upon the independent variable. In the case of our nutritional example, the independent variable is the particular diet.

Experiments may also have what are termed **covariates**. Covariates are variables that may impact the dependent variable (much like an independent variable) but are not the variables under direct investigation. For instance, if for some reason we suspected that the king's diet was particularly good for people who got abundant sleep we might include sleep as a covariate in our experimental design. This could be achieved through a second experimental manipulation: of the 100 men assigned to the veggie diet, half could be allowed 12 hours each day for sleep while the other half (randomly assigned) might only be allowed six hours for sleep. Likewise, the 100 men in the king's diet would be randomly assigned to either the six-hour or the 12-hour sub-condition. With such an experimental design, the effect of diet and sleep (and any diet-sleep interaction) on weight could be investigated. Diet would be the independent variable, sleep would be the covariate and weight would be the dependent variable.

Often, however, covariates are not experimentally manipulated but simply measured. In the case of our example this would mean that instead of assigning the men to sleep conditions, each man's amount of sleep would be measured. Then, using statistical techniques, the effect of diet on weight, statistically controlling for the impact of sleep, could be determined. This use of statistical control on covariates is particularly common when covariates cannot be experimentally manipulated, as in age, sex, ethnicity and so forth. Were Daniel's experiment to be conducted using contemporary research standards, we would randomly assign 100 people to each condition (the experimental manipulation) and also measure each for sex, age, ethnicity, beginning weight, height, average hours of sleep, amount of exercise and any other covariate that we suspect might either mediate or interfere with the impact of diet on weight. Including such covariates can often improve the precision of conclusions drawn.

Variables

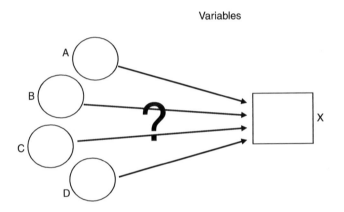

Variables A, B, C and D are non-mutually
exclusive candidates as causes for Variable X

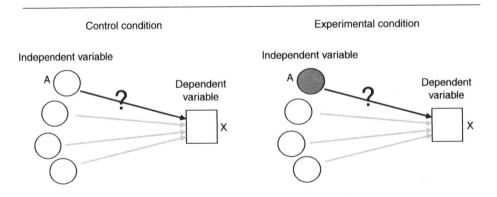

In an experiment, one variable (A) is identified as the independent
variable and varies across conditions. Variable X is measured for change
across conditions. The remaining variables are held constant across
conditions or neutralized through randomization.

Figure 2.5.1 Anatomy of an experiment

Types of experimental designs

The two-group experiment used by Daniel illustrates the proto-typical experimental struc-ture, but experiments come in numerous different designs and with varying degrees of complexity.

Between-subjects designs are experiments in which the independent variable varies between two or more groups of subjects. For instance, in his 'Good Friday' experiment, Walter Pahnke (1970) randomly assigned volunteers to a control group or a treatment (exper-imental) group. Those in the control group were given a placebo pill and those in the treat-ment group were given a hallucinogenic drug, psilocybin. Subjects were **blind** to their condition; they did not know if they had received the psilocybin or the placebo. Both groups then participated in a worship service and the various dimensions of the resulting experience measured via self-report constituted dependent variables. The independent variable, then, was the presence or absence of the hallucinogen. Because it was manipulated between the two groups of subjects, this is an example of a between-subjects design. Those in the treatment condition reported more intense and meaningful mystical experiences.

In contrast to between-subjects designs, in within-subjects designs the subjects serve in both conditions of the independent variable. That is, the independent variable is manipulated 'within' a single group. To illustrate, in examining whether five-year-old children are able to differentiate between what God knows and what humans know, Justin Barrett *et al.* (2001) asked children whether or not God would know the contents of a closed cracker box in which the crackers had been replaced by rocks. They were also asked whether their mother would know what was inside the closed box. The independent variable was the agent in question (God or mother) and the dependent variable was their response to the question 'What would – think is inside the box?' As children provided answers for both God and mother, this constitutes a within-subjects design: subjects serve in both the control and the experimental conditions. Because subjects provide information under both conditions, the order of answering the questions may influence the answers given. That is, for every other factor to be held constant across conditions, the question about God must be preceded by the question about mother and vice versa with the same frequency. Otherwise, we cannot conclude that any difference in answer to the questions is only the result of the particular question, for it may be due to the relative position in the set of questions. Within-subjects designs, hence, frequently include counter-balancing or randomization of the tasks.

Repeated-measures designs are similar to within-subjects designs and, technically, are a sub-type of within-subject designs. In repeated-measures designs subjects are measured on the same variable repeatedly. Each subject contributes a measure on the dependent variable in both a 'control' condition and in an 'experimental' condition. The most common examples of repeated-measures designs are those with pre- and post-treatment measures. For instance, Chris Boyatzis and colleagues measured American college women's satisfaction of their own appearance on a scale (Boyatzis *et al.* 2007). This pre-test measure served as a baseline or 'control' for the subsequent measures. One week later, the subjects read a list of 15 religious statements—mostly Christian in derivation—that affirmed their bodies, such as 'Do you know that your body is a temple of the Holy Spirit within you, which you have from God?' They then looked through 16 black-and-white fashion photographs from women's magazines—a task known through previous experiments to produce appearance dissatisfaction in young women. These two activities (reading the statements and looking at the photos) constituted the 'treatment' or manipulation. Afterward, they completed the body appearance satisfaction scale again. After the 'treatment', women's evaluation of their own appearance actually increased over the pre-test, but can we safely infer that the 'treatment' increased appearance satisfaction?

One limitation of repeated-measures designs is that time necessarily passes from the initial measure to the subsequent measure. Thus, more than one factor differs between the two conditions. Additionally, when the second measure is taken, subjects have already completed the measure previously. Might the simple passage of time or of experience with the measure cause the results? These concerns lead many researchers who use repeated-measures designs to embed them in more complex, mixed experimental designs. Boyatzis' study is a case in point. His study included two other conditions—one in which instead of reading religious body-affirming statements, subjects read more vaguely 'spiritual' body-affirming statements; and another in which subjects read 15 statements about current events at their university. In contrast to the 'religious' condition and the 'spiritual' condition, this latter group showed a decrease in appearance satisfaction from the first measure to the second. We can then confidently infer that the increase in appearance satisfaction from the first measure to the second for the 'religious' condition was not only the result of the passage of time or 'practice' with the measure. Something about the treatment—particularly about the content of the 15 statements—seemed to be the most reasonable causal factor.

As the Boyatzis study illustrates, sometimes experiments require more complex designs than simple between-subjects, within-subjects or repeated-measures designs. Often these three types are combined into a mixed design. Boyatzis' experiment was a cross between repeated-measures and between-subjects designs.

John Darley and Daniel Batson's famous 'Good Samaritan' study is another example of a mixed design (Darley and Batson 1973). In this case two independent variables were manipulated 'between-subjects' and another was assessed non-experimentally through correlational techniques. Princeton Seminary students were presented with a task in one location and then asked to go to another location, passing down a walkway where a confederate of the experimenter was posing as a collapsed, ill person. The dependent variable was the degree of help offered to the confederate. The experimentally manipulated variables were how hurried the subjects were (none, a little, a lot), and whether they would be giving a talk on the Good Samaritan parable or about careers outside of ministry for which a seminary degree can prepare you. The three levels of hurry and the two levels of talk-type yielded six different conditions to which subjects were randomly assigned. The non-manipulated independent variable was 'type of religiosity' (means-oriented, ends-oriented or open/searching 'quest') as operationalized by a questionnaire. Because type of religiosity was not experimentally manipulated, the research design prevented drawing any confident conclusions about a causal relationship between type of religiosity and helping. The study did successfully demonstrate a causal relationship between hurrying people and helping: those who were in a hurry were less likely to help (in part because they were less likely to notice that someone needed help). Whether one was going to be lecturing on the Good Samaritan was not found to be related to helping in this experiment.[2]

Quasi-experiments bear many of the same marks and assumptions of true experiments but lack strict control over all potentially relevant variables. For instance, Richard Sosis and Bradley Ruffle conducted a quasi-experiment investigating the relationship between religious participation and in-group cooperation (Sosis and Ruffle 2003). Their dependent variable was cooperation with in-group members as measured by an economic game that required risking one's own money in hopes that an anonymous other would likewise incur a risk for the benefit of both parties. As religious affiliation and participation cannot be readily manipulated, Sosis and Ruffle acquired a 'naturally' occurring matched-sample: secular and religious Israeli kibbutzim. As religious kibbutzim are communities patterned after their secular predecessors, they are comparable on many variables that might be relevant to in-group cooperation. Sosis and Ruffle further tried to be sure that their secular and religious kibbutzim were comparable in terms of economic success, size, age, average education, number of households with kin and so forth. Because such matching can never be perfect, Sosis and Ruffle used measures on these various dimensions as covariates in their design and statistically factored out any influence of these factors. Though they found that religious kibbutz members were more cooperative than secular kibbutz members (especially the males), even with Sosis and Ruffle's rigorous attention to carefully matching the samples and statistical control, we can only tentatively conclude that religious participation has a causal relationship with cooperation. Finding a correlation—even after carefully matching samples and statistical control—still does not entail causation. Additional, uncontrolled factors may account for the correlation.

Limitations of experimental methods

Even though experimental designs are, perhaps, the only way for scholars of religion to draw causal conclusions,[3] and causal accounts are an important component of the study of religion, limitations on experimental methods contribute to them being rarely used to study religion. Practical and ethical considerations narrow the range of applications.

Practical challenges

Because experimental methods require the ability to systematically manipulate variables independently of others, only those independent variables that can be independently manipulated may be considered. Variables that cannot be experimentally manipulated include sex, age, religious identification, ethnicity, residency and socioeconomic status, and so we can rarely clearly and confidently identify phenomena that are caused by these variables. Higher degrees of religious commitment and participation may be associated with being female, but we cannot be certain that religious commitment is directly caused by being female.

Experimental methods also assume that the dependent variable is measurable in some inter-subjectively verifiable way. That is, if more than one person cannot agree on a measurement of it, it cannot be a dependent variable in an experiment (or indeed, any quantitative method). For instance, people's inner experiences cannot be directly measured and so they cannot be experimentally investigated. What can be investigated are reports of experiences. We assume that the report is a fair index of the experiment but such an assumption may, in various cases, be faulty.

Because experimental methods require a high degree of control over the variables at play and they require a high degree of measurement agreement, experimenters frequently use laboratory environments in which they have this control. The consequence of this decision, however, is that laboratory experiments are limited to what can be conducted in the laboratory. While it may be possible to conduct fMRI (brain imaging) measures on solitary meditators, we cannot brain scan individuals while circumambulating the Kaaba.

These practical limitations mean that rather than investigating large-scale relationships or dynamics, experimental techniques are best suited for looking at components that might make up these large-scale relationships. Experiments cannot determine whether being female causes religious participation, but can examine whether feelings of persecution, disrespect or disenfranchisement might cause stronger feelings of commitment to one's religious community.

Feelings of persecution, disrespect and disenfranchisement can be experimentally manipulated and (reported) feelings of commitment to one's religious community can be measured.

The practical limitations of experimental methods also mean that they typically use simplified, stripped down, artificial-looking analogues of real world phenomena. The price paid for precision and the ability to draw causal inferences is a degree of separation from the real world. As Batson explains, 'An experiment almost always involves a caricature; one develops a simplified, artificial model of some natural process' (Batson 1977: 414).

Ethical considerations

Experimental techniques must also face a number of ethical considerations. Perhaps most distinctively, an experimentalist must consider, just because I can manipulate some factor, should I? I may find a way to artificially make someone feel weak and vulnerable to see if the person will retreat to religious commitments and activities, but should I inflict this psychological pain on another? Experimenters subjected Catholic subjects to very painful electric shocks in a recent experiment examining whether focusing on a religious image (in this case, a painting of the Virgin Mary) has analgesic effects (Wiech et al. 2008). One might question the ethics of such an experiment, but these experiments do pass ethics review boards. How?

The increased potential risk to subjects of experimental methods carries with it an increased obligation to secure informed consent of subjects. Hence, in proportion to the potential risk, experimenters bear some obligation to explain these risks, share the general purpose of the experiment (usually with promise to explain more fully upon completion of participation), and assure the would-be subjects that they may withdraw at any time without penalty. Subjects in experiments have to know what they are getting into, and have to willingly submit to any risks of physical or psychological harm. In the context of studying religion, experimenters must consider that one potential form of harm is religious or spiritual harm. Though we may find it permissible to experimentally manipulate attitudes toward a favorite television show or a political issue, would it be permissible to experimentally manipulate attitudes toward God or the ancestors or the subject's faith community? Even if the researcher does not think there is any reality to the subject's religious metaphysics, the researcher should evaluate the ethical permissibility of such manipulations presuming the subject's religious or spiritual beliefs are true.

Because of the numerous practical and ethical limitations of experimental methods, often religion scholars resort to quasi-experiments to test hypotheses.

The epistemological basis for experimental methods

Fallible realism

Experimental methods assume that there is a real world that operates on causal regularities, and that people and their feelings, thoughts and behaviors are part of that world. This ontological realism is augmented, however, by a deep suspicion about the ability for any given individual to accurately discern these realities about the world without the help of special tools—experimental methods being among these tools.

Psychological research has demonstrated that people are generally poor at accurately detecting complex correlations, let alone complex causal relationships. Likewise, people are quick to find evidence that confirms their expectations and slow to register relevant counter-evidence, a tendency dubbed 'confirmation bias' (Gilovich 1991). As people often unknowingly allow their biases to infuse their detection of patterns, experimental techniques and accompanying quantitative methods have been developed to try to eliminate or neutralize the effects of personal biases. One of the most important research standards in this regard is that experimental methods should be described with a high enough degree of specificity that other researchers could conduct the same experiment to check that they find the same results. Experiments must be replicable by a different researcher or laboratory. This demand for **replicability** has the further product that researchers with differing commitments or backgrounds can look at the same study and agree on the findings. That is, good experimental methods yield results with high inter-subjective agreement. We may have trouble seeing the influence of their biases in coloring our own scholarship, but we are pretty good at seeing the failings of others' work.

Probabilistic causation

Experimental research as applied to human thought and behavior—including religious thought and behavior—typically assumes that the causal relationships under consideration are partial, non-deterministic and probabilistic. As experiments simplify real-world causal dynamics, they only serve to identify that one or a small number of factors bear a causal relationship on one or a small number of outcomes. Any number of additional factors may causally impact that dependent variable and any number of additional factors may impact the independent variable or mediate its effect on the dependent variable. For these reasons, the relationship detected is necessarily only a partial causal account. Returning to Boyatzis' body-satisfaction study, though the 'treatment' of having young women read body-affirming religious texts had a causal impact on their reports of body-appearance satisfaction, surely a host of other factors influenced how highly the women rated their own appearance, how long the effect of the treatment would last and so forth. Similarly, experiments identify non-deterministic, probabilistic causal relationships. Though determinists of various stripes do inhabit the experimental sciences, for all practical purposes, human experimental scientists do not offer deterministic accounts of the relationships between their independent and dependent variables. Being in a hurry does not deterministically cause seminarians to be less likely to offer help, but *on average* they will be less likely to stop and help when hurried. The conclusions of experiments in the human sciences are essentially always probabilistic.

Falsifiability

Contemporary experimental research standards require that the hypothesis being tested is **falsifiable**. That is, there must be some way in which to demonstrate that a hypothesis is false. As Batson argues:

> Literature, art, history, etc., also provide perspectives or explanations—implicit theories. But for the scientist, to have a persuasive theory is only the beginning. The theory may be wrong. The scientist immediately tries to construct a situation in which the theory can show its own falseness. If the theory is a good one, a fairly explicit statement of the falsifying conditions can be made.
>
> *(Batson 1977: 414)*

Formally, experiments are actually designed to reject a particular hypothesis rather than to affirm one. For instance, in Pahnke's psilocybin experiment, the hypothesis he attempted to reject was that taking the psilocybin would not have any influence on reported intensity of religious experiences. Evidence was sufficient to reject this hypothesis and, consequently, support the alternative that psilocybin use does have an influence on intensity of reported religious experiences. A good experiment requires enough precision in its predictions that they could, if false, be shown to be false.

Sampling and statistical analyses

If an anthropologist visits a particular remote village and reports that all of the men but none of the women participate in a certain ritual, and all of the women but none of the men participate in another ritual, we do not need any fancy mathematics or statistics to understand what is happening within this village regarding these rituals. The ethnographer's description is sufficient. In experimental methods, perhaps unfortunately, statistics can almost never be avoided.

Experimental methods almost always require some kind of sampling from a population about which we would like to draw conclusions. It is typically impractical or impossible to include each and every member of a population in an experiment. Rather, we attempt to get a representative sample of a larger population to participate in the experiment, and then draw inferences from that sample to the population as a whole. For instance, from Darley and Batson's 'Good Samaritan' study, we do not want to just draw conclusions about the (male) Princeton Seminary students who participated, but about seminarians more generally, or maybe even Christian adults more generally. To do so, we must make judgments about the representativeness of the sample (do Princeton Seminary students really represent adult Christians generally?), and then use statistics to help us determine whether the observed relationship between, say, being hurried and helpfulness would likely hold for the greater population. For this reason, experimental methods are coupled with inferential statistics.[4]

Validity

When designing experiments, researchers must attend to the validity of the study; that is, whether the study likely leads to true inferences. Validity has at least five interacting components. First, **internal validity** refers to the degree to which we can be confident that the variability on the dependent variable is a consequence of the experimental manipulation of the independent variable as opposed to some other factor that was not suitably controlled. For instance, were experimenter expectations allowed to influence the behavior of subjects or the measurement of that behavior? Second, **construct validity** is the degree to which the theoretical construct has been operationalized appropriately. Does the experiment test the theory that the experimenter claims to be testing? Third, if we have concerns that a given experiment's findings will not extend to other times, places or samples, these reduce the **external validity** of the experiment. An unrepresentative sample, for example, would threaten external validity. Fourth, we may be concerned with an experiment's representativeness of real-world situations and dynamics. If a laboratory situation is too contrived or too distant from the situation in which the phenomena under study occur in real life, it may limit the sorts of inferences we can draw. These validity concerns are captured by the label **ecological validity**. Finally, because the results of experiments are normally analyzed by use of statistical techniques, whether the appropriate statistical techniques have been used bears upon the study's validity. Experiments that have been analyzed using the right techniques may be said to have high **statistical validity**.

Table 2.5.1 Assessing experimental validity

How confident can you be in drawing valid conclusions from an experiment?
If you can answer 'yes' to these questions, the experiment has strong validity.

Construct validity	✓ Does the experiment test the theory it sets out to test?
	✓ Has the experimentalist accurately understood the theorist and created fair proxies of the variables in question?
Internal validity	✓ Are the results really caused by the experimental manipulation or have other factors interfered?
	✓ Is there an alternative explanation of the results?
External validity	✓ Is the experiment replicable?
	✓ Would the same results be found with a different sample or different relevant population?
Ecological validity	✓ Does the experiment fairly mimic real-world situations or dynamics?
Statistical validity	✓ Have the results been obtained by using appropriate statistical methods?
	✓ Have all relevant and informative statistical analyses been conducted?

An incremental approach

Because experimental methods require tightly controlled, somewhat artificial arrangements to isolate particular variables of interest, any given experiment is bound to be incomplete by itself. Experimental techniques try to address a small number of factors at a time (usually one), not because the researcher is naive to the complexity of the phenomenon that is attempting to be explained, but to make each step in the causal account secure before moving forward. Experimental approaches are incremental in their character. For this reason in experimental psychology, for instance, often several experiments are reported in the same journal article. Each experiment adds a dimension or addresses a problem that a single experiment could not cover on its own. No one experiment is perfect in its coverage but can be compared to a square of a patchwork quilt. Once several experiments are stitched together, an impressive and useful blanket-explanation can develop but any one experiment by itself says very little. For this reason, too, experiments can supplement or be supplemented by other empirical methods such as ethnographic, survey or correlational methods.

Uses of experiments in the study of religion

The use of experimental methods in the study of religion has been relatively sparse. Even in the sub-discipline where one might expect the greatest use of experimental methods, psychology of religion, the number of papers published before 1977 using experimental methods has been estimated at only two (Batson 1977). Numbers have certainly risen since then, but correlational and quasi-experimental designs have remained the preferred tools for hypothesis-testing in the study of religion. This neglect may be primarily due to the practical and ethical limitations discussed above, but may also reflect the theoretical interests of the field. Cognitive and neuroscientific approaches to the study of religion, becoming more prominent in the past decades, have brought with them increased use of experimental methods. Feeble use of experimental methods may also be a consequence of lack of familiarity on the part of religion scholars, and unawareness of the potential power and flexibility of these techniques.

Fruitfully, scholars use experimental techniques to explore causes for various religious phenomena and the effects of religious participation, identification or beliefs. Though no one 'cause' of each and every thought, feeling, social arrangement or practice that we might call 'religion' will ever be found, causes for various dimensions or aspects of religion may be discovered. For instance, to account for the ethnographic finding that sometimes people regard rituals as requiring careful control over one's thoughts and intentions whereas in other rituals performing the acts properly is more important, the present author conducted an experiment (Barrett 2002). I hypothesized that if gods have direct access to our thoughts (e.g. through mind reading) then the intentions behind performing a ritual would be judged more important than the particular actions; however, if gods have to 'read' intentions from our actions much like humans do, then performing the action correctly would be judged as relatively more important. I randomly assigned half of the subjects to the 'dumb god' condition (in which they were told that rituals were performed for a god with human-like knowledge limitations) and half to the 'smart god' condition (in which they were told about a super-knowing god). Then I presented the subjects with artificial rituals to judge their likely efficacy (dependent variable). The hypothesis was supported. Perhaps, then, whether a group of people are meticulous with regard to ritual performance may, in part, be caused by how they regard the relevant god's access to their intentions. This type of experiment, then, can help identify causes for religious phenomena.

Experimental techniques can also investigate effects of religion. Though religious commitment cannot be directly manipulated, religious subjects can be asked to either perform a religious activity versus a comparison activity and then causal effects of that religious performance can be measured. Similarly, people can be subtly reminded of their religious commitments or otherwise 'primed' to see what effects heightened awareness of one's religious commitments might cause. To illustrate, Azim Shariff and Ara Norenzayan conducted an experiment exploring whether the appearance of religion-related words in a task requiring subjects to unscramble words to form sentences was sufficient to enhance generosity in a subsequent economic game (Shariff and Norenzayan 2007). It was. Though not conclusive on its own, this type of experiment can be an important piece of a case for (at least some) religion promoting generosity because, unlike correlational studies, this experiment shows a casual relationship between activating religion-related ideas and subsequent generosity.

Priming studies such as Shariff and Norenzayan's may be particularly powerful ways to move beyond mere correlation or association and gather evidence of causal links between religion and various attitudes and behaviors. Even though we cannot experimentally assign people along dimensions of many potentially important independent variables such as being religious or not, it is possible and useful to 'remind' people of their religious beliefs, identification or commitments through priming studies and see whether doing so correspondingly changes measures on other dimensions such as being generous, helpful, harmful, tolerant or prejudiced. Likewise, it is possible to 'prime' or otherwise temporarily manipulate prejudice, tolerance, helpfulness or generosity and measure whether such changes produce corresponding changes in religious identification, beliefs or feelings. In this way both causal relationships and the direction of those relationships can be explored through experimental methods.

Another promising application for experimental studies in the study of religion is examining implicit religious thoughts, feelings, attitudes and dispositions. The examination of texts and use of interviews remain excellent techniques for studying those thoughts and feelings to which people have conscious access and upon which they can reflect and ponder. In contrast, experimental techniques may be especially well-suited for digging beneath the surface. Using subtle behavioral cues such as eye-gaze and reaction-time differences in processing information or physiological measures such as pulse-rate, skin conductance and cerebral blood flow may provide evidence regarding more automatic and reflexive religious thoughts and feelings. Such experiments are abundant in the psychological sciences, but are yet to be put to common use in the study of religion.

Developmental studies of young children may provide another especially fruitful application of experimental methods. Interviewing young children without unduly introducing bias or confusion is difficult, and knowing what children actually mean by their words is complicated by the fact that their use of concepts may differ from that of adults. For these reasons, even when using verbal responses, developmental psychologists frequently use experimental research designs. Experimental approaches can improve precision. Advances in the techniques available to child developmentalists in the past three decades have encouraged a flowering of research on religious concept acquisition in young children that does not appear to be slowing (e.g. see Astuti and Harris 2008; Rosengren *et al.* 2000; Kelemen 2004).

Like any research methods, experimental techniques carry a number of practical, ethical and epistemological limitations that restrict their range on applicability in religious studies. Most seriously, many of the dynamics that interest scholars of religion revolve around factors that cannot or should not be experimentally manipulated such as residence, nationality, ethnicity, sex, gender, socioeconomic status and religious affiliation. In spite of these limitations, because experimental methods may be the only tool religious studies scholars have for drawing causal inferences about the relationship among factors, and causal relationships are ubiquitous in religious studies, experimental methods will always have a place in the study of religion. It then behooves scholars of religion to develop and improve upon experimental techniques relevant to the study of religion and become savvy consumers of the findings these experiments yield.

Table 2.5.2 Examples of experiments in the study of religion

Citation	Cultural setting	Keywords	Experimental design
Astuti, R. and Harris, P.L., 2008. 'Understanding morality and the life of the ancestors in rural Madagascar'. *Cognitive Science* 32, 713–40.	Madagascar	Cognitive development; cross–cultural research; death; Madagascar; supernatural concepts	Between–subjects
Griffiths, R.R. *et al.*, 2006. 'Psilocybin can occasion mystical–type experiences having substantial and sustained personal meaning and spiritual significance'. *Psychopharmacology* 187, 268–83.	USA	Anxiety; mystical experience; spirituality; religion	Between–subjects
Pahnke, W.N., 1970. 'Drugs and mysticism'. In: Aaronson, B. and Osmond, H. (eds), *Psychedelics: the uses and implications of hallucinogenic drugs*. Hogarth Press, London, pp. 145–65.	USA	Hallucinogenic drugs; Psilocybin; religious experience; worship	Between–subjects
Darley, J.M. and Batson, C.D., 1973. 'From Jerusalem to Jericho: a study of situational and dispositional variables in helping behavior'. *Journal of Personality & Social Psychology* 27, 100–8.	USA	Pro-social behavior; religion; social psychology; altruism	Between–subjects (with covariate)

(Continued overleaf)

Table 2.5.2 Continued

Citation	Cultural setting	Keywords	Experimental design
Granqvist, P. *et al.*, 2005. 'Sensed presence and mystical experiences are predicted by suggestibility, not by the application of transcranial weak complex magnetic fields'. *Neuroscience Letters* 379, 1–6.	Sweden	Magnetic fields; sensed presence; mystical experiences; suggestibility	Between-subjects (with covariate)
Shariff, A.F. and Norenzayan, A., 2007. 'God is watching you: Priming god concepts increases prosocial behavior in an anonymous economic game'. *Psychological Science* 18(9), 803–9.	Canada	Altruism; dictator game; religious concepts; priming; pro-social behavior	Between-subjects (with non-manipulated covariate)
Boyatzis, C.J., Kline, S. and Backof, S., 2007. 'Experimental evidence that theistic-religious body affirmations improve women's body image'. *Journal for the Scientific Study of Religion* 46(4), 553–64.	USA	Body image/satisfaction; religion	Between-subjects, repeated-measures mixed design
Barrett, J.L., 2002. 'Smart gods, dumb gods, and the role of social cognition in structuring ritual intuitions'. *Journal of Cognition & Culture* 2(4), 183–94.	USA	Causal reasoning; God concepts; religion; ritual; social cognition	Within-subjects
Boyer, P. and Ramble, C., 2001. 'Cognitive templates for religious concepts: Cross-cultural evidence for recall of counter-intuitive representations'. *Cognitive Science* 25(4), 535–64.	France, Gabon, Nepal	Concepts; cultural transmission; memory recall; religion	Within-subjects
Newberg, A.B. *et al.*, 2006. 'The measurement of regional cerebral blood flow during glossalalia: A preliminary SPECT study'. *Psychiatry Research: Neuroimaging* 148, 67–71.	USA	Cerebral blood flow; glossolalia; single photon emission tomography	Within-subjects
Wiech, K. *et al.*, 2008. 'An fMRI study measuring analgesia enhanced by religion as a belief system'. *Pain* 4(2), 147–58.	UK	Analgesia; fMRI; pain; prefrontal cortex; religion	Within-subjects (with non-manipulated covariate)
Barrett, J. L., Richert, R.A. and Driesenga, A., 2001. 'God's beliefs versus mom's: the development of natural and non-natural agent concepts'. *Child Development* 72(1), 50–65.	USA	Child development; God concepts; naturalness of religion; theory of mind	Within-subjects (with non-manipulated covariate, age of subjects)

Notes

1 '**Subjects**' are those people or animals that are being measured in an experiment. Due to concerns over treating people as mere objects, the 1990s saw a shift to using the less negative but more ambiguous term '**participants**' when referring to human subjects. I use the more precise language here to avoid misunderstanding, but in experimental reports 'participants' is the accepted jargon in some disciplines.

2 Note that failing to find a relationship between an independent variable and a dependent variable is importantly different than finding that there is no relationship between the two variables. In this particular experiment, those in the 'Good Samaritan' condition were nearly twice as likely to offer help as those in the contrasting condition, but the small sample size prevented this difference from being greater than what might occur based on chance variation. It is probable that with a larger sample size this experiment would have shown that making seminarians think about the Good Samaritan story increased their helping behavior. This study also failed to include a non-religious comparison group.

3 Historical studies often draw particular causal conclusions that are compelling as in 'the arrival of Spaniards in the New World caused Christianity to emerge in the New World'. The causal mechanisms are obscure in this sort of statement but surely the arrival of Spaniards was causally connected to the emergence of Christianity in the New World. Nevertheless, in more complex historical accounts and when trying to produce causal generalizations from these specific cases, care must be taken as numerous potential causal variables could change from Time 1 to Time 2 and account for the change in states of affairs. Strictly speaking, historical studies are correlational and so inferring causation must be done with caution.

4 Explanation of relevant statistical techniques falls beyond the scope of this chapter, but suggested readings are listed at the end.

References

Astuti, R. and Harris, P.L., 2008. Understanding morality and the life of the ancestors in rural Madagascar. *Cognitive Science* 32: 713–40.

Barrett, J.L., 2002. Smart gods, dumb gods, and the role of social cognition in structuring ritual intuitions. *Journal of Cognition & Culture* 2(4): 183–94.

Barrett, J.L., Richert, R.A. and Driesenga, A., 2001. God's beliefs versus mom's: The development of natural and non-natural agent concepts. *Child Development* 72(1): 50–65.

Batson, C.D., 1977. Experimentation in psychology of religion: an impossible dream. *Journal for the Scientific Study of Religion* 16(4): 413–18.

Boyatzis, C.J., Kline, S. and Backof, S., 2007. Experimental evidence that theistic–religious body affirmations improve women's body image. *Journal for the Scientific Study of Religion* 46(4): 553–64.

Darley, J.M. and Batson, C.D., 1973. From Jerusalem to Jericho: a study of situational and dispositional variables in helping behavior. *Journal of Personality & Social Psychology* 27: 100–8.

Gilovich, T., 1991. *How We Know What Isn't So: the fallibility of human reason in everyday life*. The Free Press, New York.

Kelemen, D., 2004. Are children 'intuitive theists'? Reasoning about purpose and design in nature. *Psychological Science* 15: 296–301.

Pahnke, W.N., 1970. Drugs and mysticism. In: Aaronson, B. and Osmond, H. (eds), *Psychedelics: the uses and implications of hallucinogenic drugs*. Hogarth Press, London, pp. 145–65.

Rosengren, S., Johnson, C.N. and Harris, P.L. (eds), 2000. *Imagining the Impossible: magical, scientific, and religious thinking in children*. Cambridge University Press, Cambridge.

Shariff, A.F. and Norenzayan, A., 2007. God is watching you: priming god concepts increases prosocial behavior in an anonymous economic game. *Psychological Science* 18(9): 803–9.

Sosis, R. and Ruffle, B.J., 2003. Religious ritual and cooperation: testing for a relationship on Israeli religious and secular kibbutzim. *Current Anthropology* 44(3): 713–22.

Wiech, K., Farias, M., Kahane, G., Shackel, N., Tiede, W. and Tracey, I., 2008. An fMRI study measuring analgesia enhanced by religion as a belief system. *Pain* 4(2): 147–58.

Further reading

For a valuable exchange regarding the place of experimental versus quasi-experimental methods in the psychological study of religion, including discussion of practical and ethical considerations regarding the experimental study of religion, see these articles by Daniel Batson, and John Yeatts and William Asher:

Batson, C.D., 1977. Experimentation in psychology of religion: an impossible dream. *Journal for the Scientific Study of Religion* 16 (4): 413–18.

Yeatts, J.R. and Asher, W., 1979. Can we afford not to do true experiments in psychology of religion? A reply to Batson. *Journal for the Scientific Study of Religion* 18(1): 86–89.

Batson, C.D., 1979. Experimentation in psychology of religion: living with or in a dream? *Journal for the Scientific Study of Religion* 18(1): 90–93.

The following are introductory guides to understanding, designing and implementing experiments and quasi-experiments:

Field, A. and Hole, G., 2008. *How to Design and Report Experiments.* SAGE, London, Thousand Oaks, CA.

Shadish, W.R., Cook, T.D. and Campbell, D.T., 2002. *Experimental and Quasi-Experimental Designs.* Houghton-Mifflin, New York.

Numerous introductions to statistical techniques relevant to experimental methods exist. They vary on accessibility, assumed mathematical background of the reader, the computer-based statistical package one might be using and the disciplinary orientation of the reader. None exist, of which I am aware, that is specifically for scholars who study religion. I therefore recommend a statistics text that is slanted toward the social and psychological sciences rather than the biological sciences or economics. A widely used introduction to statistics is Aron et al. (2009). A good introduction to doing statistical analyses with the widely used SPSS software package happens to be written by an esteemed psychologist of religion, Lee Kirkpatrick.

Aron, A., Aron, E.N. and Coups, E.J., 2009. *Statistics for Psychology.* 5th edn. Prentice Hall, Englewood Cliffs, NJ.

Kirkpatrick, L.A. and Feeney, B.C., 2009. *Simple Guide to SPSS for Version 16.0.* Wadsworth, Belmont, CA.

The National Institutes of Health (USA) website hosts a good, brief online training course for research ethics including ethics relevant to experimental methods with human subjects. At the time of writing, this course was open to the public through a log-in system: phrp.nihtraining.com/users/login.php?l=3.

Key concepts

Between-subjects design: an experimental design in which the independent variable is varied between groups of subjects. Each subject serves in only one condition of the experiment.

Blind: being unaware of the condition one is in and/or the precise hypotheses guiding an experiment. In experimental research, subjects are typically 'blind' to their condition. Experimenters may also need to be blind to the condition of a subject so as not to influence the subject.

Construct validity: the degree to which the theoretical construct has been operationalized appropriately such that the experiment tests the theory that the experimenter claims to be testing.

Control condition: sometimes called the comparison or baseline condition, the control condition serves as a point of comparison for the experimental condition, and often represents the absence of the causal factor under scrutiny (as in the non-medicated condition of a drug treatment experiment), or the status quo.

Covariate: a variable that may have a causal influence on the dependent variable but is not the primary focus of the experimental design. Covariates may or may not be experimentally manipulated.

Dependent variable: the outcome variable that the independent is thought to causally impact. Measures of the dependent variable are hypothesized to be dependent upon the independent variable.

Ecological validity: the degree to which an experiment represents real-world situations and dynamics and thus serves as a fair proxy for those causal dynamics.

Experimental condition: the experimental condition usually features the addition or subtraction of some causal factor thought to impact the dependent variable. In a drug treatment experiment, the condition in which the drug is administered is the experimental condition. For this reason, the experimental condition is sometimes called the treatment condition.

Experimental control: using experimental methods to eliminate or neutralize the impact of all but a single or small number of independent variables on a dependent variable.

External validity: the degree to which a given experiment's findings will extend to or be replicable in other times, places or samples.

Falsifiable (-ility): being able to be empirically demonstrated to be false. Experiments test falsifiable hypotheses.

Independent variable: in an experiment, the variable that is manipulated to examine its causal relationship with the dependent variable.

Internal validity: the degree to which we can be confident that the variability on the dependent variable is a consequence of the experimental manipulation of the independent variable as opposed to some other factor that was not suitably controlled.

Participant: see Subject.

Quasi-experiment: a type of study that bears many of the same marks and assumptions of true experiments but lacks strict control over all potentially relevant variables. Naturally occurring conditions, instead of random assignment, lead to subjects being in one condition instead of another.

Random assignment: the practice of assigning subjects to either an experimental or control condition using chance. Assignment is truly random when the probability of any given subject being assigned to condition is equal. Random assignment (with large enough samples) produces comparable conditions for comparison, neutralizing the impact of covariates on the dependent variable. Random assignment should not be confused with arbitrary assignment.

Repeated-measures design: a special variation of within–subjects experimental designs in which subjects are measured repeatedly on the dependent variable (e.g. before and after a treatment) and hence serve as control subjects for themselves.

Replicable (-ility): being able to be repeated at another time and yield comparable results. Experiments should be constructed and described in such a way that they are replicable for another researcher or research team and not subject to idiosyncrasies of a researcher.

Sampling: instead of measuring an entire population, the exercise of selecting representatives from a population in order to draw inferences about the entire population. Representative sampling is generally assumed, and random sampling is the best way to ensure representative sampling. Studies that use sampling require the use of inferential statistics to draw conclusions about the population from which the sample was drawn.

Statistical validity: the degree to which the experiment's results rest on appropriate and thorough use of statistical analyses.

Subject (also participant): The human or non-human from whom data is gathered in a study.

Validity: the degree to which casual inferences can be safely drawn from an experiment. An experiment with good validity supports confident inferences. Several different perspectives on a study's validity have been described including construct, ecological, external and internal.

Within-subjects design: an experimental design in which each subject provides a measurement on the dependent variable in both the experimental and the control condition (or all conditions of comparison). The independent variable is varied within the subject sample as a whole.

Related chapters

◆ Chapter 1.2 Comparison
◆ Chapter 1.3 Epistemology
◆ Chapter 1.6 Research ethics

2.6

FACET THEORY METHODS

Erik H. Cohen

Chapter summary

- Facet theory (FT) is a systematic approach to theory construction, research design and data analysis.
- FT methods and techniques such as Smallest Space Analysis (SSA) and Partial Order Scalogram with base Coordinates (POSAC) uncover and graphically portray the underlying structural inter-relationships of data.
- FT is particularly valuable in analyzing data with non-linear relationships, common in studies of religion.
- FT has been used for decades and has proven valuable in the study of religion, religious identity, beliefs and values.
- FT tools such as SSA with external variables and POSAC are useful in comparing between sub-populations, creating typologies of respondents and identifying variables that distinguish between sub-populations.

Introduction

Empirical studies of religion using facet theory

The scientific study of religion is inherently challenging. By its very nature, religion is a complex phenomenon, difficult to measure and assess empirically. Religion and religious identity are simultaneously cognitive, affective and behavioral, with multiple social and psychological impacts on the individual and community (E.H. Cohen, forthcoming; Wulff 1997).

There have been a number of ambitious, large-scale international surveys of religious affiliations and attitudes of people around the world (Gallup International 2006; Inglehart 2004; Tos *et al.* 1999) as well as targeted surveys of national populations such as Americans (Baylor Institute for Studies of Religion 2006; Pew 2008) or religious groups such as Jews (NJPS 2003), Muslims (Moaddel 2007), and Pentecostals (Pew 2006), to name only a few major studies. These studies provide valuable data.

The analysis of such data is most often conducted based on distribution tables and graphs. Not infrequently, factor analysis has been used (S. Cohen 2005; Hall and Edwards 1996; Hood et al. 2001; Yeatts and Asher 1982). Factor analysis is a useful tool in identifying the minimum number of categories necessary to describe the pattern of relationships among selected variables.

In this chapter, I explain the value in the study of religion of a well-established and useful yet little known school of data analysis known as **facet theory** (FT). One of the strengths of FT is its ability to allow the researcher to uncover and graphically portray the structural relationship between the variables, an aspect of analysis not covered by techniques such as factor analysis (A. Cohen 2003; Guttman 1992; Maraun 1997; Maslovaty et al. 2001). FT has been used by social scientists for half a century with impressive results (for a comprehensive bibliography of facet theory publications see E.H. Cohen 2009a). Despite its proven usefulness and success, FT is still relatively underutilized, though it is growing in recognition. It is not my purpose here to champion FT over other methods, but rather to demonstrate its unique contribution. FT techniques may also be used in conjunction with other methods, validating, expanding and enriching the analysis.

Box 2.6.1 When is facet theory applicable for studies of religion?

- Is the data linear or non-linear in nature? When variables with a linear relationship are plotted in a graph they follow a straight line. Variables with a non-linear relationship may show a curve, a branching 'tree' or other forms. FT is particularly useful in analyzing non-linear data.
- How many variables are being considered? FT and the SSA technique may address many variables, yet there is no requirement for a minimum number of variables in each SSA region.
- How many observations are necessary in order to find a significant structure with SSA? Some 100 observations are generally considered sufficient.

In this chapter, I first cite some previously published examples of the application of FT in the study of religion. Then some of the main tools and techniques of FT are briefly explained. A case from a field study (not previously published) is then explored in detail, illustrating the applicability to the study of religion of FT in general, and two of its main data analysis tools: **Smallest Space Analysis** (SSA) and **Partial Order Scalogram with base Coordinates** (POSAC).

FT has been used for decades and has proven valuable in the study of religion and religious identity. As early as 1969, Laumann applied SSA to analyze friendship relations among religious and ethno-religious groups in the USA. A decade later, Marsden and Laumann (1978) used FT to uncover a social structure of religious groups.

Shlomit Levy and her colleagues applied FT methods in longitudinal studies of identity among Israelis (Levy et al. 1993, 2000, 2004). In this series of studies, a mapping sentence was designed to articulate the elements of Israelis' perceptions regarding personal and social religious and national identity. The SSA technique was used to analyze data collected among two generations of Israelis. The SSA showed a differentiation between religious and national identity and between an internal and external reference group (self/others). The same basic partitioning was found in the data from the two time periods as well as among religious and secular Israelis. This formed the basis for a subsequent comparison of Israeli and

American-Jewish youth, revealing a fundamental similarity in perception of ethnic-religious identity (Rebhun and Levy 2006).

Huismans (2003) conducted a facet analysis of religiosity. Tiliopoulos *et al.* (2007) applied SSA to data from a sample of British Christians in order to explore dimensions of religious orientations (extrinsic means and intrinsic ends).

Schwartz and Bilsky (1987, 1990) used FT techniques in the development of their typology of human values, which was used as the basis of a cross-cultural comparison of values and religiosity (Schwartz and Huismans 1995). The Schwartz model was also used as the theoretical basis for an international analysis of church-state relations among Catholics (Roccas and Schwartz 1997) and a theological and socio-psychological study conducted among Roman Catholics in Belgium (Fontaine *et al.* 2005).

Rebhun (2004) applied FT techniques (mapping sentence and SSA with external variables) to analyze data from the 1990 National Jewish Population Survey, representing the structure of ways in which Jews from various parts of the American-Jewish community conceptualize their Jewish identity. The structure showed a clear distinction between attitudinal and behavioral aspects of identity. Further, Rebhun used the external variables technique to locate sub-populations of Jews (extended Jewish population, core community, Orthodox, Conservative and Reform, etc.) within this structure.

Wiley and Levi-Martin (1999) used the POSAC technique to create a **partial order** of beliefs and attitudes. Bohm and Alison (2001) used both POSAC and SSA to create a typology of behaviors for distinguishing between benign and destructive religious sects and cults.

In my own research, I have used FT methods to analyze data sets which cover large populations and many variables. The same questionnaire items were included in a number of national and international surveys, allowing for the development of widely applicable typologies. For example, a question regarding components of Jewish identity ('I consider myself Jewish: by birth, by family, by culture, by choice, by language, by commitment, by loyalty, by hope, in reaction to anti-Semitism, in reaction to the Holocaust, in relation to other Jews, in relation to Israel') was used in surveys of participants in group youth tours to Israel from around the world, Israeli high school students, participants in US Jewish summer camps and staff members of informal Jewish educational settings around the world (E.H. Cohen 2008a, 2008b, 2004; Cohen and Bar Shalom 2006). Assessing each data set using SSA enables a comparison of the overall structure of Jewish identity as perceived and organized by various groups of co-religionists. Inserting sub-populations as external variables makes it possible to compare the Jewish identity of respondents from different home countries, levels of religiosity, etc. I used POSAC to create a typology of Jewish communities based on established indicators of Jewish identity (E.H. Cohen 2009b), a typology of religious and recreational motivations among tourists to Israel (E.H. Cohen 2003), and an axiological typology of French Jews (E.H. Cohen 2005).

Basics of facet theory

Pioneered by the late Louis Guttman (see Levy 2005), FT is a meta-theoretical framework and systematic approach to theory construction, research design and data analysis. As will be shown, FT provides valuable insights into the data. In particular, it enables a structural approach to a data set which includes numerous variables for a large survey population. FT tools represent in a readable fashion the structural relationships of the data.

There are a number of data analysis techniques which have been developed in association with FT. The most commonly used FT techniques are Smallest Space Analysis (SSA, sometimes also referred to as Similarity Structure Analysis) and Partial Order Scalogram Analysis (POSAC). In many senses, the FT techniques are similar to other types of Multidimensional Scaling (on MDS see Borg and Groenen 1997; Young and Haber 1987; for examples of its application to religious studies see Brown and Forgas 1980; Duriez *et al.* 2000; Sorenson 1997). However, FT provides a theoretical framework lacking in MDS.

Box 2.6.2 Scope of facet theory

The facet theory approach encompasses the three major components of the scientific process:

- a definitional framework (mapping sentence);
- techniques for analyzing the collected data (SSA, POSAC); and
- a hypothesis regarding correspondence between the definitional system and the structure of the data (**regionality hypothesis**).

Mapping sentence

The definitional framework is articulated through a **mapping sentence**. The mapping sentence delineates the **facets** of the study, each of which represents an aspect of the phenomenon under investigation, including population, content and the range of results. Each facet contains a number of **elements**. Each of the elements is a potential measurable variable. The facet is a set of conceptually related variables. The facets and elements should be conceptually clear so that other researchers in the field can use them in classifying observations in their own studies. Logical relations among facets should be specified in the mapping sentence (Borg 1990).

The most basic mapping sentence, which includes only one content facet, has the following format:

P   {A}   →   R
Population   Content facet   Range

A sample of a simple mapping sentence including two content facets for a hypothetical study of religion[1] might be:

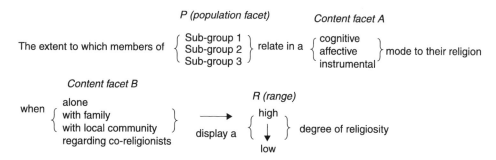

Figure 2.6.1 Sample mapping sentence 1

The facets in a comprehensive mapping sentence should completely cover the issue under consideration. An empirical study does not necessarily address all the facets and elements in the mapping sentence—it may focus on one or two, and a partial mapping sentence may be designed for a study of a specific aspect of the issue. Items in a survey questionnaire would cover the relevant facets and elements in the mapping sentence.

The mapping sentence is a flexible tool, which may be expanded or modified as research progresses. Based on the data analysis, the mapping sentence may be revised, namely by adding or deleting facets or elements within facets. By specifying and organizing facets and elements of the research observation and the relations between them, the mapping sentence helps the researcher to formulate hypotheses about the subsequent data analysis (Levy 1985).

Smallest Space Analysis

SSA graphically portrays a set of variables according to their correlations (Guttman 1968). SSA begins with the construction of a correlation matrix for the selected variables. The correlations range from −100 to +100, with 0 indicating no correlation between a pair of variables.[2] The Hebrew University Data Analysis Package (HUDAP) computer program[3] then plots the variables as points in a cognitive map (a Euclidean space called 'smallest space') in such a way that closely correlated variables are close together and weakly or negatively correlated variables are far apart. The program simultaneously takes into account the entire correlation matrix for all the selected variables. In placing the variables in the map, the program calculates the 'coefficient of alienation'—a measure of the reliability of the location of the variables based on the data in the correlation matrix. As stated by Amar (2005: 147), the coefficient of alienation expresses the degree of 'goodness of fit' of the SSA-generated map, or more precisely, 'the extent to which some distances between pairs of points in the two-dimensional space do not adhere to the rule regarding the monotone relationship between input coefficients and output distances'.

A perfect fit is indicated by a coefficient of alienation of 0; a completely imperfect fit is represented by a coefficient of alienation of 1 (these extremes are rarely found in practice). According to Guttman, a coefficient of alienation of .16 or lower may be considered highly reliable.

It should be noted that the computer program can generate a number of SSA maps in various dimensions and along various axes. The researcher may consider several possible maps to determine which shows the structure of the data most clearly. In SSA, the lower the dimensionality necessary to recognize a structure, the stronger it can be said to be. In general, it is preferable to find a structure in two or three dimensions. If the coefficient of alienation is very high, it may be necessary to consider an SSA of higher dimensionality. However, if a clear and logical structure reflecting the facets of the mapping sentence may be found an SSA map of two or three dimensions, this result may be considered reliable, even if the coefficient of alienation is moderately high (approaching .30).

Once the map is generated, the researcher looks for contiguous regions of semantically related variables. The researcher does not look for clusters defined only by distance, but regions that respond to a semantic criterion and which form a coherent overall structure. The interpretation of the map is guided by the mapping sentence. The facets, or items within facets, may be recognizable as regions in the SSA map. While the placement of the points is objective, based on the correlation between the data, the interpretation of the map is subjective, reflecting the theoretical basis of the analysis.

There are a number of possible types of structures in an SSA. Levy (1985) describes three basic structures that may be found in two-dimensional SSA maps: a *sequential* series of parallel slices (showing for example a most to least progression); a *center-periphery* structure of concentric circles and a *polar* structure consisting of pie-shaped wedges emanating from a common center and arranged in sets of oppositions. One or more of these structures may be found in the same map. In an SSA map shown in three dimensions, possible structures include a cylinder or a cone.

In looking for a structure in the SSA map, the researcher does not necessarily look for the smallest number of categories, as would be the case in a factor analysis (Guttman 1992). There is not a preference for categories containing many variables. There may be solutions in which a region is defined by a single variable, or even deduced by an empty space in a logical structure (Shye 1978; A. Cohen 2003).

SSA can be used to verify or revise the theory outlined in the mapping sentence (a 'confirmatory' SSA). The facets in the mapping sentence provide a theoretical basis in looking for regions in the SSA map. However, the regions must be contiguous and the divisions must show a clear and plausible structure. For example, excessively zig-zagging borders or island regions within other regions should be avoided, even if they correspond to the mapping sentence. The HUDAP includes an optional feature which

> permits superimposition of facet elements for each variable and produces facet diagrams to facilitate viewing regional correspondence between the empirical distribution of the variables and their faceted definition. The user can request, interactively, regionalization of the variables for Axial, Modular or Polar models.
>
> *(Amar 2005: 7)*

This may assist the researcher in looking for regions, though s/he need not be limited to the options displayed by the program.

The regionalization of SSA maps is analogous to that of geographic maps, the fixed features of which may be divided into regions according to political boundaries, natural features, population density, etc. For example, the towns of Aqaba, Eilat and Taba are situated close to each other at the northern tip of the Gulf of Aqaba, yet are in three different countries (Jordan, Israel and Egypt, respectively). Therefore, they would be included in the same region of a map divided according to natural habitat types, but in different regions in maps divided according to political boundaries. The divisions are determined according to the purpose of the map. In the case of an SSA, the divisions are determined according to the theoretical basis of the analysis as articulated in the mapping sentence. If no mapping sentence has been constructed, an SSA can be applied to the data and the researcher can look for regions as part of the process of developing a theory (an 'exploratory' SSA).

Comparing sub-populations: external variables in the SSA map

Using the graphic representation of the set of primary variables as a base, sub-groups of the survey population may be compared by introducing them as '**external variables**' (Cohen and Amar 2002). This is a unique feature of the SSA procedure, and distinguishes it from other multi-dimensional data analysis tools.

First, from a grouping variable with multiple possible responses, dichotomous dummy variables are derived, each representing a sub-population. For example, a variable with three possibilities (respondent is a member of group 1, group 2 or group 3) would be represented as three dichotomous dummy variables (the first would be: YES member of group 1/NOT member of group 2/NOT member of group 3; and so forth for the others).

A correlation array is calculated between each dummy external variable and the set of primary variables. They are then introduced into the map (which is 'fixed' so that its structure is not affected) according to the same principal of the strength of the correlation determining the location. As with the primary variables, external variables are placed in such a way that they are close to items with which they are strongly correlated and far from those with which they are weakly or negatively correlated. In placing each external variable, the computer program considers its correlation with all the primary variables simultaneously.

Box 2.6.3 Steps in conducting a Smallest Space Analysis (SSA)

1   calculation of correlation matrix between selected variables
2   placement of variables in Euclidean 'smallest space' using HUDAP program
3   analysis of resultant maps to find a logical structure based on theoretical basis of the study (as expressed in mapping sentence)

To include external variables:

1   creation of binary dummy variables from a grouping variable
2   calculation of correlation arrays between external variables and set of primary variables
3   insertion of external variables into 'fixed' SSA map

Partial Order Scalogram Analysis with base Coordinates (POSAC)

While SSA portrays the structure of the variables, POSAC ranges profiles of the surveyed individuals and portrays the structure of the profiles. A profile consists of the individual's responses to each of the selected variables. Profiles may be *comparable* or *non-comparable*. By definition (following Levy and Guttman 1994: 255), one profile is higher than another if and only if it is higher on at least one item and not lower on any other item. Such a pair of profiles is comparable. Two profiles are non-comparable if and only if one profile is higher on at least one item while the other is higher on at least one other item.

To illustrate, we will use two hypothetical profiles consisting of responses to three question-naire items in which 1 represents a negative answer and 2 represents an affirmative answer. The profile 1-1-1 (negative responses to all three items) and 2-1-1 (affirmative to the first, negative to the other two) are comparable because all of the items in the first are smaller or equal to the corresponding items in the second. The second profile is higher. The profiles 1-1-2 and 2-1-1 are non-comparable because the items vary in both directions. It is impossible to say which is 'higher' or 'lower' because the first profile contains an item that is higher and an item that is lower than the corresponding items in the second profile. Only if every pair of profiles within the sample is comparable may a *perfect order* or *scale* be found. Since perfect orders are rare, the POSAC was designed to deal with sets of comparable and non-comparable profiles by finding the best 'fit' among the profiles. This fit measures the proportion of well-represented pairs of profiles.

The profiles may be represented graphically. When *n* variables are considered, the set of profiles may be, by definition, perfectly represented a space with *n* dimensions. However, this would be a trivial result, not useful to the researcher. The goal of the POSAC program is to preserve as accurately as possible the partial order of a set of profiles in as few dimensions as possible (usually two). One dimension is sufficient only if, for a given population, all the variables considered could be reproduced by assigning each person in the population by one score or rank (Guttman 1994: 205).

The HUDAP computer program identifies which variables are most useful in discriminating between profiles. These variables serve as axes in the POSAC map. In general, two axes are selected and the structure is represented in two dimensions. These axes are the *base coordinates*. It is also possible to conduct a multi-dimensional POSAC using more than two axes. Each profile is plotted as a point in the space according to these selected axes.

When a set includes only comparable profiles, it is called a *perfect order* or *scale*. The set of comparable profiles in a perfect order can be accurately represented in one dimension; that is, ranked along a single line from 'lowest' to 'highest'. If a high proportion of pairs in a partial order (85 per cent or more) can be accurately represented in a single dimension, this may be considered sufficient. If the proportion is lower, more dimensions are necessary. For most partial orders, a two-dimensional representation (a plane with two axes, x and y) is sufficient to achieve an acceptable proportion of accurately represented pairs of profiles.

A case study using FT: symbols of Jewish identity among Jewish American youth

Now I will take results from a previously unpublished study and demonstrate, step by step, how FT may be applied. The data used are from a study conducted in Jewish summer camps in the United States. Participants in camps affiliated with Orthodox, Conservative and Reform streams of Judaism were included in the study. These three types of camps represent three major streams within contemporary American Judaism (Lazerwitz 1998). In this way, the study is an example of comparative religious studies within one religious group. Comparing the ways in which Jewish identity is expressed among the youth attending the various types of camps indicates the varying ways religious identity is understood among American Jews today.

'Jewish identity' is a multi-faceted concept, encompassing religion, culture, ethnicity and nationality. There is not simply a spectrum from religious to non-religious Jews, but rather a plurality of ways to understand what it means to be Jewish. Jews at different times and in different places have developed distinctive expressions of Jewish identity (Cohen and Horenczyk 1999; Gitelman *et al.* 2003; Wettstein 2002, among many others). Therefore, it is essential to use a wide range of variables and indicators in assessing Jewish identity. As mentioned, FT techniques are particularly useful in analyzing data sets including many variables.

During the summers of 2005–07, 731 campers completed questionnaires: 349 in Orthodox camps, 172 in Conservative camps and 210 in Reform camps. One questionnaire item presented a list of possible symbols of Jewish identity. Respondents were asked to indicate all of the symbols that represent an aspect of their personal Jewish identity.

The mapping sentence

The following mapping sentence was formulated to describe the relevant aspects of the research. The design of the mapping sentence was guided by previous research on symbols of religious and specifically Jewish identity (E.H. Cohen 2004, 2008b).

The distribution table of participants' responses to the list of symbol is given in Table 2.6.1.

There is much to be learned from the distribution table. We can see that the responses of the participants in the three types of camps were quite similar for some items, particularly the more universal symbols (peace, equality, future), while for others, such as those more specific

P *(population facet)*   *Content facet A*

Jewish youth participating in a $\left\{ \begin{array}{l} \text{Orthodox} \\ \text{Conservative} \\ \text{Reform} \end{array} \right\}$ summer camp, through $\left\{ \begin{array}{l} \text{religious} \\ \text{national} \\ \text{personal/familial} \\ \text{cultural} \\ \text{universal} \end{array} \right\}$ symbols

Content facet B   R *(range)*

which are $\left\{ \begin{array}{l} \text{central} \\ \text{peripheral} \end{array} \right\} \rightarrow$ express $\left\{ \begin{array}{c} \text{high} \\ \downarrow \\ \text{low} \end{array} \right\}$ personal Jewish identity.

Figure 2.6.2 Sample mapping sentence 2

Table 2.6.1 Responses of participants in Jewish summer camps to symbols of Jewish identity

	Participants in Reform camps	Participants in Conservative camps	Participants in Orthodox camps	Total population
Aliyah (immigration to Israel)	29%	44%	69%	52%
Bar/bat mitzvah	72%	75%	80%	77%
Brooklyn	11%	14%	11%	12%
Community	49%	60%	64%	59%
Education	79%	84%	89%	85%
Equality	46%	48%	41%	44%
Family	67%	72%	78%	73%
Freedom	78%	73%	67%	72%
Friendship	58%	68%	64%	63%
Future	52%	48%	51%	50%
God	72%	76%	85%	79%
Hebrew	63%	72%	78%	73%
History	60%	65%	70%	66%
Home	58%	57%	64%	61%
Hope	61%	58%	64%	62%
Jerusalem	60%	61%	78%	69%
Jewish foods	65%	69%	71%	69%
Jewish state	58%	70%	79%	71%
Kosher food	36%	66%	78%	63%
Memory	51%	51%	48%	49%
Moral values	60%	76%	79%	73%
Parents	66%	75%	76%	73%
Peace	69%	72%	68%	69%
Prayer	56%	66%	75%	67%
Religion	69%	72%	82%	76%
Right of return to Israel	44%	44%	63%	53%
Shoah (Holocaust)	57%	74%	80%	72%
Spirituality	40%	42%	54%	47%
Star of David	72%	58%	60%	63%
State of Israel	62%	70%	80%	73%
Success	64%	57%	62%	61%
Tolerance	33%	52%	38%	40%
Torah study	50%	60%	82%	67%
Tradition	61%	69%	76%	70%

to Jewish religious tradition, there are significant differences (i.e. Torah study, kosher food, immigration to Israel). However, it is difficult to achieve a holistic picture of the structure of the data from the table. This may be done by conducting an SSA.

The correlation matrix

To conduct an SSA, first the correlation matrix for these 34 variables was calculated, as shown in Figure 2.6.3. The non-linear monotonicity correlation (MONCO) was used. MONCO shows how much two variables vary in the same direction (increasing or decreasing). It

> expresses the extent to which replies to one question increase in a particular direc-
> tion as the replies to the other question increase, without assuming that the increase
> is exactly according to a straight line. In other words, for any two numerical values,
> when *x* increases does *y* increase or not?[4]
>
> *(Amar 2005: 117)*

It is instructive to take a brief look at the correlation matrix, in order to better understand the subsequent placement of the items in the SSA map. The two symbols *aliyah* (immigration to Israel) and Jewish State have a high correlation (80). This shows that campers who selected *aliyah* as a symbol of their Jewish identity were highly likely to also select the symbol Jewish State. The correlation between *aliyah* and Brooklyn is only 10, indicating that those who selected the symbol *aliyah* were relatively unlikely to select Brooklyn.

The basic SSA map

The HUDAP computer program places each of the variables in a map, taking into considera-
tion the entire correlation matrix simultaneously. When the map is first generated, there are no border designations. Figure 2.6.4 shows the resultant SSA without borders or regions. The maps shown here are projections in two dimensions using axes 2×3 of a map in three dimensions.[5] Clear structures (discussed below) can be recognized in this map of dimensionality 3, which has a low coefficient of alienation (.15).

Regionalization of the SSA map

The task of the researcher is to look for a structure to the items. As noted, the HUDAP offers an option for superimposing facets from the mapping sentence into the map. Alternatively, the researcher may look for semantic regions based on the mapping sentence and guided by general knowledge of the subject. While the designations of these borders are not arbitrary—that is, they are guided by knowledge of the subject, literature in the field and the mapping sentence—neither is there a rigid 'right' and 'wrong' placement of the border. The researcher must make decisions as to what will be included and specifically where to place borders between regions.

In this case, the literature on Jewish identity, including previous SSAs conducted on responses to lists of symbols and components of Jewish identity, served as a guide in creating the mapping sentence, which in turn helped in looking for regions in the current map. Figure 2.6.5 shows the same map with some preliminary borders between regions designated.

The two items in the center of the space—family and parents—are related and form the core of the structure. Their placement in the center of the map reflects their equally strong

Figure 2.6.3 Correlation matrix for primary variables (input matrix for SSA)

	1	2	3	4	5	6	7	8	9	10	11	12	13	14	15	16	17	18	19	20	21	22	23	24	25	26	27	28	29	30	31	32	33	34
1 Aliyah	100																																	
2 BarMitsva	57	100																																
3 Brooklyn	10	9	100																															
4 Community	50	64	8	100																														
5 Education	51	63	-19	71	100																													
6 Equality	32	58	22	73	72	100																												
7 Family	56	74	11	73	72	62	100																											
8 Freedom	16	45	8	47	72	72	57	100																										
9 Friendship	48	64	15	65	62	61	76	43	100																									
10 Future	37	50	-1	71	75	67	79	57	68	100																								
11 God	73	71	-4	62	65	45	75	42	62	60	100																							
12 Hebrew	65	66	-12	66	70	39	58	33	53	56	69	100																						
13 History	46	59	33	57	67	41	52	51	48	47	57	56	100																					
14 Home	40	61	13	69	68	56	80	67	67	70	67	47	51	100																				
15 Hope	41	60	-10	70	65	68	74	68	62	66	66	52	51	65	100																			
16 IsraelStat	73	71	-5	59	72	58	72	46	67	59	70	75	51	61	57	100																		
17 Jerusalem	71	69	19	59	51	36	70	29	53	51	81	59	53	59	59	84	100																	
18 JewishFood	30	53	30	47	47	30	48	53	42	43	48	53	35	41	55	55	53	100																
19 JewState	80	77	3	73	69	47	79	42	65	67	80	81	56	65	85	59	82	56	100															
20 Kosherfood	60	75	6	53	63	46	64	32	52	42	69	76	46	60	51	85	69	68	73	100														
21 Memory	36	60	20	67	65	36	70	58	65	71	57	59	48	47	64	70	46	43	63	43	100													
22 Moral	47	53	-10	71	76	47	58	38	69	51	59	63	57	48	58	50	46	30	56	58	51	100												
23 Parents	52	70	36	68	74	60	74	56	68	65	68	52	52	76	63	73	63	57	72	67	49	61	100											
24 Peace	49	66	-5	61	67	70	74	62	68	65	62	50	50	62	50	70	62	44	68	46	61	54	61	100										
25 Prayer	61	71	16	80	68	61	70	36	54	66	75	69	57	62	66	70	67	46	78	69	55	67	69	55	100									
26 Religion	70	80	5	76	73	53	84	39	63	67	84	82	68	70	64	73	82	53	82	78	60	72	78	66	85	100								
27 Return	74	59	7	67	61	58	64	38	59	54	59	65	61	56	56	75	75	37	65	77	52	70	69	59	67	77	100							
28 Shoah	68	69	-1	62	56	50	65	42	61	66	70	75	48	59	59	75	80	65	75	51	51	70	68	58	71	78	65	100						
29 Spiritual	49	55	6	50	61	32	64	56	56	70	68	56	49	66	73	59	54	27	59	40	55	72	59	61	67	70	62	63	100					
30 StarDavid	34	58	16	42	40	34	70	49	54	63	46	59	49	46	50	48	66	65	50	35	41	27	50	54	42	57	41	52	29	100				
31 Success	13	45	11	44	87	46	40	68	53	37	27	24	21	41	41	33	21	43	24	27	38	31	49	37	26	20	28	16	33	38	100			
32 Tolerance	27	46	17	70	55	56	64	47	55	46	36	36	57	56	64	49	34	31	54	42	69	73	63	67	55	50	56	57	62	25	41	100		
33 Torah	69	67	9	59	74	30	67	28	40	39	68	68	64	44	43	67	66	51	70	65	42	70	58	42	76	77	61	64	59	40	10	26	100	
34 Tradition	62	65	27	75	67	62	71	50	62	66	70	63	63	66	69	75	68	57	76	66	72	60	77	59	77	78	65	74	67	47	28	57	61	100

Figure 2.6.4 SSA of symbols of Jewish identity without regionalization

correlation with the majority of the other items. Additionally, we can see that the items on the right-hand side of the map are universal (not specifically Jewish) symbols. Most of the items on the left-hand side of the map are distinctively Jewish and religious symbols. The general items on this side of the map (i.e. history, tradition, prayer, religion, God) may be understood by this very young survey population as referring to Jewish history, Jewish tradition, etc.

Expanding upon the recognition of the core region, we can find a center-periphery structure to the symbols, as shown in Figure 2.6.6. The two symbols of parents and family form the personal core of religious identity. These symbols are shared by essentially the whole population, the common meeting point for all types and sub-groups. A study of Jewish youth in the UK found that 'the heart of this social core is the family, historically the crucible of Jewish identity and still regarded by many of our participants as the most important early influence on the development of their Jewishness' (Sinclair and Milner 2005: 101). It may be noted here that an SSA conducted on another set of data regarding symbols of Jewish identity found that people were more central in the structure of symbols than things or abstract ideas (E.H. Cohen 2008b).

Moving outward from this core another region may be designated containing symbols that are basic elements of religion, also largely shared by the population of respondents. This circle is represented by a dotted line because its borders are tentative, based on a theoretical approach and previous research into religious identity. Each of the variables in this circle represents an element in facet A of the mapping sentence: religious (religion, God), national (Jewish State), personal/familial (home), cultural (tradition) and universal (education, hope). We may find

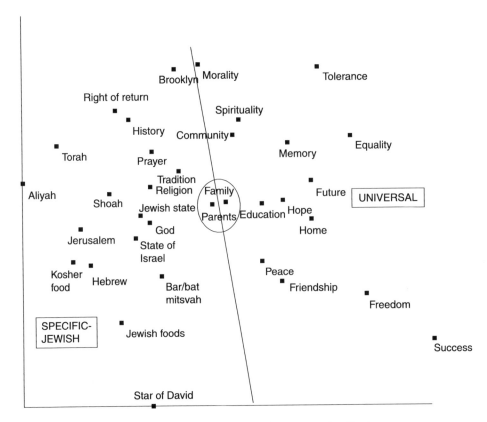

Figure 2.6.5 SSA of symbols of Jewish identity, with preliminary regionalization

support for this theoretical region of basic elements in the literature. They cover the traditional, communal and institutional elements essential to any enduring religion (Tilley 1995). Education may be considered a core element because not only is Jewish education key to transmitting the religion, but secular or universal education is also an important value to American Jews (Heilman 1992). A sense of connection to Israel as the Jewish State[6] was found to be an issue of commonality, crossing denominational boundaries among American Jews. The core symbols would need to be verified among other populations, particularly given that this survey population is so young, but it offers an insight into ways to organize the map.

Around this core is a diffuse region of symbols which are more specific and diverse. SSA treats correlations and not frequencies. Thus it must be emphasized that placement of a variable towards the center of the SSA map does *not* necessarily reflect a high response rate to this variable. Moreover, as noted previously, the HUDAP program simultaneously considers the entire correlation matrix in placing the variables. Therefore, although 'bar/bat mitzvah', for example, was selected by 77 per cent of the respondents while 'home' was selected by 61 per cent, 'home' appears closer to the center of the map. In part, this is due to the strong correlation between home and the symbols of 'family' and 'parents'. Again, though, the program considers the entire matrix at once, which is a very complex and large data set.

The map can also be interpreted as showing a polar structure of pie-shaped regions of semantically related symbols emanating from a common center. This is shown in Figure 2.6.7, superimposed over the previous divisions between core and periphery and between universal

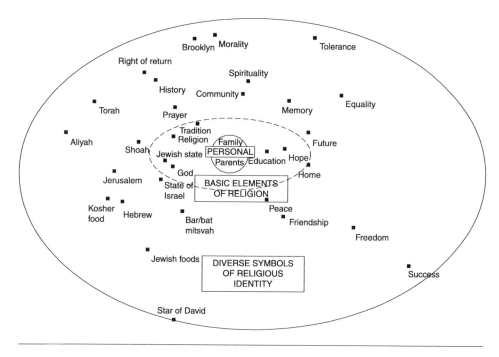

Figure 2.6.6 SSA map of symbols with center–periphery structure

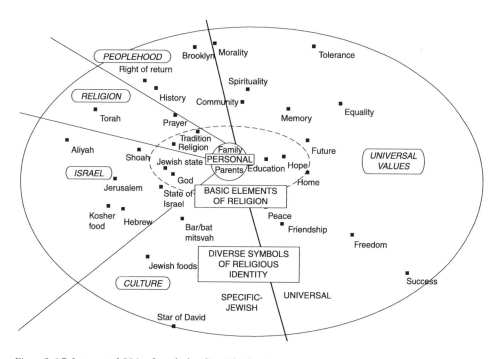

Figure 2.6.7 Integrated SSA of symbols of Jewish identity

and specific. Five regions are designated, corresponding to symbols of: Israel,[7] religion, people-hood, universal values and culture. Again, the placement of the borders is subjective, and the researcher must use discretion. For example, the items spirituality and community arguably could be considered universal values or symbols of peoplehood. Therefore, the division is drawn so that these two symbols are along the border between the two regions.

While it may seem surprising that the variable 'bar/bat mitzvah' is not placed in the religion region, this in fact accurately reflects a well-documented sociological reality. Among contemporary American Jews, particularly those outside the Orthodox community, the bar/bat mitzvah has become more of a cultural and social event that a religious one (Schoenfeld 1993, 1994), representing a type of symbolic ethnicity and religiosity (Gans 1994). Star of David, Jewish foods (as opposed to 'kosher food') and Bar/bat mitzvah seem to characterize a symbolic ethnicity.

External variables in the SSA map

Once the structure of the primary variables has been established and the regions designated, external variables may be introduced. In this case, three sub-populations of campers in each of the types of summer camps (Orthodox, Conservative and Reform) are included as external variables. This greatly increases the usefulness of the method in understanding differences between different religious groups or sub-groups of co-religionists.

First, the questionnaire item in which the respondents indicated which type of camp they attend (Orthodox, Conservative, Reform) was converted into three binary dummy variables: a participant from an Orthodox camp would be thus defined as YES Orthodox, NOT Conservative, NOT Reform (1-0-0); a participant from a Conservative camp would be defined as NOT Orthodox, YES Conservative, NOT Reform (0-1-0); and finally a participant in Reform camp would be defined as NOT Orthodox, NOT Conservative, YES Reform (0-0-1).

Next, the correlation between each external variable and the set of primary variables (the 34 most important symbols) is calculated, as shown in Figure 2.6.8. As can be seen, the Reform camp participants have negative correlations with many of the items. The strongest positive correlation is with freedom (item #8). The Conservative camp participants are also negatively correlated with many of the symbols; their strongest correlation is with the symbol tolerance (#32). The Orthodox camp participants, in contrast, have positive correlations with most of the symbols, particularly *aliyah* to Israel (#1) and Torah study (#33).

Based on these correlations, the external variables are placed in the map, as shown in Figure 2.6.9. Their placement says much about the culture of each of the camps. All three are towards the periphery of the map, highlighting their distinctive relationship to the symbols of identity. The participants in the Orthodox camps are on the specific-Jewish side of the map, specifically in the religion region, closest to the symbol 'Torah study'. The participants in the Conservative camps and Reform camps are both placed in the universal values region, but in different parts of the region. The participants in the Conservative camps are closest to the symbol 'tolerance'. The participants in the Reform camps are closest to the symbol 'freedom'. These symbols represent values that are emphasized in the distinctive cultures of each type of camp.

The POSAC typology of respondents

A POSAC was conducted to create a typology of the camp participants. Profiles of partici-pants were calculated according to their responses to six of the symbols.[8] The SSA guided the selection of these six symbols. Two symbols (freedom and equality) were selected from the universal values region, which comprises half the space of the map. One symbol was selected

	1	2	3	4	5	6	7	8	9	10	11	12	13	14	15	16	17	18	19	20	21	22	23	24	25	26	27	28	29	30	31	32	33	34
reform	-59	-16	-4	-28	-30	5	-22	23	-16	3	-28	-30	-18	-9	-3	-33	-28	-11	-40	-68	3	-42	-24	-1	-34	-25	-24	-46	-21	28	9	-21	-48	-28
conserv	-20	-7	15	3	-4	9	-5	4	13	-7	-13	-1	-2	-9	-11	-9	-22	1	-2	8	4	10	8	8	-4	-14	-24	6	-13	-13	-12	32	-22	-2
orthod	61	18	-9	21	30	-11	23	-20	4	3	34	27	17	14	10	35	40	8	37	57	-6	31	15	-5	32	32	36	37	26	-13	2	-8	58	26

Figure 2.6.8 Correlation arrays for external variables

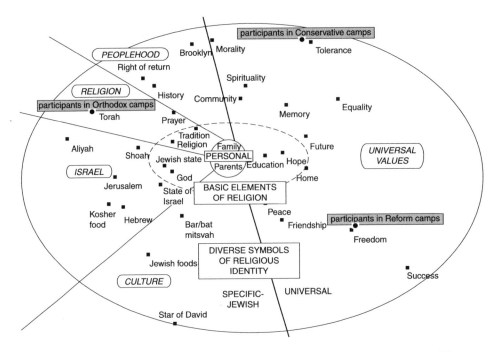

Figure 2.6.9 SSA of symbols of Jewish identity with sub-populations of campers by camp affiliation as external variables

from each of the remaining regions: Star of David (culture), history (peoplehood), freedom (universal), Torah study (religion), and Jerusalem (Israel). There were 61 different profiles among the campers. Table 2.6.2 shows as samples the five most common profiles of participants according to whether they selected each symbol (indicated by a 1) or not (indicated by 0). Profile 1 represents a camper who selected all six of the symbols. Profile 61 represents a camper who selected none of them. These two profiles are comparable with each other and with all of the others, because profile 1 is higher than every other profile, and profile 61 is lower than every other profile. The responses in each of these pairs of profiles vary in only one direction. In contrast, profiles 15 and 19 are *not* comparable with each other because the responses vary in both directions; that is, for one symbol profile 15 is higher (Star of David) and for another profile 19 is higher (freedom).

In a POSAC represented in one dimension, that is a ranging of the profiles along a single axis or straight line, only 64 per cent of the pairs of profiles were accurately represented; this

Table 2.6.2 Sample profiles

	# of respondents fitting profile	Star of David	History	Freedom	Torah study	Jerusalem	Equality
Profile 1	132	1	1	1	1	1	1
Profile 2	77	1	1	1	1	1	0
Profile 15	24	1	1	0	1	1	0
Profile 19	20	0	1	1	1	1	0
Profile 61	29	0	0	0	0	0	0

is not considered sufficient, as explained before. Therefore, we ran a POSAC which arranged the profiles in a two-dimensional plane along two axes. This yielded a higher proportion of profile pairs correctly represented, 90 per cent.

The HUDAP program for POSAC calculates the optimal pair of axes for representation of the partial order in two dimensions (x and y axes for the horizontal and vertical ranging of the variables in a plane). Table 2.6.3 shows the correlation of each of the six variables along two axes and for the diagonal joint axis ($x + y$). The symbol 'Torah study' has the highest correlation for the x axis (1.00) and the symbol 'freedom' has the highest correlation for the y axis (1.00).[9] The proportion of profile pairs correctly represented along these two axes is 90 per cent, indicating a reliable result.[10]

Table 2.6.3 POSAC results along two axes

	Axis x	Axis y	Joint axes (x + y)
Star of David	.73	.76	.83
History	.84	.76	.89
Freedom	.42	**1.00**	.90
Torah study	**1.00**	.47	.94
Jerusalem	.88	.70	.88
Equality	.54	.83	.78

Figure 2.6.10 shows the graphic representation of the profiles along the two axes of Torah (horizontal) and freedom (vertical). Profile 1 is in the upper right-hand corner, the highest along both axes; profile 61 is in the lower left-hand corner, the lowest along both. The other profiles are plotted in the map according to their partial order or 'best fit' along the two axes, as ranged by the POSAC section of the HUDAP program.

Figure 2.6.11 shows the same configuration, with the profiles labeled according to whether each includes a positive response to the symbol Torah study (indicated by a solid dot) or not (indicated by a hollow dot). There is a clear division between them along the horizontal axis. All the profiles of campers who selected the item Torah study as a symbol of their Jewish identity are on the right hand side of the map; all of those that did not are on the left side.

Figure 2.6.12 shows the same configuration again, this time with the profiles labeled according to whether each includes a positive response to the symbol freedom (indicated by a solid dot) or not (indicated by a hollow dot). Along the vertical axis, all but one of the profiles of campers who selected the symbol freedom as a symbol of Jewish identity are in the top half of the map and all but one of the profiles of those who did *not* select freedom are in the bottom half of the map. There were only two 'misplaced' profiles. Profile #20, which included a negative response to freedom and Torah and positive responses to the other four, was placed by the computer program in the top half of the map; profile #46, which included a positive response to both freedom and Torah and negative responses to the other four symbols, was placed in the bottom half.[11]

Figure 2.6.13 shows the same configuration one more time, with the space divided into four quadrants: in the upper right-hand corner are the profiles of those who selected both freedom and Torah study; in the lower right-hand corner are profiles of those who selected Torah study but not freedom; in the upper left-hand corner are profiles of those who selected freedom but not Torah study, and in the lower left-hand corner are profiles of those who did not select either of these symbols.

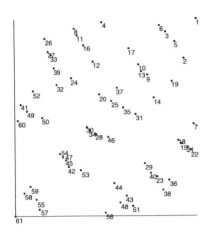

Figure 2.6.10 Representations of the profiles of the POSAC along two axes (Torah study and freedom), without regionalization

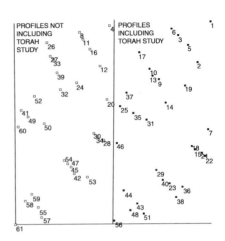

Figure 2.6.11 Differentiating between profiles of campers who did and did not select Torah study as a symbol of Jewish identity

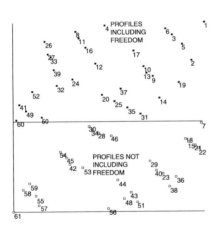

Figure 2.6.12 POSAC differentiating between profiles of campers who did and did not select freedom as a symbol of Jewish identity

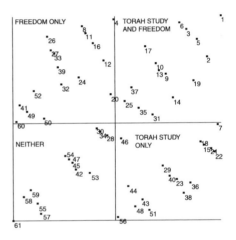

Figure 2.6.13 Representations of the profiles of the POSAC along two axes (Torah study and freedom), with regionalization

In this way, these two symbols may be used to formulate a typology of Jewish youth with four categories: those who selected Torah study but not freedom as symbols of their Jewish identity, indicating an authoritarian and traditional approach; those who selected freedom but not Torah study, indicating an autonomous approach to Jewish identity; those selecting both, indicating an approach in which traditional authority and personal autonomy co-exist; and those emphasizing neither, indicating other approaches not covered by these two symbols. The largest number of campers (353) have profiles that include both of these symbols (designed by profiles positive for both); the second largest number (144) have profiles that include the symbol freedom but not Torah; 114 campers have profiles that include only Torah study but not freedom; and 82 have profiles that include neither symbol.

It is important to emphasize that the POSAC result is not equivalent to a simple cross-tabulation between the two variables of freedom and Torah study. The POSAC simultaneously considers the responses to *all* six of the selected variables in the profile, not only the two designated as the axes. This is illustrated by the 'misplacement' of two profiles (#20 and #46). Such misplacement could not be detected in the cross-tabulation which considers *only* whether or not campers selected these two variables.

The POSAC base coordinates usually have a substantive meaning for the partial order, as we can see in the present example. The identification of these two symbols as the most useful in discriminating between sub-groups of the study population corresponds to sociological observations about the pivotal roles of religious tradition and personal autonomy in modern life, as stated by Wasserman (2008: 41): 'The conflict between spiritual grounding and intellectual autonomy, between the meaning provided by faith and the liberty to think for oneself, is a defining conflict of modernity'.

Conclusion

The application of FT methods and techniques makes it possible to uncover the underlying structure of the data and to compare sub-populations in a holistic manner. The information presented in an SSA is also contained in distribution tables and graphs, but the inter-relations are more easily perceptible in the SSA map. Again, we may use the analogy of a geographic map. A table may present distances between various cities; the map shows in a more easily readable fashion the relative distances between all the points at once. The representation of the data in this way shows groupings of variables, ordering of variables or regions of variables, empty regions which may indicate gaps in the data or theory; these features of the structure of the data are more readily apparent than they would be from a table or a factor analysis.

This exercise of applying the SSA and POSAC methods to the data set, designating various possible structural divisions within the map and introducing sub-populations as external variables has revealed much about the ways in which the youth surveyed perceive and organize the symbols of identity. They differentiate between universal and specific Jewish symbols. They further distinguish between items related to nationality/homeland (Israel), culture, religion, peoplehood and universal values. Family and parents are central symbols. The two symbols of Torah study (representing traditional authority) and freedom are useful in discriminating between sub-groups or types of participants. These findings may be applicable to studies of symbols of religious identity conducted among other populations.

Implications for other studies of religion

The methods described in this chapter may be applied to case studies of other religious groups, or comparative studies between populations of different religions. For example, a PEW (2006) study of Pentecostal Christians in ten countries includes data on religious beliefs and practices. Comparisons of expressions of beliefs and frequency of practices between Pentecostals in various countries and other types of Christians are given in table and graph form. By conducting an SSA on this data it would be possible to uncover the structural relations between beliefs and practices among Pentecostals around the world. Further, a POSAC could be conducted. Several key variables could be selected (perhaps guided by the SSA results) and the partial order among the profiles could be represented graphically, allowing for the creation of a typology of Pentecostals.

Similarly, the data on American religious beliefs and practices collected in the Baylor Institute's survey (Baylor Institute for Studies of Religion 2006) could be analyzed using SSA and POSAC. An SSA could be conducted using responses to questions on how frequently the respondent attends religious services and other religious activities, their level of agreement with various statements regarding religious beliefs and images of God, and political views and social attitudes as they related to religious belief. This would produce a graphic representation of religious views of Americans. Different religious groups could be inserted into the SSA as external variables. A typology of Americans according to key religious beliefs and practices could be represented using POSAC.

FT methods in combination with other methods

When data have been verified as being linear in nature, factor analysis and linear regression are sufficient and highly recommended. However, when data is non-linear, as is true in the majority of cases in the social sciences, facet theory methods using a monotonous (non-linear) approach is more appropriate in revealing the nature of the data.

Often, factor analysis and the SSA method may be used in conjunction, and the results are mutually enriching. In an SSA map, it may be possible to recognize contiguous regions corresponding to factors identified in a factor analysis (see for example Cohen and Werczberger 2009). This strengthens and verifies the findings of each type of analysis. Additionally, the SSA map expands upon the factor analysis by graphically portraying the structural relationship between regions. As Maraun (1997) demonstrated, a well-established model developed using factor analysis can be expanded by applying the SSA method and uncovering the structural relationship between the categories in the factor analysis.

As demonstrated in this case study, the regions in an SSA can provide a guideline for selecting variables to be considered by the POSAC. Similarly, in Bohm and Alison's (2001) study of cults, a POSAC was performed using the variables located in a distinct region of an SSA map that corresponded to destructive beliefs and behaviors.

In summary, facet theory has much to contribute to religious studies, a multivariate subject, in which data is often non-linear in nature. It is hoped that this introduction to the subject will encourage students to explore the ways in which these tools and techniques may enrich their studies of various aspects of the field.

Acknowledgements

The data on participants in US summer camps was collected as part of a survey supported by the Lookstein Center for Jewish Education of Bar Ilan University.

Thanks to Allison Ofanansky for her help in preparing and editing the manuscript.

Thanks to Reuven Amar for his comments on a previous version of the chapter.

Notes

1 Levy *et al.* (1993: v) developed a mapping sentence for a study of religious and national identity among Israeli Jews, which included no fewer than ten facets, such as: {individual-to-God/individual-to-individual/individual-to-self}; behavior of {self/others} and with respect to {daily life/Shabbat/holidays/special occasions/unspecified} as expressed in {public/private}. This mapping sentence may serve as a useful guide to researchers developing mapping sentences for studies among other populations.

2 I have found the monotonicity correlation (MONCO) to be particularly applicable. MONCO is a regression-free, non-linear coefficient of correlation. MONCO measures whether or not two items vary in the same direction (i.e. both increase) (Guttman 1986: 80–87). It recognizes a wider variety of correlations as 'perfect', and therefore MONCO correlations are always higher in absolute value than linear correlations. An SSA may also be done successfully using the more common Pearson coefficient.

3 The Hebrew University Data Analysis Package (HUDAP) data analysis software package was developed by Reuven Amar and Shlomo Toledano, Computation Authority of the Hebrew University of Jerusalem. The package includes programs for calculating cross-tabulations, MONCO or Pearson correlations of imported data, an SSA module for producing a graphic map of correlations and inserting external variables as described in this chapter, and other data analysis techniques such as discrimination coefficient (which may be used in place of the classical analysis of variance method), and POSAC (this may be used in place of the classical discriminant analysis method). For information on obtaining HUDAP contact: Elena Canetti, VP Scientific Services, Yissum Research Development Company of the Hebrew University of Jerusalem, Hi-Tech Park, Edmond J. Safra Campus, Givat-Ram, Jerusalem PO Box 39135, Jerusalem 91390, Israel; telephone: 972-2-658-6688; fax: 972-2-658-6689. A manual on the use of HUDAP (Amar 2005) may be downloaded free of charge from: www.facet-theory.org/files/HUDAP%20Manual.pdf.

4 The Guttman weak monotonicity coefficient for a pair of ordinal or interval variables belongs to a large family of monotonicity coefficients called 'regression-free coefficients of monotonicity'. There are coefficients of strong, semi-strong (semi-weak) and weak monotonicity. This coefficient varies between −1 and +1. When the coefficient is designated as $\mu2$, then $\mu2 = +1$ implies a fully monotone relationship with positive or rising trend; and $\mu2 = -1$ implies a fully monotone relationship which is of negative or descending trend. The MONCO may be calculated using the HUDAP and the resulting matrix may be imported into the SSA module of the program (Amar 2005: 117).

5 SSA maps of other dimensionalities were generated, but were less effective in showing the structure of the data, or else required higher dimensionality. For reasons of space they are not shown here.

6 The two symbols 'Jewish State' and 'State of Israel' have slightly different connotations: the former indicates a more general concept of a Jewish nation, while the latter represents more specifically the modern political entity.

7 The symbol 'God' is in the 'Israel' region and not, as might be expected, with the religion-related symbols. Similarly, it might be expected that 'Shoah' would be with other symbols of peoplehood. It should be emphasized that the respondents are still in early adolescence. Their reactions to the symbols are likely to differ from those anticipated by adults. They are still developing understandings of the concepts alluded to by the symbols. There are other reasons to which the 'misplacement' of these items or 'noise' in the map may be attributed.

8 A preliminary POSAC was conducted using all the symbols. It was found that almost each participant had a distinctive profile: 690 different profiles among 693 individuals (38 of the 731 campers did not fully answer the questionnaire item and therefore were not considered in the analysis). This is an interesting result, highlighting the individuality of Jewish identity, but it is not helpful in developing a typology of the study population.

9 It is worth noting that in several experimental POSACs conducted with larger numbers of symbols, freedom and Torah consistently emerged as the most effective for discriminating between profiles, and therefore the symbols to be used as axes. This repeated verification of the result is very strong.

10 The reduction from six variables (the six symbols) to two inevitably results in some error in the partial order.

11 These profiles are mirror images of each other:

Table 2.6.4 Mirror image profiles

	Star of David	History	Freedom	Torah study	Jerusalem	Equality
Profile 20	1	1	0	0	1	1
Profile 46	0	0	1	1	0	0

References

Amar, R., 2005. *HUDAP Manual*. Hebrew University, Jerusalem. www.facet-theory.org/files/HUDAP%20Manual.pdf.

Baylor Institute for Studies of Religion, 2006. *American Piety in the 21st Century: new insights to the depth and complexity of religion in the US*. Baylor University, Waco, TX.

Bohm, J. and Alison, L., 2001. An exploratory study in methods of distinguishing destructive cults. *Psychology, Crime & Law* 7: 133–65.

Borg, I., 1990. *Principles of Facet Theory*. Paper for the workshop on Facet Theory at the Second International Conference on Work Values, Prague.

Borg, I. and Groenen, P., 1997. *Modern Multidimensional Scaling: theory and applications*. New York, Springer.

Brown, L. and Forgas, J., 1980. The structure of religion: a multi-dimensional scaling of informal elements. *Journal for the Scientific Study of Religion* 19 (4): 423–31.

Cohen, A., 2003. The identification of underlying dimensionality in social sciences: differences between Factor Analysis and Smallest Space Analysis. In: Levy, S. and Elizur, D. (eds), *Facet Theory: towards cumulative social science*. University of Ljubljana, Ljubljana, Slovenia, pp. 61–71.

Cohen, E.H. 2003. Tourism and religion: a case study of visiting students in Israel. *Journal of Travel Research* 42 (1): 36–47.

—— 2004. Components and symbols of ethnic identity: a case study in informal education and identity formation in Diaspora. *Applied Psychology: An International Review* 53 (1): 87–112.

—— 2005. Towards a typology of values: application of the facet theory to the study of French Jews. In: Bilsky, W. and Elizur, D. (eds), *Facet Theory: design, analysis and applications*. FTA, Rome, pp. 263–73.

—— 2008a. *Youth Tourism to Israel: educational experiences of the diaspora*. Channel View Publications, Clevedon, UK.

—— 2008b. Symbols of Diaspora Jewish identity: an international survey and multi-dimensional analysis. *Religion* 38(4): 293–304.

—— 2009a. *Facet Theory Bibliography*. Jerusalem. Online www.facet-theory.org/files/wordocs/Bibliography2009.pdf (retrieved 23 February 2010).

—— 2009b. Particularistic education, endogamy, and educational tourism to homeland: an exploratory multidimensional analysis of Jewish diaspora social indicators. *Contemporary Jewry* 29 (2): 169–89.

—— forthcoming. Jewish literacy: towards a multiple model. In: Rich, Y., Katz, Y., Mevarech, Z. and Ohayon, S. (eds), *Perspectives on Jewish Literacy and Education*.

Cohen, E.H. and Amar, R., 2002. External variables as points in Smallest Space Analysis: a theoretical, mathematical and computer-based contribution. *Bulletin de Méthodologie Sociologique* 75: 40–56.

Cohen, E.H. and Bar Shalom, Y., 2006. Jewish youth in Texas: towards a multi-methodological approach to minority identity. *Religious Education* 101 (1): 40–59.

Cohen, E.H. and Werczberger, R. 2009. Jewish normativity: an explorative study. In Elizur, D. and Yaniv, E. (eds), *Theory Construction and Multivariate Analysis: applications of facet approach*. FTA Publications, pp. 35–48.

Cohen, S., 2005. Engaging the next generation of American Jews: distinguishing the in-married, inter-married and non-married. *Journal of Jewish Communal Service* 31 (1–2): 43–52.

Cohen, S. and Horenczyk, G. (eds), 1999. *National Variations in Jewish Identity: implications for Jewish education*. State University of New York Press, New York.

Duriez, B., Fontaine, J. and Hutsebaut, D., 2000. A further elaboration of the post-critical belief scale: evidence for the existence of four different approaches to religion in Flanders-Belgium. *Psychologica Belgica* 40 (3): 153–82.

Fontaine, J., Duriez, B., Luyten, P., Corveleyn, J. and Hutsebaut, D., 2005. Consequences of a multi-dimensional approach to religion for the relationship between religiosity and value priorities. *International Journal for the Psychology of Religion* 14 (2): 123–43.

Gallup International, 2006. *Voice of the People: what the world thinks on today's global issues*. Gallup International Association, Zurich, Switzerland.

Gans, H., 1994. Symbolic ethnicity and symbolic religiosity: towards a comparison of ethnic and religious acculturation. *Ethnic and Racial Studies* 17: 577–92.

Gitelman, Z., Kosmin, B. and Kovács, A. (eds), 2003. *New Jewish Identities: contemporary Europe and beyond*. Central European University Press, New York.

Guttman, L., 1968. A general nonmetric technique for finding the smallest co-ordinate space for a configuration of points. *Psychometrika* 33: 469–506.

—— 1986. Coefficients of polytonicity and monotonicity. In: Kotz, S., Johnson, N. and Read, C. (eds), *Encyclopedia of Statistical Sciences, Vol. 7.* John Wiley and Sons, New York, pp. 80–87.

—— 1992. The irrelevance of factor analysis for the study of group differences. *Multivariate Behavioral Research* 27 (2), 175–204.

—— 1994. Personal history of the development of scale analysis. In Levy, S. (ed.), *Louis Guttman on Theory and Methodology: selected writings.* Dartmouth Publishing Co., Aldershot, Hampshire, pp. 203–10.

Hall, T. and Edwards, K., 1996. The initial development and factor analysis of the spiritual assessment inventory. *Journal of Psychology and Theology* 24: 233–46.

Heilman, S., 1992. *Jewish unity and diversity: a survey of American rabbis and rabbinical students.* American Jewish Committee, New York.

Hood, Jr, R.W., Ghorbani, N., Watson, P.J., Ghramaleki, A.F., Bing, M.N., Davison, H.K., Morris, R.J. and Williamson, W.P., 2001. Dimensions of the mysticism scale: confirming the three-factor structure in the United States and Iran. *Journal for the Scientific Study of Religion* 40 (4): 691–705.

Huismans, S., 2003. A facet analysis of religiosity. In Levy, S. and Elizur, D. (eds), *Facet Theory: towards cumulative social science.* University of Ljubljana, Ljubljana, pp. 241–50.

Inglehart, R., 2004. *Human Beliefs and Values: a cross-cultural sourcebook based on the 1999–2002 values surveys.* Siglo XXI, Mexico.

Laumann, E., 1969. The social structure of religious and ethnoreligious groups in a metropolitan community. *American Sociological Review* 34 (2): 182–97.

Lazerwitz, B., 1998. *Jewish Choices: American Jewish denominationalism.* State University of New York Press, Albany, NY.

Levy, S., 2005. Guttman, Louis. In: Kempf-Leonard, K. (ed.), *Encyclopedia of Social Measurement, volume 2.* Elsevier, Amsterdam, pp. 175–88.

—— 1985. *Components of Jewish Identity as Motivators for Jewish Identification among Jewish Youth and Adults in Israel in the Period 1967–1982.* Thesis for degree of Doctor of Philosophy Hebrew University.

Levy, S. and Guttman, L., 1994. The partial-order of thyroid cancer with the prognosis of survival. In Levy, S. (ed.), *Louis Guttman on Theory and Methodology: selected writings.* Aldershot, Hampshire, England: Dartmouth Publishing Co., pp. 253–64.

Levy, S., Levinsohn, H. and Katz, E., 1993. *Beliefs, Observances and Social Interaction among Israeli Jews.* The Louis Guttman Israel Institute of Applied Social Research, Jerusalem.

—— 2000. *A Portrait of Israeli Jewry: highlights from an in-depth study.* Guttman Center of the Israel Democracy Institute and the AVI CHAI Foundation, Jerusalem.

—— 2004. The many faces of Jewishness in Israel. In: Rebhun, U. and Waxman, C. (eds), *Jews in Israel: contemporary social and cultural patterns.* Brandeis University Press, Hanover, pp. 265–84.

Maraun, M., 1997. Appearance and reality: is the big five the structure of trait descriptors? *Personality and Individual Differences* 22 (5): 629–47.

Marsden, P. and Laumann, E., 1978. The social structure of religious groups: a replication and methodological critique. In: Shye, S. (ed.), *Theory Construction and Data Analysis in the Behavioral Sciences.* Jossey-Bass, San Francisco, pp. 81–111.

Maslovaty, N., Marshall, A. and Alkin, M., 2001. Teachers' perceptions structured through facet theory: smallest space analysis versus factor analysis. *Educational and Psychological Measurement* 61(1): 71–84.

Moaddel, M., (ed.) 2007. *Values and Perceptions of the Islamic and Middle Eastern Publics.* Palgrave Macmillan, New York.

NJPS, 2003. *The National Jewish Population Survey 2000–01: strength, challenge and diversity in the American Jewish population.* United Jewish Communities and North American Jewish Data Bank, New York.

Pew, 2006. *Spirit and Power: a 10-country survey of Pentecostals.* Pew Research Center, Washington, DC.

—— 2008. *U.S. Religious Landscape Survey.* Pew Research Center, Washington, DC.

Rebhun, U., 2004. Jewish identity in America: structural analysis of attitudes and behaviors. *Review of Religious Research* 46 (1): 43–63.

Rebhun, U. and Levy, S., 2006. Unity and diversity: Jewish identification in America and Israel 1990–2000. *Sociology of Religion* 67 (4): 391–414.

Roccas, S. and Schwartz, S., 1997. Church-state relations and the association of religiosity with values: a study of Catholics in six countries. *Cross-Cultural Research* 31: 356–75.

Schoenfeld, S., 1993. The significance of the social aspects of bar/bat mitzvah. In: Leneman, H. (ed.), *Bar/Bat Mitzvah Education: a sourcebook*. ARE Publishing, Denver, CO, pp. 325–38.

—— 1994. Recent publications on bar/bat mitzvah: their implications for Jewish education research and practice. *Religious Education* 89 (4): 594–605.

Schwartz, S. and Bilsky, W., 1987. Toward a universal psychological structure of human values. *Journal of Personality and Social Psychology* 53 (3): 550–62.

—— 1990. Toward a theory of the universal content and structure of values: extensions and cross-cultural replications. *Journal of Personality and Social Psychology* 58: 878–91.

Schwartz, S. and Huismans, S., 1995. Value priorities and religiosity in four Western religions. *Social Psychology Quarterly* 58 (2): 88–107.

Shye, S., 1978. *Theory Construction and Data Analysis in the Behavioral Sciences*. Jossey-Bass Publishers, San Francisco.

Sinclair, J. and Milner, D., 2005. On being Jewish: a qualitative study of identity among British Jews in emerging adulthood. *Journal of Adolescent Research* 20: 91–117.

Sorenson, R., 1997. Doctoral students' integration of psychology and Christianity: perspectives via attachment theory and multidimensional scaling. *Journal for the Scientific Study of Religion* 36 (4): 530–48.

Tiliopoulos, N., Bikker, A., Coxon, A. and Hawkin, P., 2007. The means and ends of religiosity: a fresh look at Gordon Allport's religious orientation dimension. *Personality and Individual Differences* 42 (8): 1609–20.

Tilley, T., 1995. *The Wisdom of Religious Commitment*. Georgetown University Press, Washington, DC.

Tos, N., Mohler, P. and Malnar, B., (eds), 1999. *Modern Society and Values: a comparative analysis based on ISSP project*. University of Ljubljana and ZUMA, Ljubljana.

Wasserman, M., 2008. The far side of freedom: Torah and autonomy. *Modern Judaism* 28 (1): 41–63.

Wettstein, H. (ed.), 2002. *Diasporas and Exiles: varieties of Jewish identity*. University of California Press, Berkeley, CA.

Wiley, J. and Levi-Martin, J., 1999. Algebraic representations of beliefs and attitudes: partial order models for item responses. *Sociological Methodology* 29: 113–46.

Wulff, D., 1997. *Psychology of Religion: classic and contemporary*. 2nd edn. Wiley and Sons, New York.

Yeatts, J. and Asher, W., 1982. Factor analysis of religious variables: some methodological considerations. *Review of Religious Research* 24 (1): 49–54.

Young, F. and Haber, R. (eds), 1987. *Multidimensional Scaling: history, theory and applications*. L. Erlbaum Associates, Hillsdale, NJ.

Further reading

Amar, R., 2005. *HUDAP Manual*. Hebrew University, Jerusalem. www.facet-theory.org/files/HUDAP%20Manual.pdf.

This highly accessible manual provides step-by-step instructions for using the HUDAP package.

Canter, D. (ed.), 1985. *Facet Theory: Approaches to Social Research*. Springer Verlag, New York.

A basic text on use of FT in social research.

Cohen, E.H., 2009. Facet Theory Bibliography. Jerusalem. Online www.facet-theory.org/files/wordocs/Bibliography2009.pdf.

This comprehensive bibliography enables students and researchers to find virtually any publication using FT in a wide variety of fields.

Levy, S. (ed.), 1994. *Louis Guttman on Theory and Methodology: Selected Writings*. Aldershot, Hampshire, England: Dartmouth Publishing Co.

An excellent compilation of the scientific contributions of Louis Guttman published throughout his long career, and covering all the major areas of facet theory.

Key concepts

Element: a potential, measurable variable. The elements in a facet should be exclusive.

External variables: a method which may be used for comparing sub-populations within the structural context of an SSA map. External variables are plotted according to their correlation with the set of primary variables.

Facet: a set of conceptually related variables. Each facet in the mapping sentence is one way of classifying the research issues. Each facet contains a number of elements.

Facet theory: a systematic approach to theory construction, research design and data analysis. The FT approach provides a rationale for a hypothesis of a correspondence between a definitional framework and an aspect of the empirical data.

Mapping sentence: a definitional framework for articulating various aspects (facets) of the subject under study and the relations between them.

Partial Order: In a set which includes both comparable and incomparable profiles, the order among them is *partial*.

Partial Order Scalogram Analysis with base Coordinates (POSAC): a data analysis tool which preserves as accurately as possible the partial order of a set of profiles in as few dimensions as possible (usually two). The POSAC graphically portrays the profiles as points in a space.

Regionality hypothesis: for each element of the facet being considered, there will be a specific and contiguous region in a geometric representation (SSA map) of the variables analyzed.

Smallest Space Analysis (SSA): a data analysis tool which graphically portrays the structure of data by plotting a set of variables in a cognitive map ('smallest space') according to their correlations.

Related chapters

- ◆ Chapter 1.2 Comparison
- ◆ Chapter 1.3 Epistemology
- ◆ Chapter 1.5 Research design
- ◆ Chapter 2.18 Structuralism
- ◆ Chapter 2.20 Surveys and questionnaires

2.7

FACTOR ANALYSIS

Kendal C. Boyd

Chapter summary

- Factor analysis summarizes complex statistical relationships among variables as an aid to conceptualization. Exploratory factor analysis is particularly helpful in developing scales and subscales.
- A factor is an important, but hidden construct that causes items we can observe to co-vary. Factor analysis shows which items belong together in important dimensions, and which items do not belong together.
- When extracting factors from items, the principal axis method is most appropriate because it assumes the items have error. The principal components method assumes there is little error among the items, which is usually not warranted.
- The number of factors to extract is an important decision, and the salient loadings criterion is a good method for determining how many factors to extract. The scree test is also an acceptable method. The eigenvalues greater-than-one method is the default method in most statistical software, but should never be used.
- The factor loadings table (Table 2.7.4) displays the relationships between the items and the factors. Factor loadings are usually correlation coefficients and can be positive or negative.
- The further a loading is from zero, the stronger the loading, and the more one can generalize from the factor to the item.
- When multiple factors are extracted, they should be rotated. If they are relatively uncorrelated, varimax is the best rotation, which forces factors to be uncorrelated; if factors are substantially correlated, promax is the best rotation, which allows factor to be correlated.
- If the factors are substantially correlated, there is likely a hierarchical factor structure, with one or more higher order factors. The hierarchical factor structure can be explored by saving the primary promax factors as variables and then factoring them in the same manner in which the items were factored.
- Scales and subscales can be reliably constructed using the factor loadings table.

The goal of **factor analysis** 'is to summarize the interrelationships among the variables in a concise but accurate manner as an aid in conceptualization' (Gorsuch 1983: 2). There is an assumption that there are important, but hidden, constructs (**factors**) causing these relation-ships. A psychotherapist can observe a client looking restless and acting irritably, hear her complain that she is easily fatigued, that she is not sleeping well and she cannot concentrate. These symptoms commonly co–occur in some clients, but psychotherapists do not say that one symptom is causing the others. Instead, they say that there is a hidden, but important thing called anxiety that is producing all of them. Here anxiety is the unseen factor that is causing the things we can actually observe, the items, to correlate.

A small group of observable variables, say three, are not difficult to conceptualize. Here are only three relationships to track. The researcher might notice that the first and last vari-able tend to co–occur, or co–vary, but the middle one seems to have its own pattern. However, add another variable and there are six relationships, or correlations; seven variables create 21 correlations; ten variables create 45 correlations, and so on. The human mind has difficulty tracking such complexity.

Statistically, factor analysis works with a correlation (covariance) matrix of all the variables, and when several variables are found to be associated, the method groups them together. Put simply, factor analysis first looks for the largest cluster of covariance between multiple variables and extracts this as the manifestation of the first factor; it next looks for the largest remaining cluster of covariance and extracts this as the manifestation of the second factor, and so on.

To travel even further afield from the statistics, imagine the variable correlation matrix to be an orange, and the covariance between the variables to be the juice in the orange. Each time the method extracts a factor it is like squeezing the orange. The juice that you get with each squeeze is less than the last, and after half a dozen or so squeezes you stop. You could always get a little more juice out, but it is a trivial amount. Since most of what is left is either bitter or flavorless, you throw it away.

It is similar with factor analysis in that the variable correlation matrix contains the variance for which the researcher is looking, trivial variance and error variance. Our under-standing of psychosocial-spiritual phenomena is never complete and we have problems with reliable measurement of it, so we compensate for this by creating multiple items that each measure a small, limited part of the phenomenon. Psychosocial researchers know their vari-ables contain error, so they are only interested in the squeezes that get the major covariance out of the matrix and discard the rest as either trivial or error. A theory that has been constructed with the use of factor analysis will be clearer than the starting idea; a theory is meant to be broadly accurate and factor analysis is very good at summarizing the major themes in the data (Gorsuch 1983).

The orange analogy quickly breaks down because each factor would be a different flavor of juice. A 'factor represents an area of generalization that is qualitatively distinct from an area represented by any other factor' (Gorsuch 1983: 2).

Uses of factor analysis

Factor analysis has three major uses. One is to search through variables for possible dimen-sions and calculate how these are related to each other. This is the general role of **exploratory factor analysis** and it is particularly useful when the amount of data to consider is vast. This is essentially a theory-building endeavor.

The second major use, which will be the focus of this chapter, is an extension of the first: using exploratory factor analysis in scale and subscale development. Factor analysis yields the best results when using reliable variables with good variance, such as subtest scores from intel-ligence tests. Questionnaire, or scale, **items** have lower reliability with limited variance.

Typically, these are statements ('I am interested in factor analysis') with a response scale that ranges from two to seven categories (such as disagree/unsure/agree, with graduated qualifiers for strength of agreement or disagreement). The limited response scale reduces the variance. Because respondents interpret items differently when they read them, item reliability is usually lower compared to most variables. Researchers make up for this by creating multiple, sometimes many, items to better measure the area in which they are interested. In spite of item limitations, exploratory factor analysis has built a long and successful history of analyzing items for developing scales.

The third major use is when a theorist judges that she understands her area well and makes a hypothesis regarding how the variables or items will group themselves in factors. After she collects data, she tests it to see how well it fits her hypothesis. This is **confirmatory factor analysis**. Readers interested in this analysis should consult other texts, such as Brown (2006).

Factor analysis in religious studies

Factor analysis has long been used in the scientific study of religion. For example, almost eight decades ago, factor analysis was used to analyze students' attitudes about God and religion (Carlson 1934), and during World War II it was employed when studying personality traits of seminarians (McCarthy 1942). Some notable psychology of religion factor analytic studies have involved people's God concept (Gorsuch 1968), religious orientation (Gorsuch and McPherson 1989), religious coping (Pargament *et al.* 2000) and religious schemas (Streib *et al.* 2010).

Allport and Ross (1967) first scientifically investigated the concept of religious orientation, or one's motivation for being religious. Later several religious orientation scales were developed, notably intrinsic, extrinsic (Feagin 1964; Allport and Ross 1967; Gorsuch and McPherson 1989) and quest (Batson and Schoenrade 1991). Religious orientation theory holds that intrinsically religious people are so because they value it for its own sake. Extrinsically religious people are religious because of either its social rewards or personal comfort. People of the quest orientation turn to religion because they are seeking universal wisdom or answers to life's existential questions. After examining the factor analyses in the Batson and Schoenrade study, three-item scales were created for the intrinsic, extrinsic-social and quest religious orientations (Gorsuch and McPherson 1989; Batson and Schoenrade 1991). A typical intrinsic item is 'I try hard to live my life according to my religious beliefs', an extrinsic-social item is 'I go to my place of worship mostly to spend time with my friends', and 'I am constantly questioning my religious beliefs' is a quest item. Religious orientation items will be used in the first factor analytic example used below.

Pargament used factor analysis in developing his religious coping scale (RCOPE), a commonly used instrument for measuring religious coping with stressful situations (Pargament *et al.* 1990; Pargament *et al.* 1992). Negative life events require coping strategies and religion is often utilized for this purpose. Pargament developed items, such as 'I saw the situation as part of God's plan', 'I tried to make sense of the situation without relying on God', and 'I did my best and then turned the situation over to God'. Using factor analysis, 21 religious coping factors were found and grouped into five main dimensions, such as using religion to find meaning, or to gain control (Pargament *et al.* 2000).

Exploratory factor analysis is a method that is included in most statistical software to which researchers have access, but there are some important decisions that a factor analyst has to make in the process. The remainder of the chapter will work through some prominent decisions using religious orientation and religious coping items filled out by a group of 90 chronic pain patients recruited at an outpatient rheumatology clinic. The sample is composed of 52 rheumatoid arthritis patients and 38 fibromyalgia patients. The average age was 49 years and all but five of the patients were women. The software in the examples is SPSS (2007).

Factor extraction

The first major factor analysis choice is the method of **extraction**, or the statistical process by which factors are derived from the item correlation matrix, shown in Table 2.7.1. The default method in SPSS is **principal components**. A component may be conceptualized similarly to a factor but the statistical method by which components are derived assumes there is little error in the variables and seeks to reproduce all the item variance in the extracted components (Gorsuch 1990). This is particularly inappropriate for items because of their lower reliability. **Principal axis factoring** is preferred because it focuses on the major variance and assumes that what is left is mostly error (Gorsuch 1990).

Number of factors

Perhaps the most important decision is how many factors to extract from the items. With these data this is not in doubt because the items were selected to form three factors, but often a researcher constructs items and then looks to see how many factors emerge. There are problems with extracting too many or too few (Wood *et al.* 1996). Some factor analysts use a subjective procedure, extracting multiple numbers of factors, examining the factor loadings tables and picking the factor number that yields the most intuitive results. One advantage to this approach is that it is probably not useful to extract factors that do not make sense to researchers who know the area, but it would be better to use a more objective procedure.

With the religious orientation and RCOPE data the number of factors is not particularly in doubt because theory and previous studies were used to select items that would most likely form three factors. However, it is often the case that the researcher constructs items and is not sure how many factors will emerge and working through some number of factors criterion in these simple data sets will illustrate procedures that will also be effective on more complex data where the number of factors is initially unknown to the researcher.

Eigenvalues greater than one criterion

The default procedure in SPSS is to extract all factors that have **eigenvalues greater than one**. **Eigenvalues** are calculated in the extraction process using matrix algebra (Gorsuch 1983), and they are a measure of the variance accounted for by a factor, relative to all possible factors. If all the eigenvalues are summed, they will equal the number of items in the analysis. The eigenvalues for the religious orientation items can be seen in Table 2.7.2. The eigenvalues greater than one criterion would say to extract three factors. However, this criterion is only accurate by chance of the ratio of number of items to factors, such as three-to-five items per factor in large samples, *and should never be used* (Gorsuch 1983; Zwick and Velicer 1986; Cliff 1988), despite the fact it happened to work in these items!

Table 2.7.1 Correlation matrix of religious orientation items

	Spend time with my friends	Helps me make friends	Enjoy seeing people	Live according to beliefs	Whole approach religion	Spend time in prayer	I value my religious doubts	Constantly questioning beliefs	Rethink religious convictions
I go to my place of worship mostly to spend time with my friends.	–								
I go to my place of worship mainly because it helps me make friends.	.65	–							
I go to my place of worship mainly because I enjoy seeing people I know there.	.59	.27	–						
I try hard to live my life according to my religious beliefs.	.01	.06	.14	–					
My whole approach to life is based on my religion.	–.18	.03	–.08	.52	–				
It is important to me to spend time in private thought and prayer.	.10	.12	.27	.46	.42	–			
It might be said that I value my religious doubts and uncertainties.	.01	.03	.04	–.14	–.13	.19	–		
I am constantly questioning my religious beliefs.	.01	.04	–.03	–.07	–.04	.17	.59	–	
My life experiences have led me to rethink my religious convictions.	.20	.11	.04	–.28	–.21	.00	.23	.23	–

Table 2.7.2 Eigenvalues[1] for the religious orientation items

Factor	Eigenvalue	% of variance	Cumulative %
1	2.188	24.3	24.3
2	2.085	23.2	47.5
3	1.680	18.7	66.2
4	0.823	9.1	75.3
5	0.759	8.4	83.7
6	0.461	5.1	88.8
7	0.412	4.6	93.4
8	0.371	4.1	97.5
9	0.221	2.5	100.0
Sum	9.000	100.0	

[1] Each eigenvalue includes variance from all items in the factor analysis, not just one, although often it is defined by one item more strongly than the others.

Scree test criterion

A better use of the eigenvalues is to graph them and do a **scree test** (Cattell and Vogelmann 1977). It is so named because it reportedly reminded the scree test's originator, Raymond B. Cattell, of the cliffs of Dover in his native England. The graphs often look like a sharp cliff, followed by some rubble, and then a gradual gentle slope down to the English Channel. The smooth gradual slope represents random variance, so the scree test's objective is to establish this line distinguishing between random and non-random variance; all eigenvalues above this line have the variance for which the researcher is looking. A straight edge should be used in this process and the line should run through as many points on the graph as possible, although it is permissible for there to be a few points scattered slightly above or below the line (Cattell 1978). The scree plot for these items is shown in Figure 2.7.1. I have drawn in a dashed line on the graph where I would establish the slope of random variance, with three eigenvalues above the line. This last sentence highlights the problem with the scree test. It is not always obvious where the line should be established and another researcher might have drawn it lower so that there were five factors above the line. Despite the occasional subjectivity, the scree test is accurate most of the time and is vastly better than the eigenvalues greater than one criterion (Cattell and Vogelmann 1977; Zwick and Velicer 1986).

The three principal axis factors are shown in Table 2.7.3. However, the term **factor loading** needs to be defined to understand the table. A factor loading is the measure of the degree of generalizability between each item and each factor; the farther the factor loading is from 0, the stronger the loading, and the more one can generalize from that factor to the item. Loadings are usually correlations that range from −1 to +1.

The items that load highly on each factor are shaded in Table 2.7.3. A good procedure is to sort the rows of the factor loadings table, note which items load strongest on a factor and then give the factor a name that is consistent with the highest loading items. The items that load highly on the first factor in Figure 2.7.1 contain the idea that people are religious primarily for social reasons, and the label of extrinsic social seems a reasonable fit to the items.

The factor loadings generally conform to the three scales they were thought to form. One item that did not load highly on any of the factors was the last Quest item. If this short scale was used in other research studies, that item should likely be dropped.

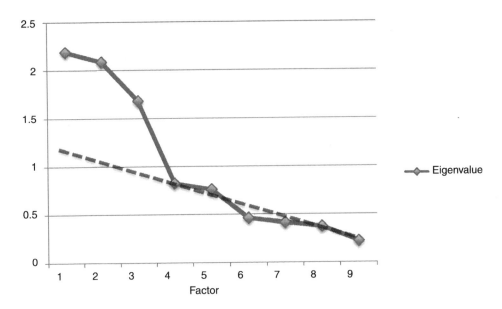

Figure 2.7.1 Scree plot of religious orientation eigenvalues, with line of random variance

Table 2.7.3 Religious orientation items factor structure

Items	Extrinsic Social	Intrinsic	Quest
I go to my place of worship mostly to spend time with my friends (ExS1)	.94	−.11	.02
I go to my place of worship mainly because it helps me to make friends (ExS2)	.61	.03	.04
I go to my place of worship mainly because I enjoy seeing people I know there (ExS3)	.60	.11	.02
I try hard to live my life according to my religious beliefs (Int1)	.08	.74	−.15
My whole approach to life is based on my religion (Int2)	−.11	.69	−.11
It is important to me to spend time in private thought and prayer (Int3)	.20	.65	.25
It might be said that I value my religious doubts and uncertainties (Que1)	.00	−.03	.77
I am constantly questioning my religious beliefs (Que2)	−.02	.03	.73
My life experiences have led me to rethink my religious convictions (Que3)	.16	−.25	.33

Principal axis extraction with varimax rotation. Coefficient alphas: Extrinsic Social = .74; Intrinsic = .72; Quest = .74.

Salient loadings criterion

A **salient loading** is an item's loading on a factor that is markedly stronger than on any other factor. There is no agreed-upon benchmark as to how strong an item should load on a factor to be considered part of it, but .40 is commonly used. In Table 2.7.4, all the shaded loadings are above .40 and are markedly stronger than the items' loadings on the other factors.

'Markedly stronger' could be defined with various standards. When trying to create a workable standard, a survey of published factor analyses found that a typical *N* was 200. The 95 per cent lower confidence interval for a loading of .40 at that *N* is .277, so 'markedly stronger' may (somewhat clumsily) be defined as being at least .13 stronger. This standard is too low in smaller samples, and too high in larger samples or with stronger loadings; however, experience has shown that it works fine as a rule.

Therefore, a salient loading may be reasonably defined as being .40 or stronger, and being at least .13 stronger than any of the item's other factor loadings. If the first part is met, but not the second, the item is said to be **cross-loaded**, or to be strongly related to more than one factor. With these definitions set, another number of factors criterion can be introduced, the **salient loadings criterion**. The author and Richard Gorsuch developed it as an adaptation of a previous, less formal guideline that he calls Wrigley's criterion (Wrigley 1960; Howard and Gordon 1963).

A significant factor has:

- At least three variables that load highest on it at .40 or greater.
- Alternatively, at least two variables that load highest on it at .50 or greater.
- Alternatively, at least one variable that loads highest on it at .60 or greater.
- In addition, none of the above loadings may have cross-loadings nearer than .13.
- A trivial factor does not have at least one, two or three variables that load highest on it at the required level without being negated by cross-loadings nearer than .13.
- More factors are extracted than will likely be kept; the scree criterion plus approximately 50 per cent more often gives a safe starting point.
- The factors are rotated to varimax (described below) and the rotated factor matrix table is inspected for trivial factors.
- If any trivial factors are noted, then the factor number is reduced by one and the process is repeated until there are no trivial factors; this is the indicated number of factors.
- Scale-builder's addendum: for a factor to be significant, its salient items must also form a scale with a Cronbach's alpha of $\geq$ .60.

This process is made easier by selecting the software option to sort the loadings table by size, and an additional option to have loadings less than .25 suppressed. Usually the last factor is the weakest. In a sorted table, these loadings will be in the bottom right-hand corner. To save time, initially investigate the last factor. If it is significant, move up the diagonal of the table checking the next-to-last factor, and so on. If this eventually leads to the extraction of a single factor, make sure to select the software option to display the unrotated factor solution. The scale-builder's addendum signifies a factor's items form a scale that is reliable enough for research or might easily be developed into such.

The salient loadings criterion is objective, simple and has proved quite accurate to date. In my studies where the number of factors was known beforehand because it was either programmed into simulated data, or the data was a normative sample of a well-established scale where there was no serious debate as to the number of factors, the salient loadings criterion performed very well. An additional selling point here is that it was developed with items in mind.

For the religious orientation items the salient loadings criterion indicated three factors should be extracted. In addition, when the salient items of the factors were added together, each of the three scales' reliability met the scale-builders addendum, seen in the note to Table 2.7.4.

Factor rotation

A factor analyst's third major decision is which factor **rotation** to use so that the item variance is appropriately spread across the factors. The SPSS default is no factor rotation, which is correct when a single factor is extracted. When more than one factor is extracted, the first factor is a general factor and often contains more than its fair share of the item variance. Statistical rotation is important to redistribute this variance. Figure 2.7.2 shows the religious orientation data graphed with the three factor vectors in space represented by arrows. The term 'rotation' comes from the fact that the factor vectors can be rotated about their point of origin to better fit the data. Originally, this was done with geometric calculations (Gorsuch, personal communication, 31 March 2011). Computer software programs now do this very simply and effectively.

The real question is whether to use a rotation that allows the factors to be correlated, such as **promax**, or one that forces them to be uncorrelated, such as **varimax**. The answer is to use the one that best fits the data. Sometimes the factors will be naturally related, and sometimes not. A pragmatic approach is to use promax to check the correlation(s) between the factors, and if the average correlation is below .30, end by using varimax because the factors are only weakly related and varimax will produce clearer results. However, if the factor correlations are high, stay with promax because using varimax will distort the factor structure. SPSS produces a factor correlation matrix in the promax factor analysis output; use the absolute value of the correlation before calculating the average. The average absolute value of the religious orientation factor correlation was only .05, so varimax rotation was used when extracting the three factors shown in Figure 2.7.1 and Figure 2.7.2, where it can be seen that the items generally cluster around the three rotated factors.

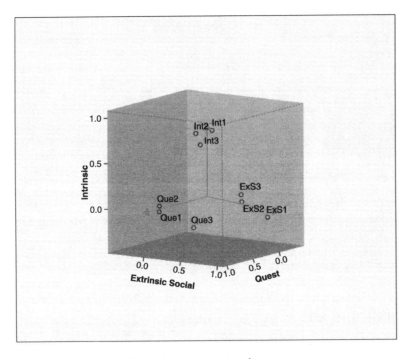

Figure 2.7.2 Religious orientation factors in varimax-rotated space

The religious orientation factors were essentially uncorrelated. When factors have substantial correlations, the process requires a few extra steps. The next example uses three short forms of the RCOPE (Pargament *et al.* 2000).

The salient loadings criterion indicated three factors, and the factor items added together formed reliable scales, shown in Table 2.7.4. The average promax factor correlation was .38. If the factors are substantially correlated, averaging above .30, there is probably a hierarchical structure to the factors with multiple **primary** factors and fewer **secondary**, or **higher order**, factors. The easiest process of performing a higher order factor analysis is to first do a primary factor analysis with promax rotation and have the software save the factors as new variables using a regression method. A new factor analysis is then done using these new variables; in other words, the researcher simply factors the primary factors. The salient loadings criterion has been shown to be accurate at this level, too. At times there can even be a tertiary level to the factors. Whatever the number of levels, when the process ends with a single, topmost factor, it is often called the **general factor**. A general religious coping factor from these data is also shown in Table 2.7.4.

Also of note in Table 2.7.4 is an item included that was not part of the RCOPE, the respondents' level of pain severity. This is conceptually different to the RCOPE factors and this is reflected in the factor loadings for this item. It does not load saliently on any of the factors. It was included in the analysis to demonstrate this point: exploratory factor analyses

Table 2.7.4 Religious coping promax factor loadings

| Items | Factors | | | |
| | Primary | | | Secondary |
	Active religious surrender	Self-directed religious coping	Benevolent religious reappraisal	General religious coping
Did what I could and put the rest in God's hands	.95	−.48	.47	.93
Did my best and then turned the situation over to God	.93	−.42	.44	.89
Took control over what I could, and gave the rest up to God	.89	−.36	.40	.83
Tried to make sense of the situation without relying on God	−.42	.95	−.27	−.63
Made decisions about what to do without God's help	−.38	.88	−.18	−.56
Tried to deal with my feelings without God's help	−.40	.86	−.23	−.58
Tried to find a lesson from God in the event	.38	−.23	.92	.60
Tried to see how God might be trying to strengthen me in this situation	.52	−.30	.87	.70
Saw my situation as part of God's plan	.36	−.15	.83	.54
Pain over the past week	.12	−.06	.12	.13

Principal axis extraction with promax rotation. Coefficient alphas: active religious surrender = .95; self-directed religious coping = .92; benevolent religious appraisal = .90; general religious coping = .89.

will reveal which items belong together in important dimensions, and which items do *not* belong in any of those dimensions.

Using factor analysis to create scales

After the factor analysis, the researcher's next task is often to use the factor-loading table to create scales or subscales by adding items together. The general process is to add all the saliently loaded items for a particular factor to create a scale. If the salient loading is negative, that item needs to be first reverse-scored; for example, if the response scale is a 1–5 ordinal response scale, a 1 becomes a 5, a 2 becomes a 4, and so on. It is common to find that no further reliability development need occur afterwards.

In summary, factor analysis yields results that further develop the researcher's knowledge and theory, and has proved to be a useful tool in helping researchers understand complex relationships between multiple variables.

References

Allport, G.W. and Ross, J.M., 1967. Personal religious orientation and prejudice. *Journal of Personality and Social Psychology* 5(4): 432–43.

Batson, C.D. and Schoenrade, P.A., 1991. Measuring religion as Quest: II. reliability concerns. *Journal for the Scientific Study of Religion* 30(4): 430–47.

Brown, T.A., 2006. *Confirmatory Factor Analysis for Applied Research*. Guilford Press, New York.

Carlson, H.B., 1934. Attitudes of undergraduate students. *The Journal of Social Psychology* 5: 202–13.

Cattell, R.B., 1978. *The Scientific Use of Factor Analysis in Behavioral and Life Sciences*. Plenum Press, New York.

Cattell, R.B. and Vogelmann, S., 1977. A comprehensive trial of the scree and KG criteria for determining the number of factors. *Multivariate Behavioral Research* 12(3): 289–325.

Cliff, N., 1988. The eigenvalues-greater-than-one rule and the reliability of components. *Psychological Bulletin* 103(2): 276–79.

Feagin, J.R., 1964. Prejudice and religious types: A focused study of Southern fundamentalists. *Journal for the Scientific Study of Religion* 4(1): 3–13.

Gorsuch, R.L., 1968. The conceptualization of God as seen in adjective ratings. *Journal for the Scientific Study of Religion* 7(1): 56–64.

—— 1983. *Factor Analysis*. L. Erlbaum Associates, Hillsdale, NJ.

—— 1990. Common factor analysis versus component analysis: some well and little known facts. *Multivariate Behavioral Research* 25(1): 33–39.

Gorsuch, R.L. and McPherson, S.E., 1989. Intrinsic/extrinsic measurement: I/E-Revised and single-item scales. *Journal for the Scientific Study of Religion* 28(3): 348–54.

Howard, K.I. and Gordon, R.A., 1963. Empirical note on the 'number of factors' problem in factor analysis. *Psychological Reports* 12(1): 247–50.

McCarthy, T.J., 1942. Personality traits of seminarians. *Studies in Psychology & Psychiatry from the Catholic University of America* 5(4): 46.

Pargament, K.I., Ensing, D.S., Falgout, K., Olsen, H., Van Haitsma, K. and Warren, R., 1990. God help me: I. Religious coping efforts as predictors of the outcomes to significant negative life events. *American Journal of Community Psychology* 18(6): 793–824.

Pargament, K.I., Koenig, H.G. and Perez, L.M., 2000. The many methods of religious coping: development and initial validation of the RCOPE. *Journal of Clinical Psychololody* 56(4): 519–43.

Pargament, K.I., Olsen, H., Reilly, B., Falgout, K., Ensing, D.S. and Van Haitsma, K., 1992. God help me: II. the relationship of religious orientations to religious coping with negative life events. *Journal for the Scientific Study of Religion* 31(4): 504–13.

SPSS for Mac, 2007. Release 16.0.1.

Streib, H., Hood, R.W., Jr and Klein, C., 2010. The Religious Schema Scale: Construction and initial validation of a quantitative measure for religious styles. *International Journal for the Psychology of Religion* 20(3): 151–72.

Wood, J.M., Tataryn, D.J. and Gorsuch, R.L., 1996. Effects of under- and overextraction on principal axis factor analysis with varimax rotation. *Psychological Methods* 1(4): 354–65.

Wrigley, C., 1960. *A procedure for objective factor analysis*. The First Annual Conference for the Society of Multivariate Experimental Psychology.

Zwick, W.R. and Velicer, W.F., 1986. Comparison of five rules for determining the number of components to retain. *Psychological Bulletin* 99(3): 432–42.

Further reading

Cattell, R.B., 1977. *The Scientific Use of Factor Analysis in Behavioral and Life Sciences* (pp. 77–86). Plenum, New York.

Cattell developed modern exploratory factor analysis after his major professor, Charles Spearman, invented it. This chapter sets the standard for training researchers in how to read scree plots.

DeVellis, R.F., 2003. *Scale Development: theory and applications*. 2nd edn. SAGE, Thousand Oaks, CA.

This appealingly thin paperback is a helpful guide through what can be a complex area. It is a volume of the Applied Social Research Methods series and demonstrates the basic process of creating reliable and valid scales.

Gorsuch, R.L., 1983. *Factor Analysis*. 2nd edn. Lawrence Erlbaum, Hillsdale, NJ.

Gorsuch was a graduate student in Cattell's lab at the University of Illinois and was an important part of the development of factor analysis. This text remains the definitive work on exploratory factor analysis. The first chapter in particular gives an excellent conceptual introduction to the area.

—— 1988. Exploratory factor analysis. In: Nesselroade, J.R. and Cattell, R.B. (eds), *Handbook of Multivariate Experimental Psychology*. 2nd edn. Plenum, New York, pp. 231–58.

In this chapter, Gorsuch addresses other technical and theoretical matters that had arisen since the second edition of his classic text. Of particular importance is his discussion of the various paradigms that guide factor analytic decisions.

Mulaik, S.A., 2009. *Foundations of Factor Analysis*. 2nd edn. Chapman and Hall/CRC, New York.

This comprehensive text is a recent treatment of current factor analytic techniques that explains the mathematics and equations behind the method. It also describes some of the procedures and options in common statistical software applications.

O'Connor, B.P., 2000. SPSS and SAS programs for determining the number of components using parallel analysis and Velicer's MAP test. *Behavior Research Methods, Instrumentation, and Computers* 32(3): 396–402.

Parallel analysis is a number of factors criterion developed by another graduate student from Cattell's lab, John Horn. It has emerged as the best procedure for determining number of factors. It is too technical to be included in this chapter's discussion but it is an extension of the scree philosophy. O'Connor has made parallel analysis much easier to use with his SPSS and SAS syntax, free for download here: people.ok.ubc.ca/brioconn/nfactors/nfactors.html.

Key concepts

Confirmatory factor analysis: a method of creating a factor model and then testing how well the data fits the model.

Cross-loading: when an item loads strongly on two different factors.

Eigenvalues: a measure of the variance accounted for by a factor, relative to all possible factors; calculated in the extraction process.

Eigenvalues greater than one: a number of factors criterion where all factors that have eigenvalues greater than one are extracted; not recommended.

Exploratory factor analysis: a method of searching through data for possible dimensions and calculating how these are related to each other.

Extraction: the statistical process by which factors are derived from a correlation matrix.

Factor analysis: a method to accurately condense the interrelationships among multiple variables to assist in the development, testing, and application of theories; can be exploratory or confirmatory.

Factor loading: the measure of the degree of generalizability between each item and each factor; the farther the factor loading is from 0, the more one can generalize from that factor to the item.

Factors: important, but hidden variables that cause relationships between observable variables.

General factor: a broad, single factor that encompasses most of the variables or items.

Items: questionnaire or scale variables, usually of lower variance and reliability so that they are often added together to create research variables.

Primary factor: a first-level factor in a hierarchical factor structure.

Principal axis factoring: an extraction method that focuses on the major variance and assumes that what is left is mostly error; recommended for items.

Principal components: an extraction method that assumes there is high reliability in the factored variables and seeks to reproduce all the item variance in the extracted components; not recommended for items.

Promax: a factor rotation method that allows the factors to be correlated.

Rotation: a statistical procedure that spreads the item variance appropriately across the factors.

Salient loading: an item's loading on a factor that is markedly stronger than its loadings on any other factor.

Salient loadings criterion: a number of factors criterion that compares salient loadings with potential cross-loadings to define significant and trivial factors; recommended for items.

Scree test: a number of factors criterion using a graph of plotted eigenvalues; the objective is to establish the line of random variance, and all eigenvalues above this line represent significant variance.

Secondary or higher order factor: a second-level factor in a hierarchical factor structure.

Varimax: a factor rotation method that forces the factors to be uncorrelated.

Related chapters

- Chapter 1.2 Comparison
- Chapter 2.20 Surveys and questionnaires

2.8

FIELD RESEARCH

Participant observation

Graham Harvey

Chapter summary

- Fieldwork is the best approach to research about the lived reality and/or performance of religion.
- The core method of fieldwork is participant observation, sometimes supported by interviews and other qualitative methods.
- Fieldwork results in rich description of religious activities that is theoretically informed and contributes significantly to academic debate.
- The history and recent practice of fieldwork in religious studies provides examples for neophyte and experienced researchers.
- Participation, presence, reflexivity and dialogue are key themes in recent discussions of fieldwork practice.
- Fieldwork approaches to religious people and activities include gaining rapport, practicing epoché, building and maintaining empathy, paying attention, being present, recording and analyzing data, dialogue about emerging understandings, and polishing the literary and other presentations of results.

Introduction

Researchers who conduct field research seek to understand religious phenomena by participating as fully as possible while observing and reflecting on what people do. More than seeking merely to describe religious activities, they are involved in a process with rich and radical implications for scholarly engagement with religion. The ideological justification of fieldwork strongly indicates that scholars should focus most on observable activities, actual events and practice, rather than on what texts, preachers or even 'ordinary' participants assert people ought to do. While they will pay attention to people's ambitions to live up to some exalted, authoritative version of what a religion should be, it is 'what people do' that engages fieldwork researchers. They may also ask questions about religious texts and the 'tradition' that forms the model of how a religion 'should be'—but the purpose of such questions will be an attempt to better understand people's experiences and interpretations. Religion, from this perspective, is not properly understood without attention to its fully embodied, materialized, local and varying practice: its vernacular or lived reality. By implication, academic understanding is best sought by scholars who are willing and able to participate reasonably fully in the field of performance and experience that they research. By entering the 'field' of religious life, performance and community, researchers seek to contribute to academic knowledge and debate. This chapter about fieldwork research among religious people uses the subtitle 'participant observation' to draw attention to the central ways of doing fieldwork.

Field researchers may draw from a suite of methods for gaining understanding of three related but not identical complexes. The first is 'what people do', what happens when people enact religion in everyday or ceremonial life. The second is what religious participants understand, say, intend and/or value about their own religious activities (and, perhaps, those of others). The third is what researchers experience as participants and as people informed by previous scholarly work that they deem or discover to be relevant in seeking understanding. In addition to various forms of observation, field researchers might also use interviews, surveys, questionnaires, video analysis and/or a suite of other techniques to increase the value of their deep engagement with a particular group, community or practice, and their reflection on the knowledge they gain by participation.

Fieldwork is conducted with a view to producing results that are not merely accurately descriptive of circumscribed phenomena, but, more significantly, contribute to relevant academic debates in significant ways. Thus, the collection of data and information in the 'field' requires researchers to attempt to get as close as they can to the 'doing' of religion while maintaining a focus on scholarly objectives. Field researchers do not aim to write about everything that religious people do or say, nor even about all the things experienced during research. Various levels of selection are applied to seeking out, observing and considering the relevance of particular events and/or practices. Then the researcher's task is to translate observations and reflections on what happens among religious people into analyzed data of value to colleagues who need to understand them but cannot be present. In practice, this can involve different ways of recording data and then re-working it into publishable outcomes. This chapter will introduce field research, say something about practicalities and techniques, discuss some of the complexities and contests around researchers' relationships with religious practitioners, and illustrate various ways in which practices have evolved from participant observation to enrich academic knowledges and debates. It is structured in a series of layers that elaborate on similar and related points to develop familiarity with important matters.

Participating and observing

Field research in the study of religion is the practice of observing religious groups, communities or activities, sometimes for sustained periods of time, sometimes in a series of shorter visits. It entails attempting to understand as fully as possible what people do, when, where, how and (possibly) why they do it. It attends in particular to the performance of religion, in both everyday and ceremonial occasions. It is open to a wide interpretation of what might be worthy of research: it is not only about religious rituals or discourses but may attend to seemingly mundane issues that impinge on people's lives, acts and ideas. (The question of what counts as 'religion' can be quite acute but it can also provoke researchers to contest the ghettoizing of their subject matter as metaphysics or 'peculiar ideas and strange rituals'.) Even when it is focused on a particular ritual, fieldwork is particularly good for seeking understanding of whole events from the preparation to the aftermath. Fieldwork requires researchers to establish sufficient **rapport** to be given access to all that this might involve. It can involve attempts to gain precise experiential, phenomenological knowledge that only participation can provide. It is also the key method for pursuing selected, focused questions about scholarly interests in religious activities and lives.

Fieldwork takes various forms that could be represented as a spectrum from observation to participation, perhaps in phases. Sometimes while in the religious 'field', among religious practitioners, researchers attempt to observe without intruding too much on what would happen if they were not there. They might watch what full participants do, but from the margins, unobtrusively, without trying to act as others do, and without acting as if they were religious themselves. On other occasions, or as practiced by other researchers, scholars in the field may appear indistinguishable from other participants. They might seek to experience everything that the people they are researching experience: the fully sensual, embodied, imaginative, ecstatic and/or ordinary performance of religious life. Perhaps researchers are more attentive than they would be if they were members of the group. Or, if not more attentive, they are at least differently attentive, considering scholarly questions even as they participate and observe. Particularly in early phases, they will seek to learn what is normal and proper behavior for the particular group. They may seek to understand what religious people take for granted or what they mean by what they do. Certainly researchers will reflect on the value, importance or significance of what they and others are experiencing.

The largely synonymous term for the most common style of field research is 'participant observation'. It was coined by anthropologists and most obviously points to the evolution of methods founded on the idea that scholars should not rely on second-hand reports but should spend time among people, gathering first-hand data. Initially, it is implied, researchers might have thought of themselves as people who observed others who were 'participants' in the observed activity or 'culture' (a term that anthropologists have argued about as much as scholars of religion have argued about 'religion'). Observation required distance and resulted in objective analysis rather than in subjective impressions or experiences. However, the full richness of people's lives or culture demanded more than observation from the margins.

Bronislaw Malinowski (1884–1942) is often considered the founder, or at least the first rigorous developer and vociferous champion of fieldwork in anthropology. Indeed, he asserted the absolute necessity of living among people for extended periods in order to learn about them and their culture, also insisting that 'by dwelling mentally for some time among people of a much simpler culture than our own we may be able to see ourselves from a distance, we may be able to gain a new sense of proportion with regard to our own institutions, beliefs, and customs' (Malinowski 1954: 145). Whether the goal of research is to understand others or ourselves continues to be discussed (and both may be properly pursued), Malinowski's example became the norm in anthropology. Doctoral students expected to spend a year, at least (in addition to any time spent learning a local or useful language), elsewhere, immersed in cultures foreign to them. In short, fieldwork researchers had to seek to 'be there' for long periods, and therefore developed ways of participating while observing, or 'participant observation'.

Fieldwork conducted by scholars of religion only rarely entails long-term dwelling among those whom researchers wish to observe. Most often it involves only periodic or regular observation of significant events or processes. (Such episodes of fieldwork may be supported by more or less formal interviews or surveys that elicit different kinds of information that can be triangulated or compared with the results of participant observation.) However, this is not to suggest that periodic visits among religious people are undertaken casually. Rather, the point is that scholars of religion rarely attempt anything comparable to the classic anthropological ambition of understanding and writing about the whole culture of a group. Even anthropologists now typically focus on specific elements of cultures. Like any kind of research, the study of religions approach to fieldwork must be suitable to the phenomena of interest. So, although religious people can or do live their whole lives 'religiously', it is common for research to focus on particular activities that can be observed in a number of visits (some lasting longer than others) over a more extended period. It is true, too, that scholars of religion perform fieldwork in order to do more than observe the brief high points of an event or ritual's denouement. They typically appreciate that the full complexity of events usually demands more sustained presence and involvement. To understand a religion as it is performed, researchers need to become thoroughly familiar with a group or community both as they prepare for or reflect on specific events and as they live out their religion more generally. The addition of 'participation' to 'observation', therefore, signals this necessity of gaining familiarity with people and their activities.

Box 2.8.1 Stages in the fieldwork process

- Deciding who/where to research
- Introducing oneself/meeting people
- Conducting a pilot study (optionally)
- Fieldwork, e.g. participant observation and recording:
  - Recording/notes and diaries
  - Turning records into drafts
  - Checking ideas with (other) participants
  - Refining ideas in dialogue
- Further phases of fieldwork
- Polishing the written and other outputs

Presence and reflection

Fieldwork and participant observation practice and theory have developed since the early 20th century. A turn towards 'writing culture' (the title of an influential book edited by James Clifford and George Marcus, 1986) from the 1970s to the early 1990s evidenced a shift from treating fieldwork and 'writing-up' as separate, sequential activities to understanding that ethnographers are, as that term indicates, people who write (or speak words) about cultures. That is, even while 'in the field' researchers are constructing literate (and eventually literary) presentations of their experiences and reflections among other people. This alteration in understanding academic activities encouraged a more fluent literary polishing of academic publications and an increase in reflections about scholarly presence in their accounts of research. This last trend resonates with other developments, e.g. the rise of feminist, anti-colonial, phenomenological and indigenous scholarship (especially since 1990), and of widespread reflection on what worked well in the field. As researchers discovered the positive benefits of more fully participative and more experiential presence, they also asserted (in their research practice and their publications) the value of **dialogical, reflexive** and discursive methods and techniques. As Kirsten Hastrup and Peter Hervik and Karla Poewe (1996) insist, 'methods of presence' will continue to be central to the 'anthropological project of comprehending the world' and, by extension, to fieldwork about religion (Hastrup and Hervik 1994: 3).

Discussion of 'reflexivity and the study of belief' in a special issue of the journal *Western Folklore* casts further light on these tensions between different ways of performing research. In introducing the issue, David Hufford contrasts reflexivity both with 'methodolatry'—which 'tries to recapture the confidence of positivism by deriving a set of rules specifying a "correct" way of doing ethnography that can yield true representations of the world'—and with postmodernism—which 'abandons notions of objectivity altogether and treats ethnographic representation as literary construction that tells about its authors rather than about the world' (Hufford 1995a: 2–3). Reflexivity achieves something else because reflexive scholars act differently to positivists and postmodernists. In seeking to understand what religious people do, think, feel and say, they reflect both on the data presented to them and on their own presence, responses, impressions, experiences and power. Hufford defines 'reflexivity' as:

> a metaphor from grammar indicating a relationship of identity between subject and object, thus meaning the inclusion of the actor (scholar, author, observer) in the account of the act and/or its outcomes. In this sense reflexivity shows that all knowledge [including that of scholars] is 'subjective'.
>
> *(Hufford 1995b: 57)*

He concludes that the application of questioning to ourselves and our scholarly 'knowledge-making' is vital to our work of explicating what we know about others. Discussion that presents our reflections on our encounters and experiences will provide a 'more accurate sense of where we are, because it will always require us to tell how we got there' (Hufford 1995b: 74). These thoughts may not meet complete agreement from every fieldworker, but they do convey a sense of what is shared by researchers committed to engaging with lived religion as reflexive scholarly participants.

To summarize the argument so far: methods of recording information, reflections and analysis are integral to fieldwork. They make explicit the selectivity, refinement or focusing that is central to the whole approach. The intentions, processes and products of fieldwork are not complete, exhaustive, final statements about a discrete entity ('religion' or 'Buddhism', for example), without remainders or exceptions. Rather, fieldworkers pay careful attention to moments and trends in ever-changing practices, experiences, representations and knowledges. By addressing defined questions (albeit while remaining open to emerging possibilities), they seek to produce outcomes that communicate matters of significance to others that will advance discussion. There is, in short, a continuous dynamic flow between the 'field', the study (or whatever venue serves for note taking, diary updating, sustained reflection, analysis and writing), and the various communities interested in the project.

Respect and drama

Especially by virtue of their close engagement with people (individuals or groups) and by willingly thinking hard about their own experiences among others, participant observers are likely to gain considerable **respect** for the people among whom they research. Many researchers come to treat such people not only as reliable informants but also as conversation partners and even as co-researchers in some respects. A recognition that religious people also reflect on their activities, experiences, ideas and interpretations (i.e. they are not merely credulous 'believers' or subservient followers of 'tradition') can create a basis for richer discussions between researchers and those among whom they research. Similarly, members of many religions are avid readers of academic publications. Indeed, many religious movements are significantly affected (if not actually created) by people's engagements with academic research (e.g. Paganism, as discussed in Harvey 2007; and Candomblé, as discussed in Engler, forthcoming). In addition to respectful dialogue with adherents of religions about academic research questions, it is increasingly common for fieldworkers to act on the understanding that their hosts deserve some benefit from the presence of a researcher. For example, there might be an attempt to establish two-way processes of knowledge transfer. Some, but by no means all, field researchers are willing to become advocates or expert witnesses supporting those among whom they have researched. In addition to resulting in peer-reviewed journal articles or monographs, field research can involve or generate advantages to the researched community.

Fieldwork is the definitive method of diverse ethnological disciplines (e.g. anthropology, ethnobotany, ethnomusicology, performance studies and the study of religion) and is increasingly practiced elsewhere (e.g. in sociology and even theology). It is particularly good for engagement with specific issues in researching religion. Fieldwork may provide rich data about people's personal experiences within a religion, particular local expressions of a religion, or specific ritual practices, but ultimately researchers present their understandings of the lived reality, performance, implications and significance of religious engagements in ways that advance critical debates of a more than local nature. This is to concur *in part* with Victor Turner's methodological preference for 'chaps not maps' (Schechner n.d.), i.e. an insistence that research should pay attention to what people do rather than being entirely determined by theoretical constructions. Then, what we write about our research should 'bring home' a sense of the **drama** of what people actually do, the drama of doing research among them, and the drama of advancing knowledge and debate. This is not to forget that large proportions of what people do 'religiously' is far from dramatic (if this suggests something theatrical or spectacular), but reminds us to attend to what people do rather than to what people or texts assert.[1] Neither does attending to the 'drama' of 'what people do' ignore the fact that researchers enter 'the field' with scholarly questions and concerns, and that they seek to test theories in relation to what they observe and experience. At its best, then, fieldwork is not 'mere' description but argument arising from close familiarity with the living reality of religious activities. This is something that ought to enthuse researchers and make their projects (if not at every moment) engaging and sometimes exciting.

We have already paid some attention to the theoretical basis of fieldwork. It has been asserted that participant observation is founded on an understanding that some experience of the lived realities or performance of religion is a necessary prerequisite for theorizing about it. This idea privileges definitions of religion as action, what people do. It resonates with Malory Nye's encouragement to talk about 'religioning' (Nye 2004: 8), itself paralleling an anthropological incitement to replace 'culture' by 'culturing' (Rapport and Overing 2004: 97). Fieldwork research protocols and outcomes invite scholars to focus on the vernacular, lived-out, actual expressions, experiences and embodied knowledges of religious people. Leonard Primiano's (1995) insistence that religion is, in fact, always vernacular is instructive: even the Pope or the Dalai Lama perform lived religion rather than demonstrating some timeless pure or abstract form. They may be elite, but what they give expression to is their current and local form of religious life and practice, not a timeless fixity. In this and various other ways, the core theme of fieldwork is that religion is what people do, and is best researched by similarly active, participatory, embodied means. Experiential encounters with lived religion result in outcomes (books, conference papers, lectures, documentaries, etc.) which demonstrate that scholarly conventions about **care** and comparability are not compromised by scholarly presence and participation when these are performed reflexively and in dialogue with the research of others.

Care, comparison and not converting in fieldwork

Care is important in relation to various aspects of fieldwork. In addition to the (hopefully self-evident) requirement that observation should be carefully attentive to significant matters and moments, 'care' is, perhaps, a twin of 'respect' when considering how researchers might be expected to approach and treat those among whom they research. In a later section about ethics it will be noted that there are arguments for and against the use of covert methods. However, another sense of 'care' is important with respect to the expected processes and protocols of the academic community. It seems right that colleagues, students and others who hear or read the conclusions drawn from research should be able to trust that they are being offered a carefully considered and justified argument. Whether everyone agrees is not the point—academia is a community of continuous debate, not a collecting point for uncontentious (and ultimately uninteresting) facts. Field researchers should take care that they have engaged as fully as possible with what interests them, seeking clarity about possible contradictions to their interpretations, presenting sufficient information ('thick' or 'rich description') not only to illustrate a point but also to demonstrate the process by which its relevance and value was ascertained. Being careful also requires researchers to show how their work enriches understanding and furthers debate. In particular, care with previous research and publications is necessary—and may be demonstrated by the proper use of citations and the discussion of considered dissent from others' theories.

A specific form of care is especially important in relation to the acts and ideas of religious people. It fuses with consideration of the role of comparison. Indeed, the idea that religious studies fieldwork is about something identifiable as 'religion' is itself both necessarily comparative and inescapably contentious. Questions about whether something common in one group is prevalent elsewhere might inspire researchers' projects. The discovery that a practice or term learnt elsewhere has misdirected attention or interpretation in one's fieldwork may cause radical re-thinking of what one is experiencing. A widespread contemporary current in the study of religion entails challenging the dominance of Protestant Christian themes promiscuously applied where they are unwarranted. Malcolm Ruel's field research in West and East Africa provides the foundation both for considerable local and comparative analysis, and for explicit rejection of the universalizing of particular religious and scholarly themes. For example, he problematizes terms that are widely used in the study of religions such as 'belief' and 'ritual'. Ruel (2005: 262–63) concludes that 'shadows' cast by unwarranted transpositions of one religion's definitive themes (such as 'belief' in Christianity) on to other traditions both 'obscures what really it is that people see or think they see' (i.e. it damages the fieldwork description that scholars might offer) and it vitiates the 'clearer, steadier gaze on the world that we share' (i.e. it debases interpretative understandings). Ruel's challenge to the centrality of 'belief' in religions other than Christianity is made more complex by the subsequent proliferation of fieldwork enriching the recognition that Christians, too, do far more than 'believe'. More generally, decisions about what 'religion' is, if it is not (only) about belief and believing, are of great importance in framing and conducting fieldwork among religious people. What, after all, is it that religious studies scholars research that is distinct from what other ethnographers (for example) study? A working definition (one that can be improved or replaced with increased study) of what counts as 'religion' for the purpose of research among a particular group seems necessary to any successful project.

A final thought about care is that a specific feature of religions (although this is common in other cultural domains too) is that religious people often invite or expect 'outsiders' to join them, to be persuaded by their rhetoric or enthused by their practice, or to 'convert'. Most religious activities are imbued with enticements to continue, commit, immerse oneself completely into the community or experience that they present and express. There are religious events intended for strangers, but they are only rarely neutral, and more commonly they are expected to have an impact on the observer, witness or as yet uninvolved. Scholarly responses to and participation in religious activities of all kinds is fraught with complex challenges. Even if researchers are not persuaded by or converted to a group, they may become so sympathetic that their published work reads more like advocacy than analysis. These difficult negotiations are regular themes in discussions of fieldwork experiences. Being clear about one's motivations, interests and purposes is likely to aid a researcher in maintaining a focus on the goal of contributing to academic debate, but all researchers can expect to be tested in some way as they engage with others.

Box 2.8.2 Key skills for fieldwork (to be continuously practiced and improved)

- Gaining rapport
- Practicing epoché
- Maintaining empathy
- Paying attention
- Being present

Conceiving the fieldwork researcher

This section surveys some of the ways in which fieldworkers have conceived of themselves and their role as field researchers. It includes common positionings such as 'methodological atheism' and 'methodological agnosticism' but also recognizes a wider range of possibilities. There are, for example, methodological ludists, guests, children, fools and neophytes. All of these develop the early reflections and practices of participant observers and the more recent emphasis on dialogical and reflexive researchers.

Scholars interested in religion have generally argued for the necessity of 'methodological agnosticism'. Peter Berger and Ninian Smart, for example, proposed an approach similar to that of phenomenologists to their subject matter. Scholars should simply not ask questions about truth (Smart 1973: 62), but should bracket out 'the ultimate status of religious definitions of reality' so that religious phenomena can be treated in a 'value-free' way (Berger 1969: 180). Although it is possible to find references to 'methodological atheism', what is intended seems little different to the 'agnostic' bracketing out of specific claims about the veracity of discourses about deities and other 'non-falsifiable postulated alternate realities' (Cox 2006: 236; Cox 2010: 21). It is legitimate, in this view, to study what people claim, but since it is impossible to scientifically test whether or not the referent of such claims are true, it cannot be academic to make the attempt.[2] Eileen Barker provides the example of an encounter with a woman who claimed to have joined a new religion 'because God directed her to the movement', and the woman's father who claimed that she 'had been possessed by evil spirits'. The sociologist, says Barker, 'cannot say which, if either, is the correct explanation—but merely reports' what these people believe (Barker 2010: 14). An interest in claims-making but not in the veracity of claims themselves is productive of accurate reportage about what people think, believe or claim. In fact, Barker is far more than a 'methodological reporter'. She demonstrates that scholarly engagement with the many ways in which people act on the basis of their claims contributes importantly to theoretically informed debates about religion.

Explorations of ways in which researchers might relate to religious people 'in the field' offer an array of positions that enhance the foundational conception of fieldworkers as 'methodological agnostics'. It is possible to draw both on previous fieldworkers and on literary and cultural critics for some provocative possibilities. These include Claude Lévi-Strauss's *bricoleur*, an adept in making available things serve new purposes; Walter Benjamin's *flâneur*, an uninvolved but fascinated observer of city life; Gilles Deleuze's 'nomad', travelling between significant points but not dwelling in them; and Julia Kristeva's 'foreigner', who recognizes that we are all strangers to one another and thus could potentially honor both difference and solidarity. In various ways, all these conceptions (and others like 'tourist', people who casually and even accidently observe religion in passing) might provide useful ways of thinking about the placement of the researcher 'in between' those among whom they research and the wider scholarly community, bringing old theories to bear on new data, sometimes fascinated by what they observe but resistant to joining and getting fixed by others' ideas and commitments. Interesting as these are, more profit is gained from considering how fieldworkers specifically interested in religion have thought about their roles and relationships, and thus of themselves and their task.

Douglas Ezzy and André Droogers both infuse their approach to phenomenological fieldwork with insights drawn from performance studies. Discussing the pivotal role of the 'suspension of disbelief' in most considerations of 'methodological agnosticism', Ezzy elaborates on the expected experience of most theatre-goers. While watching a play, the audience must willingly conspire with the actors in the fiction that they are seeing reality. Ezzy expands:

> That is to say, the focus of a hermeneutically and phenomenologically orientated ethnographic methodology is the way people tell their stories, rather than the accuracy or otherwise of the account. Neither the realities of spiritual experience, nor the integral role of social and cultural processes that shape interpretation are ignored. Rather, the focus is on the relationship between experience and interpretation, between symbolically constructed realities and their consequences.
>
> *(Ezzy 2004: 124)*

It is this methodological stance, that of the engaged audience, which underlies Ezzy's positive evaluation of research that recognizes the impact of religious interpretations on religious people. Using a range of examples, he demonstrates that religious explanations can be socially and culturally generative. Precisely by not treating religious explanations as an untouchable domain (or as only 'religious') he is able to engage with them as sociological data.

Going further, Droogers proposes a 'methodological ludism', leaving the audience and joining the performers on stage. This involves him among the players, in the midst of the action, engaged with the drama. His proposal is inspired by reflecting on traditional participant observation alongside theorization about play. He writes:

> In play, human beings are capable of dealing simultaneously with two or even more realities [. . .] By temporarily, but as completely as possible, sharing the concrete bodily experiences of the people being studied, the researcher gains in understanding the role of these experiences. Though requiring the seriousness of playing a role,

methodological ludism is [. . .] methodological [. . .] and thereby independent of the researcher's personal conviction with regard to religion.

(Droogers 2008: 455)

In practice this is not a challenge to the way most fieldwork is conducted; after all, participant observation is founded on the necessity of participation. However, Droogers supports the effort to get involved (especially in the face of challenges related to the theme of 'belief', such as the alleged gulf between 'insiders' and 'outsiders', and the potential incompatibility of a researcher's personal commitments and those of the researched community) by recognizing the strong similarities between researchers and actors performing roles. By 'sharing the concrete bodily experiences of the people being studied' researchers are likely to gain richer understanding of the embodied, sensual performances of vernacular and quotidian religion. Thus, he argues, 'we must acknowledge the role of the body as a research tool' (Droogers 2008: 456), and should recognize that bodily presence and participation, even among 'believers', will help scholars to 'understand what [particular] experiences mean to them' (ibid.: 461).

Despite his enthusiasm for close engagement with those he researches, Droogers agrees that 'the fieldworker may have some difficulty in identifying with the recruiting believer' (Droogers 2008: 461). Edith Turner, however, has expressed the hope that 'if it becomes respectable for anthropologists to admit to [actually seeing the 'spirit' forms that people suggest they can expect], it would become possible to speak from *within* a culture, rather than as an outsider' (Turner 1994: 86). It is certainly the case that most fieldworkers today do write about their experiences as an aid to conveying what certain events were like. Some do so firmly within the tradition of methodological agnosticism, noting what they observed and what they recorded other people doing. Other researchers have insisted that it is fully possible for a member of or participant in a religion to use the same skills as other scholars and to produce rich descriptive and theoretical discussions. Te Pakaka Tawhai, for example, has provided an introduction to 'Maori religion' (Tawhai 1988) that is locally and temporally bounded, and engages with ceremonies, speeches, knowledge transfers, everyday acts and his own experience. He talks of what people from his home town might understand by the word 'religion', and affirms that he is right to tell only a particular version of what is considered significant in his community, rejecting the fiction that there is one fixed thing that could be called 'Maori religion'. Another kind of partial insiderliness is the subject of Andrew Yip's reflections on 'researching British lesbian, gay and bisexual Christians and Muslims' (Yip 2005). A researcher's personal and/or social identity may provide common ground on which a dialogue can take place with members of religions to which they do not belong. Issues of belonging and difference, performing and identifying, are complex and all degrees along the 'insider/outsider' continuum can establish both bridges and barriers.

Somewhat more challengingly, Rane Willerslev's (2007) research among Yukaghir hunters in Siberia demonstrates that there are interesting parallels between the practice of fieldwork and that of hunting. In particular, researchers and hunters need to get as near as possible to their intended subject/object whilst avoiding becoming so involved with them that one not only forgets to hunt or research but becomes completely 'one of them'. (The possibility of becoming an animal is a generative theme, linked to mimesis, in Yukaghir hunters' myth-telling, hunting performance and in Willerslev's contribution to under-standing this kind of animist religious culture.) Only by joining the hunt, being taught what hunting involves among animists, and adapting his behavior to local custom, could Willerslev have had experiences that enabled his research project to succeed. Learning by doing provided insights that could be checked later (but not during the hunt if local cultural rules and roles were to be observed) in conversations and interviews. Bringing this experiential and mimetically learned understanding back to the academic world (rather than remaining a hunter in Siberia) means that Willerslev has been able to advance debate in a developing area of interdisciplinary research.

My own attempt to learn what is significant in Tawhai's multi-religious home town and among Maori living in Britain led me to conceive of fieldwork as 'methodological guesthood' (Harvey 2003, 2005). Maori have clear protocols, elaborated in a rich performative and material culture (identifiable as *powhiri*), for making strangers into guests. Field research training commonly distinguishes between 'insiders' and 'outsiders', but although this distinction might help scholars begin to think about their roles in relation to other kinds of participant, it is not so clear, convincing or productive in practice. Even before researchers arrive on the scene, religious (and other kinds of groups) are quite diverse in reality—with some holding firmly to 'core values' or teachings, others being quite flexible, and some feeling or expressing considerable doubt but enjoying the company (and so on). Researchers who are present even at the margins of an event affect what people do. When they ask questions they are likely to affect how and what people think about and express what they do or what it means. Scholars who 'belong' within the community that they research will, while performing research, attend to different actions, have different questions in mind, and experience events differently from when they are 'just' participating. There are, then, no 'insiders' who are not sometimes 'outside' to some degree in relation to those they observe. There are no 'outsiders' who are not sometimes 'inside' the event in which they participate. Like many dichotomies, this one is only heuristically useful, and then mostly before the researcher actually arrives 'in the field'. It is vital, however, for the field researcher to pay attention to whether the people who seem to tell them most (whether implicitly while being observed or explicitly as 'informants') are representative of the group of which they are members of some kind. However, within Maori protocols, being a 'guest' is not like being either an 'insider' or an 'outsider'. Guests cannot become locals, but locals cannot become hosts without guests. Culturally rich ceremonies would cease if there were no strangers seeking guesthood. Maori protocols recognize more than this. They make it possible for strangers to choose, once offered the possibility, between being enemies or becoming guests. To be an enemy might be to insist that locals are definitively wrong in what they do, or in what they understand about what they do, and that only an outside observer can authoritatively define what matters. Once a stranger has become a guest, they certainly have responsibilities but they are not expected to agree with everything their hosts might say. Indeed, Maori guest-making occasions are often followed by intense discussions and negotiations that seek mutual understanding and collaborative action but acknowledge that recognizing difference is a possible outcome. Several things become clear in using all this to think about research positions: guest-researchers can offer themselves as potential guests but it is the host's right to offer or decline access, guest-researchers do not at first know what their potential hosts know (scholars are not experts about other people, only about their own mysteries and questions), guest-researchers make a difference to locals (aka 'natives') by their presence, guest-researchers have unique (non-'native') experiences of a culture or performance in which they are guests, and fuller understanding of the relevance of local data may best arise in dialogue and interaction.

In discussing ideas about 'methodological guesthood' (often embedded in more intimate guesthood relationships) I have been offered various other religion-specific, culture-specific or rite-specific parallel or complementary perspectives. These deserve consideration because few religious groups offer anything as clear-cut as Maori guest-making protocols. Finding a

way into relationship with a community, and a way of becoming familiar and then knowledgeable about people, requires some initial positioning of oneself as a researcher. In some
contexts, children are allowed to ask questions and make mistakes until they are shown how
they should act. They may be given an appropriate, basic level of instruction on which to
build further knowledge. In other contexts, slow or dramatic processes of initiation are
required to inculcate the correct knowledge and behavior in neophytes. Researchers might,
then, conceive of themselves as children or neophytes. These are among the productive possibilities that arise from the acknowledgement that research really is about seeking understanding that scholars do not yet have about matters that are commonplace or familiar to
others.

Whether the hosts, teachers, responsible adults or initiators of such researchers are willing
to play such roles is another question. It is always possible that people might reject researchers
(whether by explicitly refusing access or by more subtly making it impossible to participate).
Jeanne Favret-Saada (1980) discovered that those from whom she sought information about
witchcraft in the French Bocage were willing to mislead her, but also that her own fairly
traditional 'observer' positioning was a barrier to understanding. She writes:

> For anyone who wants to understand the meaning of this discourse, there is no other
> solution but to practise it oneself, to become one's own informant, to penetrate one's
> own amnesia, and to try and make explicit what one finds unstateable in oneself.
> *(Favret-Saada 1980: 22)*

Her re-conception and performance of herself as a self-informant is generative of significant
insights about the popular practices, suspicions and webs of accusation that make up this form
of witchcraft. Totally immersing herself in this deeply subjective and reflexive culture arguably allowed Favret-Saada to understand 'what it felt like', and then communicate about it to
other scholars, in ways that would be hard by any means other than what can be called
'autoethnography' (Ellis 2003; Wallis 2004). However, other researchers in similar situations
might feel that there is 'another solution', namely to go elsewhere or revise their intended
project into something that can be achieved with the cooperation of others.

These various ideas about how researchers conceive of themselves and their role in relation
to the people among whom they research all, in various ways, develop out of an agreement
that fieldwork and participant observation are proper ways to conduct research. As fieldwork
practice has evolved, the question of how researchers understand and present themselves and
the results of their work has become central. Recognition of the inadequacy (conceptually
and practically) of the 'insider/outsider' dichotomy has led to a range of more participative,
reflexive and dialogical positions and performances. Most of the above examples (engaged
audience, actor, hunter, guest, child and so on) are particular versions of these developments.
They all conceive of the researcher as someone who needs more than observer status but has
to be careful about full participation. They all remain within the parameters indicated by the
collocation 'participant observation', but indicate that more precision is possible. Usually this
precision arises while in the field, trying to observe while participating and vice versa, testing
initial conceptions and ideas. To that degree, what has been set out so far has been a series of
ideas that a trainee researcher might use to develop their intention or manifesto. However,
given that these ideas come from experienced researchers, it must be clear that scholars come
to see themselves differently once they get out into the field and get involved with religious
people. The following sections, therefore, pick up the thread of the question, how is this done
in practice?

Deciding who or where to research

It seems likely that most prospective researchers already have ideas about who or where to research. They are interested in particular religions, sub-groups of religious people, communities in particular places, ritual complexes performed by specific groups, themes that cut across diverse religions or communities, or emerging trends or debates that might be examined in relation to a group or event. Sometimes a chance conversation or an apparent gap in an otherwise respected teacher's knowledge suggests a topic that might deserve investigation. My own first attempts at field research began when a new course about 'contemporary religion' was being developed at the university where I was completing my PhD about semantic fields in ancient Jewish texts. Having been brought up near Stonehenge I had been to the festival held there around the summer solstice and I had noticed, but not been particularly interested in, some Druids. Nonetheless, I volunteered to offer a session about contemporary Druidry and was taken seriously. So I set off to find out where these people were, what they did, what they intended by what they did, and what possible interest this might have for students of religion. By asking people who seemed likely to know Druids (mostly hippies and other 'alternative' people who were far from rare in the English West Country) I encountered a few groups. I introduced myself and my desire to learn about them. They were, of course, entertained by my somewhat naïve approach, some having studied degrees that led them to expect more focused questions than 'could you tell me all about yourselves?' and 'can I observe a ceremony?'

I have learnt that having a question in mind is helpful both because it provides a guide or goal for research and because it allows me to explain why I would like people to entertain my presence and interest. I do not have to ask the question of everyone involved, but I do need to be able to say what it is that motivates me. Telling them what explains my presence generally contributes significantly to conversations about why others are there too.

My later fieldwork has, then, involved attempts to engage with specific issues. There are few, if any, unresearched religious groups in the world now (or, if there are any, they are sub-groups of quite similar groups elsewhere). It is unlikely that scholars of religion will share the experience of some early anthropologists and missionaries who were the first of their kind of human to meet particular groups. More commonly, researchers interested in religion select communities to research among because it seems likely that such a group will provide the best context in which to seek understanding, or to improve knowledge, understanding or debate. Thus, a researcher seeking to define a project might select a current critical debate and ponder which group or event might most usefully be engaged with for the purpose of making an advanced contribution. For example, having heard people assert that 'Paganism is the indigenous religion of Britain' I wondered what 'religion' might be like among 'indigenous people' of the kind to which this phrase normally refers, e.g. Native Americans. Opportunities arose for me to visit a First Nation reserve in Canada for a conference about 'healing', and then a Native American reservation in the USA where some friends were visiting other friends. These brief introductions provided me with starting points for longer research projects. Somewhat serendipitous encounters and connections often lead researchers to meet with just the right people among whom the question that most interests them can be most usefully explored.

In brief, it is likely that prior interests about particular religions or a sense of intrigue about an academic issue encountered in studying religion will provide the foundation for further research. Interest and enthusiasm should not be set aside or ignored. They do not have to lead to partisanship but can be built into the foundation of the process of careful paying attention that is fieldwork in the study of religions.

Learning in the field

In introducing my suggestion that researchers might conceive of themselves as 'guests' among knowledgeable and authoritative 'hosts' I noted that it is up to others to determine whether we might be allowed access. My understanding of these possibilities, and the observations of other scholars noted above, arose while trying to act as advised by predecessors who taught or wrote about fieldwork. Many of our refinements of fieldwork positions and performance are due to the fact that what actually happens in the field is not always what is expected. As participant observation has evolved as a method and a stance with regard to others, and especially as dialogical and reflexive approaches have developed, researchers have gained confidence both in the field and in communicating what it is actually like to do research. For example, Ron Geaves describes the various senses of awe, displacement and personal change that he felt during a Naqshbandi Sufi *dhikr* in England. Realizing the number of times that similar events have occurred across the Muslim world, often involving 'some of the greatest exponents of mysticism the world has known', was awe inspiring. On then realizing that what he was participating in was happening in a British city among people who he believed familiar to him from more everyday interactions (e.g. shopping) he felt displaced and changed: he would 'never perceive [these people] through the same lens; for he had been permitted an insight into a dimension of their lives he had not formerly been aware of' (Chryssides and Geaves 2007: 240). Hard as it is to prepare for awe and displacement when participating in dramatic events or in other people's lives, researchers will be faced with questions about how to represent such experiences in what they say or write later.

If some do not encounter life-changing experiences among religionists, or if they do manage to resist their impact, they are still likely to be changed. This is not at all to suggest that scholars of religion will (let alone must) become religious. Rather it is to acknowledge that neophyte researchers will become researchers by doing research. Karen Sykes observes that an 'anthropologist getting started at fieldwork, like a kula trader getting started in ceremonial exchange, sets a chain of other transactions into play' (Sykes 2005: 214). In participant observation among one group of people or at one event, the fieldworker becomes different. It is hoped that they become more skilled. Similarly, just as the hunters among whom he researched had to 'steer a complicated course between the ability to transcend difference and the necessity of maintaining identity' as they attempted to be, to some degree, 'both human and the animals they imitate' (University of California Press 2007), so Willerslev's research required him to be both a researcher and a hunter. What may begin with mimicry becomes a visceral, deeply affecting experience of what it means to do what other people do. There is no escaping reflexivity when the task of the researcher resonates with the tasks performed by religious people when doing religion: finding out how to behave, seeking understanding, or trying to convey experience and understanding to others.

It is impossible to say what will happen to a researcher performing fieldwork. Perhaps the best possible advice is to try it while being open to possibilities and careful to allow for the unexpected. Even everyday religious activities can include surprise, and everyday research activities can include serendipitous encounters. Concentration and effort is also integral to both religious and research practice. It is hard enough, so people inform researchers, to learn to meditate, pray, sacrifice, hunt, live appropriately and so on. Observing others doing these things has its challenges, especially for researchers who seek to gain understanding by participation. On the one side there are questions of privacy and belonging, on the other there are questions about empathy, completeness and 'getting it right'.

Many religious events or activities are private or intensely personal. Being trusted enough to be shown what they involve or told what impact they have had on people is never automatic. Honesty about being there as a researcher and humility about one's ignorance might be necessary first steps towards being trustworthy. Gaining knowledge of what it is like to be taught is probably straightforward for most researchers, especially those who do not already believe themselves to be the experts or to know the whole truth already. Understanding more fully than merely recording what people say requires both experience and finding ways to check with (other) practitioners. Since reflexivity is not only about knowing how things seem to oneself, but is intended to facilitate understanding of other people, it usually involves a mixture of participatory involvement and testing with reference to other people's experiences. Participant observation, therefore, does not only mean doing what other people do and then wondering what they think they are doing. It involves dialogue with others. This might entail more-or-less intense conversations (including chatting while washing up) or more-or-less formal interviews. Knowing what is appropriate can be a challenge, especially to those who research where questions are not welcome or normal. There is always the possibility that the very fact that researchers might have to learn in different ways from other participants entails them learning different things. That is, they may not grasp exactly what it is like for non-researchers to learn about their religion. This too can be discussed with more 'insiderly' people. Indeed, the process of careful checking is another continuous exercise required of researchers as they dialogue with religionists.

Much of this can be summed up in the term 'rapport', which can be easier to define that to enact sometimes. It involves establishing and maintaining friendly relationships with people, involving trust, shared concerns and/or understandings, and some level of mutual commitment to the success of a project. It is not necessarily based on researchers agreeing with, committing to, or promoting other people's ideas and practices. It is not the same as conversion. Rather, it can involve being openly interested or even enthusiastic about what motivates and excites other people. It might be demonstrated by a willingness to turn up regularly, to pay attention, to get involved where this is possible, to be genuinely interested in others, and to talk honestly but respectfully about one's own interests. Rapport is a two-way relationship, and may involve 'informants' being willing to trust researchers enough to answer questions and to provide access to and company at events. Some people manage to make friends and establish trust easily. Similarly, some groups seem more ready to be trusting of researchers than others. Most researchers, however, find that there are times when they have to work hard at building and maintaining rapport.

Rapport may well be a result of the studied practice of **empathy**, defined by Daniel Capper as 'vicarious introspection', 'the capacity to think or feel oneself into the inner life of another person' and 'evenly hovering attention' (Capper 2003: 237–38, citing Heinz Kohut's psychology-based argument). He illustrates this with the realization that dawned on him while attempting to conduct fieldwork among American Buddhists that he was actually distancing himself from people in various ways. As Cox writes, empathy is imprecise, it is 'more like an attitude than an empirically measurable method', and 'subject to misinterpretation', so should not be treated too casually (Cox 2010: 54). Researchers have to work hard to appreciate what is ordinary and taken for granted as well as what is experienced as spectacular and inspiring by those they observe. The balancing act between observing to answer academic questions and trying to know what regular participants know is a challenge. Dialogue with others may aid researchers in checking that they really are 'getting it', appreciating what it is that others are up to. Capper's article is invaluable here. He shows that by getting more involved in tasks in the community, placing himself among others learning what was expected, and sometimes offering to do things that he was already skilled at doing, he found himself not only involved but also advancing his research. As he got 'caught' in the discourse and community, his research advanced greatly. He began to understand what others did because he was learning in the same ways as they did. He was not alone in harboring doubts and unease, so mutual sharing enriched his understanding of what it was like for others to try to become Buddhists. He found that they, too, were experimenting with different ways to understand and experience what seemed to be expected of them. Many other researchers have noted that, in addition to putting oneself in the position of other learners (children, guests or neophytes), casual conversations in kitchens and while occupied with 'mundane' work provide richer insight into a religion than any formal lecture. However, this must be attempted honestly. Raising doubts about other people's views, practice or leaders is not a good methodological gambit unless a high degree of rapport has already been established. Gaining rapport, then, is not just about entering the field, it too requires continuous negotiation. A sense of humor and a willingness to be sociable can be as helpful as trying not to take offence too easily.

Another way to think about the process of gaining entry, trust, familiarity, and eventually knowledge and understanding of a religious group is provided by thinking about Pierre Bourdieu's (1977) concept of *habitus*, taken for granted everyday or casual behaviors or demeanor, or what people expect or themselves attempt to abide by as expressed in the ways they move and act. Gustavo A. Ludueña's (2005) discussion of research among Latin American Catholic monks provides an extreme example of fieldwork among people who are hard to approach, let alone research among. Having selected a closed, silent, contemplative and ascetic order of monks as an interesting field of enquiry, Ludueña was confronted by the impossibility of actually participating in their lives. He could not even get beyond the community's guest house. However, in that place, where others visited for 'retreats', he could learn to abide by the regimes and routines of the community, albeit in a constrained and limited manner. By carrying out the silence, reading, praying and listening that is required, he gained some purchase on the permanent lifeways or *habitus* of the community. His reflections on learning the community's 'technologies of the self' (citing Foucault and those influenced by him), especially the self-surveillance implicated in the active practice of silence, permitted the emergence of an understanding of what others were experiencing. He does not claim to present to others what it is like to be a Benedictine monk, nor does he claim to have become as ascetic as them. He does, however, propose that reflection on the technologies of the self that apply inside monasteries resonate with the different kind of careful self-observation necessary if researchers are going to do more than obsess about their own preconceptions. This leads him to conclude that fieldwork is a process of 'adaptation-participation' in which researchers adjust their behavior, demeanor and practice to those of the community that they seek to understand by degrees of constrained (ascetic or adapted) participation.

Every manual on ethnology and phenomenology includes advice on the necessity and performance of **epoché**, 'the bracketing out or suspending of a researcher's previous ideas, thoughts or beliefs about the truth, value or meaning of the religion [culture, event, or community] under study' (Cox 2010: 49). That it is genuinely possible to set aside one's ideas and expectations seems unlikely, but being aware of presuppositions and one's own 'ideas, thoughts and beliefs', and being vigilant against their untested influence on one's analysis of fieldwork, is crucial. This is what the metaphor 'bracketing' intends: not rejecting or ignoring anything but finding ways to be clear and careful about what is known and what is not known. After all, some 'previous ideas' are required: research projects must begin with ideas about what information is to be sought, what debates are relevant to the selected 'field' and what potential 'meanings' are to be tested. Nonetheless, epoché, like building rapport, is a continuous fieldwork practice that checks. Its success is indicated by the ability to demonstrate the value of existing theories (from whatever source) in relation to the phenomena that present themselves.

Researchers who achieve rapport (perhaps by adjusting their habitus to that of their hosts), and practice epoché and empathy, are also likely to engage in and reflect on dialogues between their own and other people's participative acts. Put bluntly, they are likely to be interested in what other participants in religious activities understand about what happens. They are likely to discuss events and interpretations with others. Prior expectations and theories (perhaps suggested by the writings of other scholars) will have been tested by conversations and/or interviews in which the researcher says 'I think this is what happened' and 'this is how it seemed to me', and their subjects, informants, discussants or 'interpreters' (as Capper 2003 prefers to say) confirm or challenge interpretations. Then fieldworkers can say that by presence, participation and discussion they know something of what others do and understand. They may never be certain that everyone, even in a small group, has the same experiences or interpretations but they have made efforts to observe, participate, reflect on and discuss as much as is possible.

Limits

There are, nonetheless, limits to a researcher's participation in fieldwork. Beyond the difficult questions of research among potentially violent, hostile or 'deviant' groups, and the limits placed on possible research by a scholar's gender or willingness to adapt to local expectations, or by any habitual inability to achieve rapport with others, there are a few other matters that are worth noting.

A significant set of limits to the practice and value of fieldwork exist precisely because researchers do not know the field, and those in the field do. Knowing whether it is possible to ask questions is one thing. Knowing whether it is *necessary* to ask is far more difficult. While researching among the Kalahari !Kung, Richard Lee discovered that he remained ignorant and somewhat socially excluded precisely because he had not asked what was going on. He records the answer to his impassioned enquiry about why nobody had told him that he had been mocked as a way of indicating his need to act differently: ' "Because you never asked me," said Tomazo, echoing the refrain that has come to haunt every field ethnographer' (Lee 1969: 17). However, it is equally likely that Tomazo and the !Kung took it for granted that anyone but a fool or a young child would know what was happening and what was expected. Conversely, there are contexts in which the asking of questions is a certain way to close down a research project. However, ethnographies are replete with warnings about asking too many questions or, indeed, any questions at all. This can be because people become irritated by continuous interrogation or because they prefer to 'do' religion than to 'explain it'. More commonly, perhaps, people perceive researchers as asking question after question in an effort to 'explain away' or demolish practitioners' experiences or knowledges. There are also examples of religious complexes (such as Candomblé) or specific rites in which the asking of questions is deemed inappropriate. People are expected to learn by imitation and practice, or to be initiated into secrets under the authoritative direction of those who cannot be questioned. Therefore, knowing whether questions are permissible and/or necessary can set limits both to the practice and the value of research. Initial phases of research in which scholars orientate and adapt themselves to local expectations are likely to resolve these issues. However, sometimes mistakes and being corrected can be the only way to learn. Lee, for example, discovered a lot more about !Kung teaching and learning styles than if he had not been the subject of their somewhat humiliating modes of admonishment. Not only did he learn a range of hitherto unexpected rules, but he discovered the sense of social interactions he had only partially understood previously. Experiential knowledge is sometimes absolutely vital.

The asking of questions and the act of participant observation can, like all acts of observation, cause changes in that which researchers observe. Some religious people are intensely reflexive and deeply interested in understanding the meaning of what they do, but many people's first encounter with an inquisitive researcher is their first realization that anyone might worry about the 'meaning' of taken-for-granted or core activities. If *doing* a particular thing, especially if the action is one performed every day since childhood, is what it means to be counted within a group there may have been no previous reason to question it. In some respects it is true that the scholarly task (to understand religion) is quite distinct from the religious task (to do religion), even if such a claim is at the heart of Protestant Christian polemics against Catholicism, and thus lies at one fecund root of modernity. It is likely that questioning religious actions will evince more than one, often contradictory answer. It is equally likely that the 'informant' will be speaking about something that has just changed its feel, resonance, impact or even meaning for them. Negotiating this problematic area might require the researcher to dramatically curtail the asking of questions and to take considerable care in further participant observation. More likely, it could encourage the researcher to find more casual and conversational ways of eliciting knowledge of what people understand by their actions.

Similarly, questions addressed to 'ordinary' religious people are frequently answered by humble claims that 'I am not a good example, I can recommend a book or a teacher who knows more or is a better model than I'. For researchers who want to understand lived religion, this can be frustrating. Participation and reflection on experiences while acting among religious people are good means of gaining an appreciation of what is ordinary among them. However, especially given the pervasive influence of modernity globally, it is more than likely that religious people will offer researchers copious explanations of what is significant among them. That is, religious people are rarely naïve, and their religions are rarely 'pure' and untainted by experiment, doubt, reflection, questioning and debate. (This is not to suggest that they should be, but rather to parody that expectation.) Again, Paganism and Candomblé provide excellent examples of religions created and developed in more-or-less continuous dialogue with academic thought. The term 'reactivity' is one term used to label such processes. Assessments vary, but it seems proper to state that researchers should not actively set out to cause change but neither should they shy away from the inevitable fact that their presence, observation and questions will cause reactions. The thing to notice is that reactivity is not only caused by academic engagement, but religions and people are continuously adjusting and developing in reaction to their multifaceted contexts and wider relationships.

The theory of fieldwork is also haunted by the question of solipsism, the idea that people can only be certain of their own thoughts. This extreme expression of individualism can make the researcher doubt that they can possibly understand those among whom they research. Insider experience may be thought to be inaccessible or utterly personal. There are obvious links with the claims of some religious people that the core of religion is transcendent and ineffable. Equally, there are links with the claim that 'experience' is always already interpreted and never 'immediate', uninterpreted or integrated into existing patterns. If taken to extremes, such thoughts might limit the fieldworker to reporting on and analyzing only what they saw or felt, making no claims about others. They might, however, at least engage with what informants or local translators of their own experience claim to have done, felt or thought. Interviewed by Eerika Koskinen-Koivisto (2010), the folklorist Dorothy Noyes argued that:

Nothing can be communicated perfectly. Even the verbatim quotation of a verbal utterance loses tone, timbre, context. Of course it's much harder to put the taste of wine or the exhaustion of having danced all night into language: not only are you reducing the original experience, as any representation must, but you have to translate it into a completely different code. So we have to start by recognizing the inadequacy of language to reproduce experience. But the basic semiotic processes of indexicality and metaphor can still get us somewhere. We can point to the quality of experience by showing all of its observable concomitants: who was there, what the weather was like, what we drank, what music was playing. I can't give you the experience, but I can show you how I got there. And insofar as you have had comparable experiences you can get the general idea. There is also metaphor, using a familiar domain to represent an unfamiliar one: a common strategy for describing religious experience. Metaphor too relies on bodily experiences common to us as a species: being warmed by the sun or thrown into cold water, being suckled or beaten.

(Koskinen-Koivisto 2010: 4)

The probable ubiquity of metaphor in religions, and the commonality of bodily experience might provide confidence that researchers can, in fact, convey something of the experience of 'what it was like' to be among people when they did certain things. The foundational Cartesian doubt of bodily, sensate experience is unlikely to be set aside on this basis. However, perhaps skepticism and solipsism are sufficiently weakened by the setting aside of the possibility of absolute objectivity (of the kind previously attributed, intriguingly, to transcendent deities and practitioners of 'pure science') that field researchers may be encouraged to keep trying to gain participative or performative experience and to communicate thick description and phenomena-true analysis.[3]

Ethics in fieldwork

Most universities and national associations or societies devoted to the study of religion provide guidance on research ethics. Much of what concerns them has been considered in our previous discussion of various issues about establishing good relationships with the people among whom we conduct research. 'Respect' might be as good a term as any: it does not require agreement with everything people do, say or think, but it does require willingness to consider others' choices, reasons and explanations. It encourages polite explication of where one differs from 'informants' or 'insiders'. Much of this is true of any kind of research. However, there are a few issues that are specific to fieldwork research that deserve some attention.

Mathew Guest's (2002) reflections on the processes and stages of his fieldwork among different kinds of Christians usefully illustrates what university and other ethics committees encourage, i.e. 'overt' research. Not all researchers discuss the question of overt versus covert research because most assume that open identification of oneself as a researcher is the correct stance to adopt in relation to others. Guest presents the preference for overt research as having both ethical and pragmatic foundations. Ethically, he considered it proper to be honest about being there to do research, being respectful of (other) participants, giving them an opportunity to treat him differently from other participants or visitors. Pragmatically, he needed to be trusted so that people would be willing to engage in conversation and interviews. In these conversations, he notes, he responded honestly to questions about his own beliefs and affiliations, and found that this 'allowed me to gauge responses to outsiders generally' (Guest 2002: 42). Conversations about his own status, beliefs and identity contributed significantly to his understanding of the dynamics of the groups of interest. In particular, they capture the distinctive ways in which each group understands the boundaries of their communities, and how these might be variously permeated, crossed and/or policed.

Conversely, some researchers have sought to justify covert observation. There are 'soft' cases as, for example, where unobtrusive observations from the margins of a fairly public ceremony may provide rich data on what anyone would notice. This is unlikely to harm participants, and the mere attempt to gain consent from everyone would usually be impossible but anyway could seriously affect the event and, thus, the conclusions drawn from observation. It seems likely that most fieldwork involves at least some occasions of this nature. More dramatically 'hard' cases of covert research occur too. Matthew Lauder, for example, argues that that 'is a useful and necessary tool in the examination of deviant communities', citing the example of research among 'a neo-National Socialist organisation that adheres to a racial-religious worldview' (Lauder 2003: 185). Access to such groups might be difficult, but whether deceit is appropriate (let alone necessary) is likely to be variously assessed. New researchers are best advised to seek advice from their supervisors, university or subject association ethics committees before embarking on such projects. These are likely to be familiar with the difficulties, but may, in any case, suggest that potentially dangerous groups are not the right place to begin learning or developing the skills of a fieldwork researcher. There are considerable benefits in starting a research career among people one feels some positive interest in, not least of which is the increased possibility of rapport.

Another fieldwork-specific issue arises from the practice of initiation among many religious groups. In an article in which he argues for fuller 'sharing' between researchers and the researched, Douglas Ezzy (2004) cites Edith Turner's vision of ethnography as 'an endeavor shared by natives and anthropologists' (Turner 1994: 87). He illustrates his argument by referring to his edited book about Australian witchcraft (Ezzy 2003) for which he invited selected witches to write chapters. More of his argument engages a contrast between published fieldwork among British magicians by Tanya Luhrmann (1989) and Susan Greenwood (2000). Both sought and gained initiation into groups whose meetings and rituals are not open to casual observers. Neither did so covertly. Everyone involved knew they were researchers and could not be said to be harmed by being observed without their knowledge and at least tacit consent. By acting just as other people do on seeking membership of esoteric and other private or even secretive religious organizations, Luhrmann and Greenwood learnt what happens and what it feels like more fully than would be possible by other means. The contrast between their research is in their publications, with Luhrmann insisting that she never really believed in magic's efficacy, and Greenwood insisting that full religious participation can enhance rather than delegitimize a researcher's work. At the very least, as Ezzy and other scholars have responded to Luhrmann's work, there are suspicions that other participants were in fact deceived about Luhrmann's intentions and participation. Among esotericists these are central concerns, and the publication of her skepticism made it difficult for other researchers to gain access to similar groups. Conversely, Ezzy (2004: 116–24) insists that Greenwood's apparently 'insiderly' claim (that 'magical identities are structured through a psycho-spiritual interaction with the otherworld', i.e. that magicians rightly interpret their experiences) in fact generates discussion that delivers significant sociological (rather than 'religious') understanding.

Recording data

Fieldwork's most memorable moments are likely to take place in the drama of performance or the intimacy of a conversation in which understanding dawns. It is not always easy or appropriate to record events or take notes of conversations as they happen, but most people seem pleased if asked, 'do you mind if I write that down? It conveys the thing so well and I'm keen not to forget your words'. Recording the exact words used by someone is absolutely necessary if there is any intention of quoting them. Many field researchers attempt to keep a diary-style record of events and impressions, updated as frequently as possible in unobtrusive ways. These are likely to aid in the writing of rich and evocative 'thick description' that conveys the sense of what it was like to be there (even in dull, undramatic moments). Remembering that fieldwork is about analyzing experiences, it is probably of the essence that any such recorded data is reflected upon rather than treated as a 'pure', unmediated record of what happened. Notes about the relevance of what is observed are invaluable accompaniments to notes about what happened.

In considering what goes into a diary it may be helpful to consider Clifford Geertz's powerful argument in favor of 'thick description' (a phrase he credits to Gilbert Ryle) as a means of conveying both what people do and what is significant for scholars about what people do. Setting out a word-picture of what people do, describing the context of significant actions, and drawing attention to important moments and actors is not only an initial stage in presenting research to others, those who were not present when the researcher saw, heard, experienced or recorded matters. This is signaled by the subtitle of the opening chapter of his book *The Interpretation of Cultures* (Geertz 1973): 'Thick description: towards an interpretive theory of culture'. Thick description of the particular or local is a selective process in which the researcher provides rich data about lived realities in relation to which theories and debates can be tested and advanced or negated. Thus, the information in Geertz's writings about what people do and what they have told him is not there to provide colorful illustrations for detailed analytical or theoretical contributions to debates. It is already interpreted data being opened up to further consideration. Thick description is more than 'mere subjective description' or 'naïve reportage' because it is attentive to more than one person's perspective, interpretation or questions. Rather, the provision of 'thick' or 'rich' description, informed by theory and aware of debate, will contribute significantly to the continuous project of debate that Geertz says is characteristic of academia: 'The precision with which we vex each other', he says, 'along with plaguing subtle people with obtuse questions, is what being an ethnographer is like' (Geertz 1973: 29, 30). Providing other people with a sense of what is interesting, important and provocative for critical discussion begins with what is written in diaries. As with every other aspect of research, practice with diary entry writing will lead to increased fluency and the likelihood of providing oneself with material that can easily become 'thick description'.

Video and audio technologies for the immediate recording of events as they occur are now commonplace and can be immensely useful, especially in relation to religious events or rituals.[4] Viewed after the event, they can reveal details missed in the drama of the moment or while paying attention to one practitioner rather than another. Replaying episodes or seemingly significant moments can enrich understanding of their importance (whether by revealing their centrality or their marginality). Sometimes it is helpful to play recordings to other participants and ask them to say what is significant. However, if note-taking during ceremonies can be disruptive, recording equipment requires careful preparation. Notoriously, people act differently when confronted with cameras or microphones. In some contexts they are simply not allowed, perhaps on the grounds that everyone should be fully involved rather than fussing about with machinery or anticipating later viewing, or because some events are deemed too sacred or personal to permit recording. Respect for the wishes, habits or culture of informants is likely to lead to resolutions that improve the process of research. Many researchers have found that people are only disturbed by the presence of notepads, cameras or other recording devices for a short while, especially since religious events often include early efforts to concentrate on 'more important matters' and set aside all distractions. Making it possible for this to happen, and offering to share copies of (perhaps edited) recordings can be invaluable.

Although some research manuals insist on the transcription of every word of an interview and every detail of an event, few researchers have sufficient time to do so. It is, however, not only sufficient but invaluable to annotate a synopsis of all recordings (noting the time or point in the recording at which events or transitions occurred, or at which themes were raised). These will highlight the parts (which may be brief) in which the main focus of a research project is touched upon. They ought also to summarize other events or discussions because awareness may later dawn that 'this too is relevant' and also because it might contribute to a future project with different purposes.

The posthumous and controversial publication of Malinowski's private fieldwork diary (Malinowski and Firth 1989) reveals much about the process by which his ideas about field-work evolved. However, their inclusion of derogatory remarks casts doubt on whether he had sufficient respect for his hosts to have tested his personal impressions by engaging in dialogue with them. This is not (simply) a warning to take care about what to write in such diaries, rather it should serve as an encouragement to work harder at rapport, epoché, respectful attention and dialogue. It is, however, also noteworthy that any recordings, notes, diaries and publications that include information about other people must now meet the requirements of national and/or international data protection legislation. Perhaps this ought to be an auto-matic part of showing respect to those from whom we benefit greatly as researchers. Nonetheless, it is also helpful to realize that the framing of such legislation has involved considerable debate about what is useful and appropriate. In short, notes, diaries and other material that results from research among human subjects may be requested by those concerned, and must be protected from others who might misappropriate data.

More positively, the writing of notes as soon as one can, re-working them as a research diary (including at least initial interpretation and further questions to be considered), and generally writing as much as possible about everything, is valuable as a stimulation to a researcher's own reflexive and analytical tasks. Alongside recording the exact words that informants speak, noting the key stages in observed events and emphasizing significant thoughts about the research, the development of writing skills will also result in at least occa-sional realizations about what really was important. Sometimes you have to try to communi-cate something in order to understand it fully. Additionally, the fuller the notes and records are, the more likely you are to notice things that you did not expect or anticipate. If a research project really justifies the name 'research' it cannot merely confirm existing knowledge—and certainly it must do more than this if it is to result in doctoral qualifications or postdoctoral publications that advance research.

Disseminating fieldwork results

Field research tends to result in distinctive kinds of writing. It is perhaps worth repeating a point made earlier: that fieldwork involves ways of recording data that make processes of selectivity, refinement or focusing central. It is equally true that the best examples of publica-tions arising from fieldwork make the researcher's presence, participation, experiences and reflexive processes visible. Being explicit about all these key performances by the researcher is likely to enrich the presentation of results. However, research is not all about the researcher any more than it is only about the particular and local (as Geertz demonstrated in his 'thick description'). None of this is to say that all fieldwork-based publications will present the author's personal experiences or scholarly analysis in the same way. Some will only note 'presence' in acknowledging debts to those among whom the researcher spent time, or in short methodological introductions. Others will attempt to represent particularly important encounters or experiences in more extensive discussions. Following the 'writing culture' debate alluded to earlier, it is increasingly commonplace for academics to provide a richer sense of presence in their publications—after all, a researcher's participation and reflections are central to what their work actually discusses. The key point that will be conveyed in fieldwork outputs is that researchers have aimed to get involved and understand as closely as possible what they have witnessed and engaged with.

It is worth noting, too, that researchers do not only disseminate their work in the form of publications aimed at other academics. Fieldwork often builds close relationships between scholars and religious people or groups. Sometimes this results in invitations or requests to the researcher to aid the community in some way. Some are happy to serve as expert witnesses in court cases (e.g. where religious affiliation plays a role in conflicts involving divorce, child custody or inheritance). Even the fact that a book or article exists about a particular religion or local group can be cited in support or opposition of issues affecting people. Organizations such as the British Information Network Focus on Religious Movements (INFORM), and the Swedish Association for Research and Information about New Religions (FINYAR) negotiate the difficult territory between enabling 'peaceful co-existence among the diversity of religions' and challenging 'misrepresentations [that] jeopardize the human rights' of religious people (Barker 2010: 21). Others will certainly consider any such hint of advocacy to be illegitimate, perhaps preferring that religious and other social groups sought out their own difficulties without academic intervention. As during the fieldwork phase of research, so afterwards when there is data to disseminate, the question of whether 'objectivity' requires distance or some degree of participation is fraught.

Conclusion: before you go

All research methods must be fit for their purpose. Fieldwork is particularly good for getting at what lived religion is like. It is well suited to research about ritual and everyday performance. For example, a full understanding of the Roman Catholic mass requires observation, at least, of the preparation and the aftermath of the central ritual. Assertions about power, hierarchy and gender might be challenged or confirmed (or partially both of these) when the full range of participants is noted, from cleaners and cooks to ritualists and counselors. Questions about the use rather than the origins of texts, especially as read, heard, venerated, material objects, can be answered by participant observation. Finding out what 'ordinary' people (who are often extraordinary) do and think, whether or not this is what their leaders or texts decree, is well within the domain of field research.

Limits may be established both by researchers and communities. Perhaps it is the job of scholars to minimize the reasons why they could be excluded. Their inability to achieve rapport or their unwillingness to set aside preconceptions and seek to adapt themselves to a community's expected norms would be serious problems. Difficulties about whether observation, recording and/or questions are appropriate challenge the practice, especially when they cause changes that affect the nature of the phenomena of interest. Finding ways to bring into focus what is taken for granted either by the researcher or the researched is vital to the ambition to see what actually goes on rather than what is imagined or claimed about what happens.

In addition to gaining rapport and access, or meeting willing hosts, field research entails phases of participation and observation, usually simultaneously, and reflection, reporting, dialogue and further reflection to test one's interpretation, attempts to write so that the sense of presence and reflexivity are conveyed, and perhaps other modes of dissemination. It is likely, of course, that an academic will make use of their fieldwork in teaching students at all levels, benefiting them with the fruits of recent experience of the real lives of religious people.

Fieldwork, like many other tasks, is best learnt by doing it. Only so much guidance can be given before 'trying it out' is needed. Commonly, therefore, it is advisable to conduct a pilot project of limited duration and focus in order to test one's ability to gain rapport, practice reflexive analysis, determine what skills one already has and what one needs more advice about, and similar issues. Not everything that a researcher learns in one place will be useful elsewhere, but there are basics that are at the heart of fieldwork: gaining rapport, bracketing preconceptions, being empathetic, being reflexive, recording data and planning outcomes. Personal preferences, character and serendipity play significant roles in selecting topics for research, gaining access to groups, noticing or mistaking elements of value to the project, being ready to learn from others or be corrected by them, and finding colleagues with whom to discuss or collaborate. Balancing interest in a particular religion or specific group with a focus on clearly defined scholarly questions will provide secure foundations for any project.

Fieldwork is a hybrid activity, combining not only various kinds of participation and various kinds of observation, but also entailing sometimes asking questions, sometimes checking facts and impressions, sometimes wondering what an experience means. It arises from the notion that some kinds of activities require presence and participation and are better understood from within the messy living reality than from the safety of the margins. It most certainly challenges the researcher to leave the apparently safe position of a study or a library and to get involved. The question is always: how far should researchers participate, how much should they get involved and is it possible to go too far? However, there are strong arguments in favor of field research. Most importantly, if research methods should be suitable to the phenomena of interest, and if religion is an activity, practice, performance or lifeway, then researching religion requires some level of participation if it is to generate full understanding.

Before you go (out into the field), it may be good to know that, despite all his faults, Malinowski hoped that fieldwork would 'supply us with a sense of humor' (Malinowski 1954: 145). Taking one with you would be a great advantage—by that means, you are likely to enjoy the experience so much more.

Notes

1   It helps to think of 'drama' even in relation to ordinary, everyday, habitual, dull or routine acts because even these more common aspects of 'doing' or 'living' religion are elements in the full experience that researchers are trying to appreciate, understand and think sophisticated theoretically informed thoughts about.

2   The 'atheist' rhetoric is largely part of a positioning of the study of religion as something different to theology rather than a programmatic, definitive or methodological insistence on the falsehood of religion.

3   Further arguments in this direction might engage fruitfully with the work of Bruno Latour (1993, 2009) and Eduardo Viveiros de Castro (1998).

4   See Hubert Knoblauch's chapter on video analysis in this volume: Chapter 2.22 Videography.

References

Ahmadu, F., 2000. Rites and wrongs: excision and power among Kono women of Sierra Leone. In: Shell-Duncan, B. and Hernlund, Y. (eds), *Female 'Circumcision' in Africa: culture, change and controversy*. Lynne Rienner, Boulder, CO, pp. 283–312.

Babb, L.A., 1996. *Absent Lord: ascetics and kinds in a Jain ritual culture*. University of California Press, Berkeley.

Barker, E., 2010. Misconceptions of the religious 'other': the importance for human rights of objective and balanced knowledge. *International Journal for the Study of New Religions* 1 (1): 5–25.

Berger, P.L., 1969. *The Sacred Canopy: elements of a sociological theory of religion*. Doubleday, Garden City, NY.

Bourdieu, P., 1977. *Outline of a Theory of Practice*. Trans. Richard Nice. Cambridge University Press, Cambridge.

Capper, D., 2003. Scientific empathy, American Buddhism, and the ethnography of religion. *Culture and Religion* 4 (2): 233–53.

Chidester, D., 2008. Dreaming in the contact zone: Zulu dreams, visions, and religion in the nineteenth-century. *Journal of the American Academy of Religion* 76 (1): 27–53. DOI:10.1093/jaarel/lfm094

Chryssides, G.D. and Geaves, R., 2007. *The Study of Religion: an introduction to key ideas and methods*. Continuum, London.

Clifford, J. and Marcus, G. (eds), 1986. *Writing Culture*. University of California Press, Berkeley.

Coleman, S. and Collins, P., 2000. The 'plain' and the 'positive': ritual, experience and aesthetics in Quakerism and charismatic Christianity, *Journal of Contemporary Religion* 15 (3): 317–29.

Cox, J.L., 2006. *A Guide to the Phenomenology of Religion*. London: Continuum.

—— 2010. *An Introduction to the Phenomenology of Religion*. London: Continuum.

Droogers, A., 2008. As close as a scholar can get: exploring a one-field approach to the study of religion. In: de Vries, H. (ed.), *Religion: beyond a concept*. Fordham University Press, New York. pp. 448–63.

Ellis, C., 2003, *The Ethnographic I: a methodological novel about autoethnography*. Altamira, Walnut Creek, CA.

Engler, S., forthcoming. Umbanda and Africa. *Nova Religio: The Journal of Alternative and Emergent Religions*.

Evans-Pritchard, E.E., 1965. *Theories of Primitive Religion*. OUP, Oxford.

Ezzy, D., 2003. *Practising the Witch's Craft*. Allen and Unwin, Sydney.

—— 2004. Religious ethnography: practicing the Witch's craft. In: Blain, J., Ezzy, D. and Harvey, G. (eds), *Researching Paganisms*. AltaMira Press, Lanham, CA. pp. 113–28.

Favret-Saada, J., 1980. *Deadly Words: witchcraft in the Bocage*. Cambridge University Press, Cambridge.

Geertz, C., 1973. Thick description: towards an interpretive theory of culture. In: *The Interpretation of Cultures: selected essays*. Basic Books, New York. pp. 3–30.

Greenwood, S., 2000. *Magic, Witchcraft and the Otherworld: an anthropology*. Berg, Oxford.

Gruenbaum, E., 2001. *The Female Circumcision Controversy: an anthropological perspective*. University of Philadelphia Press, Philadelphia.

Guest, M., 2002. 'Alternative' worship: challenging the boundaries of the christian faith. In: Arweck, E. and Stringer, M.D. (eds), *Theorizing Faith: the insider/outsider problem in the study of religion*. University of Birmingham Press, Birmingham, pp. 35–56.

Harvey, G., 2003. Guesthood as ethical decolonising research method. *Numen* 50 (2): 125–46.

—— 2005. Performing and constructing research as guesthood. In: Hume, L. and Mulcock, J. (eds), *Anthropologists in the Field*. Columbia University Press, New York, pp. 168–82.

—— 2007. Inventing Paganisms, making nature. In: Lewis, J.R. and Hammer, O. (eds), *The Invention of Sacred Tradition*. Cambridge University Press, Cambridge, pp. 277–90.

Hastrup, K. and Hervik, P. (eds), 1994. *Social Experience and Anthropological Knowledge*. Routledge, London.

Hufford, D.J., 1995a. Introduction. *Western Folklore* 54 (1): 1–11.

—— 1995b. The scholarly voice and the personal voice. *Western Folklore* 54(1): 57–76.

Koskinen-Koivisto, E., 2010. Making sense of senses: interview with Dorothy Noyes. *Elore* 17 (1): 3–8. www.elore.fi/arkisto/1_10/haast_koskinen-koivisto_1_10.pdf.

LaFleur, W.R., 1994. *Liquid Life: abortion and Buddhism in Japan*. Princeton University Press, Princeton.

Lambek, M., 2002. *A Reader in the Anthropology of Religion*. Blackwell, Oxford.

Latour, B., 1993. *We Have Never Been Modern*. Harvester Wheatsheaf, New York.

—— 2009. Perspectivism: 'type' or 'bomb'? *Anthropology Today* 25 (2): 1–2.

Lauder, M., 2003. Covert participant observation of a deviant community: justifying the use of deception. *Journal of Contemporary Religion* 18: 185–96.

Lee, R.B., 1969. Eating Christmas in the Kalahari. *Natural History* 78 (10): 14–17.

Lewis, I.M., 1999. *Arguments with Ethnography: comparative approaches to history, politics and religion*. Athlone Press, London.

Ludueña, G.A., 2005. Asceticism, fieldwork and technologies of the self in Latin American Catholic monasticism. *Fieldwork in Religion* 1 (2): 145–64.

Luhrmann, T., 1989. *Persuasions of the Witch's Craft*. Blackwell, Oxford.

Malinowski, B., 1954. *Magic, Science and Religion and Other Essays*. Doubleday, Garden City, NY.

Malinowski, B. and Firth, R.W., 1989. *Diary in the Strict Sense of the Term*. Stanford University Press, Stanford, CA.

Meyer, B., 2008. Religious sensations: why media, aesthetics, and power matter in the study of contemporary religion. In: de Vries, H. (ed.), *Religion: beyond a concept*. Fordham University Press, New York, pp. 703–23.

Nye, M., 2004. *Religion: the basics*. Routledge, London.

Poewe, K., 1996. Writing culture and writing fieldwork: the proliferation of experimental and experiential ethnographies. *Ethnos* 3–4: 177–206.

Primiano, L.N., 1995. Vernacular Religion and the Search for Method in Religious Folklife. *Western Folklore* 54 (1): 37–56.

Rapport, N. and Overing, J., 2004. *Social and Cultural Anthropology: the key themes*. Routledge, London.

Ruel, M., 2005. Christians as believers. In: Harvey, G. (ed.), *Ritual and Religious Belief: a reader*. Equinox, London, pp. 242–64.

Schechner, R., [n.d.]. What is 'performance studies' anyway? www.nyu.edu/classes/bkg/rs2.dos.

Smart, N., 1973. *The Phenomenon of Religion*. Seabury Press, New York.

Sykes, K., 2005. *Arguing with Anthropology: an introduction to critical theories of the gift*. Routledge, London.

Tawhai, T.P., 1988. Maori Religion. In: Sutherland, S. and Clarke, P. (eds), *The Study of Religion: traditional and new religion*. Routledge, London, pp. 96–105. (Reprinted in Harvey, G. (ed.), 2002. *Readings in Indigenous Religions*. Continuum, London, pp. 238–49.)

Turner, E., 1994. A visible spirit form in Zambia. In: Young, D.E. and Goulet, J.-G. (eds), *Being Changed: the anthropology of extraordinary experience*. Broadview Press, New York, pp. 71–95.

University of California Press, 2007. *Catalog description of Willerslev 2007*. www.ucpress.edu/book.php?isbn=9780520252172.

Viveiros de Castro, E., 1998. Cosmological deixis and amerindian perspectivism. *Journal of the Royal Anthropological Institute* (N.S.) 4: 469–88.

Wallis, R.J., 2004. Between the worlds: autoarchaeology and neo-shamans. In: Blain, J., Ezzy, D. and Harvey, G. (eds), *Researching Paganisms*. Altamira, Walnut Creek, CA.

Willerslev, R., 2007. *Soul Hunters: hunting, animism, and personhood among the Siberian Yukaghirs*. University of California Press, Berkeley.

Yip, A.K.T., 2005. Religion and the politics of spirituality/sexuality: reflections on researching British lesbian, gay, and bisexual Christians and Muslims. *Fieldwork in Religion* 1 (3): 271–89.

Further reading

Fieldwork in Religion

International peer-reviewed journal publishing current fieldwork-based research including reflections on processes and methods. Published by Equinox, London. www.equinoxjournals.com/FIR.

Bailey, C.A., 2007. *A Guide to Qualitative Field Research*. Pine Forge Press, Thousand Oaks, CA.

Comprehensive guide to fieldwork from selecting a topic to publishing outcomes.

Denzin, N.K. and Lincoln, Y.S. (eds), 1998. *The Landscape of Qualitative Research: theories and issues.* SAGE, London, Thousand Oaks, CA.

An important orientation to fieldwork and other 'qualitative' (rather than 'quantitative') research, including historical, ethical and political considerations of how researchers engage with other people.

Emerson, R.M., Fretz, R. and Shaw, L.L., 1995. *Writing Ethnographic Fieldnotes.* University of Chicago Press, Chicago.

The best guide for writing notes during fieldwork and beyond.

Hammersley, M., 2008. *Questioning Qualitative Research: critical essays.* SAGE, London, Thousand Oaks, CA.

Provocative essays on continuing developments and debates about fieldwork which should be essential reading for anyone interested in the future of qualitative research—for example, debating whether our focus should be discourse or action.

Orsi, R.A., 2005. *Between Heaven and Earth: the religious worlds people make and the scholars who study them.* Princeton University Press, Princeton, Oxford.

An internationally significant scholar of religion reflects on fieldwork.

Rice, P. and Ezzy, D., 2005. *Qualitative Research Methods.* 2nd edn. Oxford University Press, Oxford.

An accessible introduction to qualitative research with a wealth of helpful advice and clear instructions.

Spradley, J.P., 1979. *The Ethnographic Interview.* Holt, Rinehart and Winston, New York.

Especially excellent on the mechanics of fieldwork, asking questions.

Spickard, J.V., Landres, J.S. and McGuire, M. (eds), 2002. *Personal Knowledge and Beyond: reshaping the ethnography of religion.* New York University Press, New York, London.

Invaluable collection of essays about how researchers come to know and present their understanding.

Wolf, M., 1992. *A Thrice Told Tale: feminism, postmodernism and ethnographic responsibility.* Stanford: Stanford University Press.

Fascinating and engagingly presented discussion of 'responsible' ways of doing fieldwork that should not only be read by feminists and postmodernists.

Key concepts

Care: Research requires various forms of care, especially towards those among whom scholars research (which may also be called 'respect') and towards the conventions and relevant debates of the wider academic community.

Dialogue: A development of participant observation in which researchers discuss their emerging interpretations and arguments with those among who they research, thus strengthening the often weak claim that such people are 'informants'. Dialogue can test whether one's observations coincide the experiences or ideas of others. It can also aid in clarifying understanding of what 'insiders' take for granted.

Drama: 'Drama' emphasizes that the 'doing' of religion (in rituals and in the mundane acts of everyday life) is the chief focus of fieldwork research. It does not imply that religion is necessarily spectacular or theatrical.

Empathy: The practice of assuming an attitude of interest in other people's lives and concerns. It is developed by feeling or thinking oneself into others' habitual and motivated lives.

Epoché: Conscious bracketing out of researchers' prior assumptions, ideologies and expectations. 'Bracketing' should not mean 'ignoring' but considered awareness of factors that might unduly influence research (while among other people or when analyzing data) and working to avoid this.

Rapport: Establishing and maintaining friendly and/or trusting relationships with others. Seeking some kind of mutual interest. Getting involved more emotionally than merely participating can imply.

Reflexivity: A development of participant observation in which researchers devote time and effort to considering the experience of being involved in religious acts. The more participatory phases of fieldwork might provide researchers with a sense of 'what it is like' to be a full participant or 'insider'. Reflecting on this provides an additional way of analyzing data and enriches the published result by enhancing description and argument.

Respect: Respect is a methodological tool, requiring effort, that can underlie and/or be expressed in care, rapport, empathy and dialogue. It need not involve liking or agreeing with those among whom one researches or those whose scholarly arguments one debates. However, it requires unprejudiced presentation of others' views and experiences, taking into account local protocols, and at least polite explication of one's reasons about disagreements.

Related chapters

- Chapter 1.2 Comparison
- Chapter 1.3 Epistemology
- Chapter 1.4 Feminist methodologies
- Chapter 1.6 Research ethics
- Chapter 2.13 Interviewing
- Chapter 2.15 Phenomenology
- Chapter 2.19 Structured observation
- Chapter 2.20 Surveys and questionnaires
- Chapter 2.22 Videography
- Chapter 3.1 Auditory materials
- Chapter 3.3 Material culture

2.9

FREE-LISTING

Michael Stausberg

Chapter summary

- Free-listing (a.k.a. list recall) is a technique to elicit data on categories, classes or cultural domains, but it can also be useful for other purposes where it is important to know the vocabulary people use to conceptualize things, events and affairs in the world.
- It can be used as part of interviews or questionnaires, and it can be used to prepare questionnaires and interview guides.
- Free-listing is relatively easy to administer and typically requires a sample size of no more than 20–30 respondents.
- Free-listing is a tool to explore salient data, i.e. data that are widely shared/distributed and considered relevant, either in terms of being distinctive and attention-grabbing or typical.

Introduction

Classification and categorization are powerful cognitive processes that pervade every domain of the human construction of reality. In the study of religion\s, the topics of classification and categorization have been a main concern—indeed one of the key issues for scholars belonging to conflicting theoretical approaches such as structuralism, post-structuralism, critical theory and cognitive/evolutionary sciences. While cognitivists have looked at how 'natural' processes of categorization have constrained the creation of religious concepts, and structuralists have analyzed religions as classificatory systems, critical theorists have pointed to the colonial, cultural, hegemonic, political, ritual and other consequences of classificatory processes in and beyond religion. The category of religion in itself has emerged as the result of specific classificatory processes. On a different level, religions have been theorized as 'powerful engines for the production and maintenance of classificatory systems' (Smith 2000: 38). Hence, the analysis of the processes of classification and the formation of cultural domains is of primary importance for the study of religion\s. The present chapter seeks to introduce a 'deceptively simple, but powerful technique' (Bernard 2006: 301) that can be used to obtain and analyze data on the vocabulary people use to refer to, or to conceptualize, a **domain** or a **category**.

This technique is known as **free-listing** (sometimes also referred to as 'list task' or 'free recall listing'). If you want to explore the categories and **concept**s the people you are studying use to refer to aspects of the world as they understand it, free-listing is one effective way to do so. One practical advantage with this technique is that it does not require a very large sample to begin with; typically, relevant (initial) findings can be achieved with a sample of 20–30 participants. Moreover, free-listing is relatively easy to conduct.

Contrary to observation in 'natural' settings,[1] free-listing is a so-called elicitation technique, which can be used in both interviews and questionnaires. Free-listing basically asks informants to provide short answers to questions such as 'what Xs are there?' or 'list all the Xs you know about'. Consider the following examples: What impure things are there? List all the commands of god you know about. What forms of blessing are there? List all the spirits you know about. What amulets are there? List all the spheres of heaven you know about. Alternatively, one can ask respondents to list examples of categories or features of concepts: e.g. list examples for 'ritual' you know of; list features of 'myth' that come to mind.

The resulting lists need to be recorded, either by the researcher or by the respondents themselves, and care must be taken to record the listed items in the sequential order in which they were produced. Of course, the technique is not quite as simple as it can seem at first sight, because phrasing the question in the right manner—so that the task is properly understood by the respondents, allowing them to provide rich and relevant information—requires some preparation (e.g. pre-testing).

Note that the general structure of the question, which asks what there is or what respondents know about what exists, hold true or take for granted about something, is important. One could potentially ask informants to list things such as their 'favourite X' (god, myth, priest, ritual, song, temple), but that would generate information about personal preferences. Information about preferences could then be analyzed systematically, where it could turn out that a given sample of respondents to some degree shares certain preferences (or not), or that they could be correlated to other variables such as age, ethnicity, gender, etc. For such correlational designs, however, much larger samples of participants are required. Free-listing can be quite useful for that type of analysis, but this is not how free-listing has generally been discussed in the literature. In the context of the study of religion\s, however, we will need to approach the issue more broadly.

Eliciting data for the analysis of domain, categories and concepts

Free-listing is typically used to elicit information on 'domains', i.e. segments of culture/ nature in the form of categories that are believed to exist 'out there'. Examples include animals, colours, forms of kinship, or types of illness. Free-listing explores the 'conceptual sphere' (Weller and Romney 1988: 9) that constitutes such a domain. The emphasis can lie on the semantic composition of the distributed yet shared knowledge about the respective 'domain' or on the lexical vocabulary used: e.g. (linguistic) terms for illness and kinship relationships or (social) forms of illness and kinship. Both aspects are to some extent interrelated, because terms are usually held to refer to something (even if this may not be the most promising way to study meaning and semantics from a philosophical point of view). The point here is that in order to understand the organization of a cultural 'domain', one is interested in what people consider or know to exist or to be the case—and not in their individual preferences or their subjective imaginations. The aim is to obtain data for culture or cultural domains (e.g. religion) or aspects of them, not primarily about individuals and their actions, attitudes, beliefs, habits, etc. A first step for an inventory of domain-relative knowledge is to map the range of words used to refer to it, and free-listing is an efficient way of doing this.

'Domain' is here understood as 'something' people know to exist and about which they have some knowledge.[2] This also includes social or cultural domains—i.e. the sort of 'affairs' (interactively constructed reality) usually studied by scholars of religion\s. As social or cultural realities, these 'affairs' or 'domains' are often normative and disputed. When extending the scope of the concept of domain, one similarly broadens the range of application of free-listing to encompass items such as (ascribed and expected) traits, features or characteristics. Obviously, this has methodological implications. When not merely listing single terms and things or object terms, which can be immediately placed in a list (such as words for animals or diseases), the researcher will eventually need to code the answers in order to sort out overlapping terms for the same or similar concepts. This implies interpretation and typically requires some knowledge of the relevant context. In particular, this is the case when the lists are generated in (one or several) foreign languages, which also raises the issue of translation.[3]

While the literature often discusses free-listing as a technique to elicit data on domains, the technique is not wedded to the concept of domains (and underlying or related theories of culture or the mind). For example, free-listing has been used as one technique (among several) in analyses of concepts in general, in particular by studies seeking to explore people's understanding of concepts. Rather than starting with theory-driven explorations, as often is the case in surveys, free-listing is a technique to elicit lay-knowledge.[4] This is especially important in fields of study, such as the study of religion\s, where concepts are important parts of the way the actors interpret and construct reality. In addition, given that the study of religion\s like many other disciplines in the humanities and social sciences, shares large parts of its vocabulary with the people it studies, it is important to understand how this scholarly vocabulary is used in non-academic contexts.

Box 2.9.1 A study of Zoroastrian priests

We used free-listing in a research project on the priesthood among Zoroastrians (Parsis) in India. All Zoroastrians we talked to agreed that priesthood is a necessary feature of the religion, and priesthood is a social reality for Zoroastrians (at least in India). Moreover, only boys born from priestly families can become priests, so that the priesthood operates under genealogical constraints and is a different social domain for the laity. The priests have the laity as their customers. Given that interactional situation, in our project we were interested not only in the activities, opinions and work situation of the priests, but also in the views of the laity regarding the priesthood (and their priests). So, we asked respondents from the laity to list characteristics of the 'good priest'. Phrasing the question in this way meant that we were not interested in their views about individual priests, nor about an ideal vision; instead, the question aimed at understanding the mixture of expectations, ascriptions, examples and experiences that are typical when evaluating a social reality. Lists from 95 respondents yielded 254 different statements, which could be coded to several main categories.

Salience and (proto-)typicality

When asking sufficiently many people to 'list all the Xs you know about' or 'what Xs are there?' (where X, for example, could be 'illnesses', 'spirits', 'commands of god' or 'character-istics of a good priest'), one may in the end come close to an exhaustive list of elements. This is, however, not what free-listing is typically used for. Instead, one hopes 'to get a list of culturally relevant items on which most of the informants agree' (Ross 2004: 90). Reportedly, what one will usually find is that 'with increasing number of informants, the number of new elements added to an aggregated list becomes smaller' (Ross 2004: 90). Moreover, the new items that emerge if one continues asking people 'tend to be more idiosyncratic' (Ross 2004: 90), meaning that the additional items are mentioned by one or few individuals only. The items recurrently listed by most respondents are apparently more familiar, better known and more widely shared by or distributed among the respondents; they can therefore be held to be the more 'typical', 'representative', or 'salient'.

In the case of our priesthood project, a somewhat different situation emerged, since our respondents kept on producing a long list of **'idiosyncratic'** items. Out of 254 different statements on the qualities of the 'good priest', only 12 (= 5 per cent) were mentioned verbatim by two or more respondents, and only five (= 2 per cent) were mentioned by at least three participants.[5] A different picture emerges when one goes beyond the verbatim level by collapsing across grammatical form and coding different statements to yield a smaller number of categories. In our case, issues of religious education and explanation and ritual performance were a recurrent concern, but were addressed by a somewhat disparate vocabulary. Some 203 of 254 statements (= 80 per cent) can be collated to six major categories, which are not in all cases mutually exclusive and can or even must be subdivided into thematically more coherent smaller (medium-range) units. Moreover, findings will vary when looking at semantic similarity (e.g. coding 'learned' as 'knowledge') rather than at lexical equivalence or slight lexical modifications (e.g. coding 'knows what he is talking about' as 'knowledge').

Salience

There are several ways to measure the **salience** of frequently mentioned items. (The 'idiosyncratic' items only mentioned by one or few respondents are not considered to qualify as salient, even if some may be quite interesting or meaningful.) To begin with, 'items recalled first are assumed to be more salient than items recalled last' (Borgatti 1999: 123); salience is here measured by which items are mentioned first, i.e. recall speed; salience thereby refers to a quality of memory recall. Conversely, if an item is likely to be mentioned frequently (i.e. by many respondents), it is also likely to be mentioned early on the individual lists. This is also what happened in our study. The two items mentioned most often were also more often mentioned in prominent positions on individual lists: honesty was listed by 17 respondents (= 18 per cent of all participants) and in 11 cases (= 65 per cent) it was listed first and in the remaining cases second; the words 'to know'/'knowledge' were used in 30 statements (with various qualifications), where it was listed first on 16 lists and second on 10 lists, while it was listed third in three cases and once in fourth position. Combining these two parameters, namely the proportion of mentions among lists and the average order of an item on individual lists,[6] can be combined to yield a salience index for all items listed. Another variable is the mean position of items on individual lists, and a so-called cognitive salience index has been proposed that combines these parameters (Sutrop 2001).

The frequency of occurrence of items on individual lists is used as the main parameter for determining the boundary of a 'domain'. Technically, one proceeds by first compiling a list of all items mentioned by more than one respondent, in order to then measure their frequency of mention. When tabulating the percentage of respondents who have listed a given item, one often notes significant breaks in frequency (comparing those items listed almost universally, or significantly more often, with the idiosyncratic ones). In other cases, one finds several 'mini-breaks', i.e. minor discontinuities in distribution curves. Typically, one defines the boundaries of a given domain along the main break or one of the mini-breaks. In our study (where the domain in a wider sense reflected the core characteristics of the Zoroastrian priest), there turned out to be one major break (in the pre-coding analysis): the core qualities of the Zoroastrian priest are 'knowledge' and [being] 'honest' (reflecting professional qualifications and attitudes), which were listed 15 and 12 times verbatim, which is significantly more often than all other items ('dedicated to work' being the third item, but only listed, verbatim, by four respondents). The literature reports that in some cases no breaks whatsoever may be apparent and then one needs to draw a line arbitrarily (Borgatti 1999: 125), or one may doubt the reliability or validity of the specific operation—in other words, there may be no clearly demarcated 'core domain' here.[7] Note also that the option to demarcate boundaries along breaks is only an indication of the existence of a break and no proof of the existence of any given natural fact. Moreover, the decision to tabulate all items listed by more than one respondent in the first place is an arbitrary decision in itself (Sutrop 2001: 265). This also recalls the issue of coding (see above).

Sample size

The confidence with which one can make such demarcations depends also on the sample size. One rule of thumb is that the greater the number of respondents, the greater the number of idiosyncratic items, and the greater the number of items not to be reckoned with when tabulating the frequency of items (Sutrop 2001: 265). In general, therefore, where greater samples can give more accurate results, the accuracy will mostly lie in the relative number of idiosyncratic items, which is largely irrelevant for the determination of a domain or for understanding its key features. According to the literature, a sample of 20–30 informants is sufficient (Weller and Romney 1988: 14), while another source refers to a minimum of 30 lists as desirable (Borgatti 1999: 122). Retrospectively, in the case of our study the prominence of knowledge and honesty became already clear after 20 individual lists (which gave 70 different characteristics of the 'good priest', with 3.5 average statements per respondent).

The adequacy of the initial sample size can be conveniently checked by the degree of achieved saturation: check the relative frequency of top-listed items after 20 lists and check again after 30 lists; if the relative frequency remains largely unchanged, there may not be a need to enlist further respondents (but if notable changes are the case, one should continue, which would have been the case in our study, given the overwhelming number of idiosyncratic items) (Borgatti 1999: 122–23). The findings, of course, can only be generalized in case of random samples: a sample of 20 priests will probably produce a structured list of deities and demons, but these figures cannot be used to infer to the non-specialist community of ordinary Zoroastrians. For more complex or arbitrary domains larger samples will be required, but that can again be tested by using the above-mentioned saturation check.[8]

In the literature on free-listing, salience is not distinguished from typicality and is often used in rather broad terms (just as 'domain' is). In some disciplines, however, the term 'salience' is given a somewhat more precise meaning.[9] In neuroscience, the salience (or saliency) of an item is a function of that quality or state which makes it stand out from neighboring items; salient items catch attention. Salience is a perceptual mechanism (for example visual salience) assumed to play an important evolutionary function, since it 'is important for complex biological systems to rapidly detect potential prey, predators or mates in a cluttered visual world' (Itti 2007). Salience is also a relevant concept in social psychology: groups or individuals can attract attention in a given social context, because they are the only exemplars of a different (ethnic, religious) group, because they stand out visually, or because they behave in unusual ways; salient people are often perceived to have greater impact on their social environment (McArthur 1981). Marketing researchers have used the term 'salience' to explore the propensity of certain brands to be noticed and to come to mind in buying situations, or to be mentioned first in memory retrieval (Romaniuk and Sharp 2004). In sum, the category of salience as used by different disciplines highlights different aspects: attention and distinctiveness; their distinctive, attention-grabbing propensities (in a given context) make salient items potentially important, be it for individual decisions, social processes, or as determinants of evolutionary success.

In order to be salient (in this sense), items need to be distinctive. In this respect, the term is different from typicality: a typical item is not particularly distinctive from other items and is therefore neither attention-grabbing as such nor especially memorable. This points to a potential ambivalence in the validity of free-listing: recall will mainly operate in terms of salience, but salient items can in theory also be somewhat untypical ones, whereas the desired exclusion of idiosyncratic items (which are potentially salient in the sense of distinct and attention-grabbing) aims at achieving a high level of typicality. One is therefore tempted to speculate that items with an extremely high salience-index (salience here understood in the broader sense) can potentially be considered as prototypical items, i.e. ones generally recognized as the most typical instances of a category (or domain). If one were to ask people in certain Western countries to list all the religions they know, Christianity would probably have a very high salience index; if the salience index were considerably higher than that of other frequently listed religions (one would expect for the so-called world religions to top the list), one could call it a prototypical item. Alternatively, analysis might seek to point to schemas, i.e. structured knowledge (or expectation) about events, objects, persons, situations, etc. For example, there may be a schema (an organized configuration of traits) for 'religion' or for 'priests' (as our case leads to suspect), etc. Note that we are, in line with the extension of the domain concept suggested above, dealing here with lists of traits rather than with lists of examples.

Prototype theory

Another relevant perspective on these issues comes from **prototype theory**. According to this theory, category systems have a vertical and a horizontal dimension. On the vertical dimension, some concepts are included in others; in general, one distinguishes between three hierarchical levels: superordinate, basic and subordinate. Moving up from the basic to the superordinate level, one asks 'to what general category does X belong' (where X is the basic category); when moving down to the subordinate level, one asks 'what are the types of X'. (Take 'ritual' as a hypothetical example for a basic-level category: the superordinate category could be 'action' and subordinate categories could include 'initiation'.) Typically, subjects list fewer attributes for superordinate categories than for the other two. The horizontal level addresses the differentiation of the category or concept on the same level. According to prototype theory, natural language concepts are structured prototypically. Prototypes are the clearest cases, best examples or key exemplars of a category or concept. According to prototype theory, categorization and conceptualization are graded; for every category, there are members that are more central (prototypical) than others, so that 'members of a category can be ordered in terms of their degree of resemblance to the prototypical cases, with members shading gradually into non-members. Boundaries between categories therefore are blurry' (Fehr 2005: 182). Similarly, there are features of concepts that are more central than others. Prototype analyses are 'undertaken to flesh out the content and structure of a particular concept' (Fehr 2005: 185) or category. Often, free-listing is used as a first step to elicit data on concepts or categories, where respondents are asked to list examples of cases or features of items. The resulting data is then analyzed by employing various techniques and methods. One typical second step is a ranking task, where a second sample of respondents are asked to rank the examples or features that were listed most frequently by the first group of respondents with regard to typicality or centrality (How good an example is A for category X? How central is feature A for concept X?).[10] Prototypical examples often share a greater number of features than less typical examples (yielding a greater 'family resemblance'). Prototype theory also predicts that respondents typically list more typical examples or more central features faster than less typical examples or less typical features; the reaction time to identify apples as a good example of fruit is less than for olives. To return to our hypothetical example, respondents would probably need more time to make up their minds whether washing is a proper case of ritual, compared to initiation. (Reaction time can be measured most precisely when respondents enter their replies on a computer.) This measure of proto-typicality thereby resonates with one interpretation of salience in the analysis of domains.

Competence

While the frequency and order of items on lists is used to determine their salience and the conceptual configuration of a domain, comparing lists of different respondents can also be used to determine the degree of their individual competence. Informants who can produce longer lists can be considered to have a greater degree of task-specific competence. If their lists, compared with those of other respondents, contain a larger number of unique (idiosyncratic) items, this is either a sign of expertise (like that possessed by religious specialists) or a sign of idiosyncratic knowledge, which may be neither relevant nor typical. In order to assess individual competence of respondents, one could therefore 'weight the items in an individual freelist by the proportion of respondents who mentions the item' (Borgatti 1999: 127). When analyzing the data, one may also, as has been suggested by consensus analysts, assign a greater weight to the lists provided by more competent respondents (Ryan *et al.* 2000: 84). Yet, a predominance of idiosyncratic items on a list cannot in itself be taken as evidence for lack of competence by the respondent, who may well have listed these items because of specific and potentially relevant experiences.

Main forms of analysis and additional variations

Free-listing produces something like membership lists in domains, or lists of traits (which in many cases will need to be coded). Such lists are sometimes called 'protocols'. One initial step of analysis is to determine the distribution of frequency of listed items. This can be done easily by setting up a 'dichotomized-respondent-by-item matrix', where the rows are the respondents and the columns are the items; one can then simply put a '1' in the cell if the respondent in the given row mentions the item in the respective cell and put a '0' if the item was not listed (which is why it is 'dichotomized'). Alternatively, a 'ranked-respondent-by-item matrix' lists the items in the columns numerically (1, 2, 3 . . .) where '1' refers to the items listed first, etc., thereby reflecting the order in which they were listed by the respondents. These matrices can be used for further analysis.

Apart from the occurrence and the order of listed items, analysis can be interested in the co-occurrence of items. This is assumed to reflect the (perceived) similarity between items. The co-occurrence of items on different lists (or protocols) can be represented in an 'item-by-item matrix', i.e. a matrix listing all items both in the columns and the row fields.

On the basis of a dichotomized-respondent-by-item matrix (as above) one identifies the number of times that a given item A was mentioned by all respondents (its frequency) and then one identifies how many times a given item B was mentioned by all the respondents who also had listed A (e.g. honesty and knowledge as characteristics of the 'good priest'). To take a hypothetical example, we have 30 respondents who have listed a total of 30 items, out of which four were listed by two or more respondents. We will then consider only these four items. Suppose item A was mentioned by 20 informants, we would write 20 in the cells identified as A both on the row and the column field; B was mentioned by 15 respondents, C by 10 and D by two respondents, respectively. Further suppose 12 respondents listed both A and B, we write 12 in the cell identified as A and B in the rows and columns respectively; if six list both A and C we write six in the cell identified as A and C in the rows and columns respectively; if both respondents who listed D also listed A we write two in the cell identified as A and D in the rows and columns respectively. Here is the hypothetical matrix: by looking at it, you may then try to identify how many protocols list B and C, or B and D, etc., respectively (i.e. the co-occurrence of these items):

Table 2.9.1 Hypothetical item-by-item matrix

	A	B	C	D
A	20	12	6	2
B	12	15	4	1
C	6	10	10	0
D	2	1	0	2

To visualize the results in a more appealing manner, numbers can be transferred into a multidimensional scaling map (MDS), which illustrates a potential core-periphery structure (Borgatti 1999: 127–29). Ryan *et al.* (2000) have exemplified analysis by using correspondence analysis.

Starting from the assumption that items listed next to or close to each other on a list are more similar than items listed far apart, one might wish to calculate the average rank distance between two items. For this, one uses a ranked-respondent-by-item matrix (as above), where one can see the implied ranking in the list (e.g. item A was listed first and an item B tenth on a list of 20 items). One then measures the distance between the two items (which would be 10–11 = 9 in this example). One can so standardize the distances (for example by dividing each distance—here nine—by the length of the respondent's list [9/20 = 0.45] and then multiplying it by 100, which would yield 45) and calculate the average distance for each possible pair, which indicates the probability that a respondent who lists A would also list B (Bernard 2006: 302–3). The generalizability of such findings depends, of course, on the sample.

Final comments

Free-listing is a potentially powerful technique for research in the study of religion\s, which can be used in combination with a variety of research methods such as discourse analysis, interviews, surveys, etc. It can elicit relevant information in a way that is relatively easy to administer. It typically produces rich and relevant data with sample sizes that are within reach even for many low-budget and small-scale projects. The technique can be employed in different stages of a project and it can be used repeatedly, in order to differentiate aspects of a category or domain (when eliciting information on, for example, its functions, effects or properties), or consecutively to fine-tune the obtained data by further free-listing of aspects that have emerged in previous stages of the analysis. Last but not least, free-listing is fun to use with students in class, be it as an exercise in teaching this technique[11] or for other purposes such as evaluation.

Box 2.9.2 Additional variations and prompting techniques

Scholars have proposed several additional variations to the original technique. One is to restrict the interviews temporally (especially in oral or online interviews). Instead of giving respondents all the time they want to complete their list, here one sets a rigid time frame (e.g. two minutes) (Sutrop 2001: 264). There also are some techniques to elicit further information (i.e. longer lists) such as *alphabetic probing*; that is, instead of asking respondents to free-list, one here takes respondents through the alphabet by asking 'what kinds of X are there that begin with the letter A?' (Bernard 2006: 302). This will be less reliable for salience, but might produce more exhaustive lists. Alternatively, one can take an item A on the original list as a starting point for probing and ask 'list all the kinds of X that are like A' (Bernard 2006: 302). This technique is known as *semantic cues* and it can increase the number of elicited items significantly. Other prompting techniques to increase the number of listed items are *nonspecific prompting*, i.e. posing a question like 'what other kinds of X are there?' once the respondent has stopped listing new items, or reading back the list that the respondent had provided to this same respondent tends to produce further items (Brewer 2002). 'These supplementary techniques may be especially valuable to apply when researchers conduct rapid ethnographic studies or have few informants with whom to work' (Brewer 2002: 116). This is not untypical for many projects conducted in the study of religion\s and should therefore be considered.

Notes

1 See Chapter 2.8 on Field research: participant observation and Chapter 2.19 on Structured observation in this volume.
2 In evolutionary cognitive studies, the term 'domain' is used in a different manner, namely to refer to stimuli or inputs to cognitive processes, so-called 'modules', which are stipulated to have developed as adaptations to address 'a range of phenomena that presented problems or opportunities in the ancestral environment of the species' (Sperber and Hirschfeld 2004: 41). Among the effects of such domains is triggering specific reactions: if something is classified as belonging to the domain of animals or physical objects, respectively, one intuitively has certain expectations with regard to their agency and properties.
3 See Chapter 2.21 on Translation in this volume.
4 For an example see the cross-cultural study of the aspects of goodness typically accessed and considered by laypersons (Smith *et al.* 2007). Free-listing was here used to elicit data for the first of two studies. The data generated by free-listing was subsequently analyzed by content analysis and regression analysis.
5 The interviews were conducted in English, which is a spoken language among the Parsis.
6 Both parameters can be conveniently presented in a table or combined in a matrix.
7 Moreover, given the relatively small sample sizes of this type of study, one must be careful when assessing the (statistical) generalizability of the findings. Statistically speaking, what looks like major

breaks in a small sample can turn out to be happenstance or a (non-significant) tendency when the sample is increased.

8 Note that 'there are no generally recognized ways to check the statistical reliability of the free listing task' (Weller and Romney 1988: 16).

9 In experimental studies, salience is often used to test the relevance of some variables. In order to explore the relevance of religion as an independent variable, for example, one might ask participants to read a text that highlights religious aspects ('priming'), whereas the control group would be given a text to read with content referring to non-religious cultural content ('salience manipulation'). The first group is then in the salience condition for religion.

10 One of the main fields of prototype analysis has been the study of concepts of emotion and of emotions such as love, commitment, embarrassment, forgiveness; for a survey see Fehr (2005).

11 When teaching the technique in class, I have asked the students to free-list the elements of the Norwegian Constitution Day, which is a national bank holiday.

References

Bernard, H.R., 2006. *Research Methods in Anthropology: qualitative and quantitative approaches.* AltaMira Press, Lanham, MD.

Borgatti, S.K., 1999. Elicitation techniques for cultural domain analysis. In: Schensul, J.J., LeCompte, M.D., Nastasi, B.K. and Borgatti, S.K. (eds), *Enhanced Ethnographic Methods: audiovisual techniques, focused group interviews, and elicitation techniques.* Altamira Press, Lanham, MD, Plymouth, pp. 115–51.

Brewer, D.D., 2002. Supplementary interviewing techniques to maximize output in free listing tasks. *Field Methods* 14 (1): 108–18.

Fehr, B., 2005. The role of prototypes in interpersonal cognition. In: Baldwin, M. (ed.), *Interpersonal Cognition.* Guilford Press, New York, London, pp. 180–205.

Itti, L., 2007. Visual salience. *Scholarpedia* 9 (2). DOI: 10.4249/scholarpedia.3327

McArthur, L.Z., 1981. What grabs you? The role of attention in impression formation and causal attribution. In: Zanna, M.P., Higgins, E.T. and Herman, C.P. (eds), *Social Cognition: the Ontario Symposium, volume 1.* Erlbaum, Hillsdale, NJ, pp. 201–46.

Romaniuk, J. and Sharp, B., 2004. Conceptualizing and measuring brand salience. *Marketing Theory* 4 (4): 327–42.

Ross, N., 2004. *Culture & Cognition: implications for theory and method.* SAGE, Thousand Oaks, CA.

Ryan, G.W., Nolan, J.M. and Yoder, P.S., 2000. Successive free listing: using multiple free lists to generate explanatory models. *Field Methods* 12 (2): 83–107.

Smith, J.Z., 2000. Classification. In: Braun, W. and McCutcheon, R.T. (eds), *Guide to the Study of Religion.* Cassell, London, New York, pp. 35–44.

Smith, K.D., Smith, S.T. and Christopher, J.C., 2007. What defines the good person? Cross-cultural comparisons of experts' models with lay prototypes. *Journal of Cross-Cultural Psychology* 38 (3): 333–60.

Sperber, D. and Hirschfeld, L.A., 2004. The cognitive foundations of cultural stability and diversity. *Trends in Cognitive Sciences* 8 (1): 40–46.

Sutrop, U., 2001. List task and a cognitive salience index. *Field Methods* 13 (3): 263–76.

Further reading

Borgatti, S.K., 1999. Elicitation techniques for cultural domain analysis. In: Schensul, J.J., LeCompte, M.D., Nastasi, B.K. and Borgatti, S.K. (eds), *Enhanced Ethnographic Methods: audiovisual techniques, focused group interviews, and elicitation techniques.* Altamira Press, Lanham, MD, Plymouth, pp. 115–51.

Useful overview; discusses also pilesorts and triads, which are not covered in the present chapter.

Fehr, B., 2005. The role of prototypes in interpersonal cognition. In: Baldwin, M. (ed.), *Interpersonal Cognition.* Guilford Press, New York, London, pp. 180–205.

A useful review of prototype analyses.

Weller, S.C. and Romney, A.K., 1988. *Systematic Data Collection*. SAGE, Newbury Park, CA, London, New Delhi.

Covers free-listing as one basic format of systematic data collection.

Key concepts

Category: a fundamental and distinct conception that groups together several concepts and serves to identify a class, group, list or set of phenomena.

Concept: basic unit of thought with corresponding meanings and representations; building blocks of categories and theories; can ideally be defined.

Domain: a segment of commonly perceived cultural/natural reality.

Free-listing: a research technique to elicit rich and relevant lexical data on categories, concepts or cultural 'domains'.

Idiosyncratic item: an item (example of a category or feature of a concept) listed by only one respondent in a free-listing study (or by very few respondents in larger samples).

Prototype theory: An alternative to classical views of definition. According to this view, natural language categories are internally structured into prototypes (best examples, clearest cases, most typical exemplars) of the category, while other members can be ordered by their degree of resemblance to the prototype(s); membership is graded and boundaries are fuzzy. Prototype analyses map the content and structure of categories and concepts by ordinary people (lay knowledge).

Salience: A concept used in different disciplines, mainly to refer to distinctive, attention-grabbing information; in a broader sense, information on categories and domains that is typical, representative and distributed.

Related chapters

- ◆ 2.8 Field research
- ◆ 2.10 Grounded theory
- ◆ 2.18 Structuralism
- ◆ 2.20 Surveys and questionnaires

2.10

GROUNDED THEORY

Steven Engler

Chapter summary

- Grounded theory (GT) is a method for the discovery of theory from the close coding and analysis of data. 'Theory' in the name of this method refers to the results of the method, not to the method itself.
- GT is also a methodology, a general position on the relation between data and theory and on how method mediates between these. As such, it has value beyond its common use as a qualitative method for studying social-interactional processes.
- One begins with the close coding of a small set of data; further data collection is informed by the concepts and categories that emerge from initial analysis (theoretical sampling); and this process spirals in toward one or more core categories.
- The point at which no significant new concepts/theory emerge (theoretical saturation) marks the conclusion of data collection and analysis.
- Relations between different variants of GT reveal fundamental meta-theoretical tensions: e.g., over the role of theory at the start of coding/analysis, over levels of theory, and over relations between theory and the boundaries of specific fields.
- There is significant similarity between the methodological characteristics of GT and holistic semantic theories: both see interpretation as always provisional, always in need of being measured against and modified in the light of emerging evidence.
- GT is relatively rare in the study of religion. Appeals to GT are often superficial and there is a common misperception that it is a generic type of qualitative analysis.

Introduction

Grounded theory (GT) aims at 'the discovery of theory from data systematically obtained from social research' (Glaser and Strauss 2009: 2). It builds theory rather than trying to verify or apply it. GT can be an effective methodological choice in three circumstances: when there is little or no literature on relevantly similar cases; when existing concepts/theories seem inadequate for aspects of the material at hand; or when one wishes to explore the possibility of alternative modes of conceptualizing a case. The first section below presents an overview of GT as a method. The second section explores some of the epistemological and semantic issues raised by the basic premise of GT, i.e. that 'theory' can emerge from or be discovered in 'data'. The third section looks at examples of GT in the study of religion.

Descriptive and analytical overview

There is no formulaic set of rules for carrying out a GT analysis.[1] GT derives concepts and categories from analyzing a data set that grows in light of that analysis itself, and it reworks and refines those concepts into more general categories and properties. The '**constant comparative method**' is another name for GT, because the researcher constantly compares data to data, and data to emerging concepts (Glaser 1965; Glaser and Strauss 2009: 101–16). It thus ends up generating theory from a highly contextualized analysis. The endpoint of this generative process is recognized by theoretical saturation.

Coding

A small set of empirical materials is first collected then subjected to an initial process of line-by-line **coding**.[2] For example, one might read closely through field notes, documents or interview transcripts, making marginal notations, filling in database fields, or making notes on index cards. Each code labels a given 'incident' (figure, theme, issue, concern, problem, perception, idea, event, mode of discourse, etc.). Subjects' own terms can serve as 'in vivo' codes (Charmaz 2006: 55). Analyzing the results of this first process of coding—e.g. looking for relations between incidents—begins to yield higher-level concepts and categories. Although usage varies, I use the terms, 'code', 'concept' and 'category' to refer to increasingly abstract and general levels of analysis (see Bryant and Charmaz 2007a: 18). **Codes** are the initial descriptive, inchoately interpretive, terms and phrase that label elements of data. **Concepts** are constructs that combine characteristics or particulars of a set of codes. **Categories** are more general classes that bring together concepts, with the latter serving effectively as properties of the former.

Three distinct types of coding are important. *Open coding* (see Box 2.10.1) involves analyzing the data to extract concepts, categories and properties: 'The aim is to produce

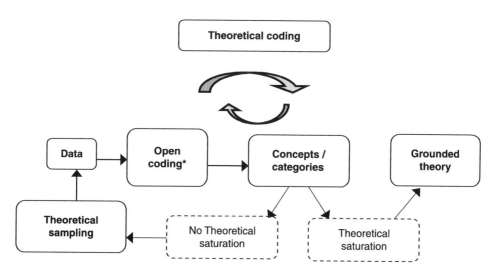

Figure 2.10.1   Grounded theory

Note: *Selective coding occupies this same position in later phases.

Box 2.10.1 An example of open coding

On the right below is an excerpt from the transcript of an interview with D., a travelling sales representative and non-professional medium, a practitioner of the hybrid Spiritist/Afro-Brazilian religion Umbanda (conducted in Brazil, 3 November 2010).[3] On the left are the codes associated with portions of text to their right.

time/family (female)	Yesterday, I said to my wife, 'G., I feel like having a glass
sudden desire/drink	of liqueur'. I just felt like it. I got a tiny glass of liqueur,
domestic space	and I sat in the sitting room. I was drinking that little
feels/not sees	glass of liqueur and I felt—I didn't see—but I felt the
family (male) spirits/home/the dead/	presence of my grandfather J. and my uncle N., at home.
holy day	That is, the 2nd of November, which is Finados [the day
Catholic (popular)/temporal and	of the dead], is the only day of the year on which the dead
normative limits/crossing-over/love/	have permission to come to the Earth to visit the beloved
bodies	beings that are still incarnate. So, I already know, inside
inner certainty	myself, look, they are here; they can come here, in my
home/boundaries	house—right?—which always has its doors open, and
crossing-in	they can come in whenever they wish. And I, I mean, I
	drank a little bit of that liqueur that was with me and [a
involuntary/Catholic (popular)	thought] came into my head, nossa! [Our Lady!], my
other's desire/drink	grandfather J. liked liqueur so much, right? And as soon
cued by recognition	as that happened, I already, I felt, at that moment, that
no coincidence	they are here. Something, it's not a coincidence, if you
	like. You're doing something else. I am there moving,
involuntary	looking, I mean, how does it come into your head
sudden desire/drink	suddenly like that, the desire to have some liqueur like
continuity of object	that, [a liqueur] that is there every day, and very rarely do
discontinuity of desire/drink	I feel a desire for it. And then, who liked liqueur? My
family (male)/other's desire	grandfather J. loved liqueur! So, there are some things, I
prayer	even think to myself that I have to give thanks to the
Christian elements/gift	Father for this opportunity that he is giving me. I grab
active reception	this with both hands.

Re-coding of this passage, in light of further rounds of coding and analysis of this and other interviews, leads to more abstract and general codes. For example, the perceived distance between the medium's own desire and that of his grandfather is coded, along with a variety of similar elements, as 'disjoint desire', and this in turn as a property of the category 'de-situated emotion', and this category appears to be an index of 'leveraged agency' (a hypothesis to be assessed by further, more focused interviewing, i.e. theoretical sampling). Popular and appropriated Catholic elements, along with beliefs in familial spirits (and other more popularly accepted types of spirits, like *encostos*), were later coded as 'matrix beliefs/practices/social forms' as properties of the category of 'matrix religiosity'. Coding, memoing and analysis is ongoing, with these emerging categories potentially in flux. A GT approach is resulting in a more contextualized set of concepts for making sense of spirit possession, one not limited to a pre-determined 'religious' and theoretical context.

concepts that seem to fit the data. These concepts and their dimensions are as yet entirely provisional; but thinking about these results in a host of questions and equally provisional answers' (Strauss 1987: 28). Line-by-line coding is frequently performed, though experienced GT researchers often filter out material that is likely to be less productive. In general, close reading of interview transcripts is likely to generate hundreds of codes. Initial coding tends to be quite descriptive, but it is already done with an eye to moving toward more general concepts, more so than is the case with standard qualitative analysis. In GT one codes with an eye to generating theory, not with the aim of simply labeling themes (Holton 2007: 272–73; Urquhart 2007: 351–52). The open coding phase is time consuming, as one immerses oneself in the growing dataset.

Selective coding proceeds on the basis of these core concepts or categories: 'The other codes become subservient to the key code under focus. To code selectively, then, means that the analyst delimits coding to only those codes that relate to the core codes in sufficiently significant ways as to be used in a parsimonious theory' (Strauss 1987: 33). Given that one is now analyzing one's material with a much smaller and more focused set of codes, this phase proceeds much more quickly.

Theoretical coding looks for relationships between the codes and extracts additional concepts, categories and properties from this process of comparison. This, in turn, may lead one to identify further conditions, properties, consequences, concepts or categories through theoretical sampling and further open coding. This is the most exciting phase of the research process, when categories emerge that one has not anticipated and that seem to pull the pieces together, pieces that often seem chaotic and disparate as coding begins. In sum, at the risk of over-generalizing, open coding organizes the empirical material with an eye to concept-building; selective coding elaborates the resulting core concepts; and theoretical coding connects these prior level of codes in order to push the analysis to more abstract and general levels.

Theoretical sampling

Further data is added to the study through **theoretical sampling**. Additional cases, samples, interviews, documents, etc. are selected on the basis of the emerging theoretical frame. Theoretical sampling aims at theory building—i.e. generating and refining concepts and categories—not at representativeness with respect to a predetermined population. For example, one might use emerging concepts to refine questions for further interviews. Generally, one begins with a small set of empirical materials, returning to the field in several later stages. However, GT can also be performed on complete data sets, beginning the coding process with a sub-set and proceeding in stages to analyze the complete set. In either case, new material is added and coded in the light of emerging conceptual work. The theorizing process thus narrows in on 'a core category which organizes the other categories by continually resolving the main concern' (Glaser 2001: 30). This very dynamic relation between data collection and analysis means that one needs consistent and ongoing access to the field where one is observing, the group among which one is interviewing, or the corpus of texts that one is analyzing.

Memoing

Memos are a crucial aspect of GT. This involves making constant exploratory notes on the emerging conceptual work at all phases of the process, e.g. notes, lists, diagrams, charts and mindmaps. They are theoretical and interpretive, not merely descriptive. **Memoing** provides the sketch pads on which conceptual and theoretical work begins to take shape (see Box 2.10.2 and Figure 2.10.2). Memos can extend, fine-tune, elaborate on and take stock of the concepts and categories that are emerging through coding; they help to explore relations and disjunctions, seeing which concepts appear most effective at capturing these relations at a higher level; they assist in grouping concepts and categories hierarchically and in families, allowing one to assess which offer more stable meta-concepts; and, as the study progresses, they offer a key tool for assessing the extent to which further data collection and coding is relatively non-productive, thus signaling the end of the process. Initial memos tend to be primarily re-descriptive. Individual memos should be dated and labeled, with a reference to the specific data element (e.g. transcript or document). The GT process is iterative, cyclical or spiral, as one moves back and forth, comparing data, codes, categories and emerging theory. Reflecting this dynamic conceptual work, sorting and rearranging memos is an important lead-up to the writing process.

Box 2.10.2 Sample memos

The following are excerpts from memos associated with the text and codes in Box 2.10.1. Italicized phrases represent early attempts to draw out concepts. Figure 2.10.2 represents a separate (graphic) memo on the same passage:

- What role does G. [his wife] play?
- The *sala* [sitting room] is a more formal space, one already oriented toward visitors, the room least integrated with the private spaces of the house. Why did D. choose to sit there? What did he know before his 'Nossa!' moment?
- Liqueur is an unusual drink. D. is a beer drinker. Why does he have it in his house?
- The 'aha!' moment is when D. sees that he is acting consistent with his grandfather's taste, not his. *Constructive recognition.* He recognizes a gap between his actions and his own desire, but sees continuity between the desire/action of his grandfather. *(Dis)continuity of desire. Discounting 'coincidence.'*
- What do the lack of fluidity, hesitations, repetitions mean? Construction of meaning? Recalling a sense of the spiritual moment? Evocation of the otherworldly? *Restaging liminality.*
- Catholic elements form a *mediating backdrop.* The encounter with these domestic/familial spirits is framed by Finados, not by D.'s 'work' [as an umbandist medium].
- Frames the narrative in the end in terms of God's agency, not his or the spirits'. *Agentic frame. Normative closure.*

Theoretical saturation

In GT data collection and analysis ends with **theoretical saturation**: the point at which no new categories or concepts emerge, or where those that do merely copy existing ones: i.e. when emergent theory changes little as the researcher adds and analyzes more empirical material. This can be defined in terms of the 'interchangeability of indicators', i.e. the point at which the new concepts and categories that are emerging are indistinguishable in their

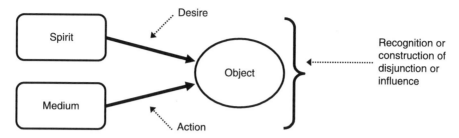

Figure 2.10.2 Sample memo diagram

analytical purchase from those already developed (Glaser and Strauss 2009: 23n23, 49, 190; Glaser 1978: 43, 64–65). Concept/theory building continues until that process stabilizes on theory that is effective at accounting for the themes and issues that have been revealed as significant in the empirical materials.

Writing

There is no specific way of writing up GT research. Trying to echo its iterative character would result in oddly structured academic texts: 'In pure form, grounded theory research would be presented as a jumble of literature consultation, data collection, and analysis conducted in ongoing iterations that produce many relatively fuzzy categories that, over time, reduce to fewer, clearer conceptual structures. Theory would be presented last' (Suddaby 2006: 637). As a result, the presentation of results generally follows standard styles. However, it is important to explicitly discuss one's procedure in sufficient detail that readers are able to assess the extent to which it has been developed fully and appropriately.

Theoretical and epistemological issues

The Discovery of Grounded Theory (2009 [1967]), by sociologists of health care Barney G. Glaser and Anselm L. Strauss, marks the origin of GT.[4] Glaser was associated with the quantitative approaches of Columbia (primarily Paul Lazarsfeld) and Strauss with the qualitative, pragmatist-influenced approaches of Chicago (W.I. Thomas, George Herbert Mead, Robert Park and Herbert Blumer). However, their early statements on GT did not emphasize continuity but rather a radical break with existing approaches.

From its start, GT manifested an uneasy tension between the idea that theory 'emerges' from data and the recognition that some conceptual and theoretical knowledge is required for getting coding and analysis off the ground. On the one hand, the researcher 'should [. . .] study an area without any preconceived theory that dictates, prior to the research, "relevancies" in concepts and hypotheses' (Glaser and Strauss 2009: 33). On the other hand, 'the researcher does not approach reality as a *tabula rasa*. He must have a perspective that will help him see relevant data and abstract significant categories from his scrutiny of the data' (Glaser and Strauss 2009: 3n3). Yet, *The Discovery of Grounded Theory* gave neither guidelines nor examples of how the researcher's previous conceptual/theoretical knowledge should inform the process of concept/theory building.

There is a similar tension in discussions of the place of literature review in GT (Bryant and Charmaz 2007a: 19–20; Dunne 2011). On the one hand, researchers should 'ignore the

---

Box 2.10.3 Elements of grounded theory method

- Codes, concepts and categories emerge from the empirical materials not from presupposed hypotheses or theories.
- *Grounding in data* (moving from data toward theory along the spectrum between these):
    - The first step is initial open coding of a small set of empirical materials.
    - Analysis proceeds through constant comparison (i.e. comparing coded elements with each other and later with the concept that emerges).
    - Prior literature review in the specific area of research is best avoided.
    - All coding should be done by the researcher(s), not delegated.

- *Concept/theory-building*

    - Data collection and analysis proceed together, with a spiraling interplay between the growing data set and the emerging conceptual/theoretical work.
    - Theorizing/concept-building becomes more general and abstract as data collection/analysis proceeds.
    - Theorizing/concept-building proceeds by induction and abduction, i.e. inference to a likely and parsimonious explanation.
    - Memo writing (beginning with the first set of empirical materials that are coded) tracks, specifies, defines and elaborates emerging concepts/categories and their inter-relations, throughout the entire research process.
    - Literature review follows and is guided by (rather than preceding and informing) theorizing/concept-building.

- *Theoretical sampling*

    - Emerging concepts/categories inform the collection of further data.

- *Theoretical saturation*

    - Data collection ends when no further concepts/categories of significance are emerging through analysis.

- *Theoretical sensitivity* (identifying theoretically relevant aspects of data).

    - The ability, developed over time and through experience, to recognize relevant data, and to use one's existing stock of heuristic concepts, e.g. theoretical and common-sense categories, to frame the emergence of (but not to force or impose) grounded categories.

---

literature of theory and fact on the area under study, in order to assure that the emergence of categories will not be contaminated by concepts more suited to different areas' (Glaser and Strauss 2009: 37). On the other hand, literature review is important at all phases of the GT process, the distinction being that one limits oneself to reading '*in a substantive field different from the research*' until the analysis is well under way: 'When the theory seems sufficiently grounded and developed, *then* we review the literature in the field and relate the theory to it' (Glaser 1978: 31, original emphasis).[5]

Glaser and Strauss proposed the concept of '**theoretical sensitivity**' to address this problematic issue of the prior place of theory in GT. The researcher should be 'sufficiently *theoretically sensitive* so that he can conceptualize and formulate a theory as it emerges from the data'. This involves one's having built up 'an armamentum of categories and hypotheses on substantive and formal levels. This theory that exists within a sociologist can be used in generating his specific theory if, after study of the data, the fit and relevance to the data are emergent' (Glaser and Strauss 2009: 46). Previous theory is a prerequisite for *recognizing* the theory that emerges from one's data, but one must avoid *applying* or forcing theory to or upon that data.

This problematic issue of the prior place of theory and the related issue of how to assess the resulting 'grounded' theory are not flaws in GT; they are challenges that necessarily follow from the basic premise that theory should emerge from data. On a related note, GT has been criticized because the same data appear to be used for both discovery and validation. These challenges are met in a number of ways: by clarifying the particular modes of reasoning—induction and **abduction**[6]—that inform the concept-/theory-building process (Bryant 2009: para. 88–100; Reichertz 2007); by exploring the centrality of 'serendipity', 'whimsy and wonder' and 'play' to theoretical sensitivity (Glaser and Strauss 2009: 2; Covan 2007: 63; Charmaz 2006: 70, 135; Locke 2007); by emphasizing the central role of reflexivity (Hesse-Biber 2007: 326; Mruck and Mey 2007); and by underlining GT's theoretical relation to pragmatism (Star 2007; Bryant 2009). More generally, proponents suggest that theoretical saturation replaces verification as measure of success in GT (Hood 2007: 161–63). The pragmatic value of the theory for producing useful analytical results with the case at hand is seen as a key measure of GT's success: Glaser emphasizes that theory that emerges from GT, done properly, 'works'; it has 'grab', 'fit', 'emergent fit', 'relevance', 'modifiability' and 'tractability' (Glaser 1978: 4).

It was primarily the attempt to clarify the meta-theoretical ground of GT itself that led to Glaser's and Straus's divergence (Kelle 2005, 2007). Glaser developed the ideas of 'theoretical coding' and 'coding families'. He elaborated 18 separate sets or families of concepts that draw upon different theoretical approaches or schools and that come into play at the level of theoretical coding: e.g. 'The Six Cs: causes, contexts, contingencies, consequences, covariances and conditions'; 'Process', including phases, progressions, passages, etc.; the 'Interactive Family', including reciprocity, interdependence, etc.; the 'Identity-Self Family', including self-image, identity, social worth, etc.; the 'Cultural Family', including social norms and social beliefs, etc.; and various types of structural, temporal and conceptual ordering (Glaser 1978: 72ff.). This emphasis on the researcher's ad hoc appeal to a wide variety of theoretical frames and resources results in a very general view of GT: it is seen not simply as a method but as 'a theory of a method which yields techniques and stages that can be used on any type of data and combination thereof' (Glaser 1998: 11). Strauss, on the other hand, consistent with his emphasis on symbolic interactionism (Strauss 1993), held a narrower view that GT is an 'approach to qualitative analysis'; it is 'not a theory but a methodology to discover theories dormant in the data' (Strauss 1987: 1; Legewie and Schervier-Legewie 2004). He and Juliet Corbin (Strauss and Corbin 1990) elaborated the idea of a 'coding paradigm' in relation to 'axial coding' (i.e. 'intense analysis done around one category at a time in terms of the paradigm items'; Strauss 1987: 32). The resulting 'paradigm model' gave pragmatism and symbolic interactionism a defining role as the meta-theoretical touchstones of GT (Strauss and Corbin 1990: 99–107).

The latter meta-theoretical frame led to GT being seen narrowly as a form of qualitative analysis, in part because Strauss and Corbin's view 'turned out much more instructive for many grounded theory users than the coding family conception' (Kelle 2007: 202), and likely also in part because Glaser revealed himself to be oddly vitriolic in defending his more general view of GT orthodoxy, as part of his self-appointed 'spiritual task as purveyor of the method' (Glaser 1998: vii). So, for example, the recent 'situational' variant of GT places exclusive emphasis on its relation to symbolic interactionism (Clarke 2005; Clarke and Friese 2007).[7]

This tendency was complicated by a related perception that the Strauss/Corbin variant of GT—a type of qualitative analysis and dominant in the 1990s—had unexamined realist/ positivist assumptions (Bryant 2009: para. 12, 53). This led Kathy Charmaz to draw an influ-ential distinction between 'objectivist' and 'constructivist' forms of GT (Charmaz 2000, 2006: 129–32). Antony Bryant similarly distinguishes between three types of GT: Glaser's, Strauss' and constructivist (Bryant 2009: para. 17).[8] This is helpful in insisting that GT take account of more epistemologically nuanced work in philosophy and the social sciences and in clarifying the sense in which it is more a 'family' of methods than a single discrete approach (Bryant and Charmaz 2007a: 11–13; Bryant and Charmaz 2007b; Dey 2007: 173). It is misleading, however, in perpetuating the commonly held misperception that GT is only appropriate when one is dealing with social/interactional processes and when one is limited to people's accounts of their experiences. Counter to that, there has been a recent tendency toward a more general stance: 'grounded theory once constituted a positivistic model of qualitative science moored in a symbolic interactionist sensitivity to the world, [. . . but it] is now often utilized as a flexible and versatile data analysis technique' (Timmermans and Tavory 2007: 495).

Sharp-eyed readers will likely be wondering just how 'data' and 'theory' are defined in the GT literature, and how the latter takes account of the view that data are always already theory-laden (see Bryant and Charmaz 2007b: 43–44). The production of a theory that covers a specific area is generally considered a necessary characteristic of a 'full use' of GT, as opposed to 'using the method to generate concepts' (Urquhart 2007: 347). However, this takes an overly rigid view. As a method, GT moves from data toward theory along a spectrum (see Figure 2.10.3). That is, GT can be considered a general technique for moving from data toward theory, without specifying a logical level of either the starting data or the final theory.

The relational nature of GT is clear in its characteristic distinction between substantive and formal theory. Substantive theory is related to a specific research setting or area of inquiry; formal theory applies across a variety of such settings or areas: the former is 'developed for a substantive, or empirical, area'; the latter is 'developed for a formal, or conceptual, area' (Glaser and Strauss 2009: 32–35).[9] However, this distinction is unclear: sometimes 'substan-tive' is correlated with 'empirical entities' and 'formal' with 'conceptual properties'; some-times the distinction is one of 'distinguishable levels of generality, which differ only in terms of degree' (Glaser and Strauss 2009: 33). The former distinction, between empirical entities and conceptual properties, is indefensible because both entities and properties vary in degrees of generalization (Alvesson and Sköldberg 2009: 70). This leaves us with a relative difference:

> [Glaser and Strauss] posit an absolute distinction—albeit with fluid boundaries— between two phenomena whose differences are in fact relative. The whole thing boils down to a matter of *a lower or higher level of generality*, and in reality there are not just two such levels, but an arbitrary number of them. Which levels are chosen will depend on the purpose of the particular investigation [. . .T]he authors' dichotomy between the substantive and the formal simply represents two possible degrees on a scale of generality.
>
> *(Alvesson and Sköldberg 2009: 70–71, original emphasis)*

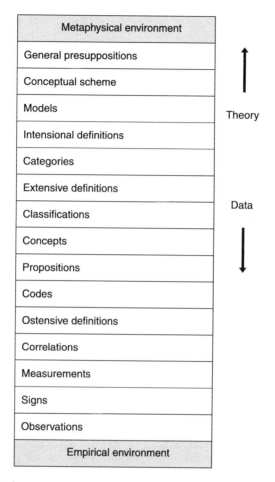

Figure 2.10.3 The data/theory spectrum

Note: Modified from Alexander (1982: 3) in light of Glazier and Grover (2002: 318). The distinction between three types of definition is significant: *ostensive* definitions point to cases or examples; *extensive* definitions list the objects that are members of a certain category; and *intensional* definitions give necessary and sufficient conditions for objects being assigned to a certain category.

The substantive/formal distinction is relational: it points to a pair of positions that move along the theory/data spectrum.

Once we recognize the relational nature of the substantive/formal distinction, some of the confusions over the starting and endpoints of GT become clearer. For example, ambivalence is reduced regarding the dynamic place of literature reviews in GT: relative to the current point of theorizing, the role of literature review is limited to providing material closer to the empirical end of the theory/data spectrum. More generally, GT does not need to begin with a certain logical level of data or to result in a certain level of theory: it is useful for concept building, for generating theory with limited application, and for building more general and abstract theories that apply to a wide variety of cases or that transcend disciplinary boundaries.

There is a tendency to discuss the meta-theoretical situation of types of GT in terms of epistemology (see e.g. Charmaz 2000; Bryant and Charmaz 2007b). The neglected issue of semantics sheds valuable additional light here.[10] That is, post-positivist and postmodernist arguments over the relations between data and the world raise questions regarding just how it is that the materials coded and analyzed by researchers actually *mean* anything.

Two issues arise here. First, the basic distinction between data and theory has been rendered problematic by philosophical work on semantics in the last century: W.V. Quine (1950) called into question the distinction between synthetic and analytic, and hence ultimately between observational and theoretical; Donald Davidson's (1984) critique of the scheme/content distinction has similar implications. In effect, this relativizes the distinction between data and theory. This is not an argument against GT but a reminder that, as noted, data and theory form a spectrum, not two categorically distinct types.

Second, Quine's thesis of the indeterminacy of translation (see Quine 1990: 44–48) and related work by other philosophers make it clear that the process of open coding—the translation of text and transcript into descriptive and analytic labels—can potentially produce an infinite number of distinct sets of codes. Glaser himself recognized that, with different researchers involved, 'coding varies over the same data' (Glaser 1978: 59; see Dey 2007: 183). Given that all of GT's concept- and theory-building work is based upon this initial act of coding, and given that different coding schemes will result in different theories, the fact that a given theory is grounded does not mean that it is unique. In a nutshell, different researchers can produce non-equivalent theories by using the same GT method on the same data set. This forces us to ask how we might argue that any such theory is more reliable, informative or true than any other.[11]

This is where the distinction between objectivist and constructivist approaches to GT seems to fall short. That distinction seems to embody a fundamental semantic distinction, between externalism and internalism. Objectivist views, as critiqued by Charmaz, seem committed to an externalist view, that meaning involves a relation between words and world (i.e. that the data are in some sense objective facts 'out there'). Constructivist views seem committed to an internalist view, i.e. one that denies that meaning is based on this sort of a relation. The latter position exacerbates the potential problem of relativism raised in the previous paragraph. A distinct axis of semantic theory—holism vs. atomism—offers a way forward here. Semantic atomism locates meaning at the level of individual words (the meaning of each word is *in* it); semantic holism locates meaning at a broader level, ranging from an indefinite network of linked units to an entire language.

There would seem to be a felicitous convergence between the methodological characteristics of GT and holistic semantic theories. First, it seems clear that GT is, by its very nature, committed to some form of semantic holism: the conceptual bootstrapping that leads from data to concepts and theory is contingent upon fleshing out the meaning of distinct elements of data in terms of their relations to other elements. GT is, in a sense, an attempt to capitalize on the view that meaning is relational. Second, thinking of the relation between data and codes as a matter of translation between two languages offers greater clarity in thinking about relations between data and theory in GT. Third, semantic holism (especially Davidson's version) underlines that interpretation is always provisional, always in need of being measured against and modified in the light of emerging evidence. Fourth, Davidson proposes 'maximal consistency' as the measure of success in the process of 'radical interpretation' that serves as the baseline for all interpretation (including that of texts); this concept appears to be closely related to 'theoretical saturation'. In sum, the coding process, the concept-building process and the endpoint of GT all seem to have a strong affinity with semantic holism. This offers a potential path for dealing with the problem of the underdetermination of theory by data that was raised above: a holistic view emphasizes that the theory-building process—like all acts of interpretation—takes place in an ongoing cycle of checking one's interpretations—one's concepts, categories and theories—against a shifting empirical context.

GT in the study of religion

There are relatively few studies that use GT to analyze religious phenomena. A review will serve to illustrate certain problems and limitations. I will focus primarily on work in the sociology of religion.

Many studies appeal to GT without actually doing it. As Marie Cornwall, editor of the *Journal for the Scientific Study of Religion* notes, 'many scholars misunderstand what constitutes qualitative research and especially grounded theory' (Cornwall 2010: iv). Roy Suddaby, editor of the *Academy of Management Journal*, drawing on his experience with such confusions over the years, has written a useful overview of 'What Grounded Theory is Not': GT is not an excuse to ignore the literature, not presentation of raw data, not theory testing, content analysis, or word counts, not routine application of formulaic technique to data, not the one true method or an easy one, and not an excuse for the absence of methodology (Suddaby 2006). Of course, as a general rule, the peer-review process should filter out, or prompt the appropriate revision of, work based in such confusions.

Work in the study of religion serves to illustrate a less problematic but still obscuring appeal to GT. A quick nod to the GT literature—generally to Glaser and Strauss's classic manifesto, *The Discovery of Grounded Theory* (Glaser and Strauss 2009)—sometimes makes a strategic, but ultimately misleading, appearance in work that neither uses nor claims to use GT. For example, Lynn Davidman and Arthur L. Greil—in their study of over 50 interviews of people who have left ultra-Orthodox Judaism—cite *Discovery* in order to support a core methodological decision: 'We left respondents free to define "leaving Orthodoxy" for themselves and let our definition evolve from the ground up' (Davidman and Greil 2007: 204). Kathleen Jenkins—in a comparative interview-based study of 'the construction and maintenance of multiracial/ethnic networks in high-boundary religious movements'—cites *Discovery* for the same reason: 'I carefully and repeatedly reviewed each data source for common themes, which informed coding categories that I then used to analyze data systematically (Jenkins 2003: 393, 395). These are both exceptional articles based on exemplary uses of interview methods. However, neither uses or claims to use GT, and neither makes any reference to the GT literature apart from the one token nod to *Discovery*.

What, then, is the function of such token citations? The answer would seem to be that a passing reference to GT is read by some as a warrant for more generic types of coding or concept building. Despite being for the most part a relatively harmless gesture, this sort of methodological metonymy is misleading: it gives the impression that one is using GT when one is not; it papers over the relation between theory and data that informs what one is in fact doing; and it obscures the distinct characteristics of GT.[12]

A second obscuring type of appeal to GT consists in claiming to use the method when one goes only part way to doing so. In some cases it is clear that the researchers used, at most, certain elements of GT. Victor Hugo Masías-Hinojosa *et al.* used 'the methodological strategy of Grounded Theory' to analyze interviews with converts to the Iglesia Metodista Pentecostal de Chile (Masías-Hinojosa *et al.* 2008: para. 27). They coded and analyzed a set of 11 life story interviews in order to arrive at a dynamic model of relations between five 'anchors' of identity. However, their method diverged from GT in two related senses: they analyzed the corpus of interviews without using theoretical sampling (e.g. without conducting further interviews in which questions were informed by the emerging analysis), and the end of data collection appears not to have been determined by theoretical saturation (i.e. line-by-line coding simply proceeded through the pre-existing corpus of interviews and then stopped).[13] In other cases, the description of methodology is insufficient to make it clear whether GT was used or not. In an important study, Mary Ellen Konieczny (2009) drew on observations and interviews to analyze the relationship between the material culture of public worship and the homes of congregants. She cites Glaser and Strauss' 1967 classic to support her claim that she 'collected data using grounded theory methods' (ibid.: 423). However, there is no evidence that theoretical sampling was used, and the explicit limitation of GT to data collection, as opposed to its integration with analysis, suggests strongly that this was not in fact a use of the method. Lene Arnett Jensen—in a study of 'how children, adolescents, and adults from religiously liberal and conservative groups conceptualize God and the Devil'—claimed to use 'a grounded theory approach' to review interviews in order to construct 'a coding manual and a qualitative database' (Jensen 2009: 128). She then formulated and tested hypotheses using a quantitative analysis of the coded results. This is not GT. The initial use of open coding bears a certain resemblance to GT, but no more so than it does to a variety of other qualitative approaches. These three examples are solid substantively and methodologically, but their methods are not GT. They suggest that appealing to GT has a certain cachet, even when one at most carries out selected aspects of the method.

Other recent examples come closer to using GT in the study of religion, but still stop short. For example, Kathleen Jenkins (2010) uses interviews to analyze the experience of divorce in religious congregations, and her use of theoretical sampling, GT coding techniques and theoretical saturation was clearly and explicitly noted. However, her findings are not presented in terms of grounded concepts, categories or theory. She writes the sort of descriptive overview that is typical in qualitative research, but without the interpretive leverage of original concepts generated through GT. Another example that comes close to GT is Richard N. Pitt's study of 'religious black gay men's neutralization of anti-gay religious messages'. The study claims to use GT and did indeed use 'inductive analysis, with no preconceived categories or hypotheses, thereby allowing the data to speak for themselves rather than serve as examples supporting or refuting existing theory', and data collection stopped with theoretical saturation (Pitt 2010: 56, 60–61). However, interviews were added using personal contacts and snowball sampling: there is no evidence of theoretical sampling. More importantly, quantitative analysis was performed on a set of 'beliefs about human sexuality, relationships and religion', and the study used 'cognitive dissonance theory as a framework' (though this view was explicitly bracketed along with all other theory during initial analysis) (Pitt 2010: 56, 61). The former could be read as an example of mixed methods, but the latter is a clear sign that this is not GT: applying an existing theory is inconsistent with using theory grounded in one's data.

Rigorous use of GT in the religious studies literature is extremely rare, narrowly speaking, and examples in the sociology of religion tend to be, at most, partial in their use of GT. There is a very valuable book-length treatment in German of qualitative methods in the study of religion, emphasizing GT (Knoblauch 2003) and a short chapter in a Swedish methods handbook (Geels 2010), but neither are available in English. Since GT began and has continued strong in the sociology of health care, it is not surprising that there are solid examples of GT studies of religious phenomena in that context (e.g. Macmin and Foskett 2004).

The lesson for readers of research on religious phenomena is to take talk of GT with a grain of salt, and the lesson for researchers is to talk GT only when they do GT. In addition, it is important to describe one's method in detail—and not only when using GT—so that readers can assess it.

Conclusion

As a methodological stance, GT offers a very general model of how method mediates between theory and data, a model that extends far beyond GT's usual limitation to qualitative research with social/interactional processes and that transcends philosophical distinctions between, for example, positivist and post-positivist stances regarding the relation between data and 'the world': there is a 'growing number of theorists who view grounded theory not as a qualitative research method but as a general research methodology occupying its own distinct paradigm on the research landscape [. . . It] transcends the specific boundaries of established paradigms to accommodate any type of data sourced and expressed through any epistemological lens' (Holton 2007: 267–68). In addition, dialogue between GT and semantic theories could potentially be very valuable, not least in the study of religion.

As a specific method, though seldom used in the study of religion, GT has great potential promise for building concepts and theories from empirical materials and as a way to assess the extent to which existing theoretical frames and categories of analysis are adequate to the empirical materials that we study. Because of its sensitivity to the context of specific elements of empirical materials, GT seems particularly useful to the study of religion, especially as researchers move away from rigid, preconceived notions of what constitutes 'religious' data. GT is time consuming and tiring, especially during the deep immersion in data that is required in the early stages of open coding and analysis and during the repeated phases of data collection that theoretical sampling demands. However, GT can be a creative process and professionally engaging, in large part precisely because the conceptual/theoretical results emerge through this intense engagement with one's materials.

Notes

1 At the same time, books that offer more of a 'how-to' manual for GT can play important roles, even if overly limiting and prescriptive. Strauss's *Qualitative Analysis for Social Scientists* (1987) and Strauss and Corbin's *Basics of Qualitative Research* (1990) were subjected to an oddly caustic yet partially justified critique from Glaser (1992), yet they were arguably responsible for the huge surge in popularity of GT in the 1990s (Timmermans and Tavory 2007: 494; Bryant and Charmaz 2011: 208). Even more rigidly formulaic overviews can serve a useful introductory role (e.g. Birks and Mills 2011). Two useful websites are Glaser's own www.groundedtheory.com and Grounded Theory Online www.groundedtheoryonline.com.

2 Researchers should do the coding themselves, not delegate it, e.g. to research assistants assigned that one task. This is due to the fact that coding and analysis proceed simultaneously and in continuous interplay, resulting in a dynamic coding *process* that undermines the possibility of any stable 'coding sheet'. For this reason, doing GT as a team can be especially effective, allowing for a cross-check between different researchers' processes of coding and concept-building (Wiener 2007).

3 This example is from my research in progress (with institutional ethics approval and participant consent). I conducted the interviews in Portuguese, did initial open coding (in English) of five recorded interviews in a three-column format similar to Box 2.10.1, with codes in one column (using a set of abbreviations), key phrases from the interview in English translation in the second, and a third tracking the time points. I then made English transcripts, for further coding, of sections identified as most likely to be analytically significant. Theoretical sampling has resulted in the transcription and closer analysis of additional parts of these five interviews, more focused (selective) coding of additional interviews already conducted, and the elaboration of further questions for the next round of interviews.

4 Many of the basic ideas were set out in an earlier article by Glaser (1965), following upon a series of articles co-authored with Strauss and culminating in their influential book, *Awareness of Dying* (Glaser and Strauss 1965).

5 A related issue is the need to use the criterion of theoretical saturation to end one's research process, rather than leaning on the familiar landmarks of existing theory as cues that one has 'arrived'. It is important to avoid the temptation to stop when one recognizes familiar concepts and categories: e.g.

noting that one's interviewees are talking about religious conversion in a manner that echoes analyses in the published literature, and concluding merely that one's own study has confirmed that prior theoretical work.

6 The use of 'abduction' in the GT literature differs from that in the philosophy of science, where it is used to justify (not generate) hypotheses by appeal to observable phenomenon and where hypotheses are viewed narrowly as causal explanations. In that context, 'abduction' is epistemological, not methodological.

7 At the same time, other theoretical allegiances are ignored. For example, GT's relation to Durkheim has passed largely unnoticed: e.g. both emphasize the centrality of comparison, begin with 'things' rather than concepts, and accept that lay beliefs can serve as the starting point for theorizing (Covan 2007: 61–65, 73n67).

8 Norman Denzin (2007) distinguishes seven distinct approaches: positivist, postpositivist, constructivist, objectivist, postmodern, situational and computer-assisted.

9 Glaser and Strauss give the following examples: substantive theory includes 'patient care, race relations, professional education, delinquency, or research organization'; formal theory includes 'stigma, deviant behavior, formal organization, socialization, status congruency, authority and power, reward systems, or social mobility' (Glaser and Strauss 2009: 33).

10 I am indebted in this section to comments and suggestions from Mark Q. Gardiner. On semantics and semantic holism in the study of religion, see Frankenberry and Penner 1999, Jensen 2004, and Engler and Gardiner 2010.

11 Appeal to the nature of abduction doesn't help: abduction aims to produce a theory/hypothesis that accounts for the data, but 'data' here are the initial set of codes, not the empirical materials themselves.

12 Glaser is less charitable: 'Jargonizing QDA [qualitative data analysis] with GT concepts has been going on so long now that it has an unquestioned historical legitimacy. It seems to have solved the creditability envy for QDA which is required to get QDA accepted in leading journals . . .' (Glaser 2009: 4). Something similar happens with uses of 'discourse' and 'construction' in the study of religion. Appeals to the former tend to simply evoke a general attention to the contextualized aspects of language and appeals to the latter a vague sense that religious phenomena reflect their social, cultural and/or historical contexts. That is, talk of 'discourse' and 'construction(s)' in the study of religion almost universally fails to connect explicitly to relevant theory (see Hjelm this volume, Chapter 2.3; Engler 2004, 2005a, 2005b).

13 There was dynamism in this study's method, but of a different sort: 'in a successive strategy, the analyses of the initial interviews aided in constructing the criteria for selecting subsequent participants' (Masías-Hinojosa *et al.* 2008: para. 29). Translations from Spanish are mine.

References

Alexander, J.C., 1982. *Positivism, Presuppositions, and Current Controversies. Vol. 1 of theoretical logic in sociology.* University of California Press, Berkeley, CA.

Alvesson, M. and Sköldberg, K., 2009 [2000]. *Reflexive Methodology: new vistas for qualitative research.* SAGE, London, Thousand Oaks, CA.

Birks, M. and Mills, J., 2011. *Grounded Theory: a practical guide.* SAGE, London, Thousand Oaks, CA.

Bryant, A., 2009. Grounded theory and pragmatism: The curious case of Anselm Strauss. *Forum: Qualitative Social Research/Sozialforschung,* no. 3. www.qualitative-research.net/index.php/fqs/article/view/1358/2850.

Bryant, A. and Charmaz, K., 2007a. Editors' introduction: grounded theory research methods and practices. In: Bryant, A. and Charmaz, K. (eds), *The SAGE Handbook of Grounded Theory.* SAGE, London, Thousand Oaks, CA, pp. 1–28.

—— 2007b. Grounded theory in historical perspective: an epistemological account. In: Bryant, A. and Charmaz, K. (eds), *The SAGE Handbook of Grounded Theory.* SAGE, Los Angeles, London, pp. 31–57.

—— 2011. Grounded theory. In: Williams, M. and Vogt, W.P. (eds), *The SAGE Handbook of Innovation in Social Research.* SAGE, London, Thousand Oaks, CA, pp. 205–27.

Charmaz, K., 2000. Grounded theory: objectivitist and constructivist methods. In: Denzin, N.K. and Lincoln, Y.S. (eds), *Handbook of Qualitative Research.* SAGE, London, Thousand Oaks, CA, pp. 509–35.

—— 2006. *Constructing Grounded Theory: A practical guide through qualitative analysis*. SAGE, London, Thousand Oaks, CA.

Clarke, A., 2005. *Situational Analysis: grounded theory after the postmodern turn*. SAGE, London,Thousand Oaks, CA.

Clarke, A.E. and Friese, C., 2007. Grounded theorizing using situational analysis. In: Bryant, A. and Charmaz, K. (eds), *The SAGE Handbook of Grounded Theory*. SAGE, Los Angeles, London, pp. 363–97.

Cornwall, M., 2010. From the editor: ten most likely ways an article submission fails to live up to publishing standards. *Journal for the Scientific Study of Religion* 49(4): i–v.

Covan, E.K., 2007. The discovery of grounded theory in practice: the legacy of multiple mentors. In: Bryant, A. and Charmaz, K. (eds), *The SAGE Handbook of Grounded Theory*. SAGE, Los Angeles, London, pp. 58–74.

Davidman, L. and Greil, A.L., 2007. Characters in search of a script: the exit narratives of formerly Ultra-orthodox Jews. *Journal for the Scientific Study of Religion* 46(2): 201–16.

Davidson, D., 1984. *Inquiries into Truth and Interpretation*. Oxford University Press, Oxford.

Denzin, N.K., 2007. Grounded theory and the politics of interpretation. In: Bryant, A. and Charmaz, K. (eds), *The SAGE Handbook of Grounded Theory*. SAGE, London, Thousand Oaks, CA, pp. 454–71.

Dey, I., 2004. Grounded theory. In: Seale, C., Gobo, G., Gubrium, J.F. and Silverman, D. (eds), *Qualitative Research Practice*. SAGE, London, Thousand Oaks, CA, pp. 80–93.

—— 2007. Grounding categories. In: Bryant, A. and Charmaz, K. (eds), *The SAGE Handbook of Grounded Theory*. SAGE, Los Angeles, London, pp. 167–90.

Dunne, C., 2011. The place of the literature review in grounded theory research. *International Journal of Social Research Methodology* 14(2): 111–24.

Engler, S., 2004. Constructionism vs. what? *Religion* 34(4): 291–313.

—— 2005a. Discourse. In: von Stuckrad, K. (with Auffarth, C., Bernard, J. and Mohr, H.) (ed.), *The Brill Dictionary of Religion*. Brill, Leiden, pp. 516–19.

—— 2005b. Two problems with constructionism in the study of religion. *Revista de Estudos da Religião (Rever)* 5(4): 28–34.

Engler, S. and Gardiner, M.Q., 2010. Ten implications of semantic holism for theories of religion. *Method and Theory in the Study of Religion* 22(4): 283–92.

Frankenberry, N.K. and Penner, H.H. (eds), 1999. *Language, Truth, and Religious Belief: studies in twentieth-century theory and method in religion*. Scholars Press, Atlanta.

Geels, A., 2010. Grundad teori. In: Svensson, J. and Arvidsson, S. (eds), *Människor och makter: En introduktion till religionsvetenskap*. Högskolan i Halmstad, Halmstad, pp. 106–9.

Glaser, B.G., 1965. The constant comparative method of qualitative analysis. *Social Problems* 12(4): 436–45.

—— 1978. *Theoretical Sensitivity: advances in the methodology of grounded theory*. Sociology Press, Mill Valley, CA.

—— 1992. *Basics of Grounded Theory Analysis: emergence vs. forcing*. The Sociology Press, Mill Valley, CA.

—— 1998. *Doing Grounded Theory: Issues and discussions*. Sociology Press, Mill Valley, CA.

—— 2001. Conceptualization: On theory and theorizing using grounded theory. *International Journal of Qualitative Methods* 1(2): 23–38.

—— 2009. *Jargonizing: using the grounded theory vocabulary*. Sociology Press, Mill Valley, CA.

Glaser, B.G. and Strauss, A.L., 1965. *Awareness of Dying*. Aldine, Chicago.

—— 2009 [1967]. *The Discovery of Grounded Theory: strategies for qualitative research*. Aldine Transaction, Piscataway, NJ.

Glazier, J.D. and Grover, R., 2002. A multidisciplinary framework for theory building. *Library Trends* 50(3): 317–29.

Hesse-Biber, S.N., 2007. Teaching grounded theory. In: Bryant, A. and Charmaz, K. (eds), *The SAGE Handbook of Grounded Theory*. SAGE, Los Angeles, London, pp. 311–38.

Holton, J.A., 2007. The coding process and its challenges. In: Bryant, A. and Charmaz, K. (eds), *The SAGE Handbook of Grounded Theory*. SAGE, Los Angeles, London, pp. 265–89.

Hood, J., 2007. Orthodoxy vs. Power: the defining traits of grounded theory. In: Bryant, A. and Charmaz, K. (eds), *The SAGE Handbook of Grounded Theory*. SAGE, Los Angeles, London, pp. 151–64.

Jenkins, K.E., 2003. Intimate diversity: the presentation of multiculturalism and multiracialism in a high-boundary religious movement. *Journal for the Scientific Study of Religion* 42(3): 393–409.

—— 2010. In concert and alone: divorce and congregational experience. *Journal for the Scientific Study of Religion* 49(2): 278–92.

Jensen, J.S., 2004. Meaning and religion: on semantics in the study of religion. In: Antes, P., Geertz, A.W. and Warne, R.R. (eds), *New approaches to the study of religion. Volume 1: Regional, critical and historical approaches.* Walter de Gruyter, Berlin, New York, pp. 219–52.

Jensen, L.A., 2009. Conceptions of God and the Devil across the lifespan: a cultural-developmental study of religious liberals and conservatives. *Journal for the Scientific Study of Religion* 48(1): 121–45.

Kelle, U., 2005. 'Emergence' vs. 'Forcing' of empirical data? A crucial problem of 'grounded theory' reconsidered. *Forum: Qualitative Social Research/Sozialforschung,* no. 2. www.qualitative-research.net/index.php/fqs/article/view/467/1000.

—— 2007. The development of categories: different approaches in grounded theory. In: Bryant, A. and Charmaz, K. (eds), *The SAGE Handbook of Grounded Theory.* SAGE, Los Angeles, London, pp. 191–213.

Konieczny, M.E., 2009. Sacred places, domestic spaces: material culture, church, and home at Our Lady of the Assumption and St. Brigitta. *Journal for the Scientific Study of Religion* 48(3): 419–42.

Legewie, H. and Schervier-Legewie, B., 2004. Research is hard work, it's always a bit suffering. Therefore on the other side it should be fun. Anselm Strauss in conversation with Heiner Legewie and Barbara Schervier-Legewie. *Forum: Qualitative Social Research/Sozialforschung,* no. 3. www.qualitative-research.net/index.php/fqs/article/view/562.

Locke, K., 2007. Rational control and irrational free-play: dual-thinking modes as necessary tension in grounded theorizing. In: Bryant, A. and Charmaz, K. (eds), *The SAGE Handbook of Grounded Theory.* SAGE, Los Angeles, London, pp. 565–79.

Macmin, L. and Foskett, J., 2004. 'Don't be afraid to tell': the spiritual and religious experience of mental health service users in Somerset. *Mental Health, Religion and Culture* 7(1): 23–40.

Masías-Hinojosa, V.H., Ramírez-Pérez, P.A. and Winkler-Müller, M.I., 2008. Construcción de identidad en personas convertidas a la Iglesia Metodista Pentecostal de Chile. *Forum: Qualitative Social Research/Sozialforschung,* no. 1. www.qualitative-research.net/index.php/fqs/article/view/336/733.

Mruck, K. and Mey, G., 2007. Grounded theory and reflexivity. In: Bryant, A. and Charmaz, K. (eds), *The SAGE Handbook of Grounded Theory.* SAGE, Los Angeles, London, pp. 515–38.

Pitt, R.N., 2010. 'Killing the messenger': religious black gay men's neutralization of anti-gay religious messages. *Journal for the Scientific Study of Religion* 49(1): 56–72.

Quine, W.V., 1950. Two dogmas of empiricism. *The Philosophical Review* 60(1): 20–43.

—— 1990. *Pursuit of Truth.* Harvard University Press, Cambridge, MS.

Reichertz, J., 2007. Abduction: the logic of grounded theory. In: Bryant, A. and Charmaz, K. (eds), *The SAGE Handbook of Grounded Theory.* SAGE, Los Angeles, London, pp. 214–28.

Star, S.L., 2007. Living grounded theory: cognitive and emotional forms of pragmatism. In: Bryant, A. and Charmaz, K. (eds), *The SAGE Handbook of Grounded Theory.* SAGE, Los Angeles, London, pp. 75–93.

Strauss, A.L., 1987. *Qualitative Analysis for Social Scientists.* Cambridge University Press, Cambridge, New York.

—— 1993. *Continual Permutations of Action.* Aldine Transaction, New Brunswick, NJ.

Strauss, A.L. and Corbin, J., 1990. *Basics of qualitative research: grounded theory procedures and techniques.* SAGE, London, Newbury Park, CA.

Suddaby, R., 2006. From the editors: what grounded theory is not. *Academy of Management Journal* 49(4), 633–42.

Timmermans, S. and Tavory, I., 2007. Advancing ethnographic research through grounded theory practice. In: Bryant, A. and Charmaz, K. (eds), *The SAGE Handbook of Grounded Theory.* SAGE, Los Angeles, London, pp. 493–512.

Urquhart, C., 2007. The evolving nature of grounded theory method: the case of the information systems discipline. In: Bryant, A. and Charmaz, K. (eds), *The SAGE Handbook of Grounded Theory.* SAGE, Los Angeles, London, pp. 339–59.

Wiener, C., 2007. Making teams work in conducting grounded theory. In: Bryant, A. and Charmaz, K. (eds), *The SAGE Handbook of Grounded Theory.* SAGE, Los Angeles, London, pp. 293–310.

Further reading

Bryant, A. and Charmaz, K. (eds), 2007. *The SAGE Handbook of Grounded Theory.* SAGE, London, Thousand Oaks, CA.

The state-of-the-art overview of the range of current issues concerning—and approaches to—GT, with examples and detailed discussions of key practical issues (e.g. coding, memoing and developing categories). The book leans toward constructionist approaches. Glaser (2009), consistent with his narrow view of 'classical' GT, argues that most of the work in this volume is not properly GT.

Charmaz, K., 2006. *Constructing Grounded Theory: a practical guide through qualitative analysis.* SAGE, London, Thousand Oaks, CA.

The most useful and up-to-date (in theoretical and methodological terms) single-volume introduction to GT. Charmaz (the key proponent of the constructivist approach) contextualizes different versions of GT, corrects common misconceptions and, most importantly, offers valuable practical guidelines for constructing grounded theory.

Dey, I., 2004. Grounded theory. In: Seale, C., Gobo, G., Gubrium, J.F. and Silverman, D. (eds), *Qualitative Research Practice.* SAGE, London, Thousand Oaks, CA, pp. 80–93.

An excellent article-length overview.

Glaser, B.G., 1998. *Doing Grounded Theory: issues and discussions.* Sociology Press, Mill Valley, CA.

A practical introduction to the Glaserian approach.

Knoblauch, Hubert. 2003. *Qualitative Religionsforschung. Religionsethnographie in der eigenen Gesellschaft.* Schöningh, Paderborn, München, Wien, Zürich.

A unique and valuable work on qualitative methods in the study of religion, with an emphasis on GT.

Strauss, A. and Corbin, J., 1990. *Basics of Qualitative Research: grounded theory procedures and techniques.* SAGE, London, Newbury Park, CA.

The classic statement of the Straussian approach (GT as qualitative analysis). This book's very practical 'how to' approach played an important role in the popularization of GT in the 1990s.

Wertz, F.J., Charmaz, K., McMullen, L.M., Josselson, R., Anderson, R. and McSpadden, E., 2011. *Five Ways of Doing Qualitative Analysis: phenomenological psychology, grounded theory, discourse analysis, narrative research, and intuitive inquiry.* Guilford Press, New York.

Useful for comparing GT to other qualitative approaches. The comparisons with phenomenological approaches and discourse analysis are especially relevant for scholars of religion.

Key concepts

Abduction: A type of logical reasoning—distinct from deduction and induction—that involves contingent inference to the best explanation/interpretation through examining and weighing alternatives that seem to fit the data.

Categories: More general classes that bring together concepts, with the latter serving effectively as properties of the former.

Codes: The initial descriptive, inchoately interpretive terms and phrases that label elements of data.

Coding: The process of labeling distinct elements of one's empirical materials, i.e. of defining what is seen as significant in the data. Coding in GT is more oriented toward conceptual abstraction than description.

Concepts: Constructs that combine characteristics or particulars of a set of codes.

Constant comparative method: Comparing elements to others at the same logical level and to the emergent more general elements at a higher logical level: e.g. data to data, data to concepts, concepts to concepts, concepts to categories, etc. This process generates increasingly abstract and general concepts, categories and theories through the process of abduction.

Grounded theory: (1) A methodology with a specific view of the relation between data and theory and of how method mediates between these. (2) One of several distinct methods instantiating this methodological stance: building concepts, categories and theories from data; with analytical work based in coding and memoing; with analysis proceeding simultaneously with data collection; and with analysis informing ongoing data collection.

Memoing: The creation of notes, lists, diagrams, tables, mindmaps, etc. during the process of GT analysis. It is a crucial step in moving past descriptive coding of the data toward the analytical generation of concepts and categories.

Theoretical sampling: The collection of further data in light of the developing analysis and in order to further develop it. It aims at further clarifying and defining emerging concepts and categories, not at representing a population.

Theoretical saturation: The point at which analysis is not producing significantly new conceptual or theoretical material. This marks the end of data collection and the beginning of the transition toward writing up results.

Theoretical sensitivity: The ability—developed through training and, especially, through experience—to reflect analytically upon data and to recognize what data are relevant to one's emerging conceptual frame. It is informed by one's existing stock of concepts and theories. It could be thought of as 'wisdom' if we were to take an Aristotelian or virtue ethic conception of research.

Related chapters

- Chapter 1.2 Comparison
- Chapter 1.3 Epistemology
- Chapter 2.3 Discourse analysis
- Chapter 2.11 Hermeneutics
- Chapter 2.13 Interviewing
- Chapter 2.15 Phenomenology

2.11

HERMENEUTICS

Ingvild Sælid Gilhus

Chapter summary

- Hermeneutics is derived from a Greek word, which means to 'express', 'translate', 'interpret'.
- Hermeneutics is both a method and a philosophy of interpretation.
- Hermeneutics is not limited to textual studies—all scientific methods presuppose hermeneutic reflection.
- Hermeneutics consists of a reading that moves back and forth between the parts and the whole of the text, between its structure and meaning, between the reader's horizon and the horizon of the text, and between the text and its contexts. These processes are different varieties of the so-called hermeneutic circle.
- Interpretation is seen as a never-ending process with emphasis on discourse and pluralism.
- Within the field of religious studies the range of acceptable readings of a text is dependent on the text's cultural and social contexts.

Introduction

Bears leave trails when they move through a forest. They scratch themselves on trees, break branches and urinate on the ground—signs that other bears find meaningful. Human beings make interpretations of the special signs that constitute their world. Examples of human signs are what people say, the facial expressions of the beloved—or the flight of birds and the liver of a sacrificial animal.

When interpretation is developed into a scientific method, it is given a Greek name—**'hermeneutics'**—a concept derived from *hermeneuein*, which means to 'express', 'translate', 'interpret'. The source material of hermeneutics is texts and other utterances, and the goal is to achieve understanding of their meanings. In religious studies the study of texts and utterances is not an end in itself, but a means to say something about religion and religious processes in a society.

Hermeneutics was developed in antiquity when a distinction was made between literal and allegorical meanings, for instance in the reading of Homer and Greek mythology and in Philo of Alexandria's interpretations of the Septuagint. Christian authors distinguished between different layers of meaning in the Bible. Origen (185–254) drew a distinction between the literal sense, the moral sense and the spiritual sense of Scripture. In practice such distinctions often boiled down to a division between the literal and the allegorical meaning. In the Renaissance hermeneutics was closely connected to philology, combined with source criticism and seen as the basic method of the humanities. With the Reformation individual Christians started to read and interpret the Bible on their own, which led to a new focus on interpretation. The Lutheran theologian Johann Conrad Dannhauer (1603–66) coined the word 'hermeneutics' and used it in the title of a book, *Hermeneutica sacra*, in 1654.

Hermeneutics was later extended to include not only Classic texts and the Bible, but texts from other cultures as well. Today hermeneutics is also applied to text-like objects such as art, drama, photography and film, and to text-analogues such as speech and non-verbal communication—in fact to any system of codes and sense-making processes (Yanow 2006: 15–16). Culture and religion can be seen as 'textual' and as webs of signs which can be analyzed by means of hermeneutical methods.

Hermeneutics consists of a reading that moves back and forth between the parts and the whole of a text, between its structure and meaning, between the reader's horizon and the horizon of the text, and between the text and its contexts. These processes are described as different varieties of a **hermeneutic circle** (see Figure 2.11.1). They presuppose a priori knowledge of the content of the text that is continually modified in reading and interpretation, adding layers of meaning and understanding in a never-ending process. No text speaks for itself and no interpretation is ever final. The hermeneutic approach is characterized metaphorically as dialogical because it presupposes a continuous exchange between the researcher and the source material.

Hermeneutics is both a method and a philosophy of interpretation. The method can neither be satisfactorily employed nor explained without being firmly rooted in theories of interpretation, because the act of interpretation should always include systematic reflection over the hermeneutical process and one's own starting points in this process. According to the philosopher Hans-Georg Gadamer (see below), hermeneutics is more basic than other types of methods because all methods presuppose hermeneutic reflection. One might even ask if hermeneutics really is a method. One answer to this question is that it is necessary to interpret texts in a methodologically sound way, which implies obeying certain rules, and thus following a method.

Hermeneutic guidelines

The first guideline in using a hermeneutic method is to read the text slowly and thoroughly. A text can be read hundreds of times—forward, backward and crosswise—yielding new information each time. In accordance with the model of the hermeneutic circle, one goes to the text with one's prejudices and then projects meanings into it. The knowledge obtained by the initial reading modifies one's prejudices and the text gets a richer interpretation in each of the following readings.

A second guideline is to apply everything one knows about the language and context of the text. The word 'text' is derived from Latin *textere*, 'weave' which is rather fitting since a text is a web of references to concepts, ideas, practices and other texts (intertextuality). A context is the interrelated conditions in which something appears or occurs. In the case of a text, the context includes especially its social and cultural background and surroundings. According to one version of the hermeneutic circle, the reader moves back and forth between the text and its context. A text always has several contexts, not only one. One example is the

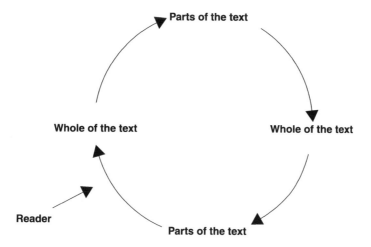

Friedrich Schleiermacher's version of the hermeneutic circle

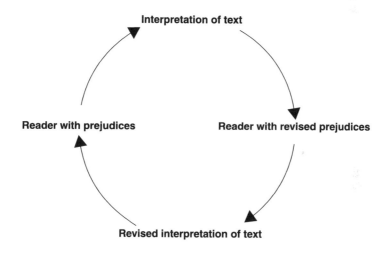

Hans-Georg Gadamer's version of the hermeneutic circle

Figure 2.11.1 Varieties of the hermeneutic circle

final instructions to the 9/11 hijackers, found after the planes had crashed into the World Trade Center. These instructions can be read in relation to the context of religion, the context of politics, the global social context, the context of terrorism, etc. The religious context could further be divided, for instance into ritual, the Qur'an and the afterlife. Meaning is in each case produced in the relation between the text and a specific context, while the text's possibility of producing meanings in relation to other contexts is simultaneously reduced.

Different contextualizations lead to different readings. When the Mithraic mysteries were studied, as Franz Cumont did, as if they had their background in Iranian religion, this led to an interpretation of the mysteries that was dominant for 70 years. After Richard Gordon and

John Hinnells criticized Cumont's thesis at the first International Congress of Mithraic Studies at Manchester University (1971), new contextualizations for the mysteries were suggested, most important Roman culture, but also astrology.

All texts speak about the world. If we know little about the world of the text, we have to find out more. For example, to make an interpretation of the *Epic of Gilgamesh* we have to be well informed about Mesopotamian religion and culture. What was the political structure? Who were the gods? What role did astrology play in this culture? How was the genre of epic poems conceived? A literary genre carries meanings that are not necessarily made explicit in a text. It will also be highly desirable to know the language of the epic, Accadic.

A third guideline is to keep an eye on the possibilities of cultural comparison. To use a hermeneutical method in the history of religions is to work within the framework of comparison. When a motif has been thoroughly analyzed in its textual and cultural context, using related comparative material from the same cultural area can inspire the interpreter to look for meanings and intentions that have been overlooked.

A fourth guideline is to be aware that textual meanings are always in flux. Texts can be studied both in relation to their origin and in relation to how various communities have used them over time. One can ask why a text was created in the first place, which questions it was meant to answer and what was the intention of the author. One can also ask why a text was kept alive. The latter question abandons the search for the original author and concentrates instead on readers and their historical and social contexts. Canonical texts, such as the Bible or the Qur'an, have accumulated layers of meaning as interpretive communities have commented on them. Interpretive activities determine what is the meaning of a text—'the text is always a function of interpretation' (Fish 1980: 341). Different persons and social groups may have changed a text and left their marks on it. It is also useful to keep in mind that texts are not always authored in a simple way. The *Bhagavadgita*, for instance, was not created by one person, but was composed by several persons before it attained its final form. Parts of older texts are sometimes combined when new texts are created.

A fifth guideline is to ask whose interests are promoted in a text. Writing texts and making interpretations of them are practices connected to groups and their interests. In the book of Genesis God commands Adam and Eve: 'Be fruitful and multiply' (Genesis 1:28 a). While marriage and reproduction were the norm in Judaism, Christian commentators made their interpretations of biblical texts so that they gave support to ascetic readings. Elisabeth Clark argues that 'early Christian writers indeed created a new asceticizised Scripture—but by interpretation, not (usually) by a literal erasure or replacement of the Biblical world' (Clark 1999: 5). Thus creative readers produced new meanings for old texts and articulated a view of religion that had Christian ascetics as its apex.

A sixth guideline is to try to pose new questions to a text. Successive modern interpreters of the *Homeric Hymn to Demeter* have seen the myth of Demeter and Kore in relation to agriculture, *rites de passage* and archetypes. In contrast to earlier readings, the classicist Helene P. Foley concentrated on the hymn's potential to say something about female experience in ancient Greece (Foley 1993). She made the reader more aware of the female roles in the text, especially the mother-daughter relationship of Demeter and Core, but also the roles of Hecate and Rhea. Foley saw the hymn as 'a female version of the heroic quest that plays a central role in Mediterranean and Near Eastern epic forms as early as the Sumerian epic of Gilgamesh' (Foley 1993: 80). To offer a new reading to a text presupposes that one masters earlier readings of it.

If we have made our interpretation in accordance with the guidelines above, how do we know that it is valid? We are on the right track when we think that everything that is said in the text is taken into account and that the different parts of the interpretation are consistent with each other and with what we already know. The approval of the scientific community is the external test on the validity of an interpretation: an interpretation that few people other than the author find convincing is most likely flawed. An interpretation must be more probable than another, for instance by giving better answers to certain questions than other interpretations do. Just as no final reading exists, there is no final verification and there are no transcendental norms.

'Come out of your tomb'

The presentation of a small text can serve as an illustration of a hermeneutic approach. In a Greek magical papyrus (PGM CXXXIII a-f) there is a short spell for childbearing (Betz 1996: 319): 'Come out of your tomb, Christ is calling you. [Place] a potsherd on the right thigh.' The spell consists of a small history and probably refers to a gospel narrative about Christ who calls the dead Lazarus to step out of his tomb. Since the spell is part of a magical text that includes several ritual formulas, it is reasonable to think that it was used for a specific purpose, in this case to speed up the birth process. The text was probably inscribed on the potsherd and placed on the woman's thigh. Giving birth is a dangerous situation in human life, and ritual power is frequently called for during the process. The story about Lazarus is by analogy made to refer to the baby (Lazarus), the womb (the tomb) and Christ (Christ/ritual expert). The text also recalls the Platonic parallel between *soma/sema*, that the body is a tomb for the soul. Rereading and musing over the words of the spell leads to the question as to whether there is a connotation to the Christian idea of a second birth: to be born by a woman is to be born to death, but to be reborn by Christ is to be reborn to eternal life. In the text above, the idea of the first birth is mixed with the idea of the second birth, likely to strengthen the possibility of a positive outcome and of a child who lives. Whose interest does the spell serve? The owner of the text is unknown, but it is likely that it belonged to a ritual expert, who probably obtained his/her livelihood and social status from trading in rituals, while the parturient and her family most likely found comfort in the ritual. Sometimes priests made a little extra by selling their services on the private market. There could also have been conflict between this type of ritual expert and the Church.

The interpretation above is the result of several readings of the spell. The various attempts at contextualization involve the magical papyrus, Christian gospels, theological interpretations, Platonic philosophy, birth, ritual experts, normative religion contra popular religion, and economy. One can pursue these perspectives and contexts further or use others, for instance a gender perspective: What is most likely the sex of the ritual expert? Does the relationship between the womb and the tomb have some misogynous connotations? The womb is usually conceived of as a life-giving organ. Does the use of the concept 'tomb' signalize a negative view of female fertility or does it only reflect that mortality rates of newborn babies in ancient societies were high?

The point is that interpreting texts involves reading and rereading, keeping a dialogue between parts and whole, posing questions and bringing in different contexts to try to tease out some of the layers of meaning that even the tiniest text always presents to its readers.

Theoretical and epistemological basis

The modern history of hermeneutics includes impulses from biblical studies, philosophy and comparative literature. It reflects the development of deeper insight into the nature of interpretation as well as conflicts over hermeneutical processes and the goal of interpretation. Among the significant names in the modern history of hermeneutics are Friedrich Schleiermacher (1768–1834), Wilhelm Dilthey (1833–1911), Martin Heidegger (1889–1976), Hans-Georg Gadamer (1900–2002) and Paul Ricoeur (1913–2005).

Friedrich Schleiermacher is called 'the father of modern hermeneutics', though this characterization occludes important predecessors (Forster 2007). Schleiermacher saw interpretation as the interplay between the understanding of words, sentences, paragraphs and the entire text. There is a continuous and never-ending movement between the interpretation of the parts and the interpretation of the whole, parallel to how words get their meaning from their opposition to other words and from their use in language. Schleiermacher's goal was to try to grasp the author's original intention.

Wilhelm Dilthey built on the contrast Schleiermacher had made between interpretation and explanation and saw hermeneutics as the central task of the humanities (understanding) and opposed to the method of natural sciences (explanation). According to Dilthey, scientists analyze the object from outside, while humanists attempt via hermeneutical methods to view the object from inside. In fact Dilthey regarded interpretation as an art.

While Martin Heidegger (*Sein und Zeit*, 1927) saw interpretation as an existential question and was less interested in linguistics than in Man's being in the world—to exist is to interpret—his pupil, Hans-Georg Gadamer, returned to the question of texts and textual interpretation. Gadamer's *Wahrheit und Methode* (Truth and Method, 1960) is a turning point in the modern history of hermeneutics. According to Gadamer the interpreter is situated historically and culturally and turns to texts with her/his prejudices. This implies that meanings are projected into the text and then modified and revised in the light of what emerges as the reader penetrates deeper into the text. This insight can be seen as a further elaboration on the model of the hermeneutic circle.

Similar to Heidegger, Gadamer found prejudices to be productive and a medium for understanding: 'Working out this fore-projection, which is constantly revised in terms of what emerges as he penetrates into the meaning, is understanding what is there' (Gadamer 1996: 267). According to Gadamer, interpretation is facilitated because past and present are connected in an historical continuity. We are part of the 'Wirkungsgeschichte' (history of effect) of ancient texts. The historicity of understanding is elevated to the status of a hermeneutic principle.

A reader approaches a text with her/his horizon of understanding, confronts the horizon of the text, modifies/opens up her/his horizon and reads the text anew with a real 'fusion of horizons'—the horizon of the text and the horizon of the interpreter. The interaction of fore-understanding and the reading of the text, as well as the interaction between reading parts of the text and reading the whole, are intrinsic to all understanding. In the new version of the hermeneutic circle the reader has moved into the circle and is no longer on the outside as s/he is in Schleiermacher's version.

Paul Ricoeur highlighted the conflict of interpretations. According to him interpreters have usually been obedient and respectful towards religious texts—especially religious interpreters. Opposed to this hermeneutics of acceptance, Ricoeur points at the **hermeneutics of suspicion** reflected in the contributions of Karl Marx (1818–83), Friedrich Nietzsche (1844–1900) and Sigmund Freud (1856–1939). Their interpretations stress hidden meanings and critiques of ideology. For these three 'masters of suspicion', interpretation is the point of departure for explanations, either of Christianity or of religion in general.

According to Ricoeur, explanation does not exhaust the possibilities for interpretation (Ricoeur 1981: 155–56). 'Ultimately, the correlation between explanation and understanding, between understanding and explanation, is the "hermeneutical circle"' (ibid.: 221). Ricoeur thus tries to unite the two approaches of interpretation and explanation, bridging Dilthey's duality.

This brief overview of the modern development of the theoretical and epistemological basis of hermeneutics shows that hermeneutics has moved from mentality, experience and the author's intention (Schleiermacher, Dilthey) to focus on language, interpretive communities, readers and conflicts of interpretation (Ricoeur, Gadamer). The dialectical process between readers and texts is always in focus, but each of the thinkers mentioned above has given the hermeneutical circle a new spin as new insights have been brought to bear. In line with the linguistic and cultural turn in the humanities during the last decades, interpretation is now seen as a never-ending process with emphasis on discourse and pluralism of interpretation.

Specific to religious studies, Joachim Wach (1898–1955) could be mentioned. In his works the problems of interpreting and understanding religion are frequently discussed (Wach 1926–33: see Klimkeit 1972; Wedemeyer and Doniger 2010).

Strengths, limitations, practical issues and challenges

Hermeneutics is important in religious studies because it deals with texts, meaning and interpretation in a theoretically reflexive way. One of the strengths of this approach is that new perspectives and contexts will invite new questions and interpretation.

We can ask what a text was intended to answer, but we can also ask questions of a text that its author never dreamed could be asked. A text is an imprint of cultural knowledge and will always tell more than its author(s) intended, because the horizon of a text is wider than that of its author. (In a similar way the author's horizon is also wider than the horizon of the text). However, even if texts can answer more questions than their authors thought, it is not possible to get an answer to every question one might want to ask of a text. The questions have to match the content and character of the texts that are interpreted.

Most of the methods outlined in this book can be combined with hermeneutics. The potential utility and range of application of hermeneutics are great. Its usefulness for philology is obvious, because of philology's traditional focus on texts and their history. Historical investigations are similarly dependent on methodologically sound interpretations and presuppose hermeneutic reflections. Since much hermeneutical work has been done on the Bible, it is representative to include one example from this field. One useful book is Manfred Oeming's *Contemporary Biblical Hermeneutics* (2006) which describes contemporary hermeneutic approaches and presents examples from different biblical texts.

As suggested above, hermeneutics is not limited to textual studies and can be combined with, for instance, anthropological methods. Clifford Geertz adopted a hermeneutic approach and used the hermeneutic circle when he described a dialectical movement between local details and global structure in his analysis of experiences of self in Java, Morocco and Bali (Geertz 1974). Armin Geertz leans on Gadamer and on Geertz's 'interpretive anthropology' when he applies the term 'ethnohermeneutics' to describe 'the bringing together of the hermeneutical horizons of the student of religion and the indigenous interpreter' (Geertz 1997: 70).

Developing skills in interpretation may counteract misunderstandings and promote intercultural respect. According to the hermeneutics of acceptance texts should be read in an empathic way with an eye to their intentions. This could, however, impose limits on interpretation, for example by reproducing the views of an elite group. According to Bruce Lincoln, those who have an idealized image of culture 'mistake the ideological positions favoured and propagated by the dominant fraction for those of the group as a whole' (Lincoln

2005: 9). To pursue a hermeneutics of suspicion usually works better because it may imply that other groups than the cultural elite are moved into focus, which also means that the empathy of the interpreter is shared between teasing out the intentions of a text and seeing how these intentions affect different groups.

One advantage of studying ancient texts is that one knows how they have been used in posterity, as well as what happened afterwards, which we do not know when we read texts from the present. To know the outcome, however, can also mean to view history in a biased way and to overlook the fact that at each moment other outcomes could have been possible.

A further aspect of the relationship between past and present is how past processes of interpretation influence hermeneutics. When we read texts transmitted from the past with a continuous history of interpretation attached to them, we might overlook how these texts were interpreted in the earlier phases of their transmission. Cultural insiders may also be blind to the obvious, for the simple reason that it is obvious to them. Comparative and cross-cultural perspectives might counteract this type of cultural blindness. If we interpret texts that are not part of a tradition known to the reader, we might encounter other types of problems, for example with making fruitful contextualization.

A hermeneutic approach to religious texts presupposes intimate knowledge about the tradition of insider interpretation within the given religion. How have texts been interpreted and commented upon, for instance in Buddhism and Sikhism? One example of successful use of hermeneutic awareness and contextualization is Jeffrey R. Timm's edited volume, *Texts in Context: Traditional Hermeneutics in South Asia* (1992), where the contributors investigate how texts have been interpreted in their individual hermeneutical contexts.

A final question: Does each and every text present an unlimited field of potential alternative constructions? In late antiquity some textual communities ('gnostics') challenged the authority of the Hebrew Bible. When God says, 'I am the only God, except for me there is no one' (e.g. Isaiah 44:6; 46:9), his challengers claimed that if he really was the only god, he had no reason to say it all the time, and they drew the conclusion that he was an imposter. This is an ancient example of how a deconstructive approach may strike at the heart of texts, give them a new interpretation and destroy their traditional authority. Texts can mean almost anything that an interpretative community wants them to (Fish 1980).

There is, however, a difference between creative uses of religious texts and scientific interpretations of them. Hermeneutists within the field of religious studies are committed to construct interpretations that they believe say something about the users of a text and of textual communities at a certain point in history. The range of acceptable readings of religious texts is thus limited and should not exceed the bounds of interpretation that are dependent on the text's cultural and social contexts.

References

Betz, H.D., 1996 [1986]. *The Greek Magical Papyri in Translation, including the Demotic Spells*. The University of Chicago Press. Chicago, London.

Clark, E.A., 1999. *Reading Renunciation: asceticism and scripture in Early Christianity*. Princeton University Press, Princeton.

Fish, S., 1980. *Is There a Text in This Class? The authority of interpretive communities*. Harvard University Press, Cambridge, MA, London.

Foley, H.P. (ed.), 1993. *The Homeric Hymn to Demeter: translation, commentary and interpretive essays*. Princeton University Press, Princeton.

Forster, M.N., 2007. Hermeneutics. In: Leiter B. and Rosen, M. (eds), *The Oxford Handbook of Continental Philosophy*. Oxford University Press, Oxford, New York, pp. 30–74.

Gadamer, H.G., 1996 [1960]. *Truth and Method.* Trans. J. Weinsheimer and D.G. Marshall. Sheed & Ward, London.

Geertz, A.W., 1997. Hermeneutics in ethnography: lessons for the study of religion. In: Klimkeit, H.-J. (ed.), *Vergleichen und Verstehen in der Religionswissenschaft.* Harrassowitz Verlag, Wiesbaden, pp. 53–70.

Geertz, C., 1974. 'From the native's point of view': on the nature of anthropological understanding. *Bulletin of the American Academy of Arts and Sciences* 28(1): 26–45.

Klimkeit, H.-J., 1972. Das Prinzip des Verstehens bei Joachim Wach. *Numen* 19: 216–28.

Lincoln, B., 2005. Theses on method. *Method and Theory in the Study of Religion* 17 (1): 8–10.

Oeming, M., 2006. *Contemporary Biblical Hermeneutics: an introduction.* London, Ashgate.

Ricoeur, P., 1981. *Hermeneutics and the Human Sciences: essays on language, action and interpretation.* Cambridge University Press, Cambridge.

Timm, J.R. (ed.), 1992. *Texts in Context: traditional hermeneutics in South Asia.* State University of New York Press, Albany.

Wach, J., 1926–33. *Das Verstehen: Grundzüge einer Geschichte der hermeneutischen Theorie in 19. Jh.* 3 vols. J.C.B. Mohr, Tübingen.

Wedemeyer, C.K. and Doniger, W. (eds), 2010. *Hermeneutics, Politics, and the History of Religions: the contested legacy of Joachim Wach and Mircea Eliade.* Oxford University Press, Oxford, New York.

Yanow, D., 2006. Thinking interpretively: philosophical presuppositions and the human sciences. In: Yanow, D. and Schwartz-Shea, P. (eds), *Interpretation and Method: empirical research method and the interpretive turn.* M.E. Sharpe, Armonk, NY, London, pp. 3–26.

Further reading

Fish, S., 1980. *Is There a Text in This Class? The authority of interpretive communities.* Harvard University Press, Cambridge, MA, London.

In this collection of essays Stanley Fish uses a reader's approach to texts and examines how interpretative communities determine the readings of texts.

Flood, G., 1999. *Beyond Phenomenology: rethinking the study of religion.* Cassell, London, New York, pp. 65–90.

Discusses the relevance of Gadamer's hermeneutics for the study of religion.

Forster, M.N., 2007. Hermeneutics. In: Leiter B. and Rosen, M. (eds), *The Oxford Handbook of Continental Philosophy.* Oxford University Press, Oxford, New York, pp. 30–74.

Presents key thinkers in the modern philosophy of hermeneutics.

Gadamer, H.G., 1996 [1960]. *Truth and Method.* Sheed & Ward, London.

Develops a theory of understanding that is dependent on language and history.

Penner, H.H., 2000. Interpretation. In: Braun, W. and McCutcheon, R.T. (eds), *Guide to the Study of Religion.* Cassell, London, New York, pp. 57–71.

Inspired by Donald D. Davidson, the author proposes that interpretation entails truth conditions, translatability and literal meaning.

Ricoeur, P. 1981. *Hermeneutics and the Human Sciences: essays on language, action and interpretation.* Cambridge University Press, Cambridge.

Examines the history of hermeneutics and formulates a concept of the text.

Key concepts

Hermeneutics: The theory of interpretation and the analysis of the principles of interpretation.

Hermeneutic circle: Describes the process of understanding meaning as a dialectic process that moves back and forth between the parts and the whole of a text, between its structure and meaning, between the text and its contexts, between the reader's horizon and the horizon of the text.

Hermeneutics of suspicion: Stresses hidden meanings and presents critiques of ideology.

Related chapters

- Chapter 1.2 Comparison
- Chapter 1.3 Epistemology
- Chapter 2.12 History
- Chapter 2.13 Interviewing
- Chapter 2.16 Philology
- Chapter 2.17 Semiotics
- Chapter 2.18 Structuralism

2.12

HISTORY

Jörg Rüpke

Chapter summary

- Historical narrative is a practice widespread in religious and non-religious groups. It typically arises in situations of conflict and contested claims. Such historicization serves purposes of legitimization, boundary drawing and formulation of identities.
- Historiography of religions shares emic history's interest in understanding the present (or past presents) as a result of past options and choices. Perspectives on the past are and were always informed by present questions and interests, so as to better deal with the future, that is, to offer orientation.
- The interests that led to past documents and narratives need not be ours. The historico-critical method is the key instrument for dealing with such 'sources'. Importance should not be given to a source's narrative plausibility, but to its access to the given data.
- Historical sources have very different medial forms. Apart from earlier historiographical texts and documents, even non-textual material is important for our understanding of past change.
- Writing a history of religion is dependent on emic narratives. It has to deal with a hermeneutic circle: it is based on earlier narratives and it must insert detailed evidence into new narratives.
- Methodologically, history has to employ many different perspectives, thus leading to the questioning of established boundaries, legitimacies and identities.

Overview

History has not been receiving good press recently in the academic study of religion. As stated at a recent conference on the History of Religion in Italy, 'Contemporary research increasingly tends to concentrate on current issues' (Spineto 2009: 47). The same point emerged from a thoroughgoing analysis of the German Study of Religion (*Religionswissenschaft*).[1] Analyses of handbooks or 'companions' for religious studies in English that have appeared in the last decade yield the same results.[2] Terms like 'history' or 'tradition' do not figure among the chapter headlines or even in the index (Kippenberg 2000; Uehlinger 2006: 380; Rüpke 2007: 15). The attempt to understand modernity by looking into its, especially religious, past led to the rise of the History of Religion (Kippenberg 2002). Now the latter has outlived its past and dedicates itself to modernity—or so it seems. This handbook does include the term 'history'. Why and to what purpose? Introductions to religious studies of the 1960s and 1970s moved directly to the two key terms of the **historico–critical method**, '**sources**' and 'source criticism'. Not without reason. Texts and monuments available for the reconstruction of the past—the 'sources'—simply do not tell us 'how it really was'. They present their view of the past and its meaning for the future. Thus it is useful to give long lists of types of sources and types of distortions of historical reality by the source's representation of it.

Working historically is not just a methodological option among others. Doing history is based on a pre-scientific conviction. The past is important for the future. This conviction is shared by popular and academic history. It is methodology that differentiates academic from popular history, and to clarify this is the aim of this chapter. Yet, frequently the differences remain small. This needs explanation and has consequences.

This chapter will thus concentrate on fundamentals. It will start by discussing what it means 'to do history', especially history of religion. Basically, it will argue that scientific history starts from personal historical experience and pre-scientific historical listings, narratives and *imaginaires*. This French word reminds us that history is not only present and presented in textual form, but in monuments, images, films or websites, as well as in complex arrangements of museums, archives and libraries. As a consequence of this framing of history as a discipline, I will then address the genesis of historical narratives (and the other media just mentioned) on religion, internal and external. Why do religions historicize themselves? Does a god have a history? Does her or his veneration have one? What is it that makes religions objects of fruitful historical analyses?

Only once we have gained a critical interest in a history that has been told and seems to pose problems, we start to look for 'sources'. How do we find relevant evidence of what we are interested in? How do we analyze contemporary documents or later representations in order to find the new history, 'our' history, the order of events that makes sense of our view of the present and future results of that development? Here, discourse analysis, hermeneutics and philological methods come into play as well as network analysis and structuralism, which will be dealt with in other chapters in more detail. Which are the broad interests that have informed historical research and yielded results?

History: a perspective and a science

Human acting is action in the present and is directed towards the future. We only occasionally 'remember' the past (some more frequently, some less), are struck by similarities between present and past persons, places or situations, reflect on differences, e.g. when sitting on a train surrounded by cellphones, remembering the old days of phone booths. Certain events regularly provoke such a look into the past. Funeral services are a sure bet, graduation ceremonies less so. In Egypt, biography and autobiography were invented as epigraphic texts on tombstones. In my experience, conversations with older generations (a stage that we will all reach, it is hoped) are more likely to result in 'histories' than would conversations with children. We historicize on occasion and on purpose. Collectively, such awareness of changeability is permanently present, even if this need not take the form of narratives, of organized **historiography**.

There is no human culture without a constitutive element of common memory. By remembering, interpreting, and representing the past, peoples understand their present-day life and develop a future perspective on themselves and their world. "History" in this fundamental and anthropologically universal sense is a culture's interpretive recollection of the past serving as a means to orient the group in the present.

(Rüsen 1996: 8)

This citation needs to be qualified. First, to speak of 'a culture' needs differentiation. I started from individual memories. Grandfather's history, the story he tells, is so interesting because it is different from the history learnt at school. Whether we agree or not with his version is secondary to that interest. Familial or ethnic groups, social movements or religious organizations tell different stories and different histories, for varying purposes. Others might or might not have a place in these histories; the histories may or may not overlap. Orientation with respect to the future might be explicit or implicit. Sometimes stories are retold when they are 'out of date'. Printed sources and libraries lack the correcting effect of human memory and oblivion. They might transmit stories that served past purposes, 'old histories' nobody would like to hear. The documents we have to deal with change their meaning over time, and they might suddenly reappear in representations of the past that they were never intended to corroborate.

Academic history (which I characterize below in terms of its methodology) does not start from scratch. It is the business of people who are raised in relation to these collective and individual memories. Even if academic history is critical by asking for clarification, more precision or total revision, it is always critical of something, not everything. In its interest, which is necessarily a present interest, it has to frame its findings, has to put them into a larger picture that needs completion and logic, typically offered by *topoi*, by things one has to use in a story, and by tropes. The former term is from ancient rhetoric and denotes the usual 'places' one has to come to in making a convincing case in pleading or speaking. Every story must have a beginning despite the permanence of change. Every story has its heroes, but such a selection is a judgment of today (or yesterday), not a fact as such. Historiography is rhetorical, too, and refers to all figurative modes of speaking and thinking, including metaphors as well as metonymy (i.e. tropes). Replacing something by something else that is similar (metaphor) or that is usually associated with it (metonymy) is to introduce fiction. Yet—and that is most important—it is not fiction for fiction's sake, but fiction for the sake of coherence, of understanding, of explanation, fiction for the sake of orientation with respect to the present and the future.

Within these limits history can become a science: History. To make it more scientific, one can try to minimize the fictitious elements. This was basically the strategy of historicism, as it blossomed in the first quarter of the 20th century. However, the later acknowledgment of the historicity of every possible point of view undermined this approach as a non-fictional perspective. It was bound to change, and hence to invalidate itself the next moment. This position led to extreme specialization, to the professionalization of methods and institutions, and to an extreme division of labor (Raphael 2003: 68). The alternative was to find a sure footing in some philosophical grounding for history, an option advocated by Joachim Wach, one of the founding figures of religious studies in Germany and (after emigration during the Nazi regime) in the United States (Rüpke 2009a). However, there is a third way, advocated by Hans-Jürgen Goertz (Goertz 2001; see Goertz 1998: 34–36). This approach admits that History is not an empirical discipline. Of course, it is referential: it tries to base its claims on 'evidence', on as many 'sources' as possible, but this evidence does not speak for itself nor does it present itself without pre-selection. History is a discipline about relationships between a present subject and a past object, both ever-changing; it is a representation selected by criteria of interest and by the historical pre-formation of the historian; and it is informed by those aspects of the historical object that come to light in a methodically controlled way, elicited by hermeneutical as well as generalizing or nomologic approaches that try to find regularities, to 'formulate laws'. Thus, in History, the process of representation and of work on the past cannot be separated: history and History are not radically separable; they differ in their degrees of reflexivity and in the explicitness of their embedded interests. The latter, History, is defined by its ethos as conforming to the standards of a science, at least as far as possible without losing its function as an orientation for a future.

Basis and frame: historiography of religion

Clearly, religious convictions contribute enormously to their adherents' or cultures' conceptualizing and narrating of the past, a past that is, in religious terms, conceived as predefined by god(s), repeating itself, a period of test or the like. Here, clearly, a large field of enquiry for any historian or historian of religion opens up. For the present purpose I will focus on a much narrower field, the history of religious groups written by themselves or attributed to them by authors external to the group.

My starting point is the claim raised in the preceding section that even methodologically controlled research is informed by previous historical accounts. While a group's account of its past and its particular recollections of itself are not the only means of achieving orientation and constructing a coherent identity, historical narratives generated by a given group seem to be important for many groups. In addition, historical narratives are furthered by academic professionals in their historiographical enterprises, popularized by best-selling books, monumentalized by large-scale public monuments, memorized in school and commemorated in public rituals. The wide range of historiographical media and practices holds true for religious groups that produce a large variety of accounts of their past. Such narratives might concentrate on a founding phase or try to integrate as much of the 'history' remembered by a society as they can. Mythology and history are not opposites but variants of historical narratives, albeit generally including very different time indicators. In scriptural societies, canonization is a frequent instrument to stabilize narrative as well as doctrinal solutions; alternative interpretations are excluded from the centre of the tradition.[3] Typically, historical narratives are triggered by conflicts and conflicting claims. There are alternatives to textual narrative, even if such narrative is crucial and probably indispensable for the generation of a concept of time and historical consciousness (see Ricoeur 1984–88). Ritual can be an important way to dramatically act out the past, in a mode of memorizing or re-presentation. Images can focus on constellations and scenes, pointing to and systematizing previous narratives, or even gaining narrative powers.[4]

As a result of these efforts undertaken by religious communities to interpret and identify themselves through their past, historians of religions have a large body of sources (see below), and these are imbued by narratives, which were produced to serve this very purpose. The task of 'emic' historiography is pursued with much ingenuity and energy by religious innovators, e.g. Buddhists arguing for continuity of their reforms by aligning themselves with one of the existing seven schools; Christian jurists legitimizing claims to power and land by appeals to the donation of Constantine; or Muslims chronographers or biographers proving the reliability of the chain of tradition (*isnad*). They all produce accounts with a dense veneer of plausibility. Thus, historians of religion—supposed to produce 'etic' accounts and striving to apply a methodology of understanding (*Verstehen*) to their scholarly objects—often uncritically adopt emic constructs and ignore the subjective and interpretive nature of these frameworks. There is no clear dividing line between emic and etic in the contents of historiography, even where authors and primary audience do not belong to the same religious group (which is often not the case and needs not be set as a norm). Whether orally or in writing, 'etic' reconstructions of a history largely depend on 'emic' narratives.

Identities and interpretations generated by religious groups are often themselves uncritically taken up by scholars as if they may safely be adopted as legitimate and valid models on the basis of which to study the history of religion. Thus, we continue to hear and read about 'the church of the martyrs' or about the 'victory' of Buddhism in its dealing with local Japanese cults in classical Japanese historiography (see Bowring 2008 for Japan), or of the 'Hellenisation of Christianity' and even about Christianity, Judaism and paganism (in the late antique Mediterranean context, for example) as if these were all separate, stable and unified entities which may or may not have influenced and interacted with each other in various ways. The concept of the 'church of the martyrs', construing the survivors as legitimate successors to those killed, is put forward by religious historiographers (most famously the fourth-century church historian Eusebius; see Grafton and Williams 2008); and in the case of the 'Hellenisation of Christianity' an extrapolation from false dichotomies and portrayals of the appearance of Christianity on the world stage as a separate and new entity is proffered by Christian historiographers. These sharply defined identities exist in contradiction to the ambiguity and ambivalences which obtain in the field of religion, but the production of boundaries by historiographers and group leaders must not be allowed to completely obscure the existence and historical significance of the vast array of shared practices in daily life. In areas of the world where multiple (or indistinct) religious identities were the norm, many functions and forms of religious practices and beliefs occurred on a shared field between and above the boundaries invoked by distinct groups.

The concept of 'religions' itself is one important and problematic consequence of the historical approach sketched so far. The units of description might be self-evident from an emic point of view, i.e., the internal discourse of a group, frequently adopted by political commentators and journalists, who all might share an interest in clear-cut boundaries, in exclusion of heretics or the inclusion of wavering allies. In the historiography of religion, 'religion' has frequently been essentialized and hence justified on the basis of such normative claims. The uncritical usage of 'a' religion and the plural 'religions' has even earned some general reserves against history of religion as the mere addition of such partial or 'confessional' histories (see Uehlinger 2006).

The academic study of the history of religion in the 19th century was characterized by a general trend towards historical research. For historicism, an important intellectual trend of the 19th and early 20th centuries, the **historicization** of religion seemed to be a matter of absolute necessity, in order to deal with the variety of religions and the criticism addressed towards them. A visible part of this pervading process of acknowledging the historical development of the present can be seen in the foundation of museums and the 'restoration' of medieval castles during that epoch. Everything was subject to change, every period had its own dignity, not simply erased by 'progress'. Everything became contingent. Yet critics of historicism looked for ways to remedy the latter consequence, so that history had to be overcome by history, as Ernst Troeltsch postulated in the first quarter of the 20th century (Troeltsch 1924; see Graf 2006): Even lasting values were to be found in history. 'History of Religion' became the dominant approach to the 'Study of Religion' (*Religionswissenschaft, sciences religieuses*) throughout this period, only slowly supplemented by anthropology and sociology. Historical accounts in the form of handbooks and lexica abounded (Hastings 1908–21; Bertholet 1925; see Stausberg 2007). The explanatory power of a genetic narrative, assessing relationships of origins, influence and chronological transitions, was highly valued. Apart from the more theologically or philosophically-minded scholars who worked towards systematic accounts of religion including the early phenomenology of religion (Rüpke 2009a), most historians of religion proceeded without further methodological ado. Philologists subjected transmitted texts to historical-critical analysis and used marginal or newly found texts as counter-histories of suppressed groups (like Manichaeans) or popular fictitious stories (like the many acts of apostles, if we think of early Christianity) in order to interpret canonical ones. However, these canonical texts—precisely those texts that are most closely attached to the identities of religious communities—still remain the standard in many overviews of history of religions, as do traditional forms of periodization and master narratives.

The boundaries construed in religious narratives, the exclusion of 'heretics' in Christianity, the chain of 'narrators' in early Islam, the genealogy and limiting of 'schools' in Buddhism, are accepted and reproduced by many scholars. In the case of Christianity, for example, by the beginning of the 20th century, Ernst Troeltsch had described a replacement for the term 'Church' with the term 'Christianity' against the backdrop of the multiplication of post-Reformation churches. Now, occasionally the plural 'Christianities' is conceded in 'Church history', but it is seldom actually put to use as a heuristic or descriptive device. Global histories of Christianity have been attempted recently, studying diffusion from a post-colonial perspective instead of the pure history of missionary activities (e.g. Mayeur and Pietri 2003–10; Childester 2004); however, in effect, globalization is treated additively, sequencing new chapters onto the religious history of different regions and continents (see, for instance, Rüpke 2009c on the first volumes of the *Cambridge History of Christianity*). Impulses from the history of mentalities or social history have claimed to be histories of piety or ritual (e.g. Angenendt 1997; Hölscher 2005; Flanagan 2001), but they typically work within the narrower boundaries of histories presupposing the established boundaries of religions and confessions (see Metzger 2010). Only recently have minority positions been reconstructed on a larger historical scale. The embedded history of Western esotericism, analyzing a strand of religious thought and practice across the boundaries of confessional histories and across the boundaries of religion, philosophy and art history is an example.[5] This is an approach that offers many more analytical perspectives than isolated treatments of 'Paganism', even if termed a 'world religion' (York 2003; Harvey 1997).

In global politics, the concepts of 'religion' and of the self-organization of social groups as 'religions' have proven to be highly successful formats for establishing oneself as a national or international agent of the 'non-governmental organization' type (Beyer 2006). This proliferation of a Western concept of 'religion' (as a parasite construct riding on the back of the notion of national identity which proliferated especially from the 19th century onwards) has brought with it the construction (or continuous cultivation) of an interpretive account of such groups and their history. This has been done to create boundaries by pointing to old feuds and differences or to forge alliances on the basis of a common ancestry ('Abrahamic religions') or of presumed shared types like 'indigenous' or 'nature religions'. For scholars of religious history, the power of emic as well as etic religious histories in international relations as well as in local conflicts today brings with it the urgent challenge of renewing and revising the manner in which the historiography of religion is approached. The direct coupling of religious identity and historiography of religion (familiar from a tradition of 'national history') in what we might term 'confessional historiography'[6] can be countered through the development of alternative and more complex histories of religion. Of course, every group is entitled to construe itself as the legitimate keeper of a tradition, but it should be the task of scientific History of Religion to highlight the selections and exclusions of positions and people implied in such emic histories. Reflecting on the biases and concealments of traditional narratives and historiography of religions and on the history of its analytical and descriptive terms is vital for any History of Religion in the 21st century.

Basic concepts: whence the knowledge?

The basis of scientific History lies in the historical-critical method. This term means that history is neither pre-eminently judged by the aesthetics of its narratives nor their narrative plausibility. Of course, both these criteria remain important: not as important as in the pre-modern period (see Grafton 2007), but probably more important than was acknowledged 50 years ago or so. The specific trait of academic history, whether in narratives or in the non-discursive form of lists and graphs, is the justification of its claims by recourse to 'sources'. These sources are formed by contemporary or later documents, textual or non-textual remains. They are not taken at face value but are carefully interpreted—here hermeneutics, the 'art of understanding' comes in—and critically evaluated, that is, subjected to source-criticism. This needs further explanation.

First, 'sources' are not isolated stones to be used for building a history, but pieces of evidence critically evaluated in the process of questioning particular points in an established narrative. To identify such 'sources', whence our knowledge flows, is a business of its own. This heuristic 'finding' of sources is intimately related to the question posed, the problem identified and the perspective chosen. The selection of material closely analyzed will limit the range of possible answers, even if the internal limitations imposed by the material treated might turn out only later. Here are three examples. (1) The analysis of theological treatises helps to clarify issues treated by intellectuals (priests, theologians, monks, judges) of a specific period but usually gives no direct access to popular beliefs. (2) The answers given by persons interrogated in trials of inquisition only occasionally offer glimpses of their personal religious convictions; instead they generally offer reactions to alternatives implicit in the questions posed by the interrogating institution. (Or will the latter have informed—via books or sermons—the world view of the former anyway?) (3) It might seem to be a good idea to value early modern Christian piety by counting the frequency of holy communion (such data exists for centuries), but low numbers might be due to heightened levels of awareness of sins (which forbid the participation in the sacrament) or due to intensive pilgrimage to nearby sanctuaries rather than attendance at the parish church.

The word 'heuristic' indicates further complications. The material might have been treated in early accounts and might have to be only retreated; it might have to be looked for in archives or some storage corner of a temple; or it might be found as a result of systematic search or casually be dig up by an archaeologist tracing the limits of a settlement. Inventiveness is a virtue of its own and is well worth thinking about. Unlike sociologists or historians working on contemporary cultures, researchers treating more remote periods cannot produce their evidence at will, e.g. by turning to interviews if they have not found anything useful in the archives. Thus, in order to reconstruct long-term changes in popular piety, one might have to turn to wax invoices, size and types of foundations, membership in cultic associations, motifs in paintings or marginalia in prayer books (see e.g. Leroy Ladurie 1976; Ginzburg 1980; Berman 2005).

As mentioned before, to speak of sources is intimately related to the historical-critical method. Starting from the analysis of former historiographic work, its basic creed is not to judge the merits of such earlier texts—earlier and hence closer to the past researched—by any apparent plausibility or coherence.

The decisive questions are:

• Where did the knowledge proffered in the text come from?
• What were the sources used?

The natural consequence is that, if these sources are still available, the use of later, secondary accounts should be replaced by the original, the surviving documents. If these are not available—and this is frequently the case for old religious traditions—one has at least to reflect about the possibility of the existence of sources:

- Could observers have existed?
- Could they have communicated their observations?
- Could written documents, which more easily span time and space, have been produced, preserved and be accessed?
- Is monumental evidence still visible or was it long ago reused?

The clue to the method is not that direct evidence is necessarily more reliable. The guess of a good traditional historiographer might be much more reliable than the misunderstanding of an uninitiated contemporary observer or the inventions of an engaged participant. The thrust of the method is to force oneself beyond judging a source's value by its mere plausibility, to replace the question 'does the account seem plausible' with 'could its producer have known about it?'

From these considerations, a whole set of questions can be derived that should be addressed to all sources:

- Who is the producer or—more specifically in the case of texts—the author (partisan, agent, victim, observer)?
- When and where did she or he write (contemporary, a diary, a recollection in old age)?
- What interests did the author have?
- What motivated the production of the source (a bureaucratic process, public communication, secret documentation)?
- What was her or his motivation (to legitimize or accuse, to contradict or affirm)?
- Who were the intended addressees (insiders or people outside a given boundary)?
- What knowledge or interests were presupposed on their part?
- How did the message reach its audience?
- How was the source used in later times?
- How did it enter tradition or archives, and why has it been preserved?

Challenges: historiography again

In many cases we are not the first to use a source. Many texts (as monuments) have a long tradition of being reproduced, re-used, re-interpreted; they have entered into historiography already and are framed by a canonized understanding. Even more, most of the desirable evidence might be lost forever. For many decisive phases of religious groupings, we have to rely on early 'historiography'. Given the priorities of processes of canonization, such historiographers have rarely received as much interest as canonized 'sacred' texts from earlier phases, even if the latter are usually read through the lenses of the former. The 'founder' of Christian universal history, Iulius Africanus, has only recently been made the object of intensive research (e.g. Wallraff and Mecella 2009), the same holds true for Eusebius, the 'father' of 'church history' (e.g. Grafton and Williams 2008).

Jewish historiography is based on a large corpus of ancient historiography. It has been flourishing anew since the 19th century, struggling with problems of a philosophy of history as well as of positioning religion within contemporary culture (Brenner 2006). In comparison to the enormous amount of research into Tanakh and Septuagint historiography, Rabbinic texts have only recently started to receive attention as historiographic literature (e.g. Neusner 1994; Gafni 1997), as is also the case for early modern chronicles focused on religion and written outside of Palestine and central Europe. Within the last ten years, Daniel Boyarin (not without serious controversy) has analyzed texts from the Rabbinic period in order to revise naïve historiographies which took the available sources as reports of facts. This resulted in a debate about the lack, or form, of historiography in Talmud and Mishna (Boyarin 2004, 2006; see Burrus *et al.* 2006). Similar issues are put in the larger context of the instrumentalization of historical narratives in the construction of identity by Jewish authors (Gardner and Osterloh 2008). In all these studies we can observe a vigorous recognition of the interpretive nature of historiographies.

Islamic historiography is focused on the life of the prophet, accessible by the Qur'an and *hadiths*, biographies of the first generations of followers of Muhammad and on the development of the legal schools and political dynasties for the subsequent period (Rosenthal 1968; Robinson 2003; Donner 1998). Reflecting the abundance of regional historiography (due to the interaction of newly established regional polities with the legitimizing resources of Arabic culture and Islam), recent accounts are characterized by regional approaches.[7] Muslim scholars, in particular from South Asia, have revisited classical ethnographic texts to establish historiographic models to describe other religions (e.g. Brodeur 2007). Source criticism in Islamic studies directs attention onto the social position and context of historiographers (Humphreys 1989).

Among Buddhist sources, systematic doctrinal accounts clearly dominate. However, Buddhist historiography (its nature and comparability is still controversial in recent research, see Schalk *et al.* 2010) has been present from early on, starting with biographies of the Buddha and chronicles (Wedemeyer 2006). Later accounts typically narrate the history and diffusion of Buddhism by tracing 'schools' dominated by heads of monasteries who were prolific writers, interpreters of earlier texts and objects of serial biography at the same time. This 'school approach' likewise informs modern accounts, even if concentrated on certain regions. For Japanese history, critique of local and national traditions in the form of divine genealogies ('Shinto') had given rise to critical historiography by the 17th century (Brownlee 1999), but geographically all-embracing accounts remain rare (Griffis 1992; Kitagawa 1966). An approach concerned with tracing the history of individual 'sects' (e.g. Machacek and Wilson 2003) dominates to the detriment of historiographic approaches aimed at analyzing the interaction of Buddhist imports and home-grown developments with local temples and patronage (Bowring 2008). The large variety of different generic forms and local intellectual traditions have been barely addressed (see Lieberman 2003 for Bangkok). Chinese historiography (Gardner 1938) has become a subject of intensive and comparative research recently. Religion, however, seems not to have been a central concern of the authors of the classical annalistic texts (Schmidt-Glintzer 1982, 2005). Comprehensive accounts of religious historiography are lacking (see Bechert 1969 for India; Appadurai 1981 in general). Future research efforts might contribute to the discussion of how historical self-consciousness became an important constituent in identity formation. The attempts of Jonathan Z. Smith (1994) to fruitfully combine historiographical and historical research have continued to be quoted, but not followed up.[8]

I have emphasized traditional religious historiography because it still dominates our scientific approaches to the history of religion to a much greater extent, probably, than the national historiographies of frequently changing political systems. Fruitful source criticism is not simply an easily reproducible technique, but a conscious effort at understanding that, first of all, must be aware of the hermeneutical circle of which it is part, of the pre-formation of one's own historical understanding by an ongoing historiographical tradition.

New fields: archaeology of religion

The contemporary changes in the media landscape have opened our eyes not only to a new understanding of classical textual materials,[9] but far beyond. Introductions to religious traditions (and hopefully continuously so) list important textual sources for these traditions, ranging from any 'sacred', often formally canonized text, commentaries and theological treatises, to ethnographic accounts of outsiders, old and new. At the same time, there is an 'archaeology' of religion that deals with religious architecture, statuary and imagery—not only from the perspective of art history. On the one hand, developments of archaeological methodology ('processual', 'new') have led to new interests and possibilities to use archaeological data in order to reconstruct rituals and inquire about belief systems underlying social action (e.g. Kyriakidis 2007 with bibliography). Religion has come to the foreground of archaeological research in international conferences and in many studies. On the other hand, history of religion has taken more and more interest in practices and everyday religion; it has focused on sanctuaries rather than gods. Hence, archaeological sources have gained in importance. Recently, for Mediterranean antiquity, the very first monographs aiming at a history of religion of individual localities that are not based on literary or primarily epigraphic sources have been published for Ostia and Pompeii (Steuernagel 2001; van Andringa 2009). Already a few books titled 'archaeology of religion' have addressed the growing interest in and necessity for textbooks and handbooks for university education. However, their use and innovative character is severely limited. Some, in a classical approach, limit their objects to preliterate societies (e.g. Steadman 2009). Others try to give short general accounts of religion with some prominence on archaeological sources (Insoll 2001). Finally, some followers of a cognitive approach towards religions try to (rather superficially) adapt archaeological material to their argumentation (e.g. Whitehouse and Martin 2004; or, more attentive to detail, Beck 2006). The cutting edge of research is clearly located in approaches to very specific areas like archaeology of ritual, of sacrifice, of death. For problems of religious experiences and expressivity, monumental sources have not yet moved to centre stage.

An example: religion in the Lex Coloniae Iuliae Genetivae[10]

The strategies of inquiry to be applied to a specific source cannot be determined in advance. Instead of some abstract rules, I offer the following extended example, which exemplifies methodical considerations and specific strategies in the analysis of a 'documentary' source. The case presented concerns one of the most important sources for our understanding of the working of ancient Roman religion in the provinces of the Roman Empire. The late republican Lex Ursonensis is one of the lengthiest inscriptions preserved from Latin antiquity, filling around 20 pages in printed editions. Found from 1870/71 onwards at the Spanish locality of Osuna, the surviving bronze fragments (González 1986; Crawford 1996) contain about one-third of all of the regulations for the Caesarian colony of Iulia Genetiva Ursonensis, founded in 44 BCE on the initiative of an unknown person who had won the support of the Roman dictator Gaius Iulius Caesar for his plan (Gabba 1988: 160–62).

As shown before, interpretation of documents depends on traditional narratives which frame our understanding. A source is hardly ever interpreted on its own. Thus, I have to briefly present the rise of the 'master narrative'. It runs like this: As part of its expansion and dominance of the Mediterranean world, the central power, Rome, had its religion, the religion of the city of Rome, exported to the empire. It aimed at fully reproducing it in the cities given the status of 'colonies' and in the military camps, but in other places partial reproductions were accepted, provided the cult of the emperor was included. Of course, the latter conditions were valid only after the fall of the republic, that is, from the late first century BCE only. This assumed historical frame is based on a single source, a passage in entertainment literature (well informed, though) from the second century BCE.

> But the relationship of colonies (to Rome) is different. For they neither come into citizenship from without, nor do they grow from their own roots, but they are developed as offshoots of the citizen body, as it were, and have all the laws and institutions of the Roman people, not those of their own devising. This condition, although it is more constrained and less free (than that of municipalities), is nevertheless thought preferable and more prestigious because of the greatness and majesty of the Roman people, of whom colonies seem to be little images, as it were, and sort-of representations. At the same time, the rights of municipalities have become obscure and largely forgotten, and hence out of ignorance they are not able to be exploited.
>
> *(Gellius, Attic nights 16.13.8–9, trans. Clifford Ando)*

As will be demonstrated, the Lex Ursonensis is easily read as a document attesting this intention to create 'little images'. A festival calendar is to be set up and priesthoods in name identical as those known from the city of Rome have to be implemented. The more sources for such institutions of Rome are quoted in 'elucidating' the text, the more the decisive questions for the historian of religion are lost. Apart from the source-critical problem of reading a text in the light of later sources, an historian of religion will ask whether religion could be assumed to make up part of such a project of multiplication of the centre. After all, the law text professes a type of legal reasoning that, by the first century BCE, is new for Roman religious thought (see Rüpke 2009d). The Roman senate and Roman magistrates had to deal with religion before. By the second century BCE, elements of explicit legislating on religion are increasingly attested, from the famous Senatusconsultum de Bacchanalibus, suppressing the Dionysiac cult (186 BCE), to the late second-century laws on augury, the most important type of political divination. All these regulations dealt with religion as part of the urban texture of power and politics. Only occasionally, for example in the repression of the Bacchanalia and Bacchants or in procuring prodigies external to Rome, did Roman politicians start to think about religion outside of Rome. Occasional interventions into foreign religious conflicts—mostly about legitimacy and resources—did not amount to a coherent body of regulations but apparently aimed at preserving or establishing internal structures on the part of the ruled provincials that were compatible to Roman aristocratic practices of policy-making (*Senatusconsulta* ('Rulings of the Senate') *de Thisbaeis, Oropiis, Aphrodisiensibus*).

These data lead to a recurrent problem of source criticism. Does the lack of earlier sources allow the conclusion that the text in hand is the earliest document of that kind? Such an *argumentum e silentio*, 'an argument from silence', is naturally weak, but frequently crucial for the understanding of one's source. As far as the Lex Ursonensis is concerned the claim that this colonial law is not a mere reproduction of an older model is corroborated by internal and external evidence. To begin with, the text is a conglomerate, a seemingly new composition out of norms that, however, might be older (see Gabba 1988: 162f. for archaic features).

Yet, it is not very probable that any encompassing legal composition had been prepared more than one or two decennia before—if there were any at all. Cicero's philosophical work 'On Laws', an attempt at a written constitution in the form of an archaizing collection of laws, dates from the 50s BCE and other systematic treatises concerning religion (Varro, Aelius Stilo)—are not much older or even younger. The surviving parts of a possible model for the Lex Ursonensis, a law referred to as Lex Iulia municipalis, do not allow to suppose a direct relationship to the Lex Ursonensis, if we identify the second part of the Tabula Heracleensis (lines 83–163) with this Caesarian law on municipies of 45 BCE.[11] We do not have any indicator that religion was a topic of this Lex Iulia municipalis, a heterogeneous collection of norms displayed at the south Italian city of Heraclea. Of course, the founding of colonies was an old business from the fourth century BCE onwards, and 'constitutional' regulations must have been part of this business, as is clearly attested from an inscription of 169 BCE (Ando 2007). If the charter of Urso was without model, it remained without successor, too. When in late Flavian times, i.e. by the end of the first century BCE, more than a century later, the Lex was republished on bronze tablets at the same time as the charters of Salpensa and Malaca (Gabba 1988: 158), the probable reason was that it had not been superseded by anything and had in the meanwhile become a prestigious model itself.[12]

It is time to reflect upon the purpose of our analysis, our interest in 'religion'. This is not a concept explicit or even implicit in the text. The surviving chapters 61–82, 91–109 and 123–34 do not have any explicit overall structure. Within the surviving fragments, the bunch of material concerning 'religion' in our sense is contained within the chapters 64–72 and 125–128. Of course, these chapters do not exhaust our notion of religion and what we know about ancient religious practices, but there is no reason to suppose that the charter contained further chapters directly addressing religious matters. As far as I know, there are no regulations on religious matters in any other colonial or municipal norm that are not included in the passages just listed, of which a selection is given below.

LXIV. Whoever shall be IIviri after the foundation of the colony, they, within the ten days next after that on which they shall have begun to hold that magistracy, are to raise with the decurions, when not less than two-thirds shall be present, which and how many days it may be agreed shall be festivals and which sacrifices shall be publicly performed and who shall perform those sacrifices. And whatever of those matters a majority of the decurions who shall then be present shall have decreed or decided, that is to be legal and binding, and there are to be those sacrifices and those festival days in that colony.

LXVI. Whichever pontiffs and whichever augurs C. Caesar, or whoever shall have founded the colony at his command, shall have appointed from the colonia, they are to be the pontiffs and they the augurs of the colonia Genetiva Iulia, and they are to be the pontiffs and the augurs in the college of pontiffs or augurs in that colony, in the same way as those who are or shall be pontiffs and augurs with the best conditions and the best status in any colony. And for those pontiffs and augurs, who shall be in each of their colleges, and for their children, there is to be exemption from military service and compulsory public service < prescribed > by what is sacred, as for a Roman pontiff, and their periods of military service are all to be credited to them. Concerning auspices and whatever things shall pertain to those matters, jurisdiction and right of judgment are to belong to the augurs. And those pontiffs and augurs at the games, whenever the magistrates shall give them publicly, and when those pontiffs and augurs shall perform the public sacrifices of the colonia

Genetiva Iulia, are to have the right and power of wearing togae praetextae. And those pontiffs and augurs are to have the right and power to watch games and combats of gladiators among the decurions.

LXVII. Whoever after the issuing of this statute shall have been chosen or co-opted according to this statute as pontiffs and augurs of the colonia Genetiva Iulia into the college of pontiffs and (the college) of augurs in the place of a man who has died or been condemned, he is to be pontiff or augur in the colonia Iulia in the college as pontiff or augur, in the same way as those who are or shall be pontiffs and augurs with the best conditions in any colony. Nor is anyone to receive or choose in replacement or coopt into the college of pontiffs, except at a time when there shall be less than three pontiffs among those who are of the colonia Genetiva. Nor is anyone to choose in replacement or coopt anyone into the college of augurs, except at a time when there shall be less than three augurs among those who are of the colonia Genetiva Iulia.

LXVIII. The IIviri or prefect is so to hold and proclaim an assembly for pontiffs and augurs, whom it shall be appropriate to appoint according to this statute, in the same way as it shall be appropriate to elect or appoint or appoint in replacement a IIvir according to this statue.

LXX. Whoever shall be IIviri, they, except for those who shall be first appointed after this statute, they during their magistracy are to organize a show or dramatic spectacle for Iuppiter, Iuno, Minerva, and the gods and goddesses, during four days, for the greater part of the day, as far as < shall be possible >, according to the decision of the decurions, and each one of them is to spend on that spectacle and on that show not less than 2,000 sesterces from his own money, and it is to be lawful to take and spend out of public money up to 2,000 sesterces for each IIvir, and it is to be lawful for them to do so without personal liability, provided that no-one take or make assignment from that sum, which sum it shall be appropriate to give or assign according to this statute for those sacrifices, which shall be publicly performed in the colony or in any other place.

LXXI. Whoever shall be aediles, during their magistracy they are to organize a show or dramatic spectacle for Iuppiter, Iuno, and Minerva, during three days, for the greater part of the day, as far as shall be possible, and during one day (games) in the circus or (gladiators) in the forum for Venus, and each one of them is to spend on that spectacle and on that show not less than 2,000 sesterces from his own money, and it is to be lawful to take from public funds 1,000 sesterces for each aedile, and a IIvir or prefect is to see that that sum is given or assigned, and it is to be lawful for them to receive it without personal liability.

(trans. Michael Crawford)

The section 64–72 presents regulations on the local definition and financing of cult (64–65), on pontiffs and augurs (66–68), the procedure for payments for ritual ingredients (69), the organization and financing of games (70–71), and the administration of money given to temples (72). The coherence of the passage is achieved by the repetition of the word *sacra*, 'cult' at the beginning and end of this passage. As usually, only by accessing the text in its original languages will we be able to make original observations. Three chapters on priest-hoods (66–68) are inserted and integrated by the frame of regulations on the financing of cult. These inserted chapters do not contain the term *sacra* nor the general notion of 'priests', *sacerdotes*. The regulations restrict themselves to talking of two specific types of Roman priests, pontiffs and augurs. The composition clearly indicates the lack of a term of or the lack of an interest in a unified concept of religion. It is the concrete public rituals, *sacra*, that form the most general concept applied. The chapters form part of a longer sequence formulating norms for the magistrates of the colony. There is no highly general conception of religion that could serve as an overall structure, as was vaguely suggested by Crawford (1996: 397). Pontiffs and augurs, grouped together with the preceding decurions, the members of the city council, are subject of chapter 91. It prescribes that any newly elected decurion or priest must own a residence at least within one thousand paces of the town that could serve as a pledge (see Crawford 1996: 440 AD loc. and translation).

In chapters 125–28 games are the subject of the regulations. Here, the context is clearer. At least from chapter 124 onwards, questions of the dignity and authority of the decurions and the magistrates are discussed. Hence three of the four chapters on games (125–27) exclusively deal with the order of seats for different status groups during different types of games; one chapter also discusses the problems of the presence of higher provincial magistrates or Roman senators and their sons (127). Chapter 128 describes the organization of all kind of religious cult by the annual appointment of magistri and their control. The presence of chapter 128 was certainly due to the intention to complete regulations of the games, but the main *raison d'être* is the continuing of the detailed discussion of the division of labor and authority between the magistrates and the decurions.

What have we learnt about the law's notion of religion? First, religion is dealt with only insofar as it is public religion. There is religion outside public religion—otherwise the author would not need to talk about the public cult of the colony, but this religion is not part of any regulation. For example, in talking about associations, there is no indication that the Lex Ursonensis (ch. 106) or the Lex Irnitana (ch. 74) have anything else in mind than the outlawing of ganging up or a riotous assembly (González 1986: 223f.). If cults formed associations, there was simply no visible interest in regulating that.

To talk of religion is to talk about rituals—as far as the author of the Lex Ursonensis is concerned. *Sacra* is the most general term employed,[13] rituals could be specified as *ludi circenses* and *scaenici*, 'games and plays', and even *gladiatores*, 'gladiators', *sacrificia*, 'sacrifices', and *puluinaria*, meals prepared for the statues of the gods.[14]

These rituals are depending on public money and the decurions' and magistrates' action. Religion comes into focus as part of the magistrates' competence only. It is, however, a primary duty, to be regulated early in their year of office: the festivals have to be defined within the first ten days (ch. 64), concrete measures and financial regulations have to be completed within 60 days (ch. 69). In the view of the Lex Ursonensis, religion is not something to be instrumentalized, to be regulated or tolerated, but part of a Roman colony's magistrates' business, an important part even.

Coming to details in the text

If religion is such an important part of towns of Roman citizens, it is important to determine its features. Festivals, time and space, the choice of gods, priesthoods and rituals could be parameters to define the 'Roman-ness' of the colony, to produce the 'little image' mentioned by Gellius in the beginning. One question to ask is whether the Roman calendar served as the temporal framework of the political and religious life in Urso. We do not know of any law prescribing the use of the Roman calendar outside of Rome. Even in the old and geographically close province of Sicily a Greek lunisolar calendar was in use in the Augustan colony of Tauromenium (Rüpke 1995: 135f.; Ruck 1996), even if in this place a centrally placed calendar informed about the relationship with the Roman calendar. The Roman government and military used Roman dates for its administrative purposes (Ando 2000: 408).

The famous Gaulish calendar of Coligny systematizes and displays an indigenous system using the technical devices of the Roman fasti and thereby attesting how widespread this calendar was in the western part of the Mediterranean.[15] Roman dates are used in norms applied to policies outside of Rome in some instances, e.g. the *kalendae Ianuariae* (1 January) and the *eidus Martiae* (15 March) in a late republican agrarian law (Crawford 1996: nr. 2,63. 70). *Kalendae Quinctiles* (1 July) was used in that part of the Tabula Heracleensis that might be quoted from the Lex Iulia municipalis (Crawford 1996: nr. 24,989).

In the Lex Ursonensis such dates appear, too. In chapter 63 the *kalendae Ianuariae* are used to define a period of service of the first attendants ever of the colony. In chapter 81 *nundinae* (market days) are presupposed; the publicity of the market days would form the best occasion for the administration of the oaths of the public scribes. However, there is no reason to identify these market days with the rhythms of eight days known from the city of Rome; they might, for example, have been organized only two times a month.[16] As the relative dating of all deadlines—'within five or sixty or similar days from their entering of office'—demonstrates, not even the periods of office are prescribed in terms of the Julian calendar. Presupposing the technical skeleton of the Julian calendar, its use in organizing the temporal structure of the colony's life is left to the colonists. The principle can be illustrated by regarding the definition of cults as formulated in chapter 64 (see Rüpke 1995: 534–46 for the following). The theological, personal and temporal structure of the public cult at Urso is subject to a majority decision.

What about the gods? While the text provides some information, a critical reading demands more than just listing the gods named. It must pay attention to selectivity and to the position of the information given within the text and has to evaluate the findings in the wider context of the document. Apart from the financial logic of chapters 64 and 65 there are no norms whatsoever as far as the selection of the deities to be venerated is concerned. The general regulations in chapters 64, 65 and 128 imply a wide range of sanctuaries, deities and rituals. Indirectly, however, two festivals are given important status. Chapters 70 and 71 oblige the highest magistrates of the colony to organize 'shows'[17] or plays: four days for the Capitoline triad by the Two Men, three days for the same deities, Jupiter, Minerva, Juno, and a fourth day to Venus by the aedils.

I suppose that the doubling of the games and the mixture of public and private spending produce a competitive situation, ensuring a high level of engagement, furthered by the definition of a minimum length and a private minimum sum to be spent.[18] Thus, the divine addressees are given ritual emphasis and a high symbolic position among an annual festival cycle that has not yet been decreed by the council. The combination of the deities assures the Roman character of the triad.[19] Flanked by Minerva and Juno, Jupiter is no Zeus and Juno could not be understood as a local mother goddess. The presence of these political deities is neither temporal nor spatial, but ritual. Thus, the symbolic link to Rome undoubtedly provided by this means is intimately tied to the top of the locally ruling elite, the highest magistracies. In terms of ritual expenditure, popularity of the upstarts is directly linked to the cult of the Roman triad. The same mechanism is applied to the deity associated with the founder of the colony, Venus, or rather Venus Genetrix, a deity cherished by late republican aristocrats (Sauron 1994).

Geographical and political contextualization is even more important and fruitful in the case of another standard feature of the concept of religion shared by us and late republican Romans. Chapters 66–68 of the Lex Ursonensis prescribe the institutionalization of two priesthoods, which by their names and specific regulations point to the city of Rome, namely pontiffs and augurs.

At first glance, the text seems to be rather straightforward. Urso is given the appearance of a Roman town by minutely transferring two of the most prestigious religious institutions of the city of Rome, the augurs and pontiffs. Gellius' 'little image' seems to include religion. The situation, however, is more complex, for the law from Urso is engaged in a controversial discourse about (public) religion.

Here is the first observation. For the founder(s) of the colony, the existence of augurs and pontiffs as colonial priesthoods, widely attested in inscriptions, must have been a matter of tradition and universal practice. The most visible symbolic honor, the priests' seating and the dressing at games, is regulated as well as the most important personal consequences, the exemption from military and public services. To my reading, this does not attest the existence of 'general regulations on priesthoods in Roman colonies' as envisaged by Crawford (1996: 434). Instead, local elites could not be denied certain privileges that they (like modern researchers) would easily find in neighboring cities (and even Rome).

Second, competences: Roman pontiffs and augurs were not only the most prestigious of public priesthoods, but the most powerful, too. Passing judgments on priestly conduct, on the religious quality of land and the gods' property, last but not least on the sacral quality of the time and—before the calendar reform in 45 BCE—intercalation, the pontiffs held a central position within the diffuse network of religious authority. The position of the supreme pontiff later became the most important and most visible religious function of the emperors (van Haeperen 2002). The augurs, by their expertise on augury, were involved into every major political decision including election of magistrates, legislation and in the battlefield (Linderski 1986; Rüpke 2005: 1441–55).

What did these priests do at Urso? We learn nothing about the pontiffs. Supervision of cults and funds is performed by the highest magistrates and the aedils, and the definition of the festival calendar fell to the decurions. A direct definition of their field of activity is given for the augurs: 'augury and the like'. What, however, was 'the like'? What sorts of augury existed in a colony? The permanent seat for divinatory bird watching (*auguraculum*) in the Roman colony of Bantia is, as far as we can see, a unique parallel (or copy) of Roman practice (Torelli 1966 = 1995: 97–129). To sum up, we do not see what the priests did at all, but they certainly did not play any role within the functioning even of the religious institutions described in the colonial law.

This is congruent, third, with those modifications of Roman rules that we can observe. At Rome a complicated procedure was followed for the election of the candidates for priesthoods nominated (and later co-opted) by the college proper (see Cicero, *On the agrarian law* 2.18). At Urso, that attempt to differentiate priests from magistrates and thereby to constitute religious authority as authority sui generis was not followed. According to the procedure described in chapter 68, priests were selected in the same manner as magistrates. The second difference concerns the number: three instead of 15 or 16 members in each college. That is no attempt to reproduce original Roman practice (thus, however, Mommsen 1875: 248 (99)), but reduces the college to the very minimum of what could be called a *collegium* at all.

Here is a fourth observation. Chapters 66–68 rule concerning augurs and pontiffs, not about priests. The generic term *sacerdotes*, 'priests', is never used in this text. The only instance of its application in chapter 91 concerns the public lists of decurions and *sacerdotes*. There were probably other priesthoods at Urso, too. They are, however, neither decreed nor granted any privileges. If they had any, it would be due to their quality as decurions, for example.

Compared to the number of public priesthoods at Rome, this list of two items only, namely pontiffs and augurs, is limited and hardly an attempt to recreate a 'little image'.

It is time for a preliminary conclusion. The analysis of the regulations concerning pontiffs and augurs does not reproduce the actual stance of Roman priesthoods during the late republic. Contrary to the reading informed by an isolated, but already ancient narrative of the relationship between the Roman center and its periphery, these traditional colleges are not positively used as symbols of the colony's Roman-ness, but, as I claim, they are accepted as unavoidable remnants of tradition. The potential political implications of the offices are restricted. With regard to the structure of public cult as developed in the other chapters, these colleges are not necessary. Against the backdrop of traditional Roman religious authority, the naming of the priesthoods held for life in the charter's chapters on religion without assigning any competences to them does not mark an integration, but their exclusion from the political fabric of the colony. The execution of public religion is given to annual 'masters', appointed and controlled by the local council as regulated in chapter 128, or is handled by the magistrates themselves.

Critical appraisal

Our analysis comes to a conclusion that goes beyond the traditional history. The model of religion as outlined by the surviving norms of the Lex Ursonensis is characterized by a two-layered structure: religious activities as financed and led by the magistrates and a realm of activities and religious specialists not even sketched. Religion has a firm place within the socio-political fabric of the colony. As public cult it is financed and organized by the council and its magistrates: the financing of the cult is the leitmotif that holds together the whole passage on religion (see chs. 65, 69–72; it is also important for 128).

It is characterized by large public rituals. The concrete content of this religion is left to the local elite and its financial power. The cult of the Capitoline triad and Venus does not seem to aim at providing a 'little image' within a foreign province. More probably, it ensures that any attempts by local magistrates to create a distinctive personal image for themselves must employ devices symbolically related to the central government, to Rome.

The existence of a second layer of religion is rather implicitly or even negatively formulated. Priesthoods, expiation, burials and the ancestor cult belong to this layer, and associations might form further elements. This layer does not form an integral part of the political structure and public religion of the colony. It is by no means illegal, but it must not interfere with political activities. The regulations concerning pontiffs and augurs attempt to transfer a traditional element of the first, public layer to the second, rather implicit layer, acknowledging this time-honored institution of public religion at Rome and depriving it of practical authority at the same time. At Urso, all priesthoods are subordinated to magisterial power. This interpretation is corroborated by chapter 72. The latter deals with private donations to temples. It should be read as a regulation that religious activities at the borderline between public and private—that is private donation to publicly defined cults—should be kept within a spatially circumscribed (and hence controlled) realm of religion. Resources legally accumulated under the umbrella of religion should not be used to interfere with the larger socio-political realm.

Now, the result of the source analysis can be summed up. The Lex Ursonensis does not offer evidence for an encompassing Roman 'sacred law'. Legal techniques are used to limit the possibilities of independent religious acting without thereby interfering with time-honored religious traditions. The Lex Ursonensis does not deny their dues to the deities, but religion is construed as social activity, subject to the priorities of public law. These findings are important with regard to methods. As often, the most important contributions of a source are those statements that are not explicit. A bundle of methods in dealing with the text—paying attention to structure, semantics and selectivity—was necessary in order to achieve a complex contextualization. Who might benefit from regulations? Who has an interest in certain institutions? Who should not be offended? Even a law, seemingly a rather straightforward type of text, is involved in discourses and attests to development. In some instances clear external evidence easily corroborates hypotheses; in others, conclusions remain hypothetical.

The viewpoint adopted by my analysis was Rome-centered. I analyzed Rome as a synthetic culture, absorbing religious traditions from immigrants and asylum-seeking people. This perspective dominated thinking about the history of religion in the Euro-Mediterranean world down to the present day. The most important handbook of Roman religion, Georg Wissowa's *Religion und Kultus der Römer* ('Religion and the Cult of the Romans'), first published in 1902, tried to structurally reproduce Varro's lost *Antiquities of Divine Things* (Rüpke 2003). Despite its massive political expansion, in religious terms Rome was considered an ever-growing center. Religious 'export' was conceptualized as reduplication of traditional Roman structures in the periphery. The centrifugal developments and their conceptual implications are only slowly informing recent research.[20]

It is our changing framework of understanding, influenced by our own experiences of globalization, that leads to a new reconstruction of history, no longer based on a generalization of Gellius' account. It is our changed framework of the history of religion that leads to altered questions and creates other supplements to our fragmentary evidence. New reconstructions of details lead to a newly nuanced overall vision. This, in fact, is what the term 'hermeneutic circle' means.

Multiple perspectives in historical approaches

My example has illustrated the historical-critical method in a rather traditional field, namely history of institutions. Recent historical research has developed a large bundle of perspectives, ranging from social history, history of mentalities and **long durée** to feminism and media history. Such approaches are highly relevant for religion, too. The importance of religion as an historical factor is undeniable, and religion is given a corresponding degree of attention in the study of general history. Within religious studies, the situation is more difficult. Research into philological or historical details in religious texts still abounds and employs a broad range of methodologies and tools of historical research. Other approaches still wait for broader reception and fruitful application. Histories addressing changes in worldviews and mentalities (e.g. Segal 2004) are supplemented by histories paying attention to the body (Bynum 1991). Social history, analyzing origins and social interest of a religious group have been supplemented by prosopographical studies, trying to reconstruct biographies of religious specialists as serial data (Neusner 1994; Rüpke 2008). History of missions and missionaries has started to analyze influences and dependencies and the large scale of exchanges in both directions, thus realizing the aims of transfer or 'entangled' history (Miller 1994; Miller 2007).

Such approaches will frequently result in micro-studies, concentrating on small groups, regions or periods. 'Comparison' is occasionally highly valued in the history of religion and has been recently advocated by scholars as different as Ugo Bianchi, Marcel Detienne, Maya Burger and Philippe Borgeaud (Bianchi 1994; Detienne 2008; contributions in Burger and Calame

2006).[21] However, it has usually been restricted to small-scale approaches, concentrating on explaining only a few phenomena. Large-scale histories of religion, however, remain rare, and they tend to reproduce the traditional patterns and boundaries generated by particular religions—'emic' or 'confessional' religious historiography as presented above. Other new models have not been established that are strong enough to overcome the constructed limits of individual religions. To order our knowledge, we are still used to think in terms of traditions and the diversity that exists within the constructed entities called religions. In transcending the boundaries of self-stabilizing traditions, history of religion still has much to offer.

Notes

1 Wissenschaftsrat, 'Empfehlungen zur Weiterentwicklung von Theologien und religionsbezogenen Wissenschaften an deutschen Hochschulen', 2010, 93 f. www.wissenschaftsrat.de/download/archiv/9678–10.pdf.
2 Taylor 1998; Braun and McCutcheon 2000; Hinnells 2005; Segal 2006.
3 For canonization see Assmann and Assmann 1987; Folkert 1989; Reinhard 2009; exemplary: Rajak 2009.
4 On narrative sequences in ancient reliefs see Torelli 1982; Hussy 2007.
5 Zander 1999; Faivre 2000; Hanegraaff *et al.* 2005; von Stuckrad 2005.
6 See the analysis of Metzger 2010; for the modern spread of the paradigm see Schmidt 2004.
7 Kennedy 1996; Levtzion and Pouwels 2000; Schulze 2000; Malik 2008.
8 A clear exception is Jewish historiography of the 19th and 20th centuries and 'Wissenschaft vom Judentum'. See Brenner 2006; Lapin and Martin 2003.
9 See e.g. Rüpke 2006 and Machado 2009 on inscriptional dedications. In general: Gumbrecht and Pfeiffer 1994.
10 The following analysis is partly taken from Rüpke 2006.
11 I follow the pragmatic stance of Crawford 1996: 362. See Cicero, *Letters to friends,* 6,18,1 for a possible date and *Inscriptiones Latinae Selectae* 5406 for the name.
12 That might be detected by anachronisms, etc. That is, if such a model existed, it must have been roughly contemporaneous to the foundation date of the colony.
13 The singular *resq(ue) diuinas,* as added to *sacra* in ch. 69, might denote the whole infrastructure of ritual, that is temples, instruments, etc.
14 See ch. 128; thus the translation of Ames 1998: 66; see Crawford 'preparing of couches'.
15 Coligny: e.g. Olmsted 1992; Monard 1999; edition: *Recueil des inscriptions gauloises* 3 (Duval).
16 Mommsen 1875: 260 (108), pointing to *Inscriptiones Latinae Selectae* 6868; for market days see Nollé 1982; Fryan 1993; Ligt 1993.
17 The term *munus* need not refer to gladiatorial shows (pace Crawford 1996: 395).
18 These expenses are rightly paralleled with *summae honorariae* by D'Ors 1986: 163. See Veyne 1976 for the financing of games and the liturgical system in general.
19 For the Roman prehistory of games to the Capitoline triad see F. Bernstein 1998.
20 Rüpke 2007, 2010a, 2010b; Ando 2008; Hingley 2010.
21 See also Chapter 1.2 on comparison (Stausberg) in the present volume.

References

Ames, C., 1998. *Untersuchungen zu den Religionen in der Baetica in römischer Zeit,* Diss. Tübingen.
Ando, C., 2000. *Imperial Ideology and Provincial Loyalty in the Roman Empire.* University of California Press, Berkeley.
—— 2007. Exporting Roman Religion. In: Rüpke, J. (ed.), *A Companion to Roman Religion.* Blackwell, Malden, Mass., pp. 429–45.
—— 2008. *The Matter of the Gods: religion and the Roman Empire.* University of California Press, Berkeley, Calif.
Angenendt, A. 1997. *Geschichte der Religiosität im Mittelalter.* Wissenschaftliche Buchgesellschaft, Darmstadt.

Appadurai, A., 1981. The past as a scarce resource. *Man* 16 (2): 201–19.

Assmann, A. and Assmann, J. (eds), 1987. *Kanon und Zensur*. Fink, München.

Astin, A.E., 1964. Leges Aelia et Fufia. *Latomus* 23: 421–45.

Beard, M., 1986. Cicero and divination: the formation of a Latin discourse. *Journal of Roman Studies* 76: 33–46.

Bechert, H., 1969. *Zum Ursprung der Geschichtsschreibung im indischen Kulturbereich*. Vandenhoeck & Ruprecht, Göttingen.

Beck, R., 2006. *The Religion of the Mithras Cult in the Roman Empire: Mysteries of teh Unconquered Sun*. Oxford University Press, Oxford.

Berman, C.H., 2005. *Medieval religion: New approaches*. Routledge, New York.

Bernstein, F., 1998. *Ludi publici: Untersuchungen zur Entstehung und Entwicklung der öffentlichen Spiele im republikanischen Rom*. Steiner, Stuttgart.

Bertholet, A., 1925. *Lehrbuch der Religionsgeschichte*. 2 vols. Mohr, Tübingen.

Beyer, P., 2006. *Religions in global society*. Routledge, London.

Bianchi, U. (ed.), 1994 *The Notion of 'Relgion' in Comparative Research: selected proceedings of the XVIth Congress of the International Association for the History of Religions, Rome, 3rd-8th Sept., 1990*. Bretschneider, Rome.

Bowring, R., 2008. *The Religious Traditions of Japan, 500–1600*. Cambridge University Press, Cambridge.

Boyarin, D., 2004. The Christian invention of Judaism: the Theodosian Empire and the Rabbinic refusal of religion. *Representations* 85: 21–57.

—— 2006. Twenty-Four refutations: continuing the conversations. *Henoch: studies in Judaism and Christianity from second temple to late antiquity* 28(1): 30–45.

Braun, W. and McCutcheon, R.T. (eds), 2000. *Guide to the Study of Religion*. Cassell, London.

Brenner, M., 2006. *Propheten des Vergangenen—Jüdische Geschichtsschreibung im 19. und 20. Jahrhundert*. C.H. Beck, München.

Brodeur, P.C., 2007 [1999]. *From an Islamic Heresiography to an Islamic History of Religions: modern Arab Muslim literature on 'religious others' with special reference to three Egyptian authors*. UMI Diss. Services, Ann Arbor (Diss. Harvard 1999).

Brownlee, J.S., 1999. *Japanese Historians and the National Myths, 1600–1945: the age of the gods and Emperor Jinmu*. University of British Columbia, Vancouver.

Burckhardt, L.A., 1988. *Politische Strategien der Optimaten in der späten römischen Republik*. Steiner, Stuttgart.

Burger, M. and Calame, C. (eds), 2006. *Comparer les comparatismes: perspectives sur l'histoire et les sciences des religions*. Archè, Paris, Milano.

Burrus, V., Kalmin, R., Lapin, H. and Marcus, J., 2006. Boyarin's work: A critical assessment. *Henoch: studies in Judaism and Christianity from second temple to late antiquity* 28(1): 7–30.

Bynum, C.W., 1991. *Fragmentation and Redemption: Essays on gender and the human body in Medieval religion*. Zone Books, New York.

Childester, D. (ed.), 2004. *Religion, Politics, and Identity in a Changing South Africa*. Waxmann, Münster.

Crawford, M.H. (ed.), 1996. *Roman Statutes*. 2 Bde. Institute of Classical Studies, London.

De Libero, L., 1992. *Obstruktion: Politische Praktiken im Senat und in der Volksversammlung der ausgehenden römischen Republik (70–49 v. Chr.)*. Steiner, Stuttgart.

De Ligt, L., 1993. *Fairs and Markets in the Roman Empire: economic and social aspects of periodic trade in a Pre-Industrial society*. Gieben, Amsterdam.

Detienne, M., 2008. *Comparing the Incomparable*. Trans. by J. Lloyd. Stanford University Press, Stanford, CA.

Donner, F.M., 1998. *Narratives of Islamic Origins: The beginnings of Islamic historical writing*. Darwin Press, Princeton.

D'Ors, A., 1986. *La ley flavia municipal (texto y comentario)*. Pontificia Universitas Lateranensis, Roma.

Duval, P.M. (ed.), 1986. *Recueil des inscriptions gauloises 3: Les calendriers (Coligny, Villard-d'Héria)*. Édition CNRS, Paris.

Faivre, A., 2000. *Theosophy, Imagination, Tradition: studies in Western esotericism*. Trans. Christine Rhone. State University of New York Press, Albany.

Feeney, D., 2007. *Caesar's Calendar: ancient time and the beginnings of history*. University of California Press, Berkeley.

Flanagan, K., 2001. Religion and modern personal identity. In: Harskamp, A.V. and Musschenga, A.W. (eds), *The Many Faces of Individualism*. Peeters, Leuven, pp. 239–66.

Folkert, K.W., 1989. The 'canons' of 'scripture'. In: Levering, M. (ed.), *Rethinking Scripture: Essays from a comparative perspective*. State University of New York Press, New York, pp. 170–79.

Fryan, J.M., 1993. *Markets and Fairs in Roman Italy: their social and economic importance from the Second Century BC to the Third Century AD*. Clarendon Press, Oxford.

Gabba, E., 1988. Reflessioni sulla Lex Coloniae Genetivae Iuliae. *Anejos de Archivo Español de Arqueología* 9: 157–68.

Gafni, I.M., 1997. *Land, Center and Diaspora: Jewish constructs in late antiquity*. Sheffield Academic Press, Sheffield.

Gardner, C., 1938. *Chinese Traditional Historiography*. Harvard University Press, Cambridge.

Gardner, G. and Osterloh, K.L. (eds), 2008. *Antiquity in Antiquity: Jewish and Christian pasts in the Greco-Roman world*. Mohr Siebeck, Tübingen.

Ginzburg, Carlo, 1980. *The Cheese and the Worms: the cosmos of a sixteenth-century miller*. Trans. John and Anne Tedeschi. Johns Hopkins University Press, Baltimore.

Girardot, N.J., 2002. Max Muller's 'sacred books' and the Nineteenth-Century production of the comparative science of religions. *History of Religions* 41 (3): 213–50.

Goertz, H.J. (ed.), 1998. *Geschichte: ein Grundkurs*. Rowohlt, Reinbek.

—— 2001. *Unsichere Geschichte: Zur Theorie historischer Referentialität*. Reclam, Stuttgart.

González, J., 1986. The Lex Irnitana: a new copy of the Flavian Municipal Law. *Journal of Roman Studies* 76: 147–243.

Graf, F.W. (ed.), 2006. *'Geschichte durch Geschichte überwinden': Ernst Troeltsch in Berlin*. Gütersloher Verlaghaus, Gütersloh.

Grafton, A., 2007. *What was history? The art of history in early modern Europe*. Cambridge University Press, Cambridge.

Grafton, A. and Williams, M.H., 2008. *Christianity and the Transformation of the Book*. Belknap Press of Harvard University Press, Cambridge, Mass.

Griffis, W.E., 1992 [1894]. *The Religions of Japan: From the dawn of history to the era of méiji*. [s.n.], [Ithaca, NY].

Gumbrecht, H.U. and Pfeiffer, L.K. (eds.), 1994. *Materialities of Communication*. Stanford University Press, Stanford.

Hanegraaff, W.J., Faivre, A., Brach, J.-P. and Broek, R.V.D., 2005 (eds). *Dictionary of Gnosis & Western Esotericism*. Brill, Leiden.

Harries, P., 2007. *Butterflies & Barbarians: Swiss missionaries & systems of knowledge in South-East Africa*. Currey, Oxford.

Harvey, G., 1997. *Contemporary Paganism: listening people, speaking earth*. New York University Press, Washington Square, NY.

Hastings, J. (ed.), 1908–21. *Encyclopædia of Religion and Ethics*. Clark, Edinburgh.

Haupt, H.G. and Kocka, J. (eds), 1996. *Geschichte und Vergleich: Ansätze und Ergebnisse international vergleichender Geschichtsschreibung*. Campus-Verlag, Frankfurt.

Hingley, R., 2010. Cultural Diversity and Unity: Empire and Rome. In: Hales, S. and Hodos, T. (eds), *Material Culture and Social Identities in the Ancient World*. Cambridge University Press, Cambridge, pp. 54–75.

Hinnells, J.R. (ed.), 2005. *The Routledge Companion to the Study of Religion*. Routledge, London.

Hölscher, L., 2005. *Geschichte der protestantischen Frömmigkeit in Deutschland*. C.H. Beck, München.

Humphreys, R.S., 1989. The Islamic world: background books. *Wilson Quarterly* 13 (4): 73–75.

Hussy, H., 2007. *'Die Epiphanie und Erneurung der Macht Gottes'. Szenen des täglichen Kultbildrituals in den ägyptische Tempeln der griechisch-römischen Epoche*. J.H. Röll, Dettelbach.

Insoll, T., 2001. *Archaeology and World Religion*. Routledge, London.

Kennedy, H., 1996. *Muslim Spain and Portugal: A political history of al-Andalus*. Longman, London.

Kippenberg, H.G., 2000. Religious history, displaced by modernity. *Numen* 47 (3): 221–43.

—— 2002. *Discovering Religious History in the Modern Age*. Trans. B. Harshav. Princeton University Press, Princeton.

—— 2003. Theologie-Religionswissenschaft: Ist komplementäre Konstruktion denkbar? In Hutter, M. *et al.* (eds), *Festschrift Karl Hoheisel*. Vandenhoeck & Ruprecht, Göttingen, pp. 289–97.

Kitagawa, J.M., 1966. *Religion in Japanese History*. Columbia University Press, New York.

Kyriakidis, E., 2007. *The Archaeology of Ritual*. Los Angelos: Cotsen Institute of Archaeology Press.

Lapin, H. and Martin, D.B., 2003. *Jews, Antiquity and the Nineteenth-Century Imagination*. University Press of Maryland, Bethesda.

Le Roy Ladurie, E., 1976. *Montaillou, village occitan de 1294 à 1324.* Gallimard, Paris.

Levtzion, N. and Pouwels, R.L. (eds), 2000. *The History of Islam in Africa.* Ohio University Press, Athens, Ohio.

Lieberman, V., 2003. *Strange parallels: Southeast Asia in global context, c. 800–1830.* Cambridge University Press, Cambridge.

Linderski, J., 1986. The Augural Law. *Aufstieg und Niedergang der römischen Welt* II.16 (3): 2146–312.

—— 1995. Römischer Staat und Götterzeichen: Zum Problem der obnuntiatio. In: Linderski, J. (ed.), *Roman Questions.* Steiner, Stuttgart, pp. 309–22.

Lorenz, C., 1999. Comparative historiography: problems and perspectives. *History and Theory* 38 (1): 25–39.

MacBain, B., 1982. *Prodigy and Expiation: a study in religion and politics in Republican Rome.* Bruxelles: Latomus.

Machacek, D. and Wilson, B. (eds), 2003. *Global Citizens: the Soka Gakkai Buddhist movement in the world.* Oxford University Press, Oxford.

Machado, C., 2009. Religion as antiquarianism: pagan dedications in late antique Rome. In: J. Bodel and M. Kajava (eds), *Dediche sacre nel mono greco-romano: Diffusione, funzioni, tipologie/Religious Dedications in the Greco-Roman World: distribution, typology, use.* Institutum Romanum Finlandiae, Rome, pp. 331–54.

Malik, J., 2008. *Islam in South Asia: a short history.* Oxford University Press, New Delhi.

Mayeur, J.M. and Pietri, L. (eds), 2003–10. *Die Geschichte des Christentums.* Herder, Freiburg.

Metzger, F., 2010. *Religion, Geschichte, Nation: Katholische Geschichtsschreibung in der Schweiz im 19. und 20. Jahrhundert—kommunikationstheoretische Perspektiven.* Kohlhammer, Stuttgart.

Miller, D., 2007. *Global Pentecostalism: the new face of Christian social engagement.* University of California Press, Berkeley.

Miller, J., 1994. *The Social Control of Religious Zeal: a study of organizational contradictions.* New Brunswick, Rutgers University Press.

Mommsen, T., 1875. Lex coloniae Iuliae Genetivae urbanorum sive Ursonensis: Data a.u.c. DCCX. In: Mommsen, T., *Gesammelte Schriften 1: Juristische Schriften 1.* [EphEp 2,108–51 (1875)]. Weidmann, Berlin, 194–240.

Monard, J., 1999. *Histoire du calendrier gaulois: le calendrier de Coligny.* Editions Burillier, Burillier Vannes.

Neusner, J., 1994. *Religion and the Social Order: what kinds of lessons does history teach?* Scholars Press, Atlanta.

Nollé, J.M., 1982. *Nundinas instituere et habere: Epigraphische Zeugnisse zur Einrichtung und Gestaltung von ländlichen Märkten in Afrika und in der Provinz Asia.* Olms, Hildesheim.

Olmsted, G., 1992. *The Gaulish Calendar: a reconstruction from the bronze fragments from Coligny with an analysis of its function as a highly accurate lunar/solar predictor as well as an explanation of its terminology and development.* Habelt, Bonn.

Pailler, J.M., 1988. *Bacchanalia: La répression de 186 av. J.-C. à Rome et en italie: vestiges, images, tradition.* Bibliothèque des écoles françaises d'Athène et de Rome 270. École Française, Rome.

Rajak, T., 2009. *Translation and Survival: the Guide Bible oft the ancient Jewish diaspora.* Oxford University Press, Oxford, New York.

Raphael, L., 2003. *Geschichtswissenschaft im Zeitalter der Extreme: Theorien, Methoden, Tendenzen von 1900 bis zur Gegenwart.* Beck, München.

Reinhard, W. (ed.), 2009. *Sakrale Texte: Hermeneutik und Lebenspraxis in den Schriftkulturen.* C.H. Beck, München.

Ricoeur, P., 1984–88. *Time and Narrative.* Trans. Kathleen McLaughlin. University of Chicago Press, Chicago.

Robinson, C.F., 2003. *Islamic Historiography.* Cambridge University Press, Cambridge.

Rosenthal, F., 1968. *A History of Muslim Historiography.* Brill, Leiden.

Ruck, B., 1996. Die Fasten von Taormina. *Zeitschrift für Papyrologie und Epigraphik* 111: 271–80.

Rüpke, J., 1995. *Kalender und Öffentlichkeit: Die Geschichte der Repräsentation und religiösen Qualifikation von Zeit in Rom.* de Gruyter, Berlin, New York.

—— 2001. *Die Religion der Römer: Eine Einführung.* C.H. Beck, München. (Engl. *The Religion of the Romans.* Polity Press, Oxford, 2007.)

—— 2003. Libri sacerdotum—Wissenschaftsgeschichtliche und universitätsgeschichtliche Beobachtungen zum Ort von Georg Wissowas Religion und Kultus. *Archiv für Religionswissenschaft* 5: 16–39.

—— 2005. *Fasti sacerdotum: Die Mitglieder der Priesterschaften und das sakrale Funktionspersonal römischer, griechischer, orientalischer und jüdisch-christlicher Kulte in der Stadt Rom von 300 v. Chr. bis 499 n. Chr.* Steiner, Stuttgart.

—— 2006. Religion in lex Ursonensis. In: Ando, C. and Rüpke, J. (eds), *Religion and Law in Classical and Christian Rome.* Steiner, Stuttgart, pp. 34–46.

—— 2007. *A Companion to Roman Religion.* Blackwell, Malden.

—— 2008. *Fasti sacerdotum: A Prosopography of Pagan, Jewish, and Christian Religious Officials in the City of Rome, 300* BC *to* AD *499. Biographies of Christian Officials by Anne Glock.* Trans. David Richardson. Oxford University Press, Oxford.

—— 2009a. History or systematic study of religion? Joachim Wach's Prolegomena. *Historia Religionum* 1: 69–76.

—— 2009b. Dedications accompanied by inscriptions in the Roman Empire: Functions, intentions, modes of communication. In: J. Bodel and M. Kajava (eds), *Dediche sacre nel mono greco-romano: Diffusione, funzioni, tipologie/Religious Dedications in the Greco-Roman World: Distribution, Typology, Use.* Institutum Romanum Finlandiae, Roma. 31–41.

—— 2009c. Early Christianity in, and out of, context. *Journal of Roman Studies* 99: 182–93.

—— 2009d. Between rationalism and ritualism: On the origins of religious discourse in the late Roman Republic. *Archiv für Religionsgeschichte* 11: 123–43.

—— 2010a. Hellenistic and Roman Empires and Euro-Mediterranean religion. *Journal of Religion in Europe* 3 (2): 197–214.

—— 2010b. Religious pluralism. In: Barchiesi, A. and Scheidel, W. (eds), *The Oxford Handbook of Roman Studies.* Oxford University Press, Oxford, pp. 748–66.

—— 2012. *Rationalization and Religious Change in Republican Rome.* University of Pennsylvania Press, Philadelphia.

Rüsen, J., 1996. Some theoretical approaches to intercultural comparative historiography. *History and Theory* 35 (4): 5–22.

Rüsen, J., Gottlob, M. and Mittag, A. (eds), 1998. *Die Vielfalt der Kulturen: Erinnerung.* Suhrkamp, Frankfurt.

Sauron, G., 1994. *Quis deum? L'expression plastique des idéologies politiques et religieuses à Rome à la fin de la république et au début du principat.* École française, Rome.

Schalk, P. *et al.* (eds), 2010. *Geschichten und Geschichte: Historiographie und Hagiographie in der asiatischen Religionsgeschichte.* Acta Universitatis Upsaliensis, Uppsala.

Scheid, J., 1988. La spartizione sacrificale a Roma. In: Amadasi Guzzo, M.G. *et al.* (eds), *Sacrificio e società nel mondo antico.* Laterza, Bari, pp. 267–92.

—— 1992. Myth, cult and reality in Ovid's Fasti. *Proceedings of the Cambridge Philosophical Society* 38: 118–31.

Schmidt, L.E., 2004. A history of all religions. *Journal of the Early Republic* 24(2): 327–34.

Schmidt-Glintzer, H., 1982. *Die Identität der buddhistischen Schulen und die Kompilation buddhistischer Universalgeschichten in China. Ein Beitrag zur Geistesgeschichte der Sung-Zeit.* Steiner, Wiesbaden.

—— 2005. *Historical Truth, Historical Criticism, and Ideology: Chinese historiography and historical culture from a new comparative perspective.* Brill, Leiden.

Schulze, R., 2000. *A Modern History of the Islamic World.* I.B. Tauris, London.

—— 2002. *A Modern History of the Islamic World.* Trans. Azizeh Azodi. I.B. Tauris, London.

Segal, A.F., 2004. *Life after Death: A history of the afterlife in the religions of the West.* Doubleday, New York.

Segal, R.A., 2006. *The Blackwell companion to the study of religion.* Blackwell, Malden.

Smith, J.Z., 1994. *Drudgery Divine: on the comparison of early christianities and the religions of late antiquity.* The University of Chicago Press, Chicago.

Spineto, N., 2009. Comparative studies in the history of religions today: continuity with the past and new approaches. *Historia Religionum* 1: 41–50.

Stausberg, M., 2007. The study of religion in Western Europe (I): Prehistory and history until World War II. *Religion* 37 (4): 294–318.

Steadman, S.R., 2009. *The Archaeology of Religion: cultures and their beliefs in worldwide context.* Left Coast Press, Walnut Creek, CA.

Steuernagel, D., 2001. Kult und Community: Sacella in den Insulae von Ostia. *Römische Mitteilungen* 108: 41–56.

Sumner, G.V., 1963. Lex Aelia, Lex Fufia. *American Journal of Philology* 84 (4): 337–58.

Taylor, M.C. (ed.), 1998. *Critical Terms for Religious Studies.* The University of Chicago Press, Chicago.

Torelli, M., 1966. Un Templum augurale d'età repubblicana a Bantia. *Rend. Accad. Naz. Lincei* 8. ser., 12, 293–315 [Repr. Id. 1995, *Studies in the Romanization of Italy*, University of Alberta Press, Edmonton, pp. 97–129].

—— 1982. *Typology and Structure of Roman Historical Reliefs*. The University of Michigan Press, Ann Arbor.

Troeltsch, E., 1924. *Fünf Vorträge zu Religion und Geschichtsphilosophie für England und Schottland: Der Historismus und seine Überwindung (1924)—Christian thought: Ist history and application (1923)*. Hübinger, G. (ed.). Kritische Gesamtausgabe 17. de Gruyter, Berlin.

—— 2009. *Schriften zur Theologie und Religionsphilosophie: (1888–1902)*. Albrecht, C., Biester, B. and Graf, F.W. (eds). De Gruyter, Berlin, New York.

Uehlinger, C., 2006. Interested companionship: a review article, *Numen* 53(3): 359–84.

Van Andringa, W., 2009. *Quotidien des dieux et des hommes: la vie religieuse dans les cités du Vésuve à l'époque romaine*. École Française de Rome, Rome.

Van Haeperen, F., 2002. *Le Collège pontifical (3ième s. a. C.–4ième s. p. C.): Contribution à l'étude de la religion publique romaine*. Brepols, Bruxelles.

Veyne, P., 1976. *Le Pain et le cirque: Sociologie historique d'un pluralisme politique*. Éditions du Seuil, Paris.

Von Stuckrad, K., 2005. Whose tradition? Conflicting ideologies in medieval and early modern esotericism. In: Engler, S. and Grieve, G. P. (eds), *Historicizing 'Tradition' in the Study of Religion*. De Gruyter, Berlin, New York, pp. 211–26.

Wallraff, M. and Mecella, L. (eds), 2009. *Die Kestoi des Julius Africanus und ihre Überlieferung*. De Gruyter, Berlin, New York.

Wedemeyer, Chr. (ed.), 2006. *Tibetan Buddhist Literature and Praxis: studies in its formative period, 900–1400*. Brill, Leiden.

Whitehouse, H. and Martin, L.H. (eds), 2004. *Theorizing Religions Past: archaeology, history, and cognition*. Alta Mira Press, Walnut Creek, CA.

Wissowa, G., 1912. *Religion und Kultus der Römer*. 2nd edn. C.H. Beck, München.

York, M., 1995. *The Emerging Network: a sociology of the New Age and Neo-pagan movements*. Rowman & Littlefield, Lanham.

—— 2005. *Pagan Theology: paganism as a world religion*. New York Univ. Press, New York.

Zander, H., 1999. *Geschichte der Seelenwanderung in Europa: Alternative religiöse Traditionen von der Antike bis heute*. Wissenschaftliche Buchgesellschaft, Darmstadt.

Further reading

Berman, C.H., 2005. *Medieval Religion: New approaches*. Routledge, New York.

Presents new thematic and methodological approaches to the European Middle Ages.

Goertz, H.J. (ed.), 1998. *Geschichte. Ein Grundkurs*. Rowohlt, Reinbek.

A sustained introduction to the historico-critical method.

Historia Religionum 1 (2009) 1–166, in particular Filoramo, G., 'What Future for a Review of History of Religion'. *Historia Religionum*, 159–66.

A discussion of the state of the art and the academic profile of 'History of Religion'.

Ricoeur, P., 1984–88. *Time and Narrative*. Trans. Kathleen McLaughlin. University of Chicago Press, Chicago.

A masterpiece of reflection on the implications of narrating the past.

Rüpke, Jörg, 2007. *Historische Religionswissenschaft: Eine Orientierung*. Kohlhammer, Stuttgart.

Discusses the difference of history and systematics in the study of religion and introduces different perspectives on historical religions; large bibliography by topics.

Wang, Q.E. and Iggers, G. (eds), *Turning Points in Historiography: A cross-cultural perspective*, University of Rochester Press, Rochester 2002.

Discusses historiographical innovations in different cultures.

Werner, M. and Zimmermann, B. 2004. *De la comparaison à l'histoire croisée*. Seuil, Paris.
Discusses important lines of transnational historiography and the integration of cultural in general history.

Key concepts

History: A form of representation, frequently narration, of the past that entails the notion of the orienting value of such a past.

Historicization: A form of appraisal of present or past institutions or even items that entails the notion of a genesis in or development, in an ordered sequence, over time.

Historico–critical method: A method of evaluating evidence not by the criterion of plausibility, but of its relationship to knowledge as a result of a form of academic 'autopsy'.

Historiography: Emic or etic accounts of a 'history', indebted to issues of legitimization and identity and to changing criteria of aesthetic plausibility and truth.

Long durée: Historical change might be disruptive and sudden, but also so slow as to be invisible to contemporaries. The French term 'long duration' refers to the latter.

Mediality: The insight that all accessible historical communication is shaped by its specific medial form, e.g. as public inscription or hidden diary.

Source: A metaphor used to characterize artifacts (frequently texts) as 'evidence' for, or as a source of, a 'flow of knowledge' from former times.

Related chapters

- Chapter 1.2 Comparison
- Chapter 1.3 Epistemology
- Chapter 2.3 Discourse analysis
- Chapter 2.11 Hermeneutics
- Chapter 2.16 Philology
- Chapter 2.21 Translation
- Chapter 3.3 Material culture
- Chapter 3.5 Visual culture

2.13

INTERVIEWING

Anna Davidsson Bremborg

Chapter summary

- Interviewing is a good method for researching people's beliefs and religious experiences.
- Interviewing results in rich and complex data.
- Contemporary epistemological developments encourage a dynamic view of knowledge as created in the interview situation between the interviewer and the interviewee.
- Interviews have a scientific and ethical frame and must be distinguished from ordinary conversations.
- The interview process includes preparations, sampling procedures, recording, transcribing, coding, categorizing, analyzing and report writing.

Introduction

Interviewing is a way to create data by orally asking people questions. How this is done, however, can vary greatly. Some interviews are highly structured and resemble spoken questionnaires. Such interviews often aim at collecting data for quantitative research. Other interviews are largely unstructured, with the interviewee freely telling his or her story. Most interviews, though, are semi-structured: they start with specific themes and issues but remain open for new questions to come up. This chapter will primarily deal with the latter, as used in qualitative studies.

Within religious studies the qualitative interview is a very useful method, since people's beliefs are diverse and multifaceted, aspects that can be hard to catch in quantitative studies. Qualitative interviews result in rich, complex and nuanced data.

Interviews are often used in combination with other methods, especially in ethnographic field studies; this reflects so-called methodological triangulation. In my study of pilgrimages (Davidsson Bremborg 2010), I started with a questionnaire that was distributed to participants on ten pilgrimages. From the respondents I recruited interviewees who provided more complex insights into their thoughts and experiences, but also made me re-evaluate some of the results from the survey. Then, I made field observations on almost 30 pilgrimages. Though the field studies included many conversations with pilgrims, I did not use these conversations in the same way as the interviews. The conversations deepened my knowledge, thus informing the overall analysis, but I did not refer to these pilgrims specifically or provide any quotations in books and articles. For this purpose, the structured form of an interview is preferable as it maximizes mutual ethical consent for the conversational frame.

Epistemology

Qualitative interviews have similarities to the hermeneutical tradition within textual analysis. One of the main purposes of qualitative interviews is to understand and interpret people's thoughts, beliefs, ideas and conceptions. The method starts with people's experiences in the world and seeks to get to the bottom of them. The philosophical approach is phenomenological, which means that it is people's experiences of the world that are to be explained, not the world in itself. Interviews are also often carried out in order to explain statistical correlations and observed changes, differences or tendencies.

Though many would say that the interviewee is the main source of knowledge, there are different epistemological conceptions of how knowledge is actually collected—and created—in the interview situation and in subsequent interpretation. Kvale uses two metaphors to describe contradictory epistemological conceptions (Kvale and Brinkmann 2009: 48–49). The first metaphor is the interviewer as a miner: knowledge is like a buried metal that needs to be detected and uncovered. Knowledge is something hidden within the **interviewee**, and the **interviewer** only has to put the right questions to get hold of it. The second metaphor is the interviewer as a traveler: the researcher travels to unknown places to collect stories from those who he or she meets. Knowledge consists in the stories collected and interpreted by the traveler. While the mining metaphor has a static view of knowledge, the travel metaphor acknowledges the production of new knowledge and the possibility that the traveler (researcher) might change during the journey. The two metaphors are epistemological ideal types. The mining metaphor has a positivistic epistemological viewpoint, seeing knowledge as given, waiting to be discovered. The travel metaphor offers a postmodern constructive epistemological understanding of knowledge as something being produced, interpreted and constructed.

The postmodern approach rejects any universal meta-story that could explain everything (Lyotard 1984); instead knowledge is viewed as constructed, achieving meaning through relations. On this view, knowledge emerges between the subject and the object, in relations between the interviewee and the interviewer, as well as between producers and readers of texts (reports). This more recent epistemological view has brought the interviewer as a person into focus. The interviewer's background, pre-understanding and personality are all seen as having significance for the result. In 1981 the feminist researcher Ann Oakley criticized the positivistic epistemology that lay behind attitudes towards interviews at that time and argued for an alternative view of the researcher. Her experiences as a female researcher interviewing women differed from how interviews were described in methodological literature. The women she interviewed asked *her* questions and were interested in her personally. She could not, as recommended, neglect to answer these questions. Instead she found that a more non-hierarchal and intimate relation between the interviewer and the interviewees contributed to richer material. The women were also active in contacting her for additional information and interviews. They were not just objects from whom she gathered material; together they were jointly *creating* material. Today, several of Oakley's ideas have been integrated into general qualitative interview methodology and research ethics. At the same time, a more integrated view of qualitative and quantitative methods as complementary and not contradictory has emerged (Oakley 1998), and different methods are often mixed in research designs (Morse and Niehaus 2009).

The main feature of qualitative interviews is the possibility of collecting nuanced and complex material. Meredith McGuire describes in her book, *Lived Religion* (2008), how she was confronted, early in her research, with the fact that people's religion was so much more complicated than she had thought. Interviews with people led to an insight in their religious lives that former studies of affiliation and organized religion had not shown. 'Realizing the complexities of individuals' religious practices, experiences, and expressions, however, has made me extremely doubtful that even mountains of quantitative sociological data (especially data from surveys and other relatively superficial modes of inquiring) can tell us much of any value about individuals' religions' (McGuire 2008: 5). The same result has come from other researchers using interviews (e.g. Ahlstrand and Gunner 2008; Rosen 2009), who have shown that statements about Northern Europe as the world's most secular place (e.g. Zuckerman 2008) are too narrow-minded and do not fully capture people's relations to religion.

Different forms of interviews

Interviews can be made in different ways and with different purposes. One kind of interview is the expert interview, carried out with key persons in a given field. They are usually made early in the study process in order for the researcher to get general knowledge about that field. Experts have an overview over the field and can present an analytical insight. Key persons are persons in a leading position, in one way or another. When doing interviews, key persons may also have the role of gatekeeper, someone with the power to 'open the door'. A common example in religious studies is first to interview a leader in a given religious community, in order both to learn about the group and to get access to the group. If bypassing the leaders, the research study can easily be perceived beforehand as being critical in a negative sense, which can obstruct the study. This is especially relevant for religious groups, which often have an especially hierarchical structure.

Though key persons are important, they have a tendency to speak for other persons. However, letting key persons represent third persons is not optimal. If this kind of data is used, it is important to make clear distinctions between these interpretations and non-expert views. Key persons and other respondents must be kept apart, as the interviews usually have different purposes. Another trap is that the interview might end up as a 'lecture', far from the original questions, as key persons often want to tell the researcher 'how it is'. Sometimes it is better to see interviews with key persons as background information and not to include them in the analysis.

As stated already in the introduction, interviews can be more or less structured. This chapter refers mainly to semi-structured qualitative interviews. The semi-structured interview has a frame consisting of some main themes that should be touched upon, but new questions and themes can be brought up during the interview, both by the interviewer and the interviewee. The interview usually follows a thematic scheme, called an interview guide, with the main questions and some alternative follow-up questions blocked out ahead of time. Though this chapter mainly deals with semi-structured interviews, two other kinds of interviews will first be briefly mentioned, because they fall into qualitative research methods and could be useful alternatives depending on the research aim.

Narrative or ethnographic interviews are more or less unstructured interviews where the interviewee's story is in total focus. These are often used for life stories in which the interviewee talks about his or her life in chronological order, from childhood to the contemporary situation, though the story often jumps back and forth in time. During the interview, photographs and other personal objects might be brought out and included in the story. In the unstructured interview, the interviewee steers the interview, while the interviewer's role is to create an inviting, open atmosphere and to only ask questions when needed to facilitate the story-telling (Atkinson 1998). Vähäkangas (2009) conducted life story interviews among childless couples in Tanzania. She describes how she could use just one starting question to receive most of the information; she just said: 'Would you tell me about your life?' In most cases the questions she wanted to hear about—those of marital life, questions of adoptions, life of a childless couple—were touched upon in the narrative the interviewee told; if not, she guided the interview into these questions during the story. An ethnographic study might even centre on one person's or a few people's life stories, such as McCarthy Brown's (2001) portrayal of Mama Lola, a Vodou priestess living in Brooklyn.

Focus groups are a kind of group interview with their own logic and epistemology (Fern 2001). A focus group usually consists of four to eight persons and a 'moderator'. In the group the moderator introduces a discussion topic, but then the group may talk more or less freely. Unlike the one-to-one interview, where the respondent directly answers a question, the participants in the focus group can be both stimulated and challenged by other people's stories. Focus groups can be a good alternative to one-to-one interviews, for example if the respondents lack experience in talking about the topic and would be helped by input from others, or if the topic is hard to talk about due to external circumstances. Furthermore, a focus group gives rich insight into how meaning is negotiated, how arguments are defended and re-evaluated, and into interpersonal relations. This was the reason for Rosen (2009) to choose focus groups when she wanted to study how Danish people understand the concept 'religion'. While field observations or one-to-one interviews were potential alternatives, she chose focus groups because she wanted to see how people construct and negotiate meanings and worldviews. In the focus group discussions, aspects of the concept 'religion' were more fully talked about than would have been the case in a single-person interview, as the participants had to refine their answers and re-evaluate them. The sample consisted of 12 focus groups, and in each the participants had a common social context, such as working place or affiliation with the same (non-religious) organization.

Another example where focus groups were used successfully is Gunilla Hallonsten's study among HIV positive Christians in Swaziland.[1] In this context HIV and AIDS are taboo topics connected with shame and exclusion from congregations. To get women talking about their experiences, Hallonsten used focus groups. In the groups, the women found confidence and safety, because they met other women with similar experiences of stigmatization. However, male participants in the study had to be interviewed one by one, as the patriarchal structures would not let the 'strong' men expose themselves in front of others.

Sampling

When doing an interview study, two urgent questions arise: who and how many? There is an important epistemological difference between a quantitative and a qualitative study when it comes to sampling. For a quantitative study the question of representativeness is solved by having a statistically representative sampling. For a qualitative study the issue of sampling is related to the theoretical question: have I found all the empirical data that could be found in order to make my analysis and develop a theory? Glaser and Strauss (1967) refer to this as **theoretical sampling**. Unlike statistical sampling, it is not possible to know in advance how many persons you have to interview or where you could find them. The sampling strategy and the selection of each new respondent are based on the assumption that he or she can contribute with relevant knowledge. When nothing new of significance emerges from the interviews, **theoretical saturation** of a category or group has been reached. To reach this goal, it is possible to start with a stratified sampling strategy, which is based on different variables that might have importance for the research questions: age, gender, ethnicity, religious affiliation or social position. The aim with the first stratified sampling is to get a wide and broad entrance into the material. After the first analysis, which should be done after a couple of interviews, new respondents can be chosen.

There are several ways to find respondents. You can make announcements, send requests to persons from a membership list or other kind of register, ask questionnaire respondents if they are willing to participate in an interview study, just ask individuals personally (e.g. when encountered in field studies), or ask those you have interviewed about other persons. The last alternative is called snowball sampling. All sampling methods have their advantages and disadvantages, and the main question is not who will be reached, but who will not be included. Are there opinions that have not been included? A continuous reflection about who will be interviewed next is of main importance.

With snowball sampling there is a risk of bias if the respondents only come from a group of friends, but if the group is small and hard to find, this might be the only way to find respondents. One way to reduce the risk of bias is to spread one's entrances into the group. Nordin (2004) used the snowball method in her study among Chilean migrants in Sweden in order to find interviewees. She started with one contact person in four different congregations. Each of them got a request to ask someone else if they might agree to an interview. After having got a positive answer, the contact person gave the name and phone number to Nordin. The same procedure was made with the next interviewee, who then asked the next respondent.

The sampling process might differ when doing qualitative research, but even here the goal is to arrive at theoretical saturation. The number of interviews needed for saturation is a constant question within qualitative research. Many studies show saturation between 12 and 30 interviews. Kvale and Brinkmann (2009) hold that most interview studies tend to have between five and 25 interviews, but they also conclude that, in general, it is better to have fewer but better prepared and more thoroughly analyzed interviews. To test the degree of saturation, Guest *et al.* (2006) made continuous saturation tests on their data, which finally consisted of 60 interviews. Already after six interviews general concepts and themes were distinguished, and by 12 interviews 92 per cent of the final analysis had been revealed. Their experiment suggests that if the group is rather homogenous, if the research question does not involve comparisons of several variables or sampling groups, and if the domain of inquiry is well defined, then 12 interviews are enough. Typically, large-scale projects make use of a much larger number of interviews; for example, Ammerman's (1997) study of 18 congregations was based on 317 interviews, field observations and a questionnaire. In my own study among funeral directors (Davidsson Bremborg 2002), I searched for younger and older persons, women and men, employers and employees, in the contexts of smaller and larger funeral homes, smaller and larger communities, regions with different religious traditions, and different areas of the country. Even though there were many variables included, it was obvious when saturation was reached. In total, 29 interviews were made.

Interview guide

Before the interview is carried out, an interview guide should be developed. The interview guide consists of the main questions and themes that are to be included in the interview. It is a template and an aid for the interviewer, though in semi-structured interviews new questions and themes can arise during the interview. The interview guide can be compared to a tree with many branches. The large limbs are the main questions. They force the interview into different directions that ought to be covered. The smaller twigs are different follow-up questions. They are used if needed or if relevant. Then there are new sprouts, new themes and ideas that just come up and might develop. You do not know when and how far they will grow, but they might change the interview. It is not easy to find the right questions, and often the questions have to be reformulated after having been tested on some respondents. Since semi-structured interviews tend to go their own way, with sidesteps and new questions, it is not possible to prepare all questions in advance. The only solution is to become a good interviewer, a role that needs practice and reflection.

There are different types of questions. First we have the introductory questions that aim to make the respondent comfortable with the situation and get him or her to begin talking. Therefore it is important that the first questions are easy to answer but also engaging. When it comes to questions within the field of religious studies, it is often rewarding to let the person start talking about his or her life and thoughts. Some interviewers choose to start the interview with some background questions, such as age and family situation. My personal experience is that this can lead to the conversation being perceived more as interrogation than interview; at the very least, it does not create a dynamic atmosphere. Usually background information comes up during the interview, and complementary questions can be asked afterwards. An alternative is a small questionnaire that the interviewee fills in directly after the interview. This procedure diminishes an emphasis on these 'hard' facts, and separates them from the recorded interview.

It is a good idea to know the main questions by heart but, during the interview, to occasionally consult the guide to verify that all questions have been covered. Usually not all questions need to be posed, since answers may already have been articulated. There is no simple formula for how questions should be asked. Some recommendations are:

- Ask one question at a time.
- Avoid questions that are easily answered with a yes or a no.
- Avoid words that are hard to understand/expert words/analytical words.
- Avoid long questions.
- Repeat the question in other words or in a new way if the interviewee does not seem to understand the question.
- Avoid normative, provocative or confrontational questions (if that is not the research aim).
- Do not be afraid of silence.
- Take your time and don't rush through the questions.
- Be polite, interested and attentive.

It is important that the interviewer is relaxed and actively listening. Silence can be an important tool in the interview. When the interviewer is comfortable with silence, the interviewee often continues and deepens the answer without having been interrupted by a new question.

Since the interviewee can explore the theme rather freely in the semi-structured interview, a common problem (usually not discovered until the analysis process starts) is to not get clear enough answers. The interviewer must be observant to follow up on what is said, for example with questions like: 'do you mean . . .?'; 'could you give an example . . .?' At the same time, ambivalence and indistinctness can be important information. For example, people's religious beliefs and conceptions should not necessarily be expected to be clear and coherent.

Interviewing in a foreign language is demanding for the interviewer, but in order to achieve rich data it is best to make the interview in the language the interviewee prefers and to which he or she is accustomed. When Nordin (2004) made her interviews with the Chilean migrants, some preferred Spanish and others Swedish, but she found a mix of languages in each interview.

Recording and transcription

The best way to document the interview is audio, or audiovisual, recording, which has become easy with new technology. Obtaining explicit permission for recording is standard practice in accordance with ethical guidelines. Even if you or the participants might feel awkward having a microphone or a video camera, recording the dialogue in the beginning, people tend to forget it after a while. Check the technology while recording (e.g. be sure there is sufficient tape or memory space, check batteries and have spares on hand, make sure the microphone is not blocked, etc.)! These may seem trivial points, but most researchers have returned home with a bad or partial recording or, in the worst case, with no recording at all. During the interview the environment has to be quite silent. Clattering coffee cups or traffic noise can easily drown the voices and make it difficult or impossible to afterwards hear what has been recorded. When interviewing in such environments, it is best to also take rich notes.

Directly after the interview you should write down some reflections about the interview: How did it go? Where did it take place? How did you feel during the interview? Did anything interrupt the interview? As soon as possible after the interview it should be transcribed. (Full transcriptions are common, but initial coding of the audio/video can highlight specific passages to be transcribed.) If only notes have been taken, a fuller transcription should be done immediately. Transcribing one hour of recorded interview takes between five and eight hours, and even longer if linguistic or conversation analysis requires that each pause and repetition be marked. The time needed depends on the quality of the recording as well as on how the respondent speaks. Spoken language differs largely from written language, which becomes obvious when transcribing. Even when you make strong efforts to transcribe as closely to the spoken language as possible, you will probably miss words or repetitions, but if you plan to work with an analysis based on the content, you could accept a 'good enough' version.

Some researchers send the transcription to the interviewees. This procedure might increase the reliability, as corrections could be made. Maybe some answers were misunderstood, or there is something the interviewee wants to add? Responses from the interviewees can differ largely. At the same time as I did my research on funeral directors (Davidsson Bremborg 2002), a colleague made interviews with persons involved in New Age activities (Löwendahl 2002). We followed this procedure with interviews, sending the transcriptions of each of some 30 interviews to the respondents. I received one response: a call from a funeral director who told me how much he had laughed while reading the interview, because he realized how different the spoken language is. However, he had nothing to comment upon regarding the content. My colleague, on the contrary, received from half of the interviewees shorter and longer complementary additions to the answers that had been given during the interview. She had to evaluate how to treat these additions, as they sometimes added new questions and themes. The differences between the two groups became clear in unexpected ways. From an ethical perspective it is good practice to share the transcription with the interviewee (this underlines the value of obtaining full contact information for participants). When doing interviews in the field, this cannot always be done and is not expected by the respondents either.

Analysis and report writing

When a couple of interviews have been transcribed, the first round of analysis should begin. The material will have to be analyzed several times, as new perspectives will probably arise until saturation is reached. Analysis could be done according to specific methods, such as grounded theory (Glaser and Strauss 1967) which aims specifically at developing new theories abductively, or content analysis (Krippelberg 2004), which is a way to quantify a qualitative material. What will be described here is a bricolage approach of analyzing interviews (Kvale and Brinkmann 2009).

The first step is to just read through the interview to get an overall impression. The next step is **coding**. Coding is the process by which the text (the transcribed interview) is classified into meaning units. Traditionally, this was made by cutting paper copies into separate pieces, and sorting them into envelopes or a card index. Using different color pens was also common and is still applied. Today, however, a variety of computer programs make it easy to code, recode and search. It is possible to apply some categories already from the beginning, but the point of the coding procedure is generally to develop new categories and subcategories. In grounded theory no predetermined categories should precede the coding process. A category ought to be on a more theoretical level, in contrast to the respondents' concrete answers and the codes. After the coding procedure, the codes need to be reconstructed by comparing the codes, finding higher-order categories, and searching for patterns and relations in a **categorizing** process. In this step the immediate text is set aside for a while and the essential question is the theoretical development.

In Table 2.13.1, there is a coding example from my own study of pilgrimages, an interview conducted in 2005, originally in Swedish, translated here by me.[2] First, the interviewee, a male participant, talks about pilgrimages as something in which not everyone takes part. His words 'there are certain kinds of people' are coded as 'exclusiveness'. (In Table 2.13.1, passages in italics refer to the related codes.) The first coding separates the meaning units 'searching' and 'wanting to have experiences', though in the text it is unclear if these words are two separate units or one, nor is it obvious if he means religious experiences or general experiences. A follow-up question could have clarified his meaning. On the other hand, an interruption from the interviewer could also have disturbed the flow in the interviewee's answer, because he continues with a deeper reflection. Assuming that he talks about two different aspects, we could create on overarching category: motives. He does not use this word, but that is what he talks about. During the pilgrimage he has also learned about another motive: remedy. This leads him to think of how some people, maybe more fragile, need special help from the leader. Here a new category is revealed, the role of the leader, who the interviewee believes should act professionally and responsibly. From the pilgrimage he brings with him new knowledge of people, another category. In this way a structure is built, and when all interviews have been coded, and new categories created, further analysis can be made on the basis of this. Finally, an overarching theory might be developed. Research questions emerging from this example might be: Who takes part in pilgrimages? What do the pilgrims want to achieve during the pilgrimage? What demands are there on the leaders?

Table 2.13.1 Sample coding of an interview

The interviewee	Categories	Codes
There is one thing that surprised me with this group that I had not thought of. But I think *there are certain kinds of people* who go on pilgrimages. We want to go because we are *searching* and *wanting to experience something more.* But it is possible to believe, and I do, that there were several in the group who came because *they were unhappy.* That they were looking for *remedy* for something, an illness, an accident or something like that. And *I had not thought of that before.* But now I think that exists in this context. And then you need *professional leaders* on these hikes. It is a heavy *responsibility.* And *I do not think the persons who led this one managed that.* They did not have that competence.	Motives Own experiences/ knowledge Role of the leader	Not for all/exclusiveness Searchers (religious?) Experiences (experience tourism?) Cure Knowledge of people Professionalism (lack of) Responsibility (lack of)

Coding text into pieces poses a risk of losing sight of the context and totality. It is important to go back to the original text once in a while, to see if later interpretations fit the original meaning. Quotations should always be checked. Another way to analyze interviews is to search for linear connections, for examples, stories over time or causal relations. The coding of meaning units can be combined with these analyses in order to produce a more contextual analysis.

After the analysis, a report has to be written, typically a thesis, a book or an article. There are two different modes to handle the interviews and the interviewees. One has a strong focus on the interviewees as persons. The interviewees are presented with some attributes and a code name. Then throughout the report their thoughts and ideas come forth, either in edited text with reference to the person, or with quotations from the interview. This way to present the material and the analyses was done in a study of Swedish female Muslim converts (Månsson 2002). The nine interviewed women are presented in a personal way in the beginning, and throughout the book the author returns to each of them at length (three to ten pages) while discussing different themes. In that way the reader can follow each case.

The other mode of presenting the analysis places greater emphasis on the theoretical content than on the individuals. General categories or research questions are in focus, and the interviewees receive at most a short, statistical presentation, for example range of age, gender distribution, religious affiliations. Quotations are used to show examples of different theoretical-driven themes, but there is no ambition to let the reader follow an interviewee's thoughts from one chapter to another. Quotations might have a reference to an interviewee number, but often references are excluded altogether. This is how Frey (1998) used her interviews in an ethnographic study among pilgrims to Santiago de Compostela. Quotations from different people are interwoven in the text, some with short presentations like 'a German carpenter', 'a Swiss pilgrim', others with a name and a little longer presentation.

Regardless of presentation style, quotations must be carefully selected. They should be not too long nor too many, and they should be understandable. It is easy to 'fall in love' with your own interviews, but the report should be written with the eyes of the reader. A quotation should clarify or deepen the text. No explanation should be needed in order to understand how the quotation relates to the analysis in the text. Neither should quotations stand alone, without any comment or analytical reference. The aim of quotations is not to verify the analysis but to exemplify the analysis.

Usually quotations need some kind of editing to increase readability, if it is not a linguistic analysis or conversation analysis. No major changes should be made, but a totally unedited quotation might portray the interviewee in a negative light and obstruct the aim of the quotation. To remove 'hm', 'well', and repetitions of words facilitates reading and does not change meaning. If the interview has been done in a language in which the interviewee is not fully fluent, special care must be taken with quotations. A poor understanding of language might obscure the intended meaning. Another problem might arise with interviews made in mixed languages: should certain parts then be translated or can you expect readers to know the language?

Potential, limitations and ethical issues

Qualitative interviews within religious studies are useful for studying people's complex conceptions of religion and beliefs. They allow individuals to express their personal and intimate views and thoughts in substantial ways. The method allows us to have a dynamic and exploratory attitude, with new knowledge being brought into theory building. In contrast to standardized quantitative approach, new answers and new questions can arise.

The most common objection to qualitative interviews is the degree of generalization. While generalization in a statistical sense cannot be obtained, if theoretical saturation is achieved it is possible to infer that the results are valid for a group larger than the interviewees. This, however, does not mean that you can make a statistical analysis of the data. If it is a qualitative study and analysis (and not a content analysis), then statistics of different variables, such as 'one-third of the interviewees thought . . .' should be avoided. Similarly, if your research question starts with 'how many?' or 'how often?', then you should avoid qualitative methods of analysis.

Another objection is the risk of subjectivity with regard to both the interviews and the analysis. To be a good interviewer, training is needed. Novices need to practice, to listen to recorded interviews, and to reflect before going out in the field. An interview is not a common conversation! In order to strengthen the validity of the analysis, two researchers should ideally analyze the material, and any discrepancies should be discussed and lead to recoding and re-categorizing. Having two researchers independently code selected transcripts is also a useful check.

However, there are also limitations related to the content, what people are able or wanting to talk about. They might lie on purpose, but they might also have untrustworthy or incomplete memories or idiosyncratic perceptions. In my own studies I have, for example, found it hard to ask people about what they do. Actions can be difficult to describe, and people are not conscious about when they do things and how. To study these questions, field observations or time diaries (where actions are noted each time they are performed) could well be better methods. More pragmatically, interviews have limitations because they are time consuming, and because it is easy to end up with lots of data, which can be challenging to structure and analyze.

As the specific purpose of interviews is to come close to individuals, their thoughts and minds, several ethical issues arise. The main ethical issue comes before the interview starts: the respondent must be aware that the situation is an interview. An interview is not a common talk; it is a way of creating data for analysis. The interviewee has the right to get information about the aim of the study, who is responsible, how the interview will be used, and when and where the result can be expected to appear. The respondent also has the right to withdraw from the study. To let the interviewee sign an informed consent, with all information, is the best way to clarify the ethical issues. The interviewer keeps one copy and the interviewee the other.

As a researcher it is important to be aware of the power that lies in both analysis and quotation. It is an important ethical rule to give the reader a fair view of the interviewee. One way to equalize the power relation is to communicate with respondents before publishing the results. At the same time, such a procedure raises questions about the integrity of the research-er's interpretations. What happens if the interviewees do not agree with the analysis? Should the researcher then revise and just be a spokesperson for the interviewees? Is it not his or her task to present the interviewees' statements in a new light through theoretical lenses? What kind of loyalty does the researcher have to the respondents?

Another ethical issue concerns confidentiality. Generally, anonymity should be aimed at in the report, which could be done by giving each person a code name or a number. However, if small, specific groups are researched, it might be difficult to guarantee full anonymity when referring to situations and statements. Descriptions of social contexts that are potentially important for the understanding of the analysis might potentially reveal certain individuals' identities. The researcher needs to take these ethical aspects into consideration when deciding what needs to be described, be it about persons or the environment.

Interviewees who represent an organization or movement might be presented by their real name, if they have been informed about and consented to this. A leader of the group might be so easily identified that it is not possible to make him or her anonymous. In such cases, openness about identities can be better for all concerned. In my study of pilgrim groups (Davidsson Bremborg 2010), the participants were anonymous, while the leaders were presented by their real names. The leaders usually held an official position as a minister or deacon, and could easily have been identified, for example with a brief search on the Internet.

Notes

1 I am grateful to Hallonsten for her allowing me to cite this example from her research in progress.
2 This particular example is unpublished, though aspects of the same research project have been published (Davidsson Bremborg 2010).

References

Ahlstrand, K. and Gunner, G., 2008. *Guds närmaste stad?: en studie om religionernas betydelse i ett svenskt samhälle i början av 2000-talet* [God's nearest city? A study of the importance of religions in a Swedish community in the beginning of the 21st century]. Verbum, Stockholm.

Ammerman, N.T., 1997. *Congregation and Community*. Rutgers University Press, New Brunswick, NJ.

Atkinson, R., 1998. *The Life Story Interview*. SAGE, London, Thousands Oaks, CA.

Davidsson Bremborg, A., 2002. *Yrke: begravningsentreprenör: om utanförskap, döda kroppar, riter och profes-sionalisering.* [Occupation: funeral director: on stigmatization, dead bodies, rites, and professionali-zation]. Lund University, Lund.

—— 2010. *Pilgrimsvandring på svenska* [Pilgrimage, the Swedish way]. Arcus, Lund.

Fern, E., 2001. *Advanced Focus Group Research*. SAGE, London, Thousands Oaks, CA.

Frey, N.L., 1998. *Pilgrim Stories: on and off the road to Santiago*. University of California Press, Berkeley.

Glaser, B.G. and Strauss, A.M., 1967. *The Discovery of Grounded Theory: strategies for qualitative research.* Aldine, Chicago.

Guest, G., Bunce, A. and Johnson, L., 2006. How many interviews are enough? an experiment with data saturation and variability. *Field methods* 18 (1): 59–82.

Krippelberg, K., 2004. *Content Analysis: an introduction to its methodology.* SAGE, London, Thousands Oaks, CA.

Kvale, S. and Brinkmann, S., 2009. *Interviews: learning the craft of qualitative research interviewing.* 2nd edn. SAGE, London, Thousands Oaks, CA.

Löwendahl, L., 2002. *Med kroppen som instrument: en studie av New age med focus på hälsa, kroppslighet och genus.* [With the body as an instrument: a study of the New Age movement with a focus on health, body and gender]. Lund University, Lund.

Lyotard, J.-F., 1984. *The Postmodern Condition: a report on knowledge.* Manchester University Press, Manchester.

McCarthy Brown, K., 2001. *Mama Lola: a Vodou priestess in Brooklyn.* University of California Press, Berkeley, CA.

McGuire, M.B., 2008. *Lived Religion: faith and practice in everyday life.* Oxford University Press, Oxford.

Månsson, A., 2002. *Becoming Muslim: meanings of conversion to Islam.* Lund University, Lund.

Morse, J.M. and Niehaus, L., 2009. *Mixed Method Design: principles and procedures.* Left Coast Press, Walnut Creek, CA.

Nordin, M., 2004. *Religiositet bland migrants: Sverige-chilenares förhållande till religion och samfund* [Religiosity among migrants: Swedish-Chileans' relation to religion and congregations]. Lund University, Lund.

Oakley, A., 1981. Interviewing women: a contradiction in terms. In: Roberts, H. (ed.), *Doing Feminist Research.* Routledge & Kegan Paul, London, pp. 30–61.

—— 1998. Gender, methodology and people's ways of knowing: some problems with feminism and the paradigm debate in social science. *Sociology* 32 (4): 707–31.

Rosen. I., 2009. *I'm a Believer – But I'll Be Damned If I'm Religious: belief and religion in the Greater Copenhagen area: a focus group study.* Lund University, Lund.

Vähäkangas, A., 2009. *Christian Couples Coping with Childlessness: narratives from Machame, Kilimanjaro.* Pickwick, Eugene, OR.

Zuckerman, P., 2008. *Society without God: what the least religious nations can tell us about contentment.* New York University Press, New York.

Further reading

The following titles provide good introductions to interviews and interviewing:

Alvesson, M., 2010. *Interpreting Interviews.* SAGE, London, Thousand Oaks, CA.

Atkinson, R., 1998. *The Life Story Interview.* SAGE, London, Thousands Oaks, CA.

Gubrium, J.F. and Holstein, J.A. (eds), 2002. *Handbook of Interview Research: context and method.* SAGE, London, Thousand Oaks, CA.

Kvale, S. and Brinkmann, S., 2009. *Interviews: learning the craft of qualitative research interviewing.* SAGE, London, Thousands Oaks, CA.

Warren, C. and Karner, T., 2009. *Discovering Qualitative Methods: field research, interviews, and analysis.* Oxford University Press, Oxford.

Wengraf, T., 2001. *Qualitative Research Interviewing: biographic narrative and semi-structured methods.* SAGE, London, Thousand Oaks, New Delhi.

Consult the following titles for introductions to focus group research:

Fern, E., 2001. *Advanced Focus Group Research.* SAGE, London, Thousands Oaks, CA.

Morgan, D.L. and Krueger, R.A. (eds), 1998, *The Focus Group Kit. 6 vols.* SAGE, Thousand Oaks, CA, London, New Delhi.

Stewart, D.W., Shamdasani, P.N. and Rook, D.W., 2007. *Focus Groups: theory and practice.* 2nd edn. SAGE Publications, Thousand Oaks, CA, London, New Delhi.

Key concepts

Categorizing: the process whereby the codes are formed into theoretical units, by comparing codes, and by finding higher-order themes, patterns and relations.

Coding: the process whereby the text is sorted into meaning units.

Interviewee: a person who is interviewed.

Interviewer: a person who conducts an interview.

Theoretical sampling: choosing new interviewees by looking for different cases compared with the ones that have already been studied.

Theoretical saturation: the moment in the sampling process when no significant new information comes from new cases.

Related chapters

2.14

NETWORK ANALYSIS

jimi adams

Chapter summary

- Network analysis focuses on the patterns of relationships (present and absent) between nodes (individuals, groups, organizations, etc.) rather than on characteristics of the nodes themselves.
- Network data can be collected to represent ego, partial or complete networks.
- 'Pipes' and 'positions' represent the two primary metaphors for why people are interested in networks.
- Measurement within social network analysis can focus on individuals' positions within networks or global network structure.
- Network visualizations (or graphs) play an important role in interpreting network patterns.

Studies of religion frequently focus on religious content (e.g. theology, texts, etc.), individuals' beliefs and practices (e.g. prayer, participation, etc.) or on religious organizations (e.g. congregations, denominations, faith traditions, etc.). While they may shift across levels, scholars' approaches generally focus on studying characteristics of these texts/people/groupings. Other chapters of this book detail many approaches for capturing relevant characteristics of these and a variety of other questions—including how those characteristics change over time, how they relate to other outcomes, and how these differing levels of analysis interact with each other (e.g. how a single mosque's available activities relates to its adherents' religious commitment or reported religious importance). A common thread in each of these is that the scholar's gaze is focused on particular entities as the units of analysis—whether tenets, individuals or collectivities. To represent any of these entities we can use single points (see Figure 2.14.1)—known as **'nodes'** in networks terminology and vary the points' traits to correspond to various node characteristics.

The approach described in this chapter shifts the gaze from these nodes and their characteristics to the spaces between them. Network analysis is primarily concerned with the presence or absence of relationships in these spaces, and provides a theoretical framework and methods for analyzing the patterning of those relationships within any given study population. Thus a **'network'** is a collection of relationships—referred to as ties or **'edges'**—that

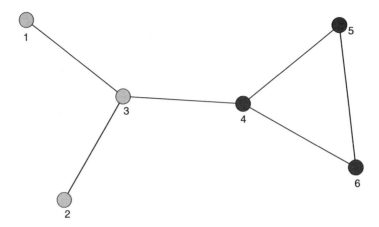

Figure 2.14.1 Exemplar graph

connect nodes, whether individuals or aggregates of individuals (e.g. small groups or congregations). To represent ties, network visualizations use lines between the connected nodes. Network studies can vary their focus to accommodate relationships between each node type described above, and can incorporate a wide variety of relationship types that are relevant to studying religion—including friendship, authority relationships, conversations.

In this chapter, I will describe the two major perspectives within the network approach regarding how and why networks matter, outline three primary strategies for studying and analyzing networks, briefly overview some of the classes of measures used in network analyses and touch on some of the previous research using networks to study religion. In doing so I will demonstrate the paradigmatic shift that arises from moving the focus from nodes in a way that allows us directly to examine religion's *social* aspects (Wellman and Berkowitz 1988).

Two network frameworks

The fundamental assumption in network analysis is a common one in many social science fields—that structure matters (Wellman 1988). For a network analyst, structure is primarily concerned with using the patterning of ties in a population to explain differences between nodes according to positions they occupy in the network; between ties, identifying how some are more/less important than others for particular outcomes; and for differentiating between entire networks.

While there are a variety of reasons analysts are interested in studying networks, the vast majority of those reasons fall under two primary overarching frameworks. For simplicity, those perspectives can be thought of as aligning with two metaphors that think of networks as important because they represent potential 'pipes' or 'positions' within a population (Borgatti *et al.* 2009).

The connectionist, or 'pipes', metaphor addresses ties between nodes as representing potential pathways through which various 'bits' can pass through a population. For example, this perspective is concerned with how relationships between nodes provide direct conduits for the diffusion of information, resources or diseases. Within this perspective, networks are analyzed to determine how the arrangement of relationships serves to hinder or promote that diffusion process.

The importance of networks in the topological, or 'positions', metaphor stems from the ability of network ties to reveal differences or similarities in actor status/roles with respect to others. A perhaps familiar notion of this aspect of networks comes from a widely studied topic—kinship networks (White 1963). While my aunt is not your aunt, my aunt is related to me in the same way that yours is to you—she is my (/your) parent's sister. As with this example, network analysis building on the 'positions' metaphor is primarily concerned with identifying positions within networks or network configurations that identify particular network signatures that allow network analysts to differentiate amongst classes of nodes, ties or networks.

Primary data collection strategies

Gathering and analyzing network data has become increasingly popular in a wide variety of settings. Many population-based studies gather **ego network data** from their samples to get a sense of the size and composition of individuals' personal networks. A common template for these sorts of questions comes from the US General Social Survey (similar questions are available on the International Social Survey Programme), which asks 'From time to time, most people discuss *important matters* with other people. Looking back over the last six months— who are the people with whom you discussed matters important to you?' (Burt 1984; McPherson *et al.* 2006: 355, original emphasis). Following this question, each respondent— or '**ego**'—is asked a variety of questions about each of the persons to whom they are connected—their '**alters**'. These questions capture characteristics of each alter, the nature of the relationship between ego and each alter, and ego's estimate of the relationships among each pair of alters. This **important matter network** question has been adapted into a wide variety of study designs and settings (adams and Trinitapoli 2009; Bearman and Parigi 2004; Marin 2004), while other ego network approaches generate alter lists from other types of ties, such as ego's (close) friends (Moody 2001; Smith 2003), which can then follow the same three steps used to gather information about 'important matter networks'.

In many study contexts, however, the network analysts' interests require strategies that differ substantially from the common approaches in population-based studies in the social and behavioral sciences. In particular, the ego network approach described above rarely captures ties that bridge across sampled ego networks. If the research question is about how messages pass through a population, this would be insufficient for modeling that diffusion process. **Partial network data** collection starts with a sample of respondents and follows the ego network approach described above, but then subsequently recruits some portion of those alters into the study and also asks them about their relationships. This pattern of 'link-tracing' can be repeated as many, or few, times as desired. You can think of 'link tracing' as providing a means to follow the flow of a particular 'bit' through a population. It was developed by epidemiologists to trace the spread of a disease through a population, but could just as easily be used to trace a new theological idea through a congregation. Additionally, such partial network designs are particularly helpful for identifying and studying hard to identify or hard to reach populations—those for whom no appropriate sampling frame likely exists (Heckathorn 1997; Salganik and Heckathorn 2004).

A final approach—known as **complete network data** defines the boundaries of the study's target population, then attempts to enumerate and describe all of the relationships that fall within that boundary. Due to the vast time necessary to gather complete network data (both for the researcher and research subjects) this strategy is often limited to well-bounded, small populations (e.g. school classrooms, single organizations, islands). Each of these strategies comes with its own strengths and limitations both as a data collection strategy and for how the data can be analyzed. Researchers must carefully consider how these trade-offs affect their primary research questions (Marsden 1990; Morris 2004; Wasserman and Faust 1994).

Analyzing network data

A wide variety of measures exist for analyzing networks, which can roughly be classified into those concerned with local network composition, those intended to capture the position of nodes or edges within a given network, or those that describe the overall structure of an entire network.

Local network analysis frequently aims to describe an ego's local network composition—in terms of the characteristics of the alters to whom ego is connected and the composition of ego's ties themselves. A simple example is the count of how many ties ego has of a particular type—known as 'degree'. Composition measures can focus on how many alters an ego has with particular characteristics (e.g. religious affiliation, race, gender, etc.) or the relative proportions of such groups among egos' alters. Often composition measures such as this are examined in relation to their homophily—tendency for similarity among ties (McPherson *et al.* 2001)—with respect to ego (i.e. what proportion are of the same class as ego) (e.g. in Figure 2.14.1 67 per cent of node 4's ties are the same color as 4, while 100 per cent of node 6's ties are). Density of local networks is also often examined. This measure captures the number of ties observed, stated as a proportion of all possible ties. Similarly, local composition measures can focus not on ego's alters, but directly on the characteristics of ego's ties (e.g. how many ties are strong versus weak). Alternately, local network analysis can also focus on the dyad—the tie linking two nodes—as its primary unit of analysis (e.g. sampling marriages), which would turn the focus of these composition measures to those characteristics of the dyad rather than of the nodes in the dyad (i.e. analyses would focus on characteristics of marriages, not characteristics of those who are married).

Much of the focus in network analysis is on describing the positions of nodes in relation to other nodes, and their position in the entire network. Distance is a common measure of this type, capturing the number of steps on a path between two nodes (Wasserman and Faust 1994). As seen in Figure 2.14.1, there can be multiple paths connecting any two nodes (e.g. 3–4–5, 3–4–6–5). The *shortest* of these is known as the geodesic distance (the geodesic distance from 3 to 5 is 2). This measure is important because information is known to travel more successfully over shorter distances.

A core concept of potential importance for studies of religious organizations is centrality, which is thought to capture the relative importance of nodes. Centrality is measured in a number of different ways including the number of ties a node has (degree centrality), the relative distance of a node to all other nodes in a network (closeness centrality), and the proportion of geodesic paths connecting each pair of nodes in a network that includes a particular node (betweenness centrality). If considering the potential for spreading news of a new event within a mosque through the 'pipes' among its adherents, these various measures of centrality can differentially capture a node's potential to spread the message (degree), hear the message (closeness), or constrain the passage of the message among nodes (betweenness) (e.g. 3 can keep nodes 1 and 2 from sending or receiving a message). A key insight in network studies is that many individual position measures are not directly related to each other—even within a single class of measures like centrality (i.e. having many friends is not the same as having the 'right' friends) (Freeman 1979).

Equivalence is a class of concepts that captures varied levels of similarity in connections to other (types of) nodes (Friedkin 1984). For example, 'structural equivalence' describes different nodes who have the same ties to the same alters (e.g. in Figure 2.14.1, nodes 1 and 2 are structurally equivalent). 'Automorphically equivalent' nodes have ties to nodes with the same position, but not necessarily to the same other nodes (e.g. in Figure 2.14.1, nodes 5 and 6 are automorphically equivalent, because both are tied to node 4 and *different* nodes connected to 4; they are not structurally equivalent because 5 is tied to 6, while 6 is not, and vice versa).

There are also classes of network measures that capture patterns of connectivity in the entire network. Several classes of these graph-level measures are concerned with identifying meaningful subgroups within a population. Block-modeling identifies equivalence classes across a network—grouping together nodes that have similar patterns of connections to similar types of alters (e.g. all religious education teachers may have ties to their different students and to the same religious education coordinator). Alternately, measures of 'cohesion' identify communities within a population as indicated by those who have more ties within the group than to nodes outside the group. Cohesive subgroups can be important for identifying pockets of support for or resistance to potentially controversial issues within a congregation.

Network analysts have also discovered several common local network patterns that aggregate in ways that have strong implications for potential full network connectivity patterns. One such example is that networks are known to form with higher than expected levels of triadic closure, which is the proportion of i-k pairs for which a tie exists given the presence of ties between i-j and j-k (Holland and Leinhardt 1972). This is the common tendency of a friend of a friend to also be a friend (e.g. in Figure 2.14.1, given the ties between 1–3 and 2–3, triadic closure would expect to see a tie also between 1–2, as with the closed triangle 4–5–6). For most classes of network measures, there are variants for use with undirected relationships (e.g. had a conversation) separately from directed ties (e.g. gave money to, taught).

Visualization

The sections above include three of the core elements that Lin Freeman argues have contributed to the consolidation of the 'new paradigm' of social network analysis (SNA): (a) a focus on structural properties of the patterned links between actors, (b) that are derived from empirical studies, and (c) can best be described and analyzed with complex mathematical or computational strategies (Freeman 2004). The fourth is an aspect of network analysis for which it is well known—the use of graphical illustrations to represent networks. These graphical depictions can be used to illustrate patterns unveiled in the data, or as a preliminary means to assist in the discovery of those patterns. Visualizing networks has evolved into a cottage industry of its own. Recently, the strategies used for representing networks have become increasingly concerned with means for displaying dynamic networks (Bender-DeMoll and McFarland 2006). There are numerous software platforms available—among the most commonly used are UCINET (Borgatti *et al.* 1999), Pajek (Batagelj and Mrvar 2001) and various platforms (e.g. Csárdi and Nepusz 2006; Handcock *et al.* 2008) available within the open source software environment R (R Development Core Team 2010), each aiming to optimize the display of meaningful patterns in the data. For example, Figure 2.14.2 shows the networks derived from a modified version of the 'important matter networks' conducted in two religious congregations in New York City. These two graphs demonstrate some clear

Organization A

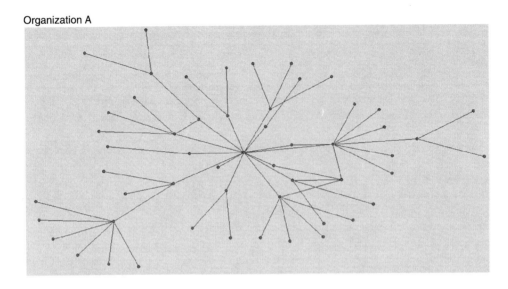

Organization B

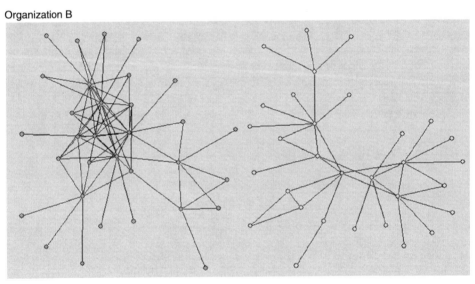

Figure 2.14.2 Two religious organizational networks

differences between the two organizations. While organization A seems to be organized around a single central individual (the node in the middle of the graph is highest on degree, closeness and betweenness centrality), organization B has no single similarly central actor. This would suggest that the central person in A can potentially wield more authority than can any single node in B. Further, Organization B is separated into two completely disconnected subgraphs, while everyone in A is connected in one large connected component. This would suggest that the dissemination of any message within B must start with a minimum of two nodes to potentially be able to reach to the entire organization, whereas in A a single seed node would potentially suffice.

Networks in research on religion

Many of the insights available via SNA have been slow to influence research not explicitly focused on networks. When incorporating network approaches into research on religion—similar to many other substantive research areas—the disproportionate focus has been on ego-network designs incorporated into population-based samples. For example, the National Study of Youth and Religion (NSYR), which focused on religious development and other socio-behavioral issues among emerging adults, included a network module gathering some detailed ego network data about each respondent's close friends (Denton and Smith 2003). Similarly, the National Congregations Study (NCS), which gathered data on a nationally representative sample of congregations, focuses on congregations as the primary unit of analysis. The NCS included a series of organization-level ego network queries about a variety of organizational ties, ranging from co-sponsorship of events to speakers sent to and received from a variety of other organizational types (Chaves 2004).

Drawing on the friendship network data in the NSYR, Vaisey and Lizardo (2010) demonstrate that religious factors and other elements of individuals' worldviews substantially influence the ways in which their social networks evolve over time—including a trend towards shifting their networks towards increasing homophily (i.e. they add ties to people with similar worldviews or lose ties to those with dissimilar worldviews more often than the inverse). Drawing on a unique sample that includes large numbers of Muslims, Buddhists, Hindus and Jews along with Christians, Wuthnow and Hackett (2003) show that individuals representing each of these religious traditions have ego networks that integrate them into their local communities to remarkably similar levels (the lone exception being that non-black Muslims are slightly more isolated than other groups). Regarding the religious heterogamy of these ego networks, *all* non-Christian groups have more frequent social interaction with members of other traditions, than do Christians.

Few studies of religion have used partial network designs. One notable exception comes from D. Michael Lindsay's research on evangelical elites. While he initially used his partial knowledge of the network structure as a strategy to gain access to a hard-to-reach population, Lindsay also carefully detailed his in-depth strategy of personal referrals (Lindsay 2007). This subsequently allowed him to analyze some characteristics of the pattern of relationships among this population (Lindsay 2006). In particular, he shows that members of the so-called evangelical elite were able to gain a place at the political table for key members of the movement by drawing on their existing ties to increasingly legitimate their position in new realms of leadership and subsequently point out the (lack of) distance between evangelical leaders and those of the wider political community they were joining.

Researchers have a longstanding interest in the conversion of individuals from one religious tradition to another (Bibby and Brinkerhoff 1973, 1983, 1994). While most of these 'market share' studies did not explicitly model religious transfers as networks, these patterns could easily be conceptualized as network questions, considering traditions as nodes, and people transfers as the *directed* links between them. A recent call suggests similar analyses may be of interest to religion researchers—particularly with an explicit inclusion of network reasoning in the new models (Vasquez 2008).

A more likely site for implementing a networks perspective to religious research is in individual (or small-N) organization-based studies. The boundary specification task, which all research must consider, is particularly problematic in network studies, which makes institutional settings especially attractive for gathering complete network data (Marsden 1990). As networks become increasingly integrated into religious research, we may come to expect to see the mapping of relationships within religious organizations an increasingly common component of congregational studies. The example discussed above with Figure 2.14.2 is drawn from one such approach—adapting the 'important matter' networks for a complete network study design in a study of Chinese immigrant congregations in New York City. This simple example demonstrates several potentially informative uses of capturing information about intra-organizational ties for examining a congregation.

Where do we go from here?

Within the field of network analysis, the primary current developments are focused on extending analytic capabilities for the study of dynamic networks (Moody 2009) and further developing statistical methods for analyzing network patterns (Snijders *et al.* 2006). While these advances will also likely be useful in studying religious networks, at this stage the more important goal is simply to get the network perspective on the radar of more religion-focused data collection projects. In particular, organization-based studies could likely readily incorporate estimates of ties among the members of studied organizations (as seen in the example in Figure 2.14.2 above), while other population-based samples could readily incorporate some variants of existing ego-network approaches. Many questions of interest to religion scholars have implicit network elements to them, but rarely explicitly investigate the network elements of the questions. Perhaps the future will see further integration of networks into religious research.

References

adams, j and Trinitapoli, J., 2009. The Malawi religion project: data collection and selected analyses. *Demographic Research* 21: 255–88.

Batagelj, V. and Mrvar, A., 2001. *PAJEK*. See vlado.fmf.uni-lj.si/pub/networks/doc.

Bearman, P. and Parigi, P., 2004. Cloning headless frogs and other important matters: conversation topics and network structure. *Social Forces* 83: 535–57.

Bender-DeMoll, S. and McFarland, D.A., 2006. The Art and Science of Dynamic Network Visualization. *Journal of Social Structure* 7(2). www.cmu.edu/joss/content/articles/volume7/deMollMcFarland.

Bibby, R.W. and Brinkerhoff, M.B., 1973. The circulation of the Saints: a study of people who join conservative churches. *Journal for the Scientific Study of Religion* 12: 273–83.

—— 1983. Circulation of the Saints revisited: a longitudinal look at conservative church growth. *Journal for the Scientific Study of Religion* 22: 253–62.

—— 1994. Circulation of the Saints 1966–90: new data, new reflections. *Journal for the Scientific Study of Religion* 33: 273–80.

Borgatti, S., Everett, M.G. and Freeman, L.C., 1999. *UCINET V for Windows: Software for social Network Analysis*. Analytic Technologies, Natick, MA.

Borgatti, S.P., Mehra, A., Brass, D.J. and Labianca, G., 2009. Network analysis in the social sciences. *Science* 323: 892–95.

Burt, R.S., 1984. Network items and the General Social Survey. *Social Networks* 6: 293–339.

Chaves, M., 2004. *Congregations in America*. Harvard University Press, Cambridge, MA.

Csárdi, G. and Nepusz, T., 2006. The igraph software package for complex network research. *International Journal of Complex Systems* 1695. igraph.sf.net.

Denton, M.L. and Smith, C., 2003. *Methodological Issues and Challenges in the Study of American Youth and Religion*. National Study of Youth and Religion, Chapel Hill, NC.

Freeman, L.C., 1979. Centrality in social networks: conceptual clarification. *Social Networks* 1: 215–39.

—— 2004. *The Development of Social Network Analysis: a study in the sociology of science*. Empirical Press, Vancouver, BC.

Friedkin, N.E., 1984. Structural cohesion and equivalence explanations of social homogeneity. *Sociological Methods and Research* 12: 235–61.

Handcock, M.S., Hunter, D.R., Butts, C.T., Goodreau, S.M. and Morris, M., 2008. Statnet: software tools for the representation, visualization, analysis and simulation of network data. *Journal of Statistical Software* 24: 1–11.

Heckathorn, D.D., 1997. Respondent-driven sampling: a new approach to the study of hidden populations. *Social Problems* 44: 174–99.

Holland, P.W. and Leinhardt, S., 1972. Some evidence on the transitivity of positive interpersonal sentiment. *American Journal of Sociology* 72: 1205.

Lindsay, D.M., 2006. Elite power: social networks within American Evangelicalism. *Sociology of Religion* 67: 207–27.

—— 2007. *Faith in the Halls of Power: how Evangelicals joined the American elite.* Oxford University Press, Oxford, New York.

McPherson, M., Smith-Lovin, L. and Brashears, M.E., 2006. Social isolation in America: changes in core discussion networks over two decades. *American Sociological Review* 71: 353–75.

McPherson, M., Smith-Lovin, L. and Cook, J.M., 2001. Birds of a Feather: Homophily in Social Networks. *Annual Review of Sociology* 27: 415–44.

Marin, A., 2004. Are respondents more likely to list alters with certain characteristics? Implications for name generator data. *Social Networks* 26: 289–307.

Marsden, P.V., 1990. Network data and measurement. *Annual Review of Sociology* 16: 435–63.

Moody, J., 2001. Race, school integration, and friendship segregation in America. *American Journal of Sociology* 107: 679–716.

—— 2009. Network dynamics. In: Hedstrom, P. and Bearman, P.S. (eds), *The Oxford Handbook of Analytical Sociology.* Oxford University Press, Oxford, New York.

Morris, M., 2004. *Network Epidemiology: a handbook for survey design and data collection.* Oxford University Press, New York.

R Development Core Team, 2010. *R: A Language and Environment for Statistical Computing.* R Foundation for Statistical Computing, Vienna, Austria. ISBN 3-900051-08-9, Version 2.11. www.R-project.org.

Salganik, M.J. and Heckathorn, D.D., 2004. Sampling and estimation in hidden populations using respondent driven sampling. *Sociological Methodology* 34: 193–240.

Smith, C., 2003. Religious participation and network closure among American adolescents. *Journal for the Scientific Study of Religion* 42: 259–67.

Snijders, T.A.B., Pattison, P.E., Robins, G.L. and Handcock, M.S., 2006. New specifications for exponential random graph models. *Sociological Methodology* 36(1): 99–153.

Vaisey, S. and Lizardo, O., 2010. Can cultural worldviews influence network composition? *Social Forces* 88(4): 1595–618.

Vasquez, M.A., 2008. Studying religion in motion: a networks approach. *Method and Theory in the Study of Religion* 20: 151–84.

Wasserman, S. and Faust, K., 1994. *Social Network Analysis: methods and applications.* Cambridge University Press, Cambridge, New York.

Wellman, B., 1988. Structural analysis: from method and metaphor to theory and substance. In: Wellman, B. and Berkowitz, S.D. (eds), *Social Structures: a network approach, Vol. 2, structural analysis in the social sciences.* Cambridge University Press, Cambridge, pp. 19–61.

Wellman, B. and Berkowitz, S.D., 1988. *Social Structures: a network approach, Vol. 2, structural analysis in the social sciences.* Cambridge University Press, Cambridge.

White, H.C., 1963. *An Anatomy of Kinship.* Prentice Hall, Englewood Cliffs, NJ.

Wuthnow, R. and Hackett, C., 2003. The social integration of practitioners of non-western religions in the United States. *Journal for the Scientific Study of Religion* 42: 651–67.

Further reading

Thematic /historical overviews

Barabási, A.-L., 2003. *Linked: how everything is connected to everything else and what it means.* Plume, New York.

Christakis, N.A. and Fowler, J.H., 2009. *Connected: The Surprising Power of Our Social Networks and How They Shape Our Lives*. Little Brown & Co., New York.

Freeman, Linton C. 2004. *The Development of Social Network Analysis: a study in the sociology of science*. Empirical Press, Vancouver, BC.

Watts, D.J., 2003. *Six Degrees: the science of a connected age*. W.W. Norton and Company, New York.

Brief technical overviews

Degenne, A. and Forse, M., 1999. *Introducing Social Networks*. SAGE, London, Thousand Oaks, CA.

Hanneman, R. and Riddle, M., 2005. *Introduction to Social Network Methods*. faculty.ucr.edu/~hanneman/nettext.

Knoke, D. and Yang, S., 2004. *Social Network Analysis*. 2nd edn. SAGE, London, Thousand Oaks, CA.

Scott, J., 2000. *Social Network Analysis: a handbook*. SAGE, London, Thousand Oaks, CA.

In depth technical treatments

Carrington, P.J., Scott, J. and Wasserman, S., 2005. *Models and Methods in Social Network Analysis*. Cambridge University Press, Cambridge.

Scott, J. and Carrington, P.J. (eds), 2010. *Handbook of Social Network Analysis*. SAGE, London, Thousand Oaks, CA.

Wasserman, S. and Faust, K., 1994. *Social Network Analysis: methods and applications*. Cambridge University Press, Cambridge.

Key concepts

Alter: the nodes to whom an ego is connected.

Complete network data: network data collection that defines a population of interest then attempts to enumerate all of the ties within that population boundary.

Edges: ties connecting nodes within a network.

Ego: the focal node in any network discussion.

Ego network data: network data collection that asks a particular respondent (ego) about the ties they have, characteristics of the alters to whom they are linked with those ties, and (potentially) the connections among their alters.

'Important matter' networks: the General Social Survey name generator that is a common tool for gathering ego-network data.

Network: a collection of relationships (edges) connecting the nodes in a particular sample.

Node: the endpoints of a connection; typically representing particular entities—whether individuals, organizations or other units of analyses.

Partial network data: network data collection that starts with a sample of respondents, asks them about their ties, then samples some of their alters to subsequently recruit for study; a process that can be repeated as many times as desired.

Related chapters

- Chapter 2.8 Field research: Participant observation
- Chapter 2.18 Structuralism

2.15

PHENOMENOLOGY

James V. Spickard

Chapter summary

- Phenomenology is a powerful, yet underused method in the study of religion—in part because too many scholars misunderstand what it entails.
- In its pure form, phenomenology seeks to describe experience as it presents itself to subjective consciousness. It is thus distinct from—and conceptually prior to—a subject's interpretations of that experience, though experiences and interpretations inevitably collide.
- Conscious bracketing allows at least a partial separation, which lets experience-near descriptions of religious phenomena emerge.

Introduction

This chapter outlines an empirical phenomenological method for exploring subjective experiences in religious settings. This method does not allow one to weigh the 'truth' of such experiences, much less gauge their 'real' referent. Instead, it allows one to enter into an aspect of the informants' religious world as it presents itself to their consciousness. From this, one may draw conclusions about their religion as it is actually lived—what some scholars are calling '**lived religion**'.

The most important, yet overlooked, question in social research is a simple one: 'What is the nature of the thing one seeks?' Different research projects look for different kinds of things. These can be simple or complex, shallow or deep, observable or matters of inference. They can lie on the surface of reality, so to speak, or they can be hidden patterns invisible to ordinary insight. Whatever the case, this nature stands at the junction of two key relationships that structure all research. One's research question specifies what one is looking for; that looked-for object determines how one must try to find it. In shorthand, Question determines Object and Object determines Method. For researchers, this is the Law and the Prophets.

One might, for example, be interested in people's religious affiliations. Depending on how strongly these are held, they could be matters of allegiance, of core identity, or just of preference. One could tap them at a relatively shallow level by means of two survey questions:

- 'What is your religious affiliation? Is it Protestant, Catholic, Jewish, some other religion, or no religion?'
- 'Would you call yourself a strong [*name of religion*], a moderate [*name of religion*], or a not very strong [*name of religion*]?'

Most Americans (and many others) could answer these questions easily. Indeed, this is why they work well on social surveys, which cannot have people confused about what is being asked. Getting a more nuanced picture, however, calls for much more penetrating questions and a lot of them. In fact, it calls for a reflective interview, which allows its respondents to qualify their attitudes toward their religious affiliations in much greater detail. Such interviews provide rich data, capable of distinguishing between such things as 'allegiance', 'identity' and 'preference' along multiple dimensions. (I may, for example, be 'Catholic' by allegiance, 'Christian' by identity and 'pantheist' by preference.) In-depth interviews allow us to collect a complex picture, but at the cost of covering a much smaller segment of the population.

Either research project is interesting. What differentiates them is the depth of view that is sought. Shallow and deep views are different **research objects**, which call for different research techniques—surveys and interviews, respectively.

The first question to ask about phenomenology in the study of religion, then, is 'What sort of thing does phenomenology seek?' If Question drives Object and Object drives Method, what kind of research object do phenomenological methods produce? What sorts of research questions call for this kind of object? I shall start with a discussion of these matters, then I shall provide some examples that show how phenomenology works. Finally, I shall explore some of the current controversies surrounding this method for the study of religions.

Toward subjective experience

I must begin with a caveat: the term 'phenomenology' has been wildly misused, and not just in religious studies. Indeed, I am periodically tempted to abandon it altogether, much as Charles Sanders Peirce abandoned 'pragmatism' for 'pragmaticism', a term he called 'ugly enough to be safe from kidnappers' (Peirce 1934: 414).[1] Still, it is worth exploring its history, if only to let us specify what can and cannot be accomplished with this research tool.

In the study of religion, the term 'phenomenology' draws us toward the experiences that are supposed to underlie religious life. The call to experience gained scholarly prominence in the late 17th century, with Friedrich Schleiermacher's (1799) attempt to justify Christianity against Enlightenment rationalism. Roughly put, he argued that religion is best grounded in emotional experiences, not in ideas. Some experiences point beyond the natural realm. People experience, for example, a sense of utter dependence—something that cannot be comprehended within the bounds of the everyday world. As they reflect on this experience, they develop the idea of an all-powerful, benevolent God, the only possible source such an experience might have. This idea is an 'over-belief', to use William James's later term: an intellectual deduction from and elaboration of the experience itself. In James's (1961: 424) words, religious ideas 'presuppose immediate experiences as their subject matter. They are [. . .] consequent upon religious feeling, not coordinate with it, not independent of what it ascertains'.

Unlike Schleiermacher, James tried to describe people's religious experiences without regard for their truth—the basic phenomenological technique of '**bracketing**' or epoché. His psychological phenomenology continues to be a significant influence on the American study of religion, but philosophical phenomenology—and the **empirical phenomenology** based on it—is better traced to the work of Edmund Husserl (1973, 1954), writing in the same period.

Husserl began his philosophy with conscious experience. He noted that consciousness is lived rather than just thought—i.e. that it has duration. He also noted that consciousness is always consciousness of something, whether it be a tree, playing chess, a lover's kiss or a memory of things past. Phenomenology involves the thick description of such subjective experiences in order to locate their structures. We may find, for example, that playing chess involves, for most of us, imagining future moves, thinking through alternatives and, ultimately, losing track of them before making what seems the best move at the time. Chess masters, on the other hand, visualize directly the line of play without focusing on individual pieces. To quote one such master, if one does see the pieces during play, then:

> the bright arcs of relations that weld the pieces into a phalanx, that make one's defense a poison-tipped porcupine shiver into filaments. The chords dissolve. The pawn in one's sweating hand withers to mere wood or plastic. A tunnel of inanity yawns, boring and bottomless. As from another world comes the appalling suggestion [. . .] that this is, after all, 'only a game.' If one entertains that annihilating proposition even for an instant, one is done for.
>
> (*Czikszentmihalyi 1975: 45, quoting Steiner*)

This describes subjective experience. Phenomenology seeks patterns in such descriptions, without imagining that they refer to anything but subjective consciousness.

Husserl's student Martin Heidegger developed phenomenology is a somewhat different direction by noting that subjective experience is not isolated. Instead, it is always situated in a pre-existing world. Not only is experience always of something, but the things presented to the experiencer are always presented in a context that shapes both parties to the action. Most of us, for example, experience a hammer not as a wooden object with a metal cross-piece, but as a tool with which to pound a nail. We do not experience the wooden-object-with-metal first, then label it 'a hammer' later; we experience it as a hammer unreflectively, because that is the context in which both we and it exist. Thus both the phenomena and the being experiencing them are constituted, at least in part, by their contexts, including by their histories. Heideggerian phenomenology explores the role that such contexts play in constituting both the experience and the experiencer.

Where Heidegger focused on context, Maurice Merleau-Ponty focused on the experiencing body. Like context, the body is a permanent, unavoidable condition of experiencing. Because the body is both the mechanism of consciousness and one of its objects, inextricably, bodily perception is the one point at which consciousness *per se* cannot be separated from consciousness-of-something. Subjective consciousness is always filtered through the body's state of being-in-the-world—whatever that state happens to be.

A passage by the psychologist (and non-phenomenologist) Susan Blackmore makes Merleau-Ponty's point concretely. As I sit at my desk in ordinary consciousness, she says, my experience:

> consists of self and the world—well divided from each other. 'I' consist of a stable body image with arms and legs, a model of myself as someone working, a lot of modeling of the substance of what I am writing. 'I' have plans for future actions (I must tidy up) and wishes that things were different (I wish I could concentrate harder) [. . .] The world around consists of the room, the sounds outside; the birds (Oh there are some birds singing. Don't they sound nice? I wonder what sort of birds

they are . . .); children [playing] (I wish they'd be quiet), the radio (I hate the noise) . . .

(Blackmore 1986: 83)

Here, world, body and mind present themselves to consciousness as separate, though in a rather jumbled state. Blackmore's description highlights this jumble, and shows how body and mind interact to present it. Now, she says, see me meditating:

I am still. The birds are singing outside, there are sounds of children playing a long way away, and a distant radio. The muddle on my desk and the room full of things are filled with stillness. There is me sitting. The sounds are full of silence. I hear a woodlouse crawl across the floor.

(Blackmore 1986: 83)

This time, body-mind-world presents itself to consciousness unitarily. The difference is striking. Merleau-Ponty's phenomenology seeks to describe such differences, seeing them as differences in what we might call 'the lived body'. Experience is always an embodied experience, embedded in a lived, embodied world. This form of phenomenology inevitably places the body at the center of religious life.

From the foregoing, it should be obvious that the work of religious studies scholars like Mircea Eliade and Ninian Smart was not 'phenomenology' in any rigorous sense of the term. As James Cox (2006: 204–5) points out, they and others used 'themes that have been associated with phenomenology—bracketing out prior assumptions, employing a fully empathetic approach, identifying typologies, [. . .] and insisting that religion comprises a category in its own right'. They advocated the systematic study of religions, emphasized that religion involved more than just ideas, and treated it as something that needed to be lived, but their approach did not focus on the subjective experiences of religious subjects, bracketed from all interpretation. Instead, their approach might be better seen as describing the religions of various times and places really, really well. Its bracketing involves an abstention from judging the truth or falsity of various religious worlds.[2]

Contemporary empirical phenomenology seeks to do something quite different. It seeks to grasp the world as people experience it, shorn of their interpretations of those experiences. Those who follow Husserl emphasize the dynamic of consciousness and consciousness-of. Heidegger's followers emphasize the simultaneous experience of object and context. Merleau-Ponty's emphasize the embodied nature of all experiencing. All, however, seek to capture subjective consciousness. This is the Object toward which the phenomenological method is directed.

How to do it

Psychologists Amedeo and Barbro Giorgi (Giorgi and Giorgi 2003) have developed a clear model of how to use phenomenological methods in empirical research. As the Giorgis point out, this calls for a translation of (mainly) Husserlian and Pontian methods of philosophical description into a form suitable for social-scientific investigation. Otherwise, one would be producing philosophical rather than empirical description, which is not quite the same thing.

For the scientific analysis, one first obtains descriptions of experiences from others, then one enters into a scientific phenomenological reduction while simultaneously adopting a psychological perspective[3] of the experience, then one analyzes the raw data to come up with the essential structure of the experience, which is then carefully described at a level other than that of the original description.

(Giorgi and Giorgi 2003: 247)

Stripped of its abstractness, the process goes as follows:

Step one: one needs data from a reasonable number of individuals about a particular experience. Seeking testimony from a number of people who are familiar with a particular experience avoids accusations of bias—a justifiable concern. How can I guarantee that my reflections on my own experiences are not unconsciously shaped by what I hope to find? Interviewing a number of others may not protect one from error, but it can help. It also allows outside review of the data, which is crucial to the scientific process.

Step two: one engages in **phenomenological reduction**. Concretely, this means that the described experiences 'are taken exactly as they present themselves [to consciousness] except that [. . .] the claim that what is present [. . .] actually exists [. . .] is not affirmed' (Giorgi and Giorgi 2003: 249). To take a trivial example: I can describe how I experience holding my morning cup of coffee, and my interviewee can help me delve into how that experience presents itself to my consciousness, without either one of us worrying about whether the coffee or my cup actually exists. Beyond the warmth of the porcelain, its heft in my hands, there is the slip of warm liquid down my throat, the slight but growing buzz as the caffeine enters my system, and so on. I can describe this without ever postulating that I, the cup or the coffee are 'real'. The goal is to describe pure experiencing.

Let me take an example from my own early fieldwork, with the American members of the Church of World Messianity in San Francisco, California, in the mid-1970s.[4] As I have written elsewhere (Spickard 1991a, 1995, 2004b), the chief sacred activity of this Japanese new religion is *johrei*, the channeling of 'divine light' to clean the clouds from people's spiritual bodies. Phenomenally, the channeler perceives a slight tingling in the middle of the palm, often a bit of warmth, somewhat similar to the feeling a qigong or tai-chi practitioner has when holding a ball of chi-energy. Some, not all, also feel a sense of warmth at the top of the head and a sense of opening in the chest. The recipient may feel nothing, may feel warmth or pressure at the point where the light is 'aimed', or may feel oneself to be sitting more erect. Those who have experienced particularly strong channelers report more sensations; one of my informants described the *johrei* he received from the head of the Japanese church as 'like being hit on the head by a board'.

Note that these descriptions do not say what is 'really' happening. Nor are they concerned with the participants' theological views about what is happening. These are different research objects. Personally, I found it fascinating that the members of the San Francisco church placed *johrei* at the center of three overlapping but different theologies, but this discovery was ethnographic, not phenomenological (Spickard 1991a, 1995). Phenomenology is concerned to describe subjective experience, without regard to its 'reality' and without regard to its interpretation.

Step three: once one has collected descriptions, one analyzes them to come up with the basic structures of the experience—something that I have just done for holding coffee and channeling *johrei*. This is harder than it seems, because one needs to have good enough interview material to determine which features of the experience are idiosyncratic and which are central. One must read beneath each person's account to find the patterns that it represents. Some accounts will have extra material in them; other accounts may use idiosyncratic language while still exhibiting a common structure. One must decide which elements are central and which are not, and must be able to justify this by reference to one's data.

Step four involves a re-description of the experience focused on this common structure. This abstracts from each individual description, without losing the common thread. The point is to describe the experience so that a 'native' can recognize it, without taking on board any of those natives' particular interpretations of what is going on. The description must be 'experience-near', though one is not limited to using just the informants' own words.[5]

Throughout this process, one must be alert to the possibility that one is dealing with two or more different phenomena rather than with a single one. As Roger Walsh (1995) points out, psychologists long equated shamanic spirit-flight with schizophrenia because they never examined the experiences closely enough to see their clear differences. Phenomenology is designed to avoid such mistakes, which means the analysis must be done very carefully. Thus, I can describe the *johrei* experience with some confidence, but I cannot say that it is the same as experiencing *reiki* (another Japanese healing technique). I have not done sufficient research on the latter to know whether their basic structures converge.

Box 2.15.1 Four steps in phenomenological method

1   Locate and interview informants who have shared a particular experience.
2   Help your informants focus on exactly how this experience presented itself to their conscious-
    ness, leaving aside what they (or you) think was 'really' happening.
3   Compare and analyze these accounts to identify the basic structures of the experience.
4   Redescribe/summarize the experience, boiled down to these basic structures.

Some examples

Walsh's (1995) article provides a useful, if partially rendered, example of how empirical phenomenology works. He focused on mapping the experiences encountered during various forms of the 'shamanic journey' and distinguishing that journey from other states of consciousness. For data, he used descriptions from the literature on shamanism, interviews with native Balinese and Basque practitioners, interviews with Westerners who were trained by shamans from various traditions, and several years of personal experiences under the guidance of Michael Harner, a former anthropologist well-versed in South American shamanism. Elements on Walsh's map included the entrance into a trance state, an experience of separating from the body, vivid sensory input in the spirit world, a partial ability to control the altered state of consciousness (especially entering and leaving it), and a continuing sense of a separate self. He did not walk the reader through all steps of his analysis, but he did provide enough details to differentiate the experience of the shamanic journey from schizophrenia, on the one hand, and from various Buddhist and yogic meditation states on the other.

Put briefly, Walsh's study showed that schizophrenic experiences lack the sense of control common in shamanic journeys, are typically disorganized rather than organized, and exhibit the dissolution of the ego rather than an enhancement of it. The meditation states he reviewed share the sense of control, but do not involve out-of-body experiences, nor do they maintain a separable sense of self. There are similarities, of course, but these states' basic structures differ enough that they can only be called different experiences.

Note that Walsh nowhere said what is 'really' happening in any of these states. He did not reduce schizophrenia to brain-wave malfunction, nor did he claim that the shaman 'really' leaves her or his body during trance. His phenomenological exercise focused on mapping and comparing the basic structures of the various experiences he reviewed. That is the point of empirical phenomenology: to chart subjective experience with as much discipline as possible.

Phenomenology need not be a purely psychological exercise, however; it can also have socio-logical uses. My own investigations of how people experience religious rituals highlight certain patterns that can reveal a good deal about those rituals' workings (Spickard 1991b, 2005).

My first (Spickard 1991b) foray into the phenomenological analysis of ritual involved analyzing Navajo healing ceremonies through the lens of Alfred Schutz's (1964) account of experiencing music. I argued that these ceremonies are like music and poetry, in that they cannot be grasped conceptually. Instead, they are experienced polythetically as they unfold in time. Over five, seven or nine days, they lead participants from disorder to order, from sickness to healing, by guiding participants' sensory experiences. The repetition of words, the rhythm of the ceremony and the flow of attention shape an experience in which harmony—the Navajo source of healing—is restored. This takes place within a Navajo conceptual universe, but the rituals cannot be reduced to that universe. They are matters of experience, rather than just of thought.

My second ritual analysis was based on 13 years of part-time ethnographic fieldwork in and around a Los Angeles radical Catholic community (Spickard 2005). The question that posed itself was how these activists maintain their social commitment in the face of near constant failure. From their point of view, the world is beset with greed and violence, their own Church is corrupt, and God's work does not seem to be making much headway in the world. How do they maintain their sense of pursuing a worthy cause in this situation?

I found that the community's Wednesday evening masses provided an experience of healing that went beyond mere symbolism. Seen as events unfolding in time, these masses shaped participants' attention, leading them from discouragement to renewal—and they did so experientially and emotionally, not just conceptually. Sticking to the highlights, the mass began with an extended conversation, opened by the prayer leader, about the horrible things happening in the world. This reminded people of what was going wrong. It produced a sense of depression, but also an emotional link to the community: here was the faithful remnant, gathered together to celebrate God's Will in the midst of the chaos. The readings continued this spiral, as did a group homily, but the mood changed at the Passing of the Peace, when the ritual stopped for a full ten minutes while each person in the room hugged every other person present. This was no symbolic greeting. It actually produced an experience of communal solidarity. This grew during the rest of the ceremony, during the potluck dinner that followed, and during the after-dinner trip to the streets to serve soup to homeless people living on Los Angeles' Skid Row. As I describe in my 2005 article, the whole evening became in effect a double-mass, in the second part of which the community became priests distributing the Body and Blood of Christ—as soup, bread and water—to the multitudes. However, it was the experiential dimension that mattered. The event took community members from an emotional low point to a high point and subsequently to a point of inward reflection, reminding them of their togetherness and the reason for their service. It structured their attention in the flow of time. It heartened them for their further journey.

Where is the phenomenology in this? You have gotten it. My account, here, is actually step four in the Giorgis' analysis: the redescription of the basic structure of the ritual, based on years of observation and interviews with participants. I have, in fact, presented an ideal-typical model of the ritual, as it was experienced during the years I attended. As reported in my article, I continued my fieldwork for an additional year after the ritual began to change shape, just to make sure that I had gotten the (now former) structure right.

The point is that the phenomenological analysis of rituals like these sheds light on an aspect of religious life that is often ignored. Religion is more than just concepts; it has an experiential dimension as well.

A different approach

Anthropologist Thomas Csordas (1994, 1997, 2002) has developed a different sort of phenomenology, based in Merleau-Ponty's emphasis on the lived body. Bodily experience is based in **perception**, and perception is not something static, an interior grasping of a pre-existing 'out-there', as was the case for Cartesian philosophy. Instead, perception is a constitutive process, which creates objects as end-points rather than assuming them as beginnings. Experience is primary; it:

> is concrete, material, embodied, and not abstract, interior, or mentalistic. It is immediate both in the sense of its concreteness, its subjective openness, its breakthrough to the sensory, emotional, intersubjective reality of right now; and in the sense in which it is unmediated, unpremeditated, spontaneous, or unrehearsed upwelling of raw existence.
>
> *(Csordas 2004: 5)*

This is not to say that perception is somehow pre-cultural. The point of phenomenology, for Csordas, is not to get 'behind' culture, as if culture were a screen that separated us from objects that existed independently of our perceiving them. Instead, phenomenology asks us to start where we in fact do start: as socially and personally habituated bodies that encounter a world with our senses, turning that world into a set of culturally elaborated objects. Csordas cites Merleau-Ponty's example of a boulder, which perception grasps not in-itself but as a culturally defined object—e.g. as something to be climbed over. It:

> is already there to be encountered, but [it] is not perceived as an obstacle until it is there to be surmounted. Constitution of the cultural object is thus dependent on intentionality (what would make one want to surmount the boulder?), but also upon the givenness of our upright posture, which makes clambering over the boulder a particular way of negotiating it (an option even if one could walk around it).
>
> *(Csordas 2002: 62)*

Members of more aesthetically oriented cultures than our own may encounter boulders as pleasing shapes and textures rather than as climbing structures, but a close examination of experience shows us that this happens in the perceiving moment, not as a conceptual afterthought. For Csordas and Merleau-Ponty, perception is always tentative, partial and indeterminate; there is always more present than we realize. Our perceptions nonetheless present us with a facticity that we cannot deny.

Anthropologists are notoriously interested in understanding 'culture'—the socially learned, habitual patterns that differ from society to society. Csordas argues that culture is not some superorganic entity (Kroeber 1917), which acts itself out through human automatons. Neither is it a mere toolkit, on which people draw to understand and guide their experiences (Swidler 2000: 39). Culture does shape our perceptions, but it does not do so, as it were, behind our backs. Csordas' contribution is to note that culture is embedded and sustained in our body-bound perceptual experiences. We do not first perceive, and then interpret, as

William James' (1961) 'over-belief' model supposes. Instead we perceive-interpret simultaneously. Put otherwise, we are not science-fiction homunculi operating passive/receptive sense-machinery from deep inside our heads. Instead, we perceive preobjectively—i.e. spontaneously and without preordained content—but in a form constituted by our cultural way-of-being (Csordas 2002: 66).

Csordas uses this approach to examine two areas of religious experience: Charismatic ritual healing and Navajo healing, both of which operate at the intersection of religion and the body. His work is too extensive to do more than illustrate here, but it is well worth serious study.

Take, for example, his study of a Navajo man with a cancerous brain lesion (Csordas 2002: 219–37). Unable to speak after his injury, this man experienced his struggle to regain speech as a religious quest—one which he understood in traditionally Navajo terms. The Navajo sense of the holiness of exact language (Witherspoon 1977) led him to experience his recovery as something holy—a hard-fought return to a socially valued state of being. Csordas describes how this man's efforts to heal himself into speech grew into a wish to become a medicine man or a minister and thus heal others. This was not, at root, a *post hoc* cultural interpretation laid over an experience. Nor, as Csordas put it, was 'the patient's search for words [. . .] thematized as religious [. . .] because religious experience is reducible to a neurological discharge [in a particular brain region]' (Csordas 2002: 287). Instead, the man grasped his bodily experience as religious in itself, fixing its inherent indeterminacy, as 'a strategy of the self in need of a powerful idiom for orientation in the world' (ibid.: 287).

Similarly, Csordas' (2002: 58–87) study of Charismatic rituals of deliverance from evil spirits shows how these spirits are not over-beliefs or labels (mis)attributed to bodily arousal, as Wayne Proudfoot (1985) claimed.[6] Based on both observations and interviews, Csordas concludes that:

> the preobjective element of this [spirit deliverance] rests in the fact that participants [. . .] experience these manifestations as spontaneous and without preordained content. The manifestations are original acts of communication which nevertheless take a limited number of common forms because they emerge from a shared *habitus*.
>
> *(Csordas 2002: 66)*

This, says Csordas, explains the healers' stress on the 'release' from bondage to the evil spirit rather than the language of demonic 'expulsion' common in the European Christian tradition. North American culture emphasizes control in many areas of life. Charismatic healers promote images of 'loss of control to demonic influence, healing as a release from bondage to that influence, and health as surrender to the will of God, whose strength helps restore self-control' (Csordas 2002: 67). This is a matter of perception, not attribution, and is experienced as spontaneous, not contrived. Culture and bodily sensation work together to constitute an experienced world.

How can we fit this into the Giorgis' methodological framework, outlined above? Their second step calls for the analyst to 'enter into a scientific phenomenological reduction while simultaneously adopting a *psychological* perspective of the experience' (Giorgi and Giorgi 2003: 247, emphasis added). They expect other disciplines to take other perspectives (ibid.: 250). Thus Csordas focuses on the anthropological elements in perception while I focus on the sociological ones. We are not viewing perception (as experience) through particular lenses, as some sort of analytic over-belief. Instead, experiences (including perceptions) are multi-faceted in their very constitution.

A simple example shows how cultural habits help constitute our perceptions. When Americans of my generation hear Rossini's 'The William Tell Overture', we can't help but envision horse-riders galloping through the deserts and plains of the American South-West. That music was the theme of 'The Lone Ranger' television series, a fact now embedded in my generational culture. It's not that we hear the music, then think, 'Oh yes! That reminds me of the Lone Ranger'. Instead, music and image occur simultaneously, viscerally.[7] Cultural habits shape perception, prereflectively, even before we have had time to turn our perceptions into objects. One of the strengths of Csordas' work is to demonstrate how this happens in the religious realm.[8]

Problems

Careful readers will have noticed something odd about the last few paragraphs. There seems to be a contradiction at the heart of the phenomenological project. On the one hand, phenomenology is supposed to investigate pure experiences, bracketing away the interpretations that people make of them. On the other hand, anthropological, psychological and sociological phenomenologies produce different accounts of these experiences. How do we know that these three approaches—and potentially others—are not just (possibly) conflicting interpretations?

Csordas' answer—and Merleau-Ponty's—is a philosophical one. They point out that to claim that we first experience phenomena, then interpret them, presupposes an insupportable dualism between subject and object. It requires that the world be made up of pre-existing objects and subjects, the former of which present the latter with sense data, out of which the latter construct an image of the world. Both Csordas and Merleau-Ponty deny this dualism, arguing that we have no actual evidence for it. Indeed, the close analysis of experience shows no such separation. For them, both subjects and objects are constructed in the process of perception. Phenomenology shows that this construction has cultural, psychological, social and perhaps other dimensions. It is, indeed, multi-faceted. Why posit pre-existing subjects and objects, in a philosophically questionable attempt to reduce those facets to one?

I shall not pursue this question here, in part because I may lack the philosophic skill to do so. I note, however, that it raises a second issue that is of real concern to practical researchers. As David Yamane (2000) noted in a trenchant critique of my work on Navajo rituals, researchers do not have unmediated access to other people's experiences. What they have— what *any* interview study has—is a set of narratives about experience. That is, phenomenological researchers get their data by interviewing informants about what has happened to them. In response, they get stories. People say 'this happened, then this happened, it took such-and-such shape, etc.' This is not direct experience; it is narrative. We know that people are highly susceptible to narratives, often retrospectively retelling their experiences according to culturally valued scripts of one kind or another. David Bromley (1998) and Sarah Pike (2009), among others, have noted how Americans often construct 'captivity narratives' to explain supposedly normal people's participation in so-called 'cults', shootings, etc. How do we know that our informants are not reconstructing the experiences about which they tell us in their phenomenological interviews?

The short answer is 'We don't', though the care with which the Giorgis ask us to bracket our informants' interpretations of their own experiences is designed to minimize such problems. Indeed, all serious phenomenological researchers wrestle with this issue—one of the reasons that phenomenology is one of the hardest research methods to use properly. We must always be alert to narratives getting in the way. Titus Hjelm's chapter (Chapter 2.3) in this volume shows us some of the ways in which we can learn to detect narratives (or 'discourses') in operation. Every budding phenomenologist should read his article with care—and then dive in, for the phenomenological project is still possible.

The fact remains that phenomenology is the only research technique that seeks to understand experience *per se*—as something separate from the interpretations that people place on it. If that is the Object that will answer one's research Question, then phenomenology is the right Method to use.

Notes

1 This may be the impetus for the new term 'phenomenography'; see Svensson (1997).
2 Social scientists have made similarly partial appropriations of the phenomenological project, missing its central focus on subjective experience. See, for example, Knibbe and Versteeg (2008), Moustakas (1994).
3 The Giorgis are psychologists, though they argue that a parallel approach would work as well for sociological, anthropological and other researchers (Giorgi and Giorgi 2003: 250).
4 *Sekai Kyusei-kyo* is one of some 700 new religions founded in Japan during the 20th century. Part of the Omoto group of religions, it emphasizes spiritual healing and the cultivation of beauty as means for aiding the transition to the coming 'Age of Fire'. Over the last 20 years the American organization has split into several groups, including the Johrei Centers, the Izunome Foundation and the Mokichi Okada Association. See Spickard (2004b) for information about these organization shifts.
5 This is a different 'experience-near' approach than the one advocated by Clifford Geertz (1974). In his words, "'Love' is an experience-near concept, "object cathexis" is an experience-distant one'. True, but from the phenomenological point of view, both are concepts, not experiences *per se*.
6 For a critique, see Spickard (2004a).
7 This is not true for later generations. Nor do all members of my age cohort share this particular prereflective response. A portion of that cohort, however, also has a visceral response to the first ten notes of Cream's 'Sunshine'—though with a different content.
8 I noted that Catholic colleagues who attended the Los Angeles house masses responded differently than did Protestants to certain ritual prayers. Their later reports led me to believe that this was a matter of perceptual culture, but one which I, as a non-Catholic, could not personally explore.

References

Blackmore, S.J., 1986. Who am I? Changing models of reality in meditation. In: Claxton, G. (ed.), *Beyond Therapy*. Wisdom Publications, London, pp. 71–85.

Bromley, D.G., 1998. The social construction of contested exit roles: defectors, whistleblowers and apostates. In: Bromley, D.G. (ed.), *The Politics of Religious Apostasy*. Praeger, Westport, CT, pp. 19–48.

Cox, J.L., 2006. *A Guide to the Phenomenology of Religion*. T&T International, London.

Csordas, T.J., 1994. *The Sacred Self*. University of California Press, Berkeley.

—— 1997. *Language, Charisma, and Creativity*. University of California Press, Berkeley.

—— 2002. *Body/Meaning/Healing*. Palgrave Macmillan, New York.

—— 2004. Healing and the human condition: scenes from the present moment in Navajoland. *Culture, Medicine, and Psychiatry* 28(1), 1–14.

Czikszentmihalyi, M., 1975. *Beyond Boredom and Anxiety*. Josey-Bass, San Francisco.

Geertz, C., 1974. 'From the Native's Point of View': On the Nature of Anthropological Understanding. *Bulletin of the American Academy of Arts and Sciences* 28(1): 26–45.

Giorgi, A.P. and Giorgi, B.M., 2003. The descriptive phenomenological psychological method. In: Camic. P.M. *et al.* (eds), *Qualitative Research in Psychology*. American Psychological Association, Washington, DC, 243–73.

Husserl, E., 1973 [1900–01]. *Logical Investigations*. Trans. J.N. Findlay. Routledge, London.

—— 1954 [1913]. *Ideas: general introduction to pure phenomenology*. Trans. W.B. Gibson. Allen and Unwin, London.

James, W., 1961 [1903]. *The Varieties of Religious Experience*. Modern Library, New York.

Knibbe, K. and Versteeg, P., 2008. Assessing phenomenology in anthropology. *Critique of Anthropology* 28(1): 47–62.

Kroeber, A.L., 1917. The superorganic. *American Anthropologist* 19: 163–213.

Moustakas, C., 1994. *Phenomenological Research Methods*. SAGE, London, Thousand Oaks, CA.

Peirce, C.S., 1934. *Collected Papers of Charles Sanders Peirce, Vol. 5*. Hartshorne, C. and Weiss, P. (eds) Harvard University Press, Cambridge, MA.

Pike, S.M., 2009. Dark teens and born–again martyrs: captivity narratives after Columbine. *Journal of the American Academy of Religion* 77(3): 647–79.

Proudfoot, W., 1985. *Religious Experience*. University of California Press, Berkeley.

Schleiermacher, F., 1958 [1799]. *On Religion: speeches to its cultured despisers*. Trans. J. Oman. Harper & Row, New York.

Schutz, A., 1964 [1951]. Making music together: a study in social relationship. In: *Collected Papers II*. Brodersen, A. (ed.) Martinus Nijhoff, Dordrecht, pp. 159–78.

Spickard, J.V., 1991a. Spiritual healing among the American followers of a Japanese new religion: experience as a factor in religious motivation. *Research in the Social Scientific Study of Religion* 3: 135–56.

——— 1991b. Experiencing religious rituals: a Schutzian analysis of Navajo ceremonies. *Sociological Analysis* 52(2): 191–204.

——— 1995. Body, nature, and culture in spiritual healing. In: Johannessen, H. *et al.* (eds), *Studies of Alternative Therapy 2: bodies and nature*. INRAT/Odense University Press, Copenhagen, pp. 65–81.

——— 2004a. Charting the inward journey: applying Blackmore's model to meditative religions. *Archiv Für Religionpsychologie* 26: 157–80.

——— 2004b. Globalization and religious organizations: rethinking the relationship between church, culture, and market. *International Journal of Politics, Culture, and Society* 18(1): 47–63.

——— 2005. Ritual, symbol, and experience: understanding Catholic worker house masses. *Sociology of Religion* 66(4): 337–58.

Svensson, L., 1997. Theoretical foundations of phenomenography. *Higher Education Research & Development* 16(2): 159–71.

Swidler, A., 2000. *Talk of Love: why culture matters*. University of Chicago Press, Chicago.

Walsh, R., 1995. Phenomenological mapping: a method for describing and comparing states of consciousness. *Journal of Transpersonal Psychology* 27(1): 25–56.

Witherspoon, G., 1977. *Language and Art in the Navajo Universe*. University of Michigan Press, Ann Arbor.

Yamane, D., 2000. Narrative and religious experience. *Sociology of Religion* 61(2): 171–89.

Further reading

Csordas, T.J., 1994. *The Sacred Self: a cultural phenomenology of healing*. The University of California Press, Berkeley, Los Angeles, London.

An extended study of Charismatic healing and ritual, from an experiential point of view.

———. 2002. *Body/Meaning/Healing*. Palgrave Macmillan, New York

A collection of Csordas' most significant articles on embodiment, on Charismatic healing, and on Navajo healing.

Giorgi, A.P., 2009. *The Descriptive Phenomenological Method in Psychology: a modified Husserlian approach*. Duquesne University Press, Pittsburgh, PA.

A recently published 'how to'-oriented elaboration of Giorgi's approach to phenomenology. Crucial reading.

Rehorick, D. and Valerie, B. (eds), 2008. *Shifting Our Lifeworld: transforming self and professional practice through phenomenology*. Lexington Press, Lanham, MD.

A series of lively and accessible examples of phenomenological work.

Schutz, A., 1964. The Stranger; making music together; Don Quixote and the problem of reality. In: *Collected Papers II*. Brodersen, A. (ed.) Martinus Nijhoff, Dordrecht.

Classic sociological phenomenology, accessible and well written.

Vaitkus, S., 2000. Phenomenology and sociology. In: Turner, B.S. (ed.), *The Blackwell Companion to Social Theory*, 2nd edn. Blackwell, Oxford, pp. 270–98.

A theoretically rich but dense outline of phenomenology as it has influenced the social sciences. A useful corrective to lesser work.

Van Manen, M., 1990. *Researching Lived Experience*. State University of New York, Albany.

An accessible approach, useful for practical researchers, though with occasional conceptual missteps.

Walsh, R., 1995. Phenomenological mapping: a method for describing and comparing states of consciousness. *Journal of Transpersonal Psychology* 27 (1): 25–56.

An accessible example of phenomenology applied to states of consciousness.

Key concepts

Bracketing: the process of removing layers of interpretations surrounding a particular experience, ideally until one has reached a description of the subjective experience itself. This involves more than just refusing to judge the 'truth' or 'falsity' of such experiences; it involves separating experience from all interpretation.

Empirical phenomenology: the study of direct experience, as it is subjectively encountered; contrasted with ideas about experience.

Lived religion: religion as it is actually lived by its participants; this includes both experiences and ideas, along with people's actual practices.

Perception (in the Pontian/Csordasian sense): the process by which a person subjectively constitutes the objects that she or he experiences. For Merleau-Ponti and Csordas, perception is culturally constituted, even in its raw experiencing.

Phenomenological reduction: the process of describing how an experience presents itself to consciousness, separate from any consideration of that experience's imagined referent.

Research object: the (metaphysical) kind of thing called for by a given research question, which can be captured by a particular research method. For example, some questions ask for shallow opinions, which survey research can provide; other questions call for deep opinions, which can be found by interview research; still other questions ask about people's experiences, which phenomenology brings to the surface.

Related chapters

2.16

PHILOLOGY

Einar Thomassen

Chapter summary

- All use of source material that has a linguistic form involves philology.
- Philology is a necessary part of source criticism in religious studies.
- Textual criticism aims at establishing the most reliable text.
- Linguistic competence is indispensible for interpreting texts with precision.
- Philological criticism and interpretation cannot be separated from the study of the subject matter of the text, its historical context and its literary form.

Introduction

The word 'philology' is commonly used to refer to two distinct albeit variously inter-related areas of scholarly pursuit. On the one hand, it can be a type of study whose primary object is language; on the other hand, it is a name for the methodical investigation of texts.[1] The difference between the two roughly corresponds to the distinction made by linguists between language as a system and language in use (or *langue* vs. *parole*, as Saussure says). The study of language as a system includes such topics as lexicography and grammatical structures; actual, recorded instances of the use of words and phrases may be quoted for the purposes of illustration or documentation, but the study of those instances is not a goal in itself. The latter, however, is precisely the purpose of the philological study of texts: here the description and the interpretation of the individual linguistic utterance in the form a document is the principal object of interest.

Philology as linguistics

'Philology' in both senses of the word may be practised by students of religion. Language as such provides important evidence for certain kinds of historical investigation. Especially important in this regard is lexicography. Indo-European languages, for example, possess a common stock of words related to the religious sphere. Thus, the Latin word for 'god', *deus*, is related to *deva* in Sanskrit and to *daēva* in the language of the Avesta (where, however, it means 'demon' or 'false god'). The reconstructed Indo-European prototype is *deiwos, a word the basic meaning of which seems to have been 'shining' and which was associated in particular with the sky. The proper names of certain gods derive from the same root: the old Vedic Dyaus pitar, 'Father Sky', the Greek Zeus, the Roman Jupiter (< Diespiter) and (probably) the Old Norse Týr. Similar etymological relationships may be traced for several other names of deities and other religious terms across the wide Indo-European terrain from Asia to Scandinavia. Such etymologies give valuable leads for understanding the nature and history of the Indo-European gods. They also enable scholars to form hypotheses about common mythological themes and inherited ritual practices: Yama/Yima, the primordial human or king of Indo-Iranian mythology seems related to the Old Norse Ymir and may somehow involve the notion of 'twin' (cf. Latin *geminus*); the Roman priestly title of *flamen* appears to be cognate to *brāhman*, and so on. However, since religious terms change their meaning in the course of history no less than what happens to other lexical items, such comparative studies require considerable caution. An Iranian *daēva* is not the same as an Indian *deva* or a Roman *deus* (Lincoln 2005; Jackson 2002).

Other linguistic areas are fields for similar kinds of studies. Scholars of the Hebrew Bible, for instance, may turn to comparative Semitic lexicography for the interpretation of difficult passages. Is the spirit [or wind?] of God 'moving upon' the waters in Gen 1: 2 actually compared to a bird 'brooding over' its eggs, in accordance with a meaning attested in Syriac for the verb used in the Hebrew text? Another example is the question of the foreign vocabulary of the Qur'ān. The fact that the word *qur'ān* itself seems to be based on the Syriac *qeryānā*, which means the recitation of scripture in a liturgical context, offers a potentially important insight into what kind of text the Qur'ān was originally intended or perceived to be (Jeffery 1938; Carter 2006).

Philology as textual studies

These are a few examples that show the interest and importance of linguistic studies in the history of religions. Even more important, however, is philology in the sense of working with texts. Since texts constitute the most significant class of source material in most types of research on religion, methodological awareness in the use of texts is crucial. From this point of view, philological method is really a sub-division of source criticism in general. It may be worth pointing out that, in religious studies, philology is not a goal in itself. Texts are primarily interesting to us because of the information they may offer *about* religious beliefs and practices. Texts in themselves are not religion; rather, they may express religion and can be sources for knowing about it. In strict philological disciplines, such as classical philology or the study of Arabic, Chinese, etc., editing texts, and reading them with understanding, appreciation and enjoyment, are respectable scholarly pursuits in their own right. In religious studies, however, such activities are, in principle, ancillary to the study of religion as something 'behind' the text and for which the text serves as evidence. A general principle of source criticism applies here too, i.e. that there is no such thing as a 'source' in itself. Something becomes a source, or 'evidence', only in relation to specific questions that are being asked about the thing studied, and the answers one claims the evidence provides. In religious studies those questions and answers are determined by the special focus of interest that defines the discipline as such: 'religion'.

If a text is to be relied upon as a source, however, in other words as 'evidence', two major conditions have to be fulfilled, which can be framed as the following questions: (1) Is the text as such reliable? (2) Is the proposed interpretation of the text reasonable? These two questions correspond to the canonical division of philology into 'criticism' and 'hermeneutics', which was made by German classical scholars in the heyday of philology as a 'science' in the 19th century. Criticism in this context means **textual criticism**: establishing a reliable text. Hermeneutics, on the other hand, is the art of accurately understanding the text.[2]

Textual criticism

The need for textual criticism arises from the fact that written sources are not always accurately reproduced. This often happens, of course, when texts are copied by hand. Scribes may be negligent, inattentive or fail to understand what they are copying. Or they may be dissatisfied with what they read and try to 'improve' the text. In this way errors and modifications will accumulate as the text is transmitted across the centuries from one scribe to the next. (In principle, the same situation obtains with printed texts, which may display variation from one edition to another.) The history of transmission of a given text may thus be compared to a family tree, starting from the 'autograph', the manuscript that was once penned (or dictated) by the author himself and which is the putative common ancestor of all the later copies. The descendents of this *Ur*-text then branch out into different 'families' distinguished by the particular errors or other modifications that each scribe once committed as he was copying the text and were inherited by those who later copied his manuscript. This genealogical model is called a *stemma*. Evidently such stemmas can hardly ever be completely reconstructed, since many of the links in the chain will be missing and must be hypothetically postulated, but the model nonetheless retains its fundamental value as a heuristic tool.

The identification of errors or secondarily effected changes in the text may emerge from the comparison ('collation') of different manuscripts of the same text. Hence the need to collate as many manuscripts as possible (or as may be found useful). The decision as to which variant is the more original and correct will be based on critical judgement: it yields a better sense, or it is easier to explain how variant *b* was corrupted from variant *a* than vice versa, etc. However, textual critics often do not shy away from suspecting error in the text even if no variant is attested in another manuscript. In such cases an 'emendation' will be based on 'conjecture'.

Box 2.16.1 An example of textual criticism

In John 1: 18 one group of ancient manuscripts reads 'No one has ever seen God; the only (begotten) Son (*monogenēs hyios*), who is in the bosom of the Father, he has made him known' (New Revised Standard Version). Other manuscripts, however, offer 'the only (begotten) God' (*monogenēs theos*) instead of 'the only (begotten) Son', and this is accepted by many modern translations. In this case, one may argue that 'Son' gives better sense than 'God' (note the pair Son/Father, and consider that the adjective *monogenēs* fits better with *hyios* than with *theos*). In addition, one may suspect that a scribe (probably in Alexandria, since this text is particularly well attested in writers connected with that city) here deliberately changed the text (replacing '*hyios*' with '*theos*') because he wanted to stress the divinity of Jesus Christ (Ehrman 1993: 78–82).

Textual criticism is concerned not only with single words and individual passages, but also with larger units of text. The fact that the end of the Gospel of Mark (16: 9–20), recounting the post-resurrectional apparitions of Jesus, does not appear in the oldest manuscripts, has led to the conclusion that it must be a later addition (see e.g. Metzger and Ehrman 2005: 226–28). The addition of smaller or larger elements to an existing textual tradition ('**interpolation**') is a relatively frequent phenomenon. When a text is extensively modified in this way, it may be described as 'rewritten' rather than just copied. It also often happens that originally independent texts are combined so as to form a new work. In such cases one may speak of the new work as a 'redaction'. The detection of older texts used as sources in the composition of a work has been called 'higher criticism' and was a major feature of 'the historical–critical method' that developed in the 19th century.

In biblical studies the practice of higher criticism has produced lasting, even if not unanimously accepted, results, most famously with the identification of the different sources of the Pentateuch in the Old Testament, and with the two-source theory of the synoptic gospels in the New Testament. In principle, the same type of operations can be performed upon texts transmitted in other traditions. 'Canonical' texts in particular have very often come into being as compilations of older materials, and they often acquire further additions as well in the course of their being adopted and used by various subgroups. Critical philological work may be able to sort out distinct components in such texts and identify various layers in the transmission, based on linguistic criteria, stylistic features, the occurrence of characteristic vocabulary and observations about textual coherence. For the historian of religion, the importance of such work lies not least in its potential for estimating the date when the various parts of the texts may have originated and, by implication, the date of the religious ideas contained in them.

Tracing the history of transmission of texts by detecting the corruptions and modifications they have undergone from one manuscript copy to the next can be interesting and illuminating in itself. Most often, however, such work is carried out with a further object in mind: the reconstruction of the original text. Such reconstruction results in a **critical edition** of the text, where the text is presented to the reader purged of all the distortions perpetrated by the copying scribes, as well as of later additions. It goes without saying that this is an ideal that in practice can only be approximated. Even the texts of the New Testament, which are far better documented (more than 4,000 manuscripts), and have been the object of more text-critical research than any other textual corpus from Antiquity, still cannot be reconstructed with absolute certainty. The standard critical edition of the New Testament (Nestlé-Aland, now in its 27th (!) edition) is still, in terms of the logic of science, no more than a scholarly hypothesis—albeit a relatively very well argued one. Because of the uncertainties that inevitably remain, the presented text is therefore accompanied by a *critical apparatus*. There, variant readings from the manuscripts are noted that are considered to be competing candidates for representing the original text of a particular passage (as well as some readings that may have historical interest even if they almost certainly are secondary).

Box 2.16.2 'Manuscript' and 'text'

The two concepts of 'manuscript' and 'text' are not infrequently confused by fresh students. It is therefore worth pointing out that a particular manuscript is not, strictly speaking, the same as a 'text'. Rather, a manuscript is only a 'witness' (as the philologists say) to a text. The 'text' as such is to be understood as the original source, no longer extant, which lies behind the various manuscripts. Unlike the latter, the text is not available to us as a physical object, but is something that may be hypothetically reconstructed in the form of a critical edition. It is thus incorrect, for example, to say that the *Gospel of Thomas* is a 'text' from the fourth century. The correct way to express this is to say that the text of this apocryphal gospel is witnessed by a (Coptic) *manuscript* from the fourth century, though the original (Greek) *text* was probably composed sometime in the second century. Fragments found of Greek manuscripts of this gospel can be dated on palaeographical grounds (the study of historical styles and customs of writing) to ca. 200–250, and the gospel is mentioned by Christian authors in the same period.[3]

The example of John 1: 18 (see Box 2.16.1) shows how textual criticism also carries interest for the history of theological ideas. Sometimes text-critical issues can trigger a major theological controversy, as in the case of the famous 'Comma Johanneum' (1 John 5: 7–8), a passage which clearly testifies to the doctrine of the Trinity, but which already in the early modern age was suspected of being an interpolation. The Catholic Church in 1897 declared the belief in its authenticity to be incumbent on all believers, a position that was later abandoned. Controversies over later additions contained in 'canonical' texts are not unknown in other traditions either. In China, for instance, scholars since the 17th century have been annoying the Confucian establishment by detecting spurious texts in the 'Classics' (Elman 2001; Pollock 2009: 953–54). These examples show how textual criticism may turn into cultural critique in a wider sense by exposing the untenable textual basis for important received ideas.

In a number of cases the textual transmission is such that it is no longer feasible to isolate an original core text from later accretions. This is often the case, for instance, with Buddhist *sutras*, which were rewritten as they spread from one region to another and were translated into other languages (Lancaster 1979: 220–28), and with Jewish mystical texts (Schäfer *et al.* 1981; Abrams 2011). In such cases the editor must often be content with editing separately the different versions ('recensions') of the text, or even the individual manuscripts, which may be presented in parallel columns. This happens with the so-called New Testament Apocrypha as well, where the history of a text often cannot be confidently reconstructed from its various recensions. In such cases, where neither the relative chronology of the different versions of the text nor their precise dates in absolute terms can be established, scholars are prevented from answering important questions about the genesis of the texts and the environments in which they originated or were modified, and they must often restrict themselves to studying the ways the texts were later received and used.

Recovering 'the original text', even when this can be done with reasonable assurance, is in any case not the only purpose of textual criticism. Later versions of a text are interesting in their own right, as testimonies to what was believed at a certain time in a particular region, or as texts that were being used by communities and referred to by religious personalities. It is obviously important for the history of religious ideas to be able to form an opinion about what the apostle Paul actually wrote, or what the historical Buddha or Zarathushtra spoke. If that is your focus of interest, textual criticism of the Pauline corpus, the *gathas* and the earliest *sutras* must be taken seriously. If you are interested instead in how the texts have been read and used by particular people down through history, later versions of those texts and translations of them will be much more relevant for your research.

Whereas some texts have been preserved in multiple copies, from which a history of transmission may be reconstructed, other texts may be attested by a single manuscript that has survived more or less by accident. A large number of important sources for the history of religions are of this kind, including some rather spectacular discoveries made in modern times: the Dead Sea scrolls, the Coptic Gnostic library from Nag Hammadi, the Buddhist and Manichaean manuscripts from Turfan, and so on. In such cases, particularly close attention will be given to the unique manuscripts themselves. Making them speak to us requires a combination of skills such as codicology (finding out how the book was constructed), palaeography (understanding the script) and the linguistic competence enabling the scholar to translate it and (to some extent) reconstruct damaged portions of the manuscript's text. In a case such as the Turfan manuscripts, some of the texts were written in previously unattested Iranian languages, and the experts had to work to reconstruct the grammar and vocabulary of those languages themselves before reliable editions and translations of the texts could be produced. Without such painstaking philological efforts, those sources would have remained closed to the history of religions.

The student relying on the published translations of such sources should nevertheless be constantly aware of the many uncertainties they still contain. In principle, the serious student should acquire some (or, rather, as much as possible) of the relevant philological skills oneself in order to use the sources in a professional manner. Moreover, in addition to the material and linguistic difficulties involved in reconstructing and understanding the manuscript itself, the very fact that a text is preserved in a single manuscript, and thus cannot be controlled by other witnesses, means that the original form of the text often remains dubious. The well-known 'gospels' of Thomas and Judas, for instance, both originally written in the second century, are each known only through a Coptic translation preserved in a single manuscript from the fourth century. There is no doubt that the texts have been changed and to some extent distorted during their transmission, but many of those changes and distortions can today no longer be positively identified.

Interpreting the text

Using a text with source-critical awareness means not only that you have to refer to a critically assured form of the text, but also that you need to understand it correctly. In the context of philology, the notion of correct interpretation means, above all, linguistically competent understanding. In short, you have to be familiar with the language in which the text is written. Translations are enormously useful for getting to know the contents of a text, and often constitute significant scholarly contributions in their own right as efforts to make texts accessible. However, a translation cannot be blindly relied upon to be used as evidence in professional research. All languages possess, for example, more than a single word for such important religious ideas as 'god', 'spirit', 'sacrifice' or 'priest'. Which native term is used in a given passage is not necessarily revealed by a translation. You have to be able to check the original text and look the word up in a dictionary to see exactly what is meant. You also need to know enough of the grammar to be able to see where the emphasis lies in the passage and what may be just an aside, in order to confidently use the text as evidence.

The word *magoi* in the nativity story in Matt 2: 1, for example, is hardly possible to translate accurately into a modern language. The usual translation as 'wise men' fails to convey the fact that the Greek term is actually a designation for Iranian priests, which, at the time when Luke was writing, also had acquired the meaning of 'magicians', and the word could be used to refer to other practitioners of specialized and/or esoteric knowledge as well, including astrology. No modern translation is able to reproduce the range of connotations the word would have carried to Matthew's Greek readers in Antiquity.

Knowing the language in a strictly linguistic manner is not sufficient, however, for sound philological interpretation. Since the object of interpretation is language in use and not language as a system, dictionaries and grammars can only help us part way towards understanding a particular passage in a text. Back in the 19th century, the classical philologist and philological theoretician August Boeckh (1886) listed four factors that had to work together in the mind of the interpreter:

- language
- historical context
- the individual author
- genre

351

That is, the interpreter must, in addition to being trained in the language as such, be apprecia-tive of the historical situation in which a text was written, including such things as political institutions or elements of material culture to which it may allude. One should also be aware of the linguistic peculiarities and style of writing belonging to the individual author, and of the genre conventions according to which the text was composed: the rules of versification in poetry, rhetorical schemata in prose, etc. These are all highly relevant points that have lost none of their validity since the time they were made. It should be observed, however, that they describe a *practice*—how sound philological **interpretation** is actually done—rather than a set of rules: they cannot be easily operationalized as a positive methodical procedure. It is very often the case, however, that *criticism* of a proposed interpretation is made with refer-ence to one or another of these four factors: e.g. the interpretation has failed to take suffi-ciently into account either the intra-textual or the extra-textual context of a passage, the usage of the particular author, the requirements of the genre and so on.

Thus, to appreciate Matthew's story of the *magoi*, it is also highly relevant to realize that the star announcing the birth of the Messiah is an allusion to the prophecy made by Bileam in Num 24: 17. It is, moreover, characteristic of Matthew as an author that he constructs his narrative by making constant references to Messianic prophecies in the Jewish scriptures, and one does well to bear in mind that the author writes in a situation where he is concerned to convince Jews and to assure Christians that Jesus is indeed the expected Messiah.

Here is another, recent example that shows the need to combine linguistic with contextual knowledge: In the *Gospel of Judas*, published for the first time in 2006, Jesus calls Judas 'you thirteenth *daimon*!' (44.21). On the assumption that Judas is a positive character in this text, the first editors took *daimon* to mean 'divine spirit', in accordance with the normal meaning of the word in classical Greek. However, in Christian texts, including all the so-called Gnostic texts to which the *Gospel of Judas* may be compared, the word universally carries negative connota-tions: it means an evil spirit. In some of those Gnostic texts, moreover, the number 13 also has an unfavorable meaning, referring to the highest level of the cosmic rulers that dominate humanity in the physical world. Finally, other passages in the text, which were taken to imply a promise of salvation for Judas, on closer examination, taking into account Coptic idiom and the rules of Coptic syntax, turned out to say the opposite of what the first editors had thought (Painchaud 2006; DeConick 2007). In consequence, Judas cannot be a positive character in the text, but is rather, indeed, a demonic figure. This example shows how linguistic competence needs to be supplemented by precise knowledge about the subject matter expounded in the text, and familiarity with similar types of documents, if a text is to be understood correctly.

It follows from this that the philological interpreter needs to be broadly trained. It is not enough to 'know the language'; you need to know about the things to which the words in the text refer and the situation in which they are used: the world of ideas and practices lying behind the text, historical events, social structures, material culture, the relevant additional literary sources, inscriptions, archaeology and art . . . No wonder Boeckh described the work of the philologist as an unending task (Boeckh 1886: 15, 86; Poiss 2009)!

Concluding remarks

The two main dimensions of philological work, textual criticism and the linguistically informed interpretation of texts, are distinct operations, but nevertheless mutually related, since judgements about the authenticity of variant readings in the manuscripts presuppose a degree of interpretation of the text, and interpretation of the text must take into account the variations in its transmission. Philological interpretation presupposes in turn, as we have seen, a familiarity with the ideas contained in the texts and with their wider contexts. The study of those ideas, on their part, cannot be done without considerations about their textual documentation. In this way, an epistemological and methodological continuum is created that ranges from textual criticism over philological interpretation to the special disciplines that use the texts as sources—including the history of religion. This explains why there cannot exist a clear division of labor between philologists and historians. In other words, knowledge about religion is necessary for philological work on religious texts. Excellent linguists have sometimes produced editions and translations of religious texts that were unsatisfactory because they lacked the necessary familiarity with the world of ideas contained in the texts. For this reason, historians of religion have not infrequently undertaken to perform such work themselves, applying their special knowledge to produce sources that others can use with confidence.

The philological work of editing and translating therefore has a necessary and rightful place within the discipline of religious studies itself. On the other hand, if historians of religion were to restrict themselves to such work, the profession would easily disintegrate into a series of specialities, and important perspectives intrinsic to it as a distinct field of knowledge might be lost from sight: i.e. the cross-religious work of comparison, conceptualization and generalization, for which the sources made available by philology provide data that can be used as examples, beyond the interest they command as objects of study in their own right.

Notes

1   The first of these meanings seems to be the most common in English; in other languages, the second meaning predominates.
2   See Chapter 2.11 on Hermeneutics in this volume.
3   For an accessible, recent introduction to this apocryphal gospel, see Plisch 2008.

References

Abrams, D., 2011. *Kabbalistic Manuscripts and Textual Theory: methodologies of textual scholarship and editorial practice in the study of Jewish mysticism.* The Hebrew University Magnes Press, Jerusalem.

Boeckh, A., 1886. *Enzyklopädie und Methodenlehre der philologischen Wissenschaften.* Bratuscheck, E. (ed.) B.G.Teubner, Stuttgart.

Carter, M., 2006. Foreign vocabulary. In: Rippin, A. (ed.), *The Blackwell Companion to the Qur'ān.* Blackwell, Malden, MA, pp. 120–39.

DeConick, A.D., 2007. *The Thirteenth Apostle: what the Gospel of Judas really says.* Continuum, London, New York.

Ehrman, B., 1993. *The Orthodox Corruption of Scripture.* Oxford University Press, Oxford.

Elman, B.A., 2001. *From Philosophy to Philology: intellectual and social aspects of change in late imperial China.* 2nd edn. University of California Press, Los Angeles.

Jackson, P., 2002. Light from distant asterisks: towards a redescription of the Indo-European religious heritage. *Numen* 49 (1): 61–102.

Jeffery, A., 1938. *The Foreign Vocabulary in the Qur'ān.* Oriental Institute, Baroda.

Lancaster, L. 1979. Buddhist literature: its canons, scribes, and editors. In: O'Flaherty, W.D. (ed.), *The Critical Study of Sacred Texts.* University of California Press, Los Angeles, pp. 215–29.

Lincoln, B., 2005 [1987]. Indo-European religions: an overview. In: Jones, L. (ed.), *Encyclopedia of Religion,* 2nd edn. Macmillan Reference, New York, vol. 7, pp. 4452–57.

Metzger, B.M. and Ehrman, B.D., 2005. *The Text of the New Testament: its transmission, corruption, and restoration.* 4th edn. Oxford University Press, New York.

Painchaud, L., 2006. À propos de la (re)découverte de l'Évangile de Judas. *Laval Théologique et Philosophique* 62: 553–68.

Plisch, U.-K., 2008. *The Gospel of Thomas: original text with commentary.* Deutsche Bibelgesellschaft, Stuttgart.

Poiss, T. 2009. Die unendliche Aufgabe. August Boeckh als Begründer des Philologischen Seminars. In: Baertschi, A.M. and King, C.G. (eds), *Die Modernen Väter der Antike*, Walter de Gruyter, Berlin, pp. 45–72.

Pollock, S., 2009. Future philology? The fate of a soft science in a hard world. *Critical Inquiry* 35 (4): 931–61.

Schäfer, P. *et al.*, 1981. *Synopse zur Hekhalot-Literatur.* Mohr, Tübingen.

Further reading

Philology is a craft, which must be learned through practice, as part of academic training in reading, and critically using original texts in their various languages. Introductory books on philology typically focus on specific linguistic areas, such as Greek and Latin, Arabic, Indian, Chinese studies, etc. The following more general and relatively recent works may nevertheless be found stimulating; they also provide further bibliography:

Chang, K. *et al.*, Forthcoming. *World Philology.* Harvard University Press, Cambridge, MA.

Greetham, D.C., 1994. *Textual Scholarship: an introduction.* Garland, New York.

Gumbrecht, H.U., 2003. *The Powers of Philology: dynamics of textual scholarship.* University of Illinois Press, Urbana, IL.

Modiano, R. *et al.*, 2004. *Voice, Text, Hypertext: emerging practices in textual studies.* University of Washington Press, Seattle.

Schaps, D.M., 2011. *Handbook for Classical Research.* Routledge, London.

Thomassen, E., 1999. Is philology relevant? In: Ahlbäck, T. (ed.), *Approaching Religion: based on papers read at the symposium on methodology in the study of religions held at Åbo, Finland, on the 4th-7th August 1997.* Part 1. Donner Institute for Research in Religious and Cultural History [Donnerska institutet för religionshistorisk och kulturhistorisk forskning] Almqvist & Wiksell International, Åbo, Stockholm, pp. 243–52.

Key concepts

Critical edition: Attempted reconstruction of the original version of a text, purged from later distortions and additions, accompanied by a critical apparatus informing about important variants in the manuscript record and justifying the preferences made by the editor.

Interpolation: The insertion of an element, small or large, into an existing text.

Interpretation: Philological interpretation takes account of the linguistic characteristics and the non-linguistic contexts of the analyzed text.

Textual criticism: Practice that aims at establishing a reliable text from the variant manuscripts; it is a basis for interpretation and source criticism.

Related chapters

2.17

SEMIOTICS

Robert A. Yelle

Chapter summary

- Semiotics adopts an approach to religion as a form of human communication.
- Semiotic analysis matches the form of a discourse to its social function.
- The core data for semiotic analysis is a text or ritual performance reduced to textual form.
- Semiotic analysis begins from the cataloguing of iconic and indexical relationships among segments of a text or ritual performance, then considers what these relationships contribute to the pragmatic function of a text or ritual in its context of performance.
- While religious texts may be analyzed like any others, some forms of religion and especially of ritual exhibit a heightening of poetic form that signals their status as culturally effective modes of rhetorical performance.
- In addition to a careful etic study of discourses, attention must be paid to the emic semiotic ideologies that inform such discourses. Semiotic analysis is not a predictive science, but a valuable aid to the study of cultural forms.

Overview: contemporary applications of semiotics within the study of religion

Depending on the definition one adopts, semiotics is either a broad discipline with an ancient pedigree, or a highly discrete field that has developed only within the last few decades. Defined broadly as a 'science of signs', semiotics refers to a range of methodologies developed to theorize and systematize our intuitive understandings of communication, signification, meaning and interpretation. The study of signs has an ancient pedigree. No comprehensive philosophy or systematic technique of rhetoric can afford to be without a theory of the sign. Contemporary semiotics has antecedents in classical rhetoric and philosophy, which were centrally concerned with persuasion and demonstration; and in the study of tropes, metaphors and poetry more generally.

Semiotics in this broad sense overlaps with several other methodologies addressed by other chapters in this *Handbook*, including particularly those on conversation analysis (Chapter 2.2), discourse analysis (Chapter 2.3), hermeneutics (Chapter 2.11), philology (Chapter 2.16), and especially structuralism (Chapter 2.18). Other new approaches that have been applied to religion, including cognitive science and aesthetics, also converge to some degree with semiotics.

The present chapter focuses on the methodologies more centrally identified with the discipline of semiotics as elaborated in the last several decades, sometimes in contradistinction to these other fields. Even under this narrower definition, semiotics is commonly understood to embrace a range of methodologies:

- The 'semiotic' of Charles Sanders Peirce (see Parmentier 1994);
- the structuralist 'semiology' of Ferdinand de Saussure (1966);
- the structuralist analyses of myth developed by Claude Lévi-Strauss (1967);
- poststructuralist theories of discourse (Barthes 1972; Murphy 2000, 2003);
- certain types of discourse analysis developed in linguistic anthropology (Silverstein and Urban 1996; Silverstein 1998);
- more recent studies within anthropology of linguistic or semiotic ideologies (Schieffelin *et al.* 1998; Keane 2007).

The focus of this essay will be certain types of analysis developed within the tradition of Peircean semiotics. Within the discipline of semiotics thus circumscribed, our focus shall be further narrowed to consider the intersection of that approach with religious phenomena, and especially with the analysis of ritual.

Despite the absolute generality of semiotics, which has elaborated totalizing theories of the sign that claim to apply equally and indifferently to all types of sign in every domain of culture and even in the natural order, there is nevertheless a special connection between semiotics and religion. The elaboration of theories of signification and interpretation played a central role in Christian typological and allegorical interpretations of scripture and of pagan myth. Protestant literalism challenged many of these traditional typological interpretations of scripture, while deepening the Christian claim to have displaced Jewish and pagan symbolism. Protestants articulated a profound critique of the semiotic dimensions of ritual, particularly of image-worship, the 'vain repetitions' of Catholic prayer, and the obscurity and 'arbitrariness' of Jewish ceremonial. Enlightenment thinkers inherited and extended a number of these critiques. While championing the arbitrary (rather than God-given) nature of linguistic signs, they also engaged in efforts to construct a universal language to overcome the problem of **arbitrariness** (see Eco 1995). Responding to such attacks on traditional symbolism, Romantics and Surrealists advocated a return to nature as well as to mythology and the intensity of aesthetic experience, and asserted a connection, through symbol and poetry, between literary and religious experience. Mircea Eliade's (1954) concept of the 'archetype' and its displacement, which has been heavily criticized (e.g. Juschka 2008), represented a late form of Romanticism.

A study of signs, including religious signs, that aims to be scientific as opposed to theological or Romantic has developed in more recent decades through the combination of certain concepts and techniques of analysis developed in the traditions of Saussure and Peirce. Although arguably, among these traditions of semiotics, it is Lévi-Strauss's structuralism that has had the deepest influence on the study of myth and ritual by both anthropologists and historians of religion, given that structuralism is covered elsewhere in this *Handbook*, little shall be said about structuralist methodologies except what is required to distinguish them from what is being described here under the rubric of a semiotics of religion.

The use of Peircean semiotic, as opposed to Saussurean structuralism, to analyze and explain religious phenomena is more recent and less widespread. Saussure emphasized binary oppositions in language and their role in constructing meaning. Structuralist analyses of myth have retained the orientation toward semantics. In contrast, Peircean semiotics emphasizes

pragmatics—the manner in which signs 'do' things—and has had more impact on the study of ritual. While structuralist analyses focus on difference, semiotic analyses focus on the concept of the 'index' or **'indexical icon'** (see Table 2.17.1) as a quasi-causal relation that is performative in the twin sense that it is (1) constructed through ritual **performance**, and (2) entails, if only virtually, certain pragmatic effects.

The application of Peircean semiotic to religious phenomena has occurred primarily in anthropology (e.g. Parmentier 1994; Silverstein 1998; Silverstein and Urban 1996). Stanley Tambiah (1985: 128) applied the Peircean category of the 'indexical icon' to account for the manner in which rituals 'perform'. He combined this with the colloquial sense of a dramatic performance, and with the philosopher J.L. Austin's (1975) observation that some statements are primarily not about meaning, but about doing something, or bringing about a certain state of affairs. (An example is 'With this ring, I thee wed'.) Tambiah argued that rituals deploy a series of formal features such as repetition, formality, and the combination of different sensory registers to heighten and accentuate this performance. More recently, cognitive theorists have referred to this phenomenon in ritual as 'sensory pageantry' (e.g. McCauley and Lawson 2002: 114).

The notion of indexical icon has been developed by the anthropologist Michael Silverstein (1998), who followed his teacher Roman Jakobson in combining Saussurean semiology with Peircean semiotic (Yelle 2003: 71–73). According to Silverstein, ritual is a heightened case of a more general poetic function of language, in which repetition and metricalization in discourse communicate both the 'entextualization' of the discourse—its emergence as a text—as well as its 'co(n)textualization' within the pragmatic context of the discourse, with which such metricalization establishes relations of presupposition and entailment of a quasi-causal nature (Silverstein and Urban 1996).

The concept of the indexical icon bridges the gap between the analysis of the structural (i.e. phonetic, morphological, semantic and syntactic) features of a text or ritual performance and the analysis of the interaction between such a text and its context.

Semiotic analysis

To appreciate the concept of the 'indexical icon' and how it can be used to analyze texts and ritual performances, we must first learn some basic concepts of Peircean semiotics. Peirce elaborated a typology of different signs, which depended upon the fundamental triad of icon, index and symbol.

Although Peirce's triadic typology has sometimes been deployed rigidly, the fact is that almost all signs are complex and fall into more than one of these three categories. For example, a red traffic light is a conventional index that signals us to stop at an intersection. The

Table 2.17.1 Types of sign (after Peirce)

Sign Type	Basis	Examples
Icon	Similarity, including structural resemblance ('diagrammatic icon')	Portrait, statue, metaphor, onomatopoeia or 'sound symbolism' (arguably)
Index	Co-occurrence, spatio-temporal contiguity, or causal relation	Smoke for fire (and vice-versa), a weathervane, metonym
Symbol	Convention; arbitrary determination	A red light for a traffic stop, (almost all) language

Table 2.17.2 Example 1: analysis of magic

Frazer's Laws	Ritual action	Sign relation	Intended goal
1 Law of Similarity	a) voodoo doll's foot injured	index	a) victim's foot injured
	b) water poured on ground	$\rightarrow$ motivated by metaphor/iconicity	b) rain falls
2 Law of Contact/ Contagion	a) hair of victim burned	index	a) victim burns
	b) weapon anointed	$\rightarrow$ motivated by metonymy/pars pro toto/indexicality	b) wound heals

Reproduced from Yelle 2003: 76.

property of signs as complex becomes important in the analysis of rituals, especially of the magical variety, where certain icons or indices may be taken as causal indices of events in their context, such as the goal of the ritual. This provides our first example of semiotic analysis.

Earlier discussions of sympathetic magic by E.B. Tylor (1903: 115ff.) and James Frazer (1951: 12ff.) already noted the use of resemblance and contiguity in spells and magical operations; more recent scholars including Thomas Sebeok (1976: 31–32, 76–77, 131–32) have pointed out that these types of magic coincide with the Peircean categories of icon and index. Such types of sign, unlike purely arbitrary symbols, 'motivate' or reinforce the indexical relationship between a magical ritual and its goal.

In the case of the preceding examples, there is a rather straightforward sign-relation between the ritual performance and the event in context that it indexes. Yet many rituals require a more complex analysis, one that attends to the unfolding performance of the ritual and the manner in which this augments the ritual as an index. Similar to Lévi-Straussian structuralism and Jakobsonian poetics (Jakobson 1960), the methodology applied in such analyses begins with a general segmentation and notation of patterns evident in the emerging event of discourse. Sequences of text, or of language or other semiotic modalities converted into text, are broken down into their phonetic, semantic and syntactic components, which are then correlated with events and patterns in their extra-linguistic context. A simple illustration of this technique appears in Table 2.17.3; phonetic and semantic parallelisms and appositions between segments of discourse are indicated by the use of capital letters.

Table 2.17.3 Example 2: analysis of a folk charm

Text	Phonetic apposition/iconicity	Semantic apposition/iconicity and antithesis
Rain, rain, go away, Come again some other day!	rAIn–rAIn–AwAy–AgAIn–dAy cOME–sOME	GO–COME [not NOW–but THEN]

Reproduced from Yelle 2003: 77. Although technically this may not be a folk charm, it does illustrate features common to such charms. For further illustrations, see Yelle 2002.

The unfolding pattern of icons and antitheses creates a recognizable text that bears also a pragmatic relation to its context (i.e. bad weather). The multiple indices thus formed—including imperative verbs and deictics—add up in a way that enhances the overall force of the spell as an index of its goal. This illustrates also the complex character of such signs, which are simultaneously icons and indices (hence 'indexical icons') and in which icons may be 'taken as' indices, and even regarded as signals or actual causes of events in context.

Example 3: analysis of a Cheremis charm (after Sebeok)

In a classic study of Cheremis charms, Thomas Sebeok (1964) used such techniques to show how these spells deploy multiple forms of poetic parallelism and repetition. Sebeok's translation of the recipe for a charm to cure a wound is: 'As the apple-tree blossoms forth, just so let this wound heal! (All blossoms must be mentioned.) When water can blossom forth, only then overcome me!' The first and third sentences are both indices, of the 'if-then' variety. The first sentence harnesses the healing of the wound to the blossoming of a tree, a naturally occurring event that is as sure as the seasons. The second sentence—which is in parentheses because it is not spoken as part of the charm, but rather instructs the speaker to repeat the first sentence naming all types of blossoms in turn—illustrates how repetition on both the formal and semantic levels of a spell can enhance its function as an index. The third sentence is a counterfactual index, which translates roughly as 'Let me die only when Hell freezes over!' This combines with the earlier indices of healing to enhance the overall force of the spell.

As Sebeok proceeds to note, such semantic patterns are complemented by a dense network of phonetic repetitions and morphological symmetries. Cheremis charms, like those of many or even most cultures, deploy such poetic devices as alliteration and rhyme. These poetic associations may be interpreted as semantic (Sebeok 1964: 364; Jakobson 1960) or even pragmatic. As suggested in Example 2 above (Table 2.17.3), poetic devices can create relationships of presupposition and entailment within the structure of a ritual performance, which can then be transferred to the goal of the ritual itself. Such redundancies serve a dual role: (1) they are techniques of ritualization that announce the status of a ritual formula as an effective act of communication, and (2) they may accumulate to augment the overall indexical or pragmatic force of the ritual.

Example 4: analysis of Hindu tantric mantras

Some of these ideas help to account for the poetic features of Hindu tantric mantras, which employ repetition, alliteration and reduplication, together with other devices, to augment the power of the mantra (Yelle 2003).

An example would be:

Om hrim srim klim amukam mama vasyam kuru kuru klim srim hrim om.
(*Om hrim srim klim*, Make, make so-and-so my slave, *klim srim hrim om*).

In this example, the repetition of imperative verbs—already a kind of index—strengthens the force of the spell, while the apparently nonsensical 'seed' (*bija*) mantras such as *hrim* add poetic and rhythmic force. The use of quasi-palindromes (i.e. repeating the same syllables both forwards and backwards at the beginning and end of the mantra) is a way of constructing the mantra as an icon of various processes of creation, such as the cosmogony and sexual reproduction, which in the Hindu tradition are conceived as having an in-and-out or back-and-forth shape.

Table 2.17.4 Example 4: analysis of Hindu tantric mantras

Mantra	*om hrim srim klim*	*make, make so-and-so my slave*	*klim srim hrim om*
Sequence of mantra	Bija (seed) mantras, in forwards order	Sadhya (goal)	Bija (seed) mantras, in reverse order
Abstract schema	a–b–c–d	X	d–c–b–a
Sequence of creation	language →	material goal	
Ibid.	creation/evolution →	stability/stasis →	destruction/involution
Ibid.	birth →	life →	death

The goal of such imitative **diagrams** or diagrammatic icons of creation is to make the mantra more creative, rhetorically speaking: to strengthen the force of the mantra so that its goal is accomplished (*siddha*). Iconicity is harnessed to the production of indexicality.

Despite sharing superficial similarities with Frits Staal's (1996) syntactical analysis of mantras and other rituals, the above approach contests or qualifies his claim that the proliferation of repetitive patterns in ritual and ritual discourse signifies 'meaninglessness'.[1] In this case, **redundancy** makes the language of the mantra both more meaningful and more powerful, by invoking and mirroring the act of creation.

Example 5: analysis of a talionic formula (after Jackson)

Such palindromic or chiastic patterns are frequently found also in the law of talion (*lex talionis*), in which a substantive or verbal resemblance between crime and punishment serves to make the latter more 'fitting' (see Yelle 2001, 2010). The most familiar example of this principle is the biblical formula 'an eye for an eye' (Deuteronomy 19:21; Exodus 21:23–24). An elaborate instance is Leviticus 24:13–23, which contains, as some scholars have noted (e.g. Jackson 2000: 291–95), an extended chiasmus, i.e. a sequence of discourse in which there is a repetition of elements in reverse order, indicated below by the letters to the left of each verse:

A1 13 And the Lord said to Moses,

B1 14 'Bring out of the camp him who cursed; and let all who heard him lay their hands upon his head, and let all the congregation stone him.

C1 15 And say to the people of Israel, Whoever curses his God shall bear his sin.

D1 16 He who blasphemes the name of the Lord shall be put to death; all the congregation shall stone him;
the sojourner as well as the native, when he blasphemes the Name, shall be put to death.

E1 17 He who kills a man shall be put to death.

F1 18 He who kills a beast shall make it good, life for life.

G1 19 When a man causes a disfigurement in his neighbor, as he has done it shall be done to him,

H 20 fracture for fracture, eye for eye, tooth for tooth;

G2 as he has disfigured a man, he shall be disfigured.

F2 21 He who kills a beast shall make it good;

E2 and he who kills a man shall be put to death.

D2 22 You shall have one law for the sojourner and for the native; for I am the Lord your God.'

C2 23 So Moses spoke to the people of Israel;

B2 and they brought him who had cursed out of the camp, and stoned him with stones.

A2 Thus the people of Israel did as the Lord commanded Moses.

The overall chiastic structure of this passage is reinforced by the inclusion, at its center, of a familiar version of the talionic formula: 'fracture for fracture, eye for eye, tooth for tooth'. Although such poetic forms may serve both a rhetorical and a mnemonic function, in this case, where the chiasmus would be evident only upon a backward scanning of the written text, its main function appears to be to reinforce the idea of retribution as an index of divine justice, and a representation of successful communication between the heavenly and earthly realms.

Theoretical and epistemological basis

Both structuralist approaches to religious phenomena and those approaches based on Peircean semiotic focus on the analysis of sequences in language and other behaviors regarded as texts. To this extent, these approaches depend on an analogy between language and religious phenomena. In some cases this analogy is relatively uncontroversial: myth and ritual language, for example, are obviously forms of language, although they exhibit special properties. The structuralist analysis of myth depends on the further contention that the deeper, unconscious and intertextual levels of a myth are structured in a manner similar to its obvious linguistic levels. Similarly, the semiotic analysis of a spell or folk charm depends on the further contention that such forms of language exhibit a heightening of a '**poetic function**' found also in ordinary language.

The categories of Peircean semiotic, including icon and index, depend on the recognition or projection of similarity and contiguity, categories that are basic to human cognition and communication. There may be a cognitive or biological basis for such categories. It should be possible in principle to conduct scientific experiments that demonstrate the effects of the deployment of such devices; arguably Pavlov's famous experiments with dogs demonstrated the creation of indices elsewhere in the animal kingdom. However, considering the variability of human cultures and the mediating influences of **semiotic ideologies** on human cognition and behavior, the semiotics of religion is not a predictive science and cannot be reduced to either behaviorism or neuroscience.

Strengths

The semiotic method outlined above has several distinct advantages over some competing methodologies. In the first instance, it helps to account for the proliferation of certain types of signs in ritual, in cases (such as magic spells) where icons strengthen the pragmatic force of the ritual as an index of its goal.

Such features of ritual are better explained by the concept of the indexical icon than by some other approaches. The concept of 'ritualization' (e.g. Bell 1992) holds that ritual cannot be defined through any particular set of features, but is constituted by its sheer difference from ordinary discourse, a difference that may be signaled by an almost infinite variety of techniques. The concept of ritualization is an extension of structuralism and post-structuralism, with their emphasis on binary oppositions and the construction of difference. Similarly, poetry, literature and other domains of culture have been said to be based on a process of distinction and opposition. The concept of ritualization does not help us much to distinguish ritual from these other genres, nor to explain the heightening of poetic function in ritual and its contribution to the pragmatics of ritual performance, which has been illustrated in the preceding examples.

A semiotic approach also has several distinct advantages over theories of religious transmission promoted by some cognitive scientists (e.g. Whitehouse 2000).[2] These theories characterize the purpose of ritual as self-propagation. The poetic features of ritual ostensibly contribute to its memorability and dissemination. This is a partly correct but rather truncated view of the form and function of ritual. As illustrated in the above examples of semiotic analysis, the poetic features of ritual do contribute to the rhetorical power of ritual, and thus to its memorability and transmission; however, they do not only promote retrospective recall, but also contribute to the persuasiveness of ritual as an index of events in the future or the immediate present.

Limitations

A consistent objection to semiotic approaches, as to structuralist approaches, has been that they read certain structures into the texts that they purport to interpret; they arguably lack any 'quality control' that would establish a consistent principle of selection. A further objection is that such semiotic methodologies are fundamentally unhistorical.

The basic triad of icon, index and symbol appears to refer to universally available ways of constructing sign-relations, which Peirce claimed to derive from a rigorous logic, and which presumably depend on fundamental properties of cognition and of the human mind. The Peircean typology is, to this extent, un- or even anti-historical. The question of whether a given sign is an icon, index or symbol—or, more likely, some combination of the above, depending on how it is viewed—is partly in the eye of the beholder. Indeed, the notion of indexical icon depends to some extent on the misrecognition of an icon as an index: for example, a voodoo doll that merely resembles the intended victim is interpreted as having a direct causal effect on the victim.

Formalizing methodologies need to be balanced against a careful study of cultural and historical differences, as reflected in texts and traditions. Fortunately, the semiotic method is sufficiently flexible that it can be adapted in different cultural contexts. In recognition of the importance of cultural differences and theoretical pluralism, anthropologists have in recent years paid increasing attention to the study of linguistic or semiotic ideologies, theories of the sign or normative theories of communication held by different cultural traditions (Schieffelin *et al.* 1998; Bauman and Briggs 2003). This concept has been developed in recognition of the fact that cultures not only produce rich semiotic data—such as myths and rituals—but also more or less explicit theories of signification, which also shape the semiotic forms produced. A study of the semiotic ideology within a given culture is therefore an important step in interpreting its signs and symbols; in the case of tantric mantras, for example, this requires a study of the Sanskrit tantras and a knowledge of Hindu cosmology.

Webb Keane (2007) has examined the impact of certain Protestant presuppositions on the semiotic ideology of modernity. As an example of the importance of attending to such ideological differences, one might point out that the very types of rhetoric deployed in Hindu mantras were dismissed by many British colonialists as 'vain repetitions'. Protestants going back to John Calvin rejected such formulas, beginning with the Hail Mary, as a form of rhetoric, magic and idolatry. In Peircean terms, they denied the ability of such poetic repetitions to function as an index of either real-world effects or sincere communication with the deity. As this example indicates, a semiotic analysis of ritual should never be deployed rigidly, without attention being paid to the cultural traditions in question.

Conclusion

Although significant work continues on the semiotics of religion within the fields of socio-cultural and linguistic anthropology—as evidenced particularly by recent attention to semiotic ideologies—semiotic methodologies have had little influence within religious studies, with some exceptions (e.g. Jackson 2000; Yelle 2003). Scholars of religion have custody of a wealth of material amenable to semiotic analysis, yet have rarely exhibited an interest in systematically developing this material. This is partly due to the dominance of descriptive philology, ethnology and area studies as approaches to the study of religion. Yet it is to be hoped that, spurred by the longstanding if sporadic concern of our discipline with symbols, scholars of religion will engage with semiotic methodologies, not only to better describe particular religious phenomena, but also to provide a history of religions that can articulate a typology of religions considered as semiotic ideologies.

Notes

1   For critiques of Staal's semiotic interpretation of ritual, see Yelle 2003: 19–21, 54; Michaels 2006; Kreinath 2006: 451–56.
2   For a semiotic critique of cognitive approaches, see Yelle 2006.

References

Austin, J.L., 1975. *How to Do Things with Words.* Harvard University Press, Cambridge.

Barthes, R., 1972. *Mythologies.* Trans. A. Lavers. Farrar, Straus and Giroux, New York.

Bauman, R. and Briggs, C.L., 2003. *Voices of Modernity: language ideologies and the politics of inequality.* Cambridge University Press, Cambridge.

Bell, C., 1992. *Ritual Theory, Ritual Practice.* Oxford University Press, New York.

De Saussure, F., 1966. *Course in General Linguistics.* Trans. W. Baskin. McGraw-Hill, New York.

Eco, U., 1995. *The Search for the Perfect Language.* Trans. J. Fentress. Blackwell, Oxford.

Eliade, M., 1954. *The Myth of the Eternal Return: or, cosmos and history.* Trans. Rosemary Sheed. Princeton University Press, Princeton.

Frazer, J., 1951. *The Golden Bough: a study in magic and religion.* Macmillan, New York.

Jackson, B., 2000. *Studies in the Semiotics of Biblical Law.* Sheffield Academic Press, Sheffield, UK.

Jakobson, R., 1960. Closing statement: linguistics and poetics. In: Sebeok, T. (ed.), *Style in Language.* MIT Press, Cambridge, pp. 350–77.

Juschka, D.M., 2008. Deconstructing the Eliadean paradigm: symbol. In: Braun, W. and McCutcheon, R.T. (eds), *Introducing Religion: essays in honor of Jonathan Z. Smith.* Equinox, London, pp. 163–77.

Keane, W., 2007. *Christian Moderns: freedom and fetish in the mission encounter.* University of California Press, Berkeley.

Kreinath, J., 2006. Semiotics. In: Kreinath, J., Snoek, J. and Stausberg, M. (eds), *Theorizing Rituals: issues, topics, approaches, concepts.* Brill, Leiden, pp. 429–70.

Lévi-Strauss, C., 1967. The structural study of myth. In: *Structural Anthropology,* Vol. 2. Trans. C. Jacobson and B.G. Schoepf. Doubleday, New York, pp. 206–31.

McCauley, R.N. and Lawson, E.T., 2002. *Bringing Ritual to Mind: psychological foundations of cultural forms.* Cambridge University Press, Cambridge.

Michaels, A., 2006. Ritual and meaning. In: Kreinath, J., Snoek, J. and Stausberg, M. (eds), *Theorizing Rituals: issues, topics, approaches, concepts.* Brill, Leiden, pp. 247–61.

Murphy, T., 2000. Discourse. In: Braun, W. and McCutcheon, R.T. (eds), *Guide to the Study of Religion.* Continuum: London, pp. 396–408.

—— 2003. Elements of a semiotic theory of religion. *Method & Theory in the Study of Religion* 15 (1), 48–67.

Parmentier, R., 1994. *Signs in Society: studies in semiotic anthropology.* Indiana University Press, Bloomington.

Schieffelin, B., Woolard, K. and Kroskrity, P., 1998. *Language Ideologies: practice and theory.* Oxford University Press, New York.

Sebeok, T., 1964. The structure and content of Cheremis charms. In: Hymes, D. (ed.), *Language in Culture and Society.* Harper and Row, New York, pp. 356–71.

—— 1976. *Contributions to the Doctrine of Signs.* Indiana University Press, Bloomington.

Silverstein, M., 1998. The improvisational performance of culture in realtime discursive practice. In: Sawyer, R.K. (ed.), *Creativity in Performance.* Ablex Publishing, Greenwich, CT, pp. 265–311.

Silverstein, M. and Urban, G., 1996. *Natural Histories of Discourse.* University of Chicago Press, Chicago.

Staal, F., 1996. *Ritual and Mantras: rules without meaning.* Motilal Banarsidass, Delhi.

Tambiah, S., 1985. *Culture, Thought, and Social Action.* Harvard University Press, Cambridge.

Tylor, E.B., 1903. *Primitive Culture.* 4th edn. John Murray, London.

Whitehouse, H., 2000. *Arguments and Icons: divergent modes of religiosity.* Oxford University Press, Oxford.

Yelle, R., 2001. Rhetorics of law and ritual: a semiotic comparison of the law of talion and sympathetic magic. *Journal of the American Academy of Religion* 69 (3): 627–47.

—— 2002. Poetic justice: rhetoric in Hindu ordeals and legal formulas. *Religion* 32 (3): 259–72.

—— 2003. *Explaining Mantras: ritual, rhetoric, and the dream of a natural language in Hindu tantra.* Routledge, London, New York.

—— 2006. To perform or not to perform?: a theory of ritual performance versus cognitive theories of religious transmission. *Method & Theory in the Study of Religion* 18 (4): 372–91.

—— 2010. Hindu law as performance: ritual and poetic elements in Dharmasastra. In: Lubin, T., Davis, D.R. and Krishnan, J.K. (eds), *Hinduism and Law: an introduction.* Cambridge University Press, Cambridge, pp. 183–92.

Further reading

Engler, S., 2009. Ritual theory and attitudes to agency in Brazilian spirit possession. *Method & Theory in the Study of Religion* 21(4): 460–92.

An interesting application of Peirce's notion of the index to analyze questions of agency in possession rituals.

Kreinath, J., 2006. Semiotics. In: Kreinath, J., Snoek, J. and Stausberg, M. (eds), *Theorizing Rituals: issues, topics, approaches, concepts.* Brill, Leiden, pp. 429–70.

Provides an excellent overview within the tradition of Peircean semiotic anthropology of some of the key issues in the semiotic analysis of ritual.

Struck, P.R., 2005. Symbol and symbolism. In: Jones, L. (ed.), *Encyclopedia of Religion*, 2nd edn, vol. 13, Macmillan Reference, New York, pp. 8906–15.

A survey of historical approaches to the symbol in religious studies that is useful despite lacking a semiotic perspective.

Key concepts

Arbitrariness: the fundamentally arbitrary nature of linguistic and other human signs, as recognized by both Saussurean structuralism and the Peircean concept of the symbol; the condition that requires the motivation of such signs for pragmatic effects; the recognition of such arbitrariness, as opposed to the naturalized view of signs indigenous to many semiotic ideologies.

Diagram or diagrammatic icon: a type of icon that depends on a structural resemblance between qualitatively different domains and/or behaviors, and that may be unfolded, like a map, in performance.

Indexical icon: a concept developed in Peircean semiotic analysis to describe the deployment of iconic relations, both internal and external to a text, in such a manner as to announce or reinforce relations of indexicality between a text and its context.

Performance: the pragmatic dimension of verbal and ritual expression, including both the orchestration of the expression itself and its range of effects such as intersubjective communication, cultural transmission, social influence and rhetorical persuasion.

Poetic function: the deployment of metricalization, repetition or metaphor in the syntactic sequence of language and other behaviors, with attendant semantic and pragmatic effects.

Pragmatics: the branch of linguistics and semiotics that focuses on the interaction between discourse and context; as contrasted with semantics and syntactics.

Redundancy: the deployment of repetition and diagrammatic icons to coordinate multiple semiotic modalities and enhance the pragmatic force of a message.

Self-referentiality: the manner in which discourse announces or refers to itself as an event of discourse, as demonstrated by metricalization and other aspects of the poetic function, and by ritualization.

Semiosis: the process of signification.

Semiotic (or linguistic) ideology: the more or less articulated theories of signification in a culture that affect the semiotic forms produced and their interaction with other domains of culture.

Related chapters

- Chapter 1.3 Epistemology
- Chapter 2.2 Conversation analysis
- Chapter 2.3 Discourse analysis
- Chapter 2.11 Hermeneutics
- Chapter 2.16 Philology
- Chapter 2.18 Structuralism

2.18

STRUCTURALISM

Seth D. Kunin

Chapter summary

- Structuralist theory suggests that all cultural objects will be shaped by unconscious underlying structure, analogous to language.
- Structuralist methodology has largely been applied to myth, but it is equally applicable to all aspects of religion and culture.
- It is useful to distinguish three different levels of structures: culture specific, culture group specific, and universal.
- Issues of transformation and agency raise important theoretical questions: the former raises the relative distinction between cold and hot societies; the latter is usefully addressed by the concept of jonglerie.
- Structuralist methods are analogous to excavation, with a central role for categorization and examining the relation between categories.

Introduction

French (or classical) **structuralism** (henceforth structuralism) provides a fascinating approach to the study of religion and culture.[1] Rather than discussing or explaining the details of particular practices, structuralism explores the abstract structures or rules that allow religions and cultures to work and to communicate meaningfully. Using the analogy of language, structuralism explains how meaningful cultural objects can be created, just as the study of grammar and syntax explain how meaningful sentences can be created. Structuralism allows for the understanding of a system as a whole, that is, how all the parts of the system work, rather than focusing on and attempting to explain any single part of the system.

Over the past 50 years structuralism has been applied to a wide range of mythological and cultural material—from Egypt to Amazonia. For example, much of the ground-breaking work of Lévi-Strauss was based on ethnographic material from North and South America; this work collectively known as the *Mythologiques* remains one of the most comprehensive structuralist analyses.[2]

While utilization of material from a wide range of cultures and ethnographic contexts would illustrate the applicability of structuralism, in this chapter we focus primarily on one ethnographic context—the biblical and Jewish. I do this for both a technical and non-technical reason. Structuralism seeks to provide a basis of explanation on an abstract level of a culture as a whole. This comprehensive aspect is best illustrated by using material from a single cultural context. Structuralism is also very useful as a comparative methodology—comparing abstract structures. The biblical/Jewish material provides a good basis for comparison with related religious traditions as for example Christianity and Mormonism. These comparisons also allow us to explore issues of transformation and restructuring.

The non-technical reason relates to the level of ethnographic or narrative information needed to understand the examples. If we were to use examples from a wide range of contexts, a significant amount of ethnographic contextualization would be required for each example. By using the much more familiar biblical/Jewish material much of this contextualization can be dispensed with.

Thus, in our theoretical and methodological discussions we introduce a range of examples from biblical/Jewish ethnography.[3] The examples taken singly provide an exemplification of the theoretical and methodological points. Taken as a whole they provide a wider analysis of biblical/Jewish underlying structure.

At its simplest level structuralism proposes that the mind is a structuring tool. As it engages with the world it provides abstract systems of order that allow the world to become comprehensible and meaningful. This process of structuring occurs as a collective process; structuralism assumes that human beings are inherently communal animals, and underlying structure is an artifact of the collective rather than the individual. This is not to say that individuals on their own would not engage in a structuring process, rather that structuralism is interested in the outcome of the collective rather than the individual processes. Each culture (or perhaps groups of cultures) will have a shared structure, which provides a fundamental basis for all of their cultural creations, including their way of conceptualizing the world both natural and supernatural. It is the structure that allows coherent and meaningful, communicative cultural objects to be both created and understood.

Levels of structure

While Lévi-Strauss never distinguishes between different levels of underlying structure, at least three levels are implicit in his work. I have found them useful in both the understanding of the theory as a whole and in its application to particular ethnographic material. Before moving into the levels themselves it is necessary to expand on the basic definition of structuralism given above.

Structuralist theory suggests that all cultural objects will be shaped by unconscious underlying structure. This proposition raises an important question about the source and nature of these structures. Given that a culture itself cannot literally think, its process of unconscious thinking must be an emergent phenomenon from the individual minds that make up that culture—thus underlying structure ultimately arises from a process of mind.[4] In using the word mind we are focusing on the non-biological aspects of the brain. Some structuralists, particularly Lévi-Strauss himself, have seen the structuring process as emerging from the biological structure of the brain (often focusing on its binary structure). While this may be the case, my approach is more provisional. It sees the mind as inherently structuring—and indeed this may be the most essential function of mind—leaving the question of the relation with the biological to future analysis and evidence. By focusing on mind rather than brain, we are able to see structure as more fluid and plastic, and move away from the binary aspect that has been the focus of many discussions.

As in the analogy with linguistics, structuralism focuses on the rules that organize and articulate simple elements (phonemes in the case of linguistics and **mythemes, cultemes** or **ritemes** in the case of structuralism) into more complex forms. Although structuralist methodology has largely been applied to myth it is equally applicable to all aspects of religion and culture. It is important in understanding this process to emphasize that it is independent from meaning—at its deepest level structuralism analyzes the organization of categories that are abstract and contentless. Structure refers to the articulation and relation between categories rather than the meaning of the categories or the elements included within them. This pattern, however, is fundamental to meaning. The particular structural pattern provides the basis for meaningful things to be said and understood—it creates the logical possibilities of meaning.

We can now move to a more technical discussion of these levels. A specific ethnographic example, Israelite food rules is introduced to clarify the role of the structural levels within the theoretical analysis and methodology. The biblical texts, particularly Leviticus and Deuteronomy, provide detailed discussions of Israelite food rules (mixed in with discussions of purity and sacrifice).

In a series of ground-breaking works, Mary Douglas developed a structuralist analysis that particularly explored the categorization of animals and the reasons why animals were considered *kosher* (fit for eating) or *treif* (forbidden for eating).[5] Our discussion here will draw on and develop some aspects of her analysis.

The **N(narrative)** level—technically not a level of structure—is the specific cultural object or set of objects being studied. It can be myths, stories, rituals or even everyday cultural practices. Both myths and rituals and many cultural practices have a diachronic aspect—the myth as a story has a certain narrative development and the ritual must be done in a certain order at a certain time. This diachronic aspect is a feature only of the N level. The levels of underlying structure are synchronic, i.e. without narrative progress or movement. The structure provides logical relations rather than temporal relations. The N level is highly cultural and context specific. It relates to the particular interests and needs of its time and place. As contexts change N changes to fit the new cultural context. This type of transformation, however, does not relate to underlying structure—the content changes but its structuring remains or may remain constant.

Depictions of the N level of Israelite food rules are found in *Leviticus* and *Deuteronomy*. These texts provide a narrative context for the laws and in some cases explanatory glosses for why a particular animal is permitted or forbidden. While our discussion focuses on the texts, the N level is also found in the Jewish ritual actions around the food rules, that is, the preparation and consuming of *kosher* food and the awareness of the rules associated with those practices.[6] N is conscious—the text consciously describes the rules. Individuals utilizing them will do so consciously and will often provide their own glosses for doing so—perhaps based on ideas of purity or wishing to act as commanded by god.

Underlying structure is divided into three levels. S^3 is the least abstract level of underlying structure. It is the level at which specific cultural content is categorized and set in relation by the more abstract levels of underlying structure. S^3 takes mythemes, ritemes or cultemes, the smallest elements out of which myths, rituals and cultural practices are created, and categorizes them based on the underlying structural rules.[7] S^3 underlies the N level, providing the elements and synchronically setting them into relation with each other (that is establishing their logical connections); this material then is put into the form of a diachronic narrative at the N level. It is important to emphasize that no individual element has a necessary meaning or value. This value is determined by the set of logical relations—in a sense the meaning of x will be different if it is the first element categorized or the second, and its meaning will also be determined by the nature of y—meaning in this context is entirely relational.

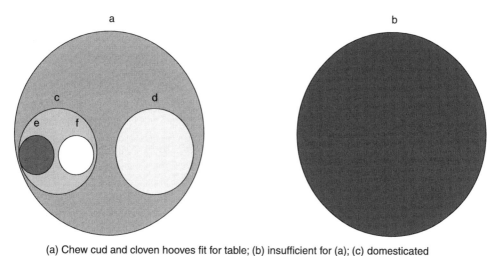

(a) Chew cud and cloven hooves fit for table; (b) insufficient for (a); (c) domesticated
(d) wild; (e) perfect–fit for sacrifice; (f) imperfect

Figure 2.18.1 Israelite food rules: land animals

N – Culture, and context specific

S3 – Culture specific
S2 – Culture Group Specific
S1 – Universal

Figure 2.18.2 Levels of underlying structure

In the context of food rules, S^3 consists of the different animals, ritemes and the relations established between them. Animals are divided into three groups—land, air and water—each of which needs to be looked at separately and each of which is structured in the same way. In the context of this discussion we will focus solely on land animals but the arguments presented work for all three groups. Within each group, animals are divided into two main categories, *kosher* and *treif*. *Kosher* land animals are clearly defined: in order to be fit for eating an animal must chew its cud and have cloven hooves. These elements are intrinsic and essential to each type of land animal. Either an animal by definition has them or it does not. All animals that have these elements are edible; all animals that lack either one or both are not. The system is defined by two categories that are by definition unbridgeable.

The narrative emphasis on the pig is an interesting, but often overemphasized aspect. While it is important on the narrative level, it is merely part of a system of categorization at S^3. The pig has cloven hooves but does not chew its cud; it is therefore by definition forbidden as food. This, however, begs the question of why the pig achieves such prominence at the narrative level. Archaeological evidence suggests that the pig was eaten in the area in which the Israelites lived. Thus, the pig represented a viable form of food and a possible means of distinguishing Israel from her neighbors on the narrative level. The pig also appears to be a bridge between the two categories. It has one necessary element but lacks the other. The pig creates the possibility that the two categories are bridgeable. By attributing to the pig significant negative value the structural aspects of the system, oppositional unbridgeable categories are emphasized, as is the opposition between Israel and her neighbors on the narrative level.

S^2 is the abstract **equation** that is given content at the S^3 level. The equation may have two or more categories that are set into relation with each other. Thus far structuralist analyses have described systems with two, three and four categories. While it may be that there are significantly more complex forms, arguably they may reduce to the simpler dyadic or triadic structures. Structuralist theory suggests that there are minimally three possible ideal relations between the categories. The concept of 'ideal type' indicates that the ideal form is an artifact of the model; each actual ethnographic example will fall along an axis of relations closer or further away from a particular ideal form.

The first form of relation is a negative relation (indicated as '–'). This relation indicates that the two categories are distinct and unbridgeable. If information x is in category A then it will never be in category B and vice versa. This is sometimes described as an oppositional relation. The second form is neutral (indicated by 'n'). In this form there is an overlap between the categories, indicating that some information in category A will also be in category B. The nature of the overlap and the value placed on movement between the categories will vary depending on the particular culture or ethnographic context. The final form is positive (indicated by '+'). In this form there are separate categories, for example A and B, but the content of the categories is identical, that is, anything in category A will also be in category B.

The key issue is not the specific content but the way in which the content is defined. Within Mormon structure, in which there are three categories (A, B and C), category A are gentiles or non-Mormons, category B is in some myths or rituals defined as 'converts to Mormonism', while category C is in these contexts defined as 'born Mormons'. The B and C categories, however, have the same content, as through the ritual of retrospective conversion all 'converts' are transformed into 'born mormons'.

Returning to the Israelite material we can move from the S^3 level to the S^2. If we abstract an equation from the material examined we can see that the underlying equation that structures the food rules is A–B, that is, anything in category A will not be in category B and vice versa, and there is no movement between the categories. Additionally we can see that there is a qualitative value placed on the two. Category A is positively **valenced** while category B is negatively valenced—this emphasizes the oppositional nature of the structure.[8]

There is, however, an additional step needed in the move between S^3 and S^2. Structuralist theory argues that the structure should be culturally pervasive, that is, most of the cultural objects in the cultural context should share the same underlying structure. Thus, we should be able to look at a wide variety of aspects of Israelite culture and find the same underlying structure.

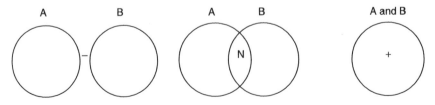

Figure 2.18.3 Ideal structural relations: negative, neutral and positive

One additional example from Israelite culture highlights the cultural pervasiveness of the structure identified here. Human beings are divided in a number of ways within Israelite thought. An initial distinction is between Israel and the nations. The nature of these categories is both intrinsic and unbridgeable. Israel is defined as being descended from Jacob via his sons. Anyone who is so descended is defined as an Israelite, anyone without this is defined as a non-Israelite.[9] Within the Israelite category the structure is replicated. Israel as a whole is divided into the Levites, defined as the descendants of the tribe of Levi and the rest of the Israelites (descended from the other sons of Jacob). As in the higher-level structure, the categories are similarly distinguished. If you are in one category you will never be in the other. This structure is further replicated within the Levites. The Levites are divided into the Cohanim (Priests) who are descended from Aaron, the brother of Moses, and the rest of the Levites. At each level the language of genealogy essentializes the categories and makes them both distinct and unbridgeable. In each case one of the categories, the Israelites, Levites and Cohanim is defined as holy, positively valenced, in relation to the other category at the same level. Thus relative to the nations Israel is holy, but relative to the Levites it is not holy. This second example suggests that the identification of A–B (with A positively valenced) is the underlying structure of Israelite society at the S^2 level.

S^1 is the universal aspect of underlying structure, that is, the common inheritance of all human beings. As we have indicated earlier in this chapter we can distinguish within S^1 both mind and brain. In relation to mind we suggest that S^1 is a general structuring principle, that is, a principle inherent in all human beings and therefore all human cultures in their interaction with the world. S^1 in relation to the brain rests on Lévi-Strauss' argument that there is a simple and abstract structure that derives from the structure of the brain, which underlies all particular structural forms. While it is possible that such a simple biologically based structure may exist, and indeed it is the holy grail of structuralism, there is not sufficient evidence to date to determine either its nature or whether it actually exists. There is, however, significant evidence for the structuring role of mind, and thus it is that aspect that I emphasize in relation to S^1.

Structural transformation and the role of agency

Two related issues are apparent with the model of underlying structure presented thus far: that of **transformation** and the role of individual **agency**. The model seems to present a static model of structure that does not provide a clear explanation of either transformation of myths or mythological elements between cultures and even more importantly within a single culture over time.

The issue of transformation between cultures is a key aspect of Lévi-Strauss' discussion in the *Mythologiques*. His analysis traces the transformation of mythemes and underlying structure between neighboring cultures within North and South America—these transformations would fit into our view of inter-related culture groups. One key aspect of his argument is that these neighboring societies in many cases share common mythemes, but due to structural differences, utilize the mythemes and the narrative level of myths (which appear on the surface to be similar) in very different structural ways.

The fundamental argument is that structure is in effect constitutive of culture (shaping and shaped by). As one moves between societies cultural changes are reflected in structural changes. The implication of this is that when one society borrows or inherits the myths of a neighboring society, the myth will be retold and restructured to fit the needs of the society in which it is found. This logic can also be extended to structure within a 'single culture' as it transforms and moves through time. As the society changes (due to internal and external pressures) the myths, rituals and cultural elements may be restructured (even if only slightly) to fit the new cultural context. I will return to the aspects of culture that facilitate transformation below.

An example of mythological elements from the Hebrew Bible helps exemplify this process of transformation between cultures. If we take the Book of Genesis from an abstract perspective, we can highlight a number of related mythemes that are found in almost every biblical narrative—e.g. divine birth/natural birth; death and rebirth. These mythemes are valenced by the emphasis on genealogy. The key figures are all born with the assistance of god—many texts emphasize the barrenness of the mother and the age of the father and mother to suggest that these are cases of divine birth without natural assistance; they also have a symbolic death and rebirth (as in the symbolic sacrifice of Isaac) and the texts emphasize the genealogical aspect of Israel's self-definition. The key aspect is the valence of each of these mythological elements—the death and rebirth are symbolic and the genealogy is real.

The same elements are found in the New Testament as key aspects of the Passion narrative—the divine birth in the virgin birth texts and the death and rebirth in the crucifixion texts. The use of these mythemes and their valence is transformed. In the New Testament divine birth is actual, Jesus is depicted as the son of god in a literal rather than a symbolic sense. Similarly the death/rebirth mytheme is also transformed from symbolic to actual. The nature of these transformations is highlighted by the valencing of kinship. In the New Testament kinship is symbolic rather than actual.

The differences in underlying structure and the relation of the mythological elements can be looked at from two different perspectives. On the cultural level the two communities have different models of self that have implications for the valencing of the mythological elements. The Israelite model is genealogical, placing strong emphasis on clear and defined lines of descent. This self understanding would be undermined if either divine birth or rebirth were real—they would deny the necessity of actual genealogical descent. Within the New Testament community symbolic kinship based on shared faith is the primary model of self. Within such a model it is useful and perhaps necessary to deny actual kinship. Thus divine birth and rebirth (resurrection) are real rather than symbolic.

We can also explain the differences utilizing the S^2 equation that can be derived from this analysis. Within both communities there is a community defined as holy, or in effect the children of god (category A). This category is defined as being either divinely born or divinely reborn. Category A is set in relation to category B—defined in opposition to A as individuals/nations who are not the children of god, that is, not divinely born or reborn. The aspects of genealogy and faith represent the relation between the categories. Genealogy is an intrinsic essentialized concept; it indicates that the categories are also intrinsic and essentialized— clearly defined and unbridgeable. Genealogy does not allow movement between categories. Faith, however, is a transformative concept. It implies movement between the categories— one gains faith, one is not born with it. Thus, the analysis suggests that while the Israelite material is defined by an A-B structure, New Testament material is defined by an A n B (that is, a neutral relation between the categories) structure. The New Testament model allows mediation between the categories and thereby facilitates movement from non-Christian to Christian.

Transformation of underlying structure as a myth or other cultural object moves between cultures is thus clearly explicable within classical structuralism. Such transformations will occur when a myth is retold in a new cultural context, and even where the myth is translated into a new language in a new cultural context. We have already suggested that diachronic cultural development will have similar impact on underlying structure. Cultural change, however, at the level of underlying structure raises some theoretical questions.

Cold and hot societies

Lévi-Strauss' work focused on societies that were perceived of as changing only slowly over time, and some of his discussions suggest that structuralism is only useful in relation to such societies. This argument is indicated by his distinction between **cold societies** and **hot societies** (see Lévi-Strauss 1966: 233–34; Lévi-Strauss 1958: 219–34). Cold societies are those that do not perceive themselves as changing. They see themselves as existing in an almost timeless space, with little change or cultural development. In line with this view they often have a circular rather than a linear understanding of history. The implication of Lévi-Strauss' discussion is that these societies change very slowly. Hot societies are those that perceive themselves to be in a constant flux. They have a strong sense of transformation in time and a linear model of history—a model of history that emphasizes change. Their self-perception is matched by rapid cultural change and thus a greater degree of structural change.

This distinction, however, has often been overemphasized. Like other similar models it presents ideal types. All actual societies will only be relatively hot or cold. In a sense cold societies are more amenable to structuralist analysis due only to the fact of relatively slower transformation. There is thus more consistent material for analysis. Hot societies are a problem as their more fluid nature makes structuralist analysis more difficult. If, however, we view structuralism as a theory of transformation and a method of explaining transformation (in light of the above discussion) then this preference for cold societies becomes unnecessary. The implication that cold societies are unchanging is equally problematic as it might prevent the analysis from seeing the transformations (even if only in emphasis) that occur both at the narrative and structural levels. Cultural transformation, whether in hot or cold societies, raises an additional question in relation to structure. If structure is unconscious and is found and replicated in all cultural objects, and shapes the thinking of the society and individuals within it, how can this structure be transformed? One clear aspect of transformation is due to external pressures. If cultural change is imposed from the outside then we might expect it to impact the nature of underlying structure if the transformation is significant and long lasting. This, however, does not explain structural transformation due to cultural changes from within a society or which come from external influence but lack imposition.

The overly static understanding of structure may arise from a rather static and monolithic understanding of culture. If culture were largely unified and bounded, then internal structural transformation and therefore significant cultural transformation would be almost impossible. If, however, we look at culture in a more dynamic way we begin to map out possible mechanisms of change. Unlike many traditional depictions of culture that emphasize the unity and cohesiveness of culture, cultures are much more complex and dynamic. They comprise a wide range of different sub-cultures and formal or informal groups. Each of these groups may have slightly different perceptions of themselves, and thus despite sharing or largely sharing the same underlying structure, they may unconsciously emphasize or de-emphasize different aspects of the structural model. These slight changes can, over time, lead to structural transformation.

The aspect of **boundedness** is also significant. Many discussions tended to see cultures as defined and bounded entities with relatively strong boundaries between neighboring cultures. Ethnographic evidence suggests that this concept of boundedness is largely artificial. The boundaries between groups are fuzzy—overlapping and moving into each other. Thus, the coming together of different structural models, particularly but not exclusively at these fuzzy boundaries, may be a strong factor influencing the possibility of structural change. It may be that the key difference between hot and cold societies is directly related to the complexity and number of these sub-cultures and fuzzy boundaries with neighboring communities.

Agency and *jonglerie*

The issue of agency is closely related to possibilities of transformation. Critics of structuralism suggested that due to the unconscious and apparently static nature of underlying structure there was little or no room for individual creativity or for individuals to be agents of change. Within, however, the model of culture proposed here agency takes on an increasingly important role. Structure includes within it several areas in which agency may play a role. All structures include a degree of fluidity. Thus, for example, even a negative relation may have a degree of mediation, areas in which overlap of categories may occur.[10] These 'fuzzy' areas can be differentially emphasized or privileged both by different groups and individuals. While this process of emphasis or privileging is unconscious, it provides a location for creativity. This 'fuzziness' is further strengthened by the nature of culture itself. The multiplication of sub-groups provides additional structural possibilities, as do the fuzzy boundaries of communities.

I suggest that *jonglerie* (Kunin 2004, 2009) is a further area in which agency and a more significant conscious aspect can come into play. This concept, which relates to the fluidity of identity, describes the process by which individuals differentially privilege aspects of their cultural inheritance (and thereby different aspects of structure), based on context, emotion and individual choice. This is not a random process, but rather one in which individuals consciously and unconsciously select aspects to emphasize or de-emphasize based on their self-understanding. *Jonglerie* is a process of structural improvisation and as such it is the pivot point between unconscious underlying structure and individual conscious self-understanding. It describes the move from the cognitive realm to that of practice—of actual lived experience. **Bricolage** is the process of unconscious creation of cultural items; *jonglerie* is the conscious/unconscious utilization and improvisation on these objects.

The nature of cultural objects as products of bricolage facilitates the range of possibilities for creativity suggested by *jonglerie*. This process can be exemplified through an ethnographic example from crypto-Judaism. Crypto-Jews are individuals who believe that their ancestors were forced to convert from Judaism to Catholicism in Spain and Portugal in the 14th and 15th centuries.[11] Despite this conversion, some aspects of Jewish identity and practices may have been passed down and have become the inheritance of their descendants living today. Modern crypto-Jews are the perfect example of fuzzy cultural boundaries. They bring together a wide range of cultures, Spanish, Mexican, American, Jewish and Catholic to name a few, and are constantly negotiating among these alternatives in the construction of self-identification. Their rituals and practice created through the process of bricolage bring together many of these cultures, and are thus fertile ground for *jonglerie*, that is, cultural improvisation.

Many crypto-Jewish families share a common practice, performed on Friday night. They describe lighting two candles accompanied by the recitation of the rosary. This practice apparently brings together the Jewish practice of lighting candles to welcome the Sabbath and the Catholic practice of recitation of the rosary. Explanations by the families helps understand the structural aspects of this ritual and the role of *jonglerie* (which in this case comes in the interpretation rather than improvisation in the act itself).

One family stated that they saw this practice as being part of their Jewish inheritance. The candle lighting was the important (privileged) aspect of the practice. They only recited the rosary, they said, to prevent any neighbors from thinking it was a Jewish practice. This interpretation clearly privileges the Jewish aspect of the practice (and identity), presenting an oppositional structure between the Jewish and Christian components.

A second family (cousins of the first) describing the same ritual stated that the Christian aspect was really the important bit. They thought that the candles perhaps reflected some remembrance of Jewish past but the important aspect was the rosary. Their depiction was in some senses structurally the opposite of the first, but there was a greater degree of mediation with the Jewish aspect not being strongly negative. Other families fell in between with greater or lesser emphasis on the two elements.

This example highlights the possibilities for improvisation and *jonglerie* inherent in a single area of ritual practice. While the example looks at variation among several different families or individuals, I have seen similar processes at work within individuals themselves. My ethnography suggests that as individual's self-understanding or identity transformed over time and context they might differentially privilege or emphasize different aspects of their past, bringing into play slightly different variations of underlying structure shaped by the conscious and unconscious articulation of identity, practice and underlying structure.

Methodology

To this point I have presented some of the key aspects of structuralist theory, exemplified by ethnographic examples. The discussion has implicitly highlighted aspects of the method of analysis. In this section I pull together these elements to highlight the key aspects of the methodology itself. I also present the analysis of four crypto-Jewish stories to exemplify the issues.

In a sense, the best metaphor for structuralist methodology is excavation. We start with the narrative level of the myth, ritual or practice and through a methodical process dig down through the levels of underlying structure. As we dig deeper we gain more fundamental information and ultimately, if successful, come to the human mind (or even brain) itself.

The N level presents us with a narrative or ritual flow in which time and character development play an important role. In order to move to issues of structural significance we need to put aside these aspects and focus on the key relations out of which the narrative/ritual is built—it is often useful as a starting point to see these relations as an individual or object and a relation (or non-relation) connecting to another individual or object. In some narratives all of the elements and aspects may be structurally significant; in others some may be added to assist the narrative or ritual flow but be structurally insignificant. Equally, one or another mytheme may be the significant defining element (the one that defines the relations with all the others). This element may relate to the apparent hero of the narrative or to another character. The narrative of the 'Sacrifice of Isaac' (Genesis 22) provides a good case in point. The narrative includes a number of characters, with Abraham being apparently the main actor in the text. If, however, we look at the focus of the action, it is all focused on Isaac, and thus in a structuralist analysis it would be important to begin with Isaac as the structural focus.

Case study[12]

Narrative 1
My grandmother told us many stories about our ancestors in Spain who had to flee to the mountains and stay there. They were hiding from the inquisitors. There was

a rule that they had to come down from the mountains to attend Mass. It was a rule. It had been a month since these two men had been to church. The two men, who were sheep-herders, that's what they could do in those days, decided not to take a bath on Sunday—they would smell just like mother nature would, the smells of sheep, horses, and whatever else they had up there. So they went to church to obey what had to be obeyed in the village. As they went into the church they saw two plates held by the angels, one on each side of the aisle as they were looking at the altar. The plates held holy water. The sheep-herders decided to act as if they were not too smart. So they said, 'ooh . . . here is a washing place'. They took off their shirts and started scrubbing their elbows, their necks and behind their ears. The sacristan said, 'Oh my goodness, it's almost time for Mass, we came to light the candles on the altar; you are disturbing us; get out of here you crazy men'. That is how they got out of attending Mass that day.

This narrative includes a number of elements that may be of structural significance. The main focus of the narrative and its key structural elements are the two sheep-herders. They are set in a number of relations in the text. The primary one is in opposition to the sacristan, as that is the key actional aspect of the text. They are also set in relation to the teller of the story as 'ancestors', both of whom are defined as belonging to the same category, that is Jews or crypto-Jews. The Christian aspects are also brought together in a higher category of 'inquisitors', which from the context is a negative category. Additionally the geographic areas in the text are set in opposition, with the mountains (perhaps nature) being identified with the Jews and the towns (perhaps culture) being identified with the Christians.

The narrative also poses a structural question that is highly relevant to crypto-Jewish identity. Can one both be a crypto-Jew and a Christian: that is the narrative expression of a structural question—what is the nature of mediation between the two categories—are they oppositional or mediated? The use of the holy water for profane purposes, the ejection from the church before the Mass indicates that the categories are oppositional rather than mediated. Though the question itself may suggest that there is a degree of ambiguity and thus some degree of mediation.

Once a preliminary analysis has been done on a single narrative, the analysis must be broadened out to look at a wider range of narrative material to determine if the structural elements highlighted are correct. Thus, for example, looking at other myths from the same culture that have very different narrative forms or looking at other forms of narrative like oral history or folktales. The analysis could then be widened to look at cultural material in the form of rituals or other practices. An individual narrative may include only part of the structure; it may also present an inverted or transformed version of the structure. Analysis of a wider range of material corrects for these possibilities. It also allows for the analysis to move beyond the S^3 level, by allowing for a greater degree of abstraction.

The method of analyzing the mythemes involves two inter-related processes: **categorization** and examination of the **relation between categories**. The first of these processes involves categorizing the mythemes as found in a number of different myths or narratives and placing them in appropriate categories. This is also analogous to looking at sentences and picking out similar parts of speech—a category of subject, objects, or perhaps nouns and verbs. The second process involves looking at the relationship between these categories: e.g., how are subjects and objects related to create meaningful sentences? The key aspect of the analysis is to determine the valency or the quality of the relations, that is positive or negative and all of the variations between these ideal types.

Narrative 2

When my great-grandmother Isabelle was born, her family lived in the mountains—there was no church nearby. They had to take her to Santa Fe to be baptized.
They got into a wagon and started the journey. On the way, they hit a bump and my
grandmother fell out—no one knew it. They got to the church and could not find
my grandmother. They had come so far, so the priest put her in the book anyway.
They started back, and there on the side of the trail was my great-grandmother, as
happy as could be. So they went home.

Narrative 3

This is about a special herb my mother gave us. When I was little we lived in
Albuquerque, and we had to go to church. We did not want anyone to know we
were Jews. Before we went to church on Sunday, our mother gave us some of the
herb from a bag; I don't know what it was. We went to church, but just before the
father gave the bread and the wine we all became violently sick and had to go out. I
guess my mother did not want us to eat that bread.

Narrative 4

A priest who had tried for a long time to convert a Jew to Catholicism is asked by
the Jew to explain the symbolism of different flowers in the priest's garden. Each
flower symbolizes a different Christian faith, and, of course, the most beautiful one
symbolizes Catholicism. When asked what a blooming cactus symbolizes, the priest
reluctantly replies that it symbolizes the Jewish religion. The Jew then remarks, 'It
may be so, but I can use all those beautiful flowers in the place of toilet paper. I dare
you to do the same with the cactus flower'.

These three narratives allow us to flesh out our understanding of the mythological elements.
Before analyzing them it is interesting to note that the first three stories, although structurally
very similar, are three different genres of narrative. The first is a folktale, the second is told as
family history and the third is a personal memory. The fourth narrative is a folktale with an
apparently different narrative form. In spite of these different forms, all are structured and,
indeed, structured in similar ways.

Narratives two and three contain similar structural elements to those found in narrative
one. In both cases the main figure is the grandmother (as baby) and the girls and their mother
are set into structural opposition to the Church. As in narrative one, there is a suggestion of
mediation, via baptism in two and the Mass in three. In both cases the mediation is denied or
downplayed—the baby is not actually baptized and the family is forced to leave prior to
communion. In narrative two we find the same structural opposition in the landscape. The
mountains are associated with the crypto-Jews and the town with the Catholics.

Narrative 4 has a very different narrative form. Its structural elements are similar. It has
two key foci, the Jew (in opposition to the Padre) and the cactus (in opposition to the other
plants). The narrative poses the possibility of mediation through the project of converting the
Jew and rejects this possibility through the narrative—like the other narratives using humor
as a means for the rejection. The plants may encapsulate the geographic opposition found in
the previous narratives with the cactus representing the wild and natural representing the
Jews, and the cultivated, cultural plants representing the Christians.

The analysis of these four stories suggests that the structural elements found in narrative
one are indeed the salient structural elements, and that similar elements and particularly a
similar underlying structure are found in other crypto-Jewish narratives, particularly those

that have a very different narrative structure. They key point is the structural relations, not the way the narrative chooses to play them out. We might extend our discussion to ritual—looking at the elements of rituals in the same way as elements of narrative. For example, the candle lighting described above. The candle lighting has the same structural elements and in one case (the first discussed) the same oppositional structure (though with some mediation). The other uses of the ritual suggest a higher degree of fluidity than comes through in these narratives.

The next stage in the analysis is one of abstraction. It brings together the material examined above and seeks to determine if there is a single structural equation that unites the material. It also seeks to determine the range of variation—how are different aspects of the equation privileged differently; what are the range of structural possibilities in the system? It is sometimes helpful to chart the categories isolated in the second phase of the analysis and examine if the chart reveals a common structuring principle.

The material examined in the case study suggest that the structural equation is composed of two categories—A and B. The first category is generally privileged while the second category is relatively oppositional, that is negatively valenced. This structure is consistent in all the narratives and in one version of the ritual. The material suggests that there is some degree of mediation but this is relatively low level and problematic. The variations on the ritual, however, suggest that crypto-Jewish culture includes a much larger degree of variation in structure than might be expected. It is possible that this is due to the diffuse nature of the community—it is highly individualistic or family oriented with very few features or structures bringing the community together on a wider level.

The analysis can then be compared with other structuralist analyses as part of the process of trying to understand the deeper cognitive or biological aspects of the structuring principle. It should be noted that the method of analysis can be used on different levels. For some research it is sufficient to stop at the identification of mythological elements and the ways in which they are related and combined, and other discussions may choose to examine the material on a more abstract level. To a degree this may depend on the questions being asked or the other approaches being used alongside. Nonetheless, structuralism is based on an understanding of the mind and of culture and any analysis of no matter what level should be informed by the theoretical implications and issues.

Notes

1 This form of structuralism refers specifically to the work of Claude Lévi-Strauss. It is, however, nuanced by other recent Structuralist analyses as for example by Mary Douglas (1978, 1984), Edmund Leach (1970; Leach and Aycock 1983), Stephen Hugh-Jones (1979), Jonathan Miles Watson (2009) and Seth Kunin (2004, 2009). Later forms are also specifically influenced by the work of Pierre Bourdieu (1977).

2 The Mythologiques refers collectively to four classic texts published by Lévi-Strauss: *Le cru et le cuit* (1964), *Du Miel aux cendres* (1966), *L'Origin des manières de table* (1968) and *L'homme nu* (1971).

3 The structuralist analyses of the biblical material come from a number of sources. The analysis of the food rules draws its inspiration from Mary Douglas (1978, 1984). The discussions of narrative and space and some aspects of the food rules derive from Kunin (1998, 2004). The material on crypto-Judaism derives from Kunin (2009).

4 Culture, however, plays a significant role in this process; it is both structured by mind and equally provides the basis for the shared structure which is then utilized by mind. We are suggesting that mind and perhaps brain provide the structuring tool. This tool is then utilized by culture, through the actions of the individuals that make up that culture to create culture specific forms of structure. Individuals who are born into the culture are enculturated into these structures, and through this process culture in effect structures mind.

5 Douglas 1978, 1984; see also Kunin 2004.

6 Jewish laws of Kashrut are based in part on biblical texts, but also largely derive from rabbinic interpretations developed over the subsequent centuries.

7 Lévi-Strauss utilizes the term bricolage to describe the process by which cultural objects are created. The *bricoleur* is analogous to the tinker. Like the tinker he collects unwanted items and saves them for later use. The items may be parts of old machines or other found objects. If at some later date he is asked to make a sewing machine he may take a bit of an airplane, a washer-dryer and a skateboard and put them together to fit the new requirement. The *bricoleur* does something similar on the cultural level. He borrows items from cultures roundabout and from his own culture's past. These elements may be narrative elements or mythemes like virgin birth or resurrection. When there is a requirement for a new myth, the bricoleur takes these found elements and puts them together in a way that relates to and is organized by the underlying structure. It is the structure that is fundamental; the objects used to give it form are merely those that were available. A key difference between the *bricoleur* and the tinker is that of consciousness. The tinker acts consciously while the cultural *bricoleur* does not. Thus the fact that a particular narrative function or form is used is largely structurally irrelevant; it is a found object.

8 The term valence is used in structuralist analysis to describe the quality of an element or a relation. Thus in an ideal sense elements can be positively or negatively valenced. The valence of an element is a factor in the nature of mediation that can be found between elements. In this sense valencing can only be used to describe a relation; it is never something intrinsic to a particular element.

9 In later developments of Israelite/Jewish culture the definition of descent moves from the patrilineal to the matrilineal lines. In spite of this change, the logic of the structure remains the same: if you are descended from a Jewish mother you are a Jew; if you are not so descended, you are part of the nations.

10 Thus, even within the strongly negative Israelite structure movement into the Israelite category through some form of conversion was possible. Although the system preserves its structure by reconceptualizing these moves as non-moves, it is possible to emphasize them differently and use them as a means of opening movement between categories.

11 Crypto-Judaism in general can refer to any individual who has Judaism as a hidden or secret aspect of identity. In the context of our discussion it refers specifically to individuals within the Spanish and Portuguese diaspora. The ethnography on crypto-Judaism is derived from Kunin (2009).

12 This material is taken from my ethnographic research among the crypto-Jews of New Mexico (Kunin 2009). The first three narratives were collected by me. The fourth narrative is taken from Juan Bautista Rael, *Cuentos Españoles de Colorado y de Nuevo Méjico: Spanish Tales from Colorado and New Mexico*, Stanford, CA 1977 [1957], p. 806.

References

Bourdieu, P., 1977. *Outline of a Theory of Practice*. Cambridge University Press, Cambridge.

Douglas, M., 1978. *Implicit Meanings: essays in anthropology*. Routledge, London.

—— 1984 [1966] *Purity and Danger*. Ark, London.

Hugh-Jones, S., 1979. *The Palm and the Pleides: initiation and cosmology in northwest Amazonia*. Cambridge University Press, Cambridge.

Hugh-Jones, S. and Laidlaw, J., 2000. *The Essential Edmund Leach: volume 2 culture and human nature*. Yale University Press, New Haven.

Hymes, D., 1977. The 'wife' who 'goes out' like a man: reinterpretation of a Clackmass Chinook myth. In: Dolgin, J. *et al. Symbolic Anthropology: a reader in the study of symbols and meanings*. Columbia University Press, New York, pp. 221–44.

Jobling, D., 1978. *The Sense of Biblical Narrative: structural analysis in the Hebrew Bible*. JSOT Press, Sheffield.

Kunin, S., 1995. *The Logic of Incest: a structural analysis of Hebrew mythology*. Sheffield Academic Press, Sheffield.

—— 1998. *God's Place in the World*. Cassell, London.

—— 2004. *We Think What We Eat: neo-structuralist analysis of Israelite food rules and other cultural and textual practices*. T&T Clark International, London.

—— 2009. *Juggling Identities: identity and authenticity among the Crypto-Jews*. Columbia University Press, New York.

Lang, B. (ed.), 1985. *Anthropological Approaches to the Old Testament*. SPCK, London.

Leach, E., 1969. *Genesis as Myth*. Jonathan Cape, London.

—— 1970. *Claude Lévi-Strauss*. Viking Press, New York.

Leach, E. and Aycock, A., 1983. *Structuralist Interpretations of Biblical Myth*. Cambridge University Press, Cambridge.

Lévi-Strauss, C., 1958. *Anthropologie Structurale I*. Plon, Paris.

—— 1962. *La Pensée Sauvage*. Plon, Paris.

—— 1964. *Le cru et le cuit*. Plon, Paris.

—— 1966. *Du Miel aux cendres*. Plon, Paris.

—— 1968. *L'Origin des manières de table*. Plon, Paris.

—— 1971. *L'homme nu*. Plon, Paris.

—— 1973. *Anthropologie Structurale II*. Plon, Paris.

Macksey, R. and Donato, E. (eds), 1970. *The Structuralist Controversy*. Johns Hopkins University Press, Baltimore.

Miles Watson, J., 2009. *Welsh Mythology: a neo-structuralist analysis*. Cambria Press, Amherst.

Pace, D., 1983. *Claude Lévi-Strauss: the bearer of ashes*. ARK, Boston.

Propp, V., 1984. *Theory and History of Folktale*. Manchester University Press, Manchester.

Rael, J.B., 1957. *Cuentos Españoles de Colorado y de Nuevo Méjico: Spanish tales from Colorado and New Mexico*. Stanford University Press, Stanford, CA.

Scholes, R., 1974. *Structuralism in Literature*, New Haven: Yale University Press.

Sturrock, J., 1979. *Structuralism and Since: from Lévi-Strauss to Derrida*. Oxford University Press, Oxford.

Turner, T., 1985. Narrative structure and mythopoesis: a critique and reformulation of structuralist concepts of myth, narrative and poetics. *Arethusa* 10(1): 103–63.

Further reading

Hugh-Jones, S., 1979. *The Palm and the Pleides: initiation and cosmology in Northwest Amazonia*. Cambridge University Press, Cambridge.

Hugh-Jones's ethnography provides an extended structuralist analysis that demonstrates the applicability of the methodology to a complex ethnographic context.

Leach, E., 1970. *Claude Lévi-Strauss*. Viking Press, New York.

Leach provides a useful introduction to structuralism which is both clear and approachable.

Leach, E. and Aycock, A., 1983. *Structuralist Interpretations of Biblical Myth*. Cambridge University Press, Cambridge.

This volume presents a range of short analyses of biblical material and highlights the range of applicability of structuralist analysis to both Judaism and Christianity.

Lévi-Strauss, C., 1963 [1958]. *Structural Anthropology*. Vol. 2, Basic Books, New York.

This volume presents some key papers on different aspects of structuralism. Chapters 9, 10 and 11 are particularly pertinent to the study of religion.

—— 1976 [1973]. *Structural Anthropology* Vol. I., University of Chicago Press, Chicago.

Part three of this volume, 'Mythology and Ritual', includes additional seminal articles.

Miles Watson, J., 2009. *Welsh Mythology: A Neo-Structuralist Analysis*. Cambria Press, Amherst.

Miles Watson presents a beautifully written monograph on Welsh mythology, which provides a fascinating introduction to that mythic system while also developing structuralist theory in new and important directions.

Key concepts

Agency: the ability of individuals to exercise conscious choice and action.

Boundedness: the extent that a culture is clearly defined and has strong external boundaries in relation to neighboring cultures. Modern anthropology increasingly sees these boundaries as largely artificial and emphasizes the fuzziness and permeability of boundaries.

Bricolage: the unconscious process whereby myths or other cultural objects are created. It is analogous to the work of a tinker, who takes elements available (mythemes, ritemes or cultemes) and organizes them in a structurally coherent pattern—this pattern is then the basis for a story, ritual or cultural object.

Categorization: structuralism is largely interested in the process by which a society organizes or categorizes different objects or elements. Thus, for example, in the context of Jewish material it is interested in the broad categories of *kosher* (fit for eating) and *treif* (not fit for eating), rather than the specific elements that are included in these categories.

Cold society: an ideal type of society that is relatively culturally unified and static and is not conscious of change or transformation.

Cultemes: the basic units out of which other cultural artifacts are made.

Equation: structuralism utilizes abstract equations to depict the structure of a given culture. This equation or structure is seen as the basis for all cultural objects within that culture. A–B is an example of this type of equation. It indicates that there are two categories, A and B, and that there is a negative relation between them. The negative relation indicates that the categories are mutually exclusive.

Hot society: an ideal type of society, which is culturally complex and dynamic and is strongly conscious of change or transformation.

Jonglerie: this refers to the process by which an individual consciously and unconsciously emphasizes different structural elements. It is largely a process of privileging or depriviliging elements depending on context and self-understanding.

Mythemes: the basic units out of which myths are constructed. The units are often composed of a relation between two elements, or an action associated with an actor.

N(narrative) level: the diachronic level of a story (or a ritual). It is the way a story develops in time from its beginning to end.

Relation between categories: structuralism sees no element or category of having intrinsic meaning, or meaning in relation to itself. Categories and elements gain meaning by being set in relation to other categories, and the meaning can change depending on the nature of the other category.

Ritemes: analogous elements that are the basic units out of which rituals are constructed.

Structuralism: the study of the abstract structures or rules that allow religions and cultures to work and to communicate meaningfully.

Transformation: the set of processes by which underlying structure changes over time. These processes are due to both internal choices and external pressures.

Valence: the quality attributed to a category—minimally positive or negative. If a category is positively valenced then its elements (and the category as a whole) will be privileged in relation to the other categories set in relation to it.

Related chapters

- Chapter 1.2 Comparison
- Chapter 1.3 Epistemology
- Chapter 2.8 Field research: Participant observation
- Chapter 2.11 Hermeneutics
- Chapter 2.17 Semiotics

2.19

STRUCTURED OBSERVATION

Michael Stausberg

Chapter summary

- Some types of actions and activities are difficult to communicate verbally, and self-recall and self-report are often not very reliable as sources of information; (structured) observation is one possible remedy.
- Structured observation is planned, scheduled observation conducted in 'natural' field settings.
- It requires a standardized observation protocol (coding scheme).
- The development and subsequent use of the observation protocol is part of the research process (typical stages of which are described).
- Structured observation works with different roles in the field, and some fields provide 'natural' observer roles.
- There are two main conditions of structured observation: open/overt and unobtrusive (sometimes covert) observing.
- Structured observation, especially in the covert form, raises research ethical issues concerning informed consent and privacy.
- Structured observation focuses on selected aspects of totalities.
- Units of observations are acts, actors, objects and places.
- Observation is either made continuously or in given periods (time sampling).
- Shortcomings and problems include forms of observer bias, the use of scarce resources (time and energy), the selected character of data and its dissociation from the meaning of the observed data.
- Structured observation can provide highly valuable data, but typically works best in combination with other methods.

Introduction

Like comparing, observing is a fundamental human activity, and just as comparison, observation is embedded in several research methods. Observing is part of live interviews (even if the observation part is rarely addressed in the transcriptions, eventual citations and analysis) and focus groups; it is crucial for many experimental studies (for the most part covertly). Participant observation is the core activity in fieldwork. In the arena of fieldwork, fieldworkers have increasingly left their position of uncommitted marginal observers to become engaged participants.[1] The observational part of fieldwork and participation covers a wide range of actions and sensory perceptions that transcend the merely visual: smells, sounds, physical objects, tastes, temperature, climate and physical contact can appear more significant than visual input in given situations in the field.

In most fieldwork projects, formal interviews—be they structured, semi-structured or unstructured—make up only a minor part, sometimes even a fraction, of interaction between the fieldworker and his hosts; whereas observation, including self-observation, is an ongoing activity (documented extensively in field notes, it is hoped, with cameras, etc.). Given that actions and talk naturally go together, interviews and observation should ideally complement each other rather than being separated out from each other in research; paralinguistic dimensions of talk such as body language and displays, touching and proxemics (i.e. the distance between people as they interact), facial expression and looks, gestures, laughter and tone, speed, rate, pitch and tremor of voice can all be important carriers of meaning. In cases where talk is not of interest (as in the study of metalinguistic communication) or even absent (as among primates, young infants or in contexts where people are not supposed to talk, such as among certain monks) observation is the only available strategy (Dallos 2006: 132).

The limits of verbal communication and the distortion of self-report and recall data

There are several types of social situation that can be communicated and understood only to a limited degree, if at all, based solely on verbal information. Consider the following examples.[2] Cooking practices, games, and rituals are often very difficult to learn and transmit verbally. In education, explicit statements often do not accurately reflect actual practice, or covert messages transmitted by behavior can be in conflict with explicitly stated (overt) ideas. For these kinds of practices, observation appears to be a more promising methodological approach than verbal statements by informants. Moreover, the reliability of verbal information about actions and behaviors is often problematic. For example, verbal communication is often defensive and provides rationalizations and other types of justifications rather than mirroring actual behavior. Miscommunication based on semantic or pragmatic misunderstandings and memory distortion and selectivity are not uncommon. Memory and communication involves (re-)construction, e.g. in the interview context, as much as retrieving 'stored' information. As we all know from experience, time budgets are easily miscalculated and misreported.

Despite these problems, many studies of behavior of people, including their religious actions and activities, continue to be based on self-reports (e.g. interviews, questionnaires), even though research has shown that self-reports are notoriously problematic and even unreliable as sources for the actual behavior of people. There appears to be an error rate of between 50 per cent and 80 per cent in self-reported behavior when compared with results from direct observation (Johnson and Sackett 1998: 302). Unless the research is interested in the patterns structuring the recall of data rather than on actual past behavior, drawing conclusions based on self-reported recall of behavior can therefore be rather speculative. Hence, it should be avoided, where possible—unless one is interested more in what people think they are doing rather in what they actually do. (The latter is, of course, an important topic, since self-perceptions are critical for the emotional and psycho-somatic conditions of people and, in a feedback loop, can determine future action.) This chapter presents one strategy of observation, namely **structured observation**, which can be useful to balance this kind of almost unavoidable distortion.

Structured observation and focused observation

Structured observation should not be confused with focused observation. We can focus on a topic or event in fieldwork and usually do that in a rather systematic yet flexible manner in addition to ubiquitous, ongoing unfocused observation of what is going on (or not) in the chosen field. Structured observation, however, refers to a technique of standardized (coded) observation, or analysis of observation (when the observation itself is recorded, typically with the help of a video camera).[3] Structured observation is controlled and planned observation which proceeds by using a standardized **observation protocol** (coding scheme) listing the relevant categories of observation (see below). While sharing these elements with observation as it occurs in experiments or experimental settings, structured observation is a field technique, i.e. it is done in so-called natural field settings (social environments).[4] As every reader of ethnographic descriptions knows, ethnographic records can be quite vague and therefore potentially ambivalent with regard to the definition of forms of described behavior (Johnson and Sackett 1998: 306); structured observation, on the other hand, requires a precise definition and protocol of the observed behavior. This can make the observation measurable and increase the usefulness of the recorded observations for future scholars.

The neglect of structured observation

Structured observation can claim an important theoretical and methodological ancestry in the social sciences including behaviorism and human ethology, formal and dramaturgical sociology (Simmel and Goffman) and ethnomethodology (Garfinkel). Structured observation is quite commonplace in a variety of fields such as social psychology, educational and marketing research, and health studies, but less frequently used in others such as social research (Bryman 2008: 269).

Despite an increased attention to religion as practised, to rituals and performance, where outward behavior is of paramount importance, so far structured observation has been only marginally used in the study of religion\s.[5] Even in a field like rituals studies, where one would expect structured observation to be routine practice, it has hardly been used.[6] From my own work on Zoroastrian rituals I know that this is unfortunate, since scholars tend to jump to interpretive conclusions on the function and meaning of rituals on the ground of very partial descriptions, which is often problematic. Scholars mostly interested in wider issues such as the religious identity or attitudes of people or groups often tend to overlook a wide range of seemingly simple things.

Epistemological changes and the enhanced ethicization and politicization of research, which have resulted in scepticism or even outright rejection of the ideal of 'objective' knowledge among scholars in the humanities and the social sciences, have during the past decade contributed to drawing attention even further away from this technique.[7] The contrast often evoked, however, is problematic in principle: even structured observation conducted in 'natural' settings, of course, does not offer access to a pre-theoretic, unmediated reality.[8] Yet, there is no need to interpret this basic epistemological fact as excluding, in principle, every attempt at observing what people do and how they interact rather than what they say and believe to be doing. Moreover, advocates and practitioners of structured observations are the first to admit to the selective and biased character of observation. As we shall see, the selection of relevant aspects of behavior (relevant relative to the theoretical aims of the respective project) is part of the procedure.

Obvious and unobtrusive forms of structured observation

There are several forms of structured observation. One distinction is that between obvious and unobtrusive, or overt and covert, observations. In obvious/overt observation, which is the commonplace form, people know that they are being observed, which results in the problem of **reactivity**, i.e. that people typically, at least for some time, modify their behavior in anticipation of being observed; they do this in order to be 'good' participants of the study, which may also lead them to adopt a presumably expected role, or in order to conform their behavior to perceived socially accepted models ('social desirability bias'). However, available research indicates that reactivity effects are relatively minor, for example in studies of classroom behavior. Moreover, reactivity is affected by 'engrossment', i.e. 'the extent to which people are caught up in what they are doing, and by "habituation", [i.e.] the extent to which they have become accustomed to the presence of the observer' (Lee 2000: 47). However, the degree of reactivity also seems to vary with the level of cultural sophistication of participants (Lee 2000: 48). When turning from 'technical' evaluations of reactivity to the ethical and relational aspects of research, the fact that people actually see the researchers, and see them doing their work, may contribute to an openness of the research situation, in addition to giving people the option of asking the researchers to stop (Bernard 2006: 437). While the recognition and openness of observation is noticeable in small-scale settings or minor groups, overt observation by researchers is hardly noticeable in larger events.

This kind of situation, even if the researcher does not attempt to cover the ongoing research (beyond the usual etiquette), crosses the threshold to unobtrusive/covert observation, where the researcher remains incognito, unnoticed or invisible. Observation is covert (and not only unobtrusive), if the observer makes an active attempt to hide or to mask his or her presence.

Unobtrusive research does not entail the same risks of reactivity, but it raises a number of ethical issues in many social contexts (especially in the covert form). In some cases, however, covert research can be the only way to avoid reactivity from the outset: for example, in some contexts, the mere presence of foreign scholars attracts great attention and sometimes raises suspicions, which threatens to modify the situation to such an extent that the original purpose of the study can no longer be achieved. If one does not want to modify the research question substantially (which might also necessitate renegotiations with supervisors, sponsors, ethics committees, etc.), moving to a less prominent/visible situation in the field, for example by placing oneself in a shop adjacent to the scene one wants to study, may be one strategy of avoiding the undesirable modification of the focus area (see Beer 2003, who reports on her own study among the Ati in the Philippines).

Main problems with structured observation (not limited to but especially worrisome in unobtrusive situations) are the violation of the principle of informed consent and the invasion of privacy. Violating informed consent is unavoidable when the observation is done in public settings, where it is practically impossible to obtain informed consent from all participants (for example when studying public celebrations or festivals). So far, this is not considered ethically problematic by most, but the situation has to be evaluated critically by each scholar, and by taking into account the legal constraints defined by sponsors, research institutions and the country where the study is to be conducted. Often, the private domain is considered to be a threshold that must not be crossed, a 'no go' domain, where unobtrusive research is not permitted as a matter of principle, unless this invasion was consented to in an informed and open manner, where participants are assured the right to drop out. However, even public areas should not be regarded as necessarily free grounds for observation; ethical considerations, for example with regard to anonymity, privacy and potential harm to the people being observed, may impose limitations. This has been discussed extensively in the literature with regard to research designs of earlier studies. At the same time, the public and the private are not always clearly demarcated domains. Religious congregations, for example, to some extent cross the boundaries between the public and the private; 'the parochial' has been suggested as a term for a public space with a distinct sense of communality (Adler and Adler 1994: 388).

In some social settings such as public feasts and festivals, unobtrusive research is generally not considered a serious ethical problem, since these kinds of arenas and events allow for a range of participant roles, including 'natural' observer roles. Tourists are an example of observer-participants, and tourists are not the only ones who routinely use recording devices such as photo and video-cameras or smartphones; in fact, in many rituals (such as weddings and initiations) recording, which implies observing, is now part of the structure of the proceedings. In many cases, scholarly observers can thereby fit into a given role repertoire.

When evaluating the ethical dimensions of unobtrusive observation, it tends to be forgotten that routinely accepted methods such as philology, document and content analysis, unstructured fieldwork observations, or phenomenology are also unobtrusive and therefore raise the same sorts of concerns, even if they are not typically addressed in that way. Historians and social scientists commonly use sources that were not originally made for their use— scholars likewise study behavior that is not enacted for scholars to observe in the first place. The fact that this happens in the open and that researchers can potentially be challenged can be considered an ethical advantage with open and unobtrusive yet non-covert observation.

Even if some social settings offer roles that observers can willingly adopt for their purposes (and which do not disrupt the event and setting, nor disturb other participants, nor invade the privacy of people), structured observation does not require a specific role in the field: one can conduct this type of observation both as a complete participant, where the fieldworker plays the double role of a participant and an observer (which may lead to some practical difficulties),[9] or as an observer only, and in other positions along that continuum; all positions entail different perspectives and carry with them advantages and disadvantages or challenges (Dallos 2006: 129–31). The complete participant, for example, may experience role tensions and encounter problems of loyalty and priorities, while the complete observer has 'no opportunity to share in the experiential world of the participants' (Dallos 2006: 131).

Units of observation

While fieldwork ideally seeks to capture the totality of social groups or situations, structured observation is necessarily more selective.

Some forms of interactions studied by social scientists such as forms of greeting also involve verbal interactions. Verbal exchanges are studied by conversation analysts.[10] Structured observation typically focuses on the non-verbal aspects of behavior, or on the connections between verbal and non-verbal aspects of actions. Non-verbal aspects include (the use of) materials and objects (including clothes) or the organization of space.

One can distinguish between the following units of observation:[11]

- Acts
- Actors
- Objects
- Places and settings

All these units (which, of course, can be found in religion as much as in other social domains) are complex in their own right. Giving a detailed and exhaustive description of apparently simple acts is more difficult than many would think. In addition, all these units have different degrees of complexity; they can be described in molecular or aggregate forms. Acts, for example, can be broken down to molecular segments, or described as patterned interactions including avoidance behavior or sequences of actions such as rituals, where observation also focuses on the sequential positions, actions and activities of the different participants (actors). Structured observation can focus on components (such as steps in producing a sacred object) or longer sequences (such as the annual cycles of festivals); it can focus on short episodes (a dance) or longer states (a pilgrimage). One important area of interest has been the use and allocation of time in and for different kinds of activities. Material objects are involved in (and often constitutive of) actions. Objects are also important for communication and relevant for collective and social identities. Structured observation with a focus on objects can be a valuable strategy to explore material religion. Social scientists have conducted structured observation in places and settings such as markets, shops and shopping malls, on streets, in court rooms and classrooms, etc. More than a description of such places, structured observation is interested in these spaces as sites for actions and interactions and for the movement and circulation of objects. Below, we will sketch structured observation in a religious space.

Stages of structured observation: sampling and selection

Structured observation selects some acts, actors, objects or places, separating them out from the totality of the field, but even these units of observation cannot be studied in their totality. Selecting what to observe is a (theory-driven) act of interpretation, and every observation is selective (reductive). One cannot, and does not need to, record everything. This causes the necessity for sampling and selection.

Box 2.19.1 Typical stages and steps of structured observation

- Sampling universe (limits of study)
- Selecting units of observation
- Gaining access and permission
- From general/descriptive to focused/selective observation
- Developing observation protocol
- Scheduling observation
- Recording
- Discussion and practice with collaborators
- Determining saturation

Structured observation is a process that cannot be done right away. It requires preparations and involves a process comprising different steps and stages. To begin with, as a prerequisite, the study needs a clear focus, which implies a well-defined research question and the determination of the social, geographical and temporal boundaries of the study ('sampling universe'). The next consideration is to determine the units of observation, which depend upon the research question and the selected universe. This necessitates gaining access to the social environment, where observation is to be conducted, and gaining permission to conduct structured observation. Apart from participants or authorities in the field, this process can also formally involve research ethics review boards.

Structured observation requires the systematization and structuring of observation. This is a process that typically starts with fairly general initial overview descriptions. In a series of subsequent steps, the emerging broad picture is increasingly brought into focus at a more detailed level. Typically, features start to become clearer, and eventually the description should narrow down to what have emerged as key elements. It is these which are to be focused on in structured observation. These elements or categories will then need to be defined and operationalized as concisely as possible, so that it is clear what can count as an instance of the respective category in the observation process.

Box 2.19.2 The observation protocol

The observation protocol, observation schedule or coding scheme is developed as part of the research process and is the key element that transforms focused or systematic observation into structured observation; it is the protocol that defines the incidents to be noted in the protocol or scheme. The protocol must be easy to administer so as not to distract the observer.

The protocol/scheme has a series of fields, among them invariably a number field, a field for date and time, a field for the name or initials of the observer, and a field for potentially relevant contextual information (such as weather conditions).

The categories on the protocol/scheme must be clear and comprehensible to the coders (which necessitates some training). It is also important that the different categories do not overlap (i.e. are mutually exclusive). While some protocols/schemes seek to be exhaustive (which often necessitates a large residual category, typically 'other'), others are more selective and specific.

Typically, observers rate the frequency, duration and quality (e.g. intensity) of behavior (McCall 1984: 270). There are several kinds of measures, mainly:

- one-zero, which notes whether the behavior listed on the scheme occurs or not
- nominal, which points to qualitative differences (e.g. kneeling, standing, walking)
- ordinal, which points to degrees (e.g. sound intensity, speed of clapping)
- interval, which notes the duration of activities

Some degrees of interpretation, subjectivity and context dependence can never be fully excluded. Observation protocols/schemes should always be pre-tested. It is also advisable to include an open field so as to be able to note potentially relevant and recurrent 'new' aspects.

Researchers nowadays have a variety of technical options for recording, from pencil and paper to video and computers. Once the elements of observation have been selected, one devises an observation protocol, also known as coding scheme (see Box 2.19.2), on which the observers note down their observations, so that observing and primary coding go hand in hand. The observation protocol can conveniently be structured as a check sheet. When using video cameras the collected materials need to be coded subsequently. The development of the observation protocol transforms the broad descriptions into measurable units; the process thereby combines qualitative and quantitative procedures.

There are several strategies for scheduling observations, and to some extent these strategies depend on the selected unit of observation. Studying a site can require strategies other than those aimed at studying an event. The most ambitious and demanding, but often impractical, strategy—commonly referred to as continuous monitoring or continuous recording(s)—is to record everything all the time. This can be valuable for observing sequences of actions, or the use of things and places. When studying rituals or ceremonies, continuous monitoring can be used to cover different actors, who then need to be observed by teams of observers. Continuous monitoring is attractive and intuitive, but imposes a number of practical challenges, for example in terms of available resources, and it may produce too much irrelevant information. One alternative strategy is known as **time sampling**, meaning that observations are made (recorded) periodically. There are several alternative forms of time sampling. One option, known as fixed-interval or time-point sampling, can be used when observing actions or events: one divides a given period of observation (recording) into discrete periods and one then records observation at the transition from one period to the next. Instead of continuously observing for one hour, for example, one can make 12 instantaneous observations (recordings) every five minutes or 60 instantaneous observations per hour (i.e. one per minute). Another option, known as spot checks, spot observations, or random–interval sampling, sets up an observation schedule that specifies day and time of each observation for a given unit of observation during a certain period. (This is a strategy we used in one part of the study summarized below.)

While some research projects are run by one researcher only, projects working with structured observation are typically conducted in pairs or teams. In large-scale projects that use many observers, the different observers need to be trained in order to achieve high inter-observer reliability, i.e. that the same situation is coded as identically as possible by different observers ('raters'); this requires unambiguous definitions and shared understanding of the categories.[12] Individual or small-scale fieldwork-based projects can engage collaborators such as field assistants or friends in different stages of the process: e.g. help in gaining access and permission, the selection of units and categories of observation, the fine-tuning of the observation protocol, pre-testing the observation scheme, and subsequent discussions on the data as a means of validation.

Researchers will have to decide how many observations they need to have in order to draw conclusions with different degrees of confidence. That can be tabulated in quantitative terms (see Bernard 2006: 429, table 15.2) relative to the frequency of the observed activity in the population. Large-scale projects will need to follow formal and mathematic sampling rules here. For most small-scale projects, as typically conducted in the study of religion\s, the criterion of **saturation** will be most helpful. This refers to the realization that new data merely replicates earlier findings. (In the example sketched below, the number of possible observations was naturally restricted by opening hours of the church and the relevant season.) This, however, presupposes that the collection of data is not merely a mechanical process but that observation and (preliminary) analysis go hand in hand. In some projects, the units of observation impose limitations to the possible number of observations, especially when observing events that are temporally limited.

Problems, disadvantages and limitations

As with any method, structural observation has a series of pitfalls, shortcomings and limitations. These start with the very acts and activity of observing. Pitfalls include observer fatigue,
observer bias, prejudice and expectancies, and 'observer drift', i.e. 'that the observers come to
use certain categories more than others; this may be due to their coming to see what they
expect or, alternatively, there may be a shift through a learning effect, so that there is a greater
differentiation between observers later in the research' (Dallos 2006: 144). Sometimes there
is the tendency to focus more on the unexpected and the exotic (Beer 2003: 139). Such problems can, at least in part, be addressed by clear observation protocols and active collaboration
between researchers, and between researchers and informants.

Structured observation requires patience and is often boring. Success can also sometimes
depend on external circumstances such as the prevailing weather conditions. Depending on
the design, it can also require a large investment of time, energy and other resources. It can
also lead to social problems, for example with people becoming suspicious or even hostile to
the researchers (a risk it shares with field research in general). One general disadvantage with
structured observation is that it directs attention to a specific set of phenomena and thereby
makes the researcher inflexible with respect to following up on other potentially interesting
things that might occur in the field. On the other hand, this inflexibility—leading to one
being forced to stay at a given location—may sometimes lead to serendipity (Johnson and
Sackett 1998: 320).

Another kind of limitation refers to the kind of data produced by structured observation.
The data can appear as fragmentary and decontextualized. Moreover, the attention to the
surface comes at the expense of losing sight of the intentionality and meaning of the observed
actions and behavior. For these reasons, structured observation can rarely be used as a
mono-method; while the data it constructs can be extremely valuable, especially to accurately
establish empirical regularities, it usually works in combination with other methods such
as surveys, interviews or document analysis.[13] It can be a highly valuable component of
triangulation. In research designs, structured observation can be used in a more specific or a
more unspecific manner: it can be employed in a more exploratory manner, a 'let's look
what is going on here' strategy, which eventually may result in generating a hypothesis;
alternatively, it can be used to test hypotheses (Dallos 2006: 128). Because of its potential
value and apparent limitations, researchers should be careful not to invest too much of their
available resources in it.

A brief example: a tourist church in Bergen

As part of a larger study of the dynamic interface between religion and tourism (Stausberg
2011), in the summers of 2007 and 2008 we researched tourists visiting churches in Bergen.[14]
While we focused on one particular church in 2007 (Johanneskirke/St John's Church), in
2008 we widened the sample to include three additional churches that are regularly visited as
part of tourist itineraries in Bergen. In both stages of the project, structured observation was
part of the research design. The following summary is based on stage one only, our work at
St John's Church, a late 19th-century church built in the Gothic Revival style on one of the
hills overlooking the central part of the town. The church has the highest (and most widely
visible) tower of all churches of Bergen, and a large public staircase leads up to the church and
the surrounding plaza from an extension of the town's central square.[15] During the summer
months, a steady stream of tourists can be seen climbing the hill up to the church, which

despite its size and an impressive wooden ceiling, is not considered to be one of the main attractions of Bergen. During the summer months, the church was kept open for a couple of hours in the late morning every day and a person was hired to be present as a guard or caretaker. Apart from tourist visits and some organ recitals, the church was used occasionally for weddings or funeral services during the summer, but there were few regular services.

We mainly wanted to find out: first, how many people actually visit the church during the peak holiday season; second, what people do during their visits and how the visits are structured; third, why people visit and what they think about their visits (motivation, experience, etc.); and fourth, how church authorities respond to these visits. Having obtained research permission from the agency acting as Ethics Review Board, we interviewed the pastor and the dean in order to address the last question. In order to address question three, we conducted several in–depth interviews with individual travellers and around 200 short interviews with anonymous tourists (individuals, pairs, families and smaller groups). Hanging out in and around the church and casually observing tourists it became clear that our respondents, when talking about their visits, rarely and selectively commented on what they actually did inside the church, while they readily commented upon the impression the church made on them, their emotions and experiences, their expectations, their 'careers' as visitors of religious buildings while travelling, and the other places they visited in Bergen. They also provided self-assessments of their religiosity and spirituality and volunteered their views of these categories. While we saw that many tourists lit candles at the globe-shaped candle holder inside the church, our respondents rarely mentioned this ritual act. Yet, when asked about it, some would comment, and for many this little rite was plainly very significant.

We conducted two series of structured observations. To address our first research question, we employed random-interval sampling, i.e. we devised an observation schedule, where we would divide a day into eight two-hour periods from six in the morning to midnight, resulting in 56 potential observation periods per week. Over a period of one month, we would cover each of the 56 two-hour units once. This gave us a relatively precise idea of visitation patterns.

Since the church was only open for some hours every day, many visitors who walked up the steps were facing closed doors. The second series of observations was conducted during the open hours of the church, yet observation was not limited to the immediate church exteriors, but we would 'pick' visitors for observation from the square underneath the steps leading up to the church and follow them on their itinerary up on the hill, around the church, inside and until they left the church again. This implied a convenience sample since the next observation unit could only be started when the previous visit was over. From an ethical perspective we first hesitated to adopt this strategy because we thereby did not give people an opportunity to articulate or deny informed consent, but we decided to disregard this principle here because of an anticipated high degree of reactivity and because the research design was such that the anonymity of people would be safeguarded. Moreover, we did not want to disrupt peoples' holiday experience. While it may appear strange to follow the movement of people, the basic difference from what scholars ordinarily do in fieldwork is the systematic approach and not the fact that people are observed without their having given their informed consent. In addition, we were not interested in the people as individuals but insofar as they acted out their tourist roles and rites (such as photographing). Given the relatively large amount of people moving around the church and the fact that most tourists were observing the church or enjoying the panorama or were engrossed in their activities, the observation did not interfere with their visits. Conducting the brief interviews in front of the church, on the other hand, did attract some attention. Occasionally, however, tourists who just stayed on at the church asked us about the nature of our undertaking. The study was limited to the month that is the peak activity for incoming holiday tourism in Bergen (July to early August).

Based on systematic preliminary observation we devised an observation protocol in the form of a check sheet.[16] This started with general features such as date, time, weather, observer, number of people observed and their assumed characteristics such as age, nationality, gender, their equipment such as cameras, maps, guidebooks, etc., and an open field for possible comments. The main part of the observation protocol was divided into four main fields, relative to the location: at the beginning of the itinerary, on the way up to the church, outside the church before entering, and inside. Some people did not enter the church, and we also 'picked up' respondents who had already climbed the stairs if that was convenient and no others were in sight. On the left side of the page, each field listed the main activities we had observed during the preliminary observations plus some empty fields for 'unexpected' activities; in the centre, the protocol had a column ticked for a yes-no measurement; if yes was applicable, on the right side the exact time and duration of the activity was to be noted, and the cell would also leave room for annotations. The data we gathered in that way provided us with potentially important insights into the process and behavioral dimension of the appropriation and use of a religious building by tourists.[17] Our understanding of this process would have been much more limited if we had restricted our data to interviews.

Notes

1 See Chapter 2.8 on field research: participant observation in this volume.
2 See Whiting and Whiting (1973: 284–86), who provide an analysis of six areas where informants seem unable to provide sufficient verbal information.
3 See Chapter 2.22 on videography in this volume.
4 Sometimes it is argued that many so-called natural settings, in particular in economically poorer countries, are not natural at all, because they are subject to 'unnatural' conditions of the colonial world (Angrosino 2005: 72). It is worth recalling that every historical contingent situation can appear as 'unnatural' when measured towards the ideal of a Romantic pristine 'natural' condition; turning to this example, the conditions of the colonizers are as unnatural as those of the colonized.
5 Kuhne and Donaldson (1995) on pastoral work activities among five evangelical ministers in the USA is the only published study that has come to my notice in which structured observation is explicitly engaged as a research method in religious studies. One of the methodologically relevant findings of that paper was that it made a difference whether a categorization of pastors' roles was based on observation or on pastors' perceptions or expert opinions.
6 In their work on Bali, Mead, Bateson and Belo developed early stages of structured observation; see Whiting and Whiting (1973: 309–12).
7 This process can be observed in the history of the three editions of *The SAGE Handbook of Qualitative Research* (edited by Denzin and Lincoln), which is a benchmark publication in that field. While the first edition contained a detailed discussion of structured observation (Adler and Adler 1994), the relevant chapter in the latest edition (Angrosino 2005) reflects trends that 'question whether observational objectivity is either desirable or feasible as a goal' (ibid.: 730) and that remodel observation striving for unbiased, objective observation to 'a matter of interpersonal interaction' (ibid.: 736).
8 See also Chapter 1.1, the introductory essay to this volume.
9 Sometimes scholarly participants pretend to be part of the group (which amounts to deception and is therefore ethically not acceptable), or they keep a deliberate ambivalence about their actual or potential status (e.g. by acting as potential converts, which is ethically problematic if this entails misrepresenting the objective of research and if used as an excuse to invade privacy). Other fieldworkers actually belong to the group they study (which can have ethically problematic consequences at the time of publishing). Sometimes fieldworkers become (temporary) active members in order to be able to do fieldwork (which again raises ethical concerns), or they alter the nature of their affiliation as a result of exposure during fieldwork.

10 See Chapter 2.2 on conversation analysis in the present volume.

11 The literature proposes alternative categorizations.

12 The degree of agreement over the coding of items by two raters can be measured by using the so-called Cohen's kappa or the Scott coefficient of agreement; see Bryman (2008: 265).

13 There are spin-off options available, for example by asking informants to keep diaries for different kinds of activities, which induces systematic self-observation.

14 The research was conducted by Janemil Kolstø (who tragically passed away in 2009).

15 For some pictures, see en.wikipedia.org/wiki/St_John%27s_Church,_Bergen.

16 Given that it was written in Norwegian, it is not reproduced here.

17 Some variables could be cross-tabulated quantitatively: did visitors remain longer or behave differently when the organ was playing, or when it was more or less crowded, when they visited alone or in pairs, families, groups, etc.?

References

Adler, P.A. and Adler, P., 1994. Observational techniques. In: Denzin, N.K. and Lincoln, Y.S. (eds), *Handbook of Qualitative Research*. SAGE, London, Thousand Oaks, CA., pp. 377–92.

Angrosino, Michael V., 2005. Recontextualizing observation: ethnography, pedagogy, and the prospects for a progressive political agenda. In: Denzin, N.K. and Lincoln, Y.S. (eds), *The SAGE Handbook of Qualitative Research*. 3rd edn. SAGE, Thousand Oaks, CA, London, New Delhi, pp. 729–45.

Beer, B., 2003. Systematische Beobachtung. In: Beer, B. (ed.), *Methoden und Techniken der Feldforschung*. Dietrich Reimer Verlag, Berlin, pp. 119–41.

Bernard, H.R., 2006. *Research Methods in Anthropology: qualitative and quantitative approaches*. 4th edn. AltaMira Press, Lanham, MD, pp. 413–44.

Bryman, A., 2008. *Social Research Methods*. 3rd edn. Oxford University Press, Oxford, New York, pp. 253–72.

Dallos, R., 2006. Observational methods. In: Breakwell, G.M., Hammond, S., Fife-Schaw, C. and Smith, J.A. (eds), *Research Methods in Psychology*. 3rd edn. SAGE, London, Thousand Oaks, CA, pp. 124–45.

Johnson, A. and Sackett, R., 1998. Direct systematic observation of behavior. In: Bernard, H.R. (ed.), *Handbook of Methods in Cultural Anthropology*. AltaMira Press, Walnut Creek, CA, pp. 301–31.

Kuhne, G.W. and Donaldson, J.F., 1995. Balancing ministry and management: an exploratory study of pastoral work activities. *Review of Religious Research* 37 (2): 147–63.

Lee, R.M., 2000. *Unobtrusive Methods in Social Research*. Open University Press, Buckingham, pp. 33–62.

McCall, G.J., 1984. Systematic field observation. *Annual Review of Sociology* 10 (1): 263–82.

Martin, P. and Bateson, P., 2007. *Measuring Behavior: an introductory guide*. 3rd ed. Cambridge University Press, Cambridge.

Stausberg, M., 2011. *Religion and Tourism: crossroads, destinations, and encounters*. Routledge, London, New York.

Whiting, B. and Whiting, J., 1973. Methods for observing and recording behavior. In: Naroll, R. and Cohen, R. (eds), *A Handbook of Method in Cultural Anthropology*. Columbia University Press, New York, London, pp. 282–315.

Further reading

The works by Adler and Adler, Beer, Bernard, Bryman, Dallos, Johnson and Sackett, Lee, McCall, and Whiting and Whiting can all be used as introductions. The book by Martin and Bateson was written for the study of animal behavior, but is widely used in the social sciences as well.

Key concepts

Inter-coder reliability: the degree to which different coders or raters agree or disagree in measuring an observation.

Observation protocol: Also referred to as coding scheme, the observation protocol (typically a check sheet) specifies the categories (of behavior) to be observed; these categories need to be defined unambiguously and should be mutually exclusive.

Reactivity: the (undesired) modification of behavior of participants in a study as a result of their awareness of being studied (observed).

Saturation: the realization that new information merely confirms previous findings without adding qualitatively new data.

Structured observation: planned, scheduled and systematic observation that employs fixed rules for the observation and recording of observational data, typically with the help of an observational protocol.

Time sampling: a method of scheduling observation according to pre-determined units (points or slots) of time.

Unobtrusive research: a class of studies based on data that was gathered without the informants knowing that the information provided by them was used for scholarly purposes.

Related chapters

- Chapter 1.3 Epistemology
- Chapter 1.6 Research ethics
- Chapter 2.8 Field research: participant observation
- Chapter 2.22 Videography
- Chapter 3.3 Material culture

2.20

SURVEYS AND QUESTIONNAIRES

Juhem Navarro-Rivera and Barry A. Kosmin

Chapter summary

- A survey is a research study in which individuals are asked to report on affiliations, opinions, beliefs, behaviors or personal characteristics.
- Surveys are a powerful investigative tool for carrying out evidence-based research and collecting information on social phenomena. The data collected in surveys is analyzed using statistical tools that allow us to test and confirm (or disconfirm) hypotheses.
- A questionnaire is the main element of a survey and consists of questions or batteries of questions that the researcher(s) want the sample to answer in order to learn about the characteristics, behavior and beliefs of the target universe. A questionnaire must have questions that are simple enough to be comprehended by most, if not all, respondents.
- In the study of religion, surveys are instrumental in shaping our understanding of the place of religion in the world. Surveys (and censuses) that measure the distribution of religious groups as well as their political, religious and social behavior are fundamental for understanding how religion affects particular nations or cultures and the world at large.

Definition

What is a **survey**? In the context of this chapter a survey is a research study in which individuals are asked about their opinion, beliefs, behaviors or personal characteristics. Surveys are not, of course, limited to persons and can have institutions as subjects or respondents. Surveys also tend to count things (or people), as such we can include inventories and measurements surveys. For example, a census of churches, temples, mosques, synagogues and other places of worship is a type of survey that does not count people, though of course individuals will report on their behalf. Instead, here we will be discussing what are known as opinion surveys in which individual persons are the subject of study and from which generalizations about the behavior, beliefs and characteristics of groups can be inferred.

Surveys can include the whole population (a census), or a segment of the population (what is commonly known as a sample survey). In the case of censuses the goal is to interview the entire **population** and define **parameters**. Surveys based on segments of the population can be divided in two ways based on the type of sample selected by the researchers. Representative surveys based on a probabilistic (random) sample, when done correctly, yield results that are, to some degree, generalizable to a larger or entire population. Surveys based on convenience (non-random) samples can yield results that provide knowledge about a population or group; however, the results of these surveys are not usually generalizable to the total **universe** or population from which the sample has been drawn. Convenience samples are usually needed to study unknown, hard-to-reach or rare populations for which there are no reliable data about their size, composition or characteristics.

This essay will focus on surveys based on probabilistic samples. Still, aside from sampling issues which have an impact on the generalization of results, all the advice in this essay applies to both types of surveys.

Usefulness

Surveys are a powerful investigative tool for carrying out evidence-based research and collecting information on social phenomena. Surveys are used to compare populations in three ways. First, surveys allow researchers to compare contemporary populations in a single society. Second, these populations can be compared over time. Third, populations can be compared across countries, cultures and societies.

The purpose of using surveys in research is to study large numbers of individuals (samples) and extrapolate from these to populations (universe) in order to better understand characteristics, traits, opinions or beliefs in a population (e.g. group). Surveys provide a statistical basis for social knowledge. The data and answers collected become social facts that can be translated into metrics and numbers subject to the laws of probability. As such, creating surveys and executing research involves science, quantitative manipulation (like weighing) and a bit of art.

The use of public opinion or social surveys in social science research provides scholars with an excellent tool for measuring and comparing individuals and groups on a wide variety of attributes, attitudes and behaviors. The usefulness of surveys lies in several elements relating to how they are reported. First, surveys seem to be easy to understand by the public, the potential respondents and the sponsors. All of us in modern societies have seen surveys quoted on television, radio, newspapers and websites in order to convey a message or strengthen an argument. Usually quantitative measures or statistics (most often percentages) are cited to give a scientific imprimatur of accuracy to the findings, and graphics provide visualization of the data collected. Ideas and concepts usually can be presented more easily, clearly, economically and precisely in terms of numbers and graphics than in words. Surveys help us share information and understand better what others are thinking about the world and about themselves. Yet, behind the simplicity of the presentation of survey data there is a complicated process.

Because survey instruments can be standardized, translated and applied to different populations, cultures and linguistic groups, they are an excellent method for conducting comparative research (Harkness *et al.* 2004).

Surveys can also be misused or abused (Traugott 2008). Some misuses occur in design and reporting. A design misuse occurs when a researcher or an organization sponsoring or promoting a study deliberately writes questions in a way that they generate a desired answer from respondents. These results may contradict previous research and if not carefully analyzed distort our knowledge.

Many reporters and journalists, as well as the general public, are not familiar with statistical and research terminology and concepts. This may lead to a misunderstanding of the results of a survey. For example, reporters or the public may overestimate the differences between two figures that are within the **margin of error** of the survey because they are unfamiliar with the concept. Moreover, in the same vein, they may apply statistical differences in the wrong way and assume that the reported error (which usually applies to the whole study) applies even when the sample is subdivided into smaller subsamples. This same error applies to surveys that include a temporal component, such as time-series studies. If incorrectly reported without caveats, changes over time that are statistically insignificant can be misreported as real and significant change.

Usage in the study of religion

In the study of religion, surveys are instrumental in shaping our understanding of the place of religion in the world. Surveys (and censuses) that measure the distribution of religious groups as well as their political, religious and social behavior are fundamental for understanding how religion affects particular nations or cultures and the world at large. Religion is one of the main sources of personal and social identity for individuals and groups. In today's interconnected world, when information travels so quickly, religion and religious beliefs are the type of concepts that tend to travel with individuals. Thanks to religion surveys we know about change or transformation over time in religious loyalties and sentiments: the spread of Protestantism in Latin America (Bastian 1993), the increase on non-religious identification in the United States (Kosmin and Keysar 2006; 2009), the secularization of Europe and the resurgence of religion in formerly communist countries (Norris and Inglehart 2004).

There are two main ways in which surveys are used to study religion. These two ways have some methodological similarities but different goals.

The first way in which surveys are applied to the study of religion is to measure aggregate attitudes and opinions. This is the way most people understand the concept of surveys. In this case the survey consists of a **questionnaire** with items that measure a respondent's views and opinions on a particular subject. When studying religion these surveys focus on aspects like belonging, belief and behavior.

The second way in which surveys are applied to the study of religion is to measure institutions and institutional change over time. In this case the interest is in individual congregations, religions or religious traditions. These surveys are useful for understanding religion from an institutional perspective.

Because surveys are a snapshot of the population at a particular point in time, in order to measure religious change or stability it is necessary to have comparable data that measures these aspects over time.

The American Religious Identification Survey (ARIS) is an example of a religious survey. Because the ARIS has been conducted three times between 1990 and 2008 there are several ways in which this survey can be used. As a snapshot of religious identification in the United States, individually, the ARIS surveys provide a time capsule view of religion in three particular points in time. The results of the 1990 National Survey of Religious Identification, as the ARIS was known then, can be used to understand religious identification in the United States at that particular point in time. However, combined with the ARIS 2001 and ARIS 2008 studies, these data show trends about the flow of religious identification in the United States over two decades.

The usefulness of surveys like the ARIS series and the recent studies conducted by the Pew Research Centers is that they use large samples, which allows for an accurate picture of the distribution of religion in a particular place. Their usefulness in estimating the distribution of particular religions is akin to that of a full census, and these types of studies are particularly useful in places where censuses do not happen too often or religion questions are not asked.

Other surveys, such as those conducted by the Gallup Organization, the World Values Survey and country-based General Social Surveys, which inquire about aspects of religious life such as attendance to religious services and religious identification, can also be useful to gauge different aspects of religious behavior over time. Since many of these surveys are conducted periodically they allow us to understand how the religious practice and behavior of a population changes over time. However, given the relatively small samples (usually 1,000–2,000), many of the results cannot be generalized for some of the smaller groups in a way that larger surveys can.

Strengths and weaknesses

As with any research method, surveys have some limitations; this is particularly true in the realm of religion wherein can be controversy and where often there is a lack of consensus and precision in defining the population groups and institutions to be studied; moreover, in religious studies there is a lack of consensus about what counts as a religion. The problems encountered in survey research include non-response, wording/comprehension and sampling, among others. In surveys and questions dealing with religion many of these issues are exacerbated due to the sensitive nature of some questions in the minds of many potential respondents. For example, social desirability and social pressure might lead people to falsify answers and so provide inaccurate estimates. This is common in questions regarding attendance at religious services. In places such as the United States where church attendance is considered a positive behavior, attendance at religious services tends to be over-reported. In contrast, attendance to religious services is under-reported in places such as some European countries. In addition, the estimation of the size and characteristics of religious minorities can be affected if such minorities are persecuted or discriminated against, which makes members of that community wary about cooperating with researchers. Another problem with wording and comprehension is the issue of language translation. Particularly in diverse societies and in cross-national surveys, translations are necessary in order to allow for accurate comparisons between groups and/or societies.

A particular issue for religion surveys is that they often include theological or specialist terms unfamiliar to uneducated or uninitiated respondents. This can elevate levels of non-response (don't knows and refusals) above those normally found in more familiar areas of survey research.

Yet, despite these drawbacks the study of religion through surveys is important. Religion is a multidimensional concept that involves aspects such as belief, belonging and behavior, among others. In addition, since religion is often held to be a global phenomenon, many surveys are international and comparative in scope. However, in order to understand how people identify and practice their religion, and how religion impacts the attitudes, behavior and opinions of people, it is necessary to standardize and simplify it into terms and concepts that are easily understandable and, more importantly, comparable.

Universe and sample

The major component of a survey aside from the questionnaire, which will be discussed later, is the universe. The universe is the population that the researcher wants to reach. In the case of opinion surveys the universe is the population or units of analysis under study. However, the type of people differs according to how the universe is defined.

In the case of opinion surveys there are at least three types of universe. The first universe is the general public or members of a specifically defined population. The research goal of focusing on this type of universe is knowing the opinions of the public at large. Two examples of this universe are 'all adults', i.e. the resident national population, which is the target population for most academic and commercial opinion surveys such as those conducted by the Gallup Organization and more specific surveys such as the American Religious Identification Survey (ARIS); the second example concerns specific groups which are the target of studies regarding sub-populations such as the Barna poll of Evangelicals (USA) or even smaller studies of particular congregations or religious communities.

A second type of universe often studied in religion is elites. Here, we define elites as leaders of religious groups and organizations, i.e. the clergy, but these can also be drawn from interest groups, political, religious charities and welfare organizations. As such, surveys of elites are useful for understanding the rationale for organizational decision-making. Although elites can be considered a subset of the general population and are usually easy to identify and locate, they tend to be a tough segment of the population to get to cooperate because of calls on their time. Given the leadership role of elites, their opinions carry special weight about the direction of their organizations, but this also often means their reluctance to have their views identified. Some studies of elites include a survey of imams (Nagata 1982) and a survey of Anglican clergy in Britain (Field 2007).

Finally, the third universe comprises organizations such as denominational bodies or congregations. Although organizations certainly cannot answer for themselves, administrators are able to present views of the organizations. Another variant of this type of survey taking into account this universe is surveys or censuses of organizations, such as the study of US Congregations conducted by the Association of Statisticians of American Religious Bodies (ASARB) and compiled as the *Religious Congregations & Membership in the United States.*

When designing or evaluating surveys it is necessary to keep in mind the type of universe for which the surveys are intended. This means that results that apply to adherents do not necessarily reflect the opinion of church or religious elites and vice versa.

There are different methods to capture surveys. Each of these methods has their own advantages but also disadvantages. The use of these particular methods will yield different response rates and errors.

When defining the universe or population of interest it is important to know the description and distribution of the population. This is particularly important in surveys of religious groups because categorization is often vague and disputed both theologically and sociologically. For example, the term Protestant refers to many churches and denominations such as Methodist and Lutheran, which themselves are split into sub-groups. Religious terms are also understood or interpreted differently across different religious groups. For example, a survey targeting only Catholic adults should not include other Christians or members of other religions except where a control group is required for comparison. In the latter case, such a survey must be careful to contain wording and concepts understandable to non-Catholics. These difficulties mean that the results are liable to be contaminated and prone to **measurement error** (calculating the wrong parameters by measuring the wrong population) unless due care is given. Thus, carefully setting the limits of the population of study will allow avoiding this type of measurement error.

Knowing the extent of our population helps determine the **sample** size. An optimal sample size is about 750–1,000 respondents. The reason behind this is that this range provides the optimal amount of cases for analysis as well as cost.

The response rate is the proportion of contacts that complete an interview. This rate is variable and several factors affect it. One of these major factors is the type of interview because different types need different levels of rapport and involvement between the **respondent** and the **interviewer**. In addition, because of these different levels of involvement, the errors that can result from these different types of surveys will affect the results accordingly.

What a good **response rate** is varies but it is more important that the final sample is inclusive. This means that it includes real people in the target universe. For example, a low response rate (20 per cent) may include members of all major ethnic or social groups in a population and be a representative sample of the universe of study. On the other hand, a survey with a high response rate (70 per cent) may be skewed toward particular types of people: persons with high incomes, or telephones, or who speak a specific language.

In the case that the sample of respondents is skewed the researcher can make some corrections. If the sample's skew is noticed during the data collection (interview) process, the researchers can target members from specific under-represented groups (e.g. more women, more minorities) allowing the sample to be more representative. In addition, the researchers can add weights to the final sample. Weighting is a process used to correct samples by placing more weight on respondents with particular characteristics and make the sample look more like the general population. These procedures can also be used to correct for **non-response**. Non-response can affect a survey by also skewing samples and results.

Sampling

Successful surveys require careful and detailed preparation in which the goals are clearly defined. Scholars interested in conducting surveys must be clear about their intended target universe, what they want to know, and how to capture the information in which they are interested. In this section we will define and provide instructions on how to design a survey. These instructions include how to define a target universe, which is crucial in order to properly answer a clear research question or questions. In addition, we will discuss how to define concepts, and translate these concepts from academic jargon to a language that can be comprehended by a lay public of ordinary people. We also discuss validity and reliability issues that may affect the interpretation of the survey results. Finally, we write about miscellaneous issues in survey design and evaluation such as generalization, sampling and translation. These issues are particularly relevant for some contemporary religious research, which are a multicultural and often a multi-national affair.

A coherent survey needs a well-defined target universe. The universe consists of the population that the researcher or researchers want to study. The survey universe comprises individuals or institutions. This universe is defined by the researchers by limiting who does or does not belong. A well-defined universe is one that clearly describes the population that the researchers are interested in studying. The universe's definition includes describing who or what is subject to study and what or who is not. The demarcation of the universe has an impact on the variation of the results that the study will show.

For example, a survey of Catholic opinions on biomedical, moral and ethical issues can comprise several universes. First, the survey can include all self-identified Catholics. This is the broadest definition of the universe as it includes anyone who considers themselves Catholic, whether because of baptism, faith, culture or tradition. In contrast, the researcher(s) can define the universe to comprise just a list of those registered with a parish, of practicing (church-going) Catholics, or solely of Catholic women. These different universes might yield different patterns of answers and as such the researcher(s) must be clear as to what they want to know and what they expect from the survey.

This universe needs to be well-defined because the variation of the results depends on the extent or size of the universe. Continuing with our Catholic universe example, the broadest universe (all self-professed Catholics) will yield much more variation among the answers than a less broad universe such as church-going mass attendees (practicing Catholics). The reason for this variability is related to size. In larger universes it is expected that opinions and beliefs will be more varied.

For practical reasons, it is impossible to interview all the members of a target universe most of the time. Instead, in opinion surveys researchers ask questions from a sample. There are exceptions. For example, censuses by definition count or attempt to count all members of the target universe. In addition, some universes may be small enough that interviewing all members may be feasible. These cases are the exception and rare.

Samples consist of persons or institutions that fit the description of the target universe and are drawn from it. In order to make generalizations about the universe it is necessary that the sample is representative of the target universe. This means that the sample must be random so as not to introduce, or at least to try to minimize, selection biases.

Representative samples can be easily achieved in countries or places where a census is periodically conducted, since the demographic characteristics of the universe are generally known. Moreover, in places where public opinion surveys are common, it is possible to know the demographic characteristics of the universe since over repeated samples these values will approach the real (universe) value.

Table 2.20.1 shows the sample size required to survey populations of different size magnitudes. The margin of error is a measure of random sampling error in a survey; the larger the margin of error, the less reliable the survey results.

With a sample size of 750–1,000, most successful surveys have about a 3–4 per cent margin of error. Looking at Table 2.20.1 it is clear why this is so. The table shows different sample sizes according to population and margin of error. When the population is small, such as 100, we suggest sampling as many members as possible. The reason for this is that at this population size the difference between a 3 per cent margin of error and the full population is negligible. However, sampling a small proportion of the population introduces much uncertainty into the results.

In contrast, as the population size increases, adding more subjects to the sample (sampling points) does not necessarily increase the precision of the survey. For example, in a population of 10,000 (say a large religious congregation), the size of a sample with a 3 per cent margin of error is similar to the sample size for a national survey for a country with 1 million potential respondents. Notice that the difference between a sample with a 3 per cent and a 1 per cent margin of error means at least doubling the sample (in the case of 1,000 respondents) or increasing it eight-fold with minimal impact on the survey's precision.

Table 2.20.1 Sample size and margin of error according to population size with a 95 per cent confidence

					Population						
% error	100	500	1,000	5,000	10,000	50,000	100,000	500,000	1,000,000	5,000,000	10,000,000
10	49	81	88	94	95	96	96	96	96	96	96
5	79	217	278	357	370	381	383	384	384	384	384
3	91	340	516	879	964	1045	1,056	1,065	1,066	1,067	1,067
1	99	475	906	3,288	4,899	8,057	8,762	9,423	9,513	9,586	9,595

The margin of error is a function of the population size and the **confidence interval**. The confidence interval is a statistical principle which states that given a particular sample size, over repeated samples these samples will reflect the real population values. In surveys with a 95 per cent confidence interval (like the samples calculated in Table 2.20.1) about 19 out of every 20 results (95 percent) will fall within the determined margin of error.

To illustrate this, imagine a religious identification poll with a 3 per cent margin of error and a 95 per cent confidence interval. Suppose 25 per cent of individuals consider themselves to belong to a particular religion, say Islam. A sample with a 95 per cent confidence interval and a 3 per cent margin of error means that 19 out of 20 times the percentage of individuals identified with the Islamic religion will range between 22 per cent and 28 per cent.

The statistical principle behind this is the **central limit theorem**. Because it is costly to interview every member of the universe, sampling is necessary, as we previously discussed. In order to know the real values in the universe it is necessary to conduct repeated measures, in this case through survey research. The role of survey research then becomes two-fold: to examine the distribution of traits and characteristics in the population and to estimate its prevalence. Usually this is done by comparing survey results since these provide external validation of the survey results. This means that we are more confident about the distribution of traits, in this case religious identification, in a population when different studies yield similar results.

The confidence interval of a survey result means that over repeated measurement, it is expected that results will be similar. For example, a 95 per cent confidence interval means that 19 out of 20 times this survey is administered to a universe using repeated random samples, the results will be similar.

However, because in the case of many surveys it is hard to secure funding or resources to replicate the studies, the estimation of confidence intervals and margins of error provide researchers with a way to place their studies within the larger population context.

Selecting the sample

When selecting our sample we must be aware of other sources of error and biases that can occur. We mentioned that we must be careful to avoid including respondents who do not belong to the target population. However, other errors can occur when sampling. For example, the sample may have gender or age imbalances that may affect the results by giving too much weight to a particular gender or age group. Other types of selection biases include samples in which members of the target universe from particular geographic areas or with particular characteristics are excluded. Continuing with our previous Catholic example, in this case our universe is all self-identified Catholics. Since the sample is supposed to be representative of the universe theoretically, all members of the universe have some probability of being selected. However, imagine a worldwide survey of Catholics in which Brazil is not included. The results of such a survey will be suspicious because it does not include people from the largest Catholic country on the planet. This means that the omission of the views and opinions of a large proportion of Catholics which may differ from those of people in other countries compromises the generalizability of the study's results.

Random selection means that all possible respondents in the universe have the same probability of being selected in the sample and thus of participating in the study. For example, in a face-to-face survey in which interviewers visit respondents in their homes such as the [United States] General Social Survey, every residential address in the United States is theoretically considered to be part of the universe. In this way selection bias is avoided in the selection of the respondents since each member of the universe is theoretically given an equal opportunity to take part in the study.

There are several types of probabilistic samples. While these sample types are similar in the sense that their purpose is to cover as much of the target universe as possible, the approaches in which these types achieve widespread coverage of the universe differ.

The first type is the simple random sample (SRS). As the name suggests, the process of selecting a random sample from this universe is simple. To conduct an SRS it is necessary to know the total universe and randomly select from it. For example, a researcher wants to know the opinion of members of a particular congregation about a new pastor. In this case the universe is known and there is a list of the members who comprise the target universe. The researcher just needs to use the list and select the names at random. This can happen in several ways.

A simple way of randomizing a sample is to collect all the names in the list and place them in a hat. Afterwards the researcher can select the names out of a hat. Another way entails the researcher assigning a number to each of the members of the target universe and, after determining the sample size, select the sample based on a frequency. This is achieved by skipping or selecting every *nth* individual depending on the frequency determined by the researchers.

Another type of random sample is the cluster sample. In this case the researcher selects segments of the target universe, for example geographic units. Afterwards, the sample is randomly drawn from these different clusters. Cluster sampling is useful for selecting samples in which there is variation in the physical location of the members of the target universe. Most public opinion surveys in the United States incorporate some cluster sampling by selecting the respondents proportionally from different regions in the country. Continuing with the previous example, imagine that the researcher wants to know the opinions that churchgoers have of their clergy in one town. A way to achieve a representative random sample is to weigh the sample according to the size of each church, then survey the members of each church using the same method as in a simple random sample (assuming a membership list is readily available). In the case that there is no such list (or access to it) the researcher(s) can assemble a team to interview people as they come out of religious services (similar to the way that political exit polls are conducted).

Finally, stratified sampling is a combination of the two previous methods. In this case the researchers divide the population in different strata, then the population in those strata is divided into clusters and the final sample is selected randomly from the clusters. For example, if a national religious denomination wants to know the opinions of members across a country and expects to find differences by regions, stratifying the sample is a way to ensure that the opinions of people in all regions are taken into consideration. This is done by dividing the universe into the necessary number of strata, let's say five regions. Afterwards the researchers select their clusters, in this case individual churches. Finally, individuals from particular churches are selected at random (simple random sampling or frequency).

This process provides diversity to the sample and robustness for analytical purposes. Because random samples are necessary for generalization purposes, but coverage of the population is also important, using different methods of random sampling allows the researcher to cover most of the population and ensures that most members of the universe have a chance of being selected. Generalization means that the results from the survey can be applied to describe the larger universe from which the sample is drawn.

One thing that should be clear about the sample is that although a normal sized-survey of about 1,000 respondents provides insights into the beliefs and opinions of a larger group, the certainty to which we can learn about sub-populations is much smaller depending on population and sample size. In other words, in a country with a population of 10 million we can learn a great deal of information from 1,000 interviews. However, if we want to know about different sub-groups within the population, our ability is limited by the smaller sample sizes of people who belong to those particular sub-groups.

On a smaller scale, let's assume that we are conducting a study of three congregations in a particular town. The interest is in differences and similarities between members of various congregations on tithing and charity giving. Altogether the congregations have about 1,000 members, but given the time and money constraints we can only interview a fraction of them. In this case we will interview 300, or 100 in each church (see margin of error table).

The way we can generalize from the sample of 300 to the universe of 1,000 is by making sure that our sample is random and by knowing some *a priori* facts about the population. For example, gender distribution or age distribution are parameters (known facts about the population) that allow us to know how well our sample represents the population.

We can compare the parameter values to our sample and realize if the sample accurately reflects the population. However, if we want to further analyze the results into smaller sub-groups such as individual congregations, gender, age groups or other sub-groups, we must take into consideration that the error in those smaller groups is larger than for the whole sample on which the margin of error is based. This means that our estimates are less reliable for sub-groups than for the overall sample.

When the defined target universe consists of populations that are hard to reach or their size is unknown, it is appropriate to rely on convenience samples. Using convenience samples has its advantages and disadvantages. The main of these disadvantages is the inability to generalize to the larger target universe. There are, however, excellent reasons for conducting surveys based on convenience samples. One of these reasons is to establish a baseline for a new population to study. Examples of studies that use this type of sample include sociological and anthropological studies of marginalized populations. Marginalized populations are, in many places, persecuted because their behavior or beliefs many times is deemed illegal by the government or considered socially unacceptable in particular cultures. As a result, oftentimes there are no public sources of information providing an approximate size and composition of marginalized populations. In cases in which the universe consists of marginalized populations the researcher needs to first gain access to the people who belong to the population. This access is achievable by gaining the trust of the prospective participants (the target universe). The process of trust-building is in many cases a long one. As such, these surveys are time-consuming and it must be made clear that results will not be immediately available.

Next, we will discuss the types of surveys. There are four main types of surveys that researchers conduct today. These are face-to-face, telephone, self-administered and over the Internet (Donschbach and Traugott 2007).

Face-to-face surveys

In face-to-face surveys the interviewer is physically present when the respondent answers the survey. In fact, the interviewer applies the survey and collects the answers. While this type of survey usually yields the highest response rates because of the personal relationship between interviewer and respondent, it has some drawbacks.

The first drawback is cost. Because face-to-face interviews are conducted by people (interviewers) in the field they involve high costs such as transportation to different sites, and the cost of paying interviewers in addition to the time involved in logistics, transportation and implementation of the study must also be factored in. For large studies in large countries, face-to-face surveys may be very expensive to conduct.

In terms of errors and biases, face-to-face surveys may lead to problems with follow-up questions if the interviewers skip them or ask the wrong questions. Another additional issue regarding interviewer error is the fact that some interviewers may react, with facial or verbal expressions, to answers provided by the respondent in ways that may appear to be approving or judgmental. These actions may affect how the respondents react. For example, these approving or judgmental actions may lead respondents to hide their true opinions or beliefs if they think that the interviewer is judging him/her.

A related error is that if the survey includes sensitive questions regarding personal information it is possible that the respondent may feel inclined to lie or refuse to answer. Moreover, if there are also questions that involve unpopular opinions or behavior some respondents may feel inclined to provide answers that are socially desirable if their preferred opinions or behavior are not in line with societal norms.

In the case of religion studies, because of the international nature of religion and the various ways in which religious life is practiced in different countries, social desirability may become an issue for persons who practice or identify with minority or otherwise marginalized groups.

Face-to-face interviews are especially useful in places with low levels of infrastructure and development, particularly communications.

Telephone surveys

Telephone surveys with land lines at fixed locations have several advantages vis-à-vis face-to-face surveys. First, telephone surveys can cover larger populations at a lower unit cost per contact. In addition, they can also cover a larger geographical area at a lower cost as well. Moreover, land lines are good for sampling and analyzing different geographic areas because land lines have identifiers such as area codes and exchanges which make them easier to locate, contributing to a better sampling coverage. If a country has separate telephone exchanges or area codes for commercial and residential telephones, this is also a case for conducting telephone surveys since it simplifies sampling even further. Another advantage that telephone surveys provide over face-to-face surveys is that because of the relatively anonymous way in which they are conducted (no visual contact), they may reduce the propensity of answering sensitive questions with socially desirable answers.

However, telephone surveys have some drawbacks. While it is true that telephone surveys can cover more people and territory they also need the infrastructure to do so. In places where there is little access to telephone lines large segments of the population may be excluded from the survey. Considering the social and economic characteristics of those who lack phones in some societies it is likely that telephone surveys will have samples skewed by class.

In addition, in today's technological world the advent of cellular phones can also affect the coverage and response rates in telephone interviews because many would-be respondents will not answer their phones. This is particularly true for young people who are more likely to use cellular technology exclusively, and among those who screen their phone calls. The cell phone issue also exacerbates the lower response rates that are associated with conducting telephone surveys. Another issue with cellular phones is that because of their portability, they are not physically linked to an area code or exchange; instead they are mainly linked to an individual. This makes cellular phones less useful when trying to determine geographic indicators from their users, especially for highly localized studies like research on congregations or parishes.

Self-administered surveys

Another way to conduct a survey is using self-administered questionnaires. These questionnaires can be self-administered in three major ways which differ on response rates and costs.

The first way is mail-in surveys. These surveys are mailed to potential respondents who can answer them in the privacy of their homes. This method is particularly useful when asking sensitive questions that may tempt respondents to answer in a socially desirable way. In addition, the costs of conducting such a study are relatively low since the main costs are printing, postage and processing.

However, because the survey is self-administered it can lead to errors such as the respondent not fully comprehending the questions or skipping questions, and other problems that cannot be corrected immediately or noted by an interviewer. Mail-in self-administered surveys also have low response rates for a couple of reasons. First, these surveys depend on the willingness of respondents to mail them back. Second, these surveys can be easily forgotten, particularly in places such as the United States where people receive a lot of 'junk' mail from companies and other businesses that go usually straight to the garbage or recycling bin.

These problems can be solved in different ways. Potential respondents can be encouraged to participate by providing incentives such as the opportunity to win some prize if the survey is returned before a deadline. This will help boost response rates. Researchers can include telephone numbers where they (or trained staff) can be contacted to respond to questions regarding the survey and minimize response errors. Another way to boost response rates and counter memory lapses is to send follow-up and reminders to potential respondents.

The second way to conduct self-administered surveys is with automated telephone calls. With this method respondents are called by phone but instead of an interviewer conducting the interview, the respondent answers by dialing the responses. This method allows for more privacy, especially in the case of sensitive questions, but given the type of interaction (no human involved) it can also yield lower response rates as it is psychologically easier to hang up on a computer than a human.

The third method is to conduct self-administered surveys assisted by a computer. This is a combination of a face-to-face interview and a self-administered one. In this case the respondent is provided with a portable computer to answer the survey. This approach combines the best of all worlds with personal interaction, minimization of error (with a pre-programmed computer) and privacy for the respondent.

This final method is quite expensive since it includes both the costs of an interviewer combined with the technology costs of computer hardware, software and programming.

Internet surveys

Internet studies have become more common but there are still problems with conducting them. Two particular issues with Internet studies are coverage, since still not everybody has access to the Internet. This is especially true for less-developed countries, but even in developed countries, access to the Internet and usage varies by age, educational level and income.

Yet, there are instances in which Internet studies are feasible and useful. For example, when the members of the target population are university professors, all of whom have personal email addresses, creating a universe or sample of email addresses is feasible. Internet surveys sampled with emails can direct potential respondents to links where the survey instrument can be accessed and completed confidentially.

In addition, Internet studies can be used to conduct panel studies of people with specific characteristics. In this case the questions are customized for a particular type of individual. Recruitment, however, could be done not only by email, but also through advertisement on websites frequented by the target population(s). Another advantage of online surveys is that the results or frequencies for individual question items can be updated and viewed in real time.

Two of the main pitfalls of Internet surveys are the difficulty of generalizing to the larger population and low response rates.[1]

Cross-sectional, longitudinal and panel studies

The different types of survey can be applied in three different temporal contexts: cross-sectional, longitudinal and panel studies.

A cross-sectional study is one that studies a population at a particular point in time: it is like a still photograph with a snapshot of a society. Most surveys are cross-sectional in the sense that the results of the study can just be applied to a particular population at the time the study was applied and any analysis done in these surveys should be accompanied by the appropriate caveats.

A longitudinal study takes place over time. To continue with the metaphor, longitudinal studies are similar to a movie where we follow-up on the story. The individual surveys are cross-sectional studies: they can only be applied to a population at a particular point in time. However, over time the same study is applied to the same population to account for changes in demographics or attitudes. The American Religious Identification Survey and the World Values Survey are examples of longitudinal studies that trace changes in a population over time.

Finally, a panel study traces change over time among a group of participants, similar to how people follow a television series: a group of characters over several episodes over different seasons in which they develop and change. This type of survey is useful for understanding opinion change and decision-making among individuals over time, which in turn can help researchers understand how these processes may work among a larger population. This method allows statements about causation while otherwise other methods imply causation through correlation. Monitoring the Future, a US-based survey of adolescents, is a classic example of a panel study. The study surveys a panel of adolescents over time about health and risk behaviors.

Researchers planning to conduct surveys must take into account the pros and cons of using these different collection methods. Researchers conducting secondary data analysis of surveys must be aware of how the data was collected and possible biases in the data.

Comparisons in surveys

A critical aspect of surveys, especially those with international components, is the way they can be used to compare different populations or subsets of the population. There are different rules that apply to different facets of research in this area.

For researchers interested in conducting international or cross-national studies, one of the most sensitive aspects of research is the translation of concepts into different languages (Harkness *et al.* 2004). Because vernaculars and local variations of language are different across countries, it is necessary to have some template for translation or some network of international scholars that can help with the survey's design. For example, the World Values

Survey employs teams of researchers in the different countries where the study is conducted. This allows the study to benefit from local knowledge by researchers who know the language and culture well.

Questionnaires

The main element of a survey, a questionnaire consists of questions or batteries of questions that the researcher wants the sample to answer in order to learn about the characteristics, behavior and beliefs of the target universe. A questionnaire must have questions that are simple enough to be comprehended by most, if not all, respondents. This simplicity must be balanced with the unavoidable conceptual complexity inherent in social science research.

Selecting the items included in a questionnaire is the most delicate part of the question-naire design. The terms used to define and describe concepts must be carefully selected. In addition, the terms selected must accurately measure the concepts under study. Moreover, it is necessary that after the survey is completed the results fit our previous knowledge regarding the topic (if that exists) and if they do not there are explanations grounded in theory. Two relevant concepts to have in mind are reliability and validity.

Reliability refers to the survey instrument (questionnaire). The questionnaire is reliable if the results are consistent. This means that the results are similar after repeated testing over a period of time. Validity refers to the theoretical grounding of the instrument. In other words, that the instrument measures what it intends to.

A way to solve this problem is to use questions and concepts that have been validated from previous studies. Using them helps in at least two ways. First, it will ease the process of creating a survey since the concepts, terminology and questions have been previously tested and have reliable estimates. The second advantage of using this method is that it allows comparisons to be made with other studies that have used similar terminology. In addition, this will help to decide if attitudes, beliefs or opinions of a population have changed or also occur among other groups.

Of course, at times assessing the reliability and the validity of an instrument may be difficult because researchers are introducing new concepts or instruments and there is no way to compare them with previous research. Likewise, in some cases there are no parameters from which to take cues. In such cases the researcher will be establishing precedent but by designing and implementing the study carefully and with a rigorous methodology it is possible to protect the study from unnecessary criticism.

Researchers designing surveys need to keep in mind that answering questionnaires is an undertaking that imposes a burden and takes time away from respondents. As such, question-naires should have certain optimum characteristics in order to be effective. The three main characteristics of importance are length, clarity and variety.

Length refers to two elements of the questionnaire. The first element is the question, or questions. Lengthy and involved questions tend to confuse respondents because it takes time to process the information required to understand them. For this reason it is recommended to limit question length. In this way respondents can recollect better the information that is required from them by the researcher(s).

Designing short questionnaires allows respondents to finish the survey quickly and with a fresh mind. Moreover, shorter questions and answer categories help in one of the important aspects of religion research: international comparisons.

Because religion is regarded as a worldwide phenomenon some surveys are international in scope, not only comparing people within a community or a country, but across countries.

This means that short surveys may also help to simplify the translation process necessary to conduct many surveys in cross-national and cross-cultural settings.

The second element is clarity. This means that the concepts used in the survey should be easily understood. The wording of the questions, for example, should avoid complicated or obscure terminology. Wording that includes academic or theoretical jargon unknown to the lay public might yield inconsistent results because respondents do not understand what they are being asked about.

The third element, variety, refers to the answers (for which the first two elements apply as well). By variety we mean that answers for the questions should be rotated. This rotation or randomization applies to response categories in closed questions within respondents and across respondents. Randomization of answers within the same questionnaire respondents helps avoid response acquiescence, which refers to the action of responding to the first answer option. This behavior on the part of survey respondents is one of the main sources of survey error. When respondents are offered several questions with similar responses such as a battery of questions measuring opinions or attitudes, there is a risk that the respondent will just select the first option available. A way to avoid this is to rotate the order of the options available. For example, if the questionnaire includes a battery of questions for which the options are yes or no, the recommendation is to rotate the order of the 'yes' and 'no' options.

Oftentimes, batteries of questions are necessarily repetitive in order to probe thoroughly particular themes. Long questions, batteries of questions, and response categories can lead to respondent acquiescence. This means that respondents will respond (or acquiesce) to the first response category available in order to finish the survey. A solution to this is the randomization of questions and answer categories. Randomization means changing the order in which questions and responses are administered to different respondents.

The sequence of themes in a survey needs careful attention because it affects responses to subsequent questions. Opinions about one subject can affect opinions on other subjects. The respondent can be influenced by items or arguments implied by prior questions or topics.

The randomization of questions across respondents, on the other hand, serves to correct for respondent acquiescence in another way. Rotating questions by creating different versions of a questionnaire is recommended to correct for respondent acquiescence in the survey.

Determining what type of questions to include is essential in the design of a survey. There are generally two types of questions: **closed** and **open-ended**. Deciding which type of question to use depends on the research goals and what type of information is needed.

Closed questions have a limited and pre-determined number of answers. In closed questions the researcher determines the options available to respondents and limits the amount of information gathered. Open ended questions allow the respondent to answer in more detail and length using their own words and terms. This means that the amount of information gathered by researchers is larger and more varied.

The use of these two methods leads to different analytical strategies. In the case of closed questions, the analysis is simplified because the response categories are pre-determined and discrete. The data in closed questions, however, many times lack a larger context and nuance, which may help explain responses in other questions or how a particular case deviates from what is normal in a particular group.

The reverse occurs with open-ended questions. Answers in these questions tend to be longer and usually more nuanced, but also may contain a lot of data noise (not useful information). The coding and analysis of the data collected with open-ended questions is more complex and time consuming. The answers need to be classified into discrete and coherent categories. Still, oftentimes the depth of data collected provides insights into the minds, beliefs and opinions of individual respondents in a way that closed questions cannot.

In order to keep the questions in the questionnaire simple, a basic rule is to avoid **double-barreled questions**. These are questions that have two or more questions within them. Double-barreled questions are confusing to respondents because the intent of the question is not clear. The answers and data collected are difficult to interpret for researchers because it is not clear which part of the question respondents are answering.

Interpreting double-barreled questions can be a frustrating and futile enterprise. When two or more questions are included in one survey item and the possible answer does not explicitly provide options for answering them independently, in reality the researcher does not know how the respondent answered the question.

Think of a question that asks 'Do you think that Jesus Christ is the Son of God and the only way to salvation?' If the response categories include 1 yes, 2 no and 3 don't know, the question is double-barreled. The reason is that when a respondent answers yes or no, it is hard to know if the person agrees with both statements or just with one of them.

These types of questions should be avoided when writing a questionnaire because they create confusion among researchers, respondents and the general public. When evaluating a survey it is important to identify possible questions in which double-barrel occurs and the implications for the answers.

On the other hand, it is possible to ask more than one question providing that a wide range of answers are provided. Returning to the previous example, it is possible to provide options for both questions in a way that they are satisfactorily answered.

Researchers can ask whether the respondent thinks that Jesus Christ is (1) both, (2) just the Son of God but not the only way to salvation, (3) just the only way to salvation but not the Son of God, (4) neither, or (5) don't know.

However, while these responses provide more clarity and avoid some confusion by disaggregating both questions, it is still recommended that combining two concepts or ideas in questions be avoided (Bassili and Scott 1996: 391).

Social desirability refers to the notion by respondents that interviewers want some specific responses or that respondents want to present a better self-image of themselves (Nederhof 1985). The phrase can also mean that some respondents may feel compelled to report or to not report some behavior or opinion because these may be socially acceptable or unacceptable.

An example of the first definition is when an interviewer identifies that he/she is working for a survey sponsored by a particular religious body or church. If the survey includes questions about feelings or opinions about this particular church, it is likely that many respondents will feel compelled to express positive opinions or feelings about the church. In this way the survey results are contaminated by social desirability, in this case the fact that the respondent answers in a way he or she thinks the interviewer wants.

The second definition is of particular importance in religion surveys. In many societies being a religious person or identifying with a religion is a socially accepted behavior. Moreover, being religious is not only socially acceptable, but also expected from well-behaved, law-abiding individuals. As such, people who do not identify with a religion or have religious beliefs may feel compelled to lie when answering these questions. The same is true for societies where religion is not the norm or even societies with dominant religions in which people who belong to religious minorities may feel compelled to lie about their affiliation in order to be closer to societal expectations and to avoid religious persecution.

There are several ways of avoiding these problems when conducting a survey. In the first definition, if the survey is conducted by mail or by phone, underscore the source of the study since it can lead itself to biases and contaminate or skew the results. In the case of face-to-face interviews, tell interviewers to avoid the use of garments or accessories that might give hints about the interviewer's religious, political or social opinions.

When evaluating surveys it is necessary to examine the interview protocol in order to observe possible language that may lend itself to **social desirability** issues. This protocol includes the instructions for interviewers and provides specific rules for engaging with respondents. For example, the protocol tells interviewers the instructions to follow for each question, to skip any questions and answers in case the respondent(s) have any doubts about a particular question or term. In this sense it is important to verify questions that may lead the respondents into particular answers.

When designing questionnaires it is important to let the respondents know that they have the option of refusing to answer a question. Allowing refusals permits the interviewer to gain trust from the interviewee because the respondent can withhold answers for questions on topics where the respondent might feel sensitive or uneasy about the options.

In addition, respondents should be able to admit that they do not know a response. There are cases in which respondents honestly do not have an answer or do not know enough about a subject to provide an answer.

The issue, however, is whether researchers should provide response categories that allow for selecting a 'don't know' or 'refuse' option. While these options should be available to the respondent, the researcher should have in mind that respondents may fall back into responding repeatedly 'don't know' and 'refuse', thus providing little useful information to the study. Another way to allow respondents to refuse to answer or admit that they do not know the answer is to have the interviewer to state it so at the beginning of the interview. Including the option of refusing or answering 'don't know' as part of the instructions of the survey can help reduce the proportion of don't knows and refusals because respondents are not constantly reminded of the options. Since respondents have to volunteer their refusals, by skipping or not answering the question(s), this improves the quality of the data. It does so by reducing the number of missing cases since there is no obvious option for refusing, forcing the respondent to choose the answer closest to his or her views. This simplifies the analysis of the data by reducing the need to understand the differences between those who responded to the question and those who refused.

Oftentimes questions require the respondents to rank items or position themselves in particular scales. Two things are important when constructing these scales or rankings. First, it is important that there are definitional differences between the items in the scale. In other words, the items must be distinguishably different in order to avoid confusion of both the respondent and the researchers. Scales measure intensity of opinion, strength of affiliation or conviction and provide insights into the importance of particular subjects for a respondent. The dilemma regarding scales for researchers is how to make the most of this measuring tool. Of particular importance is whether researchers should provide a middle option in the scale or not.

Providing middle or mid-range options means that the scale has an odd number of categories of response. For example, if a questionnaire includes a question such as 'Abortion is morally wrong', the response options for a five-item scale may include two extreme positions, two opposite positions and one middle position. These may be 'strongly agree', 'agree', 'disagree', 'strongly disagree' and 'sometimes'. The middle option, 'sometimes', may be included or not depending on the researcher's goals. Some of the types of scales that researchers use in surveys include the Likert scales. These widely used scales measure intensity by asking the respondent to reply to a question placing his/her feelings or opinions on a bipolar scale. The advantage of using these scales (such as the abortion question above) is that the respondent selects from distinguishable discrete options that do not overlap. This means that the language of the response categories at the extremes opposes each other, and the feelings/opinions moderate as they move to the center categories.

In addition, researchers can use other scales such as rankings. In this case, researchers ask respondents to rank-order their feelings or opinions in order of preferences. These scales are used, for example, in the World Values Survey, where respondents mention if they like or dislike different groups in society (including religious groups). Afterward, the responses are tabulated and we have a rough estimate of how disliked a group is by others. These types of scales are useful for measuring tolerance and social cohesion.

If a researcher wants to gauge a respondent's attitude or intensity toward an issue it is recommendable that the scale consists of even-numbered options. This ploy forces the respondent to take a position on the issue.

When constructing scales it is also necessary to decide the number of options available. A 100-point scale may be too wide and the responses may fall within a particular range (such as 5-, 10- or 20-point increments). Smaller scales such as 5- or 7-point scales are more manageable with enough variation between options and more easily collapsible for simpler analysis.

Training of interviewers

A critical aspect of survey research is the implementation of the survey. Though it is possible to minimize errors in sampling and among respondents, it is equally important to minimize errors among interviewers. Sources of interviewer error include reading errors in which the interviewer skips questions or response options. Another source of error is showing bias. In a face-to-face or telephone interview the interviewer may react to responses which could affect subsequent responses.

Sources of error among interviewers include conducting themselves in a manner that affects the respondent. For example, making comments (positive or negative) about a response can lead the respondent to refrain from responding to further similar questions sincerely. In face-to-face interviews it is important for interviewers to keep a neutral stance and attitude when talking to respondents. It is recommended that they dress somewhat conservatively so as not to call attention with their clothing. Also, interviewers should be able to blend in with the population: e.g. when sent to a neighborhood, try to find interviewers who fit the ethnic or racial profile of the neighborhood (or are fluent with the language). This language component is also important during telephone interviews among diverse populations where accents and enunciation distinguish particular populations.

Finally, other errors may occur in the data entry process. When the data are entered into a computer or spreadsheet manually we recommend using two different persons, who then corroborate with each other. Spreadsheet and statistical software can be used to compare both datasets and find discrepancies.

Analysis of surveys

The statistical rules that help create the survey also apply to analyzing the study. The margin of error applies to the topline results, or the results based on the overall sample. However, when studying sub-samples the margin of error increases and, as a result, the certainty of the results decreases. This is important to realize when generalizing about small groups in a population. While the estimate of size for small sub-groups within a population can be determined for surveys with some certainty, the subsequent analysis of characteristics of small groups is less certain. This is because the error estimate will be higher among smaller groups and subdividing these groups will yield highly volatile and unreliable results. The results are volatile because in repeated samples the results will vary significantly. The wide variation of these results will render them unreliable as a result.

Ways to fix this situation entail grouping categories in order to increment their size. These aggregate categories, however, need to be theoretically justified. In other words, combined groups must have some relationship with each other so combining them makes sense from a research perspective.

When analyzing two variables it is important to understand causation and the direction of the relationship. Take two variables such as age and attendance at religious services. The dependent variable, the one we want to explain, is attendance at religious services. The independent variable, which we will use to explain the dependent variable, is age. A simple analysis such as a histogram will show that older people will attend religious services with more frequency.

However, we must be careful with how we interpret these results, particularly when ascribing causation. The example above could be interpreted like aging makes people more religious. While this may be the case, we do not know for sure. The correct and more sober interpretation is that 'older age is associated with higher levels of attendance at religious services'. In this way we provide the correct context and we are only talking about the relationship between these two particular variables.

Why can we not say that older age causes higher levels of attendance at religious services? First, we do not know if this is the case. It is possible that this result only happens in this particular survey and that in other repeated measures the relationship between both variables changes. Second, if this is a cross-sectional survey, it is wrong to say that as people age they become more religious because the relationship between age and attendance at religious services is limited to this particular survey at a particular point in time. Ergo, we do not know if young people in this sample will be more likely to attend religious services as they get older, or if the older people in the sample stop attending religious services eventually. Finally, we cannot say that older age causes higher levels of attendance to religious services because we do not know if age is the main reason why older people attend religious services more often than younger people. There may be another intervening variable that we are not measuring. For example, maybe the reason why older people attend religious services more often is not age, but free time. Many more people in this age group will be retired than younger people, and with more free time. Maybe there is a lack of social groups for older individuals to join and so places of worship function as a way for older people to socialize.

Other ways in which surveys are analyzed are through descriptive and inferential statistics. Descriptive statistics are used to illustrate simple and straightforward points about the data: e.g. the distribution of the sample, the demographic characteristics of the sample and its relation to the target population. Researchers may use descriptive statistics to show marginals and frequencies of responses and cross-tabulations of two or more variables (such as age and gender) in order to highlight differences or similarities between groups.

Descriptive statistics are useful for grasping the immediate results of the survey. For a more in-depth analysis of relationships between variables or the testing of hypotheses, it is necessary to use inferential statistics. Inferential statistics allow us to interpret with a level of certainty how the relationships between groups of variables work. The most common of these statistics in use in the social sciences today is regression analysis.

Regression analysis explores the relationship between groups of two or more variables. One of the variables is called the dependent variable and it is the variable of which we want a better understanding. For example, we may want to understand the characteristics of people who attend religious services more than once a week. If the survey includes a question on attendance to religious services, this becomes our dependent variable.

What might explain this behavior? To answer this question we would select a variable or variables that explain the dependent variable, according to some theory or observations. This variable (or variables) is called the explanatory or independent variable, because it helps to explain the dependent variable or may be associated with it. Some of these variables, such as gender or age, may vary for members of different religions, by country, or by proximity to a place of worship.

Rather than read a whole set of tabulations between the dependent variable and each independent variable, regression analysis allows the researcher to combine all of them into a single statistical model. This regression model discerns between the different independent variables, controlling for its individual effects, and then determines which variable has a greater association with the dependent variable.

There are different types of regression analysis depending on whether the dependent variable is quantitative or ordinal (such as age), or qualitative or nominal (such as a region of a country). In addition, for different types of regressions there are statistical assumptions for the model that must be met and caveats that apply in their interpretation. There are many books that explain how to conduct this type of analysis and the software that simplifies the process of analysis.[2]

Protection of subjects

A final note regards the protection of subjects. Religion researchers must face the fact that religion is a topic about which many people have very strong opinions and emotions. It is also an arena of conflict and competition in many contemporary societies. Most surveys contain personal information about respondents such as phone numbers, postal codes or addresses, as well as identifying information such as sex and age. There are several ways to deal with issues of confidentiality and protection of information. Many universities, particularly in the United States and Europe, have protocols and review boards that weigh in on the pros and cons of the study and potential harm that can come to subjects. In addition, professional survey organizations such as the American Association for Public Opinion Research (AAPOR) and the World Association for Public Opinion Research (WAPOR) have developed and published their own guidelines for conducting surveys.[3]

Finally, researchers of religion must be constantly aware of cultural issues that may affect results and response rates. For example, some religions may have rules regarding gender relations and contact between men and women. As such, the presence of a male interviewer may hinder some females from answering, or maybe men will not feel comfortable answering questions to a female interviewer, even on the telephone. Similarly, respondents may have issues with answering questions regarding biomedical or ethical issues or about personal behaviors to a member of the opposite sex or in general.

Some solutions include, in the case of face-to-face interviews, sending interviewers in opposite-sex pairs. In this way, subjects have the option of responding to the interviewer with whom they may feel more comfortable, though this process will increase the survey's production costs. In addition, interviewers must reassure subjects that their responses are confidential, or even anonymous, and avoid any gestures or language that the subjects may find offensive, in order to ensure cooperation and enhance trust.

Some particular survey methodologies that have been mentioned here such as mail, online or automated phone calls can provide some solutions to these issues by virtue of being more impersonal methods.

This type of cultural sensitivity issue demonstrates why the survey researcher who works in the field of religion requires a larger repertoire than those who engage in other areas of social and market survey research.

Finally, it is important to assure subjects of the protections (confidentiality, anonymity) that researchers provide to the data. This means telling respondents (orally or written) that their responses will be protected and their information not released, and that at any moment they can stop participation or skip any questions with which they feel uncomfortable. Gaining the trust of respondents is crucial in the success of a survey.

Table 2.20.2 Datasets and existing surveys available online for analysis

Database	Country/region	Home institution(s)	Website
Afrobarometer	Africa	Center for Democratic Development (Ghana); The Institute for Democracy in South Africa (South Africa); Institute for Empirical Research in Political Economy (Benin)	www.afrobarometer.org
American National Election Studies	United States	Center for Political Studies, University of Michigan (USA)	www.electionstudies.org
American Religious Identification Survey	United States	Institute for the Study of Secularism in Society and Culture, Trinity College, Hartford (USA)	www.americanreligion survey-aris.org
Asiabarometer	Asia	Research and Information Center for Asian Studies, Institute of Oriental Culture, University of Tokyo (Japan); Institute of Asia-Pacific Studies, Waseda University (Japan)	www.asiabarometer.org
Association of Religion Data Archives	Various	Social Science Research Institute, Pennsylvania State University (USA)	www.thearda.com
Banco de Información para la Investigación Aplicada en Ciencias Sociales (BIIACS)	Mexico	Centro de Investigación y Docencia Económicas (Mexico)	www.biiacs.cide.edu
Barómetro de las Américas	Latin America	Vanderbilt University (USA)	barometrodelasamericas.org

(Continued Overleaf)

Table 2.20.2 Continued

Database	Country/region	Home institution(s)	Website
British Social Attitudes Survey	United Kingdom	Office for National Statistics (UK)	www.statistics.gov.uk
Canadian Social Survey	Canada	Statistics Canada	www.statcan.gc.ca
East Asian Social Survey	East Asia	Academy of East Asian Studies, SungKyunKwan University (South Korea)	www.eass.info
Eurobarometer	Europe	European Commission	ec.europa.eu/public_opinion/index_en.htm
European Social Survey	Europe	Centre for Comparative Social Surveys, City University London (UK)	www.europeansocialsurvey.org
European Values Study	Europe	Tilburg University (Netherlands)	www.europeanvaluesstudy.eu
General Social Survey	United States	National Opinion Research Center, University of Chicago (USA)	www.norc.org/GSS+Website
International Social Survey Programme	Various	The B.I. and Lucille Cohen Institute for Public Opinion Research, University of Tel Aviv (Israel)	www.issp.org
Inter-University Consortium for Political and Social Research	Various	University of Michigan (USA)	www.icpsr.umich.edu
Japanese Data Archive	Japan	Roper Center for Public Opinion Research, University of Connecticut (USA)	www.ropercenter.uconn.edu
Latin American Data Bank	Latin America	Roper Center for Public Opinion Research, University of Connecticut (USA)	www.ropercenter.uconn.edu
Latin American Public Opinion Project (LAPOP)	Latin America	Vanderbilt University (USA)	www.lapopsurveys.org
Latinobarómetro	Latin America	Corporación Latinobarómetro (Chile)	www.latinobarometro.org
North American Jewish Data Bank	United States and Canada	University of Connecticut (USA)	www.jewishdatabank.org
Pew Forum for Religion in Public Life	United States	Pew Research Center (USA)	www.pewforum.org
Roper Center for Public Opinion Research	Various (mostly United States)	University of Connecticut (USA)	www.ropercenter.uconn.edu
World Values Survey	Various	Institute for Social Research, University of Michigan (USA)	www.worldvaluessurvey.org

Table 2.20.3 Useful software and tools for designing and analyzing surveys

Name	Source	Usefulness	Website
SPSS	Proprietary	Advanced statistical analysis	www.spss.com
Stata	Proprietary	Advanced statistical analysis	www.stata.com
SAS	Proprietary	Advanced statistical analysis	www.sas.com
Statcrunch	Proprietary	Simple statistical analysis (web-based)	www.statcrunch.com
R	Open Source	Advanced statistical analysis	www.r-project.org
Microsoft Office	Proprietary	Microsoft Excel and Access can be used for data entry and these formats can be easily exported to either one of the main statistical analysis software. Word and Publisher can be used to design surveys	office.microsoft.com
Open Office	Open Source	Open Office Calc and Base can be used for data entry and these formats can be easily exported to either one of the main statistical analysis software. Writer can be used to design surveys	www.openoffice.org
Google Docs	Freeware (web-based)	The Spreadsheet application can be used for data entry and the format can be easily exported to either one of the main statistical analysis software. The Document application can be used to design surveys. The Forms application is linked to a spreadsheet and particularly useful for data entry or to conduct web-based surveys	docs.google.com
Survey Monkey	Freeware (web-based). It includes free basic plans but also paid plans for larger surveys.	A useful web application for conducting online studies	www.surveymonkey.com

This list is by no means exhaustive. Its goal is to provide a quick guide for potential researchers to resources that are commonly available through many universities, either in their computer centers, or through subsidies for licences or academic discounts.

Notes

1 The 'further reading' section includes some relevant and recent books on Internet research and surveys.
2 See the 'further reading' section below.
3 These guidelines can be found in the websites of both organizations: www.wapor.org and www. aapor.org.

References

Bassili, J.N. and Scott, B.S., 1996. Response latency as a signal to question problems in survey research. *Public Opinion Quarterly* 60(3): 390–99.

Bastian, J.-P., 1993. The metamorphosis of Latin American Protestant groups: a sociohistorical perspective. *Latin American Research Review* 28(2): 33–61.

Donsbach, W. and Traugott, M.W., 2007. *The SAGE Handbook of Public Opinion Research*. SAGE, London, Thousand Oaks, CA.

Field, C.D., 2007. Rendering unto Caesar?: the politics of Church of England clergy since 1980. *Journal of Anglican Studies* 5(1): 89–108.

Harkness, J., Pennell, B.-E. and Schoua-Glusberg, A., 2004. Survey questionnaire translation and assessment. In: Presser, S., Rothbeg, J.M., Couper, M.P., Lessler, J.L., Martin, E., Martin, J. and Singer, E. (eds), *Methods for Testing and Evaluating Survey Questionnaires*. Wiley, New York.

Kosmin, B.A. and Keysar, A., 2006. *Religion in a Free Market*. Paramount Market Publishing, Ithaca, NY.

—— 2009. *American Religious Identification Survey (ARIS 2008) Summary Report*. Institute for the Study of Secularism in Society and Culture, Hartford, CT.

Nagata, J., 1982. Islamic revival and the problem of legitimacy among rural religious elites in Malaysia. *Man* 17(1): 42–57.

Nederhof, A.J., 1985. Methods of coping with social desirability bias: a review. *European Journal of Social Psychology* 15(3): 263–80.

Norris, P. and Inglehart, R., 2004. *Sacred and secular: religion and politics worldwide*. Cambridge University Press, Cambridge.

Traugott, M.W., 2008. The uses and misuses of polls. In: Donsbach, W. and Traugott, M.W. (eds), *The Sage Handbook of Public Opinion Research*. SAGE, London, Thousand Oaks, CA.

Further reading

Agresti, A. and Finlay, B., 2009. *Statistical Methods for the Social Sciences*. Allyn & Bacon, Boston.

Agresti and Finlay's Statistical Methods for the Social Sciences *is a simple primer for beginners. At the same time, the book's organization leads the reader through the process of describing and analyzing data in an intuitive manner.*

Babbie, E., 2009. *The Practice of Social Research*. 12th edn. Wadsworth, New York.

This is the classic text on research methods. One of the most comprehensive guides on research and used as a textbook in many undergraduate and graduate courses due to both its depth and ease of understanding. The Practice of Social Research *is particularly strong in survey research methods, including the latest techniques.*

Best, S.J. and Krueger, B.S., 2004. *Internet Data Collection*. SAGE, London, Thousand Oaks, CA.

This is one of the first books on Internet-based research. Best and Krueger provide a guide not only for surveys, but also for other types of data collection. Considering how much the Internet has evolved since 2004, it is a good primer and still relevant in many instances.

Dillman, D.A., 2007. *Mail and internet surveys: the tailored design method*. John Wiley and Sons, Malden, MA.

This is the book's updated second edition, given the fast-moving digital world. It is more specific to survey research and provides strategies to increase response rates, a well-known issue not only in Internet studies but also in mail-in surveys.

Fink, A., 2009. *How to Conduct Surveys: a step-by-step guide*. 4th edn. SAGE, London, Thousand Oaks, CA.

An important book in survey research methods, How to Conduct Surveys *is, as the title suggests, a 'step-by-step guide'. Fink's style is clear and reachable for different types of audiences from the specialist to the novice.*

Fowler, Jr, F.J., 1995. *Improving Survey Questions: design and evaluation*. SAGE, London, Thousand Oaks, CA.

Questions and the way they are asked are essential in survey research. Fowler's book provides a thorough guide for designing questions and the benefits and pitfalls of different types of methods and wording strategies.

Groves, R.M., 1989. *Survey Errors and Survey Costs*. Wiley, New York.

A classic written by one of the most prominent survey researchers in the United States incorporates one usually overlooked aspect of survey research: cost. The book explains how errors and their associated costs affect the quality of research.

Groves, R.M, Fowler, Jr, F.J., Couper, M.P., Lepkowski, J.M., Singer, E. and Tourangeau, R., 2004. *Survey Methodology*. Wiley, New York.

Survey Methodology *explains the basics of survey research and offers advice for decision-making in the process of designing a survey. The book brings up to date many of the advances in the field.*

Levine, D.M., Berenson, M.L., Stephan, D. and Krehbiel, T.C., 2008. *Statistics for Managers Using Microsoft Excel*. Pearson Prentice Hall, Englewood Cliffs, NJ.

An excellent resource for those with limited access to or time for learning advanced statistical software. This book teaches the reader basic statistical functions and how to conduct these functions in the widely available MS Excel program.

Salant, P. and Dillman, D.A., 1994. *How to Conduct Your Own Survey*. Wiley, New York.

An accessible guide to designing surveys, this book provides advice on how to determine which type of survey to use as well as determining costs. It also provides help with questionnaire design, sample selection and correction and avoidance of errors.

Tourangeau, R., Rips, L.J. and Rasinski, K., 2000. *The Psychology of Survey Response*. Cambridge University Press, Cambridge.

This is an excellent guide to understand the psychological processes that involve answering survey questions. The authors explore how different types of questions elicit different respondents and how question working affects the way in which respondents answer surveys.

Key concepts

Central limit theorem: a statistical concept that states that in repeated samples, the sum of a large number of independent observations will approach a normal distribution. The principles behind the CLT are used for sampling and analysis of probabilistic surveys.

Closed questions: questions in which the respondent answers from a pre-determined list of response options.

Confidence interval: is an estimated range of values between which a population parameter may fall. With repeated sampling, these estimates will reflect the population parameters.

Double-barreled questions: a type of question in which the respondent needs to respond to two or more independent questions combined in a single statement.

Interviewer: person who imparts the survey to the respondent.

Margin of error: a statistical measure of the reliability of our estimates.

Measurement error: this term applies to several types of errors (often unintentional and unknown to the researcher) which can occur during the course of fielding a study. These errors can skew the results of the survey through incorrect estimates of the true values of the population.

Non-response bias: a type of survey error in which there is difference (demographic or otherwise) between those who respond to a voluntary survey and those who do not.

Open-ended questions: questions in which the interviewee answers with his/her own words.

Operationalization: the definition of concepts that the researcher is interested to study. After these concepts are defined the researcher constructs items that measure these concepts in a reliable and valid way.

Parameter: a representation of the value of a variable in a population.

Population: an aggregate of individuals (people, institutions) that is subject to study.

Questionnaire: the collection of questions that inquire about the attitudes, opinions or observations of a population.

Random selection: The method by which a sample for a survey that is generalizable to the general population should be selected.

Respondent: an individual who responds to a survey.

Response rate: the proportion of contacts that complete an interview. It is calculated by dividing the number of completed interviews by the total number of contacts.

Sample: a selection of individuals or institutions from a larger population.

Social desirability: A tendency among survey respondents to answer questions in a manner that their responses are acceptable to others.

Survey: a research method that allows researchers to collect opinions and observations from a sample and generalize these to a particular population.

Universe: the target population of a survey. The universe is defined by the researcher according to the characteristics of the group(s) of interest.

Related chapters

- Chapter 1.2 Comparison
- Chapter 1.3 Epistemology
- Chapter 1.5 Research design
- Chapter 1.6 Research ethics
- Chapter 2.7 Factor analysis
- Chapter 2.13 Interviewing
- Chapter 3.2 The internet

2.21

TRANSLATION

Alan Williams

Chapter summary

- Translation is a creative scientific process, intrinsic to the study of religion as we attempt to understand 'the other'.
- Translation of 'sacred texts' ('sensitive texts') affords unique opportunities for methodological reflection, bringing into focus the dilemmas of the 'outsider' delving into the world of the 'insider'.
- In scholarly editions of texts translation may be so subordinated to other scholarly work of collation, editing, explanation, etc., that it fails to be sufficiently communicative in the target language.
- Since poetry is so often already a translation into metaphor in the source text, 'literalness' in poetry translation may be preferable to a translation that attempts to gloss the 'meaning' of the poetry: thus poetry is discovered, not lost, in translation.
- Translators of religious texts need to explain and amplify the context, reception history and social significance of a text as part of their job as translator.
- Translators may act as peace-makers, bridging cultures and communities.

Introduction and overview

Translation is central to the study of religion, in so far as all scholars have recourse to translating and translations, and it is also a subject that discloses major methodological problems in our field. The reason for this is most simply put thus: translating requires the closest of readings, and all of religion requires 'translating'. Until recently, translation was something done without much methodological thinking applied to it—as one senior colleague once summed-up the prevailing attitude: 'it's a matter of flying by the seat of your pants: you know a good translation when you see one'. The relatively new discipline of translation studies has made scholars of religion sit up and think about what they are doing.[1] In our business of handling and translating **sacred texts** from all over the world, we are in a uniquely privileged position to reflect on how the challenges of translation raise more general methodological issues in the study of religion. I have written elsewhere (Williams 2004) and at length on this subject and therefore shall not repeat substantially

421

the arguments and examples of that piece (see Box 2.21.1 for a summary of questions raised in that essay).

Box 2.21.1 Questions raised by translation

- What is the nature of translation?
- Is translation entirely a culturally constructed phenomenon?
- What is the status of the source text vis à vis the translated text?
- Is something always lost from the 'original' in translation?
- Is translation a kind of cultural theft?
- Can translation replace, or at least substitute, the 'original'?
- What is untranslatable?
- Does poetry present unique problems?
- What happens when translation is 'forbidden'?
- How are sacralized languages sometimes put into the service of a linguistic/cultural imperialism?
- How is translation more than a linguistic phenomenon?
- Is translation a secondary research activity in the hierarchy of scholarly work?
- Is not reading a text, even a primary text in a source language, always 'translation'?
- How far are scholars of religion aware of developments in the study of translation in past decades?
- Do academic translators still operate on unexamined assumptions about texts and translations?
- Are the gold standards of 'fidelity' and 'scientific accuracy' the most helpful guides towards the best kind of translation?
- Do the metaphors of previous centuries, of translator as civilizer or as servant of the 'original text' still prevail?
- To what extent does the postmodern, post-colonial academy pose new questions in respect of understanding the theory and practice of translation?
- What do we nowadays understand the translator to be doing?
- Why do certain texts get selected for translation, whilst others remain untranslated?
- What is the role of the translator in the selection of texts, and what is the role of the editor, publisher or, in the past, patron?
- What are the criteria for translation strategies, and how are the translations received by the readership in the target language?
- To what degree is there methodological reflection on translation in the study of religion?
- How radically, if at all, does one 'repair' a text?
- How far can a translation communicate to its target language readers the understanding of the text that source language readers have?

(Williams 2004)

In this chapter, I confine myself to reflecting on the principal theoretical and practical challenges that are posed by translating sacred texts. Religious texts include many genres, of course, including poetry, philosophy, history and theological disputation, as well as the most visible group, namely 'scriptural, revealed' texts. This last category is regarded as a uniquely sensitive genre, and in working with such material the translator is faced with problems rarely encountered in other areas.[2] In short, as much as any other subject in this book, translation opens up the whole question of what it is we do, and how we do it, in the study of religion (see Engler 2005; Engler and Gardiner forthcoming). Translation is interpretation and communication across boundaries between the self and the other. None know better than scholars of religion just how carefully patrolled and guarded, indeed just how dangerous, those boundaries are.

'Translators do it for pleasure' could be the, proverbially ambiguous, fender sticker of the profession—though, considering the labor pains experienced in the act of giving birth to a translation, 'love' may be closer to the mark. Translators certainly do not do it for money or prestige, as the translator is all too often an invisible figure—on the dust jacket and in other credits.[3] At the same time translators are vulnerable and all too often in the firing line. The Bible translator William Tyndale was strangled to death and burned at the stake for heresy in 1536—and yet his translation became the basis of the celebrated King James Version of 1611. More recently, but also for religious reasons, the Japanese scholar of Arabic and Persian litera-ture and translator of Salman Rushdie's *Satanic Verses* Hitoshi Igarashi was stabbed to death in his own university office in 1991. Rushdie's Norwegian, Italian and Turkish translators narrowly survived assassination attempts. In the war zones of Iraq and Afghanistan translators and interpreters are regularly targets for assassination. Such victimization gives a sinister new meaning to the old Italian adage *traduttore, traditore!* 'translator, traitor!' The danger is an occupational hazard, for, as one authority in modern translation studies has said, 'Translators are agents who facilitate the crossing over a boundary' (Bassnett in Engler *et al.* 2007: 300). More than merely linguistic, those boundaries are cultural, political, ideological and, most important for our discussion of translation and the study of religion, sacred boundaries. Where boundaries do not merely demarcate areas, but actually serve to protect prohibited zones, the translator is both insurgent and thief—an agent of destabilization.

'Sacred languages' as sacred precincts

In comparison with more theoretically discursive types of work that the scholar of religions may do, translations are more visible, more read, and more engaged with by the general public. Moreover, the works translated are, rightly or wrongly, claimed as the *property and heritage* of religious communities, over which they assume a duty of protection. More poign-antly, the very languages in which they are written are believed to be sacred, and in some cases the uniquely **sacred language** of the divinity itself—certain examples of this phenom-enon are well known, e.g. Qur'anic Arabic, Gāthic Avestan, Koinē Greek, biblical Hebrew of the *Tanakh/Miqra*, Syriac and Aramaic, Vedic and other forms of *śruti* Sanskrit. Such languages are interiorised by religious specialists of the traditions, namely their priests and ritual practi-tioners, as they are also the liturgical languages of the respective traditions, without which religious practice is ineffectual: the texts are learned by heart in oral as well as, or in place of, cheirographic modes of transmission. For example, referring to Alexander's destruction of Persepolis, Mary Boyce states:

> In those days, when all religious works were handed down orally, the priests were the living books of the faith, and with mass slaughters many ancient works (the tradition holds) were lost or only haltingly preserved.
>
> *(Boyce 1979: 79)*

Whereas sacred languages are believed to have a resonance, solemnity, beauty, dignity and even effective numinous and magical power, translation into secondary, vernacular and 'secular' languages is deemed to be a process that loses the authenticity of the divine speech in the sacred language. The stipulations concerning the doctrine of the Arabic Qur'an's inimitability and the impossibility of its translation are nowadays well known, but it is perhaps too often forgotten that once not so long ago the scriptural and liturgical language of the Roman Catholic church was exclusively Latin. Translations of the Bible into English by the Oxford theologian and translator John Wycliffe (1328–84) were banned by the Church and he was declared a heretic. The deep irony of the Christian Church's taking exception to translation is captured by F.E. Peters:

> Christians were at home with the notion of translation, though not always with its results. They had been given the New Testament in what was already a form of translation—Jesus taught in Aramaic, not the koine Greek of the Gospels—and there was no apparent hesitation in bundling in with those four 'translated' Gospels a series of other works, starting with Paul's letters, whose language had no connection whatsoever with Jesus' own. As for the Old Testament, the Christians inherited a translation, the Septuagint, whose purely scholarly defects were [. . .] apparent even to Jerome, whose stated purpose was a translation of a translation, to turn the Greek Septuagint into a Latin version for the benefit of his Western readers.
>
> *(Peters 2007: 214)*

Indeed such is the power of the idea of a 'sacred language' over believers and the authorities who patrol the tradition to protect its textual and liturgical precincts that it has also been allowed to become a term in the academic field of the study of religion. This is understandable if the scholars concerned are Christian or Zoroastrian priests, for example, or religious Muslims, working on the texts of their own traditions, but it is an instance where the subject of translation raises an important methodological question and highlights the tautology by which the academic field sometimes defines itself: the study of religion as the study of traditions that have 'sacred texts' in 'sacred languages'. In place of unquestioning academic acquiescence to the notion of any language being intrinsically sacred, I have suggested elsewhere that the operation of 'sacred languages vis à vis neighboring, vernacular languages within one religious tradition is tantamount to a kind of "linguistic imperialism" of the religious kind' (Williams 2008). Latin was asserted to be the true medium of holy discourse in scripture and theology and so sacred, as opposed to the vernacular European languages. Similarly Arabic is claimed to be the language of Qur'anic revelation, which is meaningful as revelation only *in* the Arabic language and which demands valid reading and liturgical practice in that language exclusively. H. Abdul-Raof, writing on 'Cultural Aspects in Qur'an Translation', addresses this problem thus:

> For Muslim scholars, the Latin Qur'an can never be a replacement of the Qur'an because translation, for them, is 'a traducement, a betrayal, an inferior copy of a prioritised original' [. . .] Their concern, however, is not justified.
>
> *(Abdul-Raof 2005: 162, citing Bassnett and Lefevere 1998: 25)*

Abdul-Raof's subtly explained essay argues, as many others have done, for the genuine possibility of Qur'an translation. Though he admits difference between the **source language** (SL, Arabic) and **target language** (TL, e.g. English), he denies that language is the problem:

ideology and poetics are, as are cultural elements that are not immediately clear, or seen as completely 'misplaced' in what would be the target culture version of the text to be translated. Abdul-Raof's recommendation is that the translator needs to be both bilingual and bicultural:

> To narrow the gap of cultural unfamiliarity [. . .] I suggest domestication of the SL expression and exegetical footnotes in order to bring home to the TL audience, increase the level of source text informativity, and maintain SL intentionality.
>
> *(Abdul-Raof 2005: 172)*

This is a laudable attempt to explain the translator's solution to the problem, presumably discovered in the course of long practical experience, namely of domestication (translating the 'foreign' SL concept in acceptably familiar TL terms) and the appending of explanatory notes to the translation. In reality, however, does such a solution adequately respond to the religious claim that the Qur'anic text cannot adequately be translated?—for this is linguistic transcendentalism. It is not equivalent to the Englishman's claim that Shakespeare, or the Russian's claim that Pushkin, can never be done justice in another language, for this is linguistic patriotism: the religious claim appeals to a higher authority: the idea of divine speech in *the* 'sacred' language. Translators must, it seems, live with this (and hopefully not die by it). More positively, the category of sacred language has necessitated that almost infinite amounts of human energy and attention have been paid to the preservation and exegesis of texts over generations of religious scholars and priests, whose work has been supplemented and adorned by the beautification of calligraphers, painters, architects and musicians. For the scholar of religion, however, translation raises the fundamental question of the difference existing between two perspectives. The perspectives may be that of temporal difference, ancient and modern, or cultural and geographical distance, but it is always all the more poignant when it involves also the difference encountered specifically in our field, namely between the believer (insider) and non-believer (outsider).

Texts, pitfalls and possibilities

In this section I shall discuss certain pitfalls that can beset one and possibilities that can open up in translation by relating some examples of translating from my own experience. One of the first things of which the academic scholar in the study of religion may become aware, upon embarking on translation of a religious text, is that he or she is poised at the edge of the emic precipice of the 'insider' source text. The translator may imagine that one has to make a giant leap across a chasmic divide in order to render it into a target language, and yet may fall to a miserable death dashed upon the rocks of etic incomprehensibility. Mercifully the novice translator is all too often unaware of the risks of translation, as was certainly the case of the present writer in his translations of a ninth-century Zoroastrian text from Pahlavi. Working on a doctoral thesis in Iranian studies, scholarly training in the relevant Iranian languages, close examination of manuscripts and the text's origins and context, and discipline with regard to observance of syntax and grammar, lexicon and structure of the text, all ensured that translation would be as 'close' as possible. Situated in a scholarly monograph comprising manuscript collation, transliteration, transcription, editing and occasionally reconstruction of the text, the translation of the 65 chapters of the Pahlavi *Rivāyat* accompanying the *Dādestān ī Dēnīg* (*PRDd*) formed only a relatively small part of a very long work.[4] Since it was written in Middle Persian, Book Pahlavi, not the Zoroastrian sacred language of 'Gāthic Avestan' with its many *hapax legomena* and prehistoric origins, I was able to compare the text and its language with many other, earlier, contemporary and later Zoroastrian works. Since the text included materials and themes that were both found elsewhere and also unique to this text, I was obliged to take account of translations and findings already established by other scholarly editors and also to be innovative in coming to my own definitions and conclusions. Though some reviewers disagreed with certain of my translations and interpretations, the book became the standard edition of the *PRDd*. My point here is that the translation was, it seems, very much a secondary element in the monograph as a whole. Scholars who consulted the work would already be familiar with Pahlavi and could decide for themselves (and presumably for the students with whom they might read the book) how to read the text. The value of its 'closeness' to the 'original' was a scholarly matter, and not—for want of a better term—translational. I have written about this subsidiarity of translation to scholarly preoccupations in a previous essay on translation in the study of religion (Williams 2004: 15–16). One thing I can see, 20 years after publishing this work, is that my translations deliberately do not make easy reading. I had unconsciously decided that since the style of the author, and the character of Book Pahlavi itself, were difficult in the original, it was therefore justifiable that the translation should *not* make easy reading, on grounds of accuracy and fidelity to the original. The method of translation adopted was preponderantly non-domesticated: technical terms and 'Pahlavisms'—even, as I can see now, in the English syntax—were carried over into the translation in abundance. It is possible that this 'difficulty' is justifiable in terms of replicating the original writer's and reader's experience of the text in the modern reader. However, as it turned out, it was a type of scholarly translation work I did not wish to repeat in future.

It was my good fortune to be invited by a celebrated literary publisher to translate the mystical poem *Masnavi-ye Ma'navi* ('Spiritual Couplets') of Jalāloddin Rumi, the 13th-century Sufi poet. I resisted the invitation to abridge the six volumes into one, on the grounds that this would require the 'filleting' of the stories from the greater body of the book and thus distorting the work—not to mention the fact that this had already been done by A.J. Arberry (1961, 1963). I embarked on translation of the first of the six *daftars* ('books') of the *Masnavi*.[5] My intention was to bring my training in Iranian linguistics together with my understanding of Sufi tradition in order to produce an accurate version suitable for a modern English literary readership. I quickly found that such translation needed not only to convey the semantic meaning of the original, but also to reflect the aesthetic beauty of one of the greatest poets in Persian—a greater challenge than I had previously met with in academic work. Many translations of Rumi's *Masnavi* had existed since Whinfield's and Redhouse's 19th-century versifications, and notably after Nicholson's magisterial translation of all six books into a highly literal prose of somewhat archaic English.[6] After preparing a first draft in what I would call poetic prose, the experience of reading my translations to a live Iranian and Western audience at a large venue in London persuaded me that what my translation lacked was rhythm and metre. I discovered that not only was it possible to translate literally into blank verse couplets (i.e. in unrhymed iambic pentameter), but that the discipline of metrification pressured me into a more creative approach to translation than I had thought possible. The 22 syllables of the *Masnavi* distych are equivalent to the 20–22 syllables of the blank verse couplet (with male or female endings). Crucially, also, the blank verse metre affords a very wide range of poetic and dramatic registers, remarkably well-suited to the varying registers of Rumi's original. The challenge of rendering a Persian rhymed verse poem into unrhymed blank verse English metre made me acutely aware of Rumi's constantly shifting 'point of view', and brought me to formulate a theory of his mystical poetics, namely *how* he achieves the effects he does in Persian. I had always agreed with Susan Bassnett's impatient dismissal of what I call 'poetry translation-deniers':

> there is a great deal of nonsense written about poetry and translation too, of which probably the best known is Robert Frost's immensely silly remark that 'poetry is what gets lost in translation', which implies that poetry is some intangible, ineffable thing (a presence? a spirit?) which, although constructed *in* language cannot be transposed *across* languages.
>
> *(Bassnett and Lefevere 1998: 57, original emphasis)*

Bassnett, contributing more recently to a roundtable discussion (Engler *et al.* 2007: 299–300), found the poet Shelley's metaphor of translation as 'effectively an organic process of trans-plantation' helpful:

> because it takes us away from discourses about translation that highlight problems of what constitutes faithfulness and unfaithfulness and moves us instead to thinking about translation as a creative act.
>
> *(in Engler et al. 2007: 299–300)*

Crucially, Bassnett adds:

> If, as Shelley proposes, translation is so close to impossible that no text can ever be the same in any other language, then we do not need to agonize about how we can determine translation equivalence. All we have to do is accept that translation is a form of transplantation, and that in new soil, the seed that has been translated will develop into another kind of plant, becoming effectively a new original.
>
> *(in Engler et al. 2007: 300)*

Whilst I like Bassnett's 'thinking about translation as a creative act' (and my experience of this kind of work is that it is immensely rewarding, in terms of pleasing parts of the brain other academic work cannot reach), for me this creative act had to be guided by several principles:

- All of the text had to be translated—I did not reshape the work by editing out verses.
- The translation was as far as possible literal, and within the constraints of the iambic pentameter line I translated all the words.
- Literalness was possible because I insisted upon leaving the 'knots' of Rumi's original metaphors tied up just as he had written them: as a mystical poet Rumi occasionally left me baffled, as perhaps he had left every other translator, by his ultimate meaning. However, since he had already translated his meaning into metaphor, my task as translator was only to put the words of the metaphor into English. In this sense, perhaps, poetry translation may be said to be strangely simpler than other kinds of translation, such as that of philos-ophy or theology, in that the translator of those genres is obliged to explain what he understands the writer to have meant. Since the poet has used already metaphor to get his meaning across, i.e. done an *intra*-lingual 'translation' into metaphor, *inter*-lingual transla-tion is relatively easier since no further explanation is necessary. Having said this, helpful exegetical notes are sometimes essential.
- I did not use end rhymes, although internal rhymes and assonance were useful to keep up with the wordplays and punning of the original.

The nicest compliment ever paid to me as a translator of Rumi's works was once made (unwittingly and unsycophantically, I should emphasize) by an Iranian mature student who, having read a passage of my published translation remarked that he now understood the original better when he re-read it. Upon reflection I saw the reason for this perhaps having partly to do with the fact that I translated the verses into a modern language, irrespective of whether it was Persian or English. Seven centuries is a long time in any language, even in one that has changed relatively little such as Persian.

In summary, translating the *Masnavi* (an ongoing project) brought to light various methodological problems for consideration. The first challenge, but not the greatest, was: how to render volatile, sometimes explosively ecstatic, mystical poetry into modern English? I learned the lesson music teachers had tried to instil in me: read carefully what is written in the score and play just that. I found that by attending closely to the associative stream and dynamic movements of Rumi's poetic imagination, I could learn to follow what he meant to say. The time required and intensity of absorption into the text, for a task as great as translating thousands of couplets into verse form, brought me to another methodological problem. Was I, as translator, becoming absorbed into the object of my study, and allowing my critical distance from my author and his work to become diminished? In sum, was I becoming a Rumiphile in my ruminations? My answer to this is 'no, not in any problematic way'. Though my admiration for Rumi as a poet is great, it is equalled by my fascination to discover *how* this poem works. This fascination has borne fruit in some ideas about how mystical intensification works in language, and even how persuasion works in religious discourse. Quite unparadoxically, in fact,[7] translating Rumi made me question assumptions about the category of religion and simplistic, essentialist understandings about the oneness of religions. This creative and, I would say, respectably academic analytical work has all come out of translating the poetry.

The third and final example of a translation project that raised for me methodological problems, and resulted in my perhaps better understanding the nature of a religious text through translation, bore fruit in a recent monograph on the Zoroastrian Persian poem *Qesse-ye Sanjān* 'Story of Sanjān' (Williams 2009). For many years I had been interested in the fact that Parsi Zoroastrians knew this story, and yet they did not know the text, and yet still again that they based much of their identity as Gujarati-speaking, Indian Parsi Zoroastrians on the main features of this story. Written in Persian verse couplets it was also surprising that their co-religionists, the Iranian Zoroastrians, did not know either the story or the text at all. Every Parsi I had ever met could regale me with a version of the *Qesse-ye Sanjān*, yet none had seen the Persian text. An oral tradition of the story was still current in the late 20th century, based upon old, partial, inaccurate and sometimes paraphrased translations. The text was not highly regarded by scholars of Iranian studies, which was perhaps more a reflection of the fact that nobody had ever done a scholarly edition of the text from the oldest manuscripts. My efforts to translate this *Qesse-ye Sanjān*—a linguistically unproblematic Persian verse text of some 430 couplets written down by an Indian Parsi priest in Navsari, Gujarat in 1599— brought to light a number of themes of interest to scholars of Zoroastrianism and, I hope, religion in general. As a document it had been written down, so its author Bahman states, to preserve the oral memory of the ancients about how the Zoroastrians abandoned Iran after the Islamic invasion, and how they came to India and were granted refuge and then land to settle in Gujarat. It is written in a fairly literary Persian, bringing together an assortment of styles ranging from a quasi sufi-cum-courtly introductory doxology, to a narrative of a long journey, to a martial epic style recording bloody battles of victory and defeat. Since Parsis generally now know no Persian and can no longer read the Arabic script I provided a romanized transcription of the text facing the translation on the opposite page, so that Zoroastrian readers could have a sense of a Persian original present with the translation and see its verse form for themselves.[8] I considered it important that readers should take full account of the fact that this text was not a folk-chronicle or sketchy outline of history, but rather a piece of religious poetry, preserved in the collective memory—no doubt partly contrived by a High Priest with some literary pretensions—as a religious poem, and hence my blank verse translation. As such, it has to have the integrity and compositional structure of an epic poem, in miniature imitation, I hope to have shown, of the vastly greater national epic of the Iranians, namely the *Shāhnāme*. My translation went through many stages of draft, and with the experience of translating Rumi's *Masnavi*, as described above, it evolved into a blank verse translation, so as better to represent its poetic composition. As well as the chapters of introduction, text and translation, and verse-by-verse commentary, I wrote about the narrative structure of the text and lastly about the mythical nature of its story, which had for well over a century been misapprehended by Parsis and some Western scholars as bad history. This translation of the *Qesse-ye Sanjān* incorporated several levels of analysis: as well as a new treatment of a previously little-known 'famous' text, in which the original text appeared alongside the English version for virtually the first time in modernity, it was necessary to include also:

- The establishing of the context of its composition, in terms of its background, manuscript tradition and history of transmission.
- An analysis of the narrative structure of the text, demonstrating that its form and its subject matter were intertwined and mutually reinforcing.
- A full commentary explaining the technical terms and intertextual nature of the *Qesse-ye Sanjān* and moreover the significance of the borrowings and references for the overall purposes of the writer.
- An explanation of the mythic nature of the text as *rite de passage* and as a text of consolation and affirmation of community identity, having abandoned Iran and found a new 'home-land', home from home as an exiled community in India.
- Lastly, an account of the various ways in which the text had been received and explained in the past.

Conclusion

Translation can be a highly intensive, all-consuming labor, and hence it has here often been illustrated by the personal experience of the present writer. The above elements in support of the translation of the *Qesse-ye Sanjān* were necessary because the text does not exist in an academic vacuum. This was expressed in a highly formalized, codified way in the Pahlavi *Rivāyat* accompanying the *Dādestān ī Dēnīg*. Such an ancient, priestly exegetical text belongs perhaps as much to the rarefied scholarly community of Zoroastrianists as it does to the religious community. The *Masnavi* of Rumi and the *Qesse-ye Sanjān*, however, can be said to belong to a greater community. To some extent, nowadays, Rumi's work goes way beyond the Sufi and Muslim communities of the Islamic world, especially in English, to a global readership of literature and (*horribile dictu*) 'spirituality'. In my own case the translation project continues for the sake of the rich material the *Masnavi* affords for the analysis of Rumi's mystical poetics. For the Zoroastrian text, working on a subject that is of concern to a contemporary living community, one is preparing a non-scholarly version of the book for publication in the Zoroastrian community of India. There will also be a Persian translation of my monograph for circulation in Iran, where interest in the Zoroastrian past of the country has reached unprecedented levels in modern times. In sum, my own philosophy of translation is that the translator must make peace not just with those upon whom he visits his translations, but also with those from whom he has derived them. As to what model of translation one employs, one can choose, for example, from such as are illustrated in Box 2.21.2. Or indeed one can, as the present writer has attempted to do, combine and move between them, learning skills and styles in each, and trying to bring the benefits of insight from one to another.

Box 2.21.2 Some models of translation

1 *Linguistic/philological*: translation as primarily a linguistic operation, incorporating philological and general linguistic analysis; may extend to sociolinguistic and psycholinguistic analysis; such methods were previously preponderant in, e.g. Arabic, Chinese, Indian and Iranian studies.

2 *Specialist*: translation for a specialist academic audience, e.g. Indian philosophy, archaeology, i.e. fields that have a highly technical language of discourse and specification.

3 *Academic exegetical*: may include the above approach but incorporates also historical, phenomenological, anthropological and other contextual analysis drawn from the wider field of the study of religion.

4 *Literary*: represents the text for a new audience and cultural context of contemporary readers, yet retaining something of the literary/stylistic qualities of the source text; ranges from the more linguistically rigorous (inclining towards 1 or 2, above) to more popular translation (inclining to 5, below).

5 *Religious exegetical*: prioritizes the source text as a more or less sacred 'original', with regard also to its status in the canon maintained by the faith community; interpretation/exegesis is based on, or continues, the hermeneutic discourse of the faith tradition and may be for dissemination to the faith community alone or for a wider audience.

6 *Popular*: often synthesized versions collated from previous examples of translations done on the above models, intended as inspirational and/or informative for a general contemporary audience.

Notes

1 See e.g. Bassnett 1980; Bassnett and Lefevere 1990, 1998; and for a survey of the subject Gentzler 1993.
2 See, e.g. the collection of articles on the translatability of 'holy' texts in Long 2005.
3 For a full discussion of all aspects of this see Venuti 1995.
4 Williams 1990, which is a two-volume work of 738 pages.
5 Published as Williams 2006, 2007.
6 Nicholson 1925–40.
7 i.e. in spite of popular misconceptions about Rumi's own 'message' of universality.
8 It has been a convention in Iranian studies for scholars to provide a transcription (and sometimes also a transliteration) of Middle and Old Iranian texts in Pahlavi, Avestan, etc., because the scripts are generally so cryptic, but not in treatments of New Persian in Arabic script. I also provided photographs of the folios of the oldest manuscript in the centre of the book.

References

Abdul-Raof, H., 2005. Cultural aspects in Qur'an translation. In: Long, L. (ed.), *Translation and Religion: holy untranslatable?* Multilingual Matters, Clevedon and New York, pp.162–72.

Arberry, A.J., 1961. *Tales from the Mathnawi.* George Allen and Unwin, London.

—— 1963. *More Tales from the Mathnawi.* George Allen and Unwin, London.

Bassnett, S. and Lefevere, A. (eds), 1998. *Constructing Cultures: essays on literary translation.* Multilingual Matters, Clevedon.

Boyce, M., 1979. *Zoroastrians: their religious beliefs and practices.* Routledge and Kegan Paul, London.

Engler, S., 2005. Translation. In: von Stuckrad, K. (ed.) (with Auffarth, C., Bernard, J. and Mohr, H.), *The Brill Dictionary of Religion.* Brill, London, vol. 4, pp. 1916–20.

Engler, S., Bassnett, S., Bringhurst, R. and DiGiacomo, S.M., 2007. Consider translation: a roundtable discussion. *Religious Studies Review* 33 (4): 299–316.

Engler, S. and Gardiner, M.Q., forthcoming. Translation. In: Segal R.A. and von Stuckrad, K. (eds), *Vocabulary for the Study of Religion.* Brill, Leiden, Boston.

Long, L., 2005. *Translation and Religion: holy untranslatable?* Multilingual Matters, Clevedon.

Nicholson, R.A., 1925–40. *The Mathnawī of Jalālu'ddīn Rūmī: texts, translations and commentaries.* 8 volumes, Luzac & Co., London.

Peters, F.E., 2007. *The Voice, The Word, The Books.* Princeton University Press, Princeton.

Redhouse, J.W., 1881. *Mesnevi of Mevlana Jelalu'd-din er-Rumi.* Trübner & Co., London.

Venuti, L., 1995. *The Translator's Invisibility.* Routledge, London and New York.

Whinfield, E.H., 1887. *Masnaví-i Ma'naví, the Spiritual Couplets of Mauláná Jalálu'd-din Muhammad Rúmí.* translated and abridged Trübner & Co., London.

Williams, A.V., 1990. *The Pahlavi Rivāyat Accompanying the Dādestān ī Dēnīg.* The Royal Danish Academy of Sciences and Letters, Copenhagen.

—— 2006. *Rumi Spiritual Verses: the first book of the* Masnavi-ye Ma'navi. London, New York, Penguin Classics.

—— 2007. *The Spiritual Verses: translated and abridged,* read by Anton Lesser, Naxos Audiobooks, London, 4 CDs.

—— 2008. The Continuum of Sacred Language: from high speech to low speech in the Middle Iranian (Pahlavi) Zoroastrian tradition. In: Green, N. and Searle Chatterjee, M. (eds), *Religion Language and Power.* Routledge, London, pp. 123–42.

—— 2009. *The Zoroastrian Myth of Migration from Iran and Settlement in the Indian Diaspora: text, translation and Analysis of the 16th century Qesse-ye Sanjān 'The Story of Sanjān'.* Brill, Leiden, Boston.

Further reading

Baker, M. and Malmkjær, K. (eds), 1998. *Routledge Encyclopedia of Translation Studies.* Routledge, London, New York.

A useful handbook on all matters of translation.

Bassnett, S., 1980. *Translation Studies.* Routledge, London, New York.

A pioneering study by one of the founders of translation studies.

Bassnett, S. and Lefevere, A. (eds), 1990. *Translation, History and Culture.* Pinter, London.

An innovative work that explores the cultural and historical context of translation.

Bassnett, S. and Trivedi, H. (eds), 1999. *Post Colonial Translation.* Routledge, London.

An important collection of essays reflecting on the theme of translation in the post-colonial world.

Bell, Roger T., 1991. *Translation and Translating: theory and practice.* Longman, New York.

A thorough study of theory for the working translator.

Gentzler, E., 1993. *Contemporary Translation Theories.* 2nd edn. Routledge, London and New York.

The best introductory textbook on theory in translation studies.

Graham, W.A., 1987. *Beyond the Written Word: oral aspects of scripture in the history of religion.* Cambridge University Press, Cambridge.

A classic study of orality and the study of religion.

Hammond, G., 1987. English Translations of the Bible. In: Alter, R. and Kermode, F. (eds), *The Literary Guide to the Bible.* Collins, London, pp. 647–66.

A concise and useful account of the history of Bible translation.

Nida, E.A. and Taber, C.R., 1969. *The Theory and Practice of Translation.* Brill, Leiden.

A seminal work in translation studies.

Ong, W.J., 2002. *Orality and Literacy: the technologizing of the word.* 2nd edn. Routledge, New York.

A perspective-changing work. Flawed though it may occasionally be, this is a book that every student of religion should read, re-read and inwardly digest.

Williams, A.V., 2004. New approaches to the problem of translation in the study of religion. In: Antes, P., Geertz A.W. and Warne R.R. (eds), *New Approaches to the Study of Religion.* Walter de Gruyter, Berlin, New York, vol. 2, pp. 13–44.

An essay that attempts to introduce translation studies to the wider audience of scholars in the study of religion, summarizing developments of theory and practice in translation, with illustrative examples taken from published translation work.

Key concepts

Sacred language: a language believed by certain groups to be divine in origin and/or uniquely capable of communicating the word of a divine being or beings.

Sacred text: a text venerated as sacred in so far as it is communicated in a sacred language, and hence the translation of which is considered impossible or sacrilegious. Both terms are still often unquestioningly accepted by modern scholars of religion as self-evidently valid terms, i.e. that such languages and texts are indeed intrinsically sacred and deserving of the respect and circumspection afforded to them by the religious communities who deem them to be sacred.

Source language (SL): the language *from* which a translator translates; so source text (ST).

Target language (TL): the language *into* which a translator translates; so target text (TT).

Translation: translation is generally thought of as primarily a linguistic act of transferring meaning from one language by finding equivalent terms in another language. As language is embedded in a cultural context, however, translation often requires finding *cultural* equivalences in order to render the meaning into the other language adequately.

Related chapters

- Chapter 1.2 Comparison
- Chapter 1.6 Research ethics
- Chapter 2.11 Hermeneutics
- Chapter 2.12 History
- Chapter 2.16 Philology
- Chapter 2.17 Semiotics

2.22

VIDEOGRAPHY

Hubert Knoblauch

Chapter summary[1]

- Videography is an interpretive method developed in the last four decades. On the basis of focused ethnographical video data collection, it comprises the sampling and coding of video data.
- As opposed to standardized video analysis, its core consists in the sequential analysis of video-recorded actions and interactions.
- Whereas sequential analysis focuses on the temporal process of action, the visual analysis also allows for addressing the context, symbols, spatial and social structure of events.
- Hitherto, this method has been widely used in other areas but there are promising ways to apply it in the field of religious studies, particularly when analyzing religious actions, religious interactions, rituals and ceremonies.

Introduction

The study of religion is often preoccupied with texts. This is due to the fact that many religions centre around texts and to the philological-historical training of many students of religion. Whereas images and films have received some interest, video has been hitherto rarely analyzed. Among religious actors, however, it has gained much interest, and it is also increasingly used in social scientific studies of religion. Video is an innovative technology of data collection to which an increasing number of studies are devoted. Within the last decades, video has been increasingly accepted as an instrument of data collection and analysis in the social sciences. To the degree that video is established as a kind of data on religion, the question of how to handle video is becoming a topic more and more urgently to be solved in the social scientific methodology. This chapter addresses this question of how to interpret and analyze video as data in the social sciences, particularly with respect to the study of religion.

Early history of video analysis

The analysis of the visual has a solid record in the history of visual anthropology and sociology. This history started already at the turn of the 20th century, when photography and film started to be used in the social sciences. By means of visual technologies, anthropology developed an independent branch of 'visual anthropology'. Like the much more tenacious development of visual sociology, it focused primarily on photography. Film was used mainly as a means of presenting results rather than as a datum to be analyzed. Famous early examples are A.C. Haddon, Baldwin Spencer or Robert Flaherty who from the turn of the 20th century used film to analyze human conduct. Anthropology produced an unprecedented collection of film data, which was mostly used to document reality instead of analyzing it. Gesell published in 1935 a book on 'cinema analysis' as a 'method for Behavior Study' in which he used frame-by-frame analysis. Somewhat later Margaret Mead and Gregory Bateson did their famous visual analysis of Balinese dance. Then Bateson and the so-called 'Palo Alto group' used film in order to analyze interaction between family members. Members of this group also initiated the famous project on the 'History of the Interview' in which the various modes of interaction were captured for the very first time (Bateson 1958). In psychology, video was used to focus on non-verbal behavior (Ekman and Friesen 1969), resulting in a series of studies conducted by using films that tried to capture behavior in a more encompassing and meaningful way. Ray Birdwhistell (1970) analyzed the interplay between non-verbal and verbal behavior in minute detail, coining the notion of 'kinesics'. In a similar vein, Albert Scheflen (1965) analyzed the role of posture in the structuring of psychotherapeutic encounters.

The development of video analysis

Until the 1970s, however, these analyses were performed on the basis of film, which is difficult to use for fine-grained analysis. Things changed with the introduction, miniaturization and technical sophistication of video. Already in the late 1970s, Thomas Luckmann and Peter Gross started a project that used video in order to develop an annotation system for interactions which was modelled on a musical score (Luckmann and Gross 1977). Since the 1970s, video analysis based on the sociological approaches of ethnomethodology and conversation analysis became more common. Conversation analysis had been supported by the use of the audio recorder, and the introduction of the camcorder helped to extend that kind of data collection. Thus, Goodwin analyzed spoken interaction in such a way as to show how visual aspects (particularly gaze) help to bestow order (Goodwin 1981). Erickson and Schultz (1982) used video in their studies of four school counsellors in their interview interaction with pupils. Heath undertook video studies since the 1970s, targeting complex social situations, i.e. medical encounters (Heath 1986).

It was also Christian Heath (1997) who first started systematic reflections on the methodology of video analysis. For the first comprehensive volume on video analysis methodology see Knoblauch *et al.* (2006) (see also Kissmann 2008).

Video analysis and religious studies

Video analysis has proven to be successful in the field of the study of work and technology (Heath *et al.* 2000). In addition, it is used in art and museum studies and in educational settings, particularly in the classroom (Heath and vom Lehn 2006). The video analysis of religion is still very much in its infancy. Yet important steps have been taken in this direction. For example, a series of conversation analysis studies have used this methodology to analyze religious forms of verbal communication, such as Ulmer (1988), Wooffitt (1992), Trix (1993) and Lehtinen (2005). The same methodology was also applied to audiovisual materials. In a pioneering study, Bergmann, Luckmann and Soeffner used video tapes to analyze how different popes performed during visits abroad. Schnettler (2001) analyzed the ways in which a female charismatic leader of a new religious movement performed her visions and auditions in front of her disciples. Martin studied the rituals of Venezuelan Spiritism using video (Martin 1997/98), and Knoblauch and Petschke (forthcoming) demonstrate the ways in which a contemporary Marian apparition is 'performed'.[2]

These studies already hint at the typical focus of video analytical investigations. As Erickson (1988: 1083) stressed, video recordings lay a focus on the 'particulars of situated performance as it occurs naturally in everyday social interaction'. In general, they analyze the kind of interactions that Goffman (1963) called 'focused', i.e. in which the participants share a common focus of attention. In the basic case, this involves two actors, but focused interactions may also extend to large social occasions, such as meetings, stage events and demonstrations. In religious studies, video analysis is therefore most pertinent when it comes to the analysis of performative forms of actions, rituals and ceremonies, and any observable processes of religious action in (interactive) time.

Interpretation and data

In general, we should distinguish between standardized and interpretive video analysis. *Standardized* video analysis is common in many fields. It consists of **coding** more or less large segments of videos. The categories of coding are derived from (more or less explicit) theoretical assumptions that follow the deductive-nomothetic model (Cicourel 1966). Stretches of video-recorded interactions, varying in length from tens of seconds to several minutes, are subsumed under categories such as 'supportive' or 'non-supportive', 'aggressive' or 'non-aggressive' behavior (Mittenecker 1987). Note that the reasons for subsuming fragments of videos under theoretical codes are not explicated, so that the process of **interpretation** remains implicit. Instead the code may be habitualized and validated by tests on 'intercoder reliability'; in recent years it may even be automatized by means of audiovisual software. Indeed, by 2002 more than 40 software programs (such as MotionPro or SimiMotion) for standardized analysis were available, most of them based on predefined categories (Koch and Zumbach 2002). Standardized methods are not restricted to experimental and quantitative studies of audiovisual conduct but are also to be found in what are self-labelled as 'qualitative methods'. Thus, Dinkelaker and Herrle (2009) suggest segmenting video-recorded interactions according to pre-defined 'segments' and 'configurations'.

Interpretive approaches start from Max Weber's methodological axiom of 'Verstehende [interpretive] Soziologie', a tradition that was elaborated by phenomenological and hermeneutic researchers and also adapted to the study of religion (Brink 1995; Geertz 1997; Knoblauch 2003). The basic methodological assumption of interpretive social science is that actions cannot be observed objectively; rather, actions are guided by meanings that must be understood by the actors themselves. In addition, scientific observers must share this understanding (interpretation) and explicate how they arrive at this understanding in their analysis (Schütz 1962). In addition, video analysis is a hermeneutic activity, as Raab and Tänzler (2006) have argued. As a hermeneutic activity, it has to account particularly for the way the data has been produced, that is, as we call it, the data sort (Knoblauch 2003).

Because of the recording potential of the technology, '*natural(ly occurring) data*' plays an important role in video analysis. By natural data we mean that the recordings are made in social situations affected as little as possible by the researchers. 'Natural data' refers to data collected when the people studied act, behave and pursue their business as they would if there were no social scientists observing or taping them. There is no doubt that the very presence of video technology may exert some influence on the situation that is being recorded, an influence commonly labelled 'reactivity'. However, most studies show that the effect of video may be neglected in many situations after a certain phase of habituation. Other sorts of data are produced by practices such as 'video diaries' (Holliday 2000) or 'video-confessions' (Renov 1996).

Focused ethnography and coding

Understanding what is going on in the videos requires that observers understand at least the typical meaning of actions in the settings. That is to say that they have to participate in the culture of the actors. Therefore, there must be prior ethnography before any video analysis (Corsaro 1981). Unless we are not studying unknown cultures, video analyses that focus on certain situations of actions, interactions and situated **performances** can often be constricted to a 'focused ethnography' (Knoblauch 2005, 2006). This means that one does not need to reconstruct the cultural stock of knowledge necessary to act adequately in the whole field. The task of the researcher is only to acquire those elements of (partly embodied) knowledge relevant to the activity on which the study focuses. By way of observation, interviews, expert interviews, focused ethnographers try to get familiar with the settings in which they make video recordings, to acquire the knowledge necessary in order to understand the audiovisual conduct in time, and also to recover the emic perspective of the natives' point of view that is needed to understand certain situations, activities and actions. In addition, focused ethnography allows us to identify if and how the recording of a situation may be possible, to determine possible sites of recording and to settle legal problems.[3]

The process of data collection and analysis can be divided into two steps that follow the pattern Silverman (2007) describes as 'mapping the woods' (ethnography) and 'chopping up the trees' (fine-grained analysis) illustrated in Figure 2.22.1:

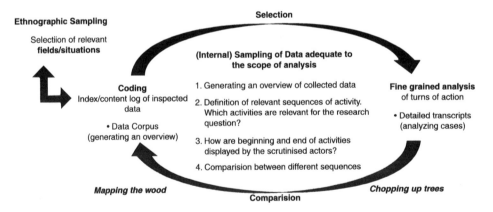

Figure 2.22.1 The process of videographic analysis

On the background of this ethnographic sampling of situations, video analysis is based on the video records made of the situation selected. What is being recorded, then, depends first on what may appear as crucial activities to be observed (and, just as important, those that are accessible) in such a field. Second, the production of audiovisual data depends on the research question that is derived from the frame of reference of one's discipline, as well as from the research context and its more general theoretical questions. Both the scientific context as well as the empirical field of research provide for the question of what to focus on. This is important especially given the fact that, if our attempt is successful, we may face a huge bulk of recorded data that cannot be subjected to the sort of fine-grained analysis discussed below. In a first step, the data that have been recorded will be coded in a (digital) content logbook. A content log contains the temporal sequence of events, a rough transcription of activities, gestures and talk, reflections and codings of sequences according to the research topic. By coding we do not mean the application of certain fixed categories of analysis to the visual, as is suggested in some video analysis books. Rather, according to grounded theory (Glaser and Strauss 1967), codes are developed within the course of the study. Note that coding is part of the internal sampling of data that leads to identifying the fragments that will be subjected to a fine-grained sequential analysis, as sketched below. It is certainly useful to make exact **transcripts** of these fragments at least with respect to the linguistic part.[4] These transcripts are typically a good reference point for **data sessions** with co-researchers on the video data, and these are highly recommended.

The selection of fragments that is dependent on the research questions (or its inductive generation) proceeds by comparisons and contrasts. One should note that data collection, selection of data and sequential analysis are not separate phases of research. Hence, the sample of data may be extended on the grounds of fine-grained analysis up to the point of saturation, i.e. when no further insights are provided by new data (Corbin and Strauss 1990).

Sequential analysis

The core of video analysis consists in the fine-grained analysis of action sequences. In general, video analysis attempts to determine certain patterns in the action and interaction sequences, be they institutionalized (as e.g. certain organizational 'problem solutions') or context dependent and situational.[5] These sequences consist of series of individual actions and of interactions between various actors, objects and technologies. Therefore, analysis tends to reconstruct the meaningful inter-relationship of these actions in the situations recorded.

Sequential analysis has been developed and applied with respect to naturally occurring data but may be extended also to other sorts of video data. It relies on particular technological facilities that are linked to video, which should basically include the following: slow motion, fast-forward and rewind, marking and zooming in. These technologies allow various practices, such as repeatedly viewing and reviewing fragments of video data, and observing in greater detail. They have been compared to the 'revolution of the tenth second' in filming, because the practices allow for the observation of actions and activities in a detail that regularly escapes the attention and memory of the actors involved (and thus are much more 'microscopic' than interviews, by means of which these activities may be reconstructed).

Sequential analysis attempts to understand what is happening and to make this understanding explicit. In doing so, it is oriented towards (at least) three analytical assumptions.[6] Given the necessity of interpreting (and understanding), analyses depend on the detailed description of what can be observed and serve as the basis of understanding.

- Since meaning cannot be 'observed', the first feature is *objectivity*. Objectivity is accounted for by the video as a technology that can by definition only record (aspects of) what has been objectified. Moreover, arguments, for example in data sessions, should not be based on general assumptions about invisible factors of actors (such as 'motives', 'subconscious desires' or 'attitudes'), but only refer to what is expressed in audiovisual conduct.

- The second feature is *reflexivity*. By **reflexivity** we refer to an often-implicit knowledge by which actors 'indicate', 'frame' or 'contextualize' what they do while they are acting. Thus actors not only ask questions, they also demonstrate that what they are doing is questioning, i.e. they reflexively show what they are doing. It is because of this reflexivity that co-actors can understand what is meant by an action. The focus of observations, then, lies in how the actions are being performed by 'investigating the methodological resources used by participants themselves in the production of social actions and activities' (Heath 1997: 184).

- *Sequentiality* is the third feature of communicative action that is exploited by video analysis. The reason for **sequentiality** lies, of course, in the basic temporality of action and interaction. That is to say that we do not simply show what kind of action we are performing when we are acting. In the temporal unfolding of our actions we also show how this action is to be understood and what kind of 'con-sequences' or 're-actions' we expect. Thus any turn in talk gains its meaning from the next turn (and this meaning can be corroborated in the next turn again).[7] As an example (see Knoblauch 1990), we may make a simple statement like 'I come'. If in the next turn someone else says 'you do not come', we are confronted with a specific contradiction that has consequences for subsequent turns (even if the actors want to avoid further argumentation, in which case they would need to 'repair' the contradiction). Thus, sequentiality is a crucial resource for interpretation in that it not only allows the actors to show their understanding, but it also makes it possible for observers to make inferences as to what these actors are doing. Audiovisual recordings are particularly prone to sequential analysis, for it is exactly the temporal feature of actions and their sequentiality that is preserved by the technological medium of video. For, like film, video is defined by the temporal sequence of pictures, and temporality is also a feature of conduct. As a result of their temporality, pictures are watched sequentially, and it is therefore sequentiality that is characteristic of video analysis. It is this feature of sequentiality that is the reason for the peculiar focus of many video analyses: actions and interactions as expressed in conduct, since this medium preserves the time structure of these processes in a way unprecedented by earlier data. (Film and audiotape both have deficiencies in this respect when compared to video.)

An example: Marian apparitions

Let us briefly consider an example from a Marian apparition that occurred in a German town close to the French border. At the same location a series of apparitions had occurred 100 years earlier, and these are memorialized by a chapel. The apparition, which was announced as witnessed by three women from the area, started in front of a chapel built to memorialize the earlier apparitions. I will try to describe the sequence in such a way that the sentences correspond to one turn of a sequence. The stills in Figure 2.22.2 illustrate the steps.

The sequence under consideration starts when the audience prays the credo. During the prayer, the head of the local Marian association (D) and the three seers stand behind one of the chapel's pillars praying (still 1), when suddenly two of the seers exchange a few words. We do not hear the words on the video tape, but sequentially seer A tells B something, who points in the direction of the camera (still 2) and moves in this direction. Seer A slowly follows her from behind the pillar (still 3). Exactly at the point where she becomes visible to the camera, she stops following B and suddenly kneels down (still 4).

Seer B stops in her movement and looks back, and seer C, who was behind A, looks at her (still 5). We now see A with a smiling face as if she were joyfully welcoming someone, while

1. A and C behind Pillar   2. A telling B who points   3. A smiles and follows B

4. A kneels down   5. B kneels down, C moves   6. D: "Mary is among us"

Figure 2.22.2 Stills from video of a Marian apparition

looking at the audience. Yet unlike greeting rituals, she does not change her expression but rather keeps the same face. While D asks C what is going on, B also kneels down at about a meter's distance, looking in the same direction. Then D and C move on until all four of them constitute a front. What is happening? Why is A smiling in such a removed way? We do not have to guess—nor must the audience. All four stand there for a short time waiting until the credo has finished. Then D announces via his microphone so that everyone can hear: 'Mary is among us, you may kneel down'.

The sequence exhibits a clear structure, as the movement of the seers is prepared by B's pointing. When A, however, 'suddenly' kneels down, no one talks to her. The 'intrusion of transcendence' in the person of Mary, as announced later, is accounted for by the fact that A does not need to account for her not following the move. Indeed, all three participants talk behind her back as if she cannot be addressed, producing in this way the 'removed' aspect of her gaze. The gaze itself is directed not to heaven (as at other apparitions) but slightly upwards, so that the gaze may meet some of the audience standing and kneeling at the bottom left of the picture. Yet again, she does not engage in such a way as to follow a greeting sequence. She rather keeps the smile and gaze that may open an encounter for the whole time, so that anyone who might think they are greeted would realize that she is not reacting to them. In this way, she indicates that she is oriented to someone else. The fact that she is not looking somewhere else must be also accounted for. As opposed to the earlier apparition, when even the Prussian police tried to find out where Mary had appeared, she does not even pretend that Mary can be seen where the gaze is. As is the case with the other seers, she does not pretend that the apparition is something occurring in the 'real life' of senses and videos. Rather, it is an 'invisible' Mary that she is addressing. Again this interpretation may be validated sequentially, for even after D announces the presence of Mary (and given that the audience knows already that A is to see Mary) no one among the audience members tries to gaze in the direction in which A is looking.

439

The lack of importance attributed to the 'real location' of Mary becomes even more visible in the next sequence of moves after the sequence illustrated by the stills. For after the announcement, D and C again start to move on, talking to A and B. Although A does not give any response signal, she stands up and follows their movement, which ends in the free space left by the audience. Having arrived there, the three women kneel down again, all three now staring to the right of the picture, exactly in the direction of the old Marian statue, the grotto and the assumed location of the 1870s apparition.

As short as the example may be, it illustrates how the situated actions themselves help to frame and define the meaning of this 'Marian apparition'. They also show to what degree the sequential order of visual conduct, bodies and movements contributes to this understanding. Finally, they also indicate the role of the context (i.e. the knowledge of the audience, the grotto, the chapel, microphones and video) that is represented in the visual aspects of the video.

The visual context

As we can see from the example, the strength of sequential analysis lies not on the side of formally given, repetitive structures; sequential analysis is much more productive with respect to what has been called performance, i.e. the situational production of meaning. Thus, the vision is not only produced by a 'removed' gaze. Rather, the removedness and the 'unexpectedness' are both a product of the concerted and coordinated actions of the participants. The sequence of action typically reflects the ways in which the actors adapt to the contingencies of the situation. However, the video represents even more. In addition to the repetitive elements of rituals that are best uncovered by comparison, videos represent visual elements, such as material objects, bodily configurations and built spaces that are not changing over the diachronic sequences subjected to fine-grained analysis. Elements like an altar, a statue or the seated audience may remain as permanent or synchronic as most elements of the decoration of actors (such as clothing, glasses or hairstyle). These elements appear as permanent on the visual representation but it would be utterly mistaken to consider them as 'background'. One way to approach these synchronic aspects of the situational in video analysis has been suggested by Goodwin (2000). He assumes that *semiotics* may be able to grasp these visual features. Thus, talk is embedded in multiple sign systems (such as graphic codes, gestures and other features of the environment).

A second way to approach the meaning of these visually permanent elements of sequences is offered by **hermeneutics**. Thus Soeffner (1997) suggests that readings of the meanings may be produced step by step by culturally competent analysts. Since hermeneutics demands that analysts dispose of or acquire relevant knowledge of the situation, we are led to the third approach, ethnography. As already stated earlier, it is the task of ethnography to uncover knowledge in order to understand the actors and their practices, e.g. by elicitation procedures, auto-confrontation, auto-ethnography or video-based interviewing.

Whereas ethnography allows for the inclusion of subjective perspectives, and not only those of the 'natives' in the situation, hermeneutics pushes us to reflect on the observer's perspective too. Together with semiotics, it provides useful tools with which to contextualize what may be seen the subject matter of video analysis in the study of religion: religious practice, i.e. actions and interactions in their original setting. Although one has to concede that video analysis is only beginning to take off in religious studies, this method may be of particular importance, given the growing importance laid on performance and participation instead of formal membership in contemporary religion.

Using videography in religious studies

Social situations, interactions and face-to-face communication lie at the focus of video analysis. With respect to religious studies, it is quite obvious that the analysis of sequences of actions touches upon rituals. Thus, instead of assuming a pre-given 'structure of rituals', **videography** looks for the meaning of ceremonies as being constituted by the 'real life' unfolding of its elements in time, the meaning of which are determined *in situ*. Thus, one may address the performance of religious experiences and emotions by individuals and groups, rituals and ceremonies, as well as whole events, such as church services, healing sessions or processions. As indicated with respect to the visual context, videography is not restricted to the analysis of temporal action processes only. Visual symbols, spatial orders and semiotic aspects (such as dress codes, interior design or technical equipment) can be analyzed in relation to the sequential structure of actions and rituals. Thus, the use of microphones or PowerPoint may affect the structure and even content of services. In addition, they may provide one feature characterizing different religious groups and milieux, so that the video analysis may form part of analyses focusing on the meso-level of social groups and organizations. Finally, symbolic events that are of importance for societies in general—even those on a global level, such as papal inaugurations or televised religious mass events—can be studied by drawing on video analysis. In all these cases, the contribution of video analysis is to be seen in the rich data it provides on a process that is produced by the actors themselves.

Notes

1 I want to thank Rene Tuma and Christoph Rechenberg for their help concerning technical matters as well as the content of the paper.
2 For an overview of video analysis in qualitative religious research see Knoblauch (2003).
3 In general, recordings are based on the principle of informed consent. For more detail see Heath *et al.* 2010.
4 For transcription see also Heath *et al.* (2010). It is suggested that these transcriptions should be made by the researchers themselves, in order to foster familiarity with the data.
5 As far as they look for patterned features, they investigate what we call 'communicative patterns', that is forms of interaction that exhibit communal structures beyond the situational actions that relate to extra-situational functions and social structures. See Knoblauch and Günthner (1995).
6 For a more detailed account of these theoretical assumptions see Knoblauch (2001).
7 See also Chapter 2.2 on conversation analysis in this volume.

References

Bateson, G., 1958. Language and psychotherapy: Frieda Fromm-Reichmann's last project. *Psychiatry* 21(2): 96–100.
Bergmann, J.R., Luckmann, T. and Soeffner, H.-G., 1993. Erscheinungsformen von Charisma – zwei Päpste. In: Gebhardt, W., Zingerle, A. and Ebertz, M. (eds), *Charisma – Theorie, Religion, Politik*. De Gruyter, Berlin, New York, pp. 121–55.
Birdwhistell, R.L., 1970. *Kinesics and Context: essays on body motion communication*. University of Pennsylvania Press, Philadelphia.
Brink, T.L., 1995. Quantitative and/or qualitative methods in the scientific study of religion. *Zygon* 30(3): 461–75.
Cicourel, A., 1966. *Method and Measurement in Sociology*. Free Press, New York.
Corbin, J. and Strauss, A., 1990. Grounded Theory Research: procedures, canons and evaluative criteria. *Zeitschrift für Soziologie* 19(4): 418–27.
Corsaro, W.A., 1981. Something old and something new: the importance of prior ethnography in the collection and analysis of audiovisual data. *Sociological Methods and Research* 11(2): 145–66.

Dinkelaker, J. and Herrle, M., 2009. *Erziehungswissenschaftliche Videographie*. Wiesbaden: VS Verlag für Sozialwissenschaften.

Ekman, P. and Friesen, W., 1969. A tool for the analysis of motion picture film or videotapes. *American Psychologist* 24(3): 240–43.

Erickson, F., 1988. Ethnographic description. In: Ammon, U. (ed.), *Sociolinguistics: an international handbook of the science of language and society*. De Gruyter, Berlin, New York, pp. 1081–95.

Erickson, F. and Schultz, J., 1982. The counsellor as gatekeeper: social interaction in interviews. In: Hammel, E. (ed.), *Language, Thought and Culture: advances in the study of cognition*. Academic Press, New York, pp. 237–60.

Geertz, A.W. 1997. Hermeneutics in ethnography: lessons for the study of religion. In: Klimkeit, H.-J. (ed.), *Vergleichen und Verstehen in der Religionswissenschaft*. Harrassowitz Verlag, Wiesbaden, pp. 53–70.

Glaser, B. and Strauss, A., 1967. *The Discovery of Grounded Theory: strategies for qualitative research*. Aldine, Chicago.

Goffman, E., 1963. *Behavior in Public Places*. Free Press, New York.

Goodwin, C., 1981. *Conversational Organization: interaction between speakers and hearers*. Academic Press, New York.

—— 2000. Action and embodiment within situated human interaction. *Journal of Pragmatics* 32 (1): 1489–522.

Heath, C., 1986. *Body Movement and Speech in Medical Interaction*. Cambridge University Press, Cambridge.

—— 1997. The analysis of activities in face-to-face interaction using video. In: Silverman, D. (ed.), *Qualitative Research*. SAGE, London, pp. 99–121.

Heath, C. and vom Lehn, D., 2006. Examining exhibits in interaction: video-based field studies in museums and galleries. In: Knoblauch, H., Schnettler, B., Raab, J. and Soeffner, H.-G. (eds), *Video Analysis: methodology and methods. Qualitative audiovisual data analysis in sociology*. Peter Lang, Frankfurt am Main, Berlin, pp. 221–45.

Heath, C., Knoblauch, H. and Luff, P., 2000. Technology and social interaction: the emergence of 'workplace studies'. *British Journal of Sociology* 51(2): 299–320.

Heath, C., Hindmarsh, J. and Luff, P., 2010. *Video in Qualitative Research: analysing social interaction in everyday life*. SAGE: London, Thousand Oaks, CA.

Holliday, R., 2000. We've been framed: visualizing methodology. *Sociological Review* 48(4): 503–21.

Kissmann, U.T. (ed.), 2008. *Video Interaction Analysis: methods and methodology*. Peter Lang, Frankfurt am Main.

Knoblauch, H., 1990. The taming of foes: informal discussions in family talk. In: Markova, I. and Foppa, K. (eds), *Asymmetries in Dialogue*. Harvester & Wheatsheaf, Hertfordshire, pp. 166–94.

—— 2003. *Qualitative Religionsforschung*. Schöningh, Paderborn.

—— 2005. *Focused ethnography*. In: Forum Qualitative Sozialforschung 6 (3), www.qualitative-research. net/fqs-texte/3-05/05-3-44-e.htm.

—— 2006. Videography, focused ethnography and video analysis. In: Knoblauch, H., Schnettler, B., Raab, J. and Soeffner, H.-G. (eds), *Video Analysis: methodology and methods. qualitative audiovisual data analysis in sociology*. Peter Lang, Frankfurt am Main, Berlin, Bern, Bruxelles, New York, Oxford, Wien, pp. 35–50.

—— 2001. Communication, contexts and culture: a communicative constructivist approach to inter-cultural communication. In: Luzio, A., Günthner, S. and Orletti, F. (eds), *Culture in Communication: analyses of intercultural situations*. John Benjamins, Amsterdam, Philadelphia, pp. 3–33.

Knoblauch, H. and Petschke, S., forthcoming. Vision and video: Marian apparition, spirituality and popular religion. In: Podolinska, T. (ed.), *Traces of Mary in Central and Eastern Europe*. Cambridge University Press, Cambridge. ·

Knoblauch, H. and Günthner, S., 1995. Culturally patterned speaking practices: the analysis of communicative genres. *Pragmatics* 5: 1–32.

Knoblauch, H., Schnettler, B., Raab, J. and Soeffner, H.-G. (eds), 2006. *Video Analysis: methodology and methods. qualitative audiovisual data analysis in sociology*. Peter Lang, Frankfurt am Main, Berlin.

Koch, S. and Zumbach, J., 2002. The use of video-analysis software in behavior observation research. *Forum Qualitative Sozialforschung/Forum Qualitative Social Research* 3(2), www.qualitative-research. net/index.php/fqs/article/viewArticle/857/1862.

Lehtinen, E., 2005. Achieved similarity: describing experience in Seventh-day Adventist Bible study. *Text* 25(3): 341–71.

Luckmann, T. and Gross, P., 1977. Analyse unmittelbarer Kommunikation und Interaktion als Zugang zum Problem der Entstehung sozialwissenschaftlicher Daten. In: Bielefeld, H.U. *et al.* (eds), *Soziolinguistik und Empirie. Beiträge zu Problemen der Corpusgewinnung und-auswertung.* Athenaum, Wiesbaden, pp. 198–207.

Martin, F.F., 1997/98. A trace of fingerprints: displacement and textures in the use of ethnographic video in Venezuelan Spiritism. *Visual Anthropology Review* 13(2): 19–38.

Mittenecker, E., 1987. *Video in der Psychologie.* Methoden und Anwendungsbeispiele in Forschung und Praxis. Huber, Bern.

Raab, J. and Tänzler, D., 2006. Video Hermeneutics. In: Knoblauch, H., Schnettler, B., Raab, J. and Soeffner, H.-G. (eds), *Video Analysis: methodology and methods. qualitative audiovisual data analysis in sociology.* Peter Lang, Frankfurt am Main, Berlin, pp. 85–100.

Renov, M., 1996. Video confessions. In: Renov, M. and Suderburg, E. (eds), *Resolutions: contemporary video practices.* University of Minnesota Press, Minneapolis, pp. 173–83.

Scheflen, A.E., 1965. The significance of posture in communication systems. *Psychiatry* 27 (1): 316–31.

Schnettler, B., 2001. Vision und Performanz. Zur soziolinguistischen Gattungsanalyse fokussierter ethnographischer Daten. *Sozialer Sinn* 8(2): 143–63.

Schütz, A., 1962. Common sense and scientific interpretation of human action. In: *Collected Papers I.* The Hague: Nijhoff, pp. 3–47.

Silverman, D., 2007. *A Very Short, Fairly Interesting and Reasonably Cheap Book about Qualitative Methods.* SAGE: London, Thousand Oaks, CA.

Soeffner, H.-G., 1997. *The Order of Rituals: the interpretation of everyday life.* Transaction, New York.

Trix, F., 1993. *Spiritual Discourse: learning with an Islamicmaster.* University of Pennsylvania Press, Philadelphia.

Ulmer, B., 1988. Konversionserzählungen als rekonstruktive Gattung. Erzählerische Mittel und Strategien bei der Rekonstruktion eines Bekehrungserlebnisses. *Zeitschrift für Soziologie* 17 (1): 19–33.

Woffitt, R., 1992. *Telling Tales of the Unexpected: the organization of factual discourse.* Harvester Wheatsheaf, Hemel Hempstead.

Further reading

Heath, C., Hindmarsh, J. and Luff, P., 2010. *Video in Qualitative Research.* SAGE: London, Thousand Oaks, CA.

Comprehensive introductory book on video analysis including methodological framework and technical instructions.

Knoblauch, H., Schnettler, B., Raab, J. and Soeffner, H.-G. (eds), 2006. *Video Analysis: methodology and methods: qualitative audiovisual data analysis in sociology.* Peter Lang, Frankfurt am Main, Berlin, Bern, Brussels, New York, Oxford, Wien, pp. 35–50.

Comprehensive overview of different approaches in video analysis.

Key concepts

Coding in video analysis: first step of the analysis of video data by which they are provisionally classified according to descriptive categories to be tested in fine-grained sequential analysis.

Data session: meeting of various participants in which video data are presented, interpretations are proposed and discussed with continuous reference to the audiovisual data.

Hermeneutics: discipline providing reflections and methods by which we interpret the intention of others' actions.

Interpretation: act by which the understanding of meanings of actions are explicated.

Performance: process in which embodied actions and interactions are enacted in time.

Reflexivity: methods, means and forms by which actors show what they are doing or saying while they are doing it.

Sequentiality: temporal ordering of actions and interactions that provides the meaningful context of each next action.

Transcript: transformation of audiovisual data into written text. Transcripts typically draw on various transcription conventions as proposed in different detail. To the degree that audiovisual technologies are refined, transcripts and visuals are increasingly coming to be fused.

Videography: combination of (focused) ethnography and sequential video analysis.

Related chapters

- Chapter 1.3 Epistemology
- Chapter 1.6 Research ethics
- Chapter 2.2 Conversation analysis
- Chapter 2.8 Field research: Participant observation
- Chapter 2.10 Grounded theory
- Chapter 2.11 Hermeneutics
- Chapter 2.15 Phenomenology
- Chapter 3.1 Auditory materials
- Chapter 3.5 Visual culture

PART III

Materials

3.1

AUDITORY MATERIALS

Rosalind I.J. Hackett

Chapter summary[1]

- An attention to the auditory domain can counteract Western aesthetic, textual and visualist biases in research on religion.
- Working with the broader category of sound, both as propagated and perceived, may be more productive for cross-cultural research than the concept of music.
- The methodological shift from musical form and content to listening practices and experiences raises new questions about religious identity, memory, authenticity and mediation.
- Scholarly trends lay more emphasis on the interplay between the senses, and on the ways in which they are embedded and embodied in particular cultural contexts.
- The soundscape concept lends itself to research on the role of music and sound in constructing or reconfiguring physical and imagined sacred spaces.
- Studying sound and music may be avoided due to lack of musical knowledge and training in formal musical or sonic analysis, but modern forms of technological reproduction and transmission of sound offer new resources for scholars of religion.
- As with the other senses, full-scale (case) studies or acoustically enhanced research are options for researchers in religious studies.

Introduction

The modern-day, comparative and historical study of religion has taken several twists and turns since its origins in the late 19th century. In the last three decades in particular, mainly in response to trends in cognate disciplines, there has been a series of transformative 'turns', such as a literary turn (applying literary theory to studies of religion), a feminist turn (paying more attention to gender issues), a spatial turn (factoring in spatial theories), a material turn (studying material culture), a visual turn (studying visual practices), a performative turn (new attention to ritual theory), a corporeal turn (incorporating bodily religious ideas and practices), a cognitive turn (applying new developments in cognitive studies), and a sensory or sensorial turn (studying the interplay of religion and the senses). Despite the significance of **sound** and **hearing** in our lives, and the emergence of an exciting, multi- and interdisciplinary body of scholarship on acoustics and audition, an **auditory** or acoustic turn in our field is only now taking shape.

Three primary reasons account for this undervaluation of sound in the academic study of religion. First, sight has been privileged over sound in Western modernity, diminishing the aural as a spiritual sense (Chidester 1992; Schmidt 2002); second, **listening** is held to be the most passive of the senses, and musical expression to be derivative rather than determinative of culture (Chernoff 2002); and third, there are a number of methodological challenges to conducting research on the **sonic** worlds of religions, even in this high-tech age. It is these challenges in particular that constitute the focus of this chapter. An overview of nascent research that adopts sound, including musical sound, as a central category of analysis in the study of religion and culture is provided by way of introduction. Then the chapter explores the methods and theoretical considerations that characterize scholarship in this area to date, by focusing on the work of some pioneering scholars. It then assesses the limitations and potential of a sonic approach to the study of religious phenomena, and considers some productive areas of application for this approach, concluding with some reflections on the practical challenges that may arise in using auditory methods and materials.

Descriptive and analytical overview

Given that sound studies is such an emergent field—both generally and in terms of those that focus on religion—it is not possible to offer a precise overview of its parameters and characteristics. In addition, the description and analysis of sound—whether in terms of how it is produced, perceived, used or transmitted—requires a variety of disciplinary perspectives from the natural, social and human sciences. As we shall see, cultural anthropologists and ethnomusicologists have been at the forefront of research on religious acoustic and auditory practices. They have underscored the risks of abstracting particular sound objects from their social contexts or utilizing Western understandings of **music** in cross-cultural settings.

It is important to clarify from the outset that the study of sound in relation to religious ideas and practices is not limited to music. Music has been defined as sound that is culturally organized and culturally meaningful (Chernoff 2002; Shelemay 2006) or 'sounds with patterned acoustical characteristics' (Ellingson 2005), yet there are languages that do not reflect the concept of 'music' as understood in Western cultures. Instead, as in Islam, they may privilege vocalized forms of expression, such as recitation. In Siberian shamanic traditions the drum and other instruments may overshadow the human voice. It is more useful, therefore, to work with an expanded notion of sound as it is variously perceived and conceptualized to mediate divine presence (Schulz 2008: 172–73). This is also more in keeping with the shift in religious studies from elitist or textual forms of religion to everyday religious practice and experience (Morgan 2009).

In terms of works by scholars of religion on sound and music, only a few have broached the subject from a comparative perspective. They tend to focus on the 'sacred music' (usually pertaining to liturgy) of selected religious traditions and how these generate communal identity and spiritual experience (Beck 2006; Sullivan 1997). There are also studies of particular religions (Friedmann 2009) or particular forms of musical practice in these religions, such as chanting in Hinduism (Beck 1993) or sacred song traditions in Christianity (Marini 2003). Some scholars prefer to address the musical dimensions of a religious landscape more generally, such as the United States (Stowe 2004), or of a specific type of religious orientation, such as esotericism (Wuidar 2010) or trancing (Becker 2004). The bulk of the research on music and sound in relation to religion is still done by historians, musicologists and anthropologists. In reflecting on her training in religious studies, Vivian-Lee Nyitray suggests that 'religion was a surprisingly quiet field of study' (Nyitray 2001). Isaac Weiner, in his valuable overview of 'Sound and American Religions' is even more pointed in his characterization of religious studies research on the sonic worlds of American religion as suffering from 'disciplinary deafness' (Weiner 2009: 897).

Use of method to date

By highlighting a few exemplary case studies, some of the methodological issues and questions confronted by the various scholars working in this area will begin to emerge. It seems appropriate to begin with the pioneering work of Leigh Eric Schmidt on the fate of Christian listening during the American enlightenment and its aftermath (Schmidt 2002). The book examines how auditory experiences and hallucinations of people 'hearing God' were re-imagined and marked with illusion. As a cultural historian, Schmidt draws on images, technical drawings, religious tracts and historical writings to develop his history of hearing in American religion. He emphasizes the need to 'broaden attention beyond preaching, communications media and musical performance to the whole of the devotional soundscape' (Schmidt 2002: 35). A study of the auditory, according to Schmidt, must take into account 'attentiveness to noises, joyful and awful' that might comprise 'sobbing, sighing, groaning, and laughing' as well as 'psalms, bells, and trumpets' (ibid.: 35). It must recognize the corporeal, dialogic and participatory aspects of hearing through examination of the historical accounts and representations of the 'rituals, disciplines, performances, and commodities' in particular cultural settings (ibid.: 36).

In the case of Hinduism, even though sound is central to Hindu theology and ritual practice, Guy Beck (1993) argues that this reality is missed by Western scholars who tend to emphasize the visual components. Hindu worship is replete with an array of instruments (drums, bells, gongs, conches, flutes) and vocalizations, and Hindu scriptures (such as the Sabda-Brahman of the Upanishads, and the Nada-Brahman of Yoga, Saivism, Saktism, Vaishnavism) talk of the cosmos being originated and permeated by sound. Beck writes as an 'insider', having spent several years learning vocal classical music in India. He went on to earn degrees in musicology and religious studies. He researches the myriad expressions of sacred sound given by Indian texts, artifacts and informants, seeking to 'penetrate beyond visual and rational surface data' by testing hypotheses about sound across a number of Hindu traditions (Beck 1993: 10–11). His work demonstrates that this 'sonic theology' constitutes an important nexus between otherwise distinct religious communities.

By virtue of his field experiences in the rich aural environments of the Bosavi people in Papua New Guinea in the 1970s, anthropologist and ethnomusicologist Steve Feld began a lifetime career of doing anthropology in and through the medium of sound (Feld and Brenneis 2004). Through his experimental sound recordings, such as 'Voices of the Rainforest' and 'Rainforest Soundwalks', he explored the relationship of sound to materiality and sociality in the Bosavi world, working with the forest-dwellers in their primary medium, which was aural. He developed the concept of an 'acoustic ecology' or 'acoustemology', a sonic way of knowing place, a way of attending to hearing, a way of absorbing that would do justice to the layered complexity of the human and environmental world of sound. Seeking to counter the notion that sound is ephemeral, he later became interested in how one can hear history and transformation in European bells.[2] He has challenged the academy to take sound more seriously in academic presentations and publishing.

In his book on listening practices among Muslim communities in Egypt, *The Ethical Soundscape: cassette sermons and Islamic counterpublics* (2006), anthropologist Charles Hirschkind demonstrates how the **soundscapes** produced through the circulation of the Qur'an and sermon tapes reshape moral aptitudes and the moral economy of revival in Cairo. His research prompts the broader question of what shifts in hearing practices in a religious tradition might reveal about that religion in its specific temporal and spatial context. Another North African study, *Traveling Spirit Masters: Moroccan Gnawa trance and music in the global marketplace* (2007), by performance studies expert Deborah Kapchan, examines how the trance music of the Gnawa transfigures musical and racial identities for this Moroccan people as well as the global musicians with whom they collaborate. Drawing on her extensive cultural and linguistic knowledge of the region, she uses interviews, observation and participation to collect her data. She provides rich analysis of both the aesthetic and affective strands of Gnawa possession trance ceremonies as well as the transculturation of trance and sacred music more generally. Some of the more interesting parts of her book are where she travels with the musicians to France and is able to compare their performances and interactions with what they do in Morocco. The work of ethnomusicologist Judith Becker also focuses on trance: she combines both scientific and cultural approaches to the study of music and emotion, and music and trancing in her book, *Deep Listeners* (Becker 2004). Becker maintains that people who experience deep emotions when listening to music are akin to those who trance within the context of religious rituals. Using new discoveries in the fields of neuroscience and biology, the book proposes an emotion-based theory of trance using examples from South-East Asian and American musics. Psychological studies generally involve self-reports of the emotions experienced by the participant while listening to music. In a more recent study, Joshua Penman and Judith Becker study physiological responses (galvanic skin response [GSR] and heart rate) among two target groups (Pentecostal Ecstatics and Deep Listeners) (Penman and Becker 2009). In sum, the works singled out above for their attention to the auditory domain demonstrate the need to employ a range of resources and methods.

Limitations of method

A range of reasons are usually adduced (Box 3.1.1) for the lack of research on sound production or perception (see Weiner 2009: 899–900).

Potential of auditory methods

Given that religious studies has developed into such a multi- and interdisciplinary field of inquiry, as evidenced by this book, it is well poised, even now compelled, to engage some of the theoretical and methodological questions generated by the 'resurgence of the ear' (Erlmann 2004). Moreover, some of the areas that scholars of religion traditionally describe and analyze, such as practice, experience, identity, liturgy, performance, mediation, embodiment and spatiality, lend themselves to aural analysis.

To begin with, there is still more research to be done on the perceived relationship between particular sounds (environmental or produced by voices or instruments) and specific divinities or spirit beings, what Ter Ellingson calls 'isoformalism' (Ellingson 2005: 6253). In this connection, Katherine Hagedorn has written on how Santería *batá* drums are critical elements of the performance process, as they are believed to speak to the *orichas* 'in their own language'. As an ethnomusicologist she has studied the use of these drums in Santería rituals in Cuba and recorded their sounds. She has also enhanced her knowledge by undergoing training from drum masters and performing herself (Hagedorn 2001). Anthropologist Rodney Needham, in his classic article 'Percussion and Transition' (Needham 1967), based on extensive reading of ethnographical literature, asks why is it so widespread that noise-making instruments and

---

Box 3.1.1 Reasons for lack of research on sound production/perception

- Sound is ephemeral, variable, fluid, promiscuous and dynamic in nature.
- Sound is difficult to capture, although there are technological improvements that have improved reproducibility and sounds can now be heard outside of ritual and performance contexts.
- The source of sound may be indiscernible or difficult to access as it may be too loud or off-limits to non-initiates.
- It is easier to see someone looking than to see someone listening.
- It can prove challenging to decide on one's research focus: the nature of sound, its generation, mediation, reception, perception, interpretation, effects, preservation, transmission, remediation, use, etc.
- The lack of technical expertise of researchers and the multi-disciplinarity required (ethno-musicology, acoustic theory, acoustic ecology, architectural and film studies, sound art, history of science, philosophy of music, neuroscience, cognitive psychology, etc.) may be a barrier.
- Historical research on sonic forms or experiences pertaining to religion can prove challenging in the absence of auditory archives. The work of aural historians such as Mark M. Smith (2004) raises pressing questions about how to reclaim the sounds of the past, whether as objective facts or as they were subjectively heard, interpreted and imagined by people in particular historical settings (see also Promey and Brisman 2010). Moreover, extraordinary and unusual sounds were more likely to be recorded, rather than the ordinary and mundane (Corbin 1995).
- The banality and ubiquity of sound in everyday life can detract from deeper research.
- It can prove challenging to investigate communal hearing practices when listening is essentially an individual act, even while shaped by social processes.
- It is difficult to write about sound, music and sonic experiences, including silence and noise.

---

devices (such as a shaman beating a drum) are deployed to establish contact with the spirit world. Through his comparative research, he discovers that the affective effects of percussive sounds are linked to rites of transition in many cultures. A similar cross-cultural example is the eerie, whirring sound of the bullroarer that has long been associated with ancestral spirits in Aboriginal Australia, Oceania and parts of Africa. Anthropologist Donald Tuzin contends that to understand the links between 'the auditory apparatus and a particular sensation that is widely interpreted as signifying a supernatural presence' (as in the case of bullroarers and large drums) the researcher needs a 'biocultural' approach (Tuzin 1984). This combines the study of the physiological impact of aural stimuli (such as the anxiety created by the unsettling sound of the bullroarer) and its religio-cultural interpretation (or resolution) in particular environmental settings (such as where thunder is prevalent).

In the contemporary American context, sociologist of popular culture Charles Brown demonstrates how Christian speed and thrash metal music has an affinity for apocalyptic ideas and imagery, and that their musical structures convey rebellion through dissonant riffing and power chords (Brown 2006: 134). He compares the sonic, visual and lyrical forms and styles of popular youth music using interviews, participant observation and secondary literature. There are many more opportunities to explore how the formal and material properties of objects and modern media technologies involved in sound (re)production relate to ideas about the divine, divinities and divineness. In addition to these more technical and theological questions it is important not to forget the social, especially gendered, dimension: who produces the sounds, and who is capable of or is allowed to hear or interpret them (Moisala and Diamond 2000).

More studies are needed on the historical and cultural factors that led to certain sounds becoming emblematic of particular religious traditions, whether vocalizations in Islam, *om* in Hinduism, throat-singing in Buddhism, the *shofar* in Judaism, or the bell in Christianity. Similarly, the lives of contemporary composers and musicians can be productively examined through (auto)biographical study and personal interviews to discern the religious and/or spiritual beliefs and practices, as well as social forces, that have shaped their music. John Cage, influenced by Indian aesthetics and Zen Buddhism and the negation of the will, was prompted to develop an aesthetic of spiritual silence in both his life and work (Kraut 2010). By situating this composition of non-music, silence, in its temporal context, it can be interpreted as a radical modernist response to the conditions of the 20th century. Scholars of American music can trace the great jazz musician John Coltrane's conviction (notably in 'A Love Supreme') that unstructured sound and improvisational music were the most effective expression of the divine to the influence of the music of the black Church in the US (Bivins 2010; Imbert 2010). Sander van Maas has deployed his theological, musicological and philosophical skills to interpret the new religious music of the 'holy minimalist' musicians such as John Tavener, Arvo Pärt and Henryk Gorecki (Maas 2008). Musicologist Joscelyn Godwin investigates the writings of poets, philosophers, astrologers, composers, musicologists and historians to develop his history of mysticism and esotericism in music (Godwin 1995).

Earlier work by scholars of religion made important contributions regarding the oral aspects and auditory interpretation of scripture (Graham 1993; Hall 1986). New scholarship on listening behavior emphasizes the complexity of the listening process, not least in relation to spirituality and religion (Schnapp 2009; Wolvin 2009). Charles Hirschkind's research on cassette-sermon audition in Cairo and the way these practices shape religious behavior and experience, and ultimately uphold forms of public life, provides a model for research on listening practices (Hirschkind 2006). Using anthropological methods of participant-observation, Hirschkind spent a year and a half meeting with those who produced and those who listened to the sermon tapes. He tracked the use and circulation of these popular media tapes in markets, public transportation and in domestic spaces. His research takes account of the fact that listening is an embodied practice that occurs in changing urban soundscapes.

The shift from 'discourse' and 'text' to a new focus on the senses as mediators of experience has been labeled a 'sensual revolution' by David Howes (2004, 2006). He, along with other scholars such as Constance Classen (1993, 1997), have been instrumental in promoting research on the cultural construction and agency of the senses.[3] Classen (1997: 401) argues that the task of the scholar is to uncover the sensory meaning and practice of particular cultures. This will entail studying how the senses are enumerated, valued and socially regulated in different historical and cultural settings, as the sensuous ethnography of Paul Stoller among the Songhay of Niger richly demonstrates (Stoller 1997, 1989). While there have been several publications on the individual senses in the Berg Sensory Formations series, of which *The Auditory Culture Reader* (Bull and Back 2003) interests us the most here, Howes emphasizes the importance of focusing on the 'interplay of the senses in cultural experience and expression' (Howes 2004: 399; see also Erlmann 2004: 4). Furthermore, in Howes' estimation, the sensorium is 'dynamic, relational and political (not the private world psychologists posit)' (Howes 2004: 400).

This is well evidenced by Marleen de Witte's call for a more embodied, tactile approach to African religious life and its sonic dimensions, rather than the more symbolic interpretations of religious sounds (de Witte 2008: 692; see also Schulz 2008). Her ethnographic studies, using participant observation and interviews with religious leaders and practitioners, of the spatial practices of sound and silence by religious groups in Accra, Ghana demonstrate the perceived power of these sounds to communicate with and access the invisible world of spirits. She advocates closer attention to the ways in which spiritual touch and embodiment can be mediated by sound (cf. Maas 2008), as has been done more recently for the visual realm (e.g. Meyer 2008).

As noted above, rather than focusing on specific sounds, some scholars now prefer to explore large-scale acoustic environments or 'soundscapes' (Schulz 2008). Music has always been known to have a 'structuring effect' and a capacity to mark boundaries or create a 'sonic frame' as with trumpet voluntaries in Christian services or conch-shell trumpet notes sounded before and after many Hindu rituals (Ellingson 2005: 6254). Alain Corbin (1998) has shown how bells serve as auditory and defensive markers in 19th-century France. Dorothea Schulz (2003) focuses on the urban soundscape in contemporary Mali, the public arena in part defined by the broadcasts of the local and national radio stations. In the course of her fieldwork and follow-up visits she has tracked the public debates over the sermons delivered by Muslim preachers, and discussed with people how they have been 'touched' by the hearing of radio broadcasts and audio-taped messages and entertainment.

The soundscape concept derives from the work of R. Murray Schafer on sonic environments (Schafer 1993). Emily Thompson (2004: 1f.) describes a soundscape as simultaneously a physical environment and a way of perceiving that environment. In other words, it is both a world and a culture to make sense of that world. Religious values, for example, can shape the relationship of listeners to their environment, as in the case of mystical Islam (Schulz 2008). Dorothea Schulz likes the way the concept underscores both the omnipresence of sound, enabled now by new acoustic and auditory technologies, and its localization (ibid.: 185). It connotes a time and space emplacement where both sound production and sound perception combine for powerful religious experience and communication with the divine (ibid.: 185). It is also productive in the quest for more multi-sensory approaches in the academy because of its ability to highlight the 'spatial and embodied dimensions of sound perception and the all-enveloping sensual experience it generates' (ibid.: 185).

Within the last decade, the study of religion has been considerably enriched by a series of publications on religion in/as media (Hoover 2006; Morgan 2007). With the new emphasis on religion as a practice of mediation (Meyer 2006; de Witte 2006), there are ample opportunities to pay more attention to aural and auditory modes of religious mediation. Many of the authors cited in the present chapter are interested in how modern media technologies amplify, transform and even re-enchant the sonic experiences and practices of religious actors. They also realize that we now have even greater opportunities to compare musical sounds across cultures and religious traditions. Szendy claims that 'our ears are outfitted as never before' (Szendy 2007: 94), with resultant new habits of listening and new agency for listeners.

The realm of healing constitutes a productive area of research for those interested in the effects of religious sounds and music. Research in this area is generally historical or anthropological. Historical inquiry into beliefs and practices relating to music's emotional and healing powers uses literary and philosophical texts, as well as medical sources (Gouk 2000). Ethnographic studies of music healing or therapy in contemporary communities focus on the discourses about sonic effects, their cosmological framing, and specific practices such as drumming and chanting (Barnes and Sered 2005). With the mass circulation of world musics, the development of radio programs[4] and websites devoted to 'sound healing', there are now new, more accessible resources for studying perceptions, practices and experiences relating to officially sanctioned or complementary healing practices that involve the sonic realm.

In contrast, an area that calls for more attention is that of conflict and noise. In an article that explores the 'sonic sacralization' of urban space in Accra, Ghana, Marleen de Witte describes the clashes between Ga traditionalists and born-again Christians over the traditional 'ban on drumming and noisemaking' (de Witte 2008: 690). Through interviews, observation and monitoring of media outlets, she explored the conflicting ways of conceptualizing sound in relation to space, personhood and spiritual power in a competitive urban soundscape (ibid.: 707). In his study of the sounds of American religious life, Isaac Weiner not only examines the ways in which music can construct religious identity and difference, but also how sound mediates contact among diverse religious communities (Weiner 2009). This is not just about how musical cultures express religious pluralism but also about how the sounds of religious others invading the public sphere can generate legal conflicts. So he focuses less on the sounds themselves and more on the discourses and negotiations that surround these auditory expressions, using both archival research, media and computer-mediated sources, interviews and legal case studies.

Practical and ethical challenges

Kay Kaufman Shelemay (2010) identifies some of the emerging ethical concerns relating to the burgeoning study of sound: how the field recording and re-inscription of sound potentially transforms it in significant ways; the unapproved circulation or transformation in cosmopolitan contexts of local, field-recorded sounds; issues of ownership and control of the sounds, as well as fair use and intellectual property. The particular volatility of music, together with technological changes and legal shifts relating to sound will necessitate, according to Shelemay, regular refinement of ethical approaches. Andrew Eisenberg relates an incident in the course of his sound-centered research on Muslim citizenship on the Kenyan coast where his recording of the *khutba* or Friday sermon raised suspicion. He underestimated how ethnographic research by someone from the global North among Muslim subjects in the global South, notably in an area fraught with contestations over communal autonomy and public space, could have generated tension. The episode stays with Eisenberg as 'a visceral reminder' that there are competing understandings of publicity, privacy, sound and space (Eisenberg (2010): 6).

The challenges of doing fieldwork on musical practices are addressed by a group of ethnomusicologists who desire more transparency and attention to experience in their field. By actively joining in a society's music-cultural practices, they believe they achieve 'truly participatory participant-observation' and the levels of dialogue and reflexivity required of post-colonial and post-modern ethnography (Cooley and Barz 2008). The majority of the contributors to Guy Beck's (2006) edited collection are also musical performers of one type or another. This raises the question of insider-outsider status with which scholars of religion are familiar (Jensen 2011). Valorizing specialized knowledge in sound and music or 'substantive participation' (Cooley and Barz 2008: 5) could have a chilling effect on this emergent sub-field in religious studies.

Doing research on globally circulating sounds or musics presents a number of obvious practical challenges to any researcher who might be interested in the therapeutic or moral effects of listening practices in diverse cultural locations. Yet computer-mediated information and communication represent great opportunities for new research while raising fresh questions about what constitutes data for auditory and acoustic inquiry in the field of religious studies.

Concluding remarks

In sum, whether one embarks on full-scale or supplementary research on the production, propagation, perception or practice relating to sound in religious traditions and communities, the results should be beneficial to scholars and students alike. While everyone may not have a Steve Feld 'rainforest experience', the time is ripe on a number of fronts, given the proliferation of sound technologies and the multi-sensory turn in several scholarly fields, for a more sonically aware religious studies.

Notes

1   The writing of this essay was aided by productive discussions with students in my Sound and Music in Religion class (spring 2011).
2   See his CD series, 'The Time of Bells', www.voxlox.net/node/41.
3   See the Concordia Sensoria Research Team (CONSERT) website: www.david-howes.com/senses.
4   e.g. Hearts of Space, www.hos.com.

References

Barnes, L.L. and Sered, S. (eds), 2005. *Religion and Healing in America*. Oxford University Press, New York.

Beck, G., 1993. *Sonic Theology: Hinduism and sacred sound*. University of South Carolina Press, Columbia, SC.

—— (ed.), 2006. *Sacred Sound: experiencing music in world religions*. Wilfrid Laurier University Press, Waterloo, ON.

Becker, J., 2004. *Deep Listeners: music, emotion, and trancing*. Indiana University Press, Bloomington, IN.

Bivins, J., 2010. 'The Lord is heavy': improvised music and religions. Paper presented at the International Association for the History of Religions XXth Quinquennial World Congress, Toronto.

Brown, D.P., 2006. *Noise Orders: jazz, improvisation, and architecture*. University of Minnesota Press, Minneapolis.

Bull, M.B. and Back, L. (eds), 2003. *The Auditory Culture Reader (sensory formations)*. Berg, New York.

Chernoff, J., 2002. Ideas of culture and the challenge of music. In: MacClancy, J. (ed.), *Exotic No More: anthropology on the front lines*. University of Chicago Press, Chicago, pp. 377–98.

Chidester, D., 1992. *Word and Light: seeing, hearing and religious discourse*. University of Illinois Press, Urbana, Chicago.

Classen, C., 1993. *Worlds of Sense: exploring the senses in history and across cultures*. Routledge, New York.

—— 1997. Foundations for an anthropology of the senses. *International Social Science Journal* 49(153): 401–12.

Cooley, T.J. and Barz, G.F., 2008. Casting shadows: fieldwork is dead! Long live fieldwork! In: Barz, G.F. and Cooley, T.J. (eds), *Shadows in the Field: new perspectives for fieldwork in ethnomusicology*. Oxford University Press, New York, pp. 3–24.

Corbin, A., 1995. *Time, Desire, and Horror: toward a history of the senses*. Trans. J. Birrell. Cambridge University Press, New York.

—— 1998. *Village Bells: Sound and Meaning in the 19th-century French Countryside*. Columbia University Press, New York.

de Witte, M., 2006. The spectacular and the spirits: Charismatics and neo-traditionalists on Ghanaian television. *Material Religion* 1(3): 314–34.

—— 2008. Accra's sounds and sacred spaces. *International Journal of Urban and Regional Research* 32(3): 690–709.

Eisenberg, A.J., 2010. Toward an acoustemology of Muslim citizenship in Kenya. *Anthropology News* 51(9): 6.

Ellingson, T., 2005 [1987]. Music: music and religion. In: Jones, L. (ed.), *Encyclopedia of Religion*. Macmillan, New York, pp. 6248–56.

Erlmann, V. (ed.), 2004. *Hearing Cultures: essays on sound, listening and modernity*. Berg, New York.

Feld, S. and Brenneis, D., 2004. Doing anthropology in sound. *American Ethnologist* 31(4): 461–74.

Friedmann, J.L. (ed.), 2009. *Perspectives on Jewish Music: secular and sacred*. Lexington Books, Lanham, MD.

Godwin, J., 1995. *Harmonies of Heaven and Earth: mysticism in music from antiquity to avant-garde*. Innert Traditions International, Rochester, VT.

Gouk, P. (ed.), 2000. *Musical Healing in Cultural Contexts*. Ashgate, Aldershot.

Graham, W.A., 1993. *Beyond the Written Word: oral aspects of scripture in the history of religion*. Cambridge University Press, Cambridge, New York.

Hagedorn, K., 2001. *Divine Utterances: the performance of Afro-Cuban Santería*. Smithsonian Institution Press, Washington, DC.

Hall, R.L., 1986. The living word: an auditory interpretation of scripture. *Listening* 21(1): 25–42.

Hirschkind, C., 2006. *The Ethical Soundscape: cassette sermons and Islamic counterpublics*. Columbia University Press, New York.

Hoover, S.M., 2006. *Religion in the Media Age*. Routledge, New York.

Howes, D. (ed.), 2004. *Empire of the Senses: the sensual culture reader*. Berg, Oxford, New York.

—— 2006. Charting the sensorial revolution. *The Senses and Society* 1(1): 113–28.

Imbert, R., 2010. The Father, the Son and the Holy Ghost: the avant-garde trinity of Coltrane, Sanders, and Ayler. Paper presented at the International Association for the History of Religions XXth Quinquennial World Congress, Toronto.

Jensen, J.S., 2011. Revisiting the insider–outsider debate: dismantling a pseudo-problem in the study of religion. *Method & Theory in the Study of Religion* 23(1): 29–47.

Kapchan, D.A., 2007. *Traveling Spirit Masters: Moroccan Gnawa trance and music in the global marketplace*. Wesleyan University Press/University Press of New England, Lebanon, NH.

Kraut, J., 2010. John Cage the mystification of musical silence. In: ter Borg, M. and van Henten, J.W. (eds), *Powers: Religion as a Social and Spiritual Force*. Fordham University Press, New York, pp. 265–74.

Maas, S.v., 2008. Intimate exteriorities: Inventing religion through music. In: Vries, H.d. (ed.), *Religion: beyond a concept*. Fordham University Press, New York, pp. 750–71.

Marini, S., 2003. *Sacred Song in America: religion, music, and public culture*. University of Illinois Press, Urbana-Champaign.

Meyer, B., 2006. *Religious Sensations: why media, aesthetics and power matter in the study of contemporary religion*. Inaugural lecture. Vrije Universiteit, Amsterdam.

—— 2008. Powerful pictures: popular Christian aesthetics in southern Ghana. *Journal of the American Academy of Religion* 76(1): 82–110.

Moisala, P. and Diamond, B., 2000. *Music and Gender*. University of Illinois Press, Champain, IL.

Morgan, D., 2007. *The Lure of Images: a history of religion and visual media in America*. Routledge, New York.

—— (ed.), 2009. *Religion and Material Culture: the matter of belief*. Routledge, New York.

Needham, R., 1967. Percussion and transition. *Man* 2: 606–14.

Nyitray, V.-L., 2001. In pursuit of active listening. *Religious Studies News* 16(2): 4–6.

Penman, J. and Becker, J., 2009. Religious ecstatics, 'deep listeners,' and musical emotion. *Empirical Musicology Review* 4(2): 49–70.

Promey, S.M. and Brisman, S., 2010. Sensory cultures: material and visual religion. In: Goff, P. (eds), *The Blackwell Companion to Religion in America*. Wiley-Blackwell, New York.

Schafer, H.M., 1993. *The Soundscape: our sonic environment and the tuning of the world*. Destiny Books, Rochester, VT.

Schmidt, L.E., 2002. *Hearing Things: religion, illusion, and the American enlightenment*. Harvard University Press, Cambridge, MA.

Schnapp, D.C., 2009. Listening in spirituality and religion. In: Wolvin, A.D. (ed.), *Listening and human communication in the 21st century*. Wiley, New York, pp. 239–65.

Schulz, D.E., 2003. Charisma and Brotherhood Revisited: Mass-mediated Forms of Spirituality in Urban Mali. *Journal of Religion in Africa* 33 (2): 146–171.

—— 2008. Soundscape. In: Morgan, D. (ed.), *Key Words in Religion, Media, and Culture*. Routledge, New York, pp. 172–86.

Shelemay, K.K. (ed.), 2006. *Soundscapes: exploring music in a changing world*. 2nd edn. W.W. Norton, New York.

—— 2010. Sounding (the) ethical. *Anthropology News* 51(9): 25.

Smith, M.M. (ed.), 2004. *Hearing History: a reader*. University of Georgia Press, Athens, GA.

Stoller, P., 1989. *The Taste of Ethnographic Things*. University of Pennsylvania Press, Philadelphia.

—— 1997. *Sensuous Scholarship*. University of Pennsylvania Press, Philadelphia.

Stowe, D.W., 2004. *How Sweet the Sound: music in the spiritual lives of Americans*. Harvard University Press, Cambridge, MA.

Sullivan, L.E. (ed.), 1997. *Enchanting Powers: music in the world's religions*. Harvard University Press, Cambridge, MA.

Szendy, P., 2007. *Listen: a history of our ears*. Trans. C. Mandell. Fordham University Press, Bronx, NY.

Thompson, E., 2004. *The Soundscape of Modernity: architectural acoustics and the culture of listening in America, 1900–1933*. MIT Press, Cambridge, MA.

Tuzin, D., 1984. Miraculous voices: the auditory experience of numinous objects. *Current Anthropology* 25(5): 579–96.

Weiner, I.A., 2009. Sound and American religions. *Religion Compass* 3(5): 897–908.

Wolvin, A.D. (ed.), 2009. *Listening and Human Communication in the 21st century*. Wiley, New York.

Wuidar, L., 2010. *Music and Esotericism*. Brill, New York.

Further reading

Beck, G., 2006. *Sacred Sound: experiencing music in world religions*. Wilfrid Laurier University Press, Waterloo, ON.

The current textbook of choice for anyone wanting to teach a course on sound and music in religion, or simply gain a comparative and historical overview of this neglected dimension of religious studies. The focus is on liturgical music, mainly chant, in the major religious traditions. Each chapter is written by someone who has both academic and performing skills in a particular tradition, and musical samples can be heard on the accompanying CD.

Bull, M.B. and Back, L. (eds), 2003. *The Auditory Culture Reader (sensory formations)*. Berg, New York.

This groundbreaking reader investigates how auditory culture impacts everyday experience. While only a few of the cultural and social theorists in this volume address the realm of religion, the multidisciplinary array of chapters points to the possibilities of research on sound(s), noise, hearing and listening.

Ellingson, T., 2005 [1987]. Music: music and religion. In: Jones, L, (ed.), *Encyclopedia of Religion*. Macmillan, New York, pp. 6248–56.

A helpful overview of the musical (and to some extent, sonic) dimensions of religion. A good, if slightly dated, place to begin thinking about possible research angles. Note: the Encyclopedia of Religion *contains several entries on music and religion in various regions of the world.*

Erlmann, V. (ed.), 2004. *Hearing Cultures: essays on sound, listening and modernity*. Berg, New York.

This book richly demonstrates the merits of the cultural and historical contextualization of auditory perception. Focusing on extramusical sounds (mainly non-religious), the contributions are theoretically sophisticated and diverse. They make a cogent case that research on sound offers new ways to examine culture and social issues.

Feld, S. and Brenneis, D., 2004. Doing anthropology in sound. *American Ethnologist* 31(4): 461–74.

Essential reading for anyone wanting to conduct research on the sonic dimensions of religious worlds. Takes the form of an interview with the father of the anthropology of sound, Steve Feld. Engaging and methodologically rich.

Hirschkind, C., 2006. *The Ethical Soundscape: cassette sermons and Islamic counterpublics*. Columbia University Press, New York.

An exemplary ethnographic study of Islamic listening practices in Egypt. Methodological contributions of this book include the importance of sensitive field research and participant-observation, and relating auditory experience to ethical dispositions and changing social and political contexts.

Schmidt, L.E., 2002. *Hearing Things: religion, illusion, and the American enlightenment*. Harvard University Press, Cambridge, MA.

A highly influential study of spiritual hearing practices in a particular historical and cultural setting. Fascinating range of examples with brilliant interdisciplinary analysis.

Schulz, D.E., 2008. Soundscape. In: Morgan, D. (ed.), *Key Words in Religion, Media, and Culture*. Routledge, New York, pp. 172–86.

The merit of this essay is that it offers a good, succinct discussion of the soundscape concept and expressly relates the concept to questions of religious mediation, sensation and practice. Includes some examples from the author's own field research in Islamic West Africa.

Weiner, I.A., 2009. Sound and American religions. *Religion Compass* 3(5): 897–908.

Vital reading for anyone contemplating research on auditory materials, or seeking to be more attuned to the sonic world of American religious life in particular. Weiner makes a cogent case for investigating how sound mediates contact among diverse religious communities. Particularly valuable are his section on 'Methodological Challenges and Theoretical Resources' and the bibliography.

Key concepts

Auditory: relating to the sense or organs of hearing.

Hearing: the sense by which sound is perceived. As in the case of the other senses, hearing mediates cultural and religious experience.

Listening: the act of hearing attentively.

Music: organized or patterned types of sounds that convey meaning within a particular cultural setting (Shelemay 2010: 4). Musical sounds are generally described as having four components: timbre, pitch, duration and dynamics. Religions vary in whether they have a concept of 'music' or 'sacred music', and whether they distinguish between vocal and instrumental music.

Sonic: of or relating to audible sound.

Sound: mechanical vibrations that have auditory effects. Sound involves propagation, transmission and perception.

Soundscape: a term coined by the Canadian composer R. Murray Shafer. It refers to an atmosphere or environment created by or with sound (musical or non-musical).

Related chapters

- Chapter 1.2 Comparison
- Chapter 1.3 Epistemology
- Chapter 1.6 Research ethics
- Chapter 2.8 Field research: Participant observation
- Chapter 2.12 History
- Chapter 2.13 Interviewing
- Chapter 2.19 Structured observation
- Chapter 3.3 Material culture

3.2

THE INTERNET

Douglas E. Cowan

Chapter summary

- Religion has been an integral part of the Internet since the popular inception of the World Wide Web in the mid-1990s.
- The Internet functions as both data and method, a site for research and a means by which research is conducted.
- Our understanding of how religion offline is affecting and affected by religion on the Internet is still fairly rudimentary and requires further research.
- Researching religion on the Internet presents a variety of ethical dilemmas, including issues of identity, disclosure and deception.
- New communications media will require an evolving understanding of the relationship between religion and technology.

Introduction

In 2010 a three-judge panel for the US Circuit Court of Appeals ruled that 'electronic ministries', organizations that conduct their activities primarily via radio, television and the Internet, do not meet the Internal Revenue Service's (IRS) criteria for tax exemption. Because they cannot pass what the panel calls the 'associational test', the requirement that members of a religious organization meet regularly in order to qualify as a 'church', they will henceforth be denied the IRS's coveted tax exemption status, usually known by its code, 501(c)3 (Qualters 2010). In the case of radio and television ministries, for example, the judges ruled that a particular program's audience does not constitute a community in a way that satisfies the law.

Although the Internet was included in the ruling, for those who seek to conduct their religious business or activity over the Internet and for researchers interested in the expansion and evolution of computer-mediated religious communication and practice, this decision poses a number of fascinating questions. In contrast to a radio or television audience, for example, does the regular meeting of a prayer group in an online chat room satisfy the associational test? If this online interaction occurs over an extended period of time and participants become emotionally involved and personally invested in each other's lives, does this then constitute a community? If it does, then why would it not satisfy the legal require-ment? If it does not—and scholars have been divided on the question of an online 'commu-nity' since the popular inception of **computer-mediated communication** (CMC) (see Cowan 2005b)—then what should we call it? More importantly, what does that mean for what some researchers consider the holy grail of online religion: a faith tradition that exists entirely and exclusively in cyberspace?

Few communications technologies have so quickly or profoundly shaped the way large numbers of people interact as the Internet. First introduced to consumers on a wide scale in the mid-1990s, the Internet and its most common component, the **World Wide Web**, have become all but ubiquitous in developed and developing countries. Once the domain of the desktop computer, the Internet is now the constant companion of hundreds of millions through laptops and netbooks, cellphones and smartphones, iPods and iPads. Indeed, for millions of people, both young and not so young, text (as in 'texting') has replaced voice as the preferred medium of communication, and social networking online has significantly augmented (and in some ways displaced) offline interaction.

Not surprisingly, since the popular emergence of the World Wide Web, scholars have sought to understand the many and varied ways that religion has figured into its usage. How have religious believers and non-believers employed the Internet and, conversely, how has computer technology altered the ways in which religious belief and practice are manifest and contested? From online prayer services to antireligious YouTube rants, from massive Web portals such as Beliefnet and Streaming Faith to tiny stand-alone homepages supporting or disputing this practice or that, and from religious interaction online to the offscreen effects of online participation, the reality is that we still know relatively little about religion on/and the Internet. Although some rather hyperbolic and unsubstantiated predictions have been made (a few of which are discussed below), considerable research remains to be done before we are close to understanding the intersection between the latest in computer-mediated technology and the oldest means of interpreting human nature.

Rather than a description of how to research religion on the Internet or how to use the Web for one's research purposes, this chapter discusses some of the ways in which scholars have approached issues of religion and the Internet. It sketches out a number of the methodo-logical problems presented both by use of the Internet as a research tool and by the World Wide Web as a research domain. Indeed, as a point of departure this particular distinction cannot be overstated, and it makes any methodological consideration of religion and computer-mediated technology somewhat different than other research approaches to religious phenomena. That is, on the one hand, the Internet presents itself as both *method* and *data*, and the researcher must be clear in which aspect—or at which point along the continuum between the two—she is working at any given time. Are we studying religion as it appears on the Internet or as it is mediated by computer technology? Are we assessing religious information presented online or observing computer-mediated communication as a venue for religious practice? Are we using computers to facilitate research into religious behavior occurring in the offline world? Or, are we operating in the liminal spaces between these points?

One of the earliest conceptions of religion and the Internet is Helland's (2000) theoretical distinction between **religion online** and **online religion**—the Internet as a vehicle for the provision of religious information and the Web as a site for religious practice and participa-tion. It quickly became apparent, however, that these were not ideal points in empirical space, but shifting activities that occur and often interpenetrate along an online continuum. That is, as advances in technology encouraged greater participation in and control over the online experience, websites blurred the distinction between information provision and visitor participation (see Helland 2005).

On the other hand, research into religion on the Internet requires awareness of more than simply the technical aspects of the World Wide Web or a simple description of what users are doing online. The ramifications of political interference with or corporate control over Internet access and content, the digital divide (which still indicates that the vast majority of the global population does not have access to the Internet), advances in technology that affect not only the means by which people communicate (e.g. hand-held devices), but the manner in which they do so (e.g. tweeting or texting), or the various ways in which participants conceptualize the computer-mediated environment—these are just a few of the concerns with which the religious researcher must contend.

From tour guides to transcendence: a brief review of claims for religion on the 'net'

Although the Internet seems at first to be an easy ground for researchers to probe, problems of research method have plagued academics for nearly two decades. Often appealing to a rather vague notion of 'phenomenology', for example, far too many articles (and not a few books) have appeared which simply describe what researchers have found on this website or that—what information is presented, what visual format is used, what others sites are hyper-linked and so forth. Rather than a critical analysis of religion in the online environment, these are little more than Internet tour guides and are frequently out of date by the time they reach the bookstore shelf. That we need to know what is on the Web is beyond question, but that is only the starting point for research and cannot pass for its conclusion. The following are just a few of the more important questions with which scholars must contend:

- Who uploaded the content and why?
- How have viewers and participants reacted to it?
- How are site visitors invited to interact with the material (if they are)?
- How is content presented and controlled in the face of contradiction or challenge?
- How does online content and participation affect religious belief and activity offline?

Other researchers, attempting more than simple description, do seek to analyze the character and consequences of online religious behavior, but they do so as though the online environ-ment can be treated in exactly the same way methodologically as research into religious tradi-tions offline. This is not necessarily the case, and researchers should not make the mistake of thinking that expertise in an offline religious tradition will translate easily or directly to an analysis of its online variant. The functionality and limitations of online activity, for example, or the inextricable relationship between the online and offline worlds, should be kept clearly in view by the researcher. Over the past decade and a half, an impressive amount of work has been done in the sociology and anthropology of the Internet, and scholars of religion who avoid this material do so at their peril.[1] Finally, some researchers have echoed industry and technophile rhetoric about the allegedly qualitative shift in consciousness facilitated by the Internet and have made unsupported and occasionally hyperbolic claims for religion on the Web. That is, rather than claims to be investigated, they have predicated arguments on untested assumptions.

In one of the first articles to address religious activity online, an analysis of text-based neo-pagan rituals taking place in electronic forums, O'Leary points out quite correctly that 'the conventional methods of academic research in religious ethnography seemed of little use'

(O'Leary 1996: 795; see also O'Leary and Brasher 1996; Paccagnella 1997). Since traditional anthropology and ritual studies have insisted on both the embodied nature of ritual practice and the physical presence of the researcher, the question of what is actually happening during text-based online interaction is considerably more difficult to answer. Among other things, O'Leary proposes that 'the textual reality of a candle as described on the screen is sufficient to ensure ritual efficacy', even though 'the cyber-flame raised in the electronic conference room has no embodiment except in text' (O'Leary 1996: 799). As I contend in *Cyberhenge*, however, the real question for a sociologist or anthropologist studying this sort of phenomenon is: *Is* it? '*Is* the word "candle," when typed on a screen in a particular Internet chat venue, "sufficient to ensure ritual efficacy"? Do participants *experience* the candle and, if so, how? And *is* such efficacy as exists sufficient to overcome the inherent difficulties of performing and participating in ritual practice through computer networks' (Cowan 2005a: 120; see Krüger 2005)? From a methodological perspective, this distinction can hardly be overstated. That is, these are questions to be investigated, not positions to be assumed.

Unfortunately, other scholars have simply embraced the commercial and enthusiast hyperbole by which the Internet has been surrounded since its inception. In *Give Me That Online Religion*, for example, Brasher claims that 'online religion is the most portentous development for the future of religion to come out of the twentieth century', and goes so far as to suggest that 'using a computer for online religious activity could become the dominant form of religion and religious experience in the next century' (Brasher 2001: 17, 19). Brasher continues that because 'it widens the social foundation of religious life, cyberspace erodes the basis from which religion contributes to the destructive dynamics of xenophobia' (ibid.: 6–7), and that 'as the latest site of cultural challenge and change, online religions (traditional and new) represent a stabilizing influence in the virtual domain' (ibid.: 13). This seems to assume that online religious participation is somehow qualitatively different—and by implication better—than religious behavior we encounter offline. There is, however, no empirical evidence to support this—indeed, quite the opposite. Because the Internet is now much more open to contribution, beyond mere consumption, prejudice is as readily available online as tolerance, and claims that the Internet will ameliorate offline tensions through increased exposure seem no more demonstrable than similar claims made for the telegraph, the telephone and the television.

Since research into religious activity on the Internet began in the mid-1990s, scholarly and popular claims have ranged from the dystopian to the utopian. As I was writing this chapter in late 2010, for example, I was contacted by a European documentary filmmaker who wanted to know about the potential of the Internet as a 'vehicle for mass mind control', something that has been debunked in the academic literature for more than a decade (Dawson and Hennebry 1999), but which still carries a certain popular resonance. My principal conclusion in *Cyberhenge*, on the other hand, was that although there are some very interesting things going on in the modern pagan Internet, much of the activity was limited to online replication of offline material and computer-mediated imitation of real-world behavior. There were occasional hints at something distinctive to the Internet, to be sure, but the vast majority of material seemed distinctly mundane and the Internet more of a delivery system than a qualitatively different magical environment. Once again, though, these are claims that depend upon research, rather than positions that can simply be assumed from the start.

A decade ago, in an early consideration of Internet methodology, Dawson proposed three principal areas that scholars needed to investigate in terms of religion on the Web: (1) 'what is on the Internet, who put it there, and for what purpose'; (2) 'how many people are using these resources'; and, most important from an academic perspective, (3) 'what influences these activities are having on the religious beliefs and practices of users' (Dawson 2000: 28).

Level 1: What?

- What kinds of religious content exist on the Internet?

Level 2: Who?

- Who produced these materials and who placed them online?
- Who is accessing or using the materials?

Level 3: How?

- How do producers or uploaders intend the materials to be used? How do they control their usage?
- How do Internet consumers use it? Do they become contributors in some way?
- How does this consumer use affect the content? Is it modified or revised to reflect usage?
- How does consumer usage affect offline religious belief and/or practice?

Level 4: Why?

- Why is this the case?
- How do we explain these patterns of Internet usage?
- What does this tell us about the nature of religion online, offline, and the relationship between them?

Figure 3.2.1 The question matrix
Source: Based on Dawson 2000: 28

To date, much of the research has focused on the first two of these concerns, while the last has gone woefully understudied. This is particularly unfortunate since it is the research most required to advance our understanding of the relationships that Dawson identifies. That is, *is* the Internet different—if indeed it is? How do offline behaviors and social networks influence online religious activity? How are they influenced by it? How do online participants conceptualize the nature of their activity and how does that affect religious relationships offline? In terms of this chapter, what are some of the methodological issues raised by these questions?

Research online: problems and promises

The advantages of computer-mediated research seem readily apparent. Since its costs are largely hidden from the end-user, the Internet appears inexpensive when compared to the cost of traveling somewhere to conduct participant-observation with a particular religious group. The Web brings us into potential contact with a considerably wider range of informants and a deeper pool of data than we might otherwise expect. Online research can save enormous amounts of time in the process of secondary literature reviews, as well as data-mining and processing. With increasingly powerful laptops we can pursue our research anywhere we have access to Wi-Fi. Put bluntly, on the surface, research that is either based on or facilitated by the Internet simply seems easier, but is it, and does it yield results that are more accurate and explanatory?

Consider, for example, the simple use of a search engine to test such things as religious vitality and growth in religious communities. I have reviewed numerous articles for publication that purport to measure the development of this or that religious tradition based on a longitudinal survey of Google returns. A researcher enters the word 'Goddess', for example, over a number of months, charting the search engine responses. On the basis of this, the argument is made that Goddess religion is growing. Or, as I noted in *Cyberhenge*, one contributor to a Yahoo!-based discussion forum wrote: 'Hey, you guys, I jus cheked out witch on the Internet and got ove a million sites! WoW! we're really out there!' [sic] (Cowan 2005a: 196). Both of these people fundamentally misunderstand two important things about the Internet:

Box 3.2.1 Questions to ask in Internet research

The easiest (and most common) way of studying religion on the Internet is simply to describe *what* one finds online:

- What does a website contain?
- Is it interactive in any way?
- Is it rudimentary or complex, well designed or not?

This is a necessary first step, but the researcher cannot stop there. She must also consider both the source(s) of online content and the material's consumer audience. This is the second level:

- *Who* is responsible for the content and for *whom* is it intended?
- Is the author of the content identified?
- Is the material original to the site or has it been re-posted from another source?
- *Who* is actually accessing, using and perhaps contributing to the content?

This leads to the third level of analysis:

- *How* is the material being used?
- *How* do content providers intend the material to be used and *how* do consumers actually use it?
- Do they re-post material elsewhere?
- *How* do providers control or manage usage?
- Do they permit open commenting, for example, or are responses to site material moderated?
- *How* does online usage affect the content over time and *how* is this reflected (if at all) in offline belief and practice?

Finally, and most important, is the question: *Why?*

- What explains this behavior?
- What can we learn from it, for example, about the relationship between religion and technology or the (d)evolution of religion in an increasingly computerized world?

It is crucial for researchers to remember that description of a phenomenon is only a first step. Critical analysis and interpretive *redescription* are the benchmarks of useful scholarship.

---

the technological and the contextual. First, Google does not return the number of websites found in response to a particular search string, but the number of times that string appears in the sites to which it has access. It may find the search string multiple times on a single page, for example, and each instance would show up in the cumulative result. Second, in the online world no less than the offline, context is everything. Web returns for the 'Goddess' could indeed indicate the online presence of Goddess-worshipping Internet users, but they could also indicate recipes for Green Goddess salad dressing, fan sites for this or that 'movie goddess', or fundamentalist Christian blogs decrying goddess worship as a tool of the Devil. These problems may seem obvious but, given some of the ways the Internet is used by both researchers and practitioners, they bear repeating.

Whether as data or method, research into religion on the Internet presents a number of more complex issues particular to computer-mediated communication and to what we might call the '**computer-conceptualized environment**', that is, how those who use computer-mediated communication understand the ideational world in which their online interaction occurs. As we consider each of these brief examples, it is important to remember that they represent interpenetrating zones of research concerns rather than discrete methodological domains, and that research into religion on the Internet is still in its formative stages. In many ways, we have more questions about what we are doing and how we are doing it than answers. To that end, consider these three areas of methodological concern: **ephemerality** and durability; identity and authority; and ethics in cyber-research. Because the Internet functions as both research site and investigative tool, each of these presents different sides of the methodological problem.

Online ephemerality and outdated durability

Similar to the Google search as a research method, the first issue is both technological and conceptual in nature, and can significantly inform the way many other issues are understood by online participants and Internet researchers. This is the paradox of *online ephemerality* and *outdated durability*, the fascinating interplay of the ways things both change and refuse to change in the online world.

On the Internet things do change—sometimes very rapidly. They are in many ways ephemeral. Witness the often frustrating fact that, for a variety of reasons, content one saw only yesterday may be all but impossible to locate today. While it is common for websites to be updated in the normal course of events, in many other cases Web content is deliberately changed to manage online impression in the face of challenge or potential conflict. In 1998 and 1999, for example, televangelist Pat Robertson was a lead voice in the conservative Christian chorus predicting the apocalypse as a result of the supposed Y2K problem (see Cowan 2003). Within weeks of 1 January 2000, however, all trace of the website that Robertson's ministry had devoted to the problem, and which he claimed was receiving well over 100,000 hits a month (quite considerable for the time), disappeared from the Christian Broadcasting Network's host portal. This illustrates both the problem of ephemerality and the issue of online impression management made possible by the ease with which Web content can be changed or consigned to archive sites such as the Wayback Machine (www.archive.org), many of which are of only limited utility.

In other cases, domain names change ownership and Web content is altered accordingly, or site operators lose interest and do not update material. These, too, can significantly affect scholarly claims about online activity. For instance, Højsgaard's search for a 'cyber-religion', one 'located primarily in cyberspace', led him to characterize a number of groups as authentic 'cyber-religions' (Højsgaard 2005: 53, n.1). As I have pointed out elsewhere, however, 'less than a year after the publication of his essay, of the thirteen sites he lists two are defunct, two have not been updated since 2000, two contain little more than the philosophical ramblings of their founders', and one—'Cyber-Voodoo'—is 'the product page for something called "Flaming Hooker Productions"' (Cowan 2007: 366). Clearly none of these would qualify as authentic religions, let alone cyber-religions, and again demonstrate the methodological problem of ephemerality.

The other side of ephemerality is what I call the outdated durability of online content: websites, blog postings, discussion threads that have not been updated in years, but which still appear in normal Internet searches and which are often treated as though they represent

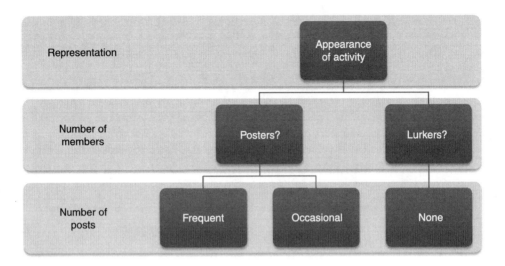

Figure 3.2.2 Membership and message traffic
Source: Based on Cowan 2005: 96–103

current information and normative conversation. This problem is exacerbated by the fact that so much material carries no identifiable date stamp and so appears up to date. I still occasionally receive emails inviting me to consider conversion to Matrixism, an alleged new religious movement founded on the principles of the 1999 blockbuster film, *The Matrix* (and the teachings of Bahaullah, the founder of the Baha'i faith). The Matrixism website, however, is very rudimentary and has not been significantly updated in several years. On the Internet, though, context is everything and unless the researcher remains aware of this—in this case of a website's provenance and history—he can easily be led to make claims that are simply insupportable.

Box 3.2.2 Assessing online participation

As I note in *Cyberhenge*, 'A useful indicator of online participation and interaction is message traffic factored against group membership and list duration. That is, over the course of its online career, how many posts does a particular group receive per month per member? On Yahoo!, fully 60 percent of the groups surveyed posted less than one message per month per member' (Cowan 2005: 97). Thus, the researcher cannot take membership numbers at face value any more than he can take the number of Google returns as an indication of anything substantive.

Identity and authority

Shifting from the experience to the participant, the most obvious—and arguably the most interesting—research problem in the online world is identity: how do we know with whom we are interacting and what does not knowing mean for our interactions? In a classic early work on social relations and identity construction on the Internet, Donath recounts the story of 'a high school student [who] claims to be an expert on viruses' and how 'patients desperate for a cure read the virtual virologist's pronouncements on new AIDS treatments, believing them to be backed by real world knowledge' (Donath 1999: 30). During my research into modern pagan use of the Web, I found numerous examples of users claiming to be a high priestess of this or high priest of that tradition, offering online classes in Wicca or witchcraft, and proclaiming themselves the leaders of Internet covens and working groups. Only very rarely was there any personal, verifiable information about these individuals. Although, obviously, this is in some ways a problem, it also opens fascinating new branches in the sociology of identity-construction and maintenance, impression management and performance, and charismatic attribution and bonding. While the work of scholars such as Harold Garfinkel and Erving Goffmann is considered out of academic fashion by some, and Max Weber's work on authority and legitimation has only rarely been invoked in research into religion online, their theoretical insights seem tailor-made for advancing our understanding of how we construct our social selves through the Internet. Identity informs the issue of authority and we are just beginning to learn how authoritative relationships are established, maintained, managed and challenged in cyberspace.

Although early studies posited the notion of a level playing field online, an anarchic dataspace in which everyone could participate equally, it is quite clear now that this is not the case. Power and authority operate as freely on the Internet as they do in real life, albeit in ways shaped both by the limitations of the technology and users' conceptualization of the online environment. Consider the following examples.

One of my students—researching a phenomenon he calls 'intervangelism' (see Bekkering forthcoming)—has discovered that the ability to control material on the Internet presents a particular problem for the maintenance of the charismatic bond. Bekkering points out that while disgraced televangelist Todd Bentley has reinvented himself as a faith healer whose computer-mediated audience is now entirely online and the vast majority of whose material is available only through the portal StreamingFaith.com. Not surprisingly, these segments are carefully edited to present him in the best possible light and any challenges to his authority that occur in the context of a healing service are simply deleted. Relatively few Bentley videos are available on YouTube, and Bekkering hypothesizes that this is because a specific feature of that site is not under his control: while YouTube allows comments (both text and video) to be shut off for any given item, the right-hand ribbon displaying contradictory items that users might find interesting.

As many researchers have noted, the technology of hyperlinking, the phenomenon of Internet replication, and our cognitive propensity toward confirmation bias all combine to accord authority online where none may exist in the offline world. With no demonstrable education in religious history or Christian theology, for example, but with seemingly limit-less amounts of time to devote to his website, Apologetics Index, Dutch fundamentalist Anton Hein has risen to become something of an authority on all things religious—at least to fellow Christians who look to his enormous website for information. As more and more people hyperlink information from his site, its prominence in a Google search for information on relevant topics increases. Since we know that relatively few people will pursue Google searches past the first few pages of returns, Hein's site becomes one of the first that users encounter, not because the information he offers is correct, necessarily, but because the nature of Internet technology makes it conveniently available. As a result, after several years, Hein has risen from a relatively obscure online presence to an authority in the conceptually enclosed world of conservative Christian apologetics. Like the issues raised by online identity, authority in computer-mediated environments presents an intriguing series of challenges to the ways in which we construe and ascribe authority, the nature, configuration and management of the charismatic bond, and implications of technology in the social psychology of online interaction. These lead quite naturally to the third concern: ethics in the conduct of research online.

Ethics in cyber-research

For several decades, two inter-related principles have grounded social scientific research into religious behavior and phenomena: disclosure and informed consent. On the one hand, the researcher has a responsibility to make both the fact and the nature of her work known to prospective subjects, while, on the other, subjects must be given the opportunity for informed consent before research begins. Except under very particular and restricted circumstances, covert research is no longer considered responsible or ethical. Over the years, of course, numerous cases in which neither of these principles has been observed (or at least were observed more in the ideal than the actual) have led to the rigorous implementation of ethical guidelines for research in most universities and as prerequisites for grant funding. The Internet, however, presents a significant challenge (and a not-insignificant temptation) to both principles. Two particular issues present themselves, one obvious, the other somewhat less so.

First, in the same way that one does not really know with whom we are interacting online—although this may change as Skype-type videoconferencing technology advances—potential research subjects do not know with whom they are communicating. While, as researchers, we can assume that many of our informants will Google us in order to under-stand who we are and what we are about while conducting research, this is only true so long as we are truthful about our identities and our projects. In addition to the ethical issue of disclosure, that we will fail to tell informants everything about who we are, a more problem-atic temptation is to invent identities as a means of covert research into marginal or secretive groups. As I pointed out in *Cyberhenge*, while researching the issue of authority in the context of modern paganism on the Internet, I could have pretended to be any number of different people: an Afro-Caribbean Santería priestess, an eager neophyte Druid anxious to find a spiritual teacher, or a New Age shaman seeking pupils for my new online school of ritual knowledge. Since, at least in the modern pagan Internet, chosen names are more common than given ones, there would be no way for respondents to know with whom they were dealing. Indeed, one modern pagan group that interacts online insists on meeting potential members offline before accepting them into the virtual coven. Although the ethical problems of covert research should be obvious, numerous conversations with colleagues over the years have convinced me that this is not the case and that this important methodological conversation must continue.

Second, most people conversant with online communications technology are familiar with the phenomenon of **lurking**: signing in to a chat room, a discussion forum, a Facebook group or a Twitter account—to name just a few of the possibilities—but neither participating nor in some cases even disclosing one's presence. It is as though we stand eavesdropping at the mall or drift from group to group at a cocktail party—observing behavior and surrepti-tiously taking notes, while hidden behind our online avatars. The ethical issues here are somewhat more complex. If users post messages on a public notice board of some kind—a publicly accessible discussion forum, a Facebook page or their own blog—can they reasonably argue for a right of privacy for their comments, or that they should expect to provide informed consent if their comments become data for some interested researcher? On the other hand, many groups require some sort of formal admission process—a note to the group's moderator, permission from the website operator, provision of personal information. Whether they are simple or sophisticated, these mechanisms represent attempts to control access to particular online venues. If operators consider these sites less than completely public, to what degree are the twin dicta of research disclosure and informed consent invoked? Given that the presence of a researcher inevitably alters both the atmosphere of the group and the potential responses he receives, the temptation to conduct online research covertly is heightened.

Twists and turns: the methodological road ahead

Just five years ago, editors of the *Online—Heidelberg Journal of Religions on the Internet* considered methodological considerations sufficiently important to devote their entire first issue to the topic. Since then, CMC technology has changed even more dramatically than in the five years since Jeffrey K. Hadden and I edited the first collection of academic essays devoted to religion on the Internet (Hadden and Cowan 2000). In 2005 threaded discussion forums such as Yahoo Groups were still enormously popular, while social networking through Facebook and MySpace and video sharing through YouTube were in their technological infancy. Blogs had made an appearance, but it was too soon to understand their contribution to the Web's overall background noise, and Twitter was not yet a gleam in its creators' eyes. Now, some data indicate that social networking is displacing (if not necessarily replacing) email as the most popular form of digital communication. While discussion threads are still important when dealing with complex issues, millions of people blog about topics ranging from the sublime to the ridiculous. Netbooks made a brief run against the popularity of laptops, only to be shown up as a bridge technology between notebook computers and media tablets such as Apple's iPad. With the advent of quantum nanocomputing, the possibility of wearable and implantable computer communications technology may not be that far in the future.

With the tremendous growth of the Internet over the past decade, the consequent increase in the background noise against which any singular online voice must compete, and the self-limiting nature of much of the search technology used to sort through one's cyber-experience, the need for awareness of context and research triangulation is greater than ever. In some ways, we must learn to evaluate an entirely new species of data. Where once people asserted with confidence, 'I heard it on the news', now they claim, 'I saw it somewhere on the Net'. Clearly, news media are not, and never have been, unbiased sources of unimpeachable information. However, given our social psychological propensity for source dissociation (our tendency to forget where we learned things with which we agree), the difference between the six o'clock news and an anonymous blog becomes less distinct— especially when the news report repeats information originally sourced to that blog. As I was writing this part of the chapter, news reports began appearing that President Barack Obama's ten-day state visit to India was costing $200 million per day and was using 10 per cent of the United States Navy. It is unclear where precisely on the Internet this absurd claim began, but numerous mainstream news media and pundits reported it as if it were accurate.

The other side of this issue is what we might call the problem of social penetration and technological familiarity, the backpressure against research as the Web becomes increasingly common. That is, as the Internet becomes more and more embedded in everyday life, as the generation that remembers card catalogues and corded telephones disappears, and as cultural expectations of Internet use and availability increase, will this mask the importance of the shift from personal- to computer-mediated communication that has happened in only two decades? As an example, although I am not aware of anyone who has done so, one could argue that the telephone was an enormously important technological element in the evolution of religion in the 20th century. It enabled shifts in the experience and delivery of religious services that range from telephone prayer trees in religious congregations to personal calls at home when one was sick. No longer did a parishioner need to wait for the minister, priest or rabbi to call in person. The religious congregation reached out electronically. The possibility of telethons and telephone banks made fundraising almost an art form for televangelists around the world. Yet, precisely because the telephone is such a ubiquitous technology, its familiarity has rendered it a piece of the cultural furniture and its central role in these phenomena has gone all but unremarked. Will the same thing happen to the Internet? As it becomes more and more a part of the background apparatus of culture, will our interest in researching its impact wane? One hopes not, because although hyperbolic claims must be tempered into empirically testable hypotheses, there is no doubt that the Internet has impacted the delivery, reception and experience of religion. How, exactly, it has done so, and what this means for the future of religion in an increasingly technologized world, remains to be seen.

Note

1   See, for example, Castells 2001; Haythornethwaite and Wellman 2002; Lanier 2010; Hine 2000; Rheingold 1993; Smith and Kollock 1999.

References

Bekkering, D., forthcoming. From 'televangelist' to 'intervangelist': the emergence of the streaming video preacher. *Journal of Religion and Popular Culture.*

Brasher, B., 2001. *Give Me That Online Religion.* Jossey-Bass, San Francisco.

Campbell, H., 2005. *Exploring Religious Community Online: we are one in the network.* Peter Lang, New York.

Castells, M., 2001. *The Internet Galaxy: reflections on the Internet, business, and society.* Oxford University Press, Oxford.

Cowan, D.E., 2003. Confronting the failed failure: Y2K and evangelical eschatology in light of the passed millennium. *Nova Religio* 7(2): 71–85.

—— 2005a. *Cyberhenge: modern pagans on the internet.* Routledge, New York, London.

—— 2005b. Online u-topia: cyberspace and the mythology of placelessness. *Journal for the Scientific Study of Religion* 44(3): 257–63.

—— 2007. Religion on the Internet. In: Beckford, J.A. and Demerath, N.J., III (eds), *The Sage Handbook of the Sociology of Religion,* SAGE, London, Los Angeles, pp. 356–76.

Dawson, L.L., 2000. Researching religion in cyberspace: issues and strategies. In: Hadden, J.K. and Cowan, D.E. (eds), *Religion on the Internet: research prospects and promises.* JAI Press/Elsevier Science, Amsterdam, London, pp. 25–54.

Dawson, L.L. and Hennebry, J., 1999. New religions and the Internet: recruiting in a new public space. *Journal of Contemporary Religion* 14(1): 17–39.

Donath, J., 1999. Identity and deception in the virtual community. In: Smith, M.A. and Kollock, P. (eds), *Communities in Cyberspace,* Routledge, London, New York, pp. 26–59.

Hadden, J.K. and Cowan, D.E. (eds), 2000. *Religion on the Internet: research prospects and promises.* JAI Press/Elsevier Science, Amsterdam, London.

Haythornethwaite, C. and Wellman, B. (eds), 2002. *The Internet in Everyday Life.* Blackwell, Oxford.

Helland, C., 2000. Online-religion/religion-online and virtual communitas. In: Hadden, J.K. and Cowan, D.E. (eds), *Religion on the Internet: research prospects and promises*, JAI Press/Elsevier Science, Amsterdam, London, pp. 205–24.

—— 2005. Online religion as lived religion: methodological issues in the study of religious participation on the Internet. *Online—Heidelberg Journal of Religions on the Internet* 1 (1), www.online. uni-hd.de.

Hine, C.M., 2000. *Virtual Ethnography*. SAGE, London.

Højsgaard, M.T., 2005. Cyber-religion: on the cutting edge between the virtual and the real. In: Højsgaard, M.T. and Warburg, M. (eds), *Religion and Cyberspace*, Routledge, London, pp. 50–63.

Krüger, O., 2005. Discovering the invisible Internet: methodological aspects of searching religion on the Internet. *Online—Heidelberg Journal of Religions on the Internet* 1(1), www.online. uni-hd.de.

Lanier, J., 2010. *You Are Not a Gadget: a manifesto*. Alfred A. Knopf, New York.

O'Leary, S.D., 1996. Cyberspace as sacred space: communicating religion on computer networks. *Journal of the American Academy of Religion* 64(4): 781–808.

O'Leary, S.D. and Brasher, B., 1996. The unknown god of the Internet: religious communication from the ancient agora to the virtual forum. In: Ess, C. (ed.), *Philosophical Perspectives on Computer-Mediated Communication*. State University of New York Press, Albany, pp. 233–70.

Paccagnella, L., 1997. Getting the seat of your pants dirty: strategies for ethnographic research on virtual communities. *Journal of Computer-Mediated Communication* 3(1), jcmc.indiana.edu/vol3/ issue1/paccagnella.html.

Qualters, S., 2010. Federal circuit: group's Internet and radio worship does not meet IRS definition of 'church'. www.law.com.

Rheingold, H., 1993. *The Virtual Community: homesteading on the electronic frontier*. The MIT Press, Cambridge, MS.

Smith, M.A. and Kollock, P. (eds), 1999. *Communities in Cyberspace*. Routledge, London, New York.

Further reading

Apolito, P. 2005. *The Internet and the Madonna: religious visionary experiences on the web*. University of Chicago Press, Chicago, London.

An interesting discussion of the effect of Internet communication on the experience of Marian apparitions and the ways in which those experiences are communicated and mediated electronically. Apolito's work is a good example of how Web chat rooms and discussion forums can shape religious discourse both online and offline.

Boellstorff, T. 2008. *Coming of Age in Second Life: an anthropologist explores the virtually human*. Princeton University Press, Princeton.

The popularity of the online role-playing world Second Life may have waned in recent years, but Boellstorff's ethnography of the virtual cultures and communities created by Second Lifers offers a wealth of methodological insight into the promises and pitfalls of online research.

Bunt, G. 2003. *Islam in the Digital Age: e-jihad, online fatwas, and cyber Islamic environments*. Pluto Press, London.

Surveying the many ways in which Muslims use the Internet for discussion, debate and activism, Bunt provides a useful model for researchers beginning their study of religion on the Internet.

Burnett, R., Consalvo, M. and Ess, C. (eds), 2010. *The Handbook of Internet Studies*. Wiley-Blackwell, Oxford.

Although too early to know for certain, this volume has the potential to be a milestone in the consideration of Internet research. Many of the pioneers in Internet research are represented and methodological consideration ranges from Web archiving to the investigation of Internet usage in everyday life.

Castells, M., 2001. *The Internet Galaxy: reflections on the Internet, business, and society.* Oxford University Press, Oxford.

Although not explicitly methodological, this is a classic synopsis of Castell's three-volume series on communication in the information age and should be part of every researcher's library. Fortunately, his method is transparent enough throughout that the careful reader will be amply rewarded.

Cowan, D.E., 2005. *Cyberhenge: modern pagans on the Internet*. Routledge, London, New York.

One of the first book-length investigations of how a new religious movement is using the World Wide Web and how that use is affecting different groups both online and offline. Contains extensive material on discussion forums as data, exploring the relationship between online and offline behavior, and the establishment and maintenance of online authority.

Jones, S.G. (ed.), 1998. *Doing Internet Research: critical issues and methods for examining the net*. SAGE, London, Thousand Oaks, CA.

Although a bit dated, Jones draws together important considerations on the importance of both quantitative and quali-tative date, the development of online surveys, discourse and rhetorical analysis, and the recurring problem of the online community.

Markham, A.N. and Baym, N. (eds), 2009. *Internet Inquiry: conversations about method*. SAGE, London, Thousand Oaks.

Written in a very approachable style, this excellent volume discusses in depth a number of issues related to the conduct of qualitative research both online and of the online environment—the Internet as data and method. The editors consider such questions as data collection, privacy issues and the question of making qualitative research theoretically meaningful.

[na] [nd] *Online—Heidelberg Journal of Religions on the Internet*. www.online.uni-hd.de.

Published since 2005 by the Institut für Religionswissenschaft at Heidelberg University, the first volume dealt entirely with issues of methodology, and the journal continues to publish many fine examples of research into religion and the Internet.

Norris, P. 2001. *Digital Divide: civic engagement, information poverty, and the Internet worldwide*. Cambridge University Press, Cambridge.

Discusses one of the most ignored and important aspects of Internet research—the simple fact that the majority of the global population does not have access to the Internet. In the midst of hyperbole over the 'connectedness' of the world, this reality cannot be overlooked by researchers.

Key concepts

Computer-conceptualized environment: an umbrella term used to describe the ways in which users of CMC understand what they are doing and the ideational environment in which their activity occurs.

Computer-mediated communication (CMC): an umbrella term used to describe any form of communication that is principally facilitated through computer technology. Note that this is not limited to the traditional understanding of a 'computer', but can include new media technology such as smartphones and text messaging devices.

Ephemerality: the tenuous nature of online material and interaction, most clearly demonstrated in the speed with which websites can change or disappear, and the experience of interrupted electronic communication due to technological breakdown or environmental interference.

Lurking: observing online activity without either participating or, in many cases, even revealing one's presence.

Online religion: religious practice that occurs online or is mediated between participants through the use of computers.

Religion online: religious information and news about religion that is available online, but which does not include participation in religious activity through the Internet.

World Wide Web: one component of the Internet, for which it is often used as a synonym, this is the most common form of computer-mediated communication.

Related chapters

- Chapter 1.5 Research design
- Chapter 1.6 Research ethics
- Chapter 2.1 Content analysis
- Chapter 3.5 Visual culture

3.3

MATERIAL CULTURE

Richard M. Carp

Chapter summary

- Material culture studies is an emerging transdiscipline with a developing methodology.
- Material culture studies is polymethodic, using and attempting to integrate an array of methods extant in other fields applied to materiality as well as some methods especially adapted to materiality.
- Religion is intrinsically material. Material culture studies enables and requires scholars to describe and interpret the material components of religion. Since material culture, unlike text, is made and used by all strata of society, studying material culture and religion allows investigation of religion among those who neither read nor write.
- Bodies both give rise to and are components of material culture. Bodies in the field of study are primary data in material culture, while scholars' bodies are the primary source of method and an inescapable methodological limitation.
- Religion and material culture raises two fundamental methodological concerns. The first involves sensory enculturation, which limits the extent to which scholars can experience others' material worlds.
- The second involves the interactions between academic and religious material cultures, since scholars must use material tools (and our bodily adaptations to them) to study religious materiality.
- Studying material culture and religion involves description and interpretation of a dynamic pattern of actions, persons, skills, technologies, social formations and artifacts.

What is material culture?

Material culture is an emerging **transdisciplinary** field integrating aspects of the disciplines of history and theory of visual and performing art and culture, archaeology, religious studies, history, anthropology, folklore, history of technology, cultural geography, psychology, sociology, materials science, conservation science and archaeometry, among others, dedicated to scholarly interpretation of material culture (Lubar and Kingery 1993: ix–xi). One advantage of **material culture studies** is that it gives us access to all strata of a culture. At most times and places, only certain elites—usually men—produced texts, while women, the poor and even slaves created material culture.

Material culture may at first seem to be the study of a collection of things—artifacts. Actually, material culture is much more than that, although the whole can be derived from artifacts, for each thing implies a set of material activities and significations that interact with the artifact and one another and which mediate a **cultural landscape**. Any artifact entails a dynamic pattern of actions, persons, skills, technologies, social formations and other artifacts whose similar patterns partially overlap with one another. The interactive panoply of these interacting arrays is a cultural landscape. One's focus need not begin with an object. One can start with actions (*salat*), a person (a *mohel*), a skill (icon making), or any other component of material culture; each will lead to the others.

Box 3.3.1 Religion and the history of technology

Robert B. Gordon (1993) writes that forward and backward linkages are crucial to interpreting artifacts in the history of technology. Backward linkages relate to origins, forward linkages to effects. In both cases they include 'skills and social structures' (ibid.: 80). How might this apply to religion? Consider the Christian Bible, not as a text, but as an artifact. As a text, the Bible has been relatively fixed since the fourth century; as an artifact, it changed with the invention of the printing press. Once irreplaceable, Bibles became reproducible; once rare, they were more common. Copyists' devotional labor was replaced by printmakers' artisanry, and calligraphy gave way to typeface, while vernacular literacy challenged Latin conventions and vernacular Bibles were printed.

Though the words in the text remained the same, the artifact and the persons and skills interacting with it changed. This new Bible helped give rise to the Protestant Reformation, founded in part on the notion that each believer (or at least each citizen, male believer) should have direct access to the Bible, without intermediaries. This idea was literally unthinkable before easily reproducible Bibles and widespread vernacular literacy, themselves results of printing technology. So we see that the history of technology can play a formative role in the development of religion. The Protestant Reformation is, in part, a forward linkage of the printing press. (Gutenberg's first press was developed in 1450. Luther's theses were posted in 1517.)

Material culture, then, refers to everything that is both perceptible and cultural, not only artifacts, but also the contexts, processes and skills of use and production that surround and interpenetrate artifacts. Thus material culture includes space (contrast, for example, Western perspectival space with Japanese *ma*) and time (contrast Western time before and after the invention of clocks). It includes all modes of perception, not merely sight and its correlate, visual culture; invisibility is not synonymous with imperceptibility. Music, for example, is material (the sound of it, as well as the instruments and bodies that make it); so is the taste of a sacred meal, the scent of incense, the feel of rosary beads in one's fingers, the proprioception of one's body in sacred postures or gestures (kneeling in prayer, for example, or making the sign of the cross) or the kinesthesia of one's body engaged in religious activity (for example *sa'y* during the *Hajj*).[1]

Methods in material culture and the study of religion

The interpenetrations of religion and material culture are complex and multidimensional; because of this, methods to study those interpenetrations are also complex and multidimensional. Three analytical distinctions are useful to clarify the field of religion and material culture: material religion; material religious influences on secular culture; and material components that pass across these boundaries. They should be understood as heuristic devices, rather than as categorical distinctions. *Material religion* is everything perceptible that is part of a religious tradition. This extends to ritual objects, images, architecture and music, but also food (and diet), scents (e.g. incense), prescribed uses of the body (kneeling for prayer, postures of exaltation), proscribed uses of the body (women hiding their hair except to their husbands, forbidden sexual practices, fasting, prohibitions on tattooing), and so forth. In every case, these must be taken to include the processes and personnel by which they are made, used, enforced and so on. Material religion extends beyond explicitly religious contexts.

> Religions discipline and interpret bodies; create and define sacred spaces through architecture; generate, adore, and study images in all media; regulate the intake of food; structure temporal experience; and in general interpenetrate and are in turn permeated by the cultural landscapes in which they exist.
>
> *(Carp 2007: 3)*

Method

Method, though often presented as a disciplined and ordered procedure for investigating data and developing knowledge, can equally validly be understood as the means by which data and knowledge are made to appear and to seem self-evident (Carp 2001: 90–104). In the study of religion, as elsewhere, methods for studying material culture involve methods of data collection and those of interpretation. For the latter, the general methodological understandings concerning hermeneutics apply:

> The study of texts has led to the conclusion that the tools by which we study them and the understanding of textuality we bring to them participate powerfully in the meanings we take from them. Just so, our embodied disciplinary practices and the material culture within and by means of which we undertake them are epistemological problems in the study of religion.
>
> *(Carp 2007: 4)*

On the one hand, entering a field in development such as religion and material culture may seem daunting, especially to emerging scholars. On the other hand, studying the intersections of religion and material culture offers scholars the chance to shape an emerging field at its genesis, as well as to correct a double oversight: that of religion in material culture studies and of material culture in religious studies. From the perspective of this book, it affords the chance to bring a field into being by developing and applying new and hybrid methods, demonstrating their effectiveness by simultaneously bringing new data sets into view, and demonstrating their significance and fecundity.[2] Despite the broad range of methods relevant to material culture studies (such as archaeometry, materials science, conservation science, historical and industrial archaeology, semiotic analysis and analysis of form), there is a reasonably small set of them that will offer junior scholars entrée into the field. My methodological work has largely centered on the implications of the interpenetrations of human bodies and material culture as they affect the study of religion. I will begin considering this at some length, and then proceed more briefly to discuss other important methods in material culture and religion.

Box 3.3.2 Systematic questioning as method

One approach to method in material culture and religion is to develop a systematic process of questioning that leads out from one's immediate point of concentration to its larger contexts (or vice versa). Consider for example a cup used for wine in Eucharist. How big is it, what is it made of, how was it made, is it manufactured or crafted? Are the size, material or creative processes significant? If so to whom? Who made it; how was making it experienced (as worship, sacred personal transformation, a business transaction, slave labor)? Who uses it (who is not allowed to)? When is it used, what actions are taken with it (filling, raising, chanting, presenting, drinking, cleansing) and why? How is it manipulated in space and time (out of sight, on a side table, on the altar, raised on high, put away) and why? What other artifacts and actions are relevant to understanding it (the symbolism of bread and wine in Eucharist; the structure of Catholic or Protestant worship space; the semiotics of altar/pulpit/lectern; officiant's vestments, including their colors; the social formations that give rise to the gender/race/class/ethnicity of the congregation and officiant)?

Body, method, material culture and religion

Studying material culture puts us in touch with our own material culture: our bodies and the physical entities, context, processes and skills with which they are enmeshed. As scholars, we become aware of the embodied aspects of scholarship, and of the material culture of the academy:

> Academic thought is produced by a specifically disciplined body, one that can tolerate sitting for hours in sterile rooms buzzing with the sound of fluorescent lights, listening to word after word of lecture after lecture. These bodies have been taught to dissociate from themselves, trained to delay elimination (and even the experience of the need to eliminate), to repress the experience of sexual desire, thirst, to still the urge for movement and kinesthetic expression for a slumberous physical stillness which is required not only for attending (conferences, classes, laboratories) but also for reading, writing and computer work.
>
> *(Carp 2002: 99)*[3]

Scholars' bodies are correlated with an array of material culture: spaces such as classrooms, conference halls, seminar rooms and laboratories; expressive forms such as books, libraries, journal articles, museums and galleries; the choreography of bodies through campuses; the transportation devices and temporary living and eating arrangements necessary for professional conferences; tools of the trade (pencils, computers and their programs, offices, desks), and so forth. Meanwhile, the research university came into being and is maintained 'with or even through an armory of little tools—catalogues, charts, tables (of paper), reports, questionnaires, dossiers, and so on' (Clark 2006: 6).

Human bodies are material entities. Because of our extreme neoteny, an infant body cannot become a competent adult body except in a socio-cultural context. For an infant, that context is every bit as real as gravity. It is a given, and the infant and developing child adapt to it. This adaptive process, which goes on throughout life, actively transforms bodies. Sensory experience, for example, is profoundly cultured (Howes 2005; Classen 1993). Skills and capacities, too, are learned. Our ability to learn skills is enabled and limited by our perceptual capacities, which are themselves shaped by our enskillment, while both perceptual capacities and the skills available and necessary to learn are affected by culture (Ingold 2000). Ordinary daily body activities such as walking, sitting and standing at rest vary cross-culturally (Downey 2005: 209; Hall 1977), while bodies adapted to different cultures differ in their muscular and skeletal development and neural architecture (Ingold 2000: 376).

Becoming competent in a culture is a complex form of physical education which shapes one's total experience of the world including oneself and one's capacities. 'Regardless of whether we realize it, we are all engaged in life-long projects of bodily self-cultivation' (Downey 2005: 33). These 'different physical techniques, broadly understood, affect a person's sensual experience, including the most basic perceptions [. . .as well as] the skills and behaviors through which they perceive' (ibid.: 210). While material culture is a human product, material culture is also an objective reality, and humans are products of material culture (cf. Berger and Luckmann 1967: 61). That is, human bodies are artifacts of material culture.[4]

Box 3.3.3 Body methods in the study of religion

- Scholars must be aware of, and make their audiences aware of, their own **bodily encultura-tion**—the extent to which and ways in which scholars' and audiences' experience is enabled and limited by their inherence in particular trajectories of material culture and the ways those trajectories shape their bodies' capacities and limitations.
- Scholars must be aware of, and make their audiences aware of, the extent to which and the ways in which scholars' bodies are further enabled and limited by the specific regimes of bodily training involved in scholarship itself. Our bodies are not only enculturated, they are also (academically) disciplined (Carp 2001).
- We would never send an illiterate scholar to study sacred texts. Why would we send scholars without dance training to study sacred dance, or without sculptural experience to study religious sculpture? This is why many art history programs require studio practice. Garner some direct experience of the practices involved in the media you want to investigate (Carp 2007; LaMothe 2008).
- Body knowledge extends beyond explicit and formal practices in particular media. Studying dance, for example, may help one understand not only sacred dance, but also everyday movement and its religious entanglements as well. Paul Stoller (1997) proposes that we train ourselves to engage in 'sensuous scholarship'. We develop our minds flexibly to enter into others' worlds to the greatest extent possible; why not our bodies as well?
- There is no substitute for apprenticeship as a method to understand the production, use and meaning of material culture (Downey 2005: 51–54). For a useful discussion of the benefits and dangers of apprenticeship in the study of religion, see Brown (1991).

Scholars' bodies are doubly produced by material culture: first by material culture in general, and second by the material culture of the academy and of particular disciplines. Our bodies are themselves the context and source of methods. 'The everyday world of cultural normalcy and the specialized world of academic knowledge are co-produced from a shared set of skills embedded in our bodies and their technical and technological extensions' (Carp 1997: 103). 'Bodies, cultures, sensing and perceiving, and knowing and believing are woven together in a net of interconnections, which cannot be cut [. . .] As knowers we find ourselves ineluctably situated in a network that both enables and limits our knowledge' (Carp 2008: 178–79).[5]

Other methodological concerns in material culture and religion

Below I will discuss several useful and important methods for studying material culture and religion (behavioral approaches, interpreting cultural landscapes, materials and material processes, forward and backward linkages, and the use of literary sources). There are several other important methods that I will not address here, because they are considered elsewhere in this volume. Their application to material culture and religion is not significantly different than to religion considered in other frames, except for the general methodological considerations discussed above. These include field research, comparison, media studies of various kinds (documents, video, internet, film, visual culture), and spatial methods.

Use

Technology 'involves a large component of nonverbal thinking that is not easily recorded in words or even by drawings' (Gordon 1993: 74). Scholars thus gain understanding by engaging with the material culture they study in terms both of its use and its creation. This may take the form of participant observation, of apprenticeship or, in the case of extinct cultures, 'experimental archaeology' (Gordon 1993: 90). Even when use is not possible, scholars should not rely solely on images or descriptions of artifacts or processes, but should experience them in person, whenever possible sufficiently frequently to become familiar with them, if at all possible on site, rather than in museums or other repositories.

Box 3.3.4 Behavioral approach to *kōlam* of South Asia

Kōlam are a widespread women's folk art in South Asia, 'beautiful and complex geometric and symmetrical designs [that] form a central component of domestic and ritual practice' to create auspicious and avoid inauspicious conditions (Mall 2007: 55). Alfred Gell studied the completed forms in the 1990s, interpreting them as artifacts for snaring demons 'by presenting them with insoluble cognitive conundrums' (ibid.: 75–76). In the 2000s Amar S. Mall supplemented Gell's method by observing women making *kōlam*, speaking with practitioners, talking with observers while *kōlam* were being drawn, reading printed guidebooks for practitioners, examining practitioners' notebooks, and making and examining videos of practitioners at work. He determined that *kōlam* (particularly the variety known as *kampi kōlam*) do not catch demons through intellectual confusion, but by engaging them in the very process of which the *kōlam* are a result, tangling demons in 'a labyrinthine mesh of threads along which all of life and existence is constrained to run' (ibid.: 76). These methods also help Mall develop new insights into South Indian folk understandings of agency and materiality (not just the meaning of what is made, but of making it, and of who makes it).

Behavioral approaches

All material culture is a manifestation of human behavior, and its ongoing uses, including its 'meanings', are human behaviors. This implies using 'specific circumstances and incorporating principles of psychological, communicative, and interactive process' [sic] (Jones 1993: 194) to understand it. Behavioral approaches may require the researcher to range away from the local community in which research is being conducted to explore artisans, clients and others in distant communities whose engagement is significant to the matter at hand.

Interpreting cultural landscapes

An interconnected array of material culture can be described as a cultural landscape. According to Lewis, a cultural landscape includes 'everything humans do to the natural earth for whatever reason' (Lewis 1993: 116). Because cultures differ, so do cultural landscapes; because cultures change over time, so do cultural landscapes, becoming 'in effect a kind of cultural autobiography' (ibid.: 116), which can be interpreted by close attention. Individual components of a cultural landscape take on their significance because of their relations with the whole, much as words take on meaning through their relations with a broader web of signification. There is no artifact or activity 'in itself'. We can and usually must cut out a limited part of a cultural landscape to study. We and our audiences are best served when we first set that limited part in the broadest context we are able and when we are conscious of and explicit about the distortions caused by our cutting out. For example, geography matters. 'To a large degree, cultures dictate that certain activities should occur in certain places and only in those places' (Lewis 1992: 181). A temple should not be studied 'in itself', as if viewed in a photograph from which all surrounding buildings and activities have been removed. Its context matters. Where it is and where it would not be allowed to be, what is and is not around it, who is there and who cannot be, and what they do (and when), as well as when and under what conditions certain activities take place, are all important clues to the temple's significance.

Box 3.3.5 Cultural landscape and religion in Indianapolis

Sacred Circles/Public Squares (Farnsley *et al.* 2004) is an excellent example of the use of cultural landscape in religious studies, telling the story of the multiple roles of religion in the public life of Indianapolis as well as the multiple effects of Indianapolis' development on religion. It is especially concerned with the dialectic between dispersive forces associated with suburbanization and integrative forces (re)asserting a civic (and religious) center. In 1840 the city center was ringed by four main line Protestant churches; today only one remains. In the interim suburbanization, economic sprawl and increasing religious and ethnic diversity have scattered religious institutions and functions throughout the built environment. *Sacred Circles* integrates history, geography, architecture, urban planning, the multiplicities of elite and popular cultures, policy, politics and collective religious, secular and political behavior into a rich discussion of the multiple interactions of religion and 'the public' in Indianapolis' cultural landscape over nearly 200 years.

The notion of cultural landscape directs us to look at 'common' as well as elite components of the built environment; the assumption is that *'all human landscape has cultural meaning'* (Lewis 1992: 176, italics in original, see also 178). Cultural landscapes have significant inertia and require wealth, energy and effort to transform. They change, as Lewis says, only 'under heavy pressure' (ibid.: 177). We know something important was going on in Indian religion in the second and third centuries CE, because of the sudden appearance of freestanding, naturalistic figural representations, first of the Buddha and then quickly of a range of indigenous deities.

Style

In considering style, we are not interested in the minds of individuals, but rather the 'matrix of feelings, sensations, intuitions, and understandings that are nonverbal or preverbal, and in any given culture many of these are [. . .] held in common' (Prown 1993: 5). Style is the key to discovering these components, where style means shared formal characteristics. 'Those resemblances or resonances constitute style' (ibid.: 4). 'When style is shared [. . .] in a time and place, it is akin to a cultural daydream expressing unspoken beliefs' (ibid.: 5), which can be uncovered by an analysis of style. Elite style can fruitfully be interrogated in terms of art forms; Jane Dillenberger's *Style and Content in Christian Art* (2005) is a classic example. The most telling investigations, however, involve style in the common material culture of everyday people in their everyday lives. Most analyses of style compare sets of artifacts to understand differing sensibilities, for example within one group as it changes over time, between groups co-existing in one cultural landscape, or between contemporary groups in different cultural landscapes.

Analysis of style can be used, however, to discover and interpret sensibilities as they are coming into being in contemporary time. This is strikingly demonstrated in the analyses of popular media in everyday lives in Africa and South America reported in *Aesthetic Formations* (Meyer 2009). The contributors are anthropologists, and their primary methods are participant observation and fieldwork. They also draw on media studies to investigate how various media engage users in differing bodily habits and social configurations, and how these, in turn, are linked to perceptual and behavioral factors. In addition, they are vitally sensitive to the appearance of style by engaging in comparison of formal qualities across a wider range of phenomena, e.g. public and private statements, dress, uses of space, alterations in ritual practice, economic habits, and uses of new and old media.[6]

Materials and material processes

'The material itself conveys messages, metaphorical and otherwise, about the objects and their place in a culture' (Friedel 1993: 43). Among the reasons materials are used are function, availability, economy, style and tradition (ibid.: 44). Scholars need to place materials in the context in which they are encountered, rather than in scholars' own contexts. Methods relevant to doing so include locating materials' distance from site of use and difficulty of procurement, placing materials and processes in the local history of technology, discerning trends in fashion in the local environment, and determining if changes in materials used results from competition from other cultures or other components of the given culture (ibid.: 45). Because materials and ways of working with them both signify, semiotic analysis of both is necessary and must be placed in the context of local systems of meaning, since values linked with materials and processes are not inherent, but circumstantial (ibid.: 46–47). Finally, scholars must distinguish between the meaning of materials and those of the things made from them (one might revere a plastic Eucharist cup while reviling plastic).

Forward and backward linkages

Backward linkages include, for example, natural and human resources necessary for the object of study to come into (or remain in) being. 'The human resources include the skills of the artisans and the social structures that have to be in place' (Gordon 1993: 81). Forward linkages include interactions with users, interactions with observers, and the effect on the cultural and ecological environment (ibid.: 81–82).

Box 3.3.6 Lineage

'Objects have a lineage, an ancestry, that is essential in understanding their roles in and reflection of society' (Lubar and Kingery 1993: xi). Jessica Rawson investigated the lineage of the bronze Chinese ritual vessels known as *ding*. Although *ding* were first cast around 1500 BCE and today grace every respectable collection of historical Chinese art, neither *ding* as a category nor any individual *ding* has been continuously available for use over that time. Buried in the Shang or Zhou periods, they were dug up by the Han or later the Song, only to be lost and rediscovered. 'The act of rediscovery has been crucial to the role of the bronzes in these later episodes' (ibid.: 54), including those only now being excavated in China (ibid.: 68).

Rawson uses backward and forward linkages, interpretation of materials and processes, use (practice), texts, new material practices (forgery), and other methods to disclose six transformations associated with the *ding*. Although the material artifacts never changed, their meaning, function and use were transformed (see also Box 3.3.1).

Literary sources

A wide array of relevant texts may provide useful information about any aspect of study: religious texts, technological treatises, guides to practice, interpretations of the object of study and so forth. Here we are talking about the informative aspects of texts, considered apart from their materiality. Considered in their materiality, texts belong to, rather than comment on or help to interpret, material culture. Scholars should be careful not to give texts undue priority in interpretation; texts may misinterpret material culture, intentionally or not. Moreover, material culture sometimes effects or signals religious developments before texts do.

Case studies

Case study one: Nanno Marinatos on Minoan religion

Nanno Marinatos' *Minoan Religion: Ritual, Image, and Symbol* (1993) is a brilliant display of the use of material culture to uncover religion where there are neither interpretable texts nor contemporary practitioners to consult.[7] In her introduction, Marinatos first provides brief descriptions of the four major periods of Minoan civilization, characterized by distinct patterns of material culture uncovered through archaeology. Then she presents line drawings and descriptions of 'Minoan cult equipment', describing the form, function, materials, processes and probable uses of each. This equipment is progressively interpreted and illuminated throughout the text. Hewing to the principle of 'layering', Marinatos begins her discussion with the earliest period. Relying on architecture, comparison, close examination of artifacts,

geographical location, material processes, extant scholarship on Minoan religion and archaeology, and anthropological theory, she demonstrates the high probability that Minoan religion originated with a cult of the dead, whose primary symbolic dimensions she was able to
articulate and interpret.

She defines the next two periods by interpreting alterations in the cultural landscape,
including new and extended agricultural practices, the appearance of palatial structures and
cities, changes in how grain was stored (and therefore distributed), and the appearance of
large numbers of cult symbols. Marinatos moves on to a detailed consideration of the 'palaces',
working with architectural description and analysis. She consults ground plans, directional
orientation and functional uses of various recurring spaces; she considers the skills involved
in making and using the buildings and the artifacts found in them; she interprets religious
functions of, for example, libation jars, sacrificial altars, promenades and votary sculptures;
she discusses those artifacts in themselves, in terms of their materials and processes, and
iconographically; she analyses the wall paintings, contemplating not only their iconography
but also, for example, why they are found in some places and not others. All this is considered
in relation to the earlier cults of the dead, and in comparison to other Minoan religious materials of the period, for example mountaintop and cave sanctuaries and small urban shrines, as
well as cult implements. She is then able to propose an answer to a longstanding question in
Minoan religion, 'where are the temples?' Her answer: the 'palaces' 'were centers of religious
activity', and the 'rulers' were at least as much 'priests and priestesses'. Moreover, given the
absence of fortifications for these sites, she concludes that the Minoans in this era were unified
by religion rather than force (Marinatos 1993: 74–75).

Marinatos then examines in detail the four types of shrine complexes in the 'palaces'. She
sets the shrines in relation to other structures in the building (e.g. storage rooms and sleeping
quarters). She considers the form, style and function of each component of each shrine, and
sets each component in relation to each other component of its shrine type (relations include
material, spatial, iconographic and functional). She analyzes archaeological remains to deduce
the existence and function of, for example, upper stories that have collapsed. She considers the
choreography imposed by the palace structure and the location, access and egress of the shrines
and of the public in and out of the complex. She reflects on the significance of the presence
and absence of various types of cult objects and symbols. She analyzes the iconography of
artifacts as well as their orientation and their formal and spatial relationships.[8] She integrates
these with prior scholarship on the Minoans and with anthropological theory and evidence
concerning ritual and other religious activity in cultures of similar size and complexity. As a
result, she argues for a continuation and transformation of the cult of the dead, interprets the
meaning and function of several architectural features, and establishes the existence of ritual
meals shared by ruling elites but viewed by larger publics. Most spectacularly, she demonstrates with a high degree of probability the existence of a ceremony involving an epiphanic
appearance of the goddess, impersonated by the high priestess (Marinatos 1993: 109).

Following this, Marinatos considers other material remains of Minoan religion which
allow her to touch on town shrines; nature sanctuaries; the priesthood; goddesses and gods;
shrines and rituals; ritual contests, hunting and rites of passage; and the relations among them.
She draws a rich and detailed picture of Minoan religious practices and beliefs and of their
integration into and mutual interaction with other aspects of Minoan life. Moreover, she is
able to distinguish folk religion from elite religion and articulate the development of interactions between them. Finally, she examines Minoan religion after the fall of the palaces. In
each case she carefully traces continuities and transformations over time. As she wrote, 'The
historical dimension must not be lost sight of' (Marinatos 1993: 146). By considering these

various elements in relation to one another, Marinatos teases out a complex story of continuity and transformation over 1,700 years.

Case study two: Diana Eck on Darśan

At the time of its publication, *Darśan* (Eck 1996) was a groundbreaking book, both in Hindu studies and in material culture and religion, for methodological as well as substantive reasons. Nevertheless, it has also been subject to substantive criticism rooted in critique of its material methods.

Eck integrates a number of methods. She chooses her object of study, *darśan*, the ritual practice of seeing and being seen by divinity embodied in an image, sometimes as humble as an animal, rock or other natural feature (ibid.: 32). She sets *darśan* in an array of material and religious contexts (painting, sculpture and folk art, pilgrimages, temples and landscapes; holy men, polytheism, festivals, creation and consecration of images, the city of Varanasi, everyday life), as well as in the context of Hindu sacred literature and theological writings, and of Western scholarship. Before going to India, she had read widely on Hinduism and become familiar with Hindu visual culture through exhibits, photographs and films, through which she 'first was drawn to the study of Hinduism and Sanskrit' (ibid.: 2). She is attentive to the religious generativity of material culture, insisting that Hindu visual culture makes original contributions to Hindu thought and experience; it is not merely illustrative (ibid.: 2). She also accounts for her (and our) enculturated body; throughout she insists that the experience and understanding of seeing in *darśan* is not how she and other Westerners customarily see. Nor does she understand *darśan* as ordinary sight for Hindus; it is 'sacred perception' (ibid.: 6). She works comparatively, especially concerning Hindu and Islamo-Judeo-Christian skills of seeing and attitudes toward imagery (ibid.: 16–22). She engages in participant observation, going to India and being present for *darśan*, although her engagement falls short of apprenticeship. She concludes that 'In India's own terms, seeing is knowing. And India must be seen to be known' (ibid.: 11). Although ideally that would mean participant observation for every student, that is impractical, so, says Eck, we have much to learn about Hinduism from art, slides and films (ibid.: 2), especially film (ibid.: 11), which she recommends as primary tool for studying Hinduism.

Sylvain Pinard challenges Eck's central premise that sight is the key to Indian religious experience and to Western scholarly understanding of it, on methodological and material cultural grounds. In particular, Pinard criticizes Eck's contention that photographic images provide special entrée into Indian religion, noting 'the fact that photographs have no taste or smell or sound' (Pinard 1991: 223, see also 230). Pinard uses the same array of methods as Eck, but he carries farther the critique of bodily enculturation, and is more sensitive to the multisensory character of experience of material culture. Although Eck writes, 'Hindu worship [. . .] makes full use of the senses—seeing, touching, smelling, tasting, and hearing' (Eck 1996: 11), she limits her own explorations to seeing, and she imagines seeing that takes place without engagement of the other senses. Pinard adds to this 'a gastronomic anthropology [. . .] India should also be tasted to be known' (Pinard 1991: 222). Eck makes a methodological claim that 'photographic images enable us to employ the senses in the process of learning' (Eck 1996: 13). Says Pinard, 'she overlooks the fact that photographs have no taste or smell or sound' (Pinard 1991: 222). Pinard shows that many instances of *darśan* involve exchanges of food, as well as sight. Eck herself notes that *prasād* (food exchanges with divinities and saints) often accompanies *darśan* (Eck 1996: 63). Pinard develops an analysis of *prasād*, even finding instances in which *prasād* is obligatory but *darśan* is not. Pinard then links *prasād* with a wide variety of other practices of taste and eating and with a swath of sacred, theo-logical, and scholarly texts. He makes a compelling case for eating, including the various stages of digestion, as key to the practice, self-understanding, and scholarly investigation of Hinduism.

Why then, despite her methodological complexity and self-awareness, did Eck 'overlook the evidence of her senses and even the texts she cites?' (Pinard 1991: 230). Two primary reasons come to mind, both cautionary examples for all Western scholars of material culture. The first is the visualism of Western culture. Increasingly since the Renaissance, and espe-cially the Enlightenment, Western senses have been trained to emphasize sight, even as Western metaphors for knowledge have become increasingly visual (Carp 2008: 178–82). Although Eck was sufficiently sensitive to her bodily enculturation to realize that *darśan* was a different practice of seeing, she was not sufficiently sensitive to realize her tendency to over-look non-visual practices and meanings, leading to 'the visual reductionism of her method' (Pinard 1991: 230). The second is her use of text as a metaphor to understand material meaning. Texts require reading, which is a visual activity, and texts can be read in the orig-inal or in copies, and in a variety of contexts, without (at least so we believe) materially affecting their meaning. Not so other material practices and the artifacts and contexts with which they are entangled. As Pinard concludes, 'It is important to be cautious of the means and metaphors we use to study other cultures, since if we are not, we can end up mistaking the map for the territory, or eating the menu in place of the meal' (Pinard 1991: 230).

Box 3.3.7 A checklist for methods in religion and material culture

1 Determine your primary focus: A cultural landscape or some components of it? An artifact or collection of artifacts? A process or processes? A person or group? A time and/or geograph-ical period? Comparison?

2 Set your object of study in a wider context. (Imagine it as the center of a bull's-eye. Set it in at least two concentric rings of context, i.e. ask a question and then a question about the question.)

3 Clarify how your physical education and academic (and religious) material culture enable and limit your access to the object of study. Account for your bodily enculturation and your scholar's body. Consider how bodies that make, use and understand your area of study differ from and resemble yours.

4 Determine the relevant academic disciplines and the methods they would use.

5 Use those methods. If you cannot, find a collaborator who can (collaboration is itself a method).

6 Investigate the intentional and unintentional meanings of your object of study (it may have both).

7 Ask how it shapes self, structures mind, manifests power and stands for place in society.

8 What is its lineage? (Michelangelo's *Pietá* has had several meanings and functions over time. None are its 'true' meaning and function.) 'Peel the onion.'

9 What is it made of and by means of what processes? (Both materials and processes themselves are meaningful. Remember that human bodies are materials.)

10 Place your object of study in the context of its cultural landscape. How does it interact with other aspects of the built environment? With sensory modalities other than the ones prima-rily associated with it?

11 How does making/using the object of study shape makers' and users' bodies (or how do the perceptual and other bodily skills of the culture affect the meanings of the object of study)?

12 Go back to question 1. Has your object of study changed as you have studied it? Re-engage each question at least once more before you decide you are done.

Conclusion

Material culture and religion is an emerging transdisciplinary field interrogating religious cultural landscapes and the presence of religion in secular cultural landscapes. It brings into relief the embodied and material character of both religion and scholarship, generating a potential critique of our prior, more immaterial and disembodied understandings of both. As an emerging field, material culture and religion requires methodological creativity and clarity. It must borrow methods from a range of adjacent fields, while integrating them in new ways and seeking new methods of its own.[9] In this way the field comes into being through a dialectic of data and method: while data determine methods which can interpret them, methods cause data to appear and demand interpretation. Thus material culture and religion offers a creative and challenging arena for investigation, especially for junior scholars and graduate students now clarifying their research interests.

Notes

1 A variety of subfields of religious studies, including some represented by chapters in this book, address aspects of material culture. For example, there is a field of visual culture and religion, there are studies of religious music, there is ritual studies. Spatial and temporal studies of religion address material culture, as do documentary studies when they consider material aspects of documents.

2 The overlap of religion and material culture has not been entirely overlooked, but it has not been solidified as a field, although there have been recent steps in that direction, especially the establishment of the journal *Material Religion* in 2005 (see Meyer *et al.* 2010 for an overview of the journal). Most studies, though, whether recent or older, tend to take on one aspect of material culture without situating it in a larger material context. There are thus studies of religion and media (Meyer 2009; de Vries and Weber 2001), religious music (Bohlman *et al.* 2006), religious architecture (Hoffman 2010), religion in the public landscape (Farnsley *et al.* 2004) and so forth. Recent work in the anthropology of the senses has resulted in scholarship focusing on sensory religion, usually concentrating on a single sense modality (Korsmeyer 2005; Drobnick 2006). An entire field, religion and visual culture, has developed around sight (e.g. Morgan 2005), while studies are beginning to appear on the religious dimensions of secular material culture (Sheffield 2006).

3 '[A]ttention to discipline is not merely a concern about institutions and professionalization; it is above all concern about bodies—human bodies. Disciplines are institutionalized formations for organizing schemes of perception, appreciation, and action, and for inculcating them as tools of cognition and communication' (Lenoir 1993: 72).

4 Of course, bodily enculturation, including its sensory dimensions, is not monolithic within a given culture. It may vary by sex, gender, age, class, ethnicity and a variety of other factors, and it changes over historical time. These factors may be important to consider in any given piece of research.

5 In our encounters with material culture, scholars must be especially sensitive to the visualist bias characteristic of Western culture and exacerbated in the academy (Howes 2005; Classen 1993; Ingold 2000). For example, there is a tendency to consider architecture as 'visual culture', although buildings are much more than visual artifacts. They have significant auditory components; they create choreographies (they structure body movement and placement) and therefore address kinesthesia; they are often olfactory. Stephen Feld (2005) has proposed that the acoustic components of culture are as important as the visual.

6 Birgit Meyer and her collaborators make evident the new styles of 'religious sensational forms' brought into being by the effects of new technologies in relation to existing material cultures in particular (often impoverished) cultural communities. These sensational forms are 'condensations of practices, attitudes, and ideas that structure religious experiences and thus "ask" to be approached in a particular manner [. . .] invoking sensations by inducing particular dispositions and practices [. . .] part and parcel of a particular religious aesthetics, which governs a sensory engagement' that is to say, a style (Meyer 2009: 13).

7 We have found Linear A tablets belonging to the Minoan culture, but we cannot read them.

8   At one point she writes, 'It remains to explore the relationship of the paintings to the space in which they were placed' (Marinatos 1993: 211). At another point she reminds us that an image on a funeral vessel at one point in time may carry different meaning than in a mural at a palace/temple at another (ibid.: 229–42).

9   The late Ninian Smart, then Chair of Religion at UC–Santa Barbara was fond of saying, 'Perhaps we're really not talking about interdisciplinarity, but about polymethodism' (personal conversation). Material culture and religion is surely a polymethodic enterprise!

References

Berger, P. and Luckmann, T., 1967. *The Social Construction of Reality*. Anchor Books, New York.

Bohlman, P.B., Blumhofer, E.L. and Chow, M.M., 2006. *Music in American Religious Experience*. Oxford University Press, New York.

Brown, K.M., 1991. *Mama Lola: a Vodou priestess in Brooklyn*. University of California Press, Berkeley.

Carp, R.M., 1997. Perception and material culture: Historical and cross-cultural perspectives. *Historical Reflections/Réflexions Historiques* 23 (3): 269–300.

—— 2002. Integrative praxes: learning from multiple knowledge formations. *Issues in Integrative Studies* 19: 71–121.

—— 2007. Teaching religion and material culture. *Teaching Theology and Religion* 10 (1): 2–12.

—— 2008. Seeing is believing, but touching's the truth. In: Watkins, G.J. (ed.), *Teaching Religion and Film*. Oxford University Press, New York, pp. 177–88.

Clark, W., 2006. *Academic Charisma and the Origins of the Research University*. University of Chicago Press, Chicago.

Classen, C., 1993. *Worlds of Sense: exploring the senses in history and across cultures*. Routledge, New York.

de Vries, H. and Weber, S. 2001. *Religion and Media*. Palo Alto, CA: Stanford University Press.

Dillenberger, J., 2005. *Style and Content in Christian Art*. Wipf and Stock, Eugene OR.

Downey, G., 2005. *Learning Capoeira: lessons in cunning from an Afro-Brazilian art form*. Oxford University Press, New York.

Drobnick, J. (ed.), 2006. *The Smell Culture Reader*. Berg Publishers: London and New York.

Eck, D.L., 1996. *Darśan: seeing the divine image in India*. 2nd edn. Columbia University Press, New York.

Farnsley, A.E., II *et al.*, 2004. *Sacred Circles Public Squares: the multicentering of American religion*. Bloomington, IN: Indiana University Press.

Feld, S., 2005. Places sensed, senses placed: toward a sensuous epistemology of environments. In: Howes, D. (ed.), *Empire of the Senses: the sensual culture reader*. Berg, Oxford, New York, pp. 179–91.

Friedel, R., 1993. Some matters of substance. In: Lubar, S. and Kingery, W.D. (eds), *History from Things: essays on material culture*. Smithsonian Institution Press, Washington, pp. 41–50.

Gordon, R.B., 1993. The interpretation of artifacts in the history of technology. In: Lubar, S. and Kingery, W.D. (eds), *History from Things: essays on material culture*. Smithsonian Institution Press, Washington, pp. 74–93.

Gruen, V., 1964. *The Heart of Our Cities; the urban crisis: diagnosis and cure*. Simon and Schuster, New York.

Hall, E.T., 1977. *Beyond Culture*. Doubleday, Garden City, New York.

Hoffman, D.R., 2010. *Seeking the Sacred in Contemporary Religious Architecture*. Kent State University Press, Kent, OH.

Howes, D. (ed.), 2005. *The Empire of the Senses: the sensual culture reader*. Berg, New York.

Ingold, T., 2000. *The Perception of the Environment: essays in livelihood, dwelling, and skill*. Routledge, New York.

Jones, M.O., 1993. Why take a behavioral approach to folk objects? In: Lubar, S. and Kingery, W.D. (eds), *History from Things: essays on material culture*. Smithsonian Institution Press, Washington, pp. 182–96.

Korsmeyer, C. (ed.), 2005. *The Taste Culture Reader: experiencing food and drink*. Berg Publishers: London and New York.

LaMothe, K., 2008. What bodies know about religion and the study of it. *Journal of the American Academy of Religion* 76(3): 573–601.

Lenoir, T., 1993. The discipline of nature and the nature of discipline. In: Messer-Davidow, E., Shumway, D.R. and Sylvan, D.J. (eds), *Knowledges: historical and critical studies in disciplinarity*. University of Virginia Press, Charlottesville, pp. 70–102.

Lewis, P., 1992. Axioms for reading the landscape: some guides to the American scene. In: Schlereth, T.J. (ed.), *Material Culture Studies in America*. The American Association for State and Local History, Nashville, TN, pp. 174–82.

—— 1993. Common landscapes as historic documents. In: Lubar, S. and Kingery, W.D. (eds), *History from Things: essays on material culture*. Smithsonian Institution Press, Washington, pp. 115–39.

Lubar, S. and Kingery, W.D. (eds), 1993. *History from Things: essays on material culture*. Smithsonian Institution Press, Washington.

Mall, A.S., 2007. Structure, innovation and agency in pattern construction: the *kōlam* of Southern India. In: Ingold, T. and Hallam, E. (eds), *Creativity and Cultural Improvisation*. Berg, New York, pp. 55–78.

Marinatos, N., 1993. *Minoan Religion: ritual, image, and symbol*. University of South Carolina Press, Columbia, SC.

Meyer, B., 2006. *Religion, Media, and the Public Sphere*. Indiana University Press, Bloomington, IN.

—— (ed.), 2009. *Sensory Formations: media, religion, and the senses*. Palgrave Macmillan, New York.

Meyer, B., Morgan, D., Paine, C. and Plate, S.B., 2010. The origin and mission of *Material Religion*. *Religion* 40(3): 207–11.

Morgan, D., 2005. *The Sacred Gaze: Religious visual culture in theory and practice*. University of California Press, Berkeley, CA.

Motokawa, T., 1989. Sushi science and hamburger science. *Perspectives in Biology and Medicine* 32(4): 489–504.

Pinard, S., 1991. A taste of India. In: Howes, D. (ed.), *The Varieties of Sensory Experience: a sourcebook in the anthropology of the senses*. University of Toronto Press, Toronto, pp. 221–30.

Plate, S.B. and Meyer, B. *et al.* (eds), 2005. *Material Religion: The journal of objects, art, and belief*. Berg, Oxford.

Prown, J.D., 1993. The truth of material culture. In: Lubar, S. and Kingery, W.D. (eds), *History from Things: essays on material culture*. Smithsonian Institution Press, Washington, pp. 1–19.

Ruprecht, L.A., 2011. *Winckelmann and the Vatican's First Profane Museum*. Palgrave Macmillan, New York.

Sheffield, T., 2006. *The Religious Dimensions of Advertising*. Palgrave Macmillan, New York.

Stoller, P., 1997. *Sensuous Scholarship*. University of Pennsylvania Press, Philadelphia.

Further reading

Arweck, E. and Keenan, W. (eds), 2006. *Materializing Religion: expression, performance, and ritual*. Ashgate, Oxford.

A cross-cultural, multi-religion investigation of lived religion through material culture, with chapters on music, architecture, festivals, ritual, artifacts, dance, dress and magic, each addressing method as well as content.

Classen, C., 1998. *The Color of Angels: cosmology, gender, and the aesthetic imagination*. Routledge, New York.

—— 1993. *Worlds of Sense: exploring the senses in history and across cultures*. Routledge, New York.

Explorations of sensory cosmology in history and across cultures, with special attention to the methodological issues raised by attempts to enter the sensory worlds of the other cultures.

Cort, J.E., 1996. Art, religion and material culture: some reflections on method. *Journal of the American Academy of Religion* 64(3): 613–32.

Somewhat dated but still excellent discussion.

Marinatos, N., 2010. *Minoan Kingship and the Solar Goddess: a Near Eastern koine*. University of Chicago Press, Chicago.

Sets Minoan religion in the context of ancient Near-Eastern religion, confirming some and altering other conclusions of Minoan Religion, while exploring mutual influences of Minoan and other religions in the region. Careful discussion of cross-cultural comparison, iconography and cultural geography in material culture studies.

Meyer, B., Morgan, D., Paine, C. and Plate, S.B., 2010. The origin and mission of *Material Religion*. *Religion* 40(3): 207–11.

A discussion by the editors of Material Religion *of its history and their guiding concepts.*

Miles, M.R., 1985. *Image as Insight: visual understanding in Western Christianity and secular culture.* Beacon Press, Boston.

A survey and analysis of the roles of imagery in Western semiotic processes from early Christianity through the 20th century, with special emphasis on women and others excluded from reading and writing. Begins with an extended meditation on methods for interpreting images and their differences with text-based methods of interpretation.

Prussin, L., 1986. *Hatumere: Islamic design in West Africa.* University of California Press, Berkeley.

A discussion of contemporary and historical material practices and artifacts that play vital roles in popular Islam in West Africa. Considers questions of method in relation to popular culture.

—— 1995. *African Nomadic Architecture: space, place, and gender.* Smithsonian Press, Washington, DC.

Displays and interprets the integration of architecture, other material culture and cosmology among women in several African cultures.

Seremetakis, C.N. (ed.), 1994. *The Senses Still: perception and memory as material culture in modernity.* The University of Chicago Press, Chicago.

Meditations on material culture as an active force in perceptual enculturation, social and personal memory and cultural difference, including significant reflections on scholars' senses as methodological concerns.

Sullivan, L.E., 1988. *Icanchu's Drum: an orientation to meaning in South American religions.* Macmillan, New York.

A detailed investigation of South American religions, thoroughly rooted in their material culture, of which Icanchu's drum is emblematic.

—— 1990. Body works in the study of religion. *History of Religions* 30 (1): 86–99.

An investigation of the methodological problematic of the body in the study of religion. Considers others' formation and transmission of religion as and by means of body experience and the challenges presented by scholars' bodies as we attempt to understand and interpret this religion.

Key concepts

Bodily enculturation: the cultural effects on the sensory capacities, muscular and skeletal architecture, neuroanatomy and other aspects of bodies. Scholars' bodily enculturation, and its differences from the bodily enculturation of others, presents a fundamental methodological issue.

Interpretation of cultural landscape: the processes involved in deciphering an interconnected array of material culture, which ideally would include the totality of physical human effects in a place.

Material culture: everything that is both perceptible and cultural, not only artifacts, but also the contexts, processes and skills of use and production that surround and interpenetrate artifacts.

Material culture studies: an emerging transdisciplinary and polymethodic field dedicated to scholarly interpretation of material culture with special attention to its complex, intertwined bodily, perceptual, social, historical, material and technological dimensions.

Transdisciplinarity: academic study that investigates phenomena not fully comprehended by any discipline or group of disciplines and that integrates multiple academic and non-academic knowledge sources and methods.

Related chapters

◆ Chapter 1.3 Epistemology

3.4

SPATIAL METHODS

Kim Knott

Chapter summary

- Spatial methods have become increasingly important in the study of religions since the 1990s but are under-documented.
- Models for the study of sacred space have been developed, but no replicable method has been devised.
- Spatial studies of religion raise theoretical issues about the primacy of religion or place and whether they are *sui generis* or socially constructed.
- Maps provide useful tools for illustrating the distribution of religions and of religious communities, places and routes.
- The mapping of religions occurs at different scales: local, regional, national and global.
- Both quantitative and qualitative methods can be used in the mapping of religions.
- Maps of religions are representations which can be replicated for other historical and geographical contexts, and then compared.
- A spatial approach to the study of religion is not a method of data collection but a series of analytical steps allied once data has been collected.
- Thinking spatially about religion helps researchers to position religious places, objects or bodies in relation to their surroundings.

Introduction

The development of spatial approaches for studying religion is a recent phenomenon, and time will tell whether they will have a lasting impact and relevance. The **geography of religion**—as a field in the sub-discipline of social and cultural geography—has a long history (Büttner 1980; Park 1994; Knott 2010a). However, whilst it has contributed to an understanding of the distribution and mapping of religions, it has failed to produce a formal methodology or practical methods of its own, but has depended on methods common across the discipline of geography or on those from other social sciences. A thematic agenda for the geography of religion has been posited by authors of books and review articles on the subject (e.g. Kong 1990, 2001, 2010; Park 1994; Stump 2008), but with no methodological principles, tools or techniques explicitly proposed. Within religious studies there has been a body of work on **sacred space**, from van der Leeuw (1938) and Eliade (1959) in the mid–20th century to Chidester and Linenthal (1995) and Macdonald (2003) more recently, but again without the overt articulation of a methodological approach. This perhaps explains why spatial and geographical approaches have rarely featured in handbooks on general approaches to the study of religions. However, as the impact of the **spatial turn** (Crang and Thrift 2000; Hubbard *et al.* 2004) of the 1990s and 2000s has become more embedded across the humanities and social sciences, this situation has begun to change. The *Routledge Companion to the Study of Religion* (Hinnells 2005, 2010) included chapters on geography and **space**, and the journal *Religion Compass* commissioned articles on spatial theory in both theology (Bergmann 2007) and the study of religion (Knott 2008).

So what is meant here by 'spatial methods'? I include those methods, tools and analytical strategies that can be used to approach data on religion (and other comparable ideological and practical systems) from the perspective of space, place or geography, and that foreground spatial location, positioning, relationships, distribution, diffusion, scale, movement, or the properties, characteristics and types of space. As a secondary feature, spatial methods may be designed to be attentive to or to enable the study of contestation and struggles in and for space, the production and reproduction of space (including sacred space), and the use and representation of space. However, whilst a number of scholars have studied religion geographically or spatially, few have sought to articulate a replicable method for doing so. It has been left to newcomers to the field to draw out useful methodological insights or models from the work of their forebears. We can see this process at work in the following historical case, which addresses the development of axioms and other principles for studying sacred space.

As Brereton (2005: 7978) noted, scholars writing on the subject have repeatedly referred back to the work of Mircea Eliade who wrote:

> [W]e have a sequence of religious conceptions and cosmological images that are inseparably connected and form a system [. . .] (a) a sacred place constitutes a break in the homogeneity of space; (b) this break is symbolized by an opening by which passage from one cosmic region to another is made possible [. . .] (c) communication with heaven is expressed by one or another of certain images, all of which refer to the *axis mundi* [. . .] (d) around this cosmic axis lies the world (= our world).
>
> *(Eliade 1959: 37)*

It is clear from later studies that Eliade's axioms were tested in relation to a variety of contexts and critical perspectives (e.g. Wheatley 1971: 411–76; Smith 1978: 91–103; Chidester and Linenthal 1995: 16–19), with his critics amending or subverting them to suit their own conditions and purposes. In their different versions the axioms acquired methodological status in so far as they could be applied and tested in other times and places. In addition, these scholars contributed other tools for use in an examination of sacred space. J.Z. Smith distinguished three cosmological 'maps' (Smith 1978: 292–302) and articulated the relationship between the sacred, place and ritual in the sacralisation of space (Smith 1987). Chidester and Linenthal reminded readers of the homologies of sacred space proposed by van der Leeuw, and added their own 'modes of symbolic engagement' in the production of sacred space: appropriation, exclusion, inversion and hybridization (Chidester and Linenthal 1995: 19–20). Stump (2008: 302–49) listed categories, forms and adherent interactions with sacred space, all of which could be used by others to examine and compare places deemed to be sacred. However, it is debateable whether any of these models constitutes a spatial method.

Spatial methods: theoretical and epistemological issues

Earlier debates between geographers and scholars of religion suggested variously that, (1) geographers should focus on the effect of religion on people, place and space, and scholars of religion on how environment affects religions; (2) that the former should concentrate on geography of religion and the latter on religious geography; and (3) that the two should be engaged in some kind of dialectical approach (Sopher 1967; Büttner 1980; Park 1994). These attempts to imagine and divide scholarly territory illustrate bi-directional orientations to religion and space. Later reviews of the field (e.g. Kong 1990, 2001, 2010) have revealed that scholars have resisted such categorizations and worked increasingly across disciplinary boundaries.

It is possible, nevertheless, to identify other distinguishing characteristics within the field which often cut across disciplinary boundaries. For example, there are scholars who favor a phenomenological approach, within both the study of religions and geography of religion, for whom religion/the sacred is understood to be *sui generis*, as well as those who believe that place has existential primacy. In addition, there are outspokenly religious geographers of religion whose faith informs their research. There are also social scientists within the study of religions for whom 'religion' and 'space' are material, social and cognitive constructions. Equally, there is a strong scientific tradition of positivistic geography focused on the distribution of religious populations, places of worship and ideas.

In noting these fault lines and divergent stances, however, we should not assume that the field is static, or that methodological developments have been or will be predictable. Recent work shows a wide range of approaches, including those that bridge apparently opposed positions, and those that innovate by challenging or building on traditional perspectives, for example, by adopting a critical realist embodied stance (Holloway 2003), by focusing on spaces of affect or emotion (Maddrell 2009), by taking a post-phenomenological perspective on spiritual landscapes (Cloke and Dewsbury 2009), or by theorizing religion spatially (Tweed 2006). Methodological accounts of such novel moves are rarely provided, however.

Mapping religion

In the 20th century the principal geographical approach to religions was the study of their distribution. In his historical overview, Park (1994: 56) cited Deffontaines and Fleure as early exponents, and noted that studies of religious distribution had focused primarily on either the national or global scale (see Table 3.4.1).

'Mapping religion' is a broad term for research conducted at various scales, using different types of data—both quantitative and qualitative—and with a variety of different purposes, including mapping change, diversity, religious demography and religion in conjunction with other variables such as ethnicity, politics or gender. What is generally meant by the term 'mapping' is the study and representation of religion(s) in a bounded space, such as a locality, region, nation or continent, or in movements across spaces (e.g. in association with mission, migration or pilgrimage). Religions may be mapped in isolation, but more often they are considered in relationship to other factors in or across those spaces. 'Mapping' may literally mean maps, charts and other visual forms of representation (cartography), or it may be used metaphorically to signal a survey, a detailed empirical description, or a study of the position and relationships between (religious) people, places, routes and other variables. As maps have traditionally been representations of places from particular standpoints (both spatial and ideological), they are also a useful metaphor for worldviews, cosmologies or orientations (e.g. Smith 1978; cf. Gardiner and Engler 2010).

Table 3.4.1 Mapping religions: case studies

Scale	Examples	Areas mapped
Global	al-Faruqi and Sopher (1974)	Atlas of world religions
	O'Brien and Palmer (2007)	Atlas of world religions
	Barrett (1982)	Data on world Christianity
	World Christian Database	Data on world religions, particularly Christianity
National	Zelinsky (1961)	American church membership
	Gay (1971)	Religion in England (since 1851)
	Gaustad (1976)	Religion in America (historical)
	Knippenberg (1992)	Religion in the Netherlands (historical)
	Henkel (2001)	German religious communities
	Jacob *et al.* (2003)	Religious affiliation in Brazil
	de la Torre and Gutiérrez Zuñiga (2007)	Religious affiliation in Mexico
	Pew Forum on Religion and Public Life	US religious landscape survey
Regional	Diez de Velasco (2009)	Religions; Canary Islands (Spain)
	Dix (2009)	Religions: Lisbon and environs (Portugal)
	Hernández and Rivera (2009)	Religions: regions in Mexico
	Krech (2009)	Religions: North Rhine-Westphalia area (Germany)
	Mikaelsson (2009)	Christianity: regions in Norway
	Repstad (2009)	Christianity: a region in Norway
Local	Knott (1998, 2009, 2010a)	Religions: Leeds, UK
	Martikainen (2004)	Religions: Turku, Finland
	Heelas and Woodhead (2005)	Religion and spirituality: Kendal, UK
	Fibiger (2009)	Religions and spirituality: Aarhus, Denmark
	Bowman (2009)	Religion and spirituality: Glastonbury, UK
	Gutiérrez Zuñiga *et al.* (2011)	Religions: Guadalajara, Mexico

Maps are valuable because they offer representations, generally fixed in time and space, which can be replicated for other historical and geographical contexts (with the proviso that the data on which they are based is comparable). These can then be used either to form a larger dataset or to enable comparisons. As Martikainen suggested,

> Whereas traditional ethnographic research is often centred on the study of a specific religious institution, community, or culture in depth (vertical research), **mapping religions** is a comparative method that aims for a horizontal understanding of some specific features among religious communities that are present within a restricted context or locality.
>
> *(Martikainen 2002: 313)*

Such mappings are undertaken in order to understand more about context, religion and their inter-relationship. Global and transnational interconnections, as well as local context, form part of this complex engagement of place and religion. The benefits of mapping religions are not restricted to the amassing of data about a place and its religions, however: such data may also provide the basis for further policy-oriented studies, in-depth analyses of particular groups, local or oral histories, and comparative projects with other places. They may provoke local debate and may stimulate an engaged relationship between researchers and local agencies and communities.

What forms have such mappings taken? They may be very different, as revealed in the approaches discussed by authors writing on religion in Western Europe. Krech (2009) presents a quantitative multi-dimensional model for measuring religious diversity and its impacts; Fibiger (2009) describes a local survey, questionnaire and interview process conducted by students; Dix (2009) examines the use of national statistics for mapping religion; Bowman (2009) presents an ethnological approach which involves repeated exposure to religion in a bounded place over time; and Diez de Velasco (2009) presents a polymethodical approach to the collection of data on multi-religiosity and religious co-existence. The size of place may differ, so may the period of time studied; researchers may employ quantitative or qualitative methods, or both. My own experience of religious mapping (Knott 1998, 2009, 2010a) is of teams of students working with local partners to produce a fieldwork-based mapping of religions in various urban and suburban neighborhoods in the city of Leeds. The local character of the neighborhood, its religious communities and groups, and their engagement with other aspects of the social, economic, political and cultural life of the area have been captured in the teams' reports and public presentations (cf. Community Religions Project). Taken together, these neighborhood snapshots comprise an emerging map of the religious life of the city over time.

As Zelinsky (1961) suggested, in a foundational article on how to map American church membership, maps, and therefore the process of mapping, are judged in part by the quality of their representation: their likeness to the original. When we map religions, are those maps deemed to be accurate by those whose lives or worldviews are spatially depicted? They are also judged on the basis of the quality of the data that support them. Maps are the result of a research process involving primary or secondary data gathering, and analytical decisions about data selection, representation, comparability and replication. Even within a small local area, and certainly at continental or global scales, information about religion and its relationship with other variables and institutions will not always be comparable. How group size is measured may differ. What membership or adherence means to different denominations or movements, whether they gather in places of worship or in each other's homes or not at all, and what variable impacts they have on local communities or environments are all likely to confound the map-maker's urge to impose order on the landscape. And this brings us to the crux of the matter: maps are constructions (Gardiner and Engler 2010). 'Mapping religion' involves constructing a representation—whether visual or textual—that other academics and participants (those who are mapped) may find compelling and useful, but which is open rather than closed, in the sense that the supporting data and process of representation are available for scrutiny and challenge, and open to replication and modification.

A spatial approach to the study of religion

The second approach for consideration was developed in order to provide appropriate scholarly tools for analyzing the location of religion in Western secular societies. Whilst it was self-evident that religions resided in their places of worship and organizations, in new movements and in accepted spiritual beliefs and practices, it was not clear where and to what extent religion was located in other, ostensibly secular, places, nor how a researcher might proceed to study it. My interest was in considering the location of religion in the fabric of the secular (Knott 2005a: 73) by analyzing various apparently non-religious places, objects, communities and organizations. My first thought experiments involved ruminating on the location of religion in the street corner by my house, my daughter's school playground and the walk to my local park. Such places had the potential to contain historical traces of religion (a Roman shrine had been discovered in the park, for example). Religious dress, images and sounds moved through them—e.g. on bodies, in cars—and iconography and buildings marked the landscape. Religious and sometimes atheist expressions, both literal and metaphorical, could be seen on posters and heard in passing conversations. These thoughts presented me with new possibilities for thinking about religion, place and space.

However, I soon realized that such an exercise would require two things: first, a theory and method for analyzing not only places themselves but the socio-spatial process of location, and, second, an operational conceptualization of religion (the object to be located). Not being satisfied with existing methods and definitions from geography or the study of sacred space, I was obliged to develop my own approach. The results are described in Part I of *The Location of Religion: A Spatial Analysis* (Knott 2005a). In Part II, they are then used to examine the presence of religious, secular and post-secular positions in contemporary representations of the left hand. Guides to this method of analysis followed (Knott 2005b, 2008), as did other case studies, of a medical center (Knott and Franks 2007), everyday ritual (Knott 2007a), the disciplinary relationship between theology and religious studies (Knott 2007b), and urban locations (Knott 2009, 2010b).

Before discussing this spatial approach, it is important to clarify the distinction between practical methods used to collect data and analytical techniques applied subsequently to examine and interpret them. The approach that I will describe here does not instruct researchers on how to gather data, but offers a systematic way of reflecting on material once it has been collected. I have used a range of methods, including ethnography, documentary methods and interviewing, but historical, participatory and other social research methods could also be used. Having spatial issues in mind during the data collection process may well help when it comes to analysis, but it is not essential. The analytical approach developed in *The Location of Religion*, which is based on my reading of the socio-spatial theories of Lefebvre, Foucault, de Certeau and the geographer, Doreen Massey, consists of a series of steps for analyzing a place, object, body or group (hereafter, 'a place')—and the location of religion therein—by means of its spatial attributes (see Figure 3.4.1). Together they constitute an *aide mémoire* for spatially interrogating a place in all its complexity. I shall describe them briefly

1. Body as source and resource for space

2. The dimensions of space
   - Physical
   - Social
   - Mental

3. The properties of space
   - Configuration
   - Extension
   - Simultaneity
   - Power

4. The aspects of space
   - Perceived
   - Conceived
   - Lived

5. The dynamics of space
   - Production and reproduction

Figure 3.4.1 Spatial method: analytical steps

Source: Knott 2005a

here, but fuller explanations can be found elsewhere (Knott 2005a, 2005b), including a case study for illuminating them, a local urban street (Knott 2008, 2009).

The body is foundational for the experience and representation of both space and the sacred. If we take the street example—for which we might have gathered data from observations, time and motion studies, and interviews—the first analytical step in considering the location of religion is to look for signs of the body. How has this place emerged with reference to the body and its parts; what discourses of the body can be seen at work within it; how are bodies used to maintain and reproduce it? Can religion be seen in these processes, expressed on or disciplining the bodies of residents and other users, for example? The second step involves an examination of the street with reference to its physical, social and mental dimensions or 'fields' (Lefebvre 1991: 410–11). Any space is the sum of its material characteristics, the people who live and work in it and move through it, and the many representations and discourses associated with it. It may be that religion is identifiable in the physical fabric, social relations and public controversies that constitute the street. This propensity to draw together physical, social and mental dimensions is the first of several 'properties of space' (Knott 2005a; cf. Foucault 1986), all of which may be discerned when we examine a given place like a street, building or object. In addition to 'configuration', they include 'extension', 'simultaneity' and 'power'.

With the term 'extension', I refer to both the sense of time flowing through a place and the way in which 'stratified places' reveal the traces of earlier times and different regimes, including religious ones (de Certeau 1984: 201). The data on our street may reveal its history, today's facade being only the most recent, with evidence of earlier temporalities uncovered by archaeology, the built environment, local and oral histories. However, as well as the extensive, diachronic nature of this place, there are also the synchronic interconnections with other sites, both those that are similar in kind (other streets in the same or different cities), and those co-existing sites, real and imagined, to which this particular street may be connected by the movement of people and capital, the flow of communications and ideas (Massey 1993: 155–56). An urban street, with its religious places, groups and occasional public practices, exhibits this property of local and global 'simultaneity'. The final spatial property is 'power': knowledge-power and social power. Space is not an empty container or backdrop in or against which life takes place, but an arena of struggle in which groups or individuals seek to express themselves (Lefebvre 1991: 417). Examining how a street is produced, contested and maintained by its residents, planners, vendors and consumers, and how it is subject to the flows of power that move through and within it can reveal much about religious struggles in the context of ostensibly secular space.

In analyzing a street with these properties in mind it becomes clear that it is not static or bound by fixed spatial co-ordinates, but repeatedly torn down and reproduced whether materially, socially or discursively. This is further underlined in the remaining analytical steps, where the focus turns to how space is perceived, conceived and lived (Lefebvre 1991: 38–40; Knott 2005a: 35–58). Lefebvre's three aspects, of 'spatial practice' (perceived space), 'representations of space' (conceived space) and 'spaces of representation' (lived space), provide useful tools for thinking about how people experience the spaces they inhabit, and how they use and represent space. A street, for example, is a site of habitual spatial practice, social interaction and popular imagining, which through intensive examination may be broken open and analyzed. Furthermore, it is a 'conceived space' (Lefebvre 1991: 38), produced by city planners and civil servants, and by corporate, technical and other institutional agents whose representations of the city may be uncovered in official documents and the built environment. Periodically, though, such a place may be transformed by the self-conscious, often resistant or discrepant, symbols and actions of those who live there. As such, the street is a 'lived space' in which the dominant spatial order may be overturned by a groundswell of local activity, effort and collective sentiment, such as a festival or carnival, demonstration or procession. All three aspects have implications for the way religion is practised, constituted and lived in such ostensibly secular places, and for how it might be studied and interpreted.

Thinking deeply with each of these steps in mind about the social, historical and documentary data one has gathered, in this case on the urban street, will generate a complex contextual picture of the space, and the place of religion within it. Small places, such as bodies and objects, and large, such as institutions, cities or national parks, can become the focus for such an analysis. However, my own preference is for the small-scale. Collecting the necessary data and then analyzing it in depth is more manageable, and the results can then be used to develop hypotheses and theories for studying other places, or scaled up to build a bigger picture. This analytical process takes time, but is rewarding because of the opportunity it provides to approach and interpret a given place from a variety of perspectives, and in relation to different scales, movements and interests.

It is important to note that the choice and application of any practical or analytical method has implications for how the object of study is conceptualised and later interpreted. In developing a spatial approach it was necessary for me to make operational decisions about what I meant by 'religion' and the 'secular' (Knott 2005a), though future users of the approach would be at liberty to adopt their own definitions. The opposite is no less true: the object speaks back to the method. In my case, I had to consider the consequences of developing a spatial approach for locating religion based on a secularist tradition of social and cultural theory (derived from the work of Marxist and poststructuralist scholars). Although this did not lead me to alter the analytical method itself, it did alert me to the need for a degree of suspicion and sensitivity when applying it to religion.

A final question we might ask is whether this spatial approach could be used for locating things other than religion. Although it was developed with religion in mind, religion is not intrinsic to it. Rather it is a systematic analytical tool for examining bounded spaces and locating things within them.

Conclusion

After a brief history of the study of sacred space and geography of religion, and an examination of some theoretical and epistemological issues, I introduced two spatial methods for studying religion. I considered their development, method of application, benefits and challenges, and examples of their use. A key difference between them is perspective. Irrespective of scale, mapping, as Martikainen (2002: 313) observed, takes a 'horizontal' approach to the research field. Spatial analysis, by focusing in depth on the location of religion within a designated place, object or body, takes a 'vertical' one, whilst remaining attentive to outward connections and relationships. Although the former affords more opportunity for the use of quantitative methods, and the latter is the more interpretive, it is arguably a spatial approach that is the more systematic of the two. For historical reasons, 'mapping religion' is a cluster of different methods and outcomes ranging from the production of literal maps developed from statistical data to metaphorical maps based on documentary or interview material. An analytical spatial method works with pre-gathered data on a particular place to produce a deep contextualisation of religion within it. The assessment I have presented here of 'mapping religion' is summative: we know about it and are able to describe it by looking at examples of the way it has been developed and applied in the past. However, my assessment of a spatial approach is formative, arising from personal experience of having developed it, of continuing to apply it, and of revising it along the way.

References

al-Faruqi, I.R. and Sopher, D.E. (eds), 1974. *Historical Atlas of the Religions of the World*. Macmillan, New York.

Barrett, D. (ed.), 1982. *World Christian Encyclopedia, 1900–2000*. Oxford University Press, Nairobi.

Bergmann, S., 2007. Theology in its spatial turn: space, place and built environments challenging and changing the images of god. *Religion Compass* 1 (3): 353–79.

Bowman, M., 2009. Learning from experience: the value of analysing Avalon. *Religion* 39 (2): 161–68.

Brereton, J.P., 2005. Sacred space. In: Jones, L. (ed.), *The Encyclopedia of Religion*, 2nd edn, vol. 12., pp. 79 78–86.

Büttner, M., 1980. Survey article on the history and philosophy of the geography of religion in Germany. *Religion* 10 (2): 86–119.

Chidester, D. and Linenthal, E.T. (eds), 1995. *American Sacred Space*. Indiana University Press, Bloomington and Indianapolis.

Cloke, P. and Dewsbury, J.D., 2009. Spiritual landscapes: existence, performance, immanence. *Social and Cultural Geography* 10 (6): 695–711.

Community Religions Project, www.leeds.ac.uk//trs/irpl/crp.htm.

Crang, M. and Thrift, N. (eds), 2000. *Thinking Space*. Routledge, London, New York.

de Certeau, M., 1984. *The Practice of Everyday Life*. Trans. S. Rendall. University of California Press, Berkeley.

de la Torre, R. and Gutiérrez Zuñiga, C. (eds), 2007. *Atlas de la diversidad religiosa en México*. CIESAS, México.

Diez de Velasco, F., 2009. Multi-religiosity in the Canary Islands: analysing processes of religious change between continents. *Religion* 39(2): 147–53.

Dix, S., 2009. Religious plurality within a catholic tradition: a study of the Portuguese capital, Lisbon, and a brief comparison with mainland Portugal. *Religion* 39(2): 182–93.

Eliade, M., 1959 [1957]. *The Sacred and the Profane: the nature of religion*. Harcourt Brace Jovanovitch, San Diego.

Fibiger, M.C.Q., 2009. The Danish pluralism project. *Religion* 39(2): 169–75.

Foucault, M., 1986 [1967]. Of Other Spaces (Des espaces autres). *Diacritics* 16(1): 22–27.

Gaustad, E.S., 1976. *Historical Atlas of Religion in America*. Harper and Row, New York.

Gay, J., 1971. *Geography of Religion in England*. Duckworth, London.

Gardiner, M.Q. and Engler, S., 2010. Charting the map metaphor in theories of religion. *Religion* 40(1): 1–13.

Gutiérrez Zuñiga, C., de la Torre, R. and Castro, C. (with Cruz, H., González, E. and Jiménez, E.), 2011. *Una ciudad donde habitan muchos dioses: cartografía religiosa de Guadalajara*. CIESAS, Mexico.

Heelas, P. and Woodhead, L., 2005. *The Spiritual Revolution: why religion is giving way to spirituality*. Blackwell, Malden MA, Oxford.

Henkel, R., 2001. *Atlas der Kirchen und der anderen Religionsgemeinschaften in Deutschland: eine Religionsgeographie*. Kohlhammer, Stuttgart.

Hernández, A. and Rivera, C. (eds), 2009. *Regiones y Religiones en México: estudios de la transformación socioreligiosa*. CIESAS, Mexico.

Hinnells, J. (ed.), 2005. *The Routledge Companion to the Study of Religion*. Routledge, London, New York.

—— (ed.), 2010. *The Routledge Companion to the Study of Religion*, 2nd edn, Routledge, London, New York.

Holloway, J., 2003. Make-believe: spiritual practice, embodiment, and sacred space. *Environment and Planning A* 35: 1961–74.

Hubbard, P., Kitchen, R. and Valentine, G. (eds), 2004. *Key Thinkers on Space and Place*. SAGE, London, Thousand Oaks, New Delhi.

Jacob, C.R., Rodrigues Hees, D., Waniez, P. and Brustlein, V. (eds), 2003. *Atlas da filiação religiosa e indicadores sociais no Brasil*. Edições Loyola, São Paulo.

Knippenberg, H., 1992. *De Religieuze Kaart van Nederland*. Assen, Maastricht.

Knott, K., 1998. Issues in the study of religions and locality. *Method and Theory in the Study of Religion* 10: 279–90.

—— 2005a. *The Location of Religion: a spatial analysis*. Equinox, London, Oakville, CT.

—— 2005b. Spatial theory and method for the study of religion. *Temenos: Nordic Journal of Comparative Religion* 41(2): 153–84.

—— 2007a. At home in the secular: a spatial analysis of everyday ritual. *Jaarboek Voor Liturgie-Onderzoek* 23: 45–62.

—— 2007b. Religious studies and its relationship to theology: a spatial analysis. *Temenos: Nordic Journal of Comparative Religion* 43(2): 173–98.

—— 2008. Spatial theory and the study of religion. *Religion Compass* 2(6): 1102–16.

—— 2009. From locality to location and back again: a spatial journey in the study of religion. *Religion* 39(2): 154–60.

—— 2010a. Geography, space and the sacred. In: Hinnells, J. (ed.), *The Routledge Companion to the Study of Religion*, 2nd edn, Routledge, London, New York, pp. 477–91.

—— 2010b. Cutting through the postsecular city: a spatial interrogation. In: Beaumont, J., Molendijk, A.L. and Jedan, C. (eds), *Exploring the Postsecular: the religious, the political, and the urban*. Brill, Leiden, Boston, pp. 19–38.

Knott, K. and Franks, M., 2007. Secular values and the location of religion: a spatial analysis of an English medical centre. *Health and Place* 13(1): 224–37.

Kong, L., 1990. Geography of religion: trends and prospects. *Progress in Human Geography* 14: 355–71.

—— 2001. Mapping 'new' geographies of religion: politics and poetics in modernity. *Progress in Human Geography* 25(2): 211–33.

—— 2010. Global shifts, theoretical shifts: changing geographies of religion. *Progress in Human Geography Online First*, 30 March 2010: 1–22.

Krech, V., 2009. What are the impacts of religious diversity? A review of the methodological considerations and empirical findings of a research project on religious pluralisation in North Rhine-Westphalia, Germany. *Religion* 39(2): 132–46.

Lefebvre, H., 1991 [1974]. *The Production of Space*. Trans. D. Nicholson-Smith. Blackwell, Oxford, Cambridge MA.

Macdonald, M. (ed.), 2003. *Experiences of Place*. Harvard University Press, Cambridge MA.

Maddrell, A., 2009. A place for grief and belief: the Witness Cairn, Isle of Whithorn, Galloway, Scotland. *Social and Cultural Geography* 10(6): 675–93.

Martikainen, T., 2002. Mapping religions. In: Pesonen, H., Sakaranaho, T., Sjöblom T. and Utriainen, T. (eds), *Styles and Positions: ethnographic perspectives in comparative religion*. University of Helsinki, Helsinki, pp. 312–29.

—— 2004. *Immigrant Religions in Local Society: historical and contemporary perspectives in the city of Turku*. Åbo Akademi University Press, Åbo.

Massey, D., 1993. Politics and space/time. In Keith, M. and Pile, S. (eds), *Place and the Politics of Identity*. Routledge, London, pp. 141–61.

Mikaelsson, L., 2009. Regional approaches to religion: Christianity in Norway. *Religion* 39(2): 117–25.

O'Brien, J. and Palmer, M., 2007. *The Atlas of Religion*. University of California Press, Berkeley.

Park, C., 1994. *Sacred Worlds: an introduction to geography and religion*. Routledge, London, New York.

Pew Forum on Religion and Public Life, [n.d.]. *US Religious Landscape Survey*. religions.pewforum.org.

Repstad, P., 2009. A softer God and a more positive anthropology: changes in a religiously strict region in Norway. *Religion* 39(2): 126–31.

Smith, J.Z., 1978. *Map is Not Territory: studies in the history of religions*. Chicago University Press, Chicago, London.

—— 1987. *To Take Place: toward a theory of ritual*. University of Chicago Press, Chicago, London.

Sopher, D.E., 1967. *Geography of Religions*. Prentice-Hall, New York.

Stump, R.W., 2008. *The Geography of Religion: faith, place and space*. Rowman and Littlefield, Lanham.

Tweed, T.A., 2006. *Crossing and Dwelling: a theory of religion*. Harvard University Press, Cambridge MA, London.

van der Leeuw, G., 1938. *Religion in Essence and Manifestation*. Trans. J. E. Turner. Princeton University Press, Princeton.

Wheatley, P., 1971. *The Pivot of the Four Quarters*. Aldine, Chicago.

World Christian Database, worldchristiandatabase.org/wcd.

Zelinsky, W., 1961. An approach to the religious geography of the United States: patterns of church membership in 1952. *Annals of the Association of American Geographers* 59: 139–93.

Further reading

There are as yet no 'how to' guides for the geographical or spatial study of religion, but the following works offer some methodological reflections on mapping religion or analyzing it spatially.

Knott, K., 2005b. Spatial theory and method for the study of religion. *Temenos: Nordic Journal of Comparative Religion* 41 (2): 153–84.

This article describes Knott's spatial approach in more detail and considers its strengths and weaknesses.

—— 2009. From locality to location and back again: a spatial journey in the study of religion. *Religion* 39 (2): 154–60.

Knott's spatial approach is discussed in the context of wider debates about locality and location, and in relation to the case of an urban street.

—— 2010a. Geography, space and the sacred. In: Hinnells, J. (ed.), *The Routledge Companion to the Study of Religion*, 2nd edn, Routledge, London, New York, pp. 477–91.

A useful introduction to geographical and spatial approaches to the study of religion.

Stausberg, M. (ed.), 2009. Special issue: perspectives on religion in Western Europe. *Religion* 39(2).

This journal issue offers plentiful examples of the mapping of religions in different European settings.

Zelinsky, W., 1961. An approach to the religious geography of the United States: patterns of church membership in 1952. *Annals of the Association of American Geographers* 59: 139–93.

An influential article on how to map church membership in the United States.

Key concepts

Geography of religion: the study of religion and its mutual engagement with landscape, environment and populations.

Mapping religions: locating, surveying and representing the presence of religions within a designated area.

Sacred space: space produced by ritual or sacralization; a place deemed to be imbued with special meaning, power and ritual significance.

Space: the dynamic and multi-dimensional arena of nature and human life; both the medium or context of action and relationships and its product.

Spatial study of religion: examining religion and religions through a spatial lens; applying a spatial approach or methodology to the study of religion.

Spatial turn: late 20th-century scholarly trend in which the concept of 'space' was redefined and reappropriated by social and cultural theorists and widely applied across the disciplines.

Related chapters

◆ Chapter 1.2 Comparison
◆ Chapter 2.4 Document analysis
◆ Chapter 2.8 Field research: Participant observation
◆ Chapter 2.12 History
◆ Chapter 2.13 Interviewing
◆ Chapter 2.20 Surveys and questionnaires
◆ Chapter 3.1 Auditory materials
◆ Chapter 3.3 Material culture

3.5

VISUAL CULTURE

John Harvey

Chapter summary

- The visual culture of religion is an interdisciplinary field of study of the tangible and perceptual (visual and mental) expressions of belief.
- The approach seeks to understand how ideas, doctrines and convictions are articulated, visually, within (and to those outside) faith communities. It also examines ways in which visual culture actively constructs and shapes religious concepts.
- The substance of study includes fine-art artifacts, craft objects and ephemera made, adapted or adopted for the purpose of worship, teaching, commemoration and propaganda (both for and against religion).
- The approach variously entails a descriptive, comparative and explanatory exegesis of visual artifacts and ideas in relation to the religion's textual referents (such as sacred scriptures); oral and aural modes of expression; cultural, geographical and historical contexts; other visual manifestations; and sites and modes of installation.
- The aim of study is to comprehend the significance of visual culture for religions and their subsets, sects, cults and emergent faith communities, both at its point of inception and as seen from a present-day perspective.
- This is with a view to also determining the commonalities and distinctions between the visual culture of different religions, movements and groups in relation to the artifacts' iconography, materiality, function, interpretation and reception.

Introduction

Religion is always realized. It is conveyed and apprehended in the sound of music, and speech uttered through prayer, rhetoric, discussion, confession and song; as text in sacred writings, commentaries and spiritual books; in the context of places and spaces created or adapted for worship; and through a diversity of visual accoutrements associated with religious observance in its broadest sense.

This chapter discusses the nature of, and approaches to studying, those aspects of religion that are either tangible to the eye or 'seen' in the imagination—its visual culture. Scholars of the visual culture of religion conduct research into methodologies, materials, 'immaterials' and theories of visuality in relation to belief and practice. They interpret the perceptible aspects of religion not only as artifacts but also as an embodiment of ideas, intents and interpretations: how religionists see themselves (self-imaging), how they wish to be seen by others (self-projection), how they are really seen by others (external perception), and how believers use visual culture to articulate and promulgate their faith (self-promotion). Scholars also examine the ways in which religionists envision what cannot be seen: for example, events and characters (living and dead, human and supernatural) encountered in sacred writings, in the form of apparitions, and in dreams and visions.

Visual culture of religion: definition and scope

Imagine that visual culture and religion are binary stars. Each has a planetary system comprising many academic subjects. Orbiting the primary light are the spheres of religious studies, philosophy, anthropology, sociology, psychology of religion and theology. Around the companion, or secondary, light revolve **art history, iconography, iconology**, semiotics, **visual cultural studies**, visual studies, visual and critical studies, and fine-art practice. To make matters even more complex, the two systems interact: the stars encircle one another, while their planets' and moons' paths intersect continually (see Figure 3.5.1). Mapping the trajectories of, and classifying, these bodies, and understanding their mutual influences, is a further responsibility of the study of the visual culture of religion. One of the interdiscipline's other objectives is to study (again, to use an astronomical analogy) the visible matter and the dark matter comprising and distributed throughout the two systems.

The 'visible matter' includes traditional fine art (architecture, book illustration, ceramics, painting, photography, print and sculpture). While all fine art is visual culture, not all visual culture is fine art. Whereas fine art is a special category of creativity, visual culture subsumes all other artifacts of material culture that are intended to be apprehended visually—from a painting by Giotto to a street artist's graffito (Box 3.5.1).[1]

Box 3.5.1 Graffiti as visual culture

There is a rudimentary, symbolic representation of the crucifixion (with caption) hand drawn on the vertical shaft of one of the 14 crosses making up the Stations of the Cross in Florence. This is as much a part of the visual culture of religion as the Crucifix (1287–88) painted by Cimabue (*c*.1240–*c*.1302) for the Basilica of Santa Croce in the same city.

Many of the images and artifacts that make up the visual culture of religion are produced by, or under the auspices of, particular religious groups and individuals in order to propagate their cause, to serve as aids to teaching and devotion, and to commemorate significant events. However, there is also a visual culture of religion that reflects an entirely antithetical set of ideals and incentives. It is produced by those who are proactively antagonistic to religion *per se* or to the claims of specific faiths. Their aim is to perpetrate visual blasphemy by contriving new, and perverting existing, images and iconography in order to vilify the deity, undermine doctrine, persecute believers and disseminate anti-religious sentiment.

'Dark matter' alludes not to the sinister motivations and concoctions of visual blasphemers, but rather to phenomenal and transcendental visual expressions of religion—visions, dreams, apparitions and other types of subjective imaginings (such as visual memory)—that may be invisible to all but the percipient, and that are immaterial. (Images are not necessarily embodied in artifacts, and visuality is not confined to a retinal experience.) In such cases, the visual percept is inaccessible and examinable only via a textual or oral account (a written or spoken testimony or some other mode of relation) or an artist's impression of a dream image or vision, after the fact, at a remove and in a different medium. The reader or hearer constructs their own version of the original percept, fleshed out—and, therefore, re-envisioned—by their own visual imagination (see Harvey 2003: 2–37). (Illustrators engage in the same process when converting a literary description into a visual image.) Some phenomena, it is claimed, are either transiently visible or else invisible to the naked eye until they are captured technologically (and thereby given permanence). One manifestation is spirit photography.[2]

Some religionists eschew any visualization of their beliefs. Two attitudes are evident: either believers want to render images invisible, or else they are sufficiently unresponsive to visuality that, for all intents and purposes, images may as well be invisible. Anti-iconicism is one manifestation of the former attitude. It is a mode of active resistance to representation derived from a religion's advocacy of scriptural prohibitions on image-making and image worship (see Besancon 2009). Iconoclasm, or the wilful destruction of religious images (such as icons, idols and monuments) is the most dramatic expression of this outlook. Like visual blasphemy, iconoclasm is an act of desecration and an attack upon the belief system via its visual representations. However, the motive derives from a sense of (perceived) righteousness rather than from a desire to ridicule. Non-iconicism exemplifies the latter attitude. This form of passive resistance is symptomatic of either an uninterested response to religious representation or the absence of a strong visual sensibility in the social and culture context in which the religion (or one of its subsets) is situated.[3] Neither anti-iconicism nor non-iconicism need have an entirely negative result. Some religious movements, while repudiating the accessories and elaborations of worship, have developed a simple dignity and a dignified simplicity, manifest in, for instance, the design and fitting of their places of worship.[4]

The study of the visual culture of religion, therefore, adopts an uncompromisingly democratic and inclusivist approach to all aspects of human (and, putatively, supernatural) visuality: from the sacred to the sensational, the beautiful to the banal, the doxological to the defamatory, life to death (and beyond), and the affirmatory to the condemnatory.

Methodologies: definition and scope

In the push and pull of the two systems, as the celestial bodies curve towards and away from one another, a number of gravitational fields of study have been formed (see Figure 3.5.1). The methodologies underpinning many of these conjunctions have been adapted from the academic study of visual culture *per se* and its many subgenres: film, television, performance, media studies, art history and fine-art practice, among others.

There is no single paradigm for a methodological enquiry into the visual culture of religion: the disciplines associated with one planetary system bring to those associated with the other distinct approaches, objectives and agendas. However, there is a conviction, shared by the participants in this field of research, that a religious culture's visible expression is as much a repository and an articulation of thought, identity, values, ideals and priorities as that culture's textual, oral and auditory representations. Furthermore, the study of this

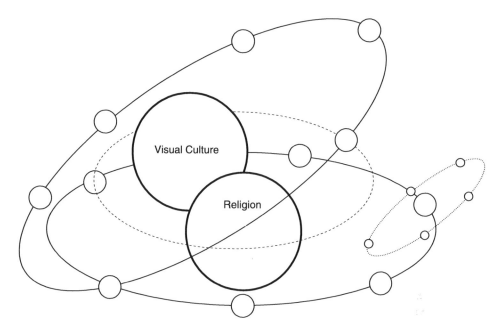

Figure 3.5.1 Religious studies and visual culture as gravitational fields of study

expression is indispensable to a fully rounded appreciation of religious life and belief. Therefore, one of the overarching ambitions of the field is to redress an imbalance in existing scholarship—one that concentrates, almost exclusively, on the literary, aural and oral culture of religion.

Case study one: dealing with religious art (William Holman Hunt, The Shadow of Death)

In your own study of religious imagery, one principle should be borne in mind: there is no 'one size fits all' approach to visual exegesis. Works of art and artifacts of visual culture are too varied in terms of their physical nature, imagery, style of execution and purpose for there to be other than general rules of engagement. (The interpretive approach is to great extent emergent, contingent and local to the image or object that is being studied.) Nevertheless, students with a limited experience of art can follow a step-by-step process of analysis and interpretation that will allow them to critique the image and discern its relationship to the literary source. The process is divided into two phases representing distinct, although not sequential, modes of perception: those of 'the innocent eye' (Phase 1) and of 'the informed eye' (Phase 2). 'The innocent eye' denotes the viewer's immediate response to the image, untutored by a knowledge of its background and the artist's/maker's intent, other relevant images, and the image's relation to a religious, in this case biblical, text. Phase 3 examines the viewer's contribution to the interpretive process.

Phase 1: One can experience an image in an instant. However, the eye cannot take in all the visual information at once, any more than one can read all the words on this page in one glance. (This is especially true of detailed or complex images.) *Step 1*: The viewer's first task is to scrutinize the image and make a mental (and written) inventory of what the image comprises, objectively, by scanning the image from left to right and from top to bottom several times.

Step 2: Second, in order to prepare to interpret the image, they must interrogate it. The following questions will serve as a starting point: What is the image's primary or principal element? (For example, in the case of representational painting, this may be a figure located at the centre of composition.) What are the secondary elements? (They may include a second and other subordinate figures.) What are the tertiary elements? (These will include the objects and the background depicted in the image.) The viewer may also pose questions in order to establish: identity (who are the characters portrayed?); relationship (why do they belong together?); action (what are they doing?); and motive and meaning (why are they doing it?). Interrogation is not interpretation, any more than problems are solutions. Rather, the strategy helps the viewer to understand what they do not yet know.

Step 3: Next, the viewer should return to observation mode and establish whether there is information ancillary to the image, such as a caption (which is often appended to a picture frame, or situated on the gallery wall, or printed alongside an illustration in a publication). The caption will indicate the name of the artist/maker, the work's title, and sometimes its medium and size too.

Let us ground this process in a concrete example: the English Pre-Raphaelite painter Holman Hunt's *The Shadow of Death* (1870–73). The primary figure is Christ. The secondary figure is his mother, Mary. The tertiary elements consist of a variety of objects associated with a carpentry workshop, principally, and the physical and geographical settings of the scene. The painting's title is significant. Indeed, the titles of most artworks are important: they serve to direct the viewer's attention to the appropriate level of meaning. In order to grasp its significance we must now move from 'the innocent eye' to that of 'the informed eye', and from observation to interpretation.

Phase 2: 'The informed eye' is a mode of perception that is enlightened by knowledge external to the image. One source of this knowledge is kindred images. Images (and their titles) interpret one another, enabling the viewer to compare like with like and to comprehend the particular in the context of the general, so as to discern what is distinctive about the image at hand and how it should be understood in the context of the tradition of the subject (that which is represented).

Step 1: For example, the title of Hunt's work, unlike that of his fellow pre-Raphaelite John Everett Millais's (1829–96) painting *Christ in the House of His Parents (The Carpenter's Shop)* (1849–50), is not descriptive. Gombrich (1985: 221) identifies three classes of titles: anecdotal, descriptive and referential. Hunt's title is referential, but to what does it refer? At this juncture, the viewer needs to access another source of external knowledge—the biblical source. The title is a text (Psalm 23: 4). However, the painting does not appear to illustrate (that is to say, to complement and visualize) the content of the psalm.[5] To what, then, does the title refer? The viewer must return to observation. There is a shadow cast on the rear wall of Christ with his arms outstretched, evoking the posture that he would assume at the crucifixion. In this way, the title and the shadow prefigure Christ's death.

Step 2: The identification of the primary element/figure as Christ is dependent upon establishing an iconographic correspondence between the way the figure is depicted in the painting and the normative tradition of Christ's portrayal in art. (Iconography is the art-historical study of, primarily, the identity, conventions and familiar of representation, and treatment of images. This is distinct from, but related to, iconology, which is the art-historical analysis of the subject matter, symbolism, imagery, style, medium and cultural-historical context of art.) There is a wide selection of reference books on the iconography of the major world religions available for students new to the study of art history (see 'further reading').

Just as an image may comprise more than a primary element, so also it can have meanings besides the dominant one. In Hunt's painting they are signified by the tertiary elements. The painted objects are not only denotations of the real things but also typological symbols of spiritual ideas. Some of the symbols are biblical in origin. Others are of the artist's making. Hunt explained their meanings in an extensive document, which he wrote as an accompaniment to the painting. (Researchers frequently have recourse to art-historical, primary-source texts, written by artists, in order to interpret religious painting.)

Step 3: Having advanced from observation to interpretation, the viewer proceeds to the final stage in the approach: application. Applicatory questions investigate: how the image was intended to be used (which may not be the same as how it was actually, or is presently, used); the contexts in which it was used; and the identity of the users. Hunt conceived of *The Shadow of Death* as a visual sermon. Protestant ministers at the time pressed the painting into service as a surrogate biblical text, exegeting its typological symbolism to illustrate spiritual and moral lessons preached at churches and chapels or published in books.

Phase 3: The viewer is not, however, encountering the painting at the time it was made but, rather, in their own time. Furthermore, a 'reading' of the image is dependent upon not only the viewer's understanding of the text and its context, and of the iconographic tradition of the text, but also the other types of knowledge ('practical, national, cultural, aesthetic' and associative) which they bring to the image (Barthes 1977: 39, 46). For this reason, the viewer should be aware that they perceive the picture through a filter of 'the informed eye' and of their cultural and personal history and cognizance of other disciplines. In so doing, they actively participate in the construction of meanings (which may be neither intended by the artist nor conceivable at the time it was made). Thus, at some level the viewer's understanding of a visual artifact will be personal and idiosyncratic and bespoke.

Methodological perspective: religious studies

Visual culture, in the context of religious studies, comprises historic and contemporary artifacts made and used within a global, an institutional and a domestic setting of piety. Using anthropological, sociological, political, philosophical, psychological and ethnographical methodologies, the discipline examines images and objects associated with doctrine and belief, religious behavior, symbolic acts, commemoration, teaching, proselytizing, worship, ceremony, ritual and liturgy of the mainstream religions and their subsidiary movements and groups, minority sects and cults, and maverick or notable individuals (whether religionists or artists/makers, or both). In so doing, scholars adopt both a broad- and small-brush approach to studying how artifacts act religiously.

Case study two: dealing with visual culture
(Protestant nonconformist banner)

Having looked at an example of biblical religious art, we turn to examine an artifact of religious visual culture: a Protestant nonconformist banner (see Plate 3.5.1 and Plate 3.5.2). A thorough account of the artifact is possible only when the trajectories of religious studies and art-historical and visual-cultural studies intersect. Therefore, the viewer

Plate 3.5.1 Protestat nonconformist banner (obverse)

needs to keep an eye on both disciplines constantly. (In the account of the artifact, the domain of each discipline's expertise is distinguished as follows: **bold type** for religious studies and regular type for art-historical and visual–cultural studies.) As in the previous case study, the process of analysis includes observation, interrogation, interpretation and application.

Step 1: Observation needs to be structured. It involves scrutinizing the artifact in two ways: first as a thing in itself; and second by situating it within a cultural matrix. These approaches do not necessarily represent distinct or consecutive phases of research. It is

Plate 3.5.2 Protestant nonconformist banner (back)

helpful to partition the observation into categories (such as one might encounter on a database) related to its physical and cultural characteristics. (The list of categories is not fixed; it can be added to or subtracted from. The accompanying text box is illustrative: a greater level of detail for several of the categories would be valuable for a fuller analysis. What is important is that the fields are serviceable and relevant to a wide-ranging description of the artifact.)

Box 3.5.2 Disciplinary analysis of a Protestant nonconformist banner

Bold type denotes religious studies; regular type denotes art–historical/visual–cultural studies.

  1 **Religious context:** *Christian > Protestant > Nonconformist > Calvinistic Methodist*

  2 **Geographical context:** *United Kingdom > Wales*

  3 **Site-specific context:** *Siloh (Calvinistic Methodist) chapel, Aberystwyth, Dyfed*

  4 **Historical context:** *19th century > 1880s–1940s > 20th century, first quarter*

  5 Mode of encounter: *direct*

  6 Place of origin: *Leeds*

  7 Artist/designer/maker/manufacturer: *E. Riley & Co.*

  8 Status of product: *bespoke adaptation of manufacturer's pattern*

  9 Medium: *oil on silk*

10 Construction: *two-sided cloth, draped and suspended over a wooden crossbar*

11 Dimensions: *5 ft (height) × 3 ft (width)*

12 Physical condition: *good; the silk is worn and torn on the bottom border*

13 Imagery: *Christ standing among children and adults (obverse); young man refusing the offer of a glass of wine (back)*

14 **Text:** *obverse:* **'Band of Hope Shiloh'**; **'Bugeilia Fy Nefaid'** *[.]* **'Ioan XXI.17'** *('Feed My Sheep' [.] 'John XXI.17')*, **'Cymdeithas Ddirwestol** *[.]* **Shiloh'.** *(Temperance Society [.] Shiloh'); back:* **'Gwatwarus Yw Gwin A Therfysgaidd Yw Diod Gadarn'** *[.]* **'Diar XX.1'** *('Wine is a mocker, strong drink is raging' [.] 'Prov XX.1')*

15 **Function:** *paraded on Whitsun walks, and set up in the chapel on the occasion of anniversaries and festivals; denominational propaganda*

16 **Classification:** *image/text-bearing artifact*

Step 2: When the categories are complete, the viewer should review their contents and begin the process of interpretation. In the course of the review, several general methodological principles need to be discerned. First, look at the artifact as a thing in itself. The 'status of the product' described in 8 may be either unique or mass-produced, or (in this case) a combination of both. The location and date of artifact (outlined in 1–4 and 15) may not be immediately discernible. (One does not always encounter the artifact in the place for which it was intended.) Second, situate the artifact within a cultural matrix. The nature, history and sociology of its function can be inferred only by accessing knowledge that lies outside of the artifact. In respect to the latter, the diagram identifies four zones of external knowledge (or situations) which pertain to the artifact (Figure 3.5.2). The 'physical context of the artifact' comprises those characteristics referred to in 1–4 and 15. The 'religious content of the artifact' includes information entered under 1, and permits scope to explore the theological and doctrinal discourse surrounding the artifact.

Step 3: In the example of the banner, these latter aspects of the study contribute significantly to an interpretation of the artifact and to understanding its application: the commissioning chapel belonged to a denomination that has its theological roots in Calvinism. Calvinist worship is distinguished by the regulative principle. This insists that only those elements that are prescribed or implied by scripture are permissible in worship (Calvin 1845: 120–33). Accordingly, Calvin prohibited the setting up of images in the 16th-century

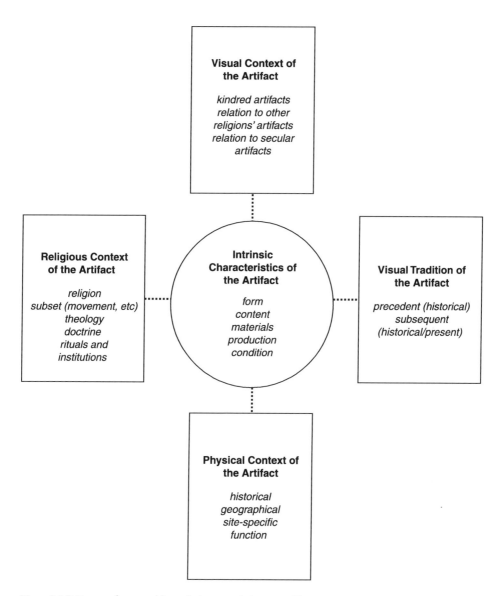

Figure 3.5.2 Zones of external knowledge pertaining to artifacts

Reformed churches in Europe. The presence of an image-laden banner in a 19th-century Calvinistic chapel in Wales, therefore, suggests an alteration in either the influence, the practice or the understanding of the regulative principle.

Step 4: Under the heading of the 'visual tradition of the artifact', one might conduct interpretive research into the precedents for the chapel banner in the visual culture of earlier Christian churches and movements, and of the Bible (Song of Songs 2: 4, Isaiah 13: 2, Psalm 20: 5). Under the heading of the 'subsequent (historical/present)' category the viewer might, following the principle of comparing like with like (explored in the previous case study), look at examples of banners produced after this one but before the present day.

Step 5: Interpretive research pursued in relation to the 'visual context of the artifact' category could involve a study of different types of banners associated with the religious subset, or the relationship of the chapel banner to other types of image- and text-bearing and propagandist artifacts used by other subsets of the same religion, or by other religions, or by secular groups (such as the trade unions).

Methodological perspective: art history, visual cultural studies and art practice

Religious studies scholars are not particularly adept at dealing with the aspects of religious artifacts that lie outside the domain of the text's narrative content, *dramatis personae* and cultural entanglements, nuances and reception. A consideration of the 'visual tradition of the artifact' and the 'intrinsic characteristics of the artifact' (the aesthetic and formal qualities: line, shape, tone, texture, size and scale), materiality, and situation (or the artifact's placement in place of worship, domestic setting or an exhibition) is either often overlooked or else regarded as superfluous. (For all intents and purposes, a printed reproduction of the artifact suffices in most cases.) This is unsurprising, given that scholars from this discipline do not possess the expertise to deal with these attributes of the artifact.

Art and visual-cultural historians appreciate that an artifact's significance extends beyond the represented subject. Traditionally, art historians have illuminated religious art iconographically, by identifying, interpreting and describing the intrinsic content (that which constitutes and signifies the represented subject). The intrinsic meaning of that content is established by mounting what could be called a visual-hermeneutical analysis. This intrinsic meaning is contingent: the product of the work's origins (or provenance), genre, stylistic tradition; the artist's/maker's biography; the period of manufacture; and the national, philosophical, religious, class, ethnic and gender values bearing upon it.[6] Consequently, apprehending the nature of an artifact (be that 'high' or 'low', 'major' or 'minor', art or visual culture) requires an attitude of attentiveness to the thing in itself, and to the contextual, situational and ideological positions of its maker and recipient (which may not necessarily concur).

Artists/makers, for their part, comprehend the artifact from the inside out: from inception, through evolution, to resolution. Biographies and autobiographies of artists provide valuable insights into these phases of creativity, as well as into the artist's ideological presuppositions, intent, decision-making process, assessment of outcomes and perception of the work's merit. (It is helpful to read artists' biographies and personal declarations if only to distinguish between their intentions and your reception of the artwork.) Artists recognize, too, that an artifact possesses a further significance, one that is as integral to the artifact's meaning and to the percipient's experience of such, as the subject it represents. The signifiers are encoded in the materials, form (color, shape, line, pattern, etc.), and the manner of their application and manipulation, the stylistic conventions, the scale and size of the artifact, framing devices, and artifact's position in relation to the site of installation and to the percipient (see Box 3.5.3). Decoding the signifiers and understanding the process of signification requires a specialized knowledge of materials and methods, art theory, practical theory, aesthetics and creative dynamics. This comes through training (in the case of artists) and study (in the case of art historians, theorists and aestheticians).

Few of these characteristics (and their psychological impact)—such as its size, materiality, surface features, detail, actual color (as opposed to its color in a reproduction, which is rarely accurate), and the context of its display (see case study three)—can be appreciated in a photographic reproduction of the work or deduced from the caption details. Where possible, a direct encounter with the work is preferable. The disparity between a direct and a mediated encounter with an artifact can be illustrated with reference to Antony Gormley's (b.1950) sculpture *The Angel of the North* (1994–98).[7] In this example, the artwork's physicality is of its essence.

If religious scholars are less able to deal with the art aspect than with the religious aspect of religious artifacts, then art historians and artists have the opposite limitation. Rarely do they possess expertise in any branch of religious scholarship. When dealing, for example, with biblical images, most do not address the source material as text, or the text itself as an image-laden, culturally and historically specific, yet constantly adaptable, representation of ideas. Instead, the scriptures are treated merely as a pool of illustratable narratives, events and characters. Again, in art-historical studies of religious artifacts, it is commonplace for art historians to discuss the artist's/maker's choice and interpretation of subject matter, themes, stories and iconography, but somewhat less often to draw attention to the doctrinal or institutional tradition they may espouse or by which they may have been commissioned.

Box 3.5.3 *The Angel of the North* (Antony Gormley, 1994–98)

Made of an amalgam of weather-resistant steel and copper, *The Angel of the North* weighs 150 tons, is 20 metres high and has a wing-span of 54 metres (just 14 metres shorter than that of a Boeing 747–48 Intercontinental aircraft). It is the largest sculpture in the United Kingdom. The work is elevated and exposed to the elements on a hill that was once the site of a colliery, at the head of the Team valley and overseeing (like a guardian) the motorways and a mainline railroad at Gateshead, England. Its physical presence, materials and manner of construction evoke the pitheads and ship- and bridge-building of Tyneside's industrial past. The artist, Antony Gormley, represents a counter-ethereal conception of an angel—it is supernatural only in scale and iconography—simultaneously grounded in the landscape and ascending into the sky. The monument is an open-ended symbol, one that embraces (like its wings) a breadth of messages and meanings, communal and individual, spiritual and historical.

Moreover, little consideration is given to the artist's convictions about a particular religion or its scriptures, that is, whether they regard the text as revelation or speculation, unitary or fragmentary, mythology or history, truth or travesty, authoritative and sacred or malleable and relative, and whether they approach it with devotion and submission or cool academic detachment. The artist's convictions can affect their intellectual and spiritual attitude to work, their sense of its significance and the degree of imaginative interpretation or variance they deem permissible. An understanding of an artist's view of religion and scripture has considerable relevance to a scholarly interpretation of their artistic intent and imagery. Therefore, academics and practitioners from both 'planetary systems' need each other and to recognize that the beliefs both of the artist or maker and of the faith must be addressed together if there is to be a balanced and an informed study of religious visual culture.

Case study three: dealing with contemporary art (*Chris Ofili*, The Upper Room)

Chris Ofili's (b.1968) controversial work *The Upper Room* (1999–2002) exemplifies not only the complex ways in which the contemporary artist can engage and unseat our expectations regarding the traditions of religious representation but also the importance of taking into account the artist's cultural, racial and geographical background.[8] The following case study 'exegetes' Ofili's piece by combining the complementary perspectives discussed above: fine-art practice, art history and visual culture and religious studies. The methodological approach entails an inquiry into: the artist's biographical background and the contextual background (the artist's *oeuvre*) (Phase 1); a description of the artwork; a description of the context of installation; a relation of the artwork to artworks by other artists (Phase 2); and an examination of the work from art historical and religious studies perspectives (Phase 3).

Phase 1: In this example, we begin by looking not at the art but at the artist. *Step 1*: Who an artist is—culturally, racially and socially—informs their work as much as do the visual influences, ideas and professional training to which they have been exposed. Artists' biographies and autobiographies, and interviews in journals or broadcasts, are prime sources for this information. Ofili is a black Briton of Nigerian descent, educated in a Roman Catholic school and at Chelsea School of Art and the Royal College of Art, London. *Step 2*: What an artwork means—in terms of its subject matter, style, and the artist's intent and approach—is deduced by examining it not in isolation but in the context of their prior and subsequent work. (The viewer should consult monographs on the artist and catalogues of their exhibitions.) Religion has been the theme of a number of his previous works, most notably the *Holy Virgin Mary* (1996). His depiction of persons and narratives from the Christian Bible is perceived by some critics and members of the public to be scandalous, sacrilegious and worthy only of censorship. Others consider his stance on religion as deliberately ambiguous, misunderstood, or refreshingly provocative in the way it pushes at the boundary between art and offence (see Adjaye and Golden 2009). Is the artist rebelling against his religious upbringing or recasting its iconography in the mould of his African visual-cultural heritage? The viewer must come to his or her own informed opinion.

Phase 2: *The Upper Room* comprises 13 paintings that were installed, between September 2005 and January 2007, at Tate Britain, an important gallery in London, in a purpose-built environment designed by the architect David Adjaye (b.1966).[9]

Step 1: Where an artwork is situated and how it is presented may be as significant as its content, and will condition how the artwork affects the viewer. The paintings are installed in a long, basilica-shaped, panelled room with a central bench for spectators to sit. (In this way, the installation invites the viewer to reflect upon the paintings, rather than merely acknowledge them and swiftly walk on.) The paintings are discreetly lit; spotlights envelop each with a soft incandescent aureole. Why has the artist illuminated the paintings in such a deliberate manner? What effect does the lighting have upon you? You might conclude that Ofili's aim is to connote an aura of sacredness by association with the aureole (the soft radiance or luminous nimbus that cocoons holy persons in religious art).

Step 2: Turning to Ofili's paintings themselves, endeavor to describe, first, their works' visual complexity and use of medium. Ofili's works strive towards sensory overload—a fullness of form achieved by superimposing image upon image, decorative complexity, multichromacy and intermediality. (They are made using oil and acrylic paint, felt-tip pen, graphite, glitter, resin and canvas.) It is possible to separate, mentally, the many layers of visual information (the tangle of colors, forms and textures). This would be an inventorial approach—like discerning individual species of plants in a dense tropical jungle, but the experience of 'jungleness' is in the totality of the general effect. Similarly, the painting is best experienced as the sum of its parts. Ask yourself: 'What immediate impression does the painting make upon me?' After you have tried to interpret the paintings' iconography

(Phase 3, Step 3), ask yourself: 'How does the manner in which the subject matter is conveyed contribute to its meaning?'

Second, note the type of artwork Ofili has made. Is this a painting in the conventional sense? Besides media, the artist combines art forms too: the works are not hung upon but leant against the wall, elevated from the floor by pedestals made of elephant-dung in a manner that implies that they are both paintings and sculptures.[10] Third, examine the imagery (or iconography). In representational art this will often yield important information about the primary subject of the work. Ofili also conjoins art referents: the motif of the monkey (in a smoking jacket and cap, holding a tumbler and tossing a ball represented by elephant dung) is based on a drawing by the American Pop artist Andy Warhol (1928–87) and inter-mingles with a kind of exotic wallpaper influenced by Art Nouveau cum Henri Rousseau (1844–1910) (the French primitive painter). In so doing, Ofili converges and harmonizes aspects of the visual cultures of Africa, North America and Europe.

Phase 3: In this phase of the inquiry, the perceptual observations made in the previous phases are placed within the disciplinary contexts of biblical studies, art historical studies, and religious studies. *Step 1*: Multiplicity, synthesis and syncretism are features of not only the work's form but also its intellectual (as opposed to visual) content. In order to tease apart the strands of this thread, we begin with the work's title and a biblical study. 'Upper room' has several biblical referents. In New Testament times, the upper room was a chamber in either the roof of a house (like a loft space) or its upper storey. In the Gospels, it was the context of the Last Supper, the occasion when Christ instituted the Eucharist and spoke of his betrayal and death (Luke 22: 1–23). In the Acts of the Apostles, Peter delivered his first sermon, Matthias was chosen to replace Judas as one of the twelve apostles and the Holy Spirit descended at Pentecost in an upper room (Acts 1: 13; 2: 1–6, 14–36). An upper room was also one of the locations for Paul's preaching and, interestingly, in connection with Ofili's install-ation, in the latter upper room, the Bible says, 'there were many lights' (Acts 20: 8). In the New Testament, therefore, the upper room was a place associated with inaugurations, exposi-tion and multiple languages and cultures mixed together—which again is apposite, given the nature of Ofili's own upper room.

Step 2: Next, we examine the artwork within an iconographical context. The association of *The Upper Room* principally (although not necessarily exclusively) with the context of the Last Supper is connoted by the number and arrangement of the paintings: 13 (one for each of the 12 apostles), in two rows of six, flanking a golden painting entitled *Mono Oro* at the end of the room. In this respect, the work resists the dominant iconography of the theme, which depicts the apostles seated behind a long table, in a row, with Christ at the centre. However, the most conspicuous departure from the normative iconographic code for the Last Supper is Ofili's portrayal of Christ and the apostles as monkeys.[11] This, coupled with the intrinsic polyvalence of visual images (their capacity to be 'read' in more than one way), constitutes the elemental gas cloud in which the stars of interpretation coalesce.

Step 3: Then, we endeavor to deduce the significance of the artwork's deviance from iconographic norms. What does the work mean and what are the artist's motives and intent? The critical and public response to these questions, as in the case of Ofili's previous religious work *Holy Virgin Mary*, is divided. Is the artist being ironic and blasphemous by implying that the founding figures of the Christian religion were a bunch of monkeys? If one's hermeneutic terms of reference are confined to Christian visual culture, then *The Upper Room* is problem-atic in this respect, particularly for Christians. In contemporary Western culture the monkey symbolizes negative characteristics such as mischief and trickery. Some of these connotations derive from medieval Christian iconography, where the primate variously symbolized the devil, heresy, paganism, lewdness, greed, gluttony and the fall of mankind (in other words, all that was contrary to god and godliness). In Albrecht Dürer's (1471–1528) *Madonna with the Monkey* (*c*.1498), an image which also places Christ and a monkey in the same picture, the animal is seen tethered by the side of the Virgin Mary and positioned beneath the Christ-child—suggesting the subjugation of all the creature stands for to the holy persons. Thus, in conflating Christ and the apostles with monkeys, Ofili would appear to be proffering an unholy alliance of good and evil.

Step 4: However, appearances can be deceptive. One needs always to situate an interpretation of the part in relation to that of the whole. The tenor of the display does not encourage an interpretation of the work in terms of either comic irony or malicious profanity. Neither does the room or its content promote a contemptuous (that is, designedly offensive or defamatory), parodic, sacrilegious or an irreverent perspective on the Last Supper. Moreover, *The Upper Room* does not demystify that which is mysterious (which is one of the principle stratagems of intentional visual blasphemy). On the contrary, the work's inscrutability promotes a sense of mystery, something that lies at the heart of religion. If, by irony, we mean that there is an incongruity between the way in which Ofili has realized the subject and what might be expected, then the answer is yes, but to what purpose is this use of irony?

Outside the iconographic and religious traditions of Judeo-Christianity, the monkey does not necessarily possess pejorative overtones. In Hinduism, for example, it is a positive symbol for the soul, and is venerated. The deity Lord Hanuman had a monkey's face, and his monkey-ness was associated with intellectual agility. The particular species that Ofili has painted is the rhesus macaque, which is native to Afghanistan, India and China. It is regarded as one of the most compassionate and intelligent animals. In this respect, the association of the monkey with Christ and the apostles is entirely apposite. Furthermore, the term 'rhesus' also refers to a human blood-group system; and blood, symbolized by wine, is an element in the Eucharist. Arguably, this dissonance between the monkey and its meaning serves to dislocate the images' discourse from the Christian religion exclusively. In conclusion, Ofili mixes religions like art media: here Christianity is blended with ethnic, mainstream and animist religions. In so doing, Ofili in his *Upper Room* provides us with a contemplative environment within which religion is encountered in the round.

Case study four: dealing with conflict (visual blasphemy)

Ofili's *Upper Room* is not designedly blasphemous. However, a superficial reading of the work might lead to an entirely different conclusion. There are two reasons for this ambiguity. First, images are polyvalent and flexible. Unlike texts, they are non-propositional and unable to 'say' anything specific, and therefore able to accommodate a variety of different 'readings'. Second, visual blasphemy can be: (1) unintentional (arising from a misunderstanding on the part of the percipient regarding the motivations behind the 'mis'-use of religious imagery, or a failure on the part of the perpetrator to appreciate the sensitivities and sensibilities of religionists, or both); or (2) deliberate (that is, with the intent of expressing irreverence or contempt towards something held to be sacred, and thereby causing offence).

Plate 3.5.3 shows an example of unintentional visual blasphemy. In a spontaneous gesture, a cuddly toy moose is hung upon a wooden cross above a child's grave in a contemporary municipal cemetery, likely by a parent or close relative. Understanding the intent is crucial. *Step 1*: Examine the sociology of death and find out whether the practice fits within known patterns of bereavement (see Robben 2004). In the United Kingdom and USA, objects either associated with childhood or belonging to the deceased are customarily placed where those

Plate 3.5.3 An example of unintentional visual blasphemy

persons are laid to rest, especially in secular working-class cultures. *Step 2*: In the light of this knowledge, the viewer is not likely to conclude that this is a defamation of the crucifixion, but, rather, an inadvertent and bizarre conjunction, an instance of visual irony that would, in all likelihood, not have occurred to the bereaved.

Plate 3.5.4 shows an example of deliberate visual blasphemy. This mode of religious visual culture ('dark matter') is often disseminated via dedicated, nefarious websites. In respect to the illustration: *Step 1*: Observe the image. Has the perpetrator altered its iconography in any

Please note the studied grace with which a naughty Jesus receives his punishment.

Plate 3.5.4 Daveman, Jesus the Masochist, from the website of 'The Christian Holocaust'

way? *Step 2*: Read the appended captions. Are they intrinsically disrespectful? *Step 3*: How do the texts modify the image, and vice versa? The illustration shows a reproduction of a painting of Christ's flagellation, which depicts the saviour tied to a pillar and beaten by his tormentor (following the established iconography of the subject) (Plate 3.5.4). The artist Daveman has retitled the reproduction 'Jesus the Masochist', and appended the caption: 'Please note the studied grace with which naughty Jesus receives his punishment'. In so doing, he has recontextualized an example of biblical art by appending inappropriate texts that exploit the images' visual-semantic ambiguity. The motive behind his 'maladjustment' of the image is unambiguous.[12]

A less straightforward case is provided by one of the most controversial, recent examples of visual blasphemy: the cartoons of the Islamic prophet Muhammad, first published in the Danish newspaper *Jyllands-Posten* on 30 September 2005. *Step 1*: Observe the images and their context. The set of 12 cartoons and the accompanying text variously satirize and critique the prophet Muhammad and Islam (and give the editors' reasons for so doing) in the belief that, post 9/11, issues about Islamist activities should be freely aired and discussed. Following the sometimes-violent protests by Islamicists and a judicial inquiry, the newspaper explained that the intent was not to offend and apologized. *Step 2*: Examine the reasons why many Muslims were humiliated and hurt by the portrayal of the prophet. Are the images of Muhammad (drawn in the manner of contemporary, Danish political cartoons) derisory or disrespectful in their adaptation of the traditional iconography for the prophet? Does the location, action and caption undermine his portrayal? What bearing do the theology of aniconism and Islamic prohibitions against insulting Muhammad have on the nature of the offence? (Shi'a Islam is generally tolerant of presentations of the prophet, while Sunni Islam forbids them, but both groups regard insulting Muhammad as a crime.) Based on the visual and textual information, and on the broader religious context, would you conclude that the caricatures are a case of unintentional or deliberate visual blasphemy?

Conclusion

Although it is still in its nascent and pioneering period, the collaboration between religion and art and visual culture has already provided reciprocal insights, including the need to develop a rich knowledge and understanding of the visual traditions of specific systems of faith, as well as a holistic and unified conception of religious visuality within a global, historical and multi-faith context. While a great deal has already been achieved in these respects, many other trajectories, orbits and intersections remain to be plotted, followed and crossed. Opportunities and responsibilities abound. One of the challenges of research into religion and visual culture is to comprehend how religious concepts, knowledge and faith mutate when they are conveyed in visual languages. We also need to understand better how the media and iconographies of representation intersect. The medium may not always be the message, but the medium always has a message—one that is either consonant or dissonant with the message of the subject.

In the future, the **interdisciplinary** study of religion and visual culture needs to speak to a context in which—post-9/11—faith has taken centre stage in the political and cultural arena. Presently, in the West, academic discussion is centred on the Judaeo-Christian traditions. Baha'i, Buddhist, Hindu, Islamic, Shinto, Sikh, Taoist and Zoroastrian perspectives on the relationship between image and text, and between visualization and theology, remain on the margins of the debate. Likewise, a rigorous taxonomy and monographic analysis of the visual culture of religious subgroups, non-orthodox movements, and belief systems such as atheism, deism, paganism, Rastafarianism, Scientology and New Christianities have yet to be undertaken. There is a need also to encourage not only a mutual understanding and appreciation of the values shared by the visual traditions of the Abrahamic faiths but also coexistence and consultation—through empathy, respect and appreciation—between a diversity of faiths and artistic communities, both at home and abroad. In this sense, the visual culture of religion will both stand as an academic interdiscipline and serve as an active intermediary.

Notes

1 Religious graffiti is one of a number of under-researched topics of the visual culture of religion. This is surprising, since its history is almost as old as Christianity; therefore, the genre constitutes the earliest visual culture of this religion. The ICHTHUS and hope and anchor symbols were inscribed on the walls of Rome prior to the *Pax Romana* (27 BC–AD 180), and served as a secret visual code to communicate between believers who met clandestinely for fear of persecution.

2 Spirit photographs show, purportedly, the appearance of the dead (alongside that of the living sitter who had posed for the photograph); in other examples, the photograph records visual manifestations of supernatural entities (see Chéroux *et al.* 2005; Harvey 2007a; Jolly 2006).

3 Indeed, scholars argue, in some cases a society's or culture's conspicuous aesthetic austerity is the consequence of its dominant religion's reticence about or resistance to representation. However, the interdict on images is rarely consistently and comprehensively applied. While visual artifacts may not be set up as an aid to, or an object of, worship, they are often used in the service of other religious ends (see above) (O'Kane 2010: 71–89; see also Harvey 2000, 2007b; Malraux 1947–49).

4 The Calvinist-inspired meeting houses and chapels in Wales during the 18th and 19th centuries are characterized by an elegant plain style, expressed in terms of a rudimentary structure, nominal decor and functionalism. The form embodied the conviction that all that was required to worship God, according to the pattern prescribed in the New Testament for the early church, was a context for oral and aural interaction: the performance and reception of preaching, singing and prayer. In my own research through art practice, I have self-consciously adapted the Calvinist embargo on religious representation and emphasis on the Word of God as a methodological process of fine-art image-making. The artworks, predominantly abstract and minimal in style, are letter-by-letter visual codifications of biblical texts (Garvan 1950: 5–13; Harvey 2000, 2007b).

5 Neither does the painting illustrate an event from the life of Christ as recorded in the gospels. The New Testament does not say that Christ was a carpenter like his father, Joseph.

6 The distinction between the terms 'artist' (in the present-day sense) and 'maker' indicates that not all artificers regard themselves as self-expressing innovators, or as creating unique works of 'art' as such. 'Makers' include artisans, craftsmen and technicians who may be highly skilled, are often anonymous, and are sometimes involved in the mass production of objects. The distinction is one of identity rather than of quality.

7 A photographic survey of the sculpture is presented at en.wikipedia.org/wiki/Angel_of_the_North.

8 Chris Ofili, *The Upper Room* (2003), Victoria Miro Gallery, London. Photographs of the installation and the individual paintings are presented by Tate Britain, London at 'Chris Ofili: The Upper Room' (www.tate.org.uk/britain/exhibitions/Ofili/default.shtm). See Adjaye and Golden 2009.

9 The work was also part of a retrospective of Ofili's work at Tate Britain from 27 January to 16 May 2010.

10 Ofili points out that elephant dung, a material used in many of his earlier works, symbolizes fertility and nurturing in some African cultures.

11 The traditional iconography for the theme is apparent, quintessentially, in Leonardo da Vinci's (1452–1519) *The Last Supper* (1495–98). The iconography (via da Vinci's work) is reconstituted in Sam Taylor-Wood's (b.1967) *Wrecked* (1996). This directorial photograph courted controversy (and accusations of visual blasphemy) for including a female and topless 'Christ' standing with her arms outstretched (thereby referencing Holman Hunt's *The Shadow of Death* (1869–73) too) (Rosenthal 1997: 172–73).

12 For an analysis of the dynamics of visual blasphemy within a cross-religious (and specifically Abrahamic) framework see Plate 2002: 1–17; Plate 2006.

References

Adjaye, D. and Golden, T., 2009. *Chris Ofili*. Rizzoli, New York.

Barthes, R., 1977. *Image–Music–Text*. Trans. Stephen Heath. Collins, Glasgow.

Besancon, A., 2009. *The Forbidden Image: an intellectual history of iconoclasm*. University of Chicago Press, Chicago.

Calvin, J., 1845 [1560]. *Institutes of the Christian Religion*. Vol. 1. Trans. Henry Beveridge. Calvin Translation Society, Edinburgh.

Chéroux, C., Fischer, A., Apraxine, P. *et al.*, 2005. *The Perfect Medium: photography and the occult*. Yale University Press, New Haven, London.

Garvan, A., 1950. The Protestant plain style before 1630. *Journal of the Society of Architectural Historians* 9(3): 5–13.

Gombrich, E.H., 1985. Image and word in twentieth-century art. *Word and Image* 1(3): 213–41.

Harvey, John, 2000. *The Pictorial Bible I: settings of the Psalms*. National Library of Wales, Aberystwyth.

—— 2003. *The Appearance of Evil: apparitions of spirits in Wales*. University of Wales Press, Cardiff.

—— 2007a. *Photography and Spirit*. Reaktion Books, London.

—— 2007b. *The Pictorial Bible Series II: seal up the vision and prophecy*. School of Art, Aberystwyth.

Jolly, M., 2006. *Faces of the Living Dead: the belief in spirit photography*. British Library, London.

Malraux, A., 1947–49. *The Psychology of Art*. Trans. Stuart Gilbert. 3 vols. Pantheon Books, New York.

O'Kane, M and Morgan-Guy, J. (eds), 2010. *Biblical Art from Wales*. Sheffield Phoenix Press, Sheffield.

Plate, S.B., 2002. *Religion, Art, and Visual Culture: a cross-cultural reader*. Palgrave Macmillan, New York.

—— 2006. *Blasphemy: the art that offends*. Black Dog, London.

Robben, A.C.G.M. and Morgan- Guy, J.(eds), 2004. *Death, Mourning, and Burial: a cross-cultural reader*. Blackwell, Oxford.

Rosenthal, N. 1997. *Sensation: young British artists from the Saatchi Collection.* Royal Academy of Arts, London.

Further reading

Mirzoeff, N., 1991, *An Introduction to Visual Culture.* Routledge, London, New York.

The book is appropriate for students of religious studies and of visual art. It gives a clear and extensive explanation of the nature of visual culture. The discussion engages a broad range of media, including fine art, film, the Internet, photography, performance and television, using a variety of postmodernist theories. The text is ideal for students who require a general introduction to the scope and methodologies of visual culture.

Morgan, D., 2005. *The Sacred Gaze: religious visual culture in theory and practice.* University of California Press, Berkeley.

This is a seminal text on the concept of religious perception as practised by a wide range of religions, across the world and over a broad period of time. The book examines how religious images and objects are appropriated, and ways in which their meanings are constructed and mutate over time, while introducing and critiquing the procedures and apparatus for examining such. The discussion provides an accessible primer for students who are new to the interdiscipline of religious studies and visual studies.

Morgan, D. and Promey, S.M. (eds), 2001. *The Visual Culture of American Religions.* University of California Press, Berkeley.

The collection of essays provides a geographical and cultural case study suitable for students of religious studies and art history. It examines the significant role that art and other visual imagery has had in shaping the consciousness, actions and material artifacts of American religious life. The texts address the theme to the cultures of evangelicalism, Judaism, Native-American religion and Roman Catholicism, among others. The book demonstrates how one might deal with the visual cultures of a variety of religions within a common geographical context.

Plate, S.B. (ed.), 2002. *Religion, Art, and Visual Culture: a cross-cultural reader.* Palgrave Macmillan, New York.

The book is a readable introduction to the nexus of belief and imagery, one that is relevant to students either of religion, art or cultural studies. It examines a variety of visual artifacts and practices from, for example, traditional icons, contemporary religious art, popular media, calligraphy, Zen gardens, architecture and religious iconography. The essays provide accessible examples of theories and approaches to interpreting the visual culture of religions such as Buddhism, Christianity, Hinduism, Islam and Judaism. As such, the book exposes students to a diversity of methodological approaches, religions and visual cultures.

Key concepts

Art history: the academic study of two- and three-dimensional art practices and objects in order to understand their historical and stylistic development, meaning and function.

Art practice: the exercise or pursuit of a creative and formal engagement with materials or other media or objects, leading to the production of artifacts with perceptual properties.

Iconography: a sub-field of art history that seeks to identify and classify subject matter in visual art with reference to its traditional and conventional treatment.

Iconology: a sub-field of art history that deals with the meaning and interpretation of subject matter, symbolism, medium and style.

Interdisciplinarity: the academic study or practice of two distinct disciplines in synthesis.

Visual cultural studies: the theoretical, historical and practical critique of visual images, objects and media with particular emphases upon understanding their cultural meaning, the concept of visuality as lived experience, and the intersection of different media systems.

John Harvey

Related chapters

- Chapter 2.4 Document analysis
- Chapter 2.8 Field research: Participant observation
- Chapter 2.11 Hermeneutics
- Chapter 2.12 History
- Chapter 2.15 Phenomenology
- Chapter 2.19 Structured observation
- Chapter 3.1 Auditory materials
- Chapter 3.3 Material culture

INDEX

Page numbers in italic refer to chapter summaries, tables, boxes and figures.